Best Editorial Cartoons of the Year

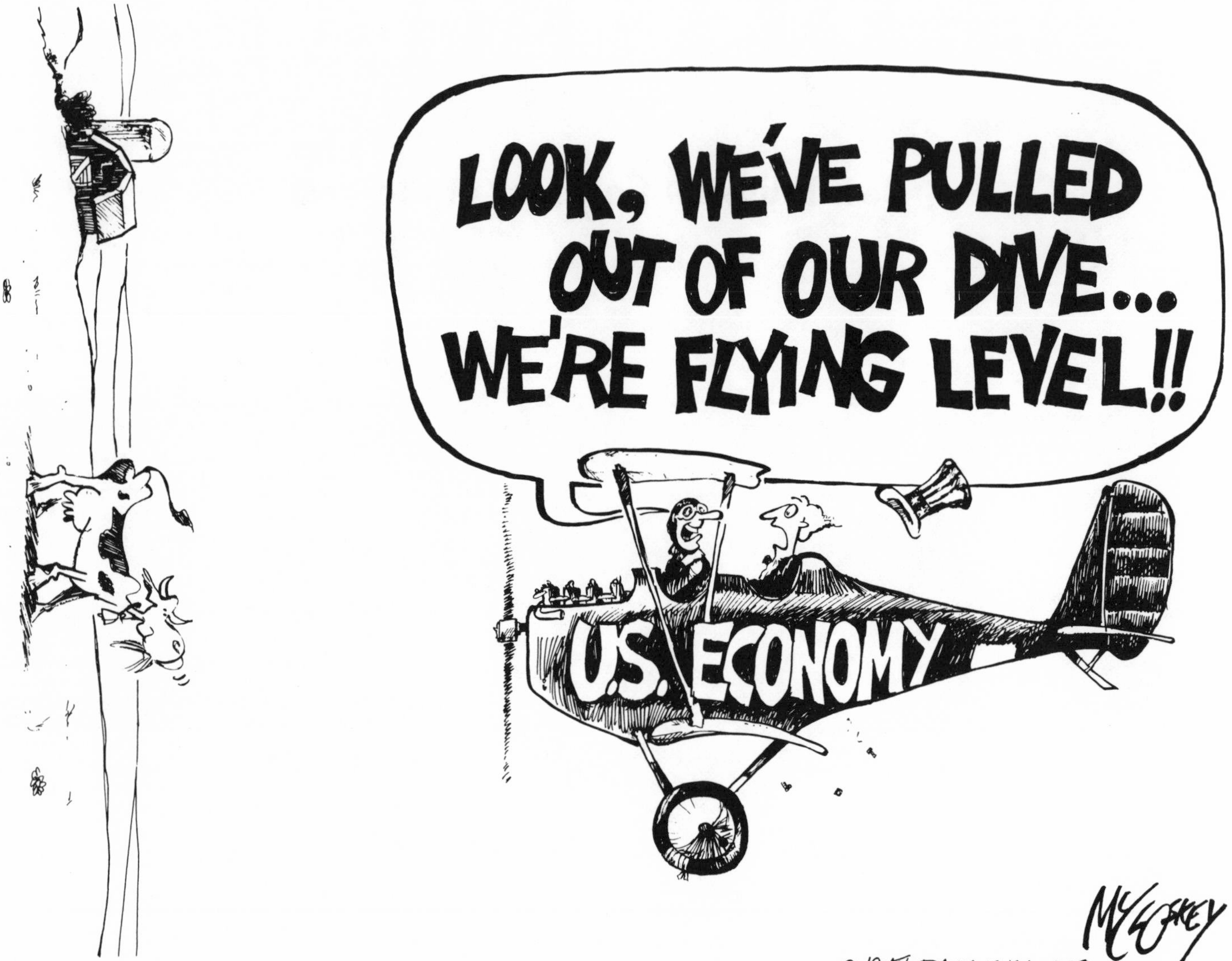
LOOK, WE'VE PULLED OUT OF OUR DIVE... WE'RE FLYING LEVEL!!
U.S. ECONOMY
McCLOSKEY
©1991 The DAILY NEWS LEADER

JIM MCCLOSKEY
Courtesy Staunton Daily News Leader

BEST EDITORIAL CARTOONS OF THE YEAR

1992 EDITION

Edited by
CHARLES BROOKS

PELICAN PUBLISHING COMPANY
Gretna 1992

Library of Congress Serial Catalog Data

Best editorial cartoons. 1972-
   Gretna [La.] Pelican Pub. Co.
   v. 29 cm. annual-
"A pictorial history of the year."

   1. United States- Politics and government –
1969 – Caricatures and Cartoons – Periodicals.
E839.5.B45   320.9'7309240207   73-643645
ISSN 0091-2220   MARC-S

Manufactured in the United States of America
Published by Pelican Publishing Company, Inc.
1101 Monroe Street, Gretna, Louisiana 70053

Contents

Award-Winning Cartoons

1991 PULITZER PRIZE

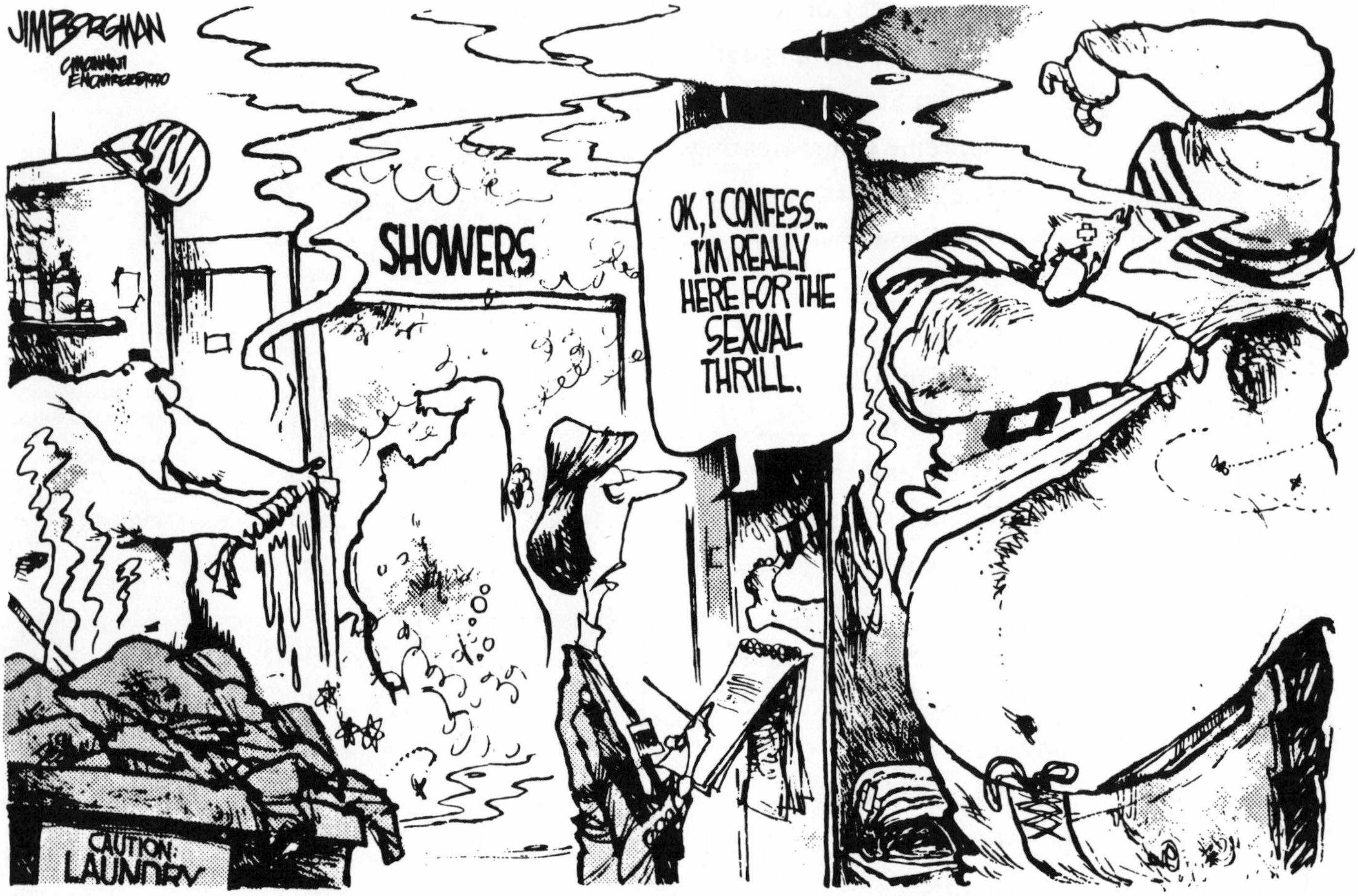

JIMBORGMAN
SHOWERS
OK, I CONFESS... I'M REALLY HERE FOR THE SEXUAL THRILL.
CAUTION: LAUNDRY

JIM BORGMAN
Editorial Cartoonist
Cincinnati Enquirer

Native of Cincinnati, Ohio; summa cum laude graduate of Kenyon College in Fine Arts, 1976; Phi Beta Kappa; editorial cartoonist for *Cincinnati Enquirer*, 1976 to present; cartoons syndicated by King Features Syndicate; author of two books, *Smorgasborgman* and *The Great Communicator*, and coauthor of a third, *The Mood of America*; winner of the Sigma Delta Chi Award for Cartooning, 1978, and the National Headliners Club Award, 1991.

1991 NATIONAL HEADLINERS CLUB AWARD

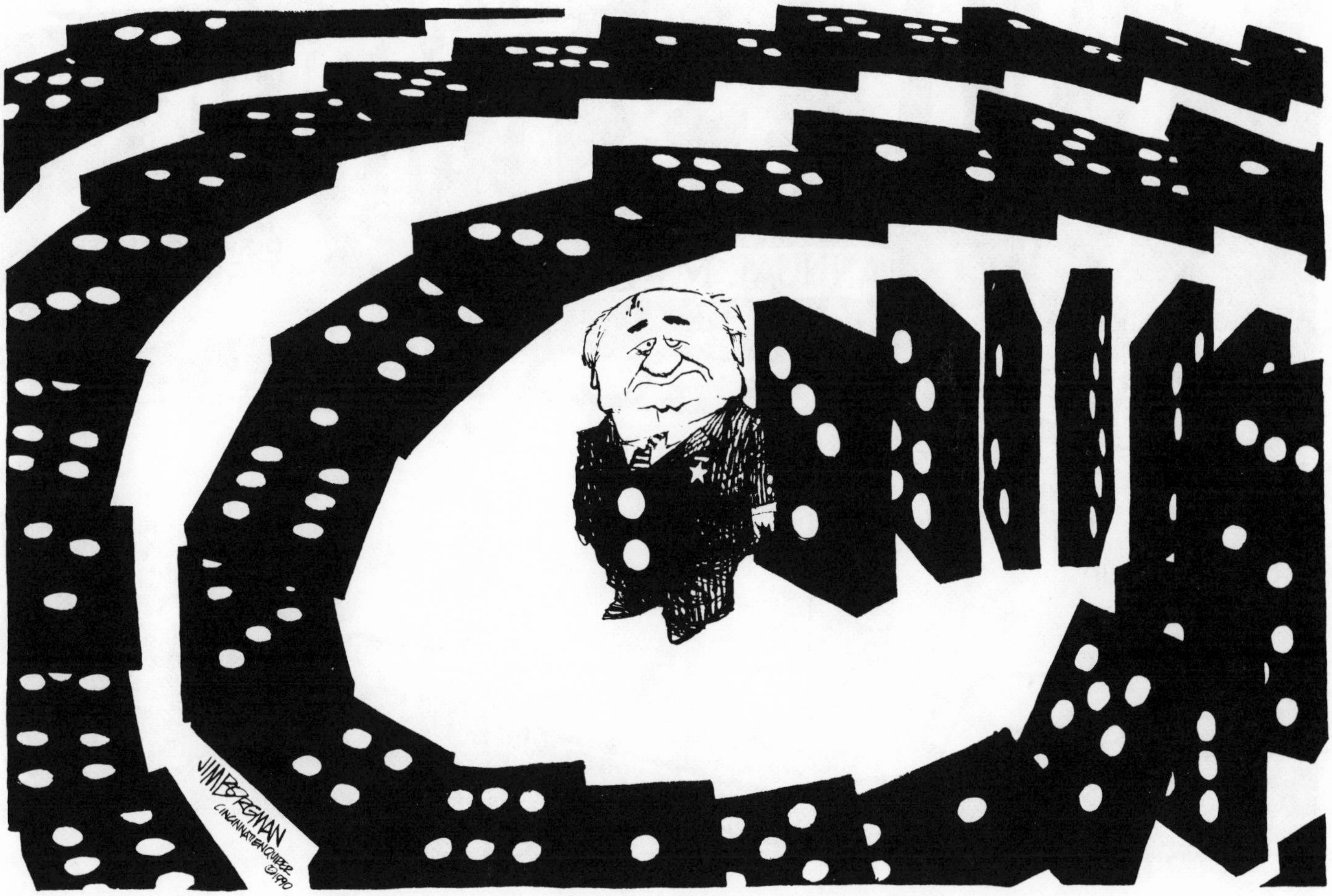
JIM BORGMAN
CINCINNATI ENQUIRER ©1990

JIM BORGMAN
Editorial Cartoonist
Cincinnati Enquirer

1990 NATIONAL SOCIETY OF PROFESSIONAL JOURNALISTS AWARD
(Selected in 1991)

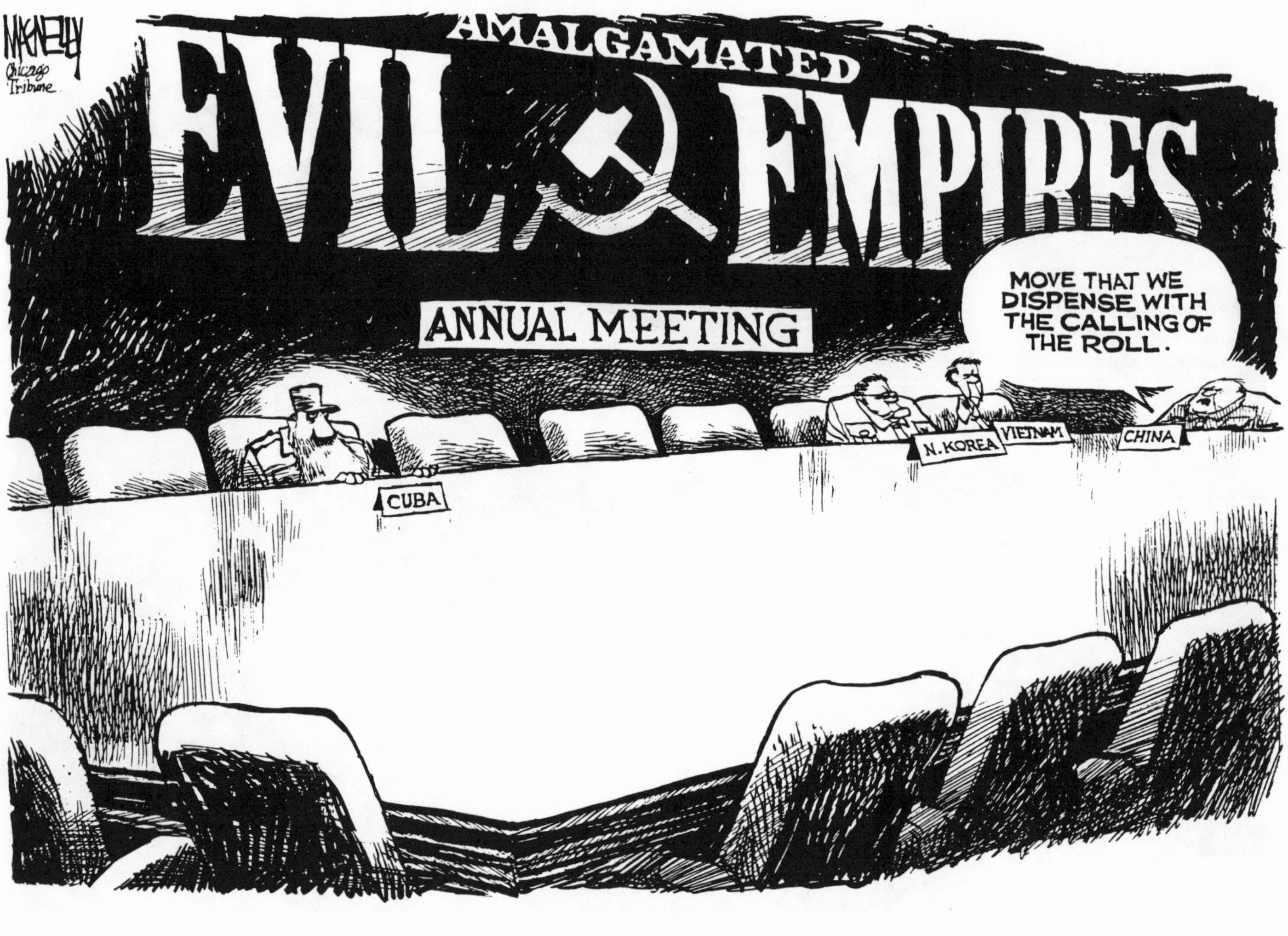
MACNELLY
Chicago Tribune
AMALGAMATED
EVIL EMPIRES
ANNUAL MEETING
MOVE THAT WE DISPENSE WITH THE CALLING OF THE ROLL.
CUBA
N. KOREA
VIETNAM
CHINA

JEFF MACNELLY
Editorial Cartoonist
Chicago Tribune

Born in New York City, 1947; graduated from Phillips Academy, Andover, Massachusetts, 1965, and attended the University of North Carolina; winner of Pulitzer Prize for Cartooning, 1972, 1978, and 1985; winner of George Polk Award, 1978; two-time winner of the Reuben Award, the top honor of the National Cartoonists Society; creator of comic strip "Shoe," carried in hundreds of newspapers; syndicated by Tribune Media Services.

1991 FISCHETTI AWARD

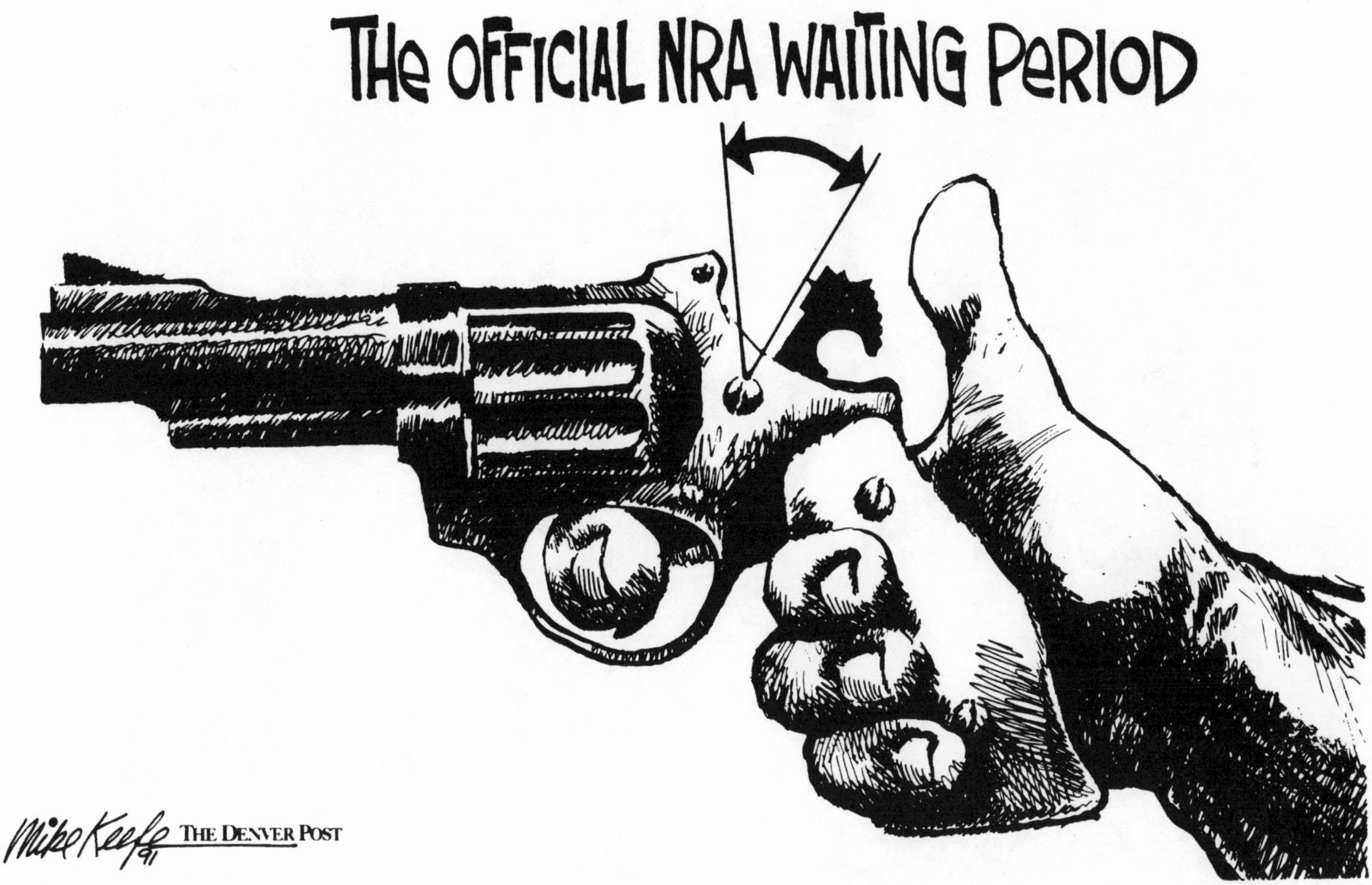
The OFFICIAL NRA WAITING PeRIOD
Mike Keefe '91
THE DENVER POST

MIKE KEEFE

Editorial Cartoonist
Denver Post

Native of Santa Rosa, California; holds master's degree in mathematics from the University of Missouri at Kansas City; editorial cartoonist for the *Denver Post*, 1975 to present; weekly contributor to *USA Today*; former president of the Association of American Editorial Cartoonists; winner of Sigma Delta Chi Award and the National Headliners Club Award, both in 1986; Knight Fellow at Stanford University, 1988-89; author of three books and coauthor of two comic strips.

1990 NATIONAL NEWSPAPER AWARD / CANADA

(Selected in 1991)

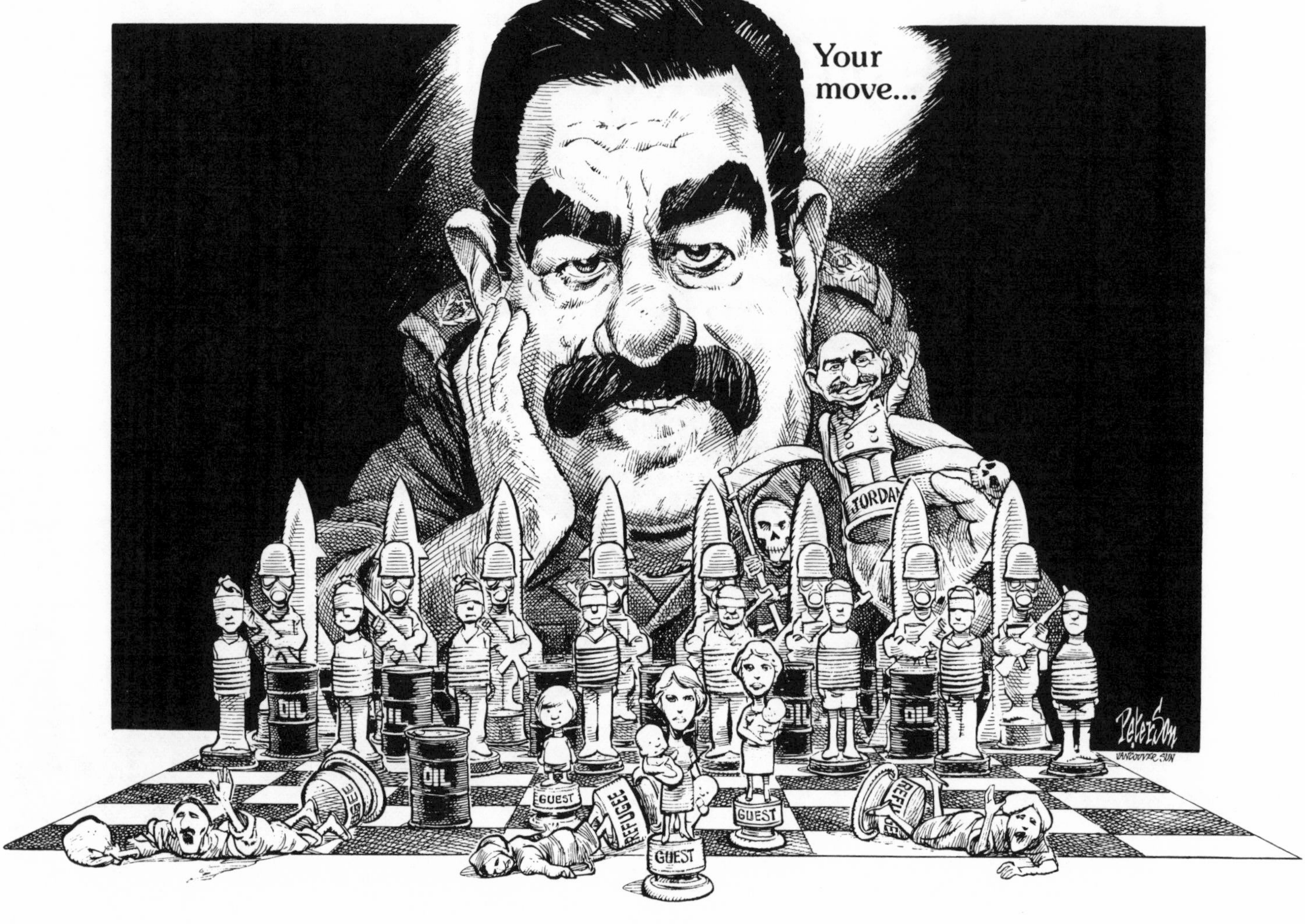
Your move...
JORDAN
OIL
OIL
OIL
OIL
OIL
OIL
GUEST
REFUGEE
GUEST
GUEST
PETERSON
VANCOUVER SUN

ROY PETERSON

Editorial Cartoonist

Vancouver Sun

Born in Winnipeg, Manitoba, 1936; editorial cartoonist for the *Vancouver Sun*, 1962 to present; former president of the Association of American Editorial Cartoonists; former president of the Association of Canadian Editorial Cartoonists; winner of Editor & Publisher North American Award, 1966; previous winner of the National Newspaper Award, 1968, 1975, and 1984; winner of Grand Prize, International Salon of Caricature, 1973; author of two books and coauthor of seven.

Best Editorial Cartoons of the Year

FRED CURATOLO
Courtesy Edmonton Sun

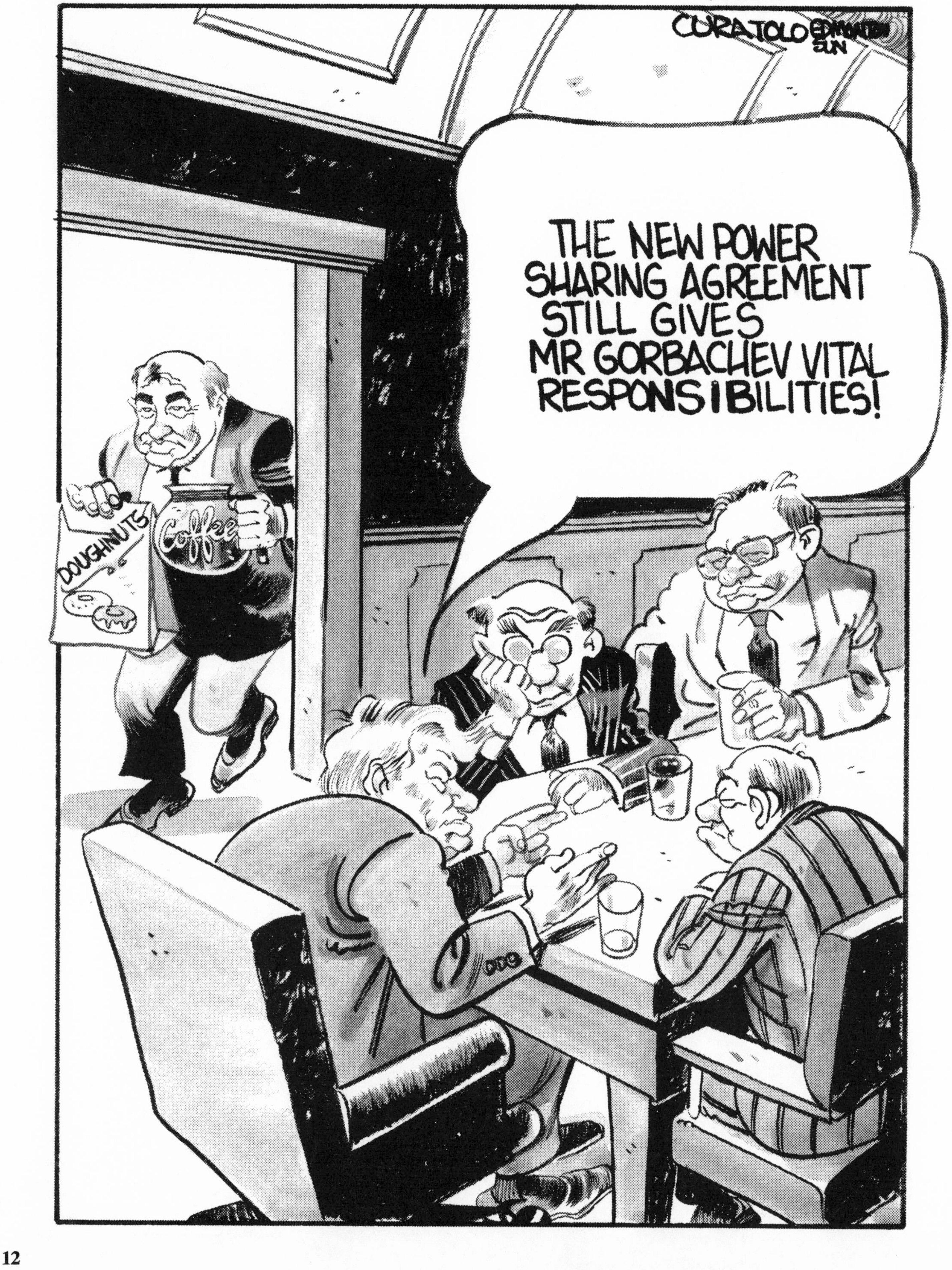
CURATOLO EDMONTON SUN
THE NEW POWER SHARING AGREEMENT STILL GIVES MR GORBACHEV VITAL RESPONSIBILITIES!
DOUGHNUTS
Coffee

The Soviet Collapse

Like a sand castle being washed away by the incoming tide, the Soviet Union was demolished in 1991. First, the Baltic states of Lithuania, Latvia, and Estonia demanded freedom from the Soviet Union, and Mikhail Gorbachev responded with troops, which served to strengthen the move toward independence. Armenia, Georgia, and Moldavia then defied the Kremlin, and striking coal miners called upon Gorbachev to step down. The cracks in the Soviet authority soon became too large to repair.

In August, there was a botched coup attempt by hardliners in the military and the government. Their timing was bad, their planning even worse, and many military units mutinied as the central government lost control of the army and the air force. When the coup began, Gorbachev was vacationing at a secluded compound overlooking the Black Sea. The hardliners failed to reckon with Boris Yeltsin, president of the Russian Republic, who led the people against the coup. Citizens took to the streets to oppose the revolt and ringed the Russian Parliament Building to protect Yeltsin from troops and tanks. By late December, Russia, the Ukraine, and several other republics had formed a commonwealth completely divorced from communism. The red flag of the communist U.S.S.R. was lowered, to be replaced in Moscow with the flag of the Republic of Russia. One of the last bastions of communism, however, refused to budge. Cuba's Fidel Castro seemed determined to await the bitter end.

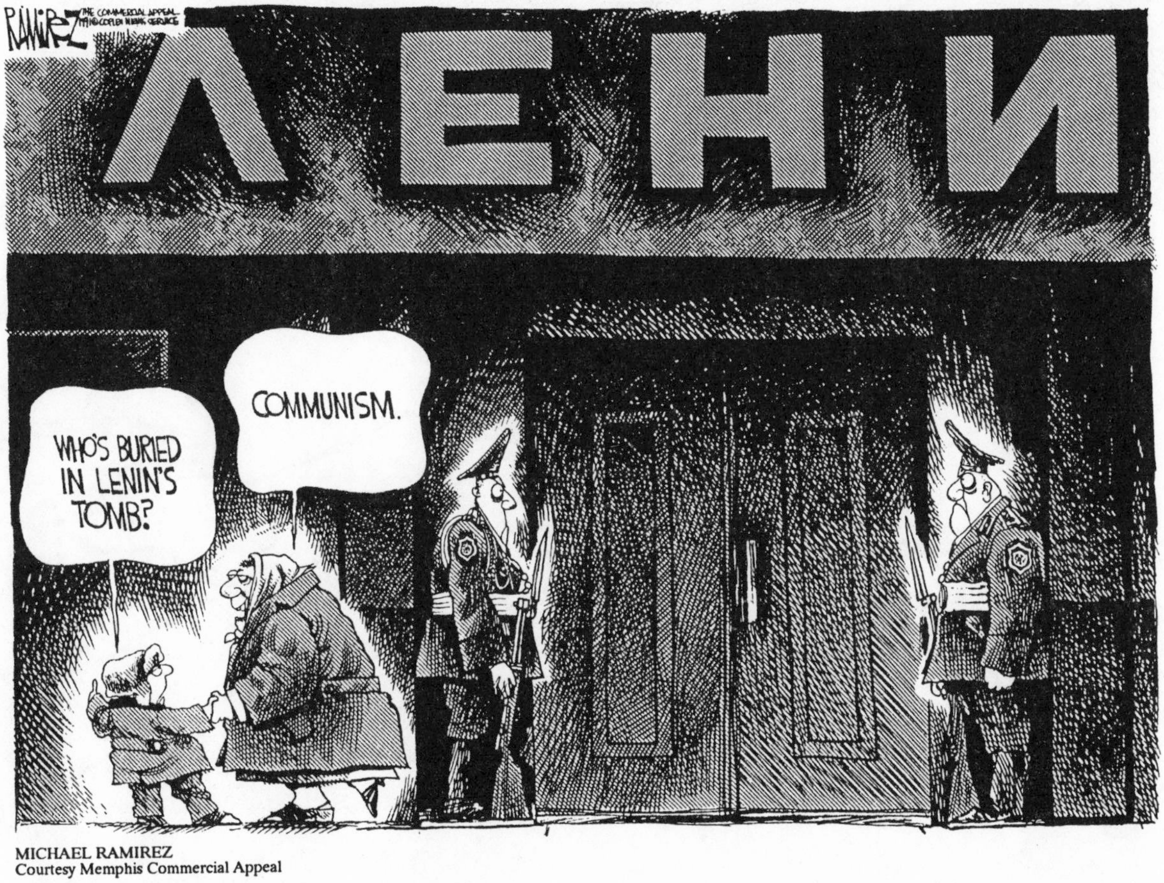
RAMIREZ
ЛЕНИ
WHO'S BURIED IN LENIN'S TOMB?
COMMUNISM.

MICHAEL RAMIREZ
Courtesy Memphis Commercial Appeal

JIM BORGMAN
Courtesy Cincinnati Enquirer

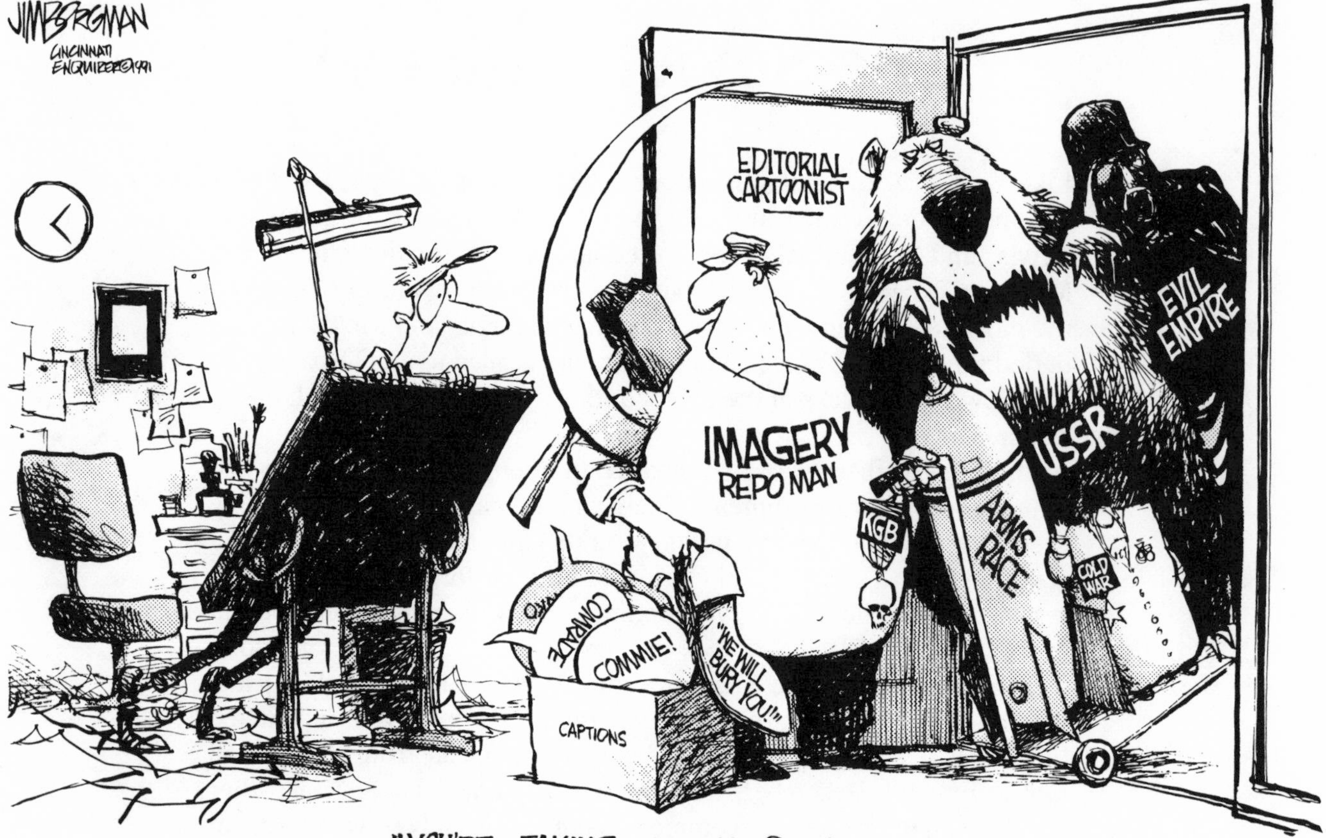

JIM BORGMAN
CINCINNATI ENQUIRER ©1991
EDITORIAL CARTOONIST
IMAGERY
REPO MAN
KGB
ARMS RACE
USSR
EVIL EMPIRE
COLD WAR
COMRADE
COMMIE!
"WE WILL BURY YOU!"
CAPTIONS

"YOU'RE.... TAKING..... IT...... ALL ?......"

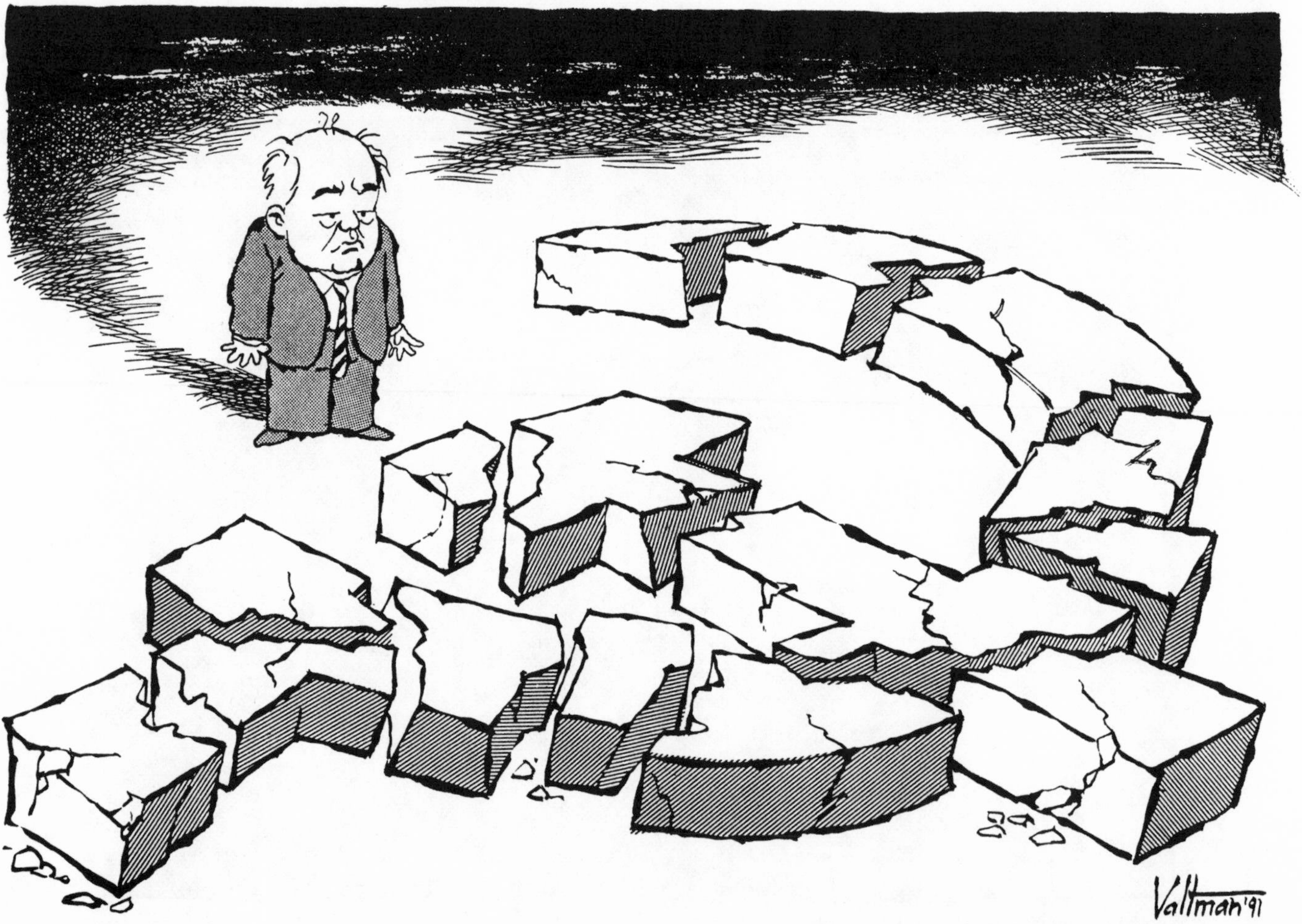

Valtman '91

EDMUND VALTMAN
Courtesy Chronicle and Middletown Press (Conn.)

BILL GARNER
Courtesy Washington Times

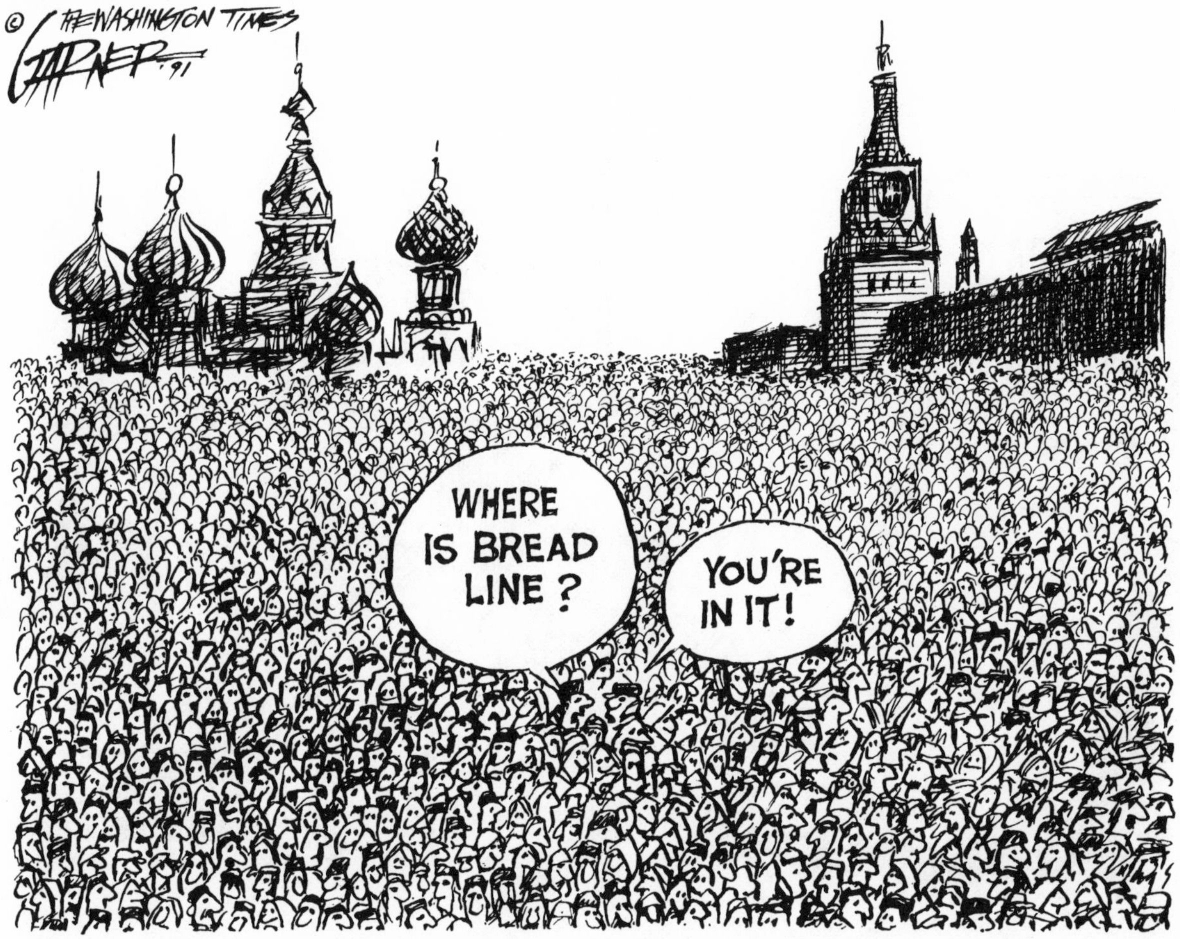
© THE WASHINGTON TIMES
GARNER '91
WHERE IS BREAD LINE ?
YOU'RE IN IT!

ETTA HULME
Courtesy Ft. Worth Star-Telegram

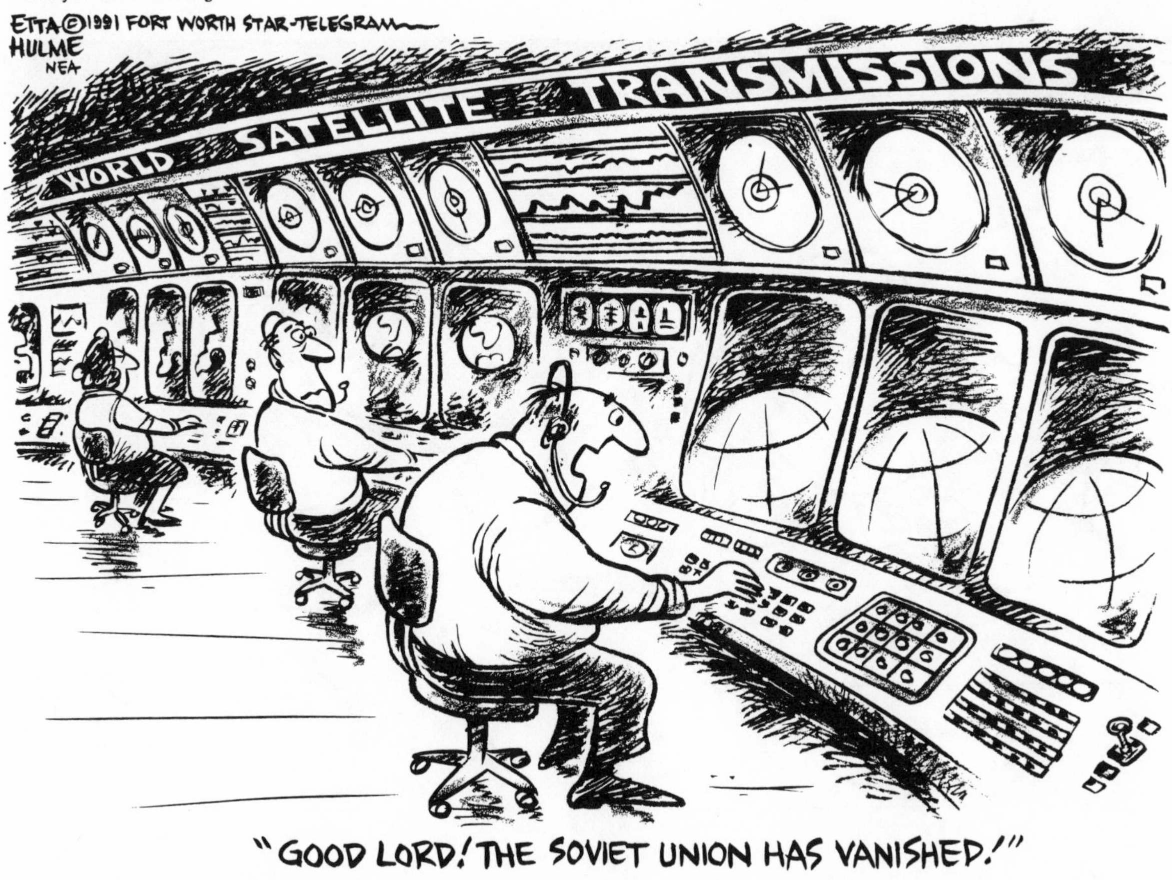
ETTA ©1991 FORT WORTH STAR-TELEGRAM
HULME
NEA
WORLD SATELLITE TRANSMISSIONS

"GOOD LORD! THE SOVIET UNION HAS VANISHED!"

LAMBERT DER
Courtesy Greenville News

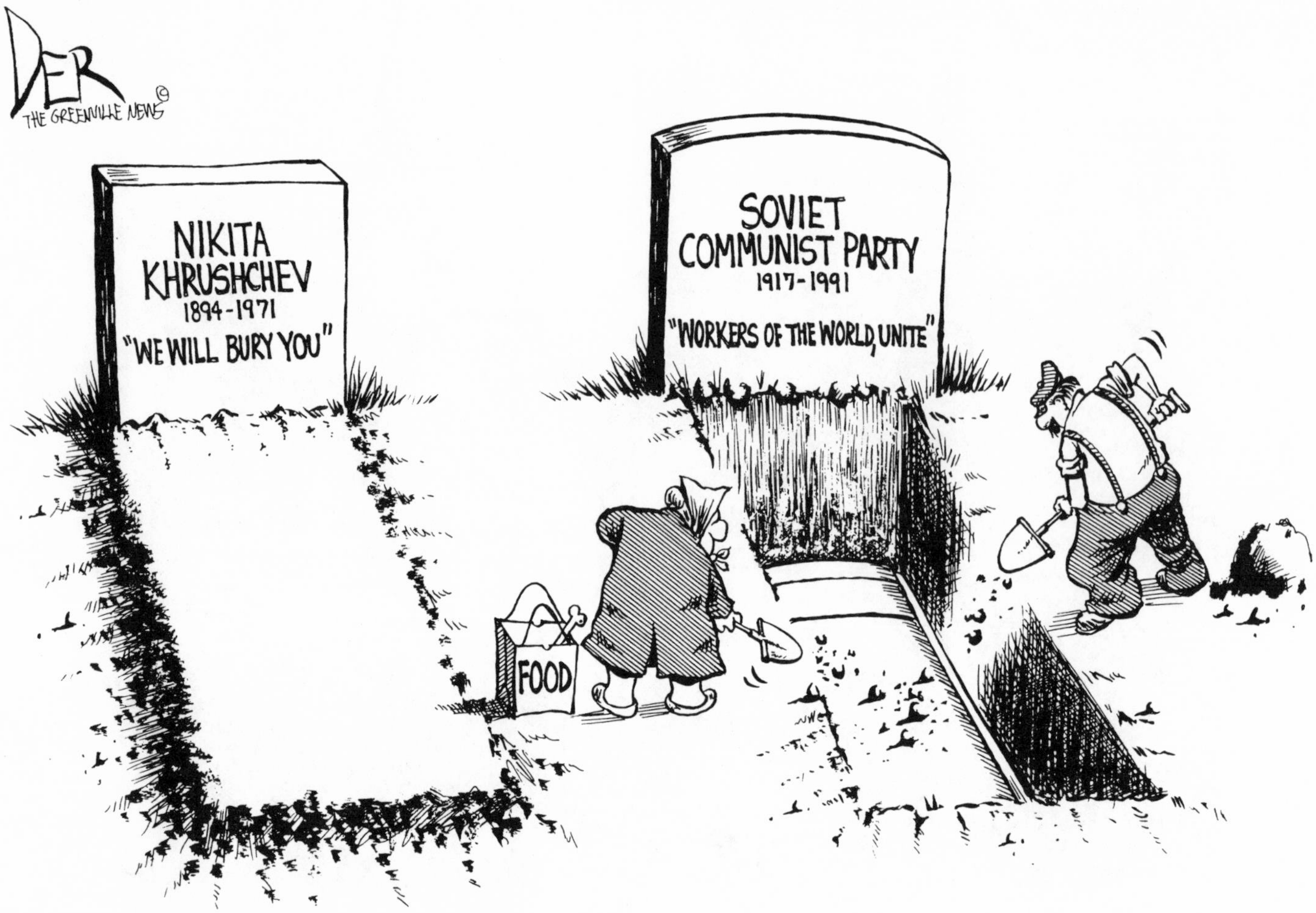

DER
THE GREENVILLE NEWS ©
NIKITA KHRUSHCHEV
1894-1971
"WE WILL BURY YOU"
SOVIET COMMUNIST PARTY
1917-1991
"WORKERS OF THE WORLD, UNITE"
FOOD

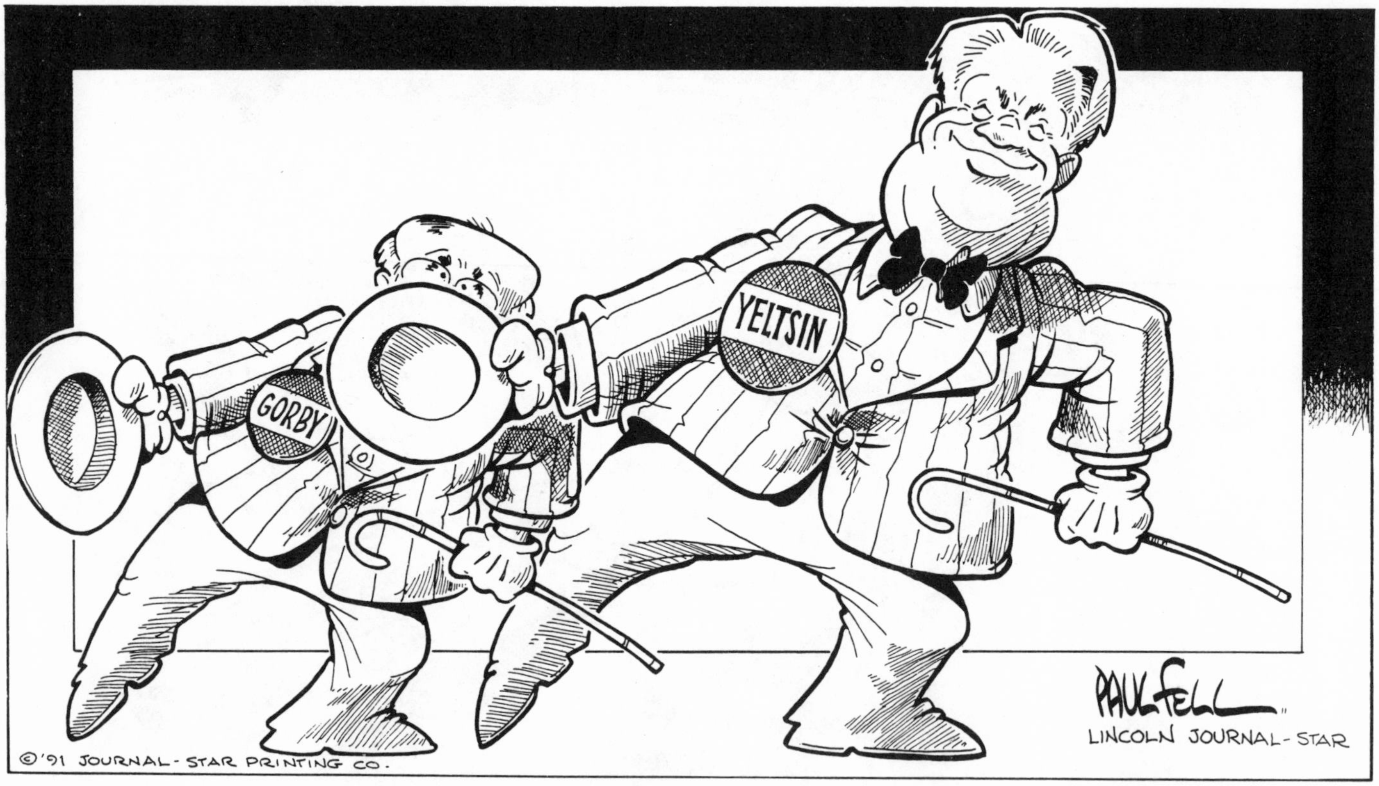

GORBY
YELTSIN
PAUL FELL
LINCOLN JOURNAL-STAR
©'91 JOURNAL-STAR PRINTING CO.

PAUL FELL
Courtesy Lincoln Journal

JEFF BRANCH
Courtesy San Antonio Express-News

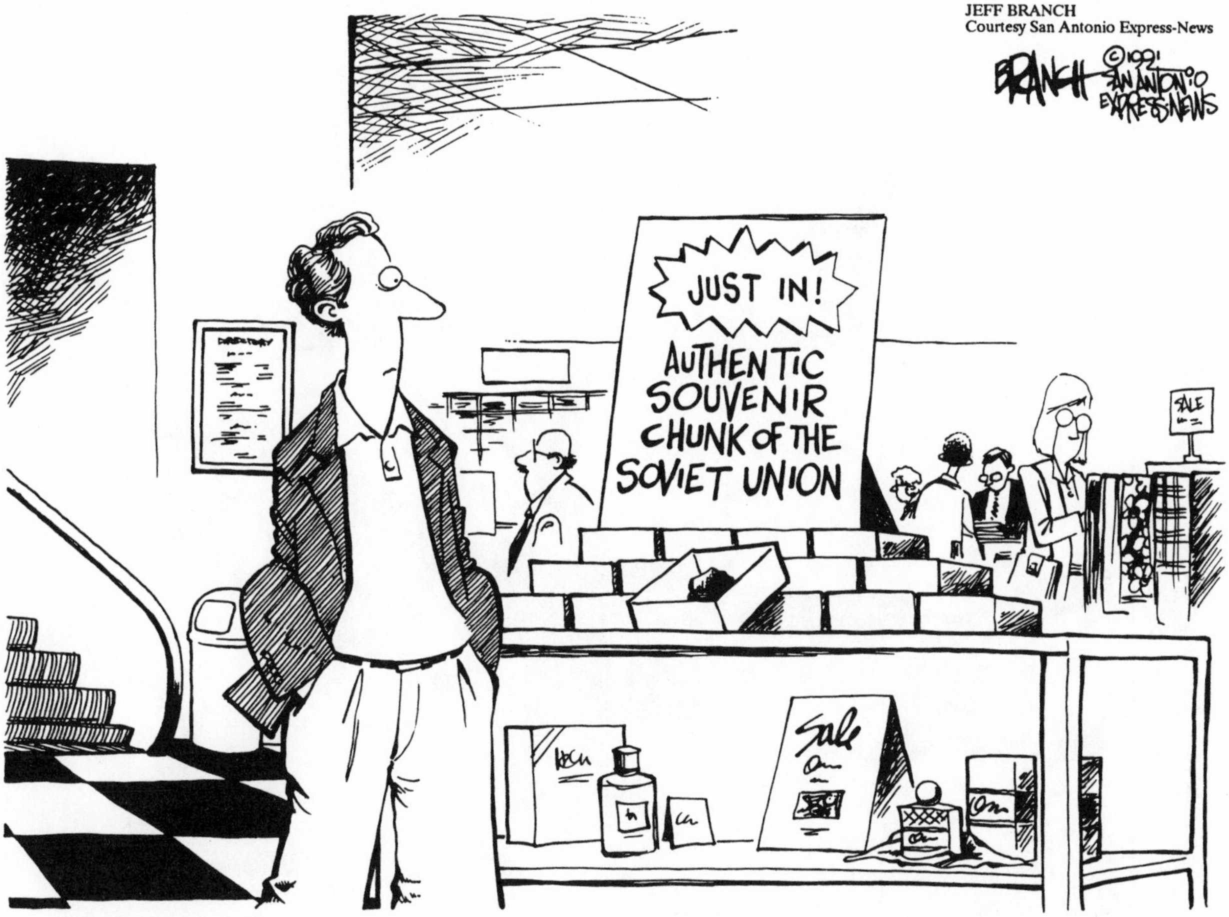
BRANCH ©1991 SAN ANTONIO EXPRESS-NEWS
JUST IN!
AUTHENTIC SOUVENIR CHUNK OF THE SOVIET UNION
SALE
Sale

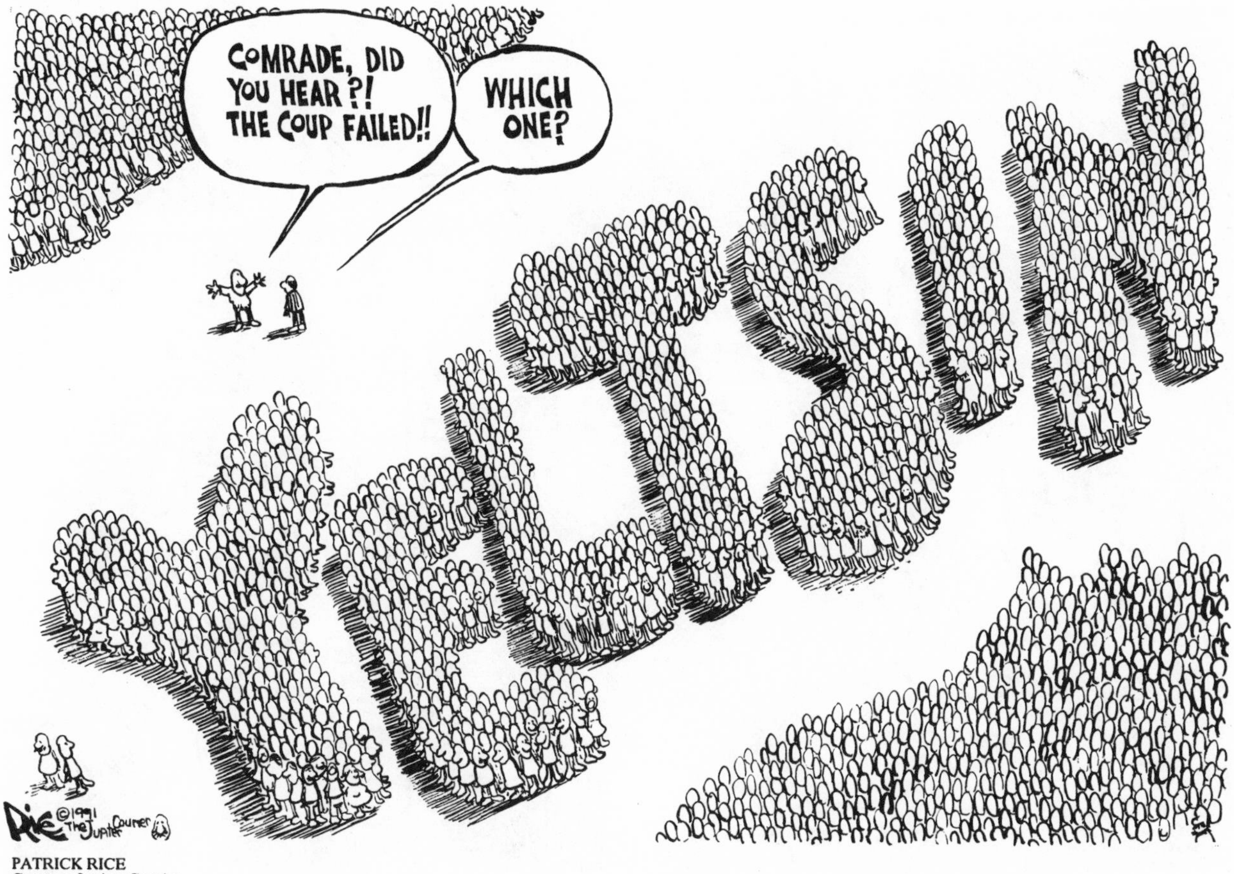
COMRADE, DID YOU HEAR?! THE COUP FAILED!!
WHICH ONE?
YELTSIN
RICE ©1991 The Jupiter Courier

PATRICK RICE
Courtesy Jupiter Courier

TOM ENGELHARDT
Courtesy St. Louis Post-Dispatch

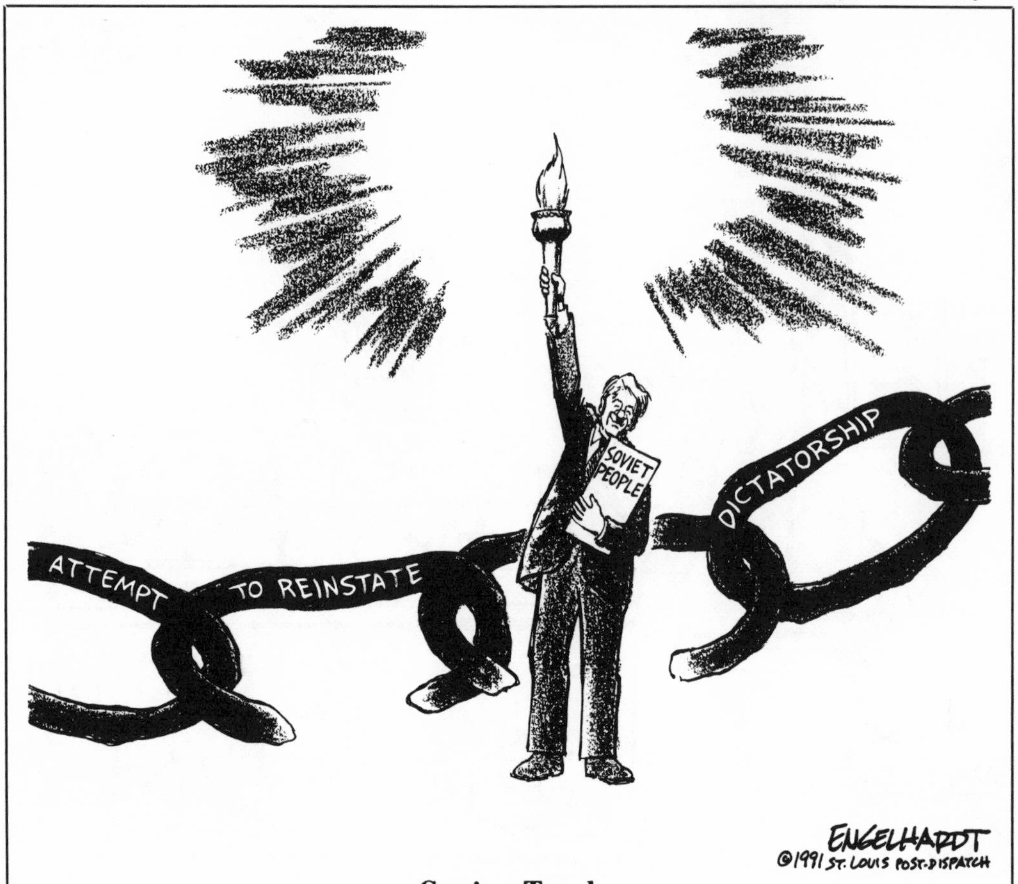
SOVIET PEOPLE
DICTATORSHIP
ATTEMPT
TO REINSTATE
ENGELHARDT
©1991 ST. LOUIS POST-DISPATCH

Cutting Torch

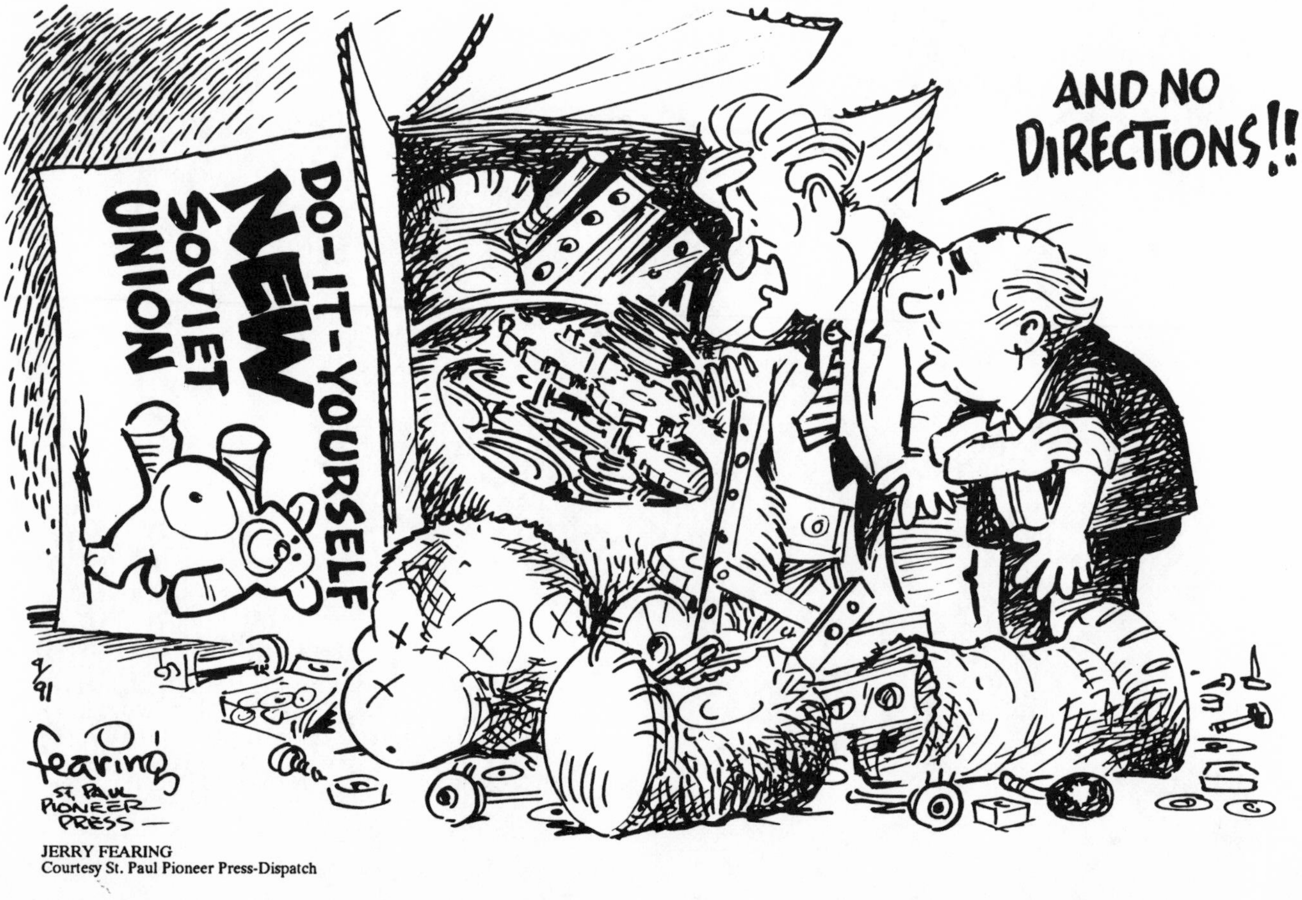
AND NO DIRECTIONS!!
DO-IT-YOURSELF
NEW
SOVIET
UNION
9/91
fearing
ST. PAUL PIONEER PRESS

JERRY FEARING
Courtesy St. Paul Pioneer Press-Dispatch

CARL MOORE
Courtesy National Review

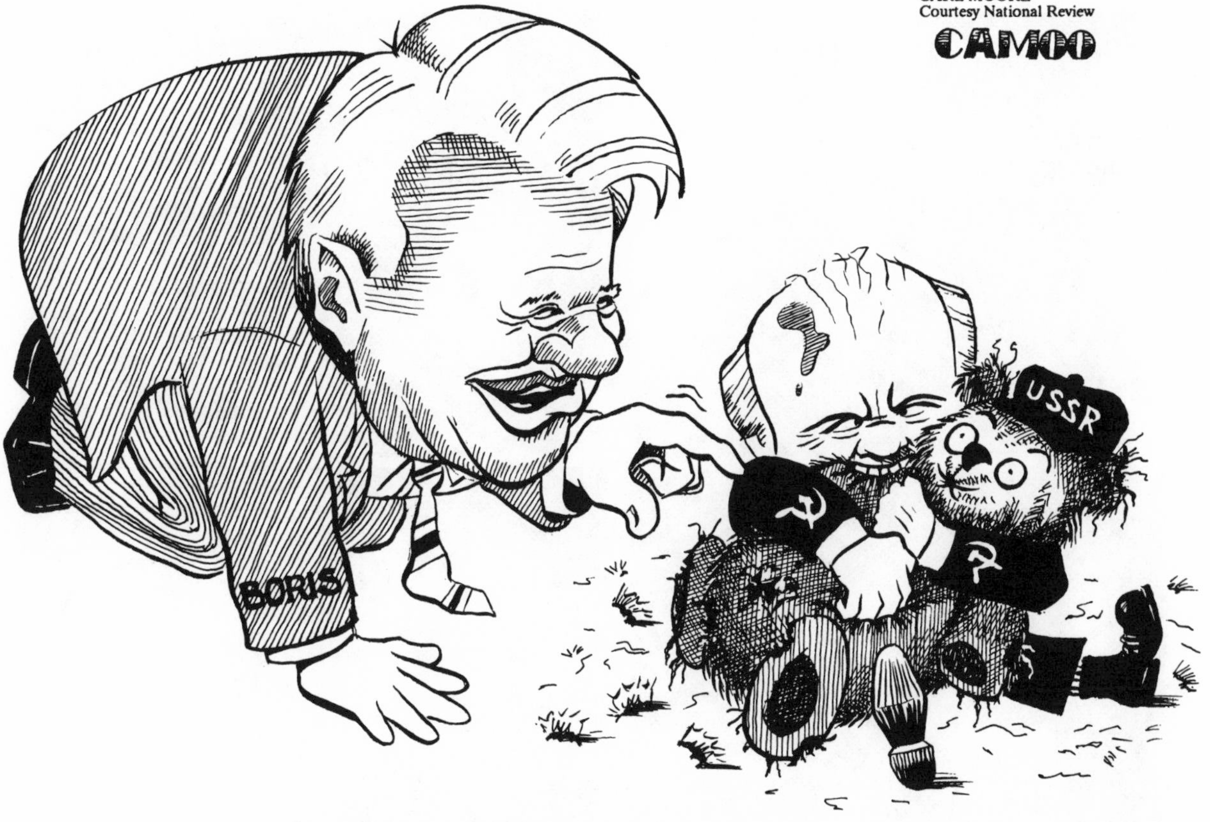
CAMOO
BORIS
USSR

"TIME TO LET GO, MIKHAIL..."

JAMES LARRICK
Courtesy Columbus Dispatch

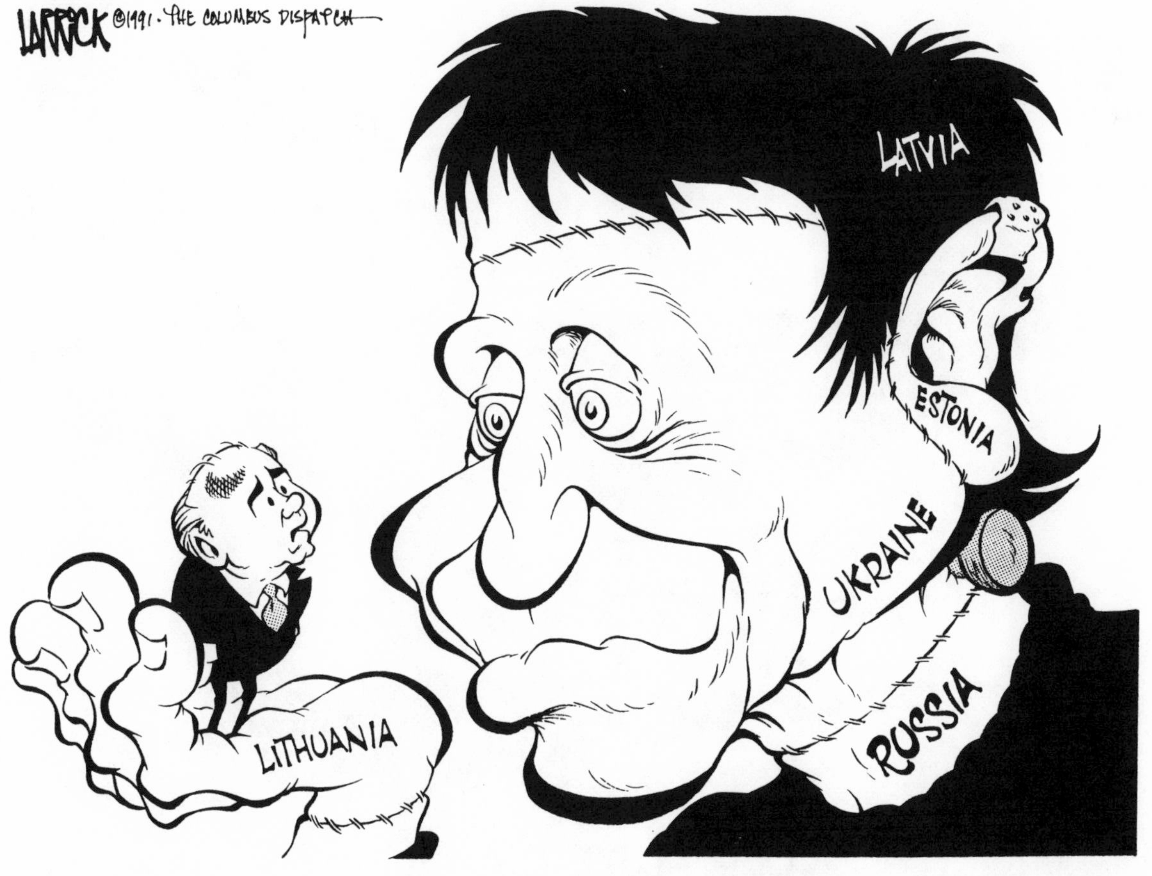
LARRICK ©1991. THE COLUMBUS DISPATCH
LATVIA
ESTONIA
UKRAINE
RUSSIA
LITHUANIA

JACK HIGGINS
Courtesy Chicago Sun-Times

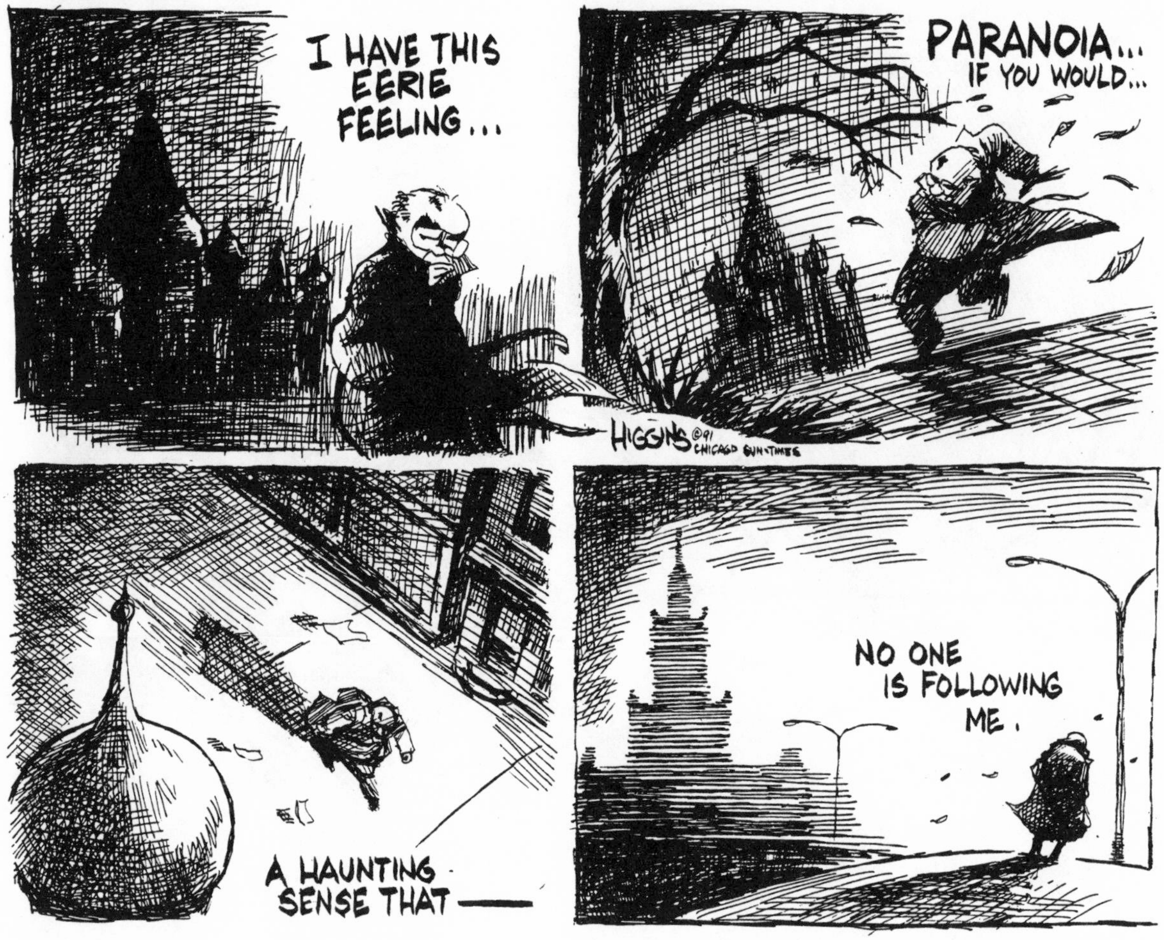
I HAVE THIS EERIE FEELING...
PARANOIA... IF YOU WOULD...
A HAUNTING SENSE THAT—
NO ONE IS FOLLOWING ME.
HIGGINS ©91 CHICAGO SUN-TIMES

BRUCE MACKINNON
Courtesy Halifax Chronicle-Herald

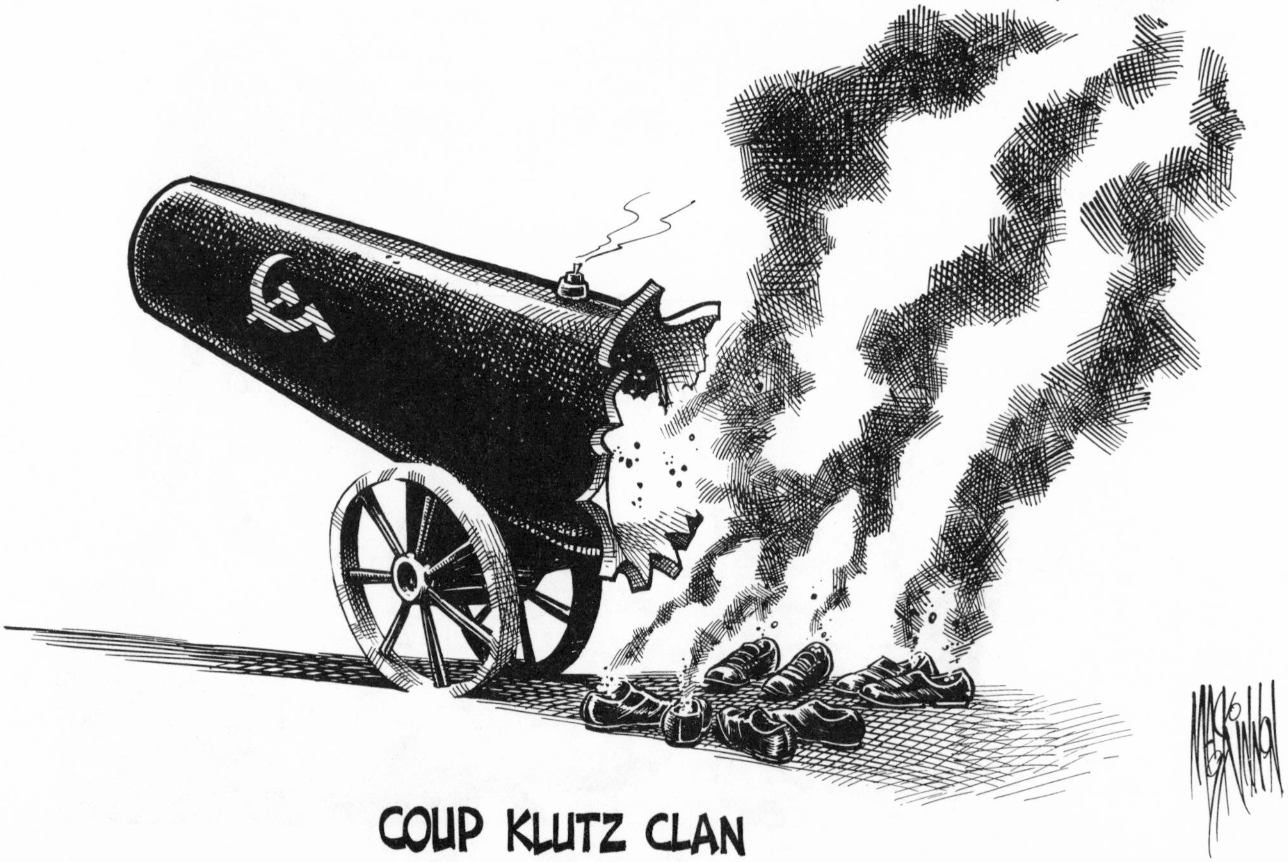

COUP KLUTZ CLAN

EDMUND VALTMAN
Courtesy Chronicle and Middletown Press (Conn.)

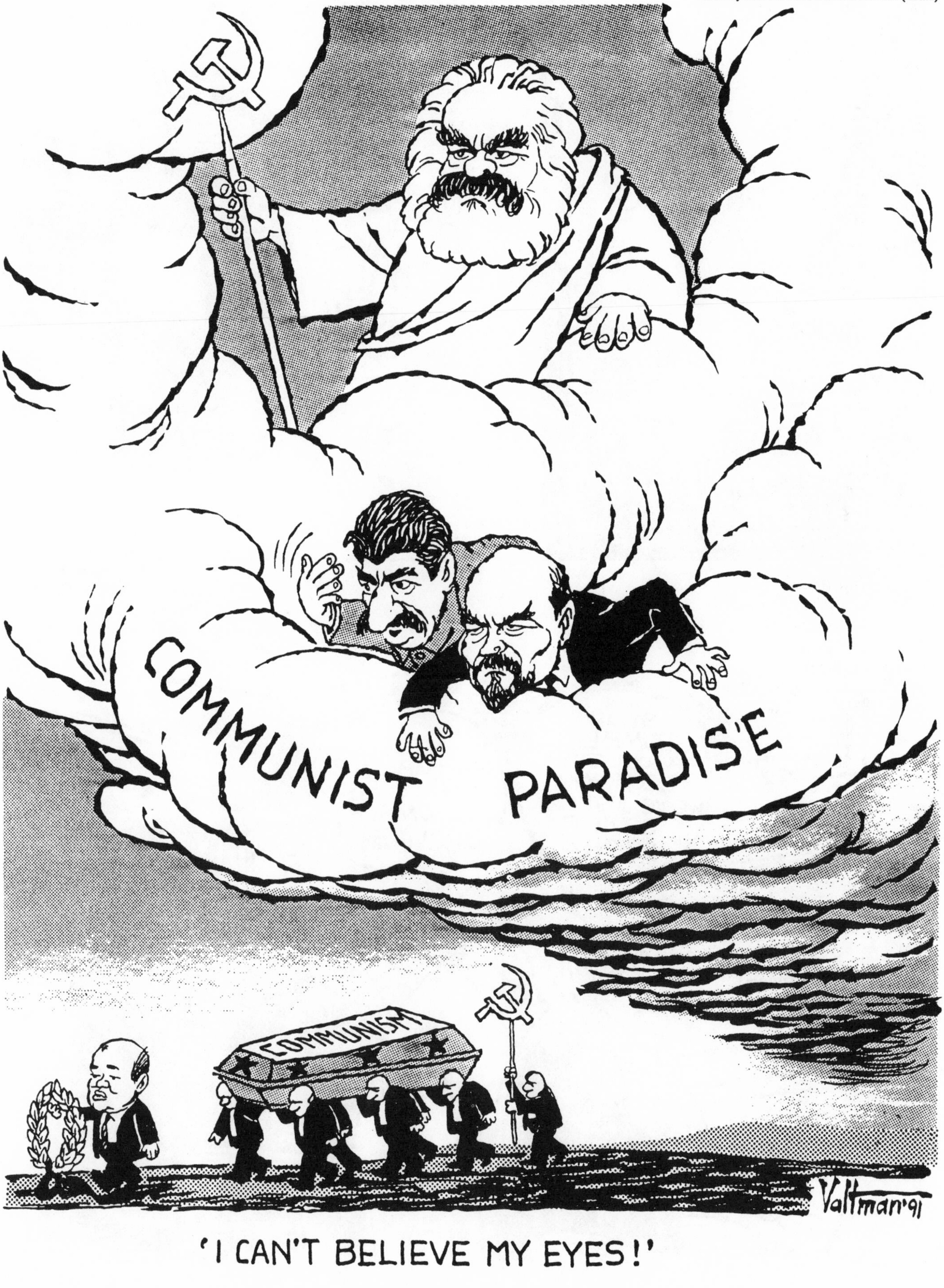
COMMUNIST PARADISE
COMMUNISM
Valtman '91

'I CAN'T BELIEVE MY EYES!'

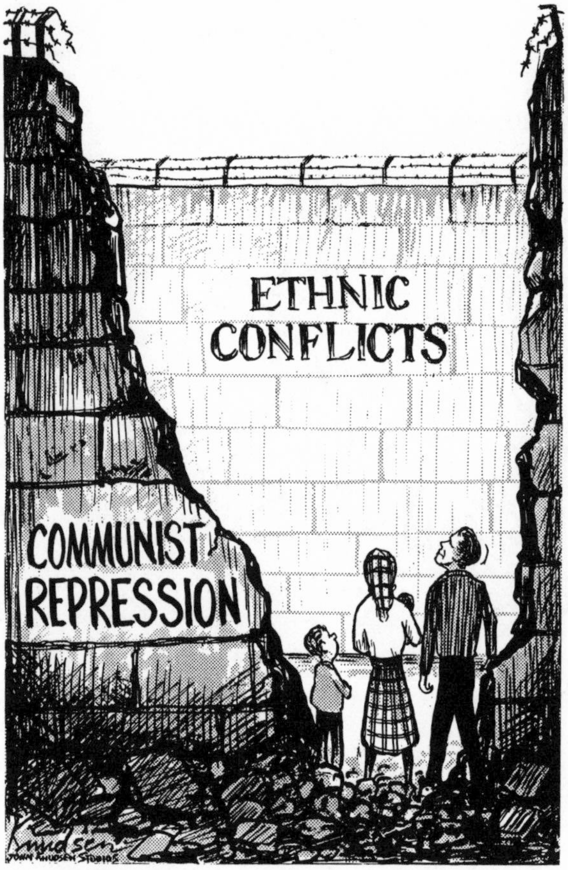
ETHNIC
CONFLICTS
COMMUNIST
REPRESSION
knudsen

JIM KNUDSEN
Courtesy The Tidings (Calif.)

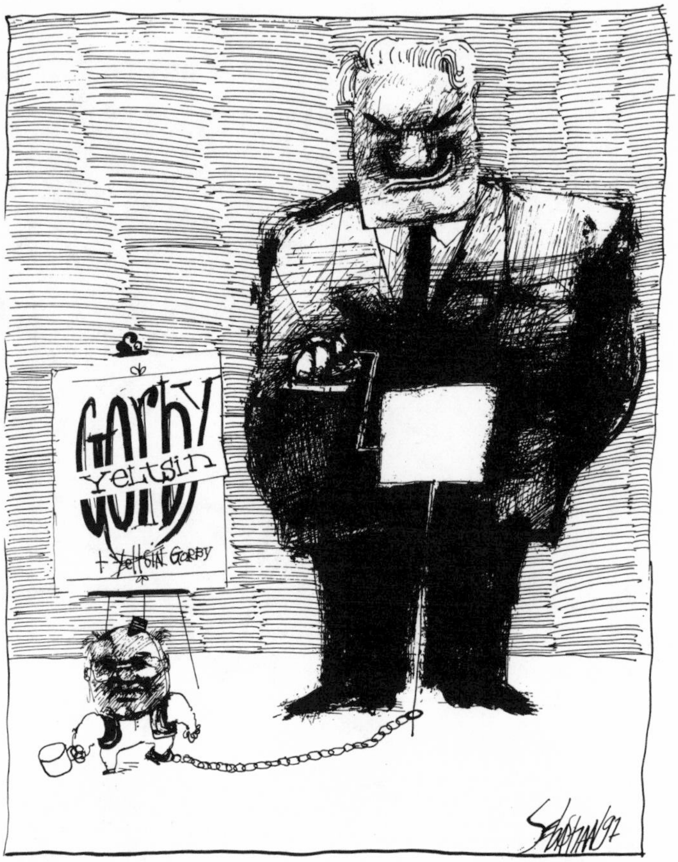
Gorby
Yeltsin
Sebastian '91

FRED SEBASTIAN
Courtesy Ottawa Citizen

GEORGE DANBY
Courtesy Bangor Daily News

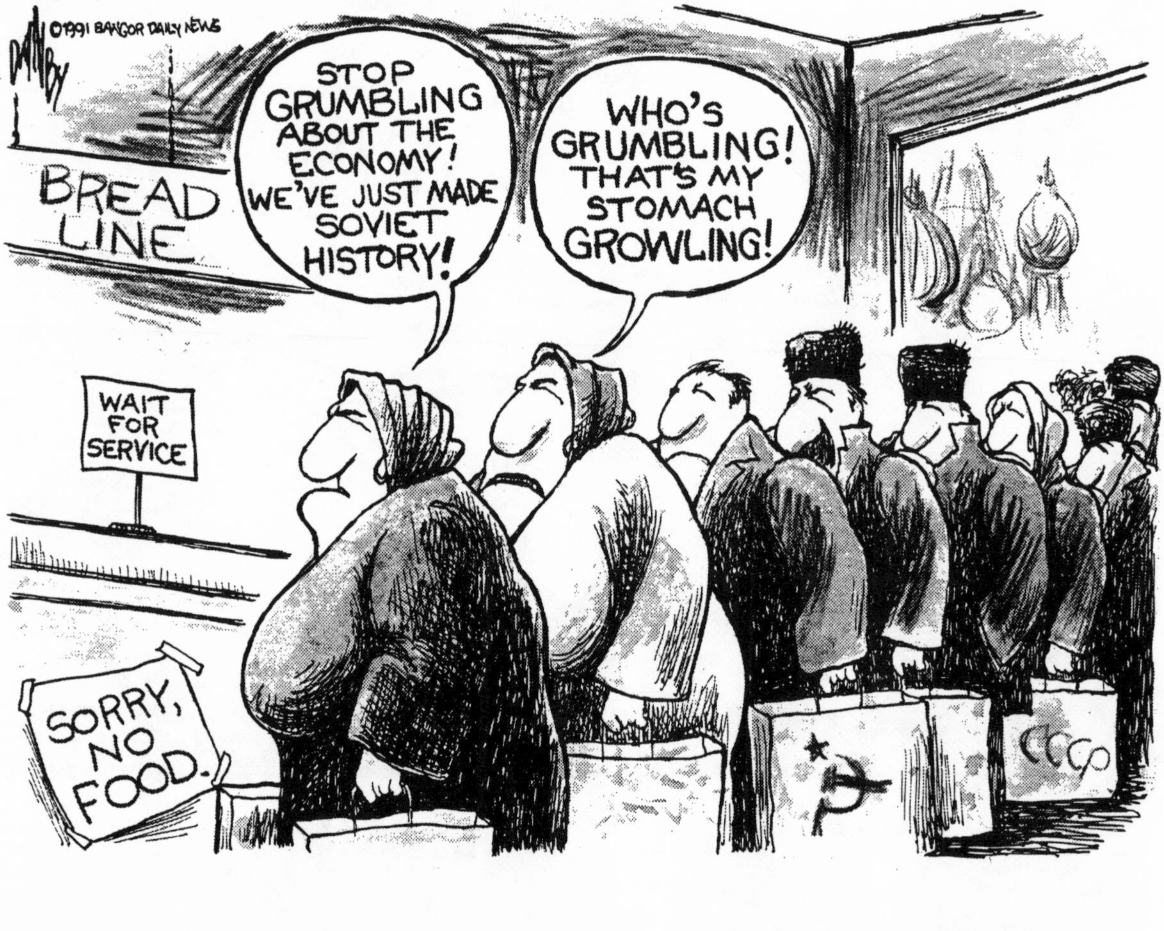
DANBY ©1991 BANGOR DAILY NEWS
BREAD LINE
STOP GRUMBLING ABOUT THE ECONOMY! WE'VE JUST MADE SOVIET HISTORY!
WHO'S GRUMBLING! THAT'S MY STOMACH GROWLING!
WAIT FOR SERVICE
SORRY, NO FOOD.
CCCP

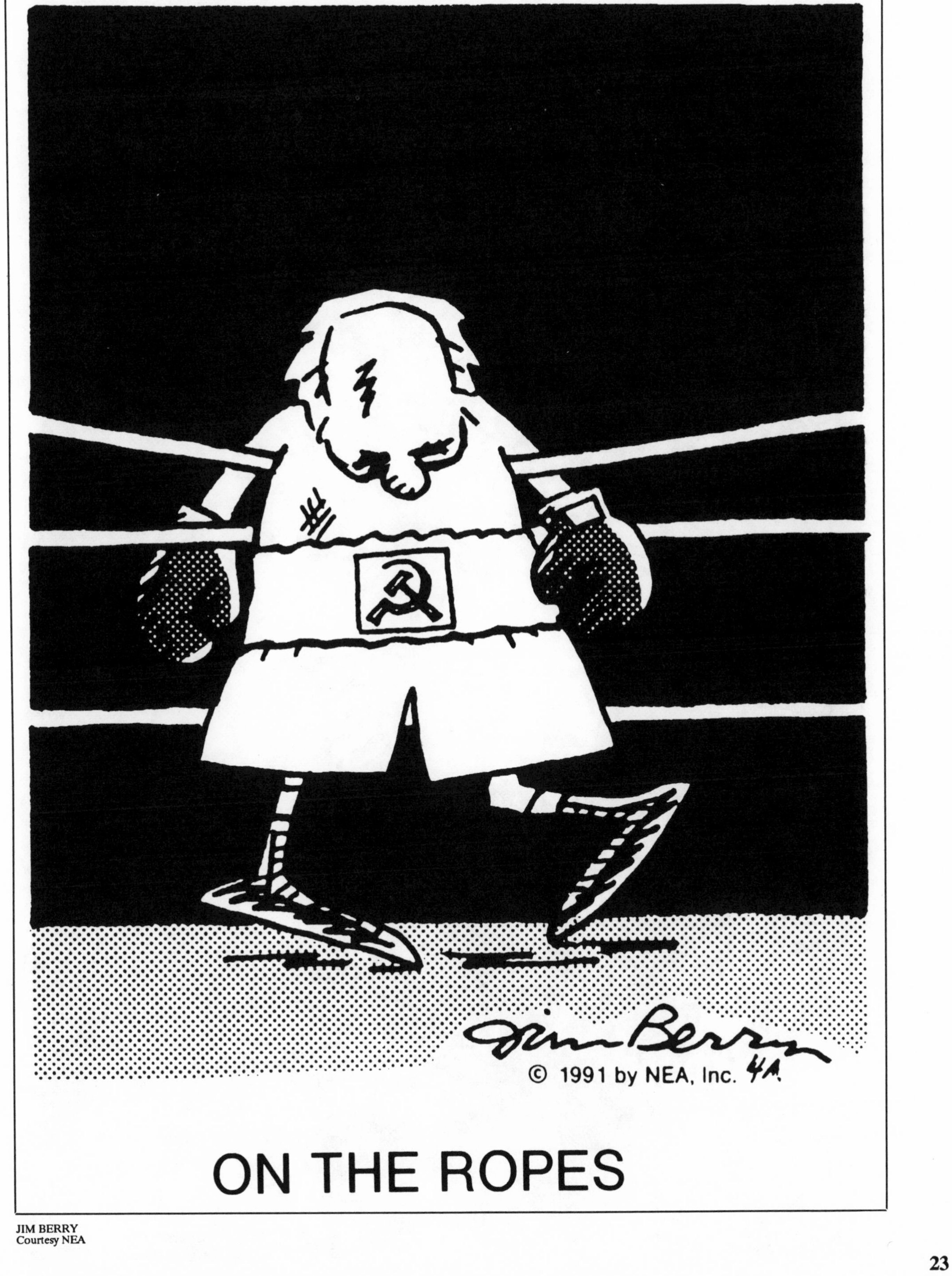
Jim Berry
© 1991 by NEA, Inc. 4A

ON THE ROPES

JIM BERRY
Courtesy NEA

BOB ENGLEHART
Courtesy Hartford Courant

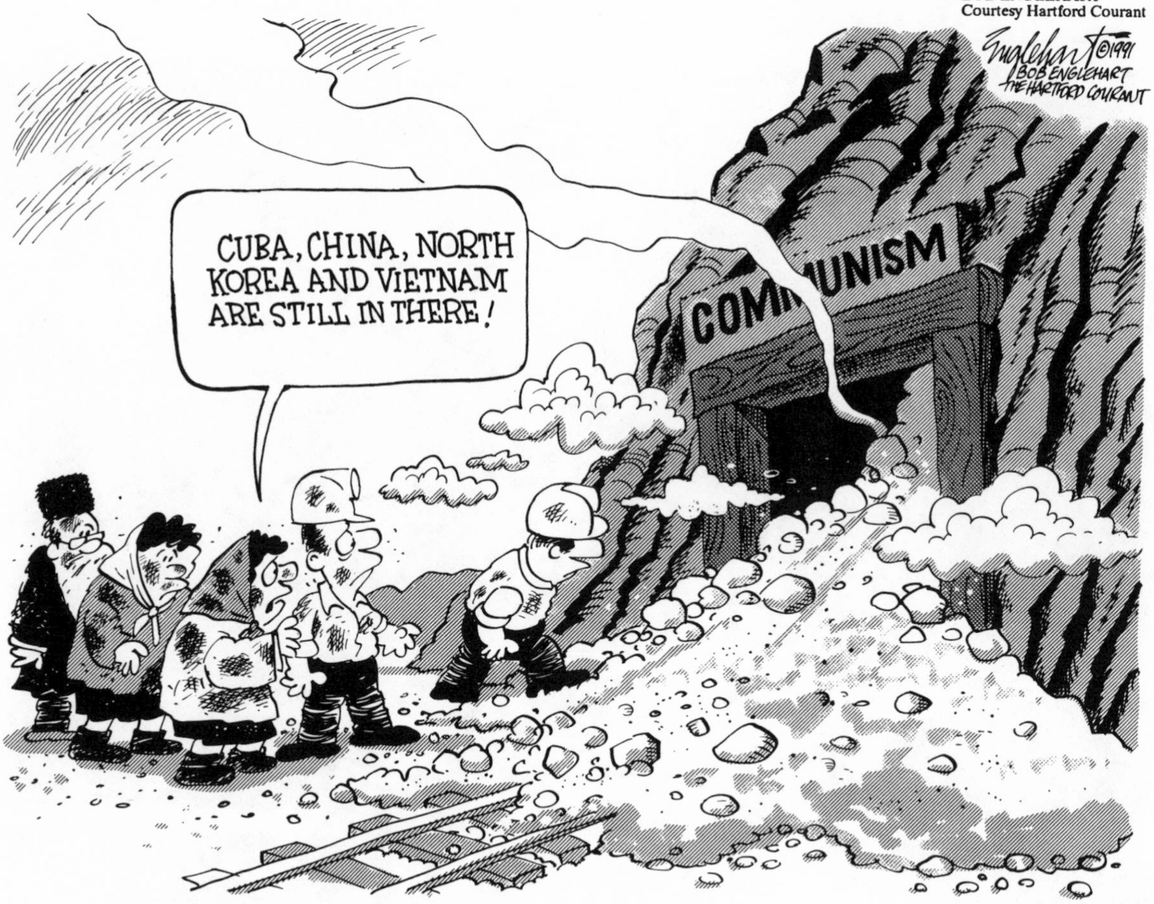
Englehart ©1991 BOB ENGLEHART THE HARTFORD COURANT
CUBA, CHINA, NORTH KOREA AND VIETNAM ARE STILL IN THERE!
COMMUNISM

WILLIAM COSTELLO
Courtesy Lowell Sun

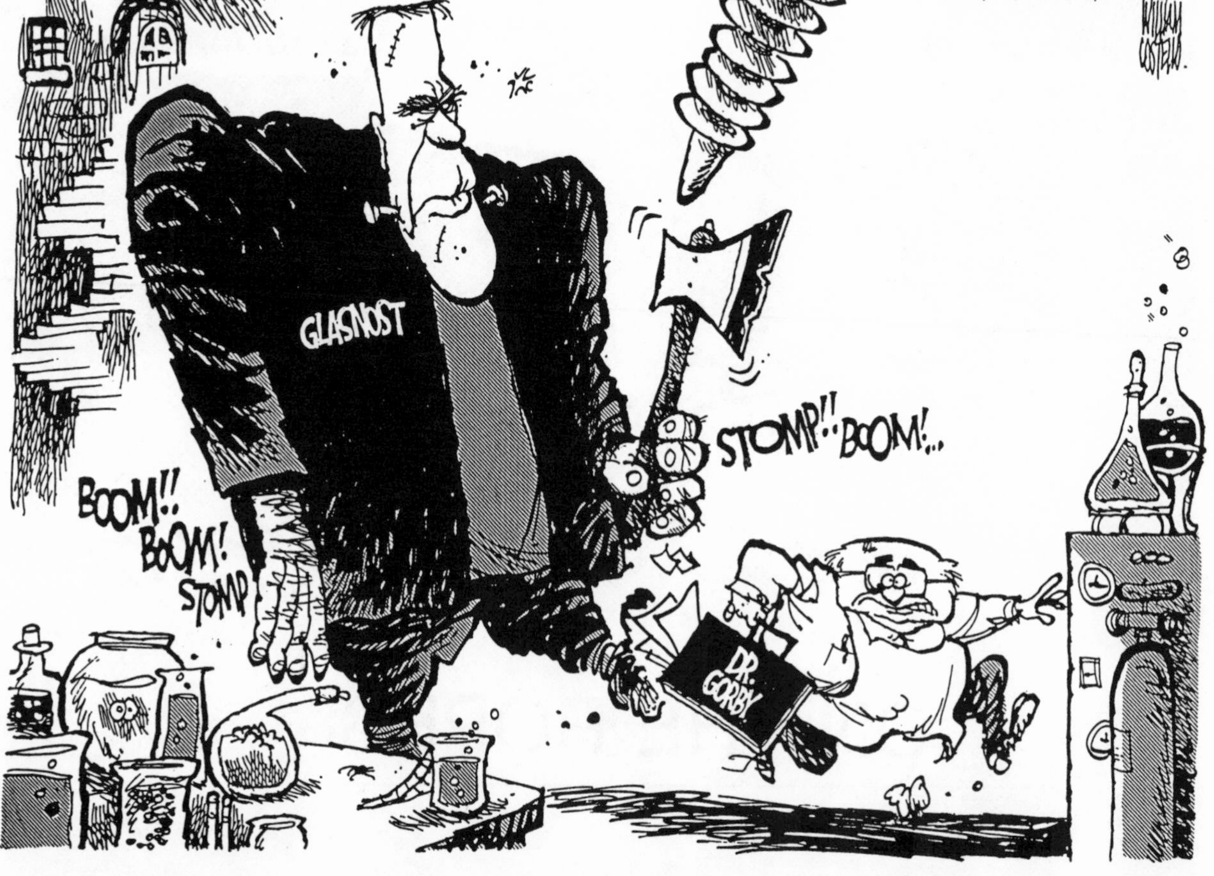
©1991 THE LOWELL SUN
WILLIAM COSTELLO
GLASNOST
STOMP!! BOOM!..
BOOM!! BOOM! STOMP
DR. GORBY

JEFF KOTERBA
Courtesy Omaha World-Herald

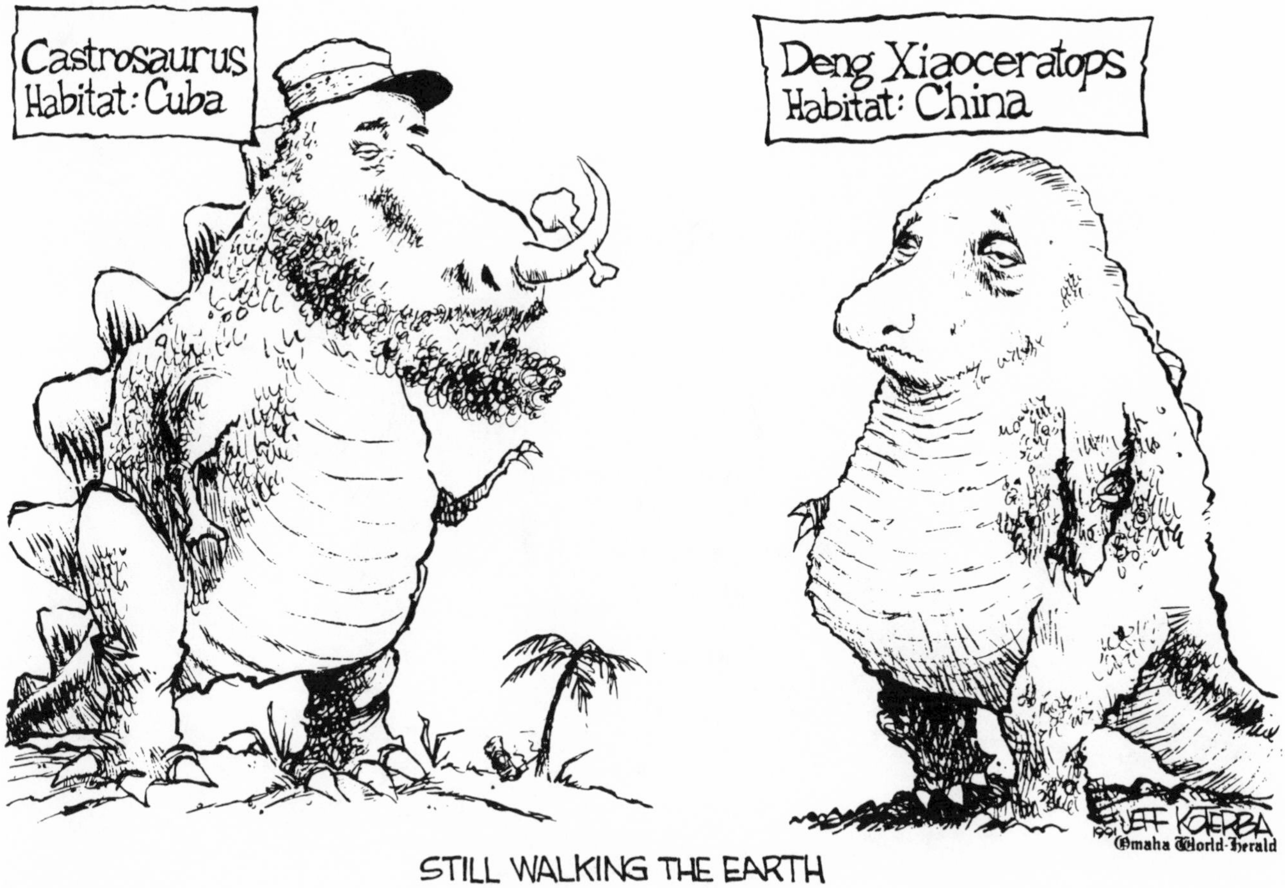
Castrosaurus
Habitat: Cuba
Deng Xiaoceratops
Habitat: China
1991 JEFF KOTERBA
Omaha World-Herald
STILL WALKING THE EARTH

JEFF MACNELLY
Courtesy Chicago Tribune and
Tribune Media Services

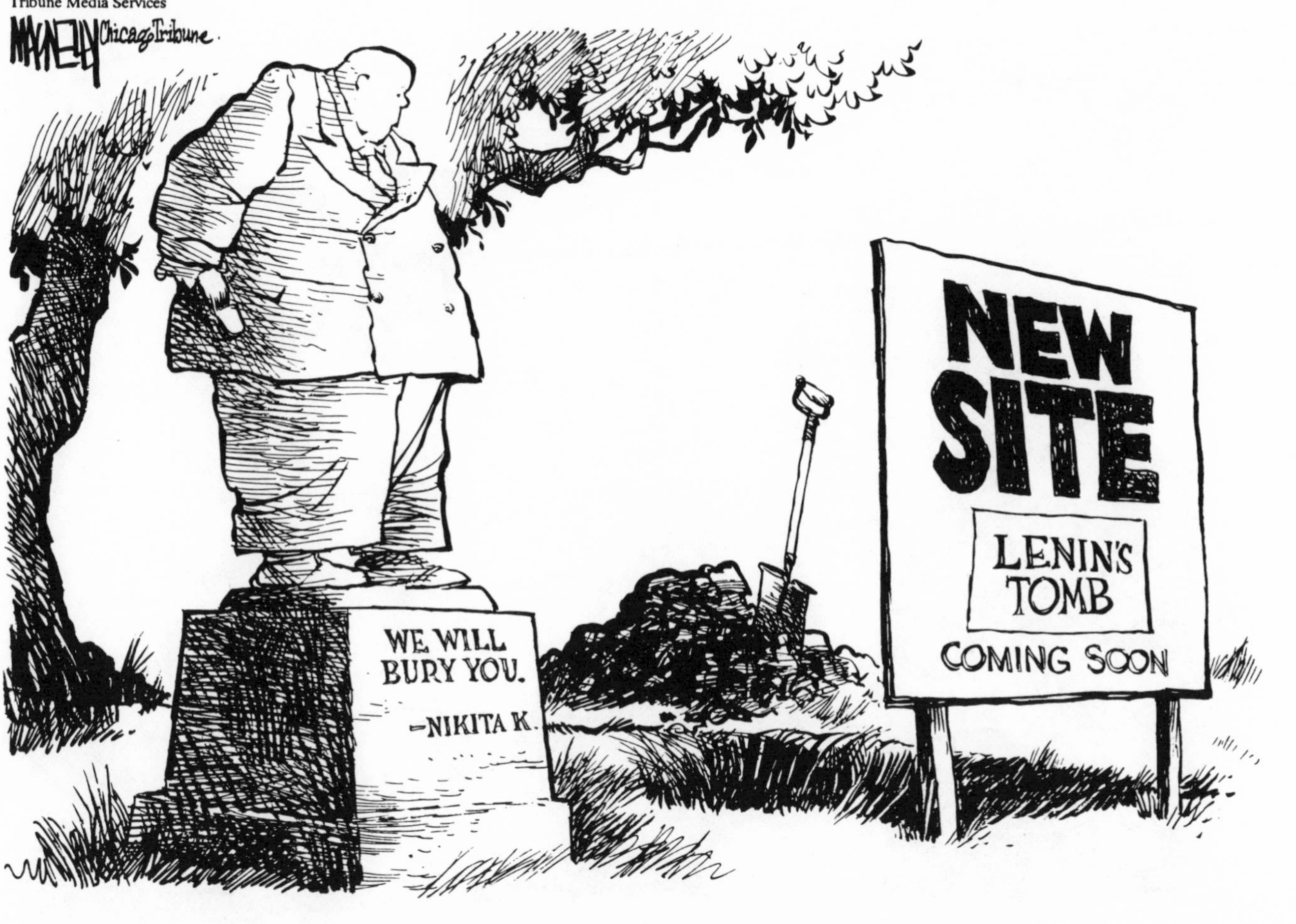
MACNELLY Chicago Tribune
WE WILL
BURY YOU.
–NIKITA K.
NEW
SITE
LENIN'S
TOMB
COMING SOON

REX BABIN
Courtesy Times Union (N.Y.)

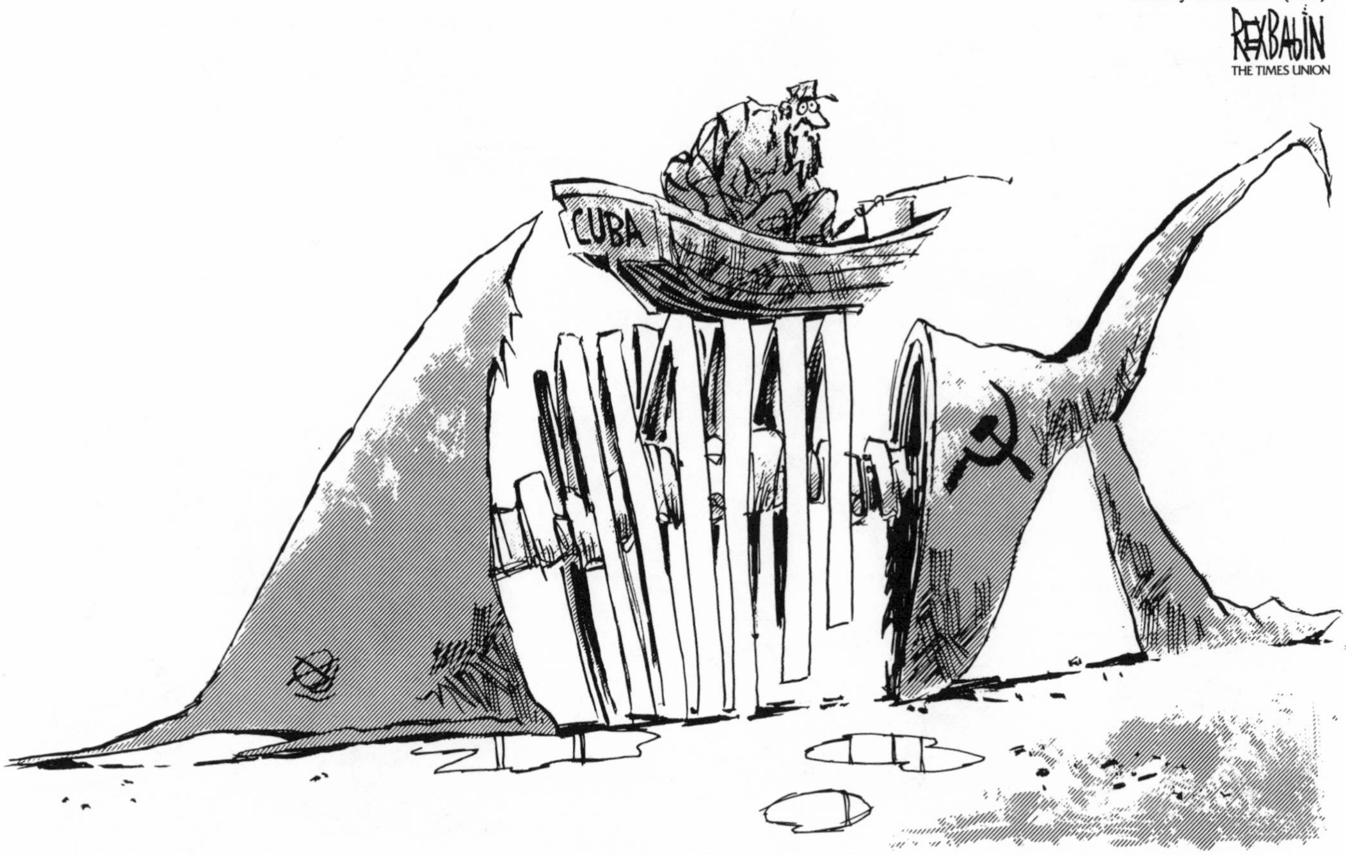
REXBABIN
THE TIMES UNION
CUBA

THE OLD MAN AND THE SEA

PAT BAGLEY
Courtesy Salt Lake Tribune

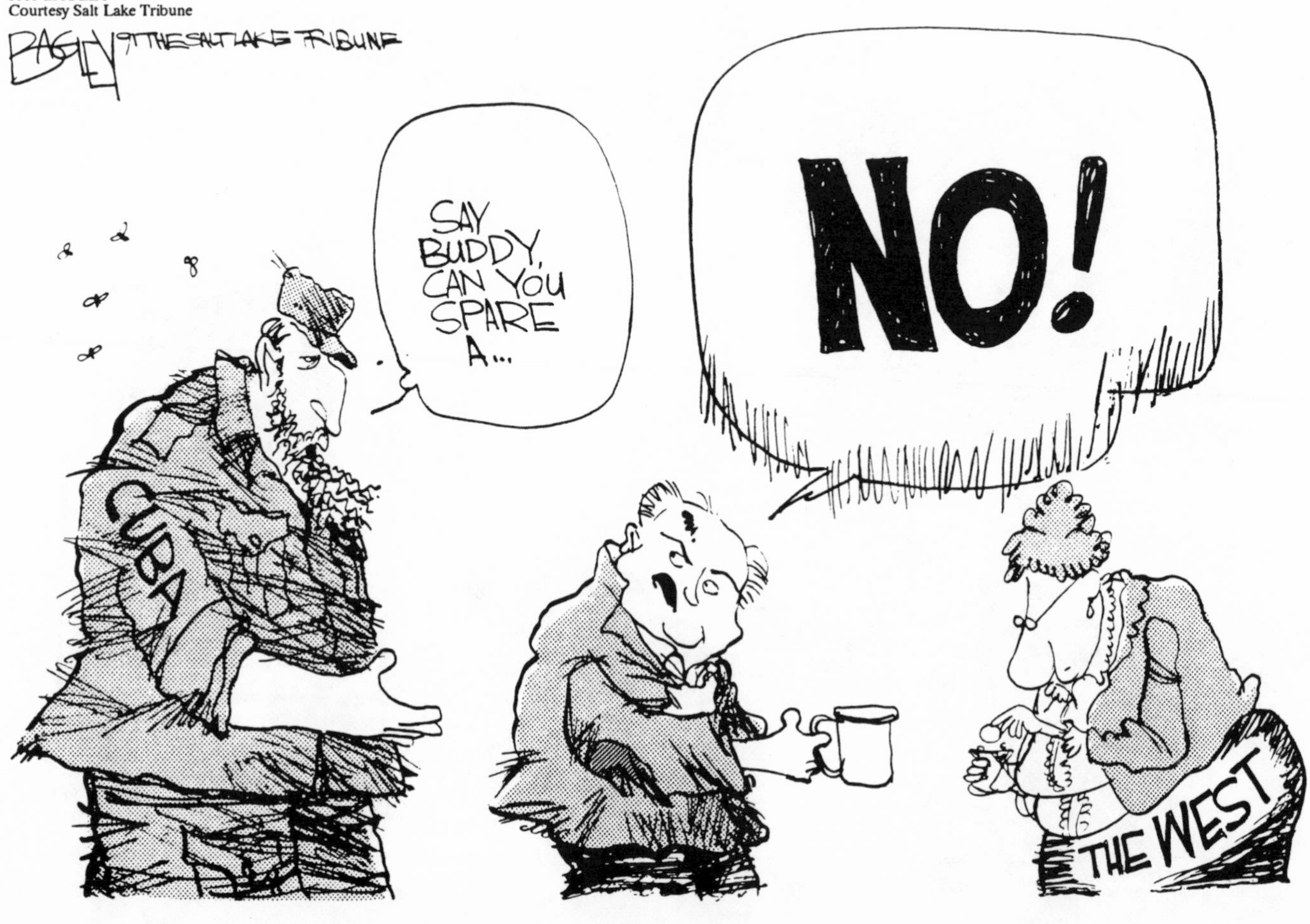
BAGLEY '91 THE SALT LAKE TRIBUNE
SAY BUDDY, CAN YOU SPARE A...
NO!
CUBA
THE WEST

VIC HARVILLE
Courtesy Arkansas Democrat-Gazette

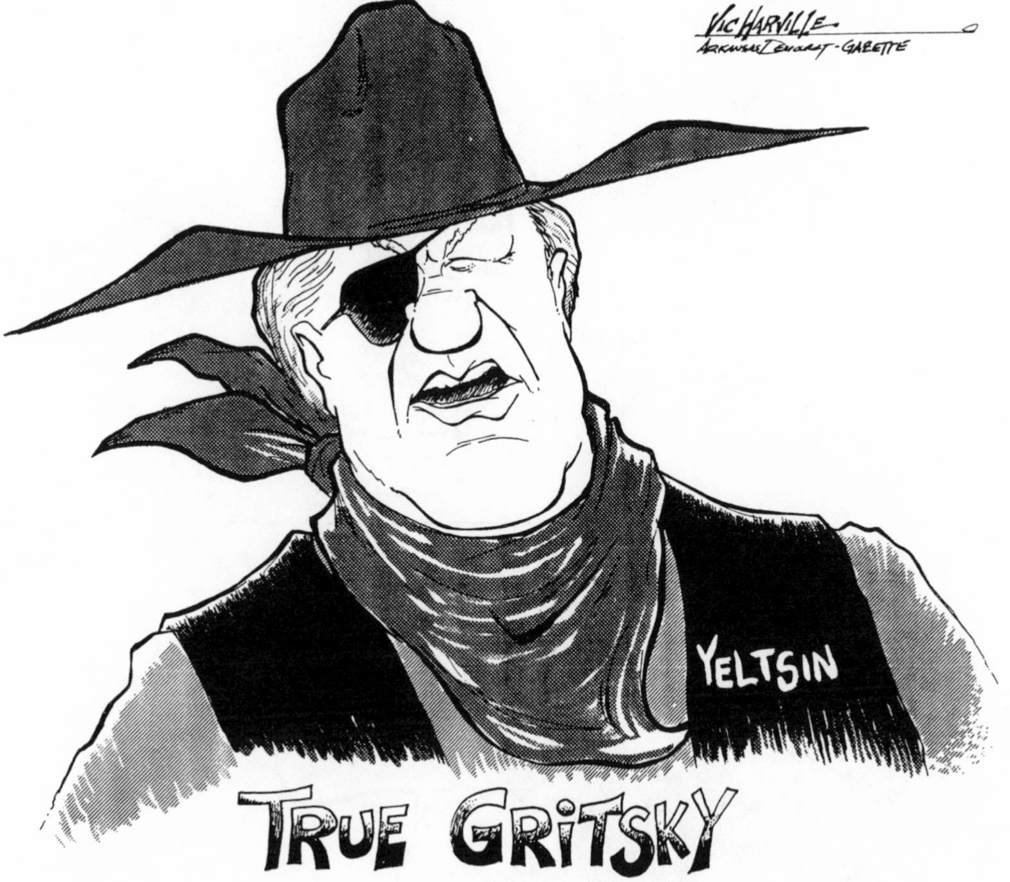
VIC HARVILLE
YELTSIN
TRUE GRITSKY

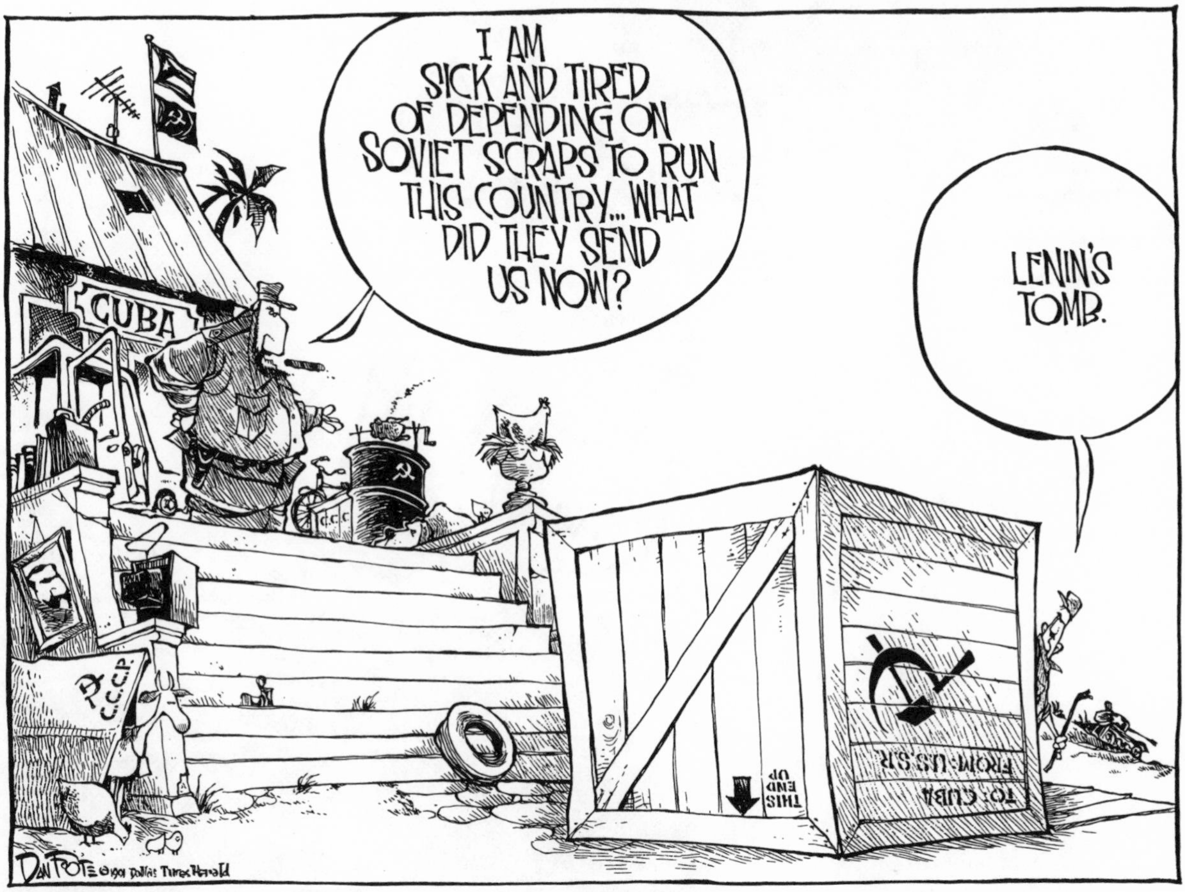
CUBA
I AM SICK AND TIRED OF DEPENDING ON SOVIET SCRAPS TO RUN THIS COUNTRY... WHAT DID THEY SEND US NOW?
LENIN'S TOMB.
C.C.C.P.
THIS END UP
TO: CUBA FROM: U.S.S.R
DAN FOOTE

DAN FOOTE
Courtesy Dallas Times Herald

HUP'HO! HUP'HO! HUP...
CUBA
SOVIETS
ASAY © COLORADO SPRINGS GAZETTE TELEGRAPH

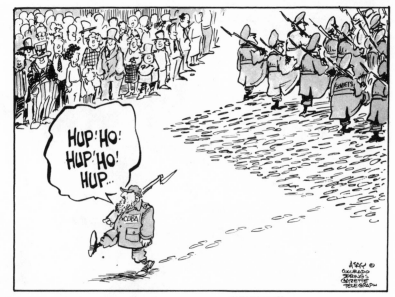

CHUCK ASAY
Courtesy Colorado Springs Gazette Telegraph

QUICKLY, FIDEL!! YOU MUST MAKE YOUR GETAWAY! THE REPO MAN IS COMING!..
CUBA MARXISM
WELLS '91 THE AUGUSTA CHRONICLE

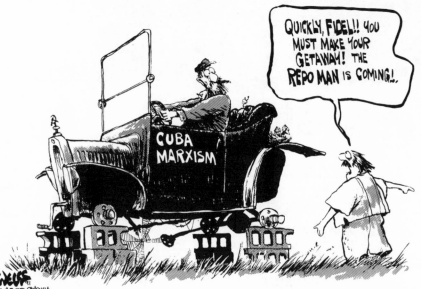

CLYDE WELLS
Courtesy Augusta Chronicle

JOHN TREVER
Courtesy Albuquerque Journal

TREVER ALBUQUERQUE JOURNAL ©1991
TAKE HER DOWN, MR. GORBACHEV!
CUBA
SOVIET AID

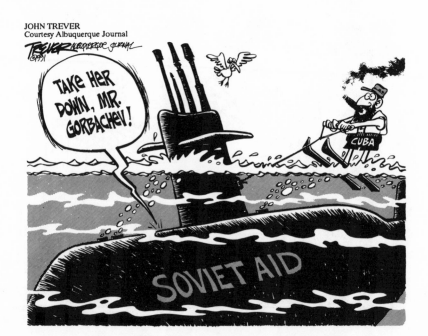

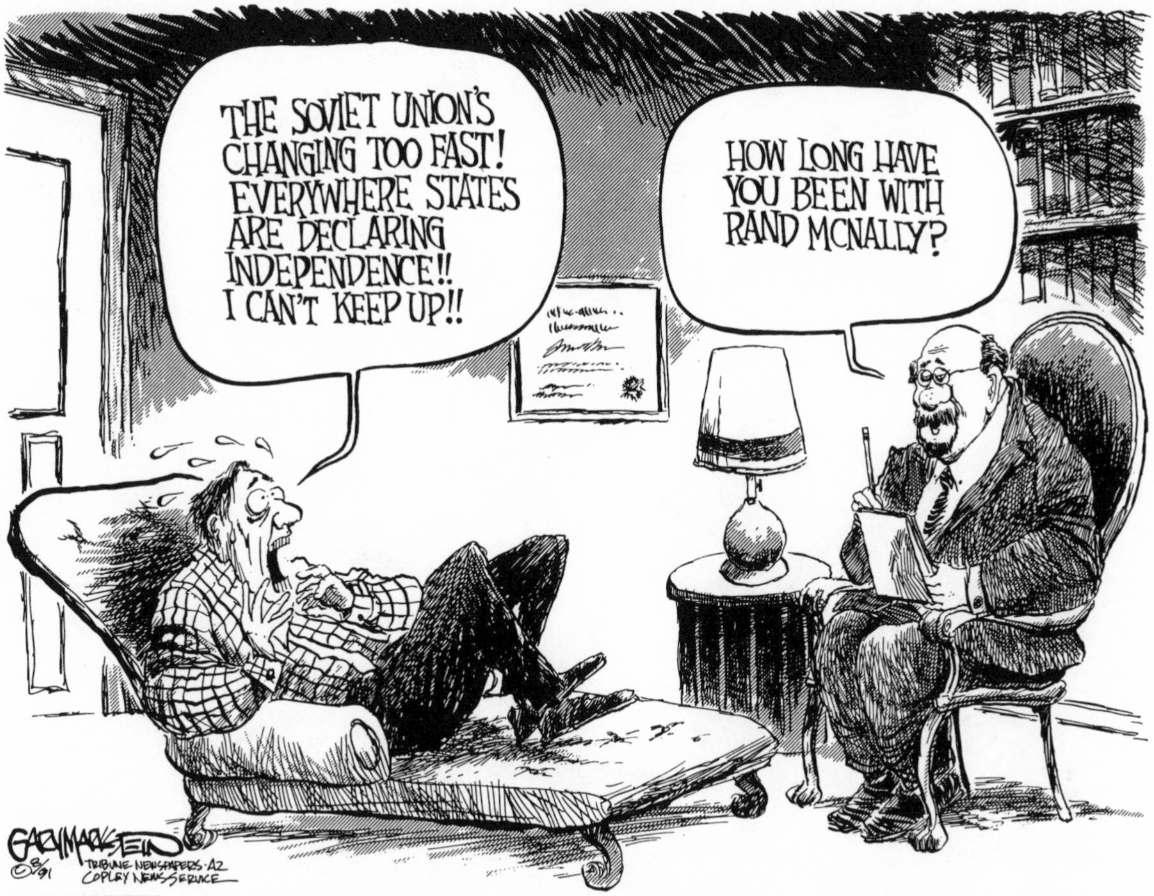
THE SOVIET UNION'S CHANGING TOO FAST! EVERYWHERE STATES ARE DECLARING INDEPENDENCE!! I CAN'T KEEP UP!!
HOW LONG HAVE YOU BEEN WITH RAND MCNALLY?
GARYMARKSTEIN
©8/91
TRIBUNE NEWSPAPERS-AZ
COPLEY NEWS SERVICE

GARY MARKSTEIN
Courtesy Tribune Newspapers

ED STEIN
Courtesy Rocky Mountain News and NEA

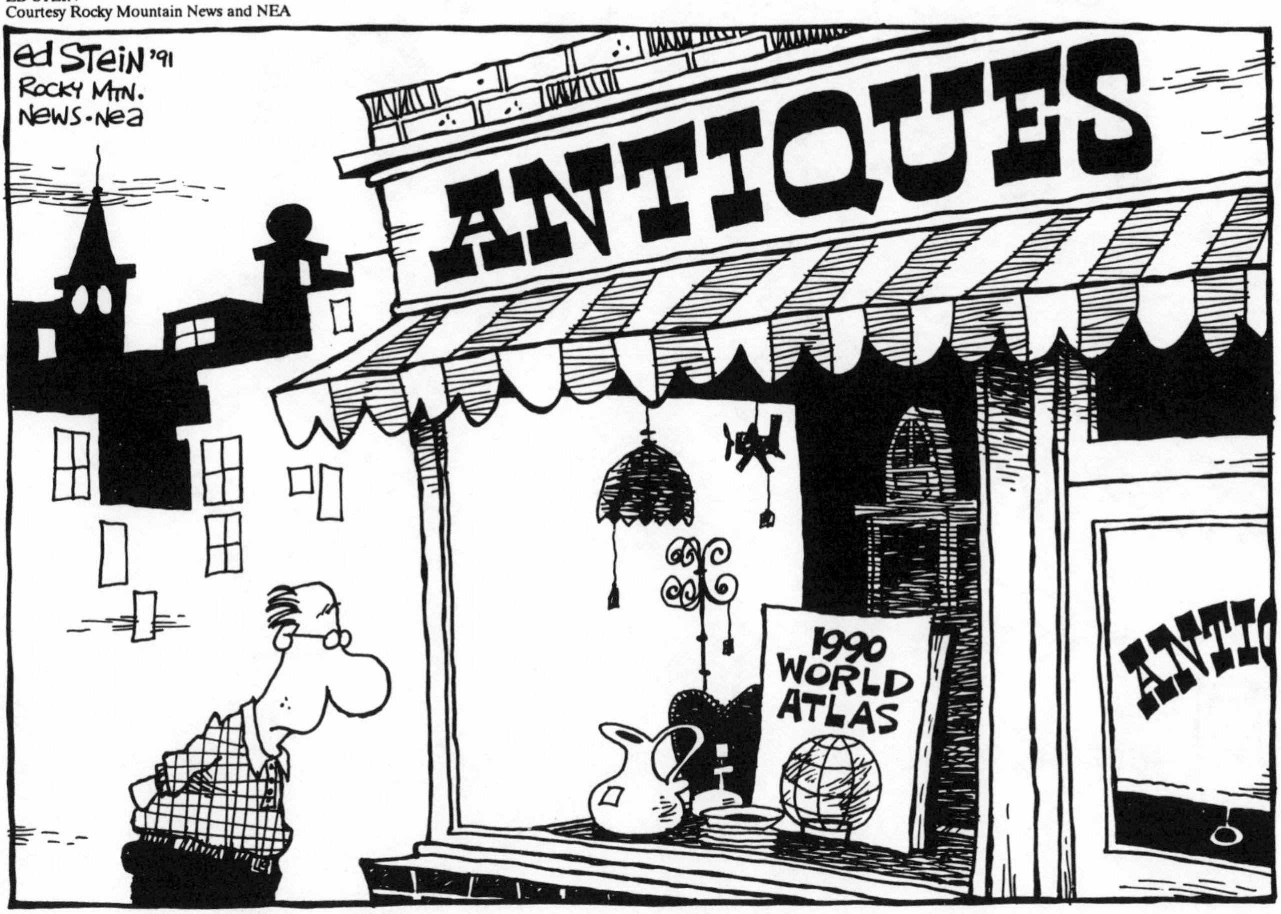
ed STeiN '91
ROCKY MTN.
NEWS-NEA
ANTIQUES
1990 WORLD ATLAS

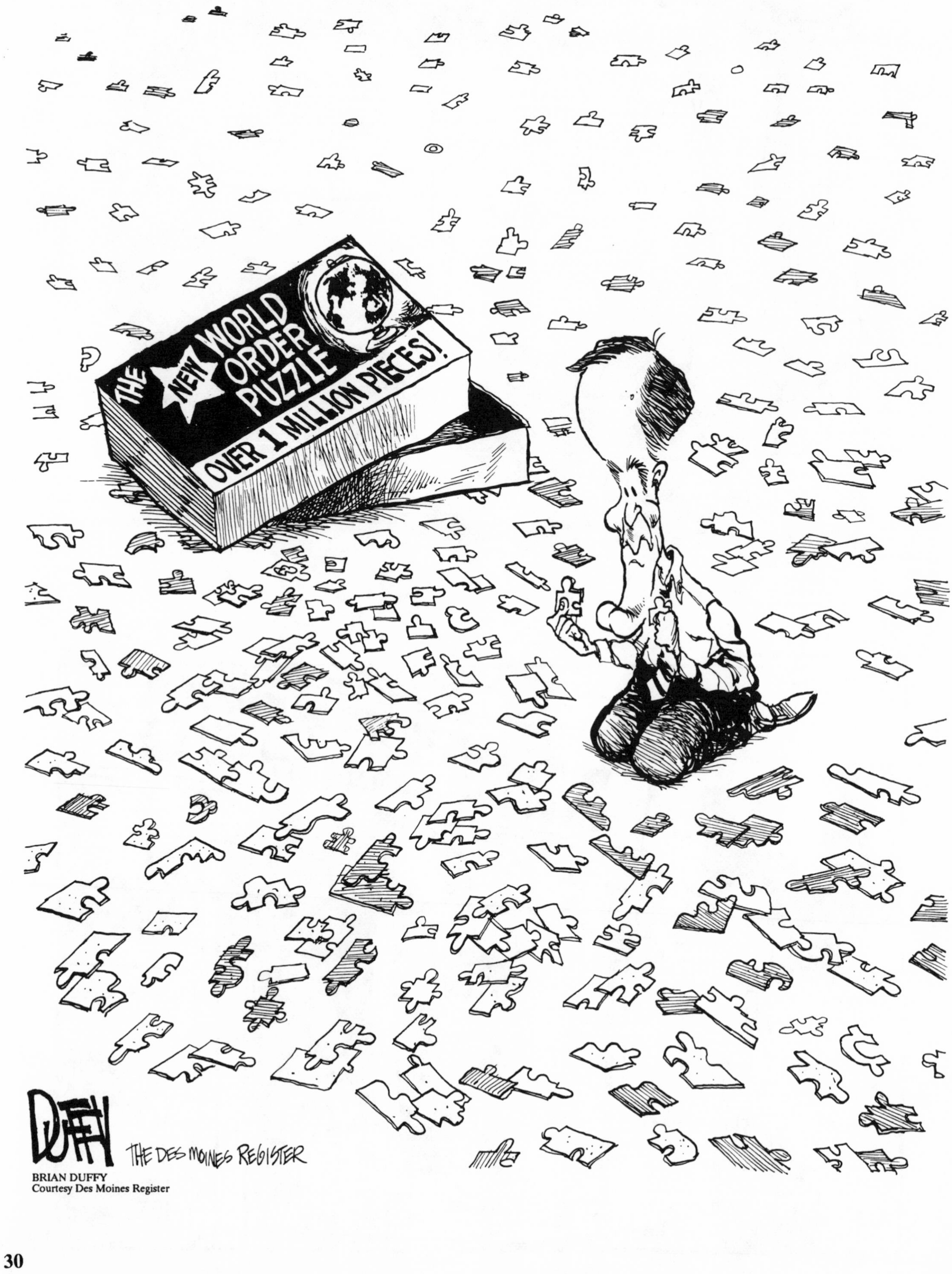
THE NEW WORLD ORDER PUZZLE
OVER 1 MILLION PIECES!
DUFFY
THE DES MOINES REGISTER

BRIAN DUFFY
Courtesy Des Moines Register

The Bush Administration

President George Bush began 1991 riding tall in the saddle. American and allied warplanes had pulverized Iraqi strongman Saddam Hussein's war machine in Kuwait, and then the soldiers of Desert Storm under Gen. Norman Schwarzkopf swiftly decimated the remainder of the Iraqi invaders. Allied casualties were remarkably light, and America welcomed the troops home with parades and jubilation. Bush's approval rating topped 90 percent, and he looked unbeatable in 1992.

But it soon became apparent that the new world order the president envisioned was not taking shape at all. It was discovered that Saddam still retained hidden nuclear materials, and the tyrant seemed as firmly entrenched as ever. And the recession deepened, despite Bush's rosy predictions, with workers being laid off by the tens of thousands. And then there was John Sununu, the White House chief of staff, whose flagrant unauthorized use of government aircraft for personal business infuriated the country. Sununu became such a liability that Bush finally fired him.

The net result was a growing domestic crisis that millions of voters felt was being ignored. Year-end polls showed that 60 percent of Americans disapproved of Bush's handling–or mishandling–of the economy. That seemed to pave the way for a spirited presidential campaign in 1992.

ED FISCHER
Courtesy Rochester Post-Bulletin

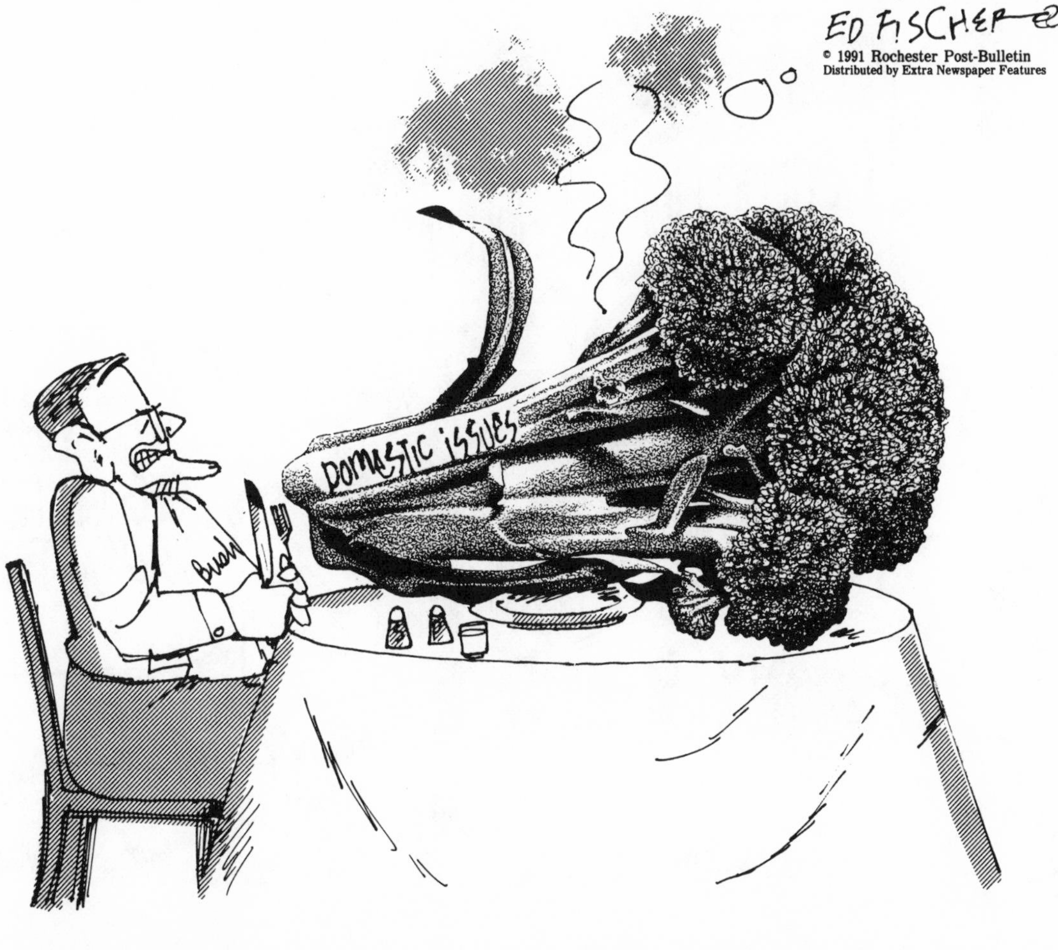
ED FISCHER
© 1991 Rochester Post-Bulletin
Distributed by Extra Newspaper Features
DOMESTIC ISSUES
Bush

JIM MORIN
Courtesy Miami Herald

MORIN
The Miami Herald
CHINA? I LOOK AT THE BIG PICTURE!!
$ TRADE
MOST FAVORED NATION STATUS
TIBET
TIANANMEN
FREEDOM

ROBERT ARIAIL
Courtesy The State (S.C.)

ARIAIL ©1991 THE STATE
RE-ELECT
George Herbert Hoover Bush
PRESI
THAT'S WALKER! GEORGE HERBERT WALKER BUSH!!
ECONOMY
SIGN CO.

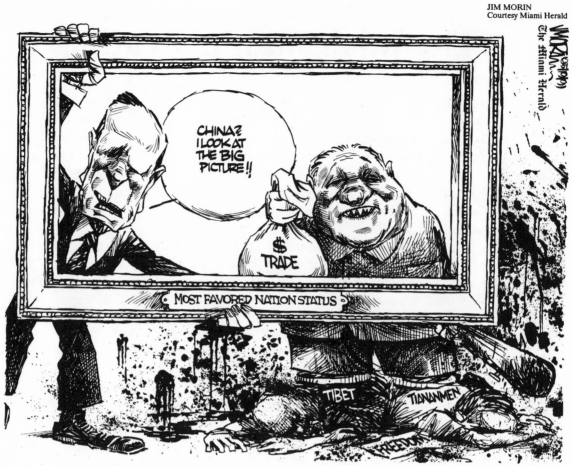

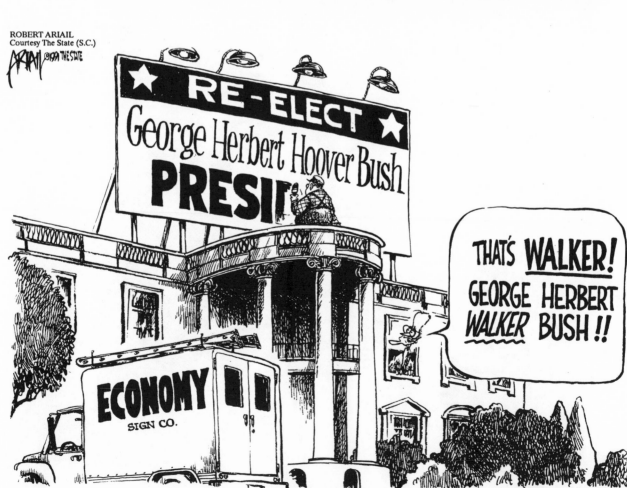

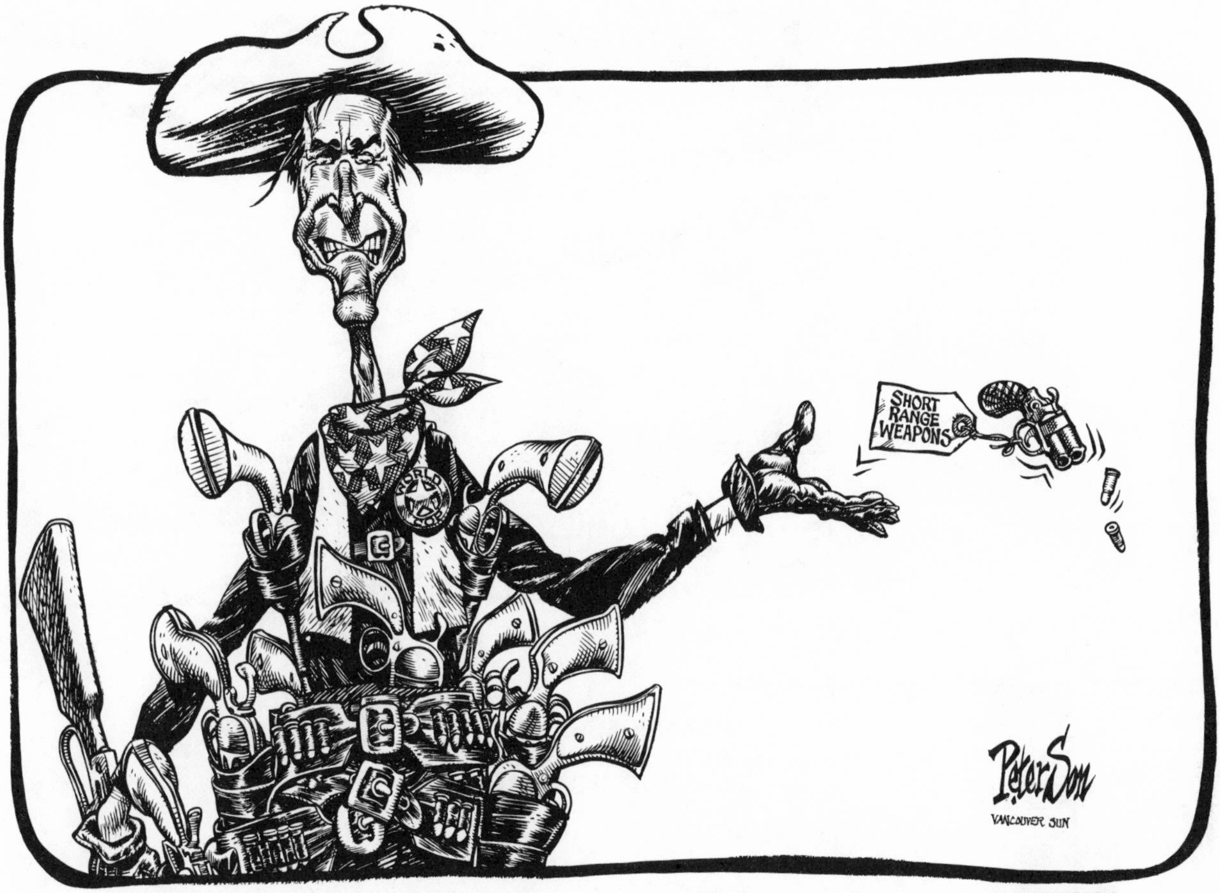
SHORT RANGE WEAPONS
PETERSON
VANCOUVER SUN

ROY PETERSON
Courtesy Vancouver Sun

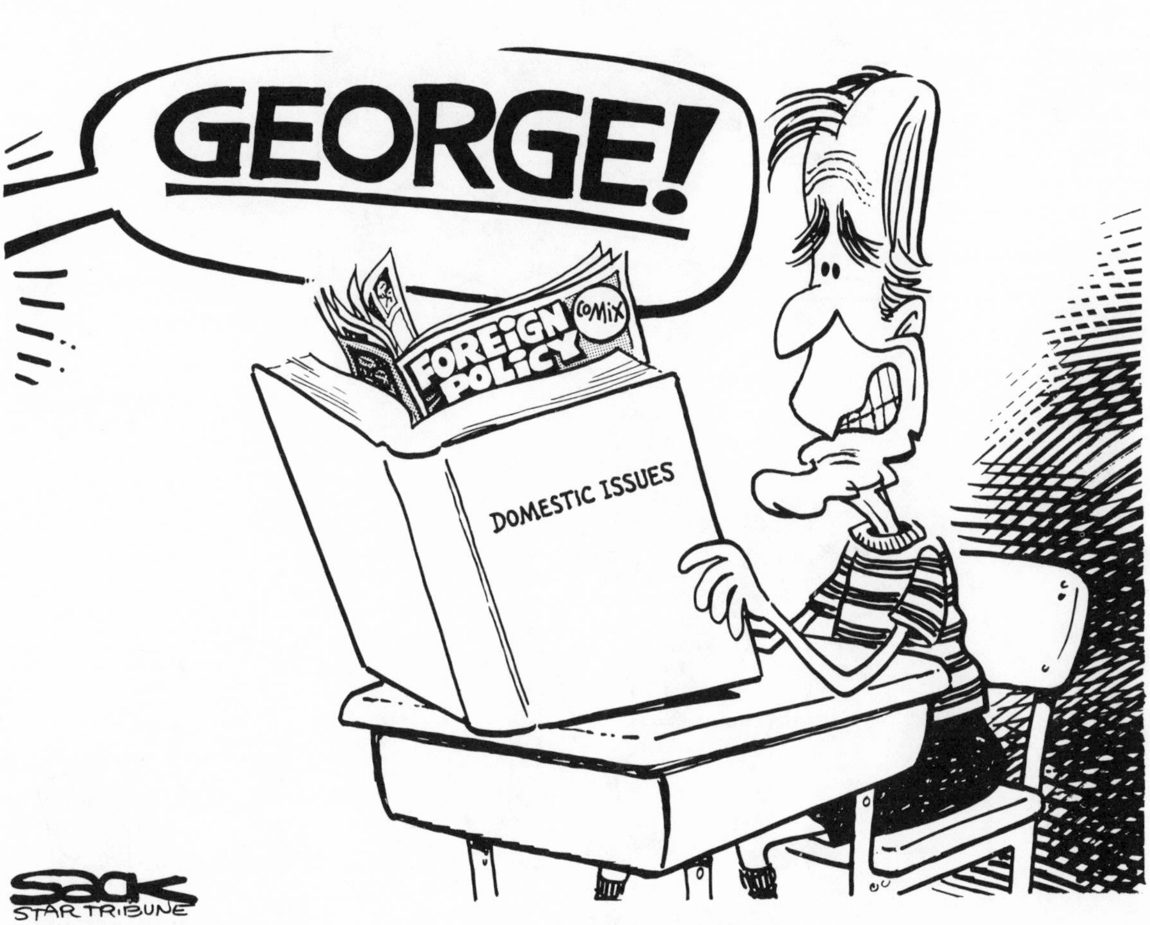
GEORGE!
FOREIGN POLICY
COMIX
DOMESTIC ISSUES
SACK
STAR TRIBUNE

STEVE SACK
Courtesy Minneapolis Star Tribune

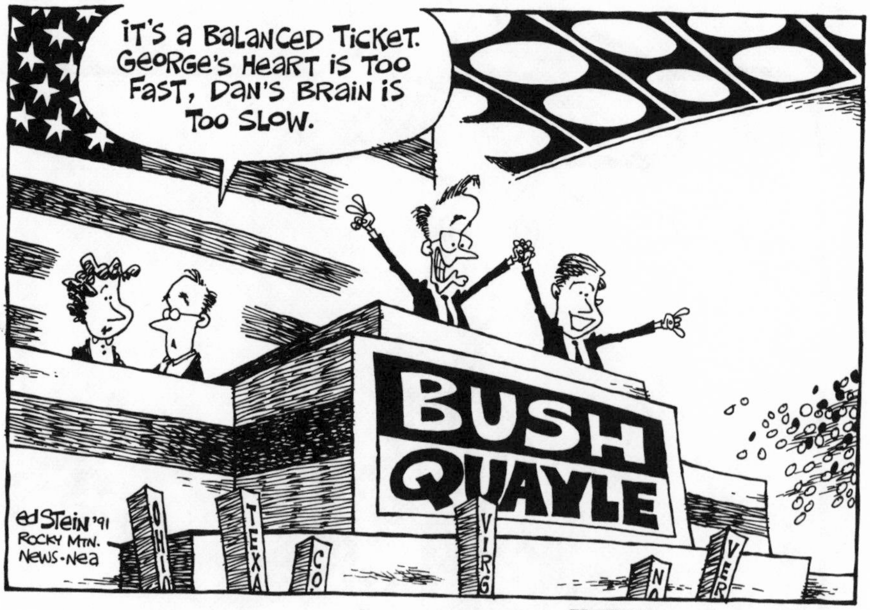
IT'S a BaLanCeD TicKeT. GeoRGe'S HeaRT iS Too FaST, DaN'S BRaiN iS Too SLOW.
BUSH QUAYLE
ed STein '91 ROCKY MTN. NEWS-NEA

ED STEIN
Courtesy Rocky Mountain News and NEA

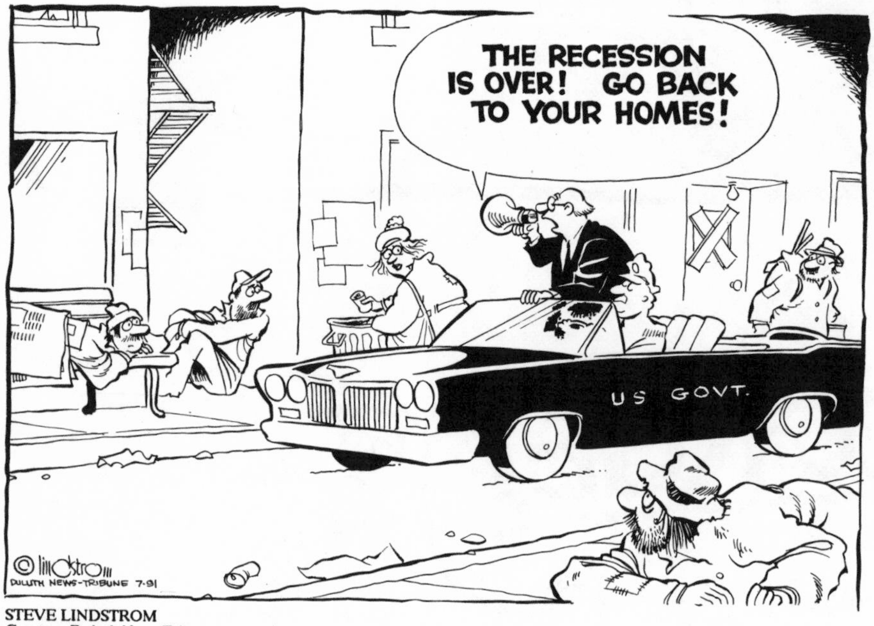
THE RECESSION IS OVER! GO BACK TO YOUR HOMES!
US GOVT.

STEVE LINDSTROM
Courtesy Duluth News-Tribune

RANDY WICKS
Courtesy Valencia Signal (Calif.)

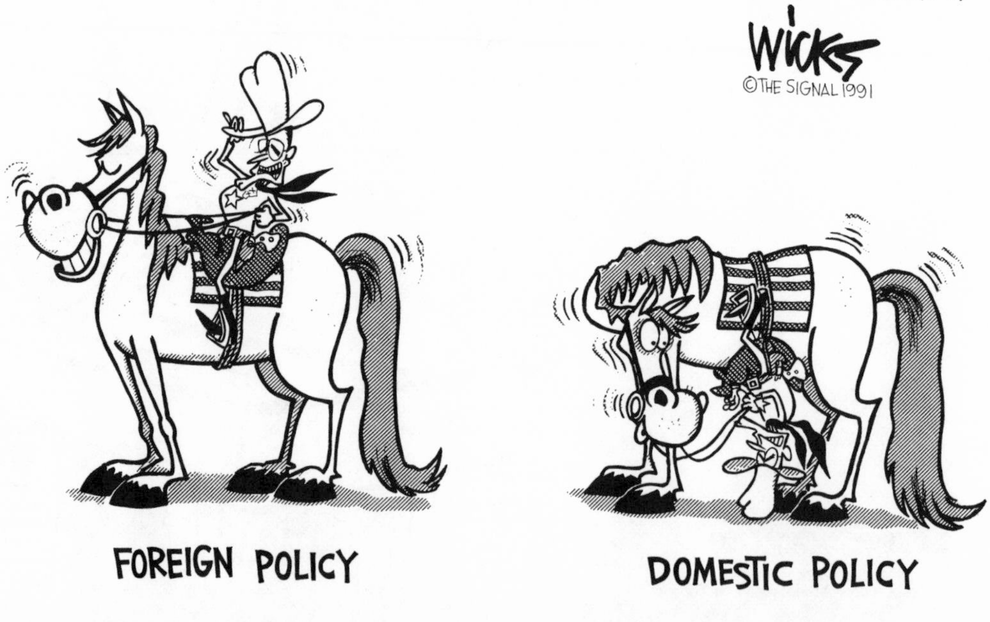
WICKS
©THE SIGNAL 1991
FOREIGN POLICY
DOMESTIC POLICY

JERRY HOLBERT
Courtesy Boston Herald

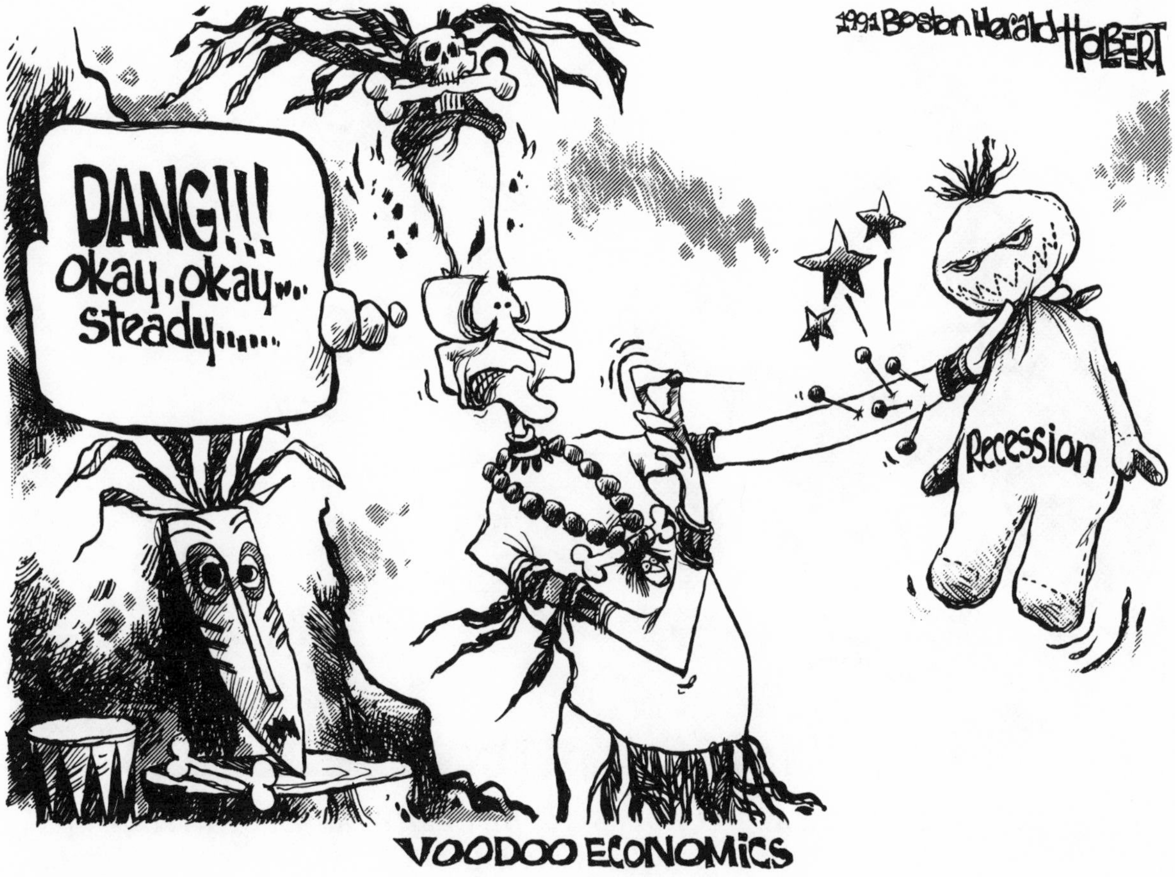
1991 Boston Herald HOLBERT
DANG!!! okay, okay... steady......
Recession
VOODOO ECONOMICS

JOHN TREVER
Courtesy Albuquerque Journal

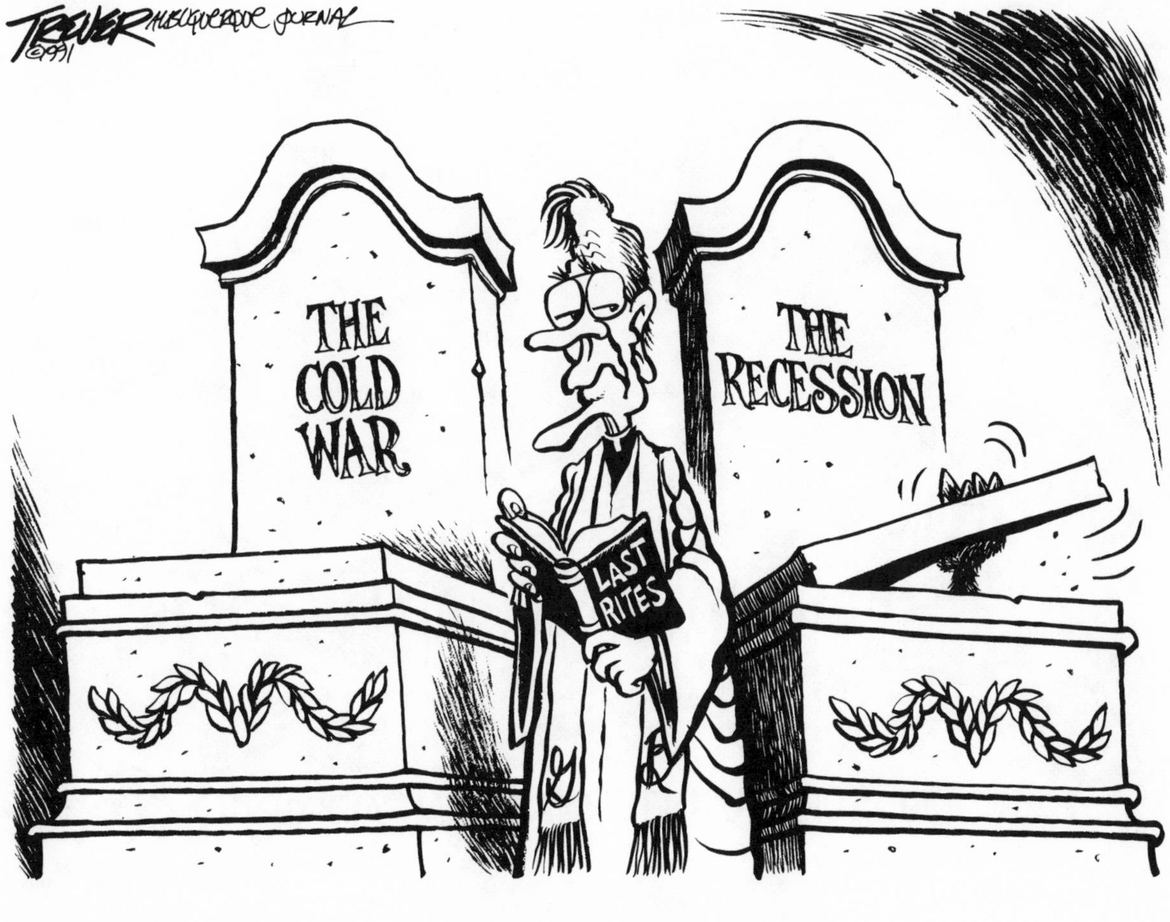
TREVER ALBUQUERQUE JOURNAL ©1991
THE COLD WAR
THE RECESSION
LAST RITES

CHARLES BISSELL
Courtesy The Tennessean

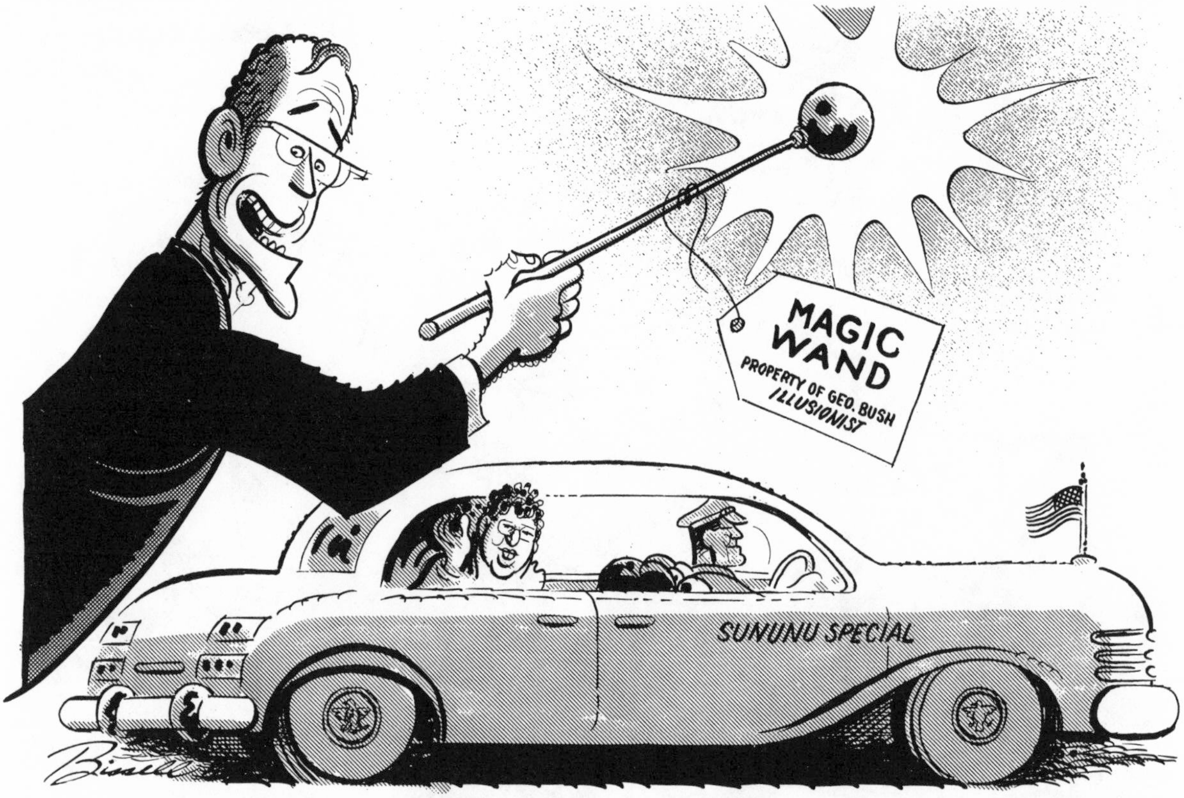
MAGIC WAND
PROPERTY OF GEO. BUSH ILLUSIONIST
SUNUNU SPECIAL
Bissell

"HE'S DOING A GREAT JOB, FOLKS . . . THE CUSHY TRANSPORTATION THING IS JUST AN APPEARANCE "

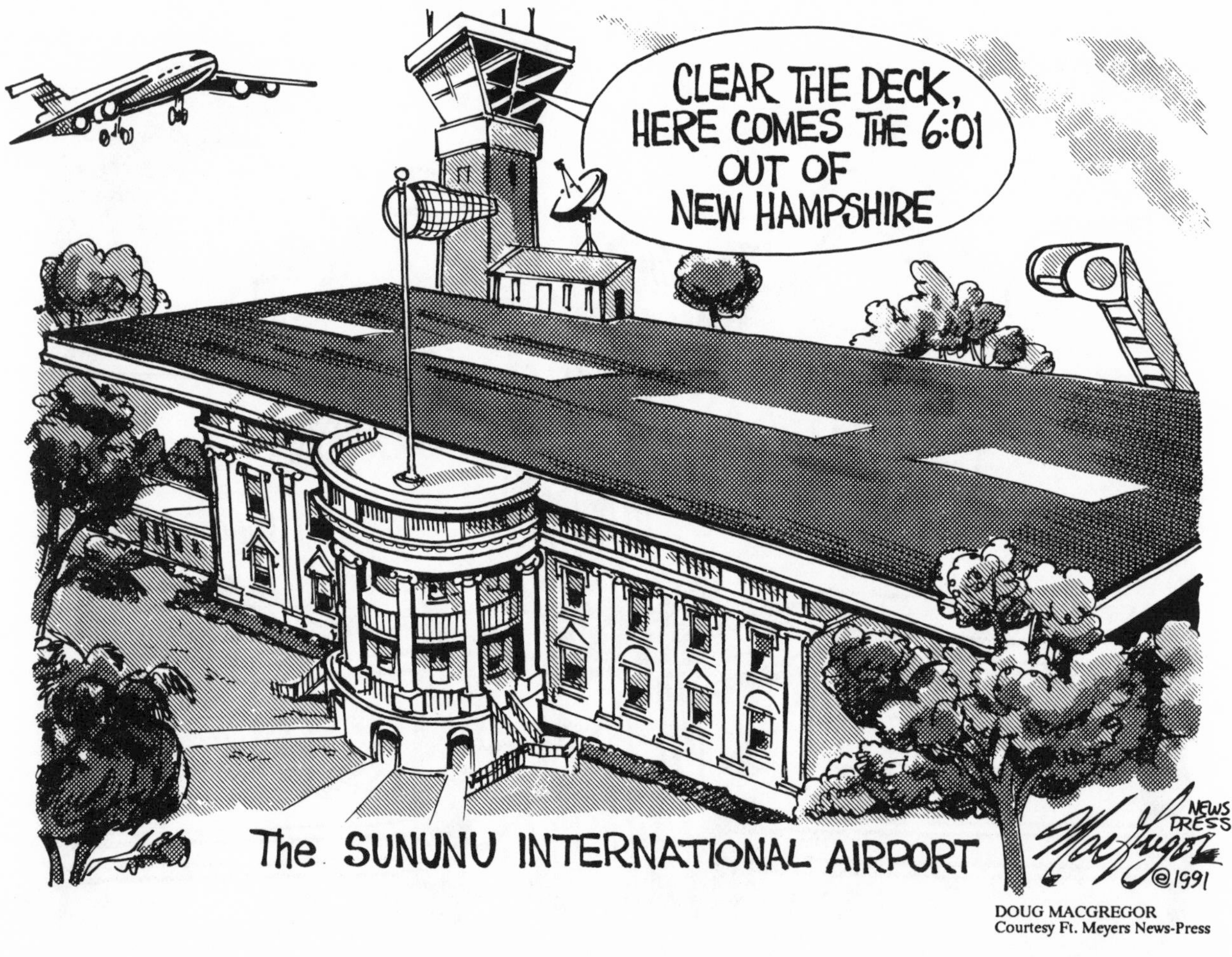
CLEAR THE DECK, HERE COMES THE 6:01 OUT OF NEW HAMPSHIRE
The SUNUNU INTERNATIONAL AIRPORT
NEWS-PRESS
MacGregor
©1991

DOUG MACGREGOR
Courtesy Ft. Meyers News-Press

JOHN DEERING
Courtesy Arkansas Democrat-Gazette

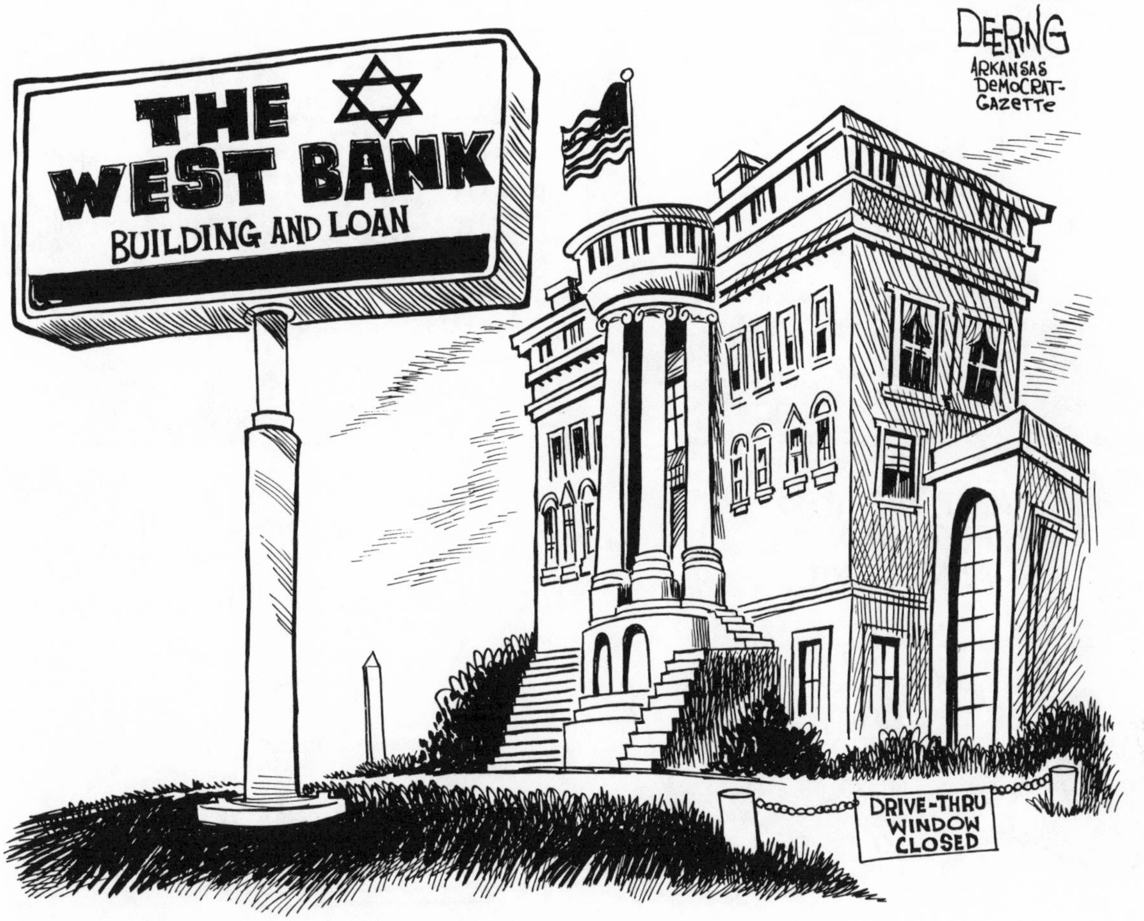
DEERING
ARKANSAS DEMOCRAT-GAZETTE
THE WEST BANK
BUILDING AND LOAN
DRIVE-THRU WINDOW CLOSED

STEVE KELLEY
Courtesy San Diego Union

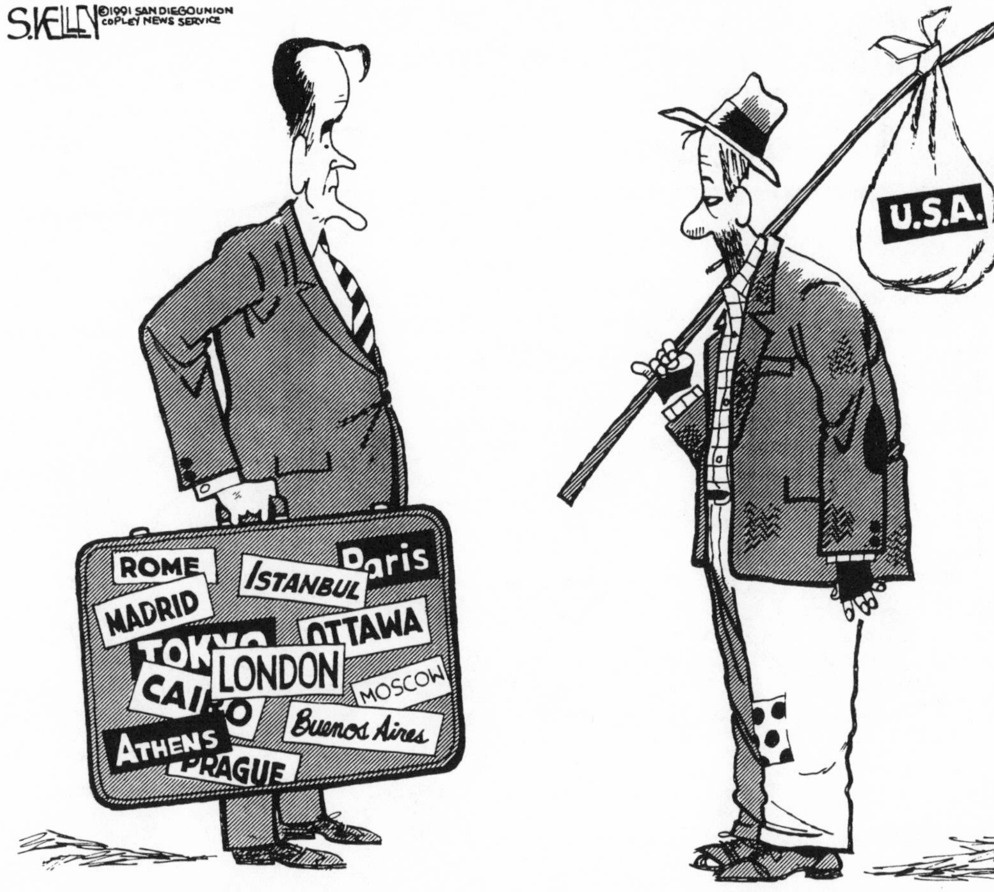
S.KELLEY ©1991 SAN DIEGO UNION COPLEY NEWS SERVICE
U.S.A.
ROME
ISTANBUL
Paris
MADRID
OTTAWA
LONDON
MOSCOW
Buenos Aires
ATHENS
PRAGUE

DANA SUMMERS
Courtesy Orlando Sentinel

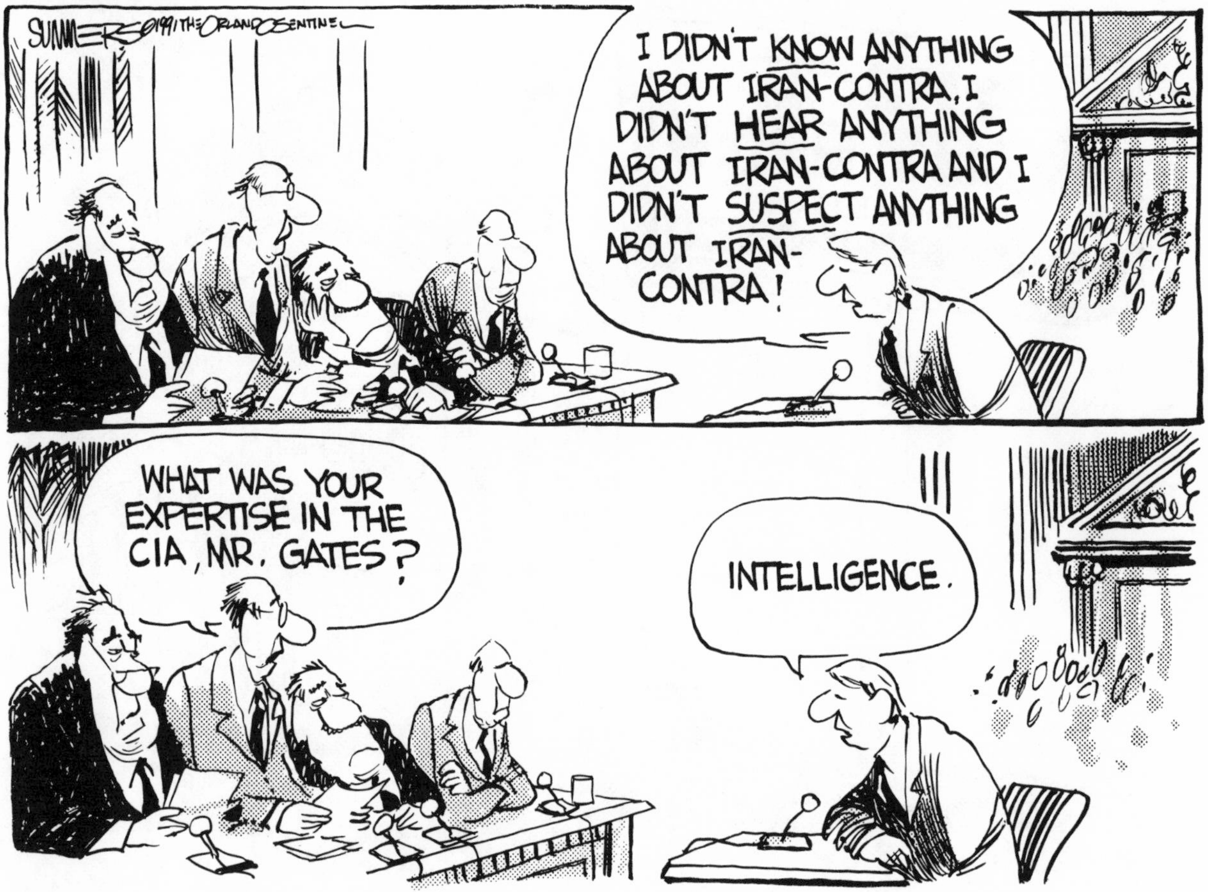
SUMMERS ©1991 THE ORLANDO SENTINEL
I DIDN'T KNOW ANYTHING ABOUT IRAN-CONTRA, I DIDN'T HEAR ANYTHING ABOUT IRAN-CONTRA AND I DIDN'T SUSPECT ANYTHING ABOUT IRAN-CONTRA!
WHAT WAS YOUR EXPERTISE IN THE CIA, MR. GATES?
INTELLIGENCE.

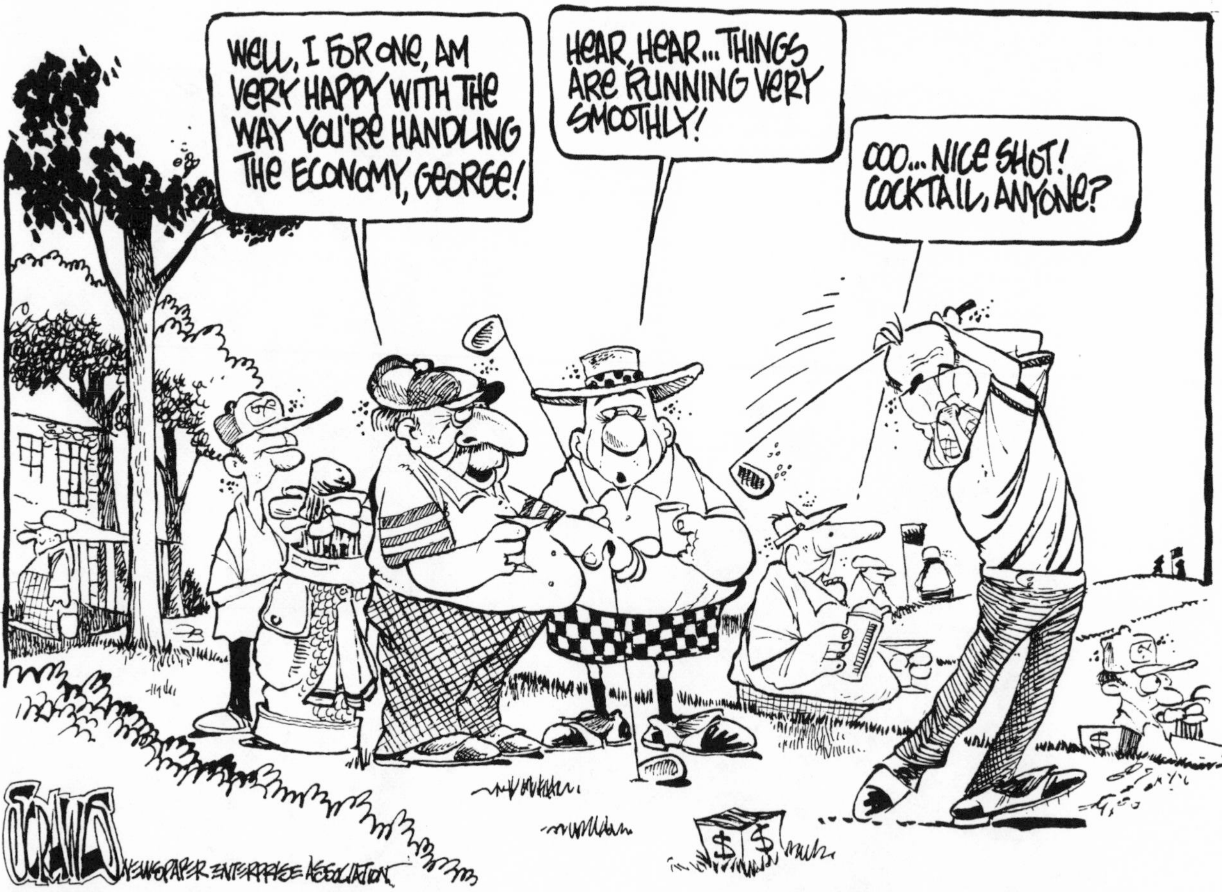
WELL, I FOR ONE, AM VERY HAPPY WITH THE WAY YOU'RE HANDLING THE ECONOMY, GEORGE!
HEAR, HEAR... THINGS ARE RUNNING VERY SMOOTHLY!
OOO... NICE SHOT! COCKTAIL, ANYONE?
RAWLS NEWSPAPER ENTERPRISE ASSOCIATION

S. C. RAWLS
Courtesy NEA

HY ROSEN
Courtesy Albany Times-Union

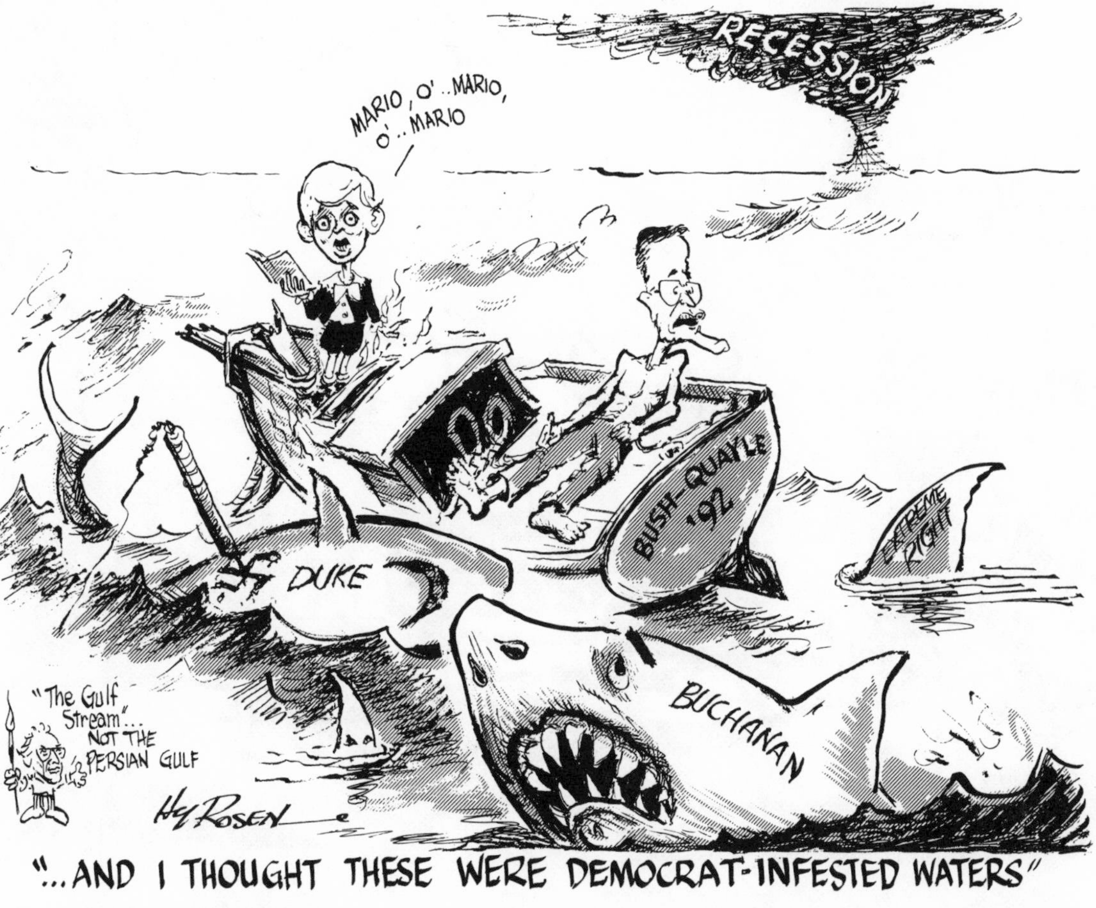
RECESSION
MARIO, O'..MARIO, O'..MARIO
BUSH-QUAYLE '92
EXTREME RIGHT
DUKE
BUCHANAN
"The Gulf Stream"... NOT THE PERSIAN GULF
HY ROSEN
"...AND I THOUGHT THESE WERE DEMOCRAT-INFESTED WATERS"

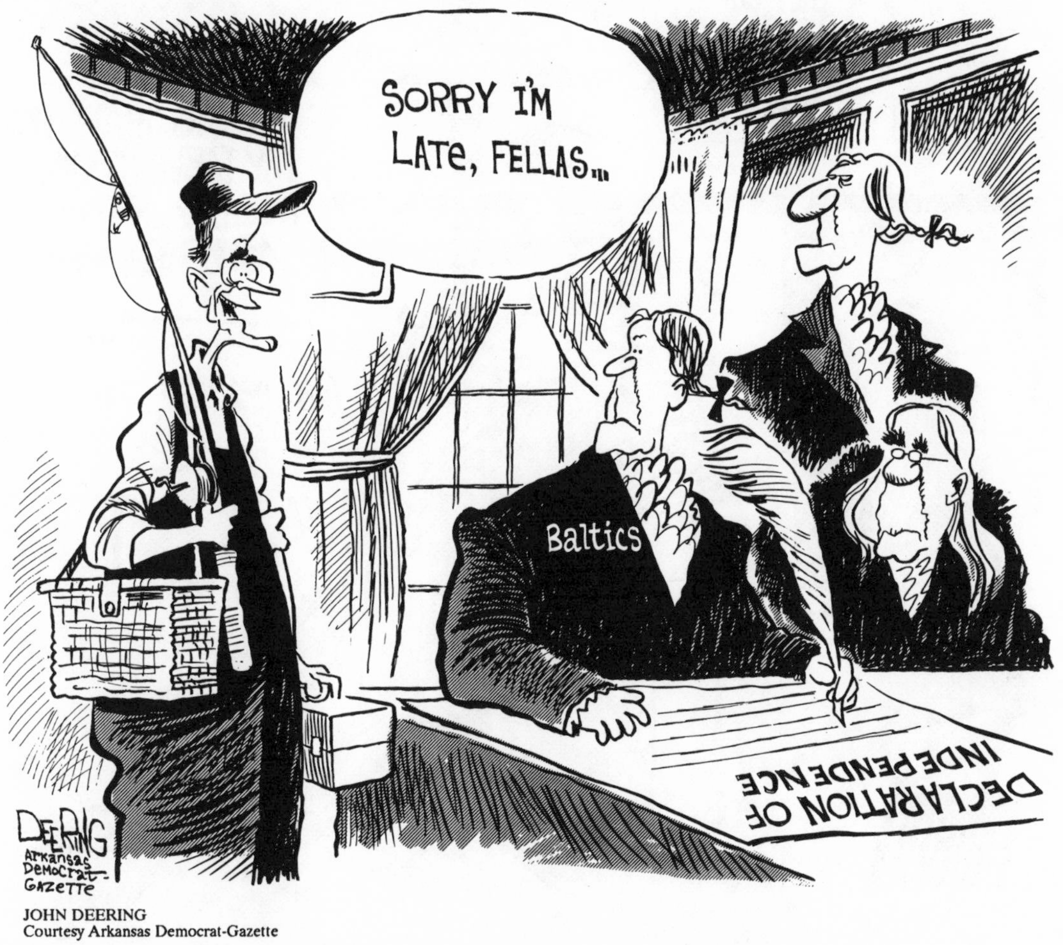
SORRY I'M LATE, FELLAS...
Baltics
DECLARATION OF INDEPENDENCE
DEERING Arkansas Democrat-Gazette

JOHN DEERING
Courtesy Arkansas Democrat-Gazette

JACK OHMAN
Courtesy Portland Oregonian

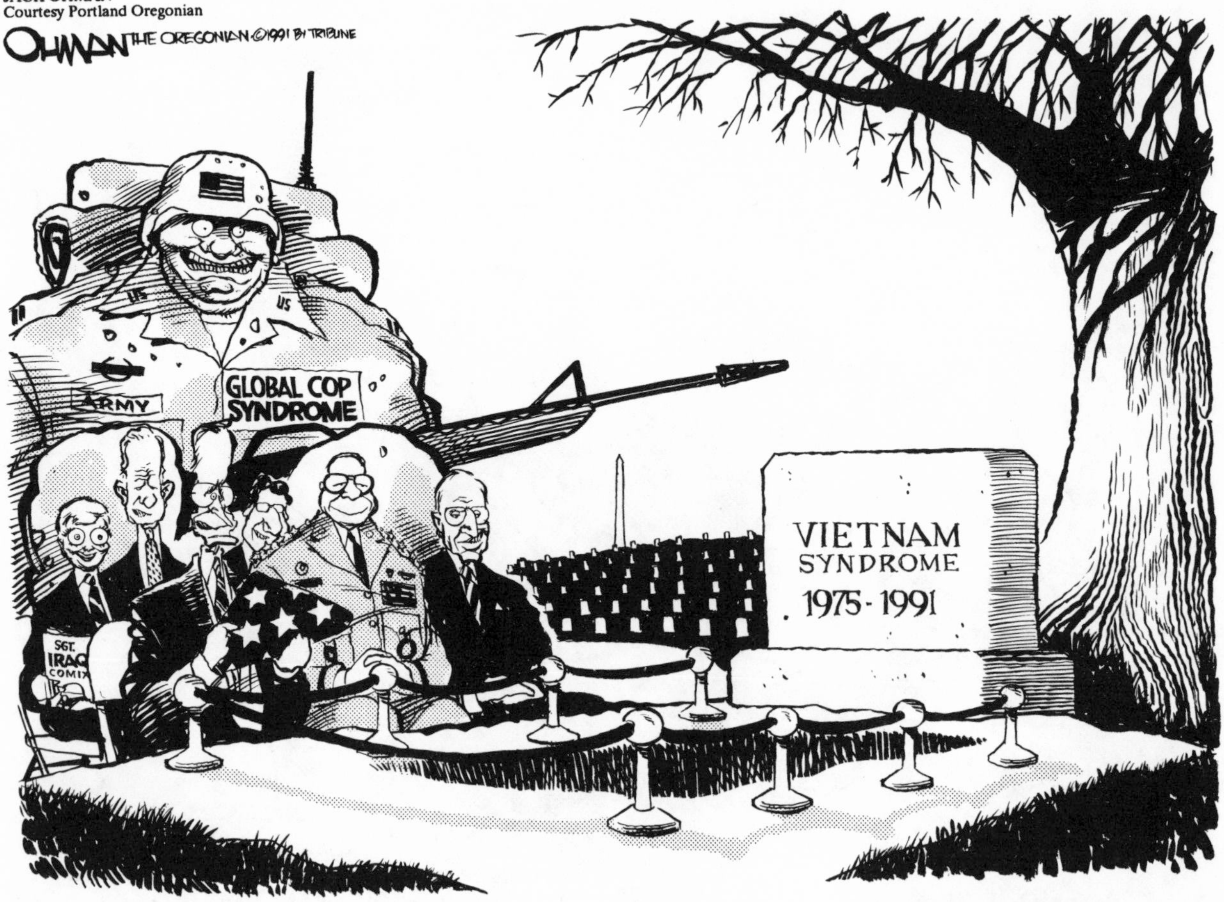
OHMAN THE OREGONIAN ©1991 BY TRIBUNE
US
US
ARMY
GLOBAL COP SYNDROME
SGT. IRAQ COMIX
VIETNAM SYNDROME 1975 - 1991

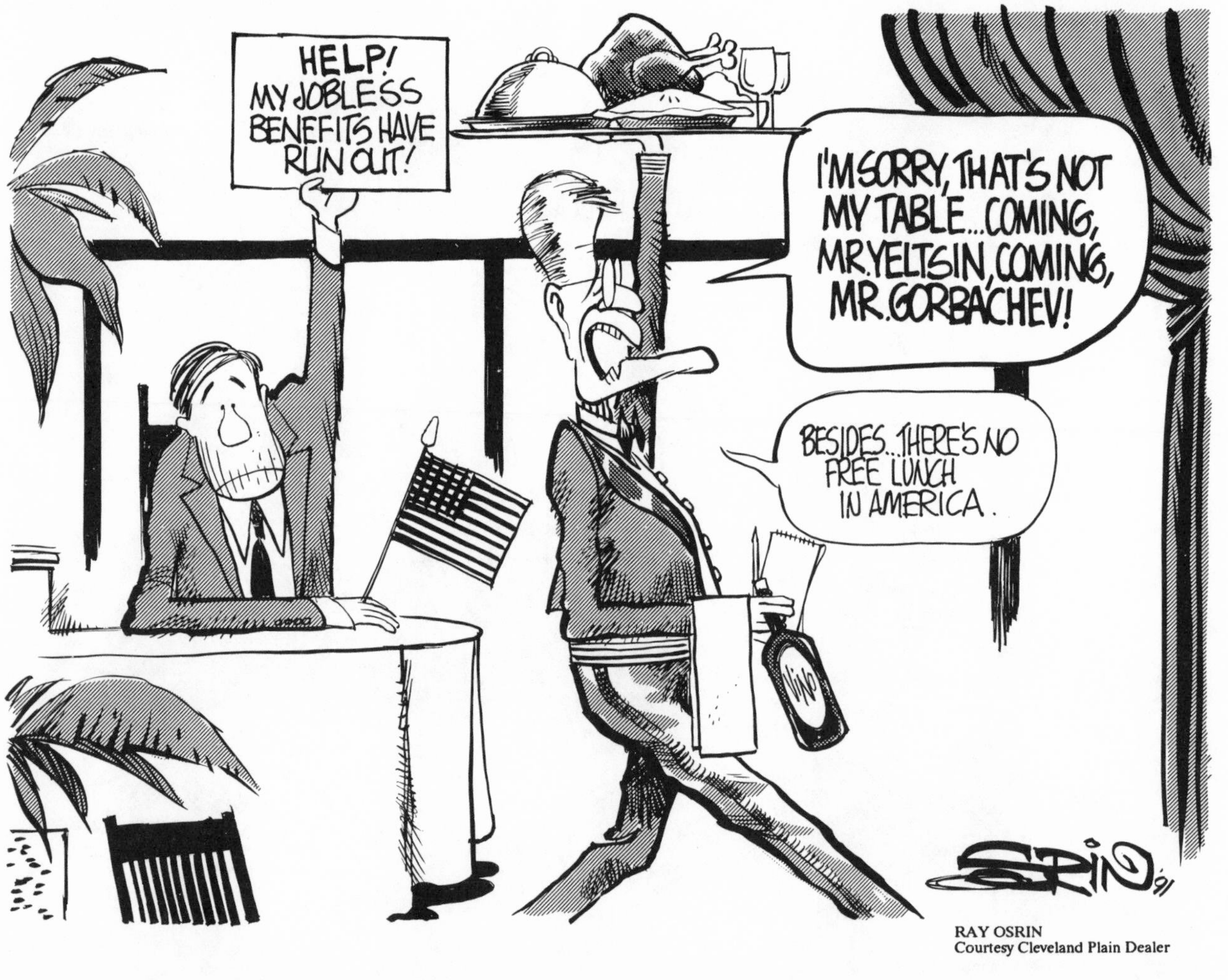
HELP! MY JOBLESS BENEFITS HAVE RUN OUT!
I'M SORRY, THAT'S NOT MY TABLE...COMING, MR. YELTSIN, COMING, MR. GORBACHEV!
BESIDES...THERE'S NO FREE LUNCH IN AMERICA.
VINO
OSRIN '91

RAY OSRIN
Courtesy Cleveland Plain Dealer

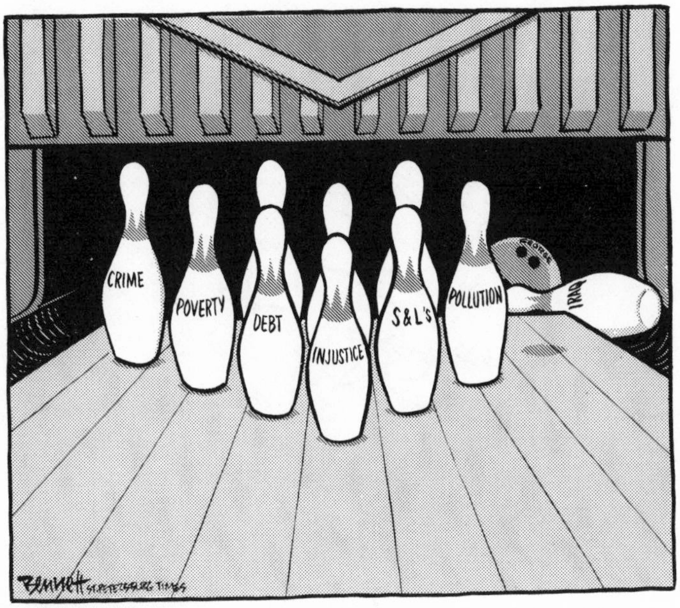
CRIME
POVERTY
DEBT
INJUSTICE
S&L's
POLLUTION
IRAQ
BENNETT ST. PETERSBURG TIMES

CLAY BENNETT
Courtesy St. Petersburg Times

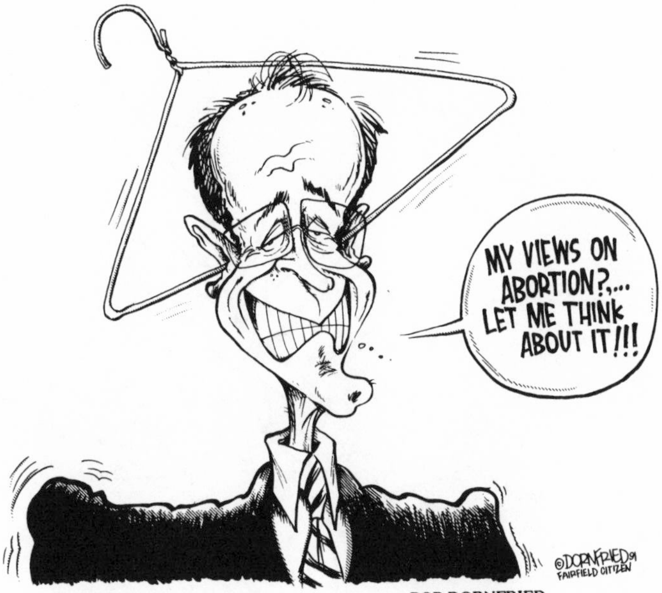
MY VIEWS ON ABORTION?,... LET ME THINK ABOUT IT!!!
©DORNFRIED 91 FAIRFIELD CITIZEN

BOB DORNFRIED
Courtesy Fairfield Citizen (Conn.)

BRUCE PLANTE
Courtesy Chattanooga Times and
Extra Newspapers Features

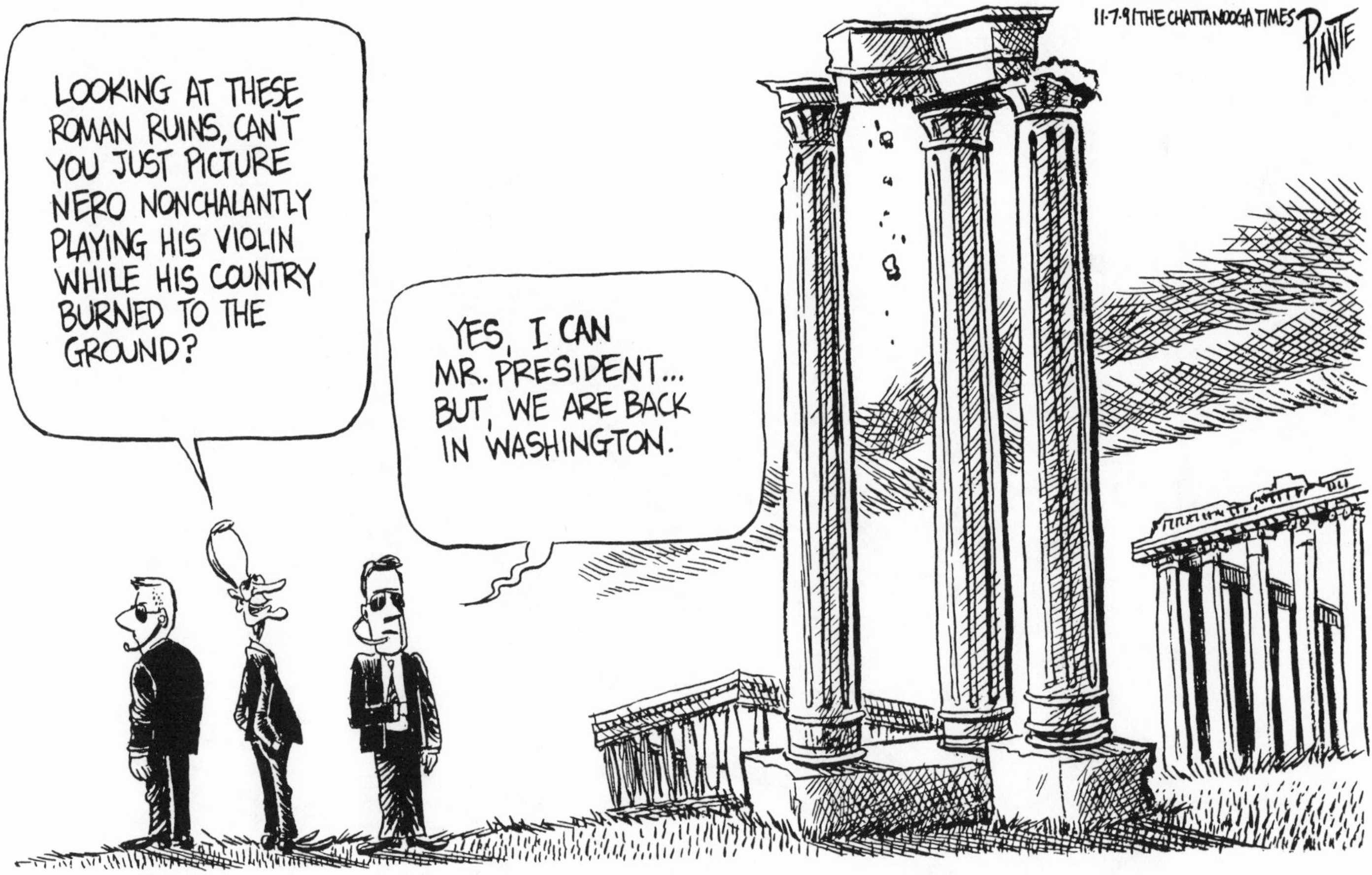
11-7-91 THE CHATTANOOGA TIMES PLANTE
LOOKING AT THESE ROMAN RUINS, CAN'T YOU JUST PICTURE NERO NONCHALANTLY PLAYING HIS VIOLIN WHILE HIS COUNTRY BURNED TO THE GROUND?
YES, I CAN MR. PRESIDENT... BUT, WE ARE BACK IN WASHINGTON.

V. CULLUM ROGERS
Courtesy Spectator Magazine

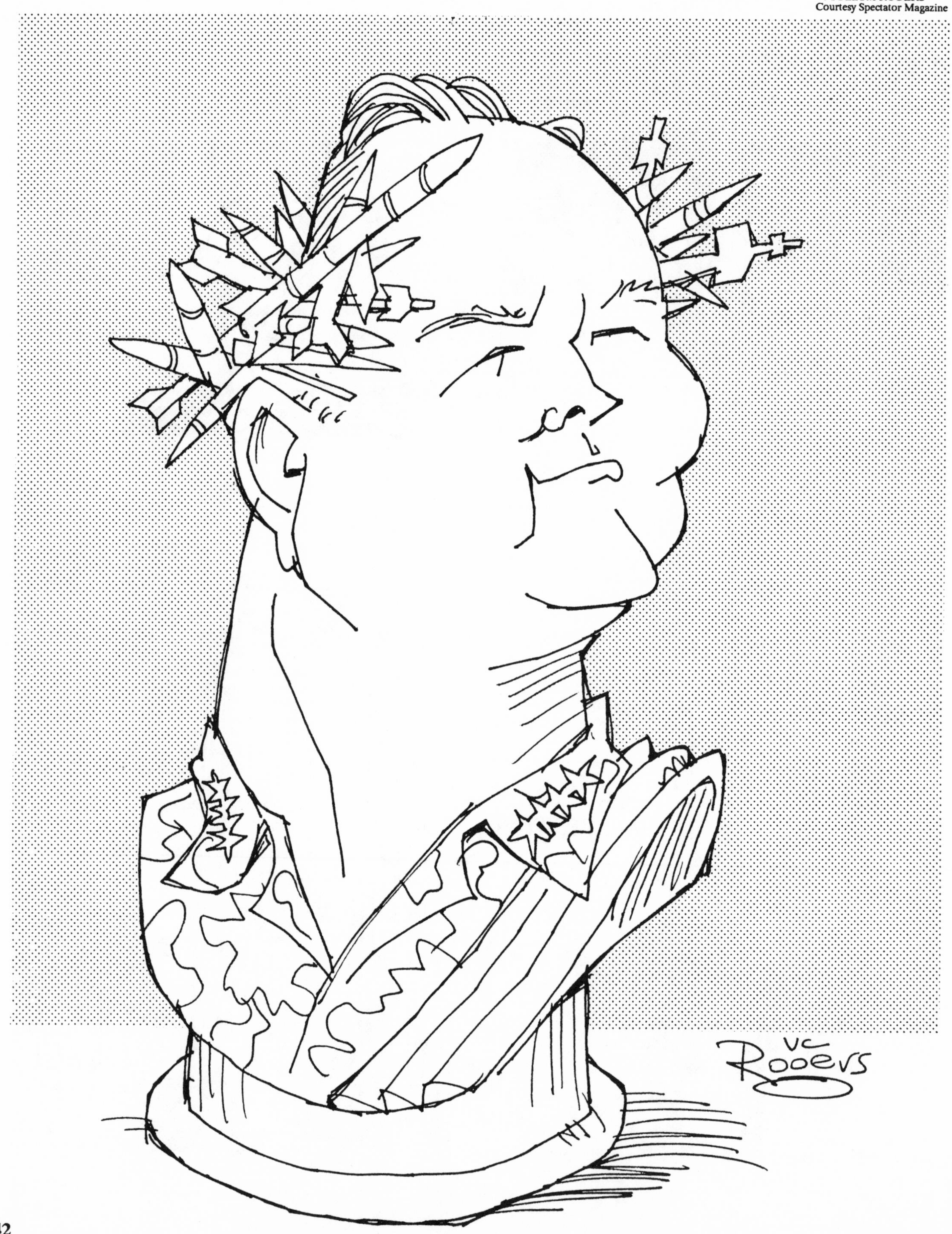
VC
Rogers

Desert Storm

The United Nations gave Iraq's Saddam Hussein a January 15 deadline to pull his invading troops out of neighboring Kuwait, and the U.S. and its allies assembled the largest military force since World War II to defend Mideast oil. When Hussein ignored the deadline, Allied troops launched massive bombing and missile strikes against Iraqi troops. Then Gen. Norman Schwarzkopf, commander of the allied forces, executed a textbook campaign, sweeping around enemy positions and cutting off their reinforcements and supplies. It was a rout, with very low Allied casualties.

The questionable decision to conclude the ground war after only 100 hours was largely due to pressure from Saudi Arabia and Egypt. The Arab Allies were concerned about the Arab world's reaction if the Allies went beyond the United Nation's directive only to liberate Kuwait. Nevertheless, Saddam's forces had set fire to more than 500 oil wells in Kuwait, slaughtered thousands of Kuwaitis, and pillaged much of the oil-rich kingdom.

Laser-guided bombs dropped by virtually invisible Stealth bombers and high-tech weapons systems made it possible to defeat Iraq quickly. But credit must be given to the leadership and resolve of the American troops. They were the best-trained ever, and some 30,000 of them were women.

JIM BORGMAN
Courtesy Cincinnati Enquirer

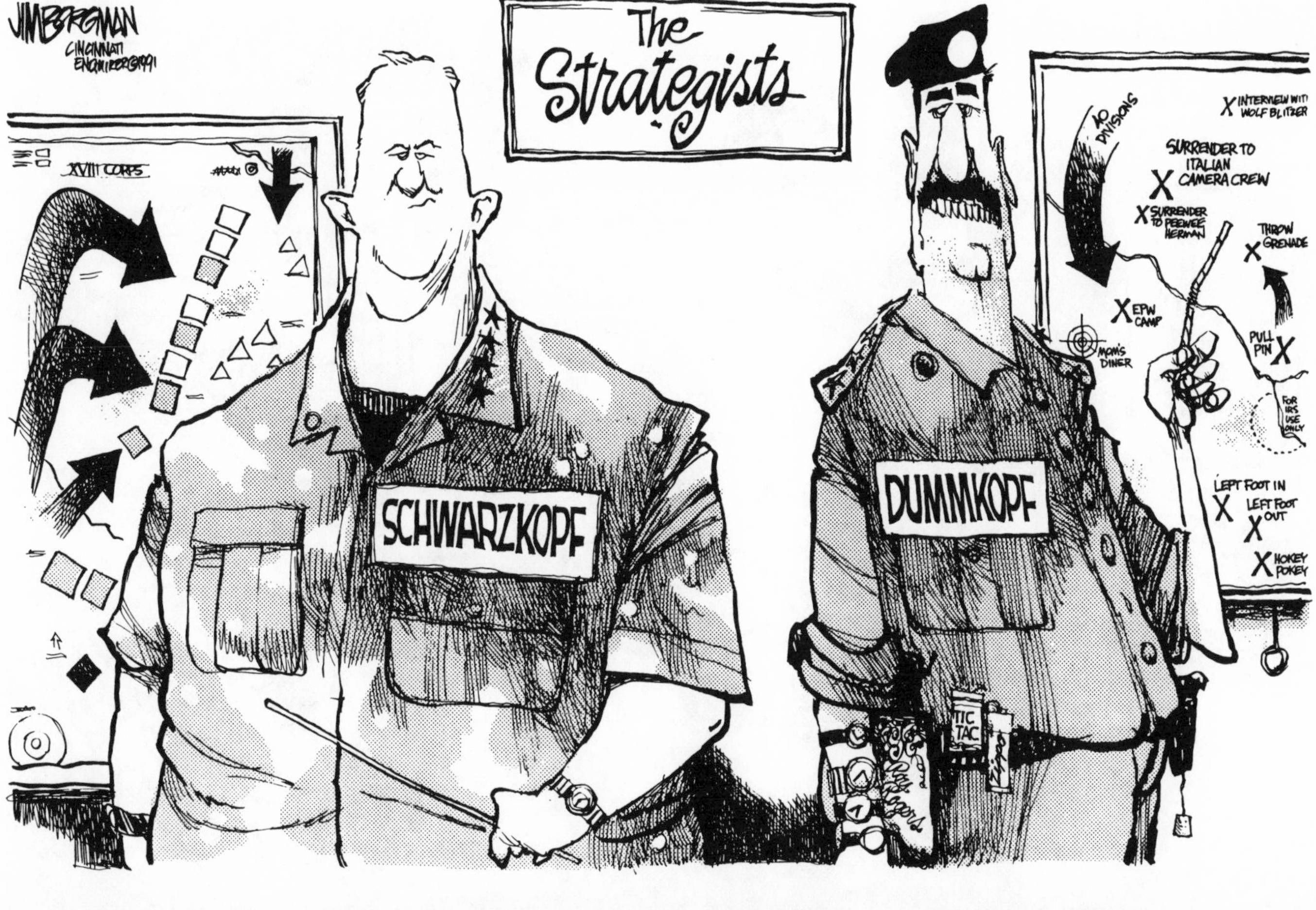
The Strategists
XVIII CORPS
SCHWARZKOPF
DUMMKOPF
INTERVIEW WITH WOLF BLITZER
SURRENDER TO ITALIAN CAMERA CREW
SURRENDER TO PEEWEE HERMAN
THROW GRENADE
EPW CAMP
MOM'S DINER
PULL PIN
LEFT FOOT IN
LEFT FOOT OUT
HOKEY POKEY
TIC TAC

PAT BAGLEY
Courtesy Salt Lake Tribune

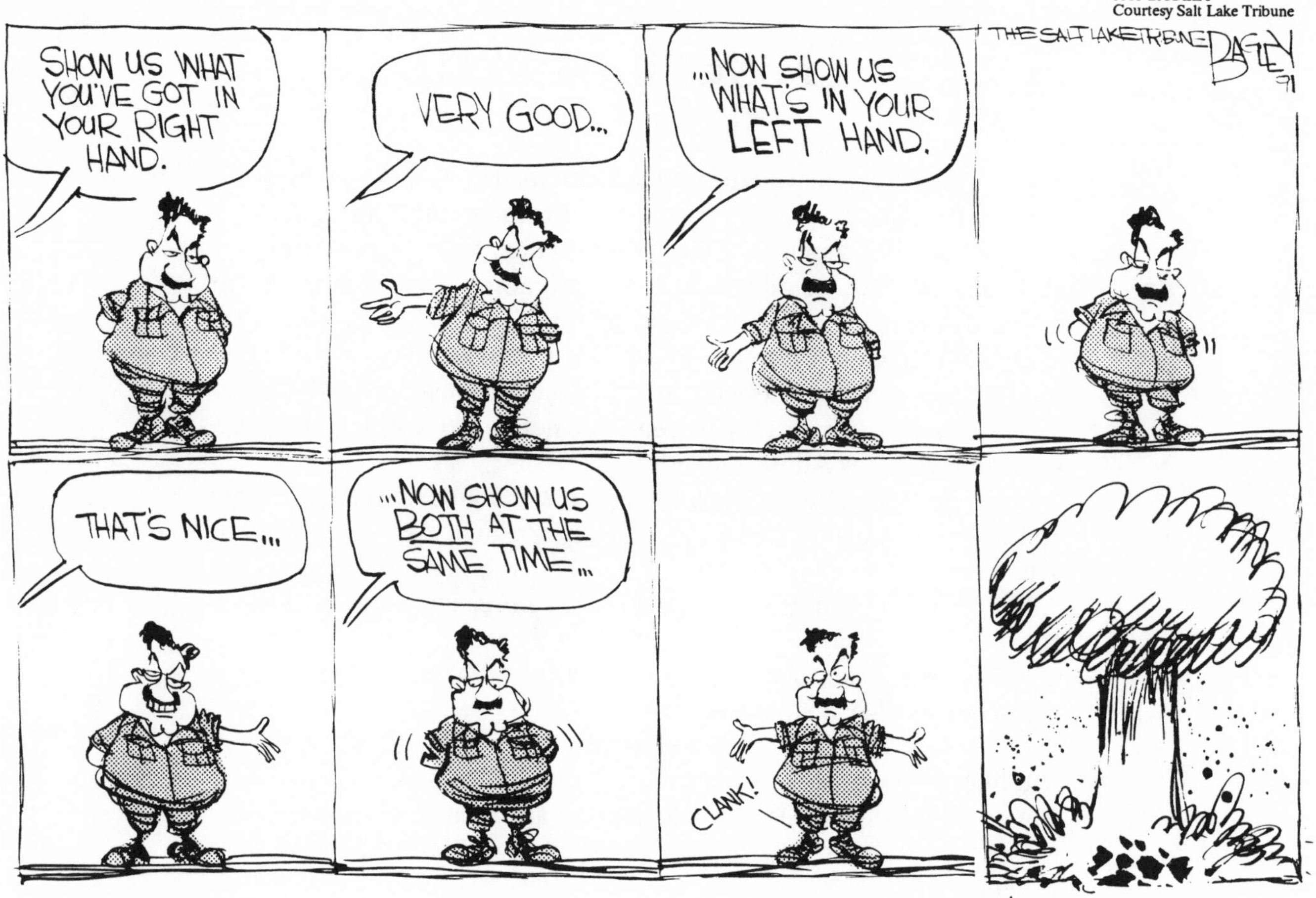
THE SALT LAKE TRIBUNE BAGLEY '91
SHOW US WHAT YOU'VE GOT IN YOUR RIGHT HAND.
VERY GOOD...
...NOW SHOW US WHAT'S IN YOUR LEFT HAND.
THAT'S NICE...
...NOW SHOW US BOTH AT THE SAME TIME...
CLANK!

MIKE KEEFE
Courtesy Denver Post

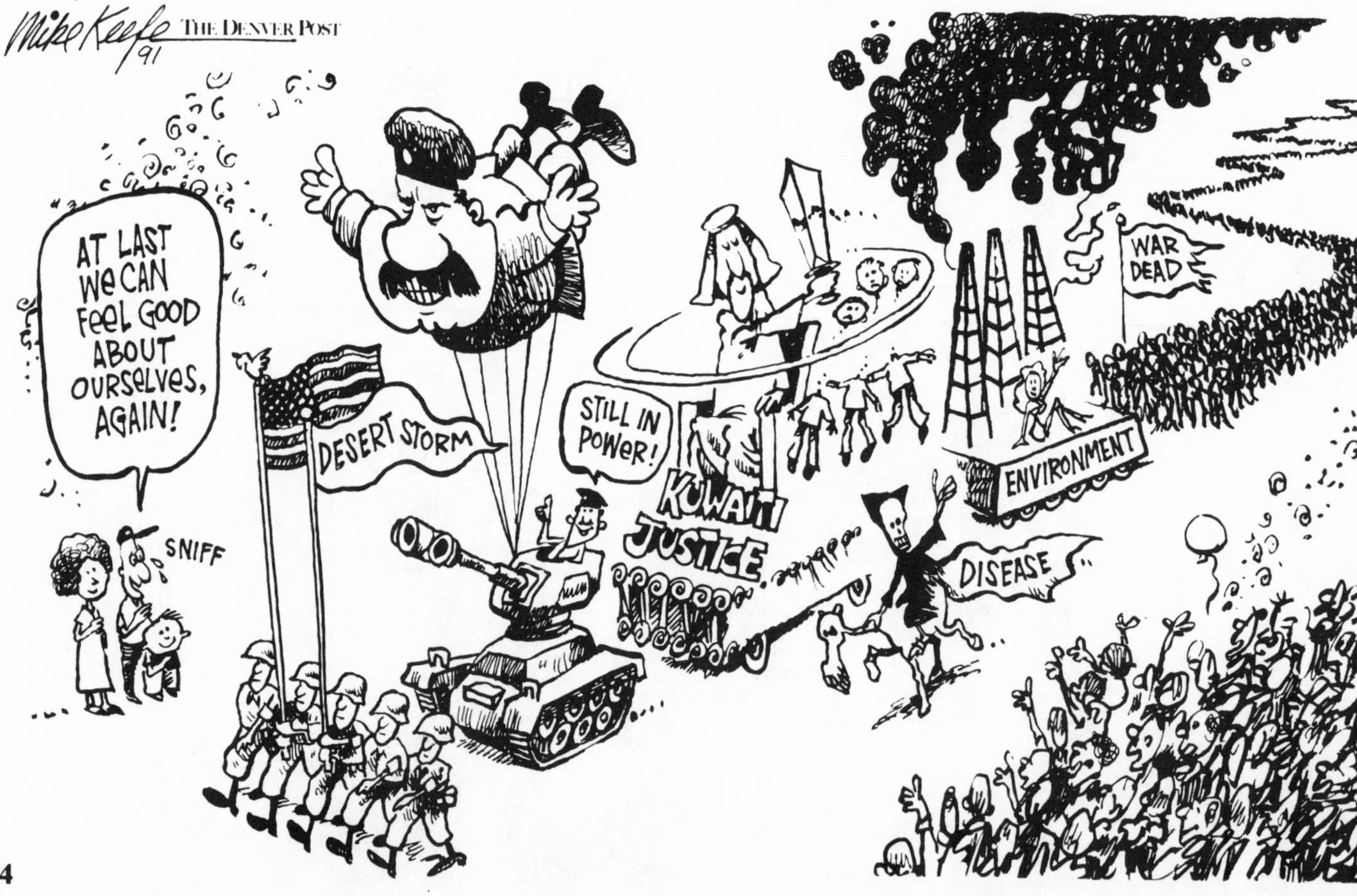
Mike Keefe '91 THE DENVER POST
AT LAST WE CAN FEEL GOOD ABOUT OURSELVES, AGAIN!
SNIFF
DESERT STORM
STILL IN POWER!
KUWAITI JUSTICE
ENVIRONMENT
WAR DEAD
DISEASE

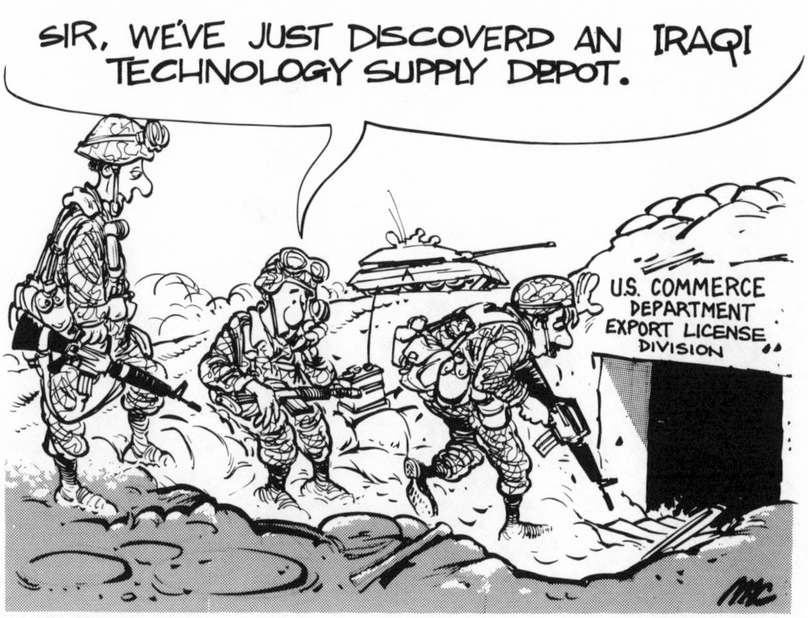
SIR, WE'VE JUST DISCOVERD AN IRAQI TECHNOLOGY SUPPLY DEPOT.
U.S. COMMERCE DEPARTMENT EXPORT LICENSE DIVISION

CRAIG MACINTOSH
Courtesy Minneapolis Star-Tribune

KEVIN SIERS
Courtesy Charlotte Observer

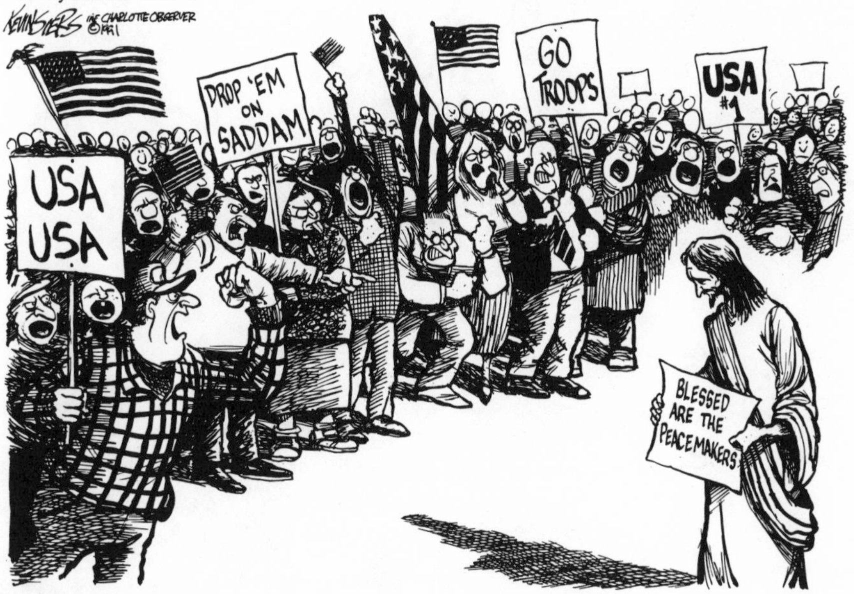
DROP 'EM ON SADDAM
GO TROOPS
USA #1
USA USA
BLESSED ARE THE PEACEMAKERS

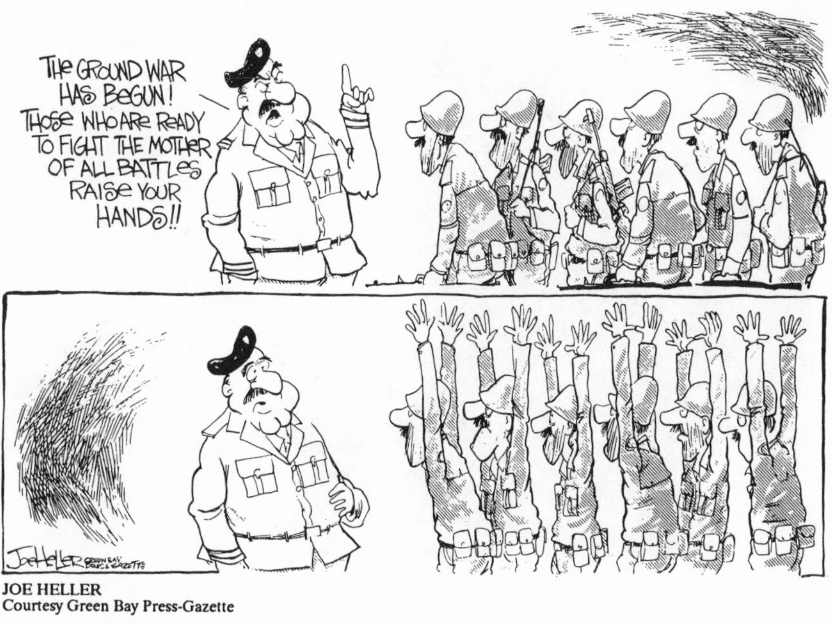
THE GROUND WAR HAS BEGUN! THOSE WHO ARE READY TO FIGHT THE MOTHER OF ALL BATTLES RAISE YOUR HANDS!!

JOE HELLER
Courtesy Green Bay Press-Gazette

PAT BAGLEY
Courtesy Salt Lake Tribune

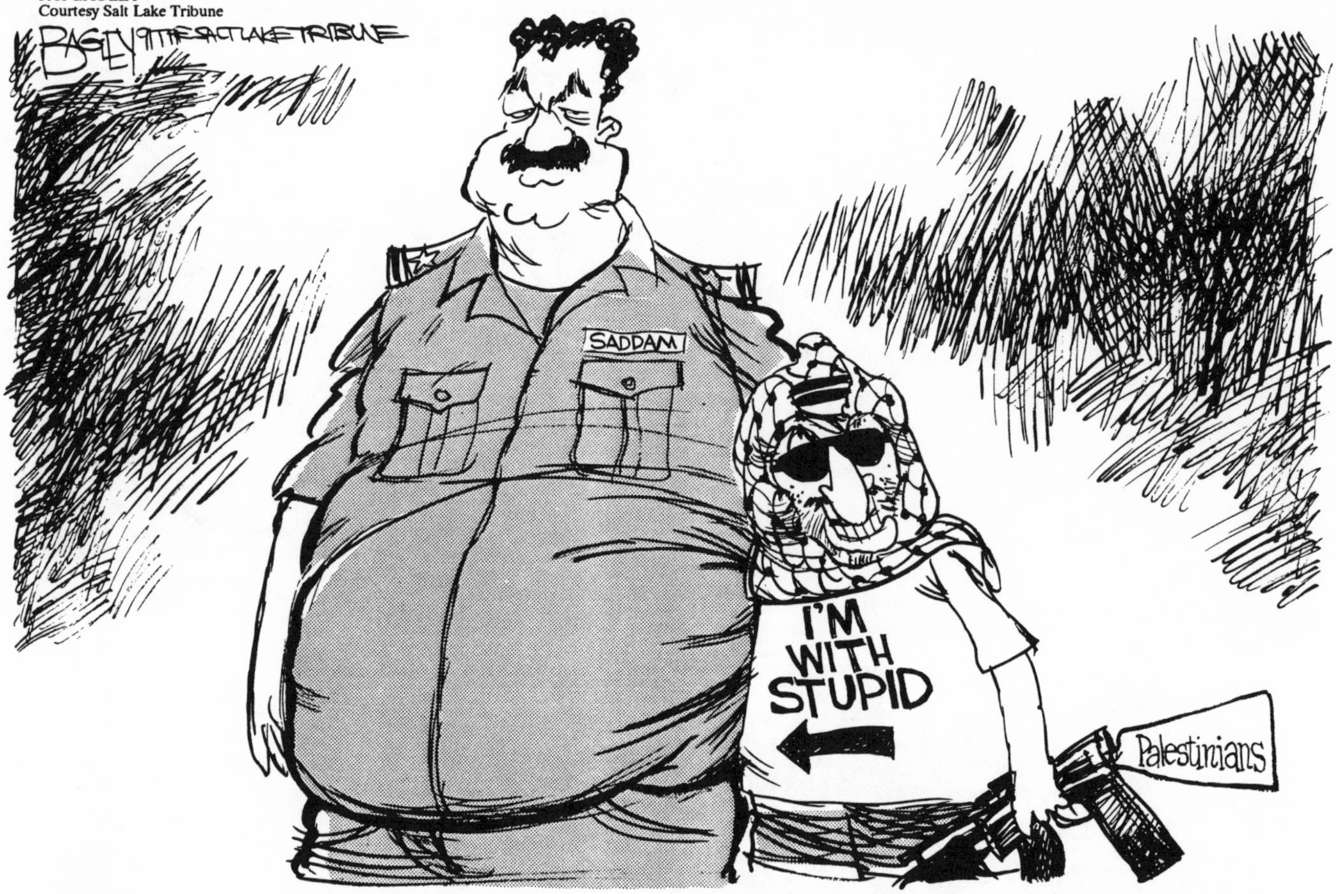
BAGLEY ©1991 THE SALT LAKE TRIBUNE
SADDAM
I'M WITH STUPID
Palestinians

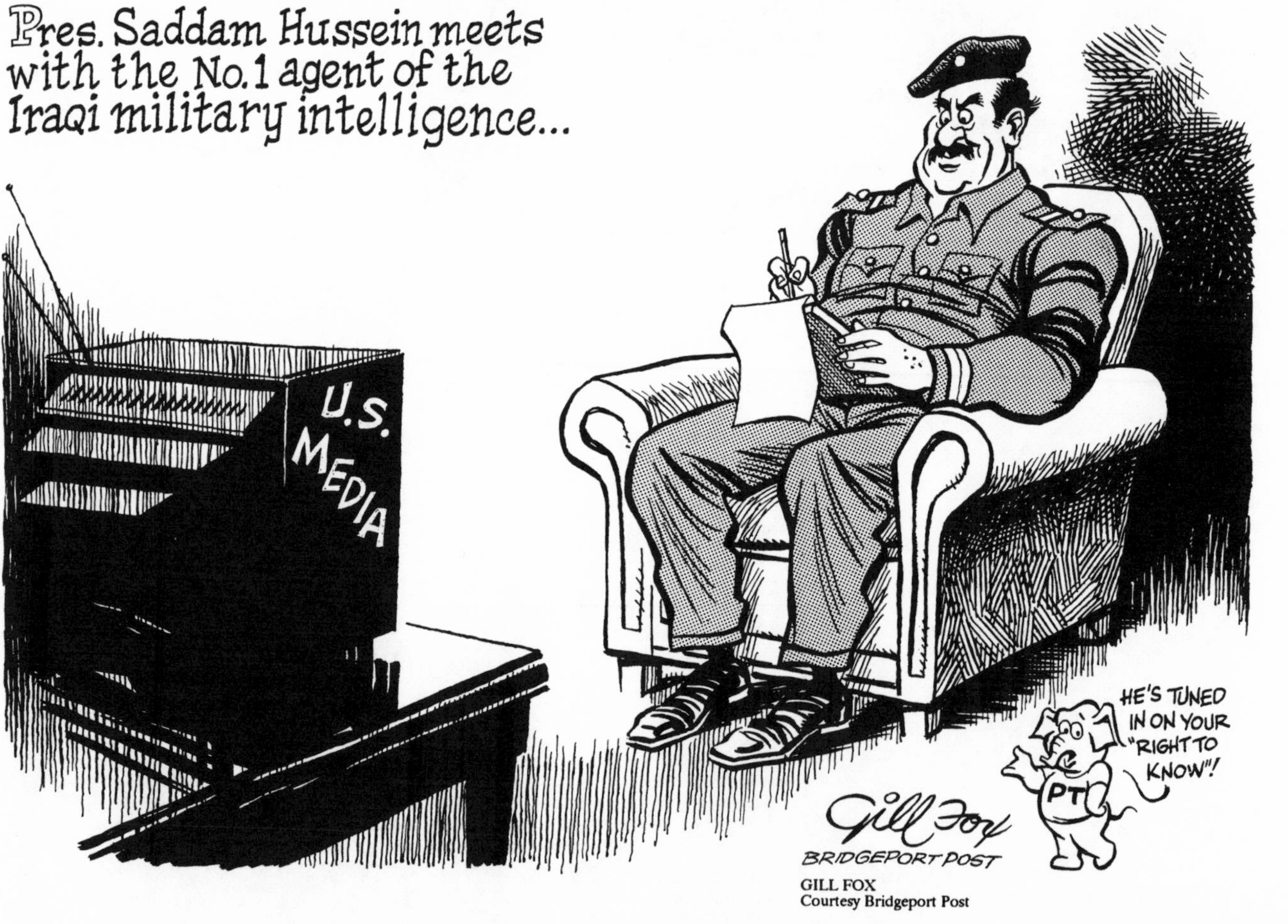
Pres. Saddam Hussein meets with the No. 1 agent of the Iraqi military intelligence...
U.S. MEDIA
HE'S TUNED IN ON YOUR "RIGHT TO KNOW"!
PT
Gill Fox
BRIDGEPORT POST

GILL FOX
Courtesy Bridgeport Post

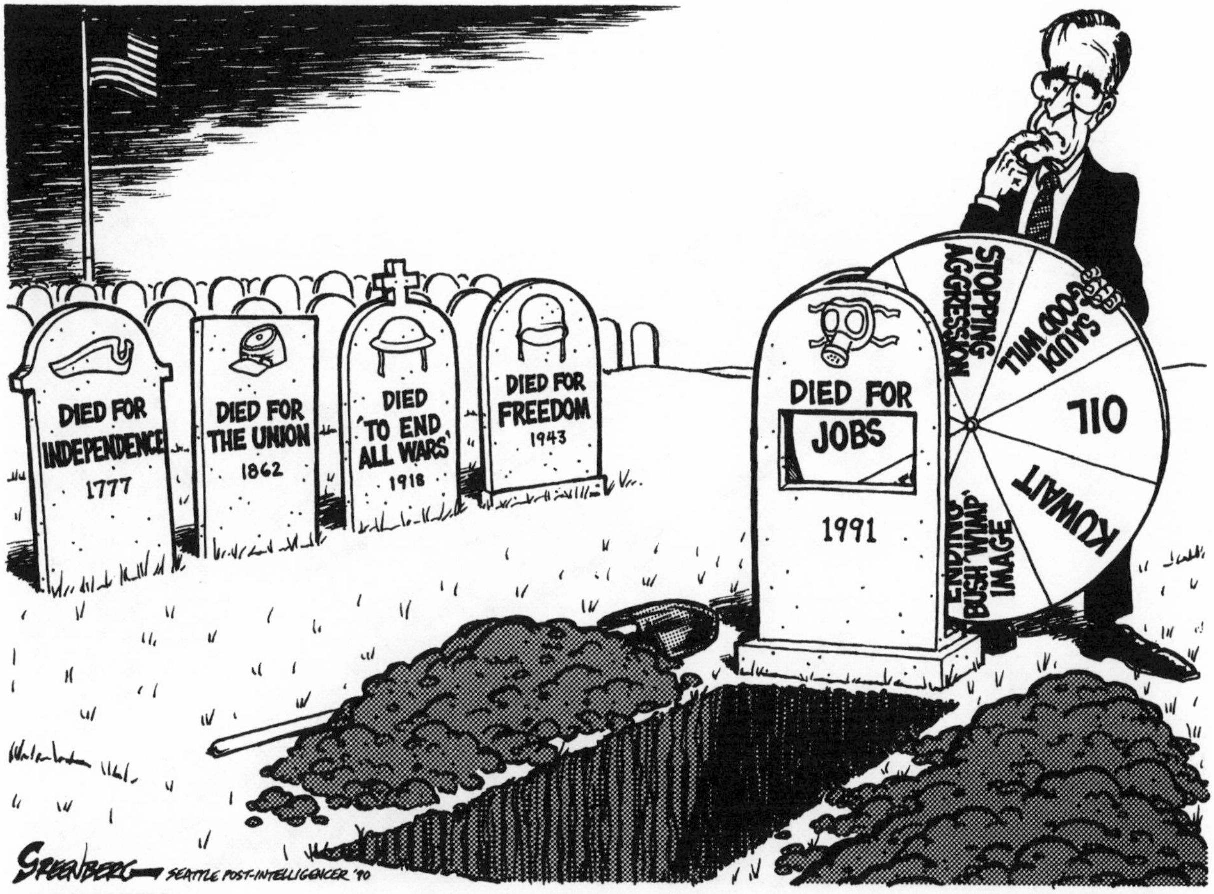
DIED FOR INDEPENDENCE 1777
DIED FOR THE UNION 1862
DIED TO END ALL WARS 1918
DIED FOR FREEDOM 1943
DIED FOR JOBS 1991
STOPPING AGGRESSION
SAUDI GOOD WILL
OIL
KUWAIT
ENDING BUSH 'WIMP' IMAGE
GREENBERG SEATTLE POST-INTELLIGENCER '90

STEVE GREENBERG
Courtesy Seattle Post-Intelligencer

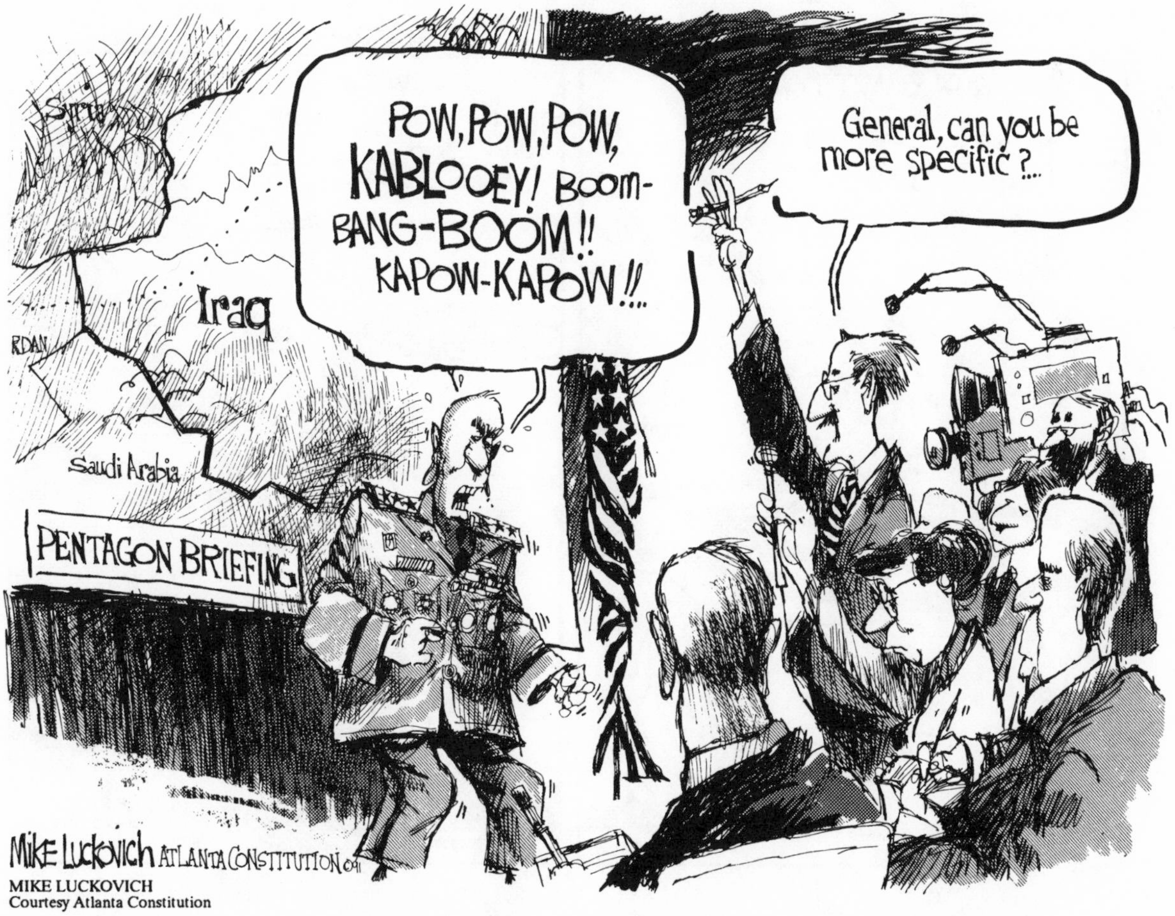
POW, POW, POW, KABLOOEY! Boom-BANG-BOOM!! KAPOW-KAPOW!!..
General, can you be more specific ?...
Syria
Iraq
RDAN
Saudi Arabia
PENTAGON BRIEFING
MIKE LUCKOVICH ATLANTA CONSTITUTION

MIKE LUCKOVICH
Courtesy Atlanta Constitution

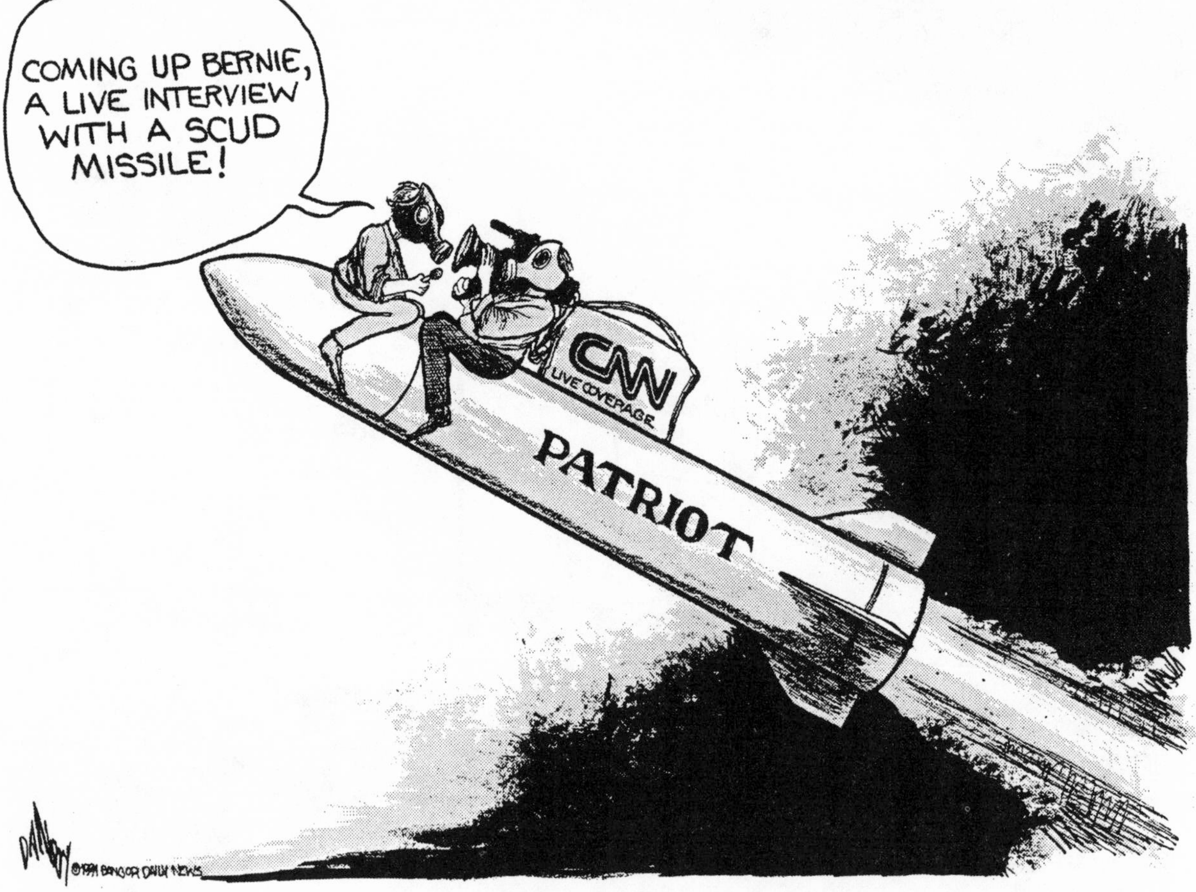
COMING UP BERNIE, A LIVE INTERVIEW WITH A SCUD MISSILE!
CNN
LIVE COVERAGE
PATRIOT
©1991 BANGOR DAILY NEWS

GEORGE DANBY
Courtesy Bangor Daily News

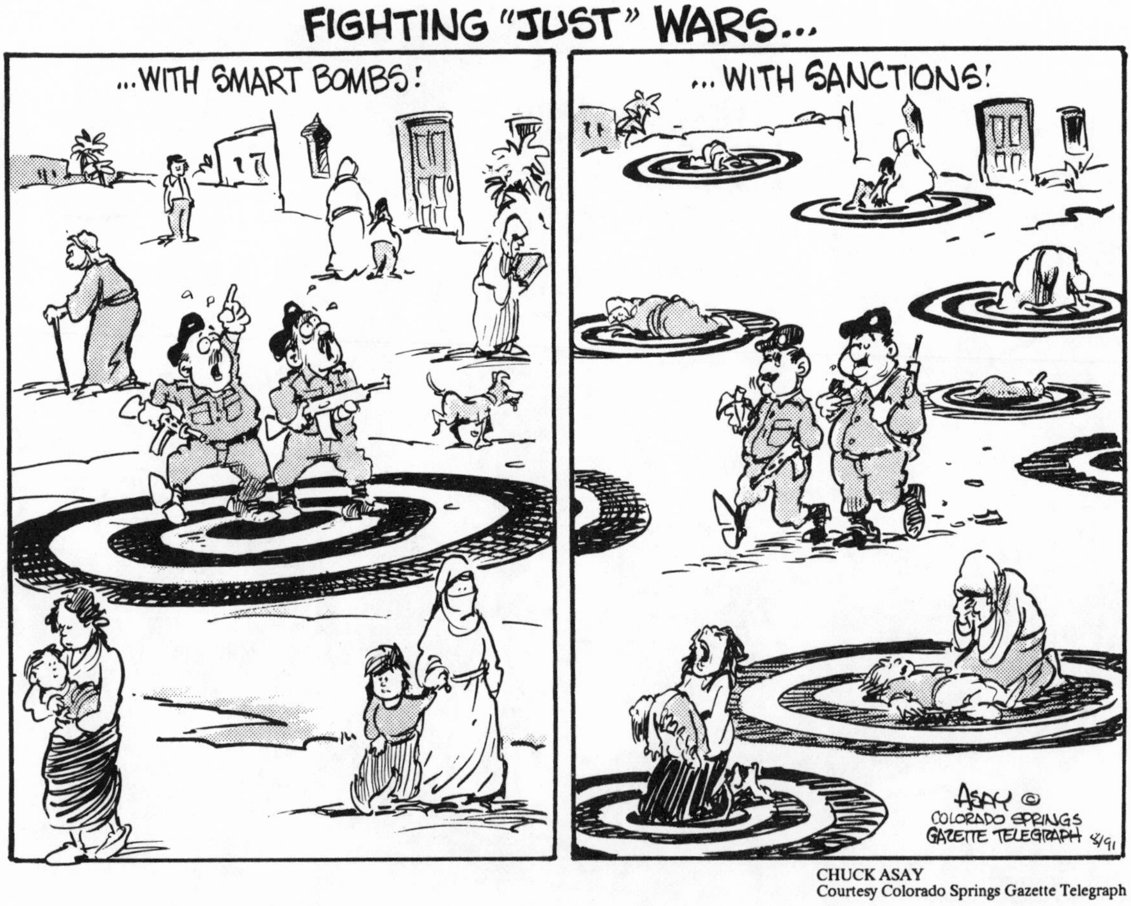
FIGHTING "JUST" WARS...
...WITH SMART BOMBS!
...WITH SANCTIONS!
ASAY ©
COLORADO SPRINGS
GAZETTE TELEGRAPH 8/91

CHUCK ASAY
Courtesy Colorado Springs Gazette Telegraph

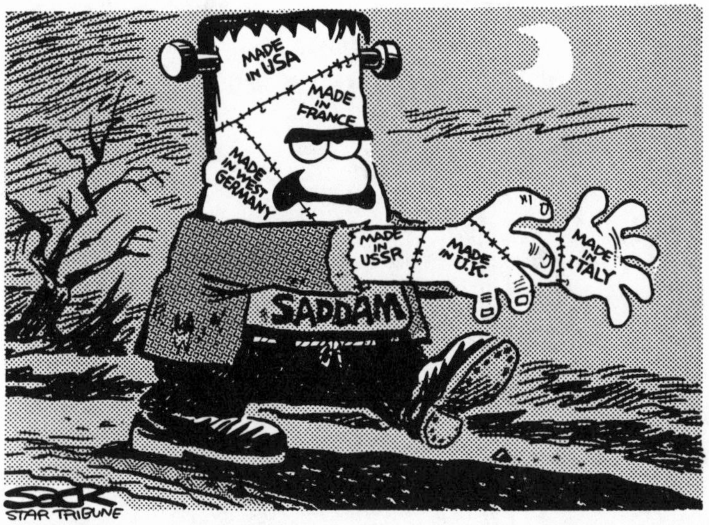
MADE IN USA
MADE IN FRANCE
MADE IN WEST GERMANY
MADE IN USSR
MADE IN U.K.
MADE IN ITALY
SADDAM
SACK
STAR TRIBUNE

STEVE SACK
Courtesy Minneapolis Star Tribune

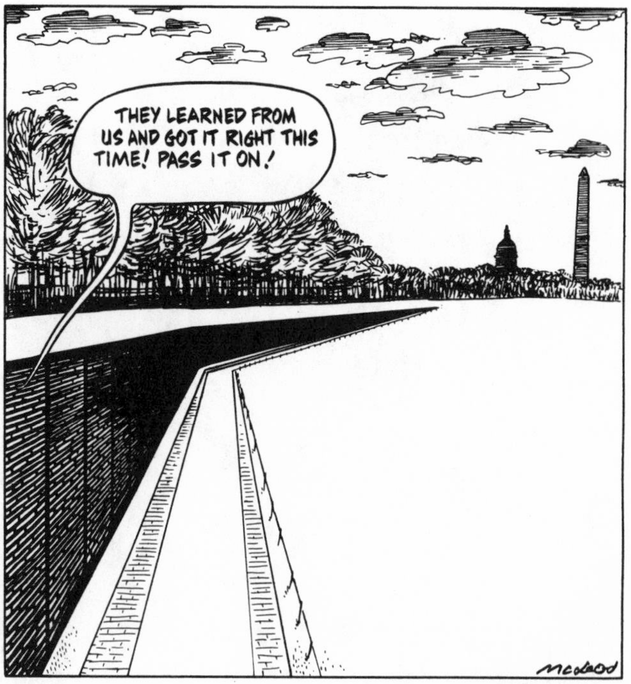
THEY LEARNED FROM US AND GOT IT RIGHT THIS TIME! PASS IT ON!
mcleod

JACK MCLEOD
Courtesy Army Times

PAUL SZEP
Courtesy Boston Globe

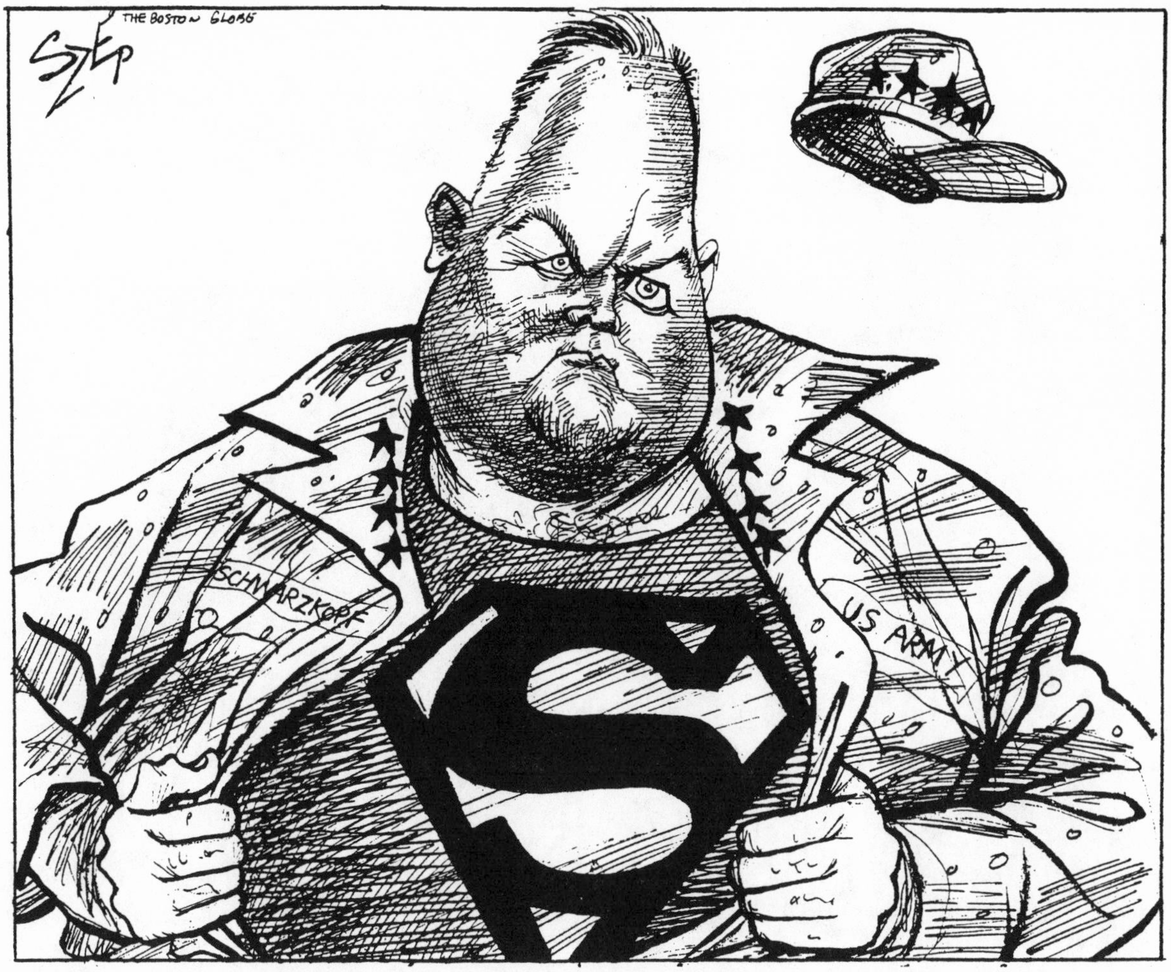
SZEP
THE BOSTON GLOBE
SCHWARZKOPF
U.S. ARMY

It's a hawk, it's a tank, it's Schwarzkopfman!

JACK OHMAN
Courtesy Portland Oregonian

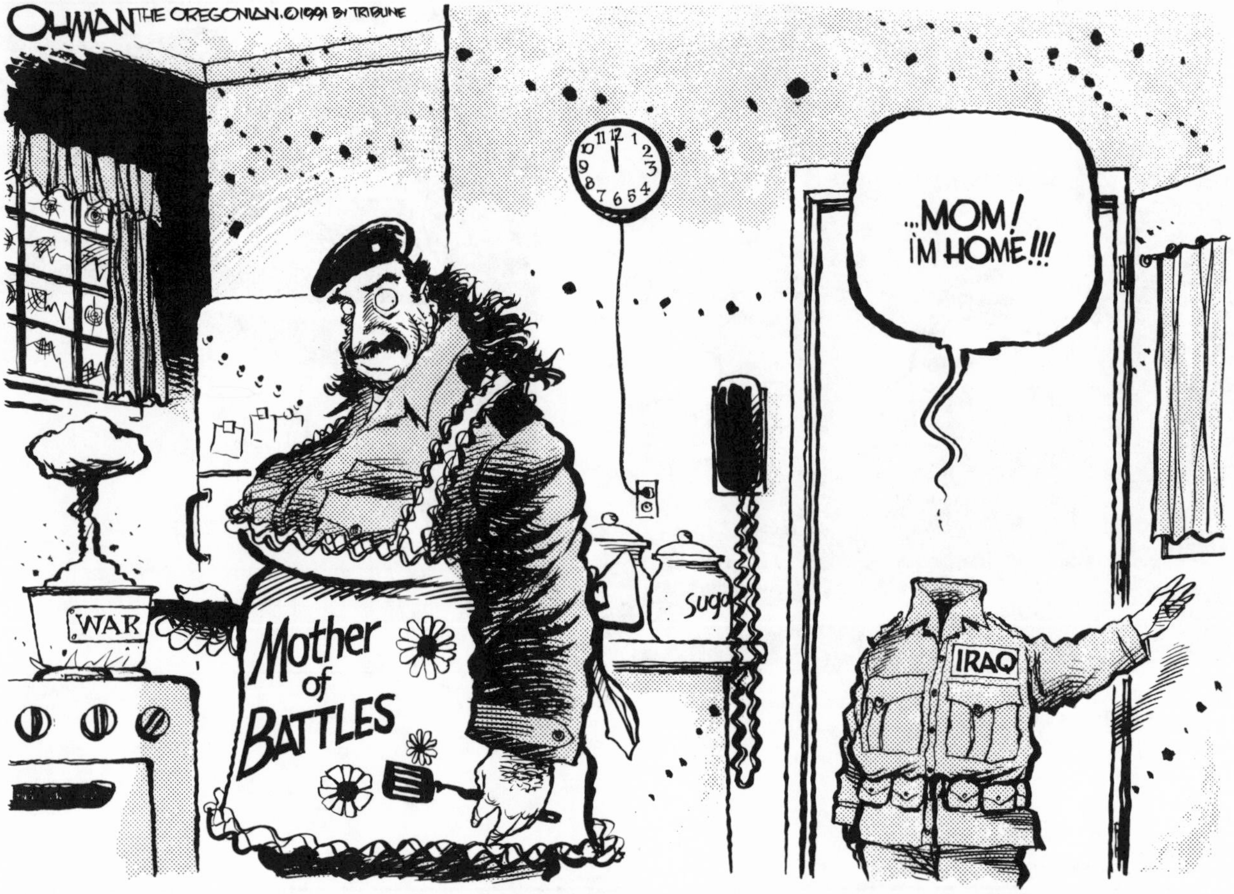
OHMAN THE OREGONIAN ©1991 BY TRIBUNE
WAR
Mother of BATTLES
SUGA
..MOM! I'M HOME!!!
IRAQ

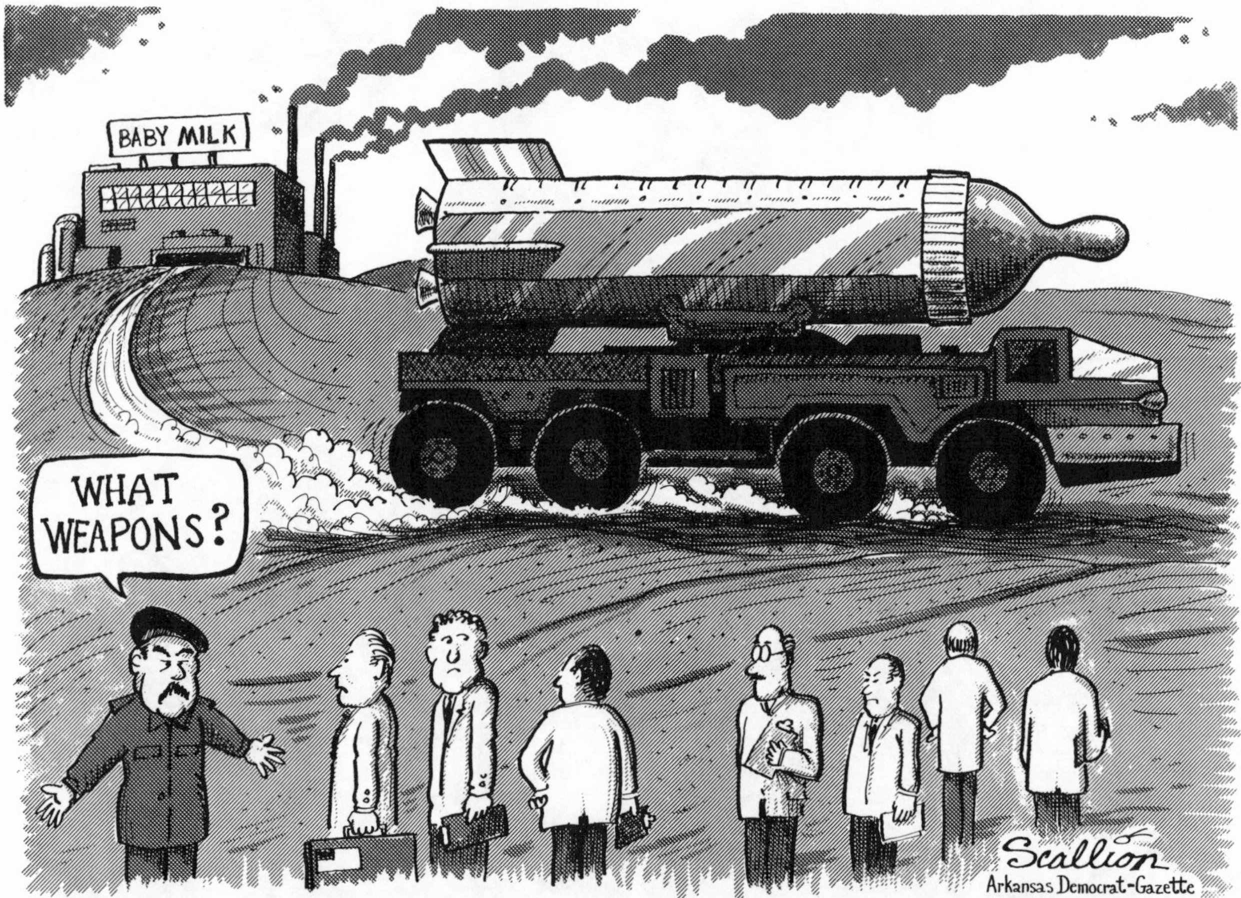
BABY MILK
WHAT WEAPONS?
Scallion
Arkansas Democrat-Gazette

STEVE SCALLION
Courtesy Arkansas Democrat-Gazette

TOM ENGELHARDT
Courtesy St. Louis Post-Dispatch

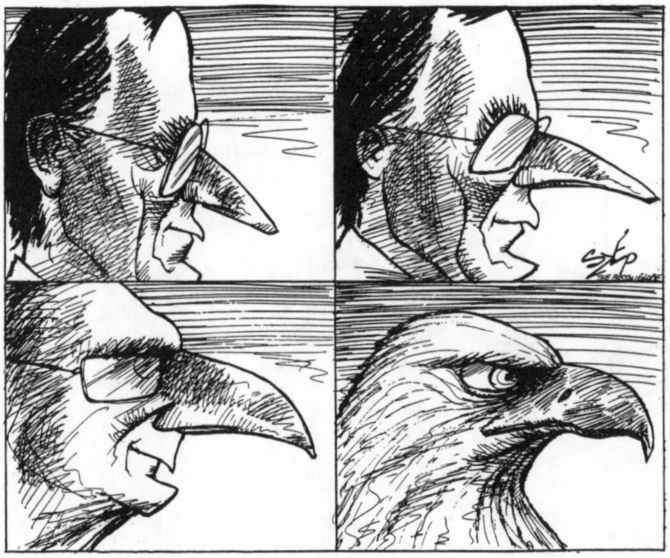

PAUL SZEP
Courtesy Boston Globe

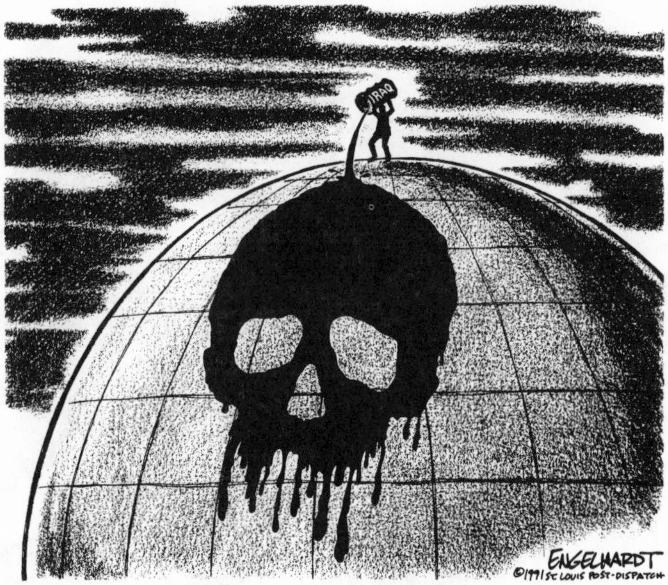
IRAQ
ENGELHARDT
©1991 St. Louis Post-Dispatch

Sneak Attack On the Planet

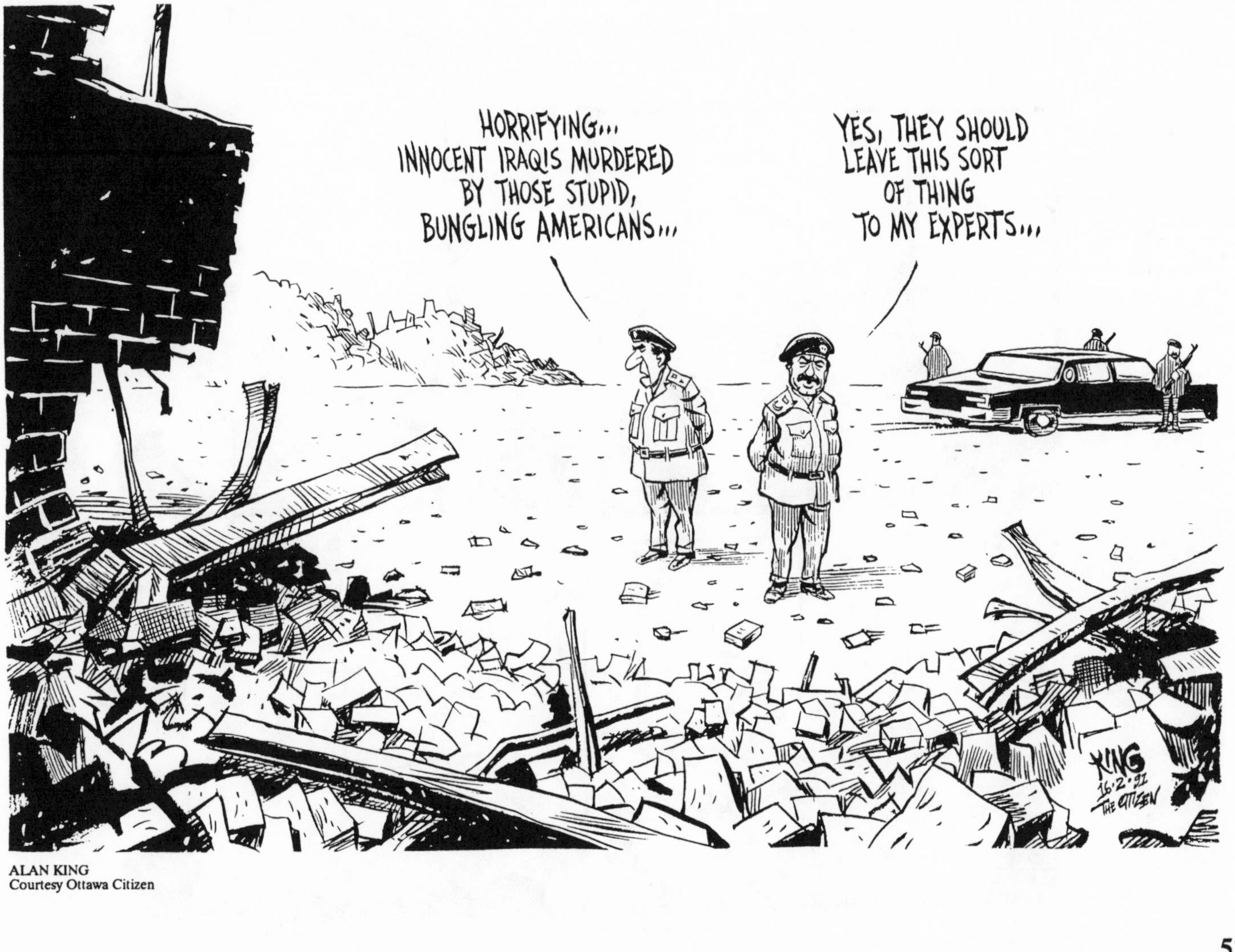
HORRIFYING... INNOCENT IRAQIS MURDERED BY THOSE STUPID, BUNGLING AMERICANS...
YES, THEY SHOULD LEAVE THIS SORT OF THING TO MY EXPERTS...
KING 16·2·91 THE CITIZEN

ALAN KING
Courtesy Ottawa Citizen

JERRY HOLBERT
Courtesy Boston Herald

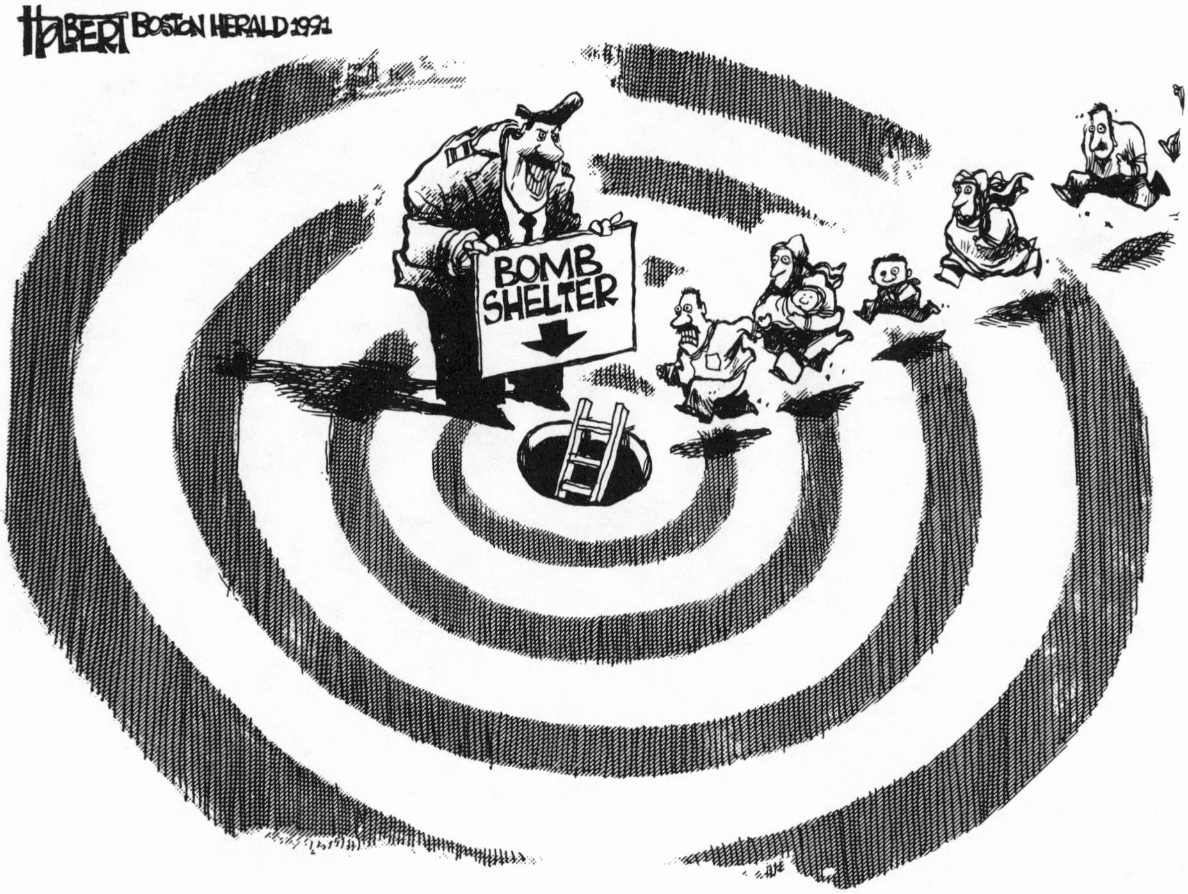
HOLBERT BOSTON HERALD 1991
BOMB SHELTER

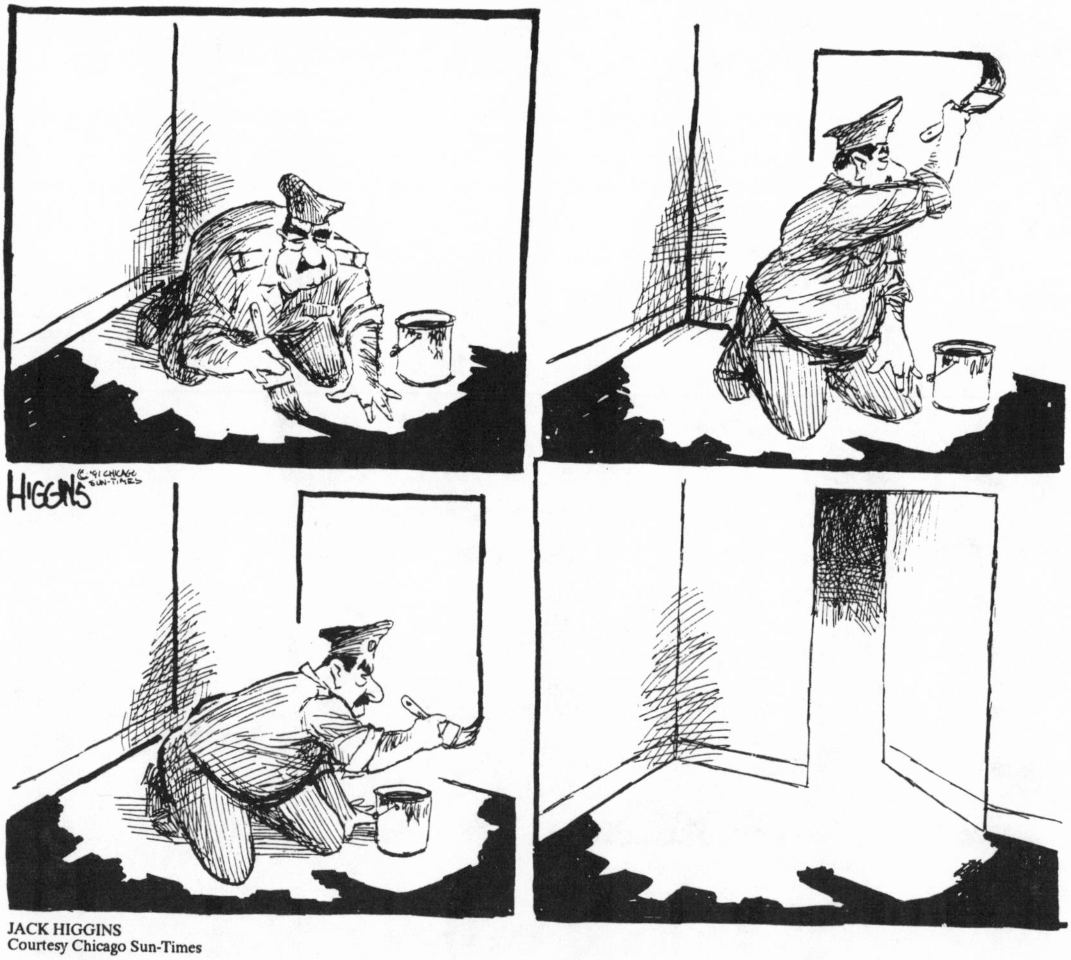
HIGGINS ©'91 CHICAGO SUN-TIMES

JACK HIGGINS
Courtesy Chicago Sun-Times

WALT HANDELSMAN
Courtesy Times-Picayune (N.O.)

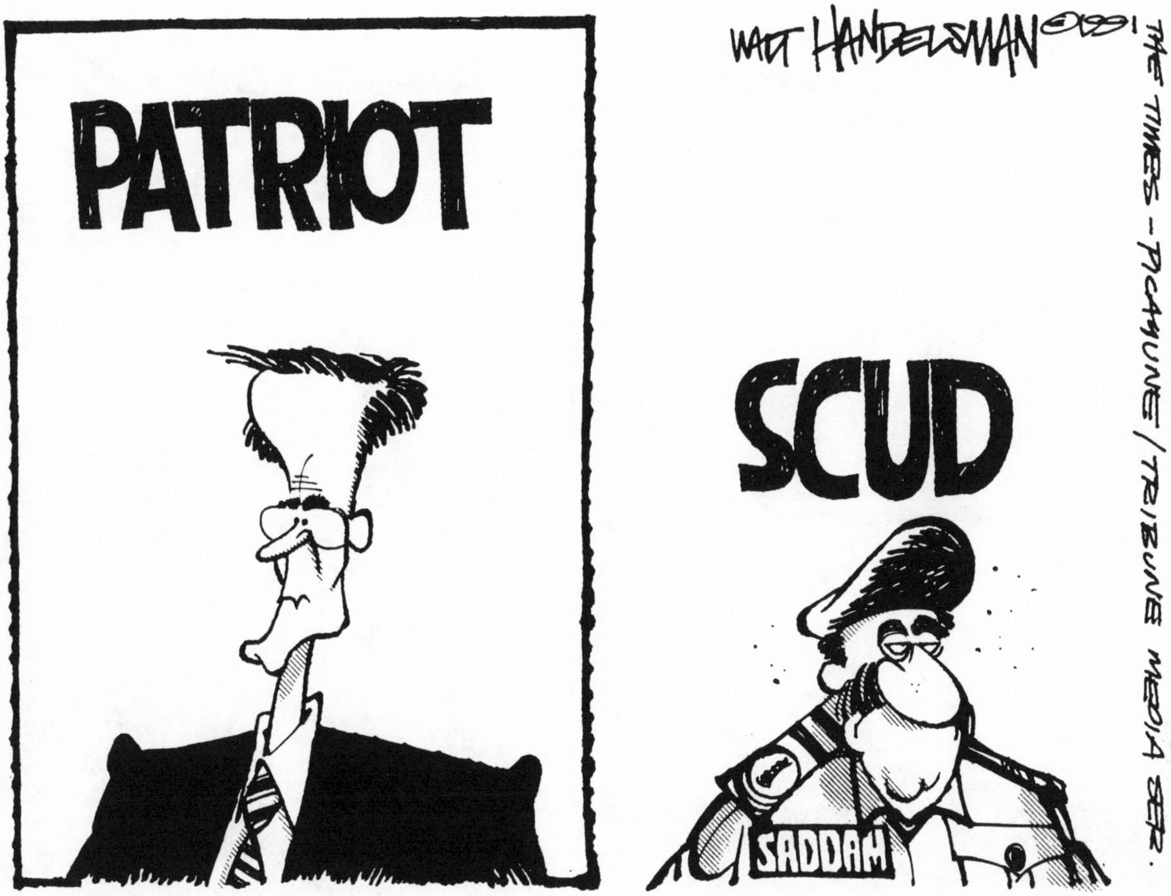
WALT HANDELSMAN ©1991
THE TIMES-PICAYUNE/TRIBUNE MEDIA SER.
PATRIOT
SCUD
SADDAM

CHUCK AYERS
Courtesy Akron Beacon Journal

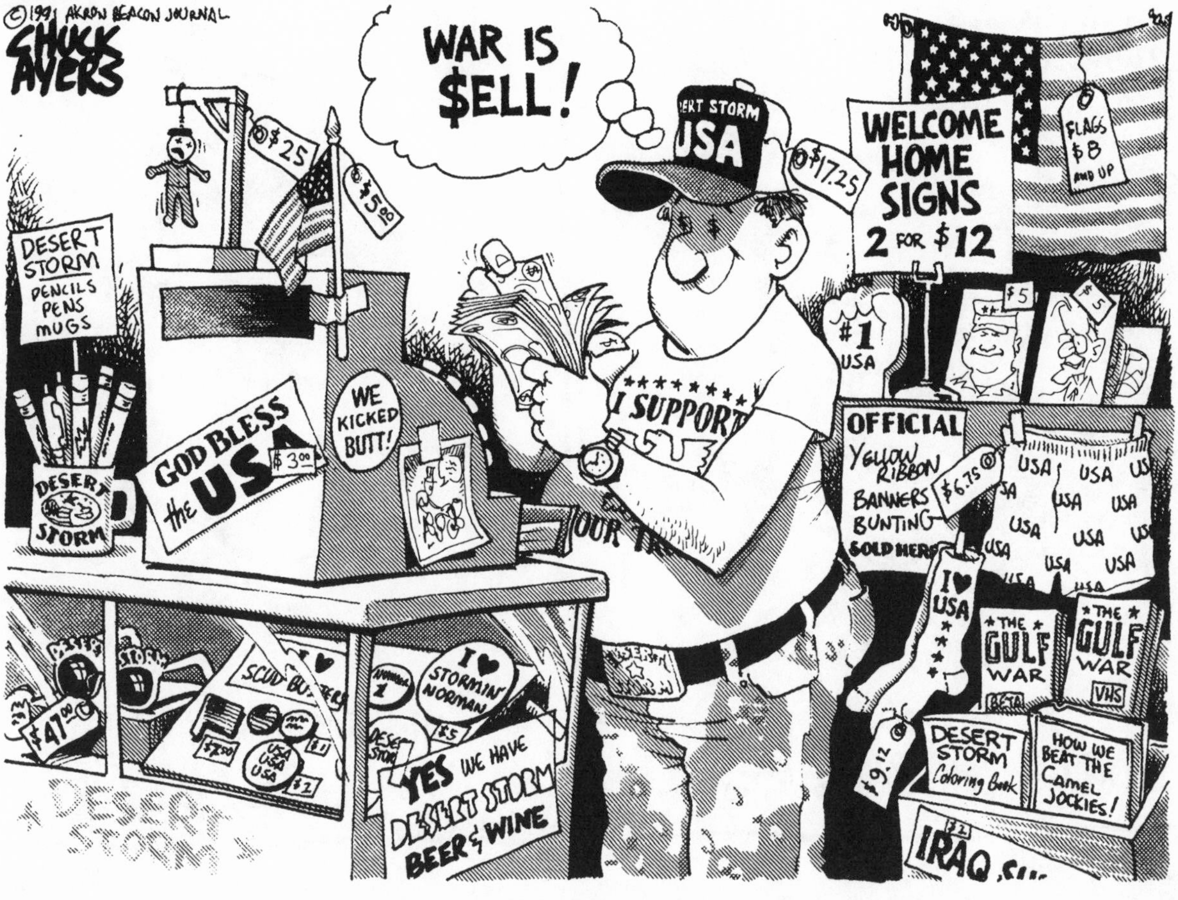
©1991 AKRON BEACON JOURNAL
CHUCK AYERS
WAR IS $ELL!
DESERT STORM USA
$17.25
WELCOME HOME SIGNS 2 FOR $12
FLAGS $8 AND UP
$25
$5.00
DESERT STORM PENCILS PENS MUGS
#1 USA
$5
$5
I SUPPORT
WE KICKED BUTT!
GOD BLESS the USA
$3.00
DESERT STORM
OFFICIAL YELLOW RIBBON BANNERS BUNTING SOLD HERE
$6.75
USA
I ♥ USA
THE GULF WAR
BETA
THE GULF WAR
VHS
SCUD BUSTERS
I ♥ STORMIN' NORMAN
$47.00
YES WE HAVE DESERT STORM BEER & WINE
DESERT STORM Coloring Book
HOW WE BEAT THE CAMEL JOCKIES!
$9.12
IRAQ
DESERT STORM

DICK LOCHER
Courtesy Chicago Tribune

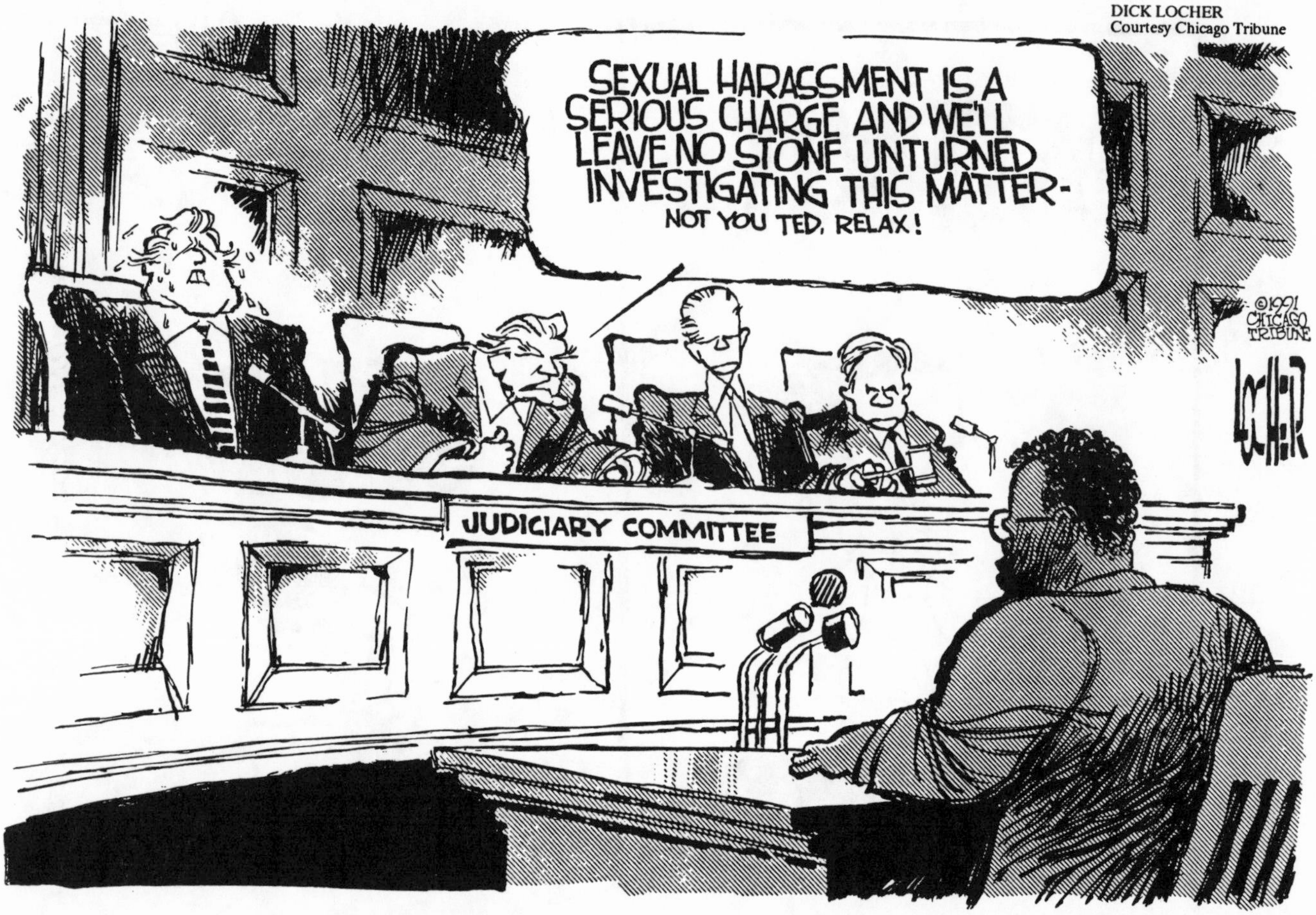

SEXUAL HARASSMENT IS A SERIOUS CHARGE AND WE'LL LEAVE NO STONE UNTURNED INVESTIGATING THIS MATTER-
NOT YOU TED, RELAX!
©1991 CHICAGO TRIBUNE
LOCHER
JUDICIARY COMMITTEE

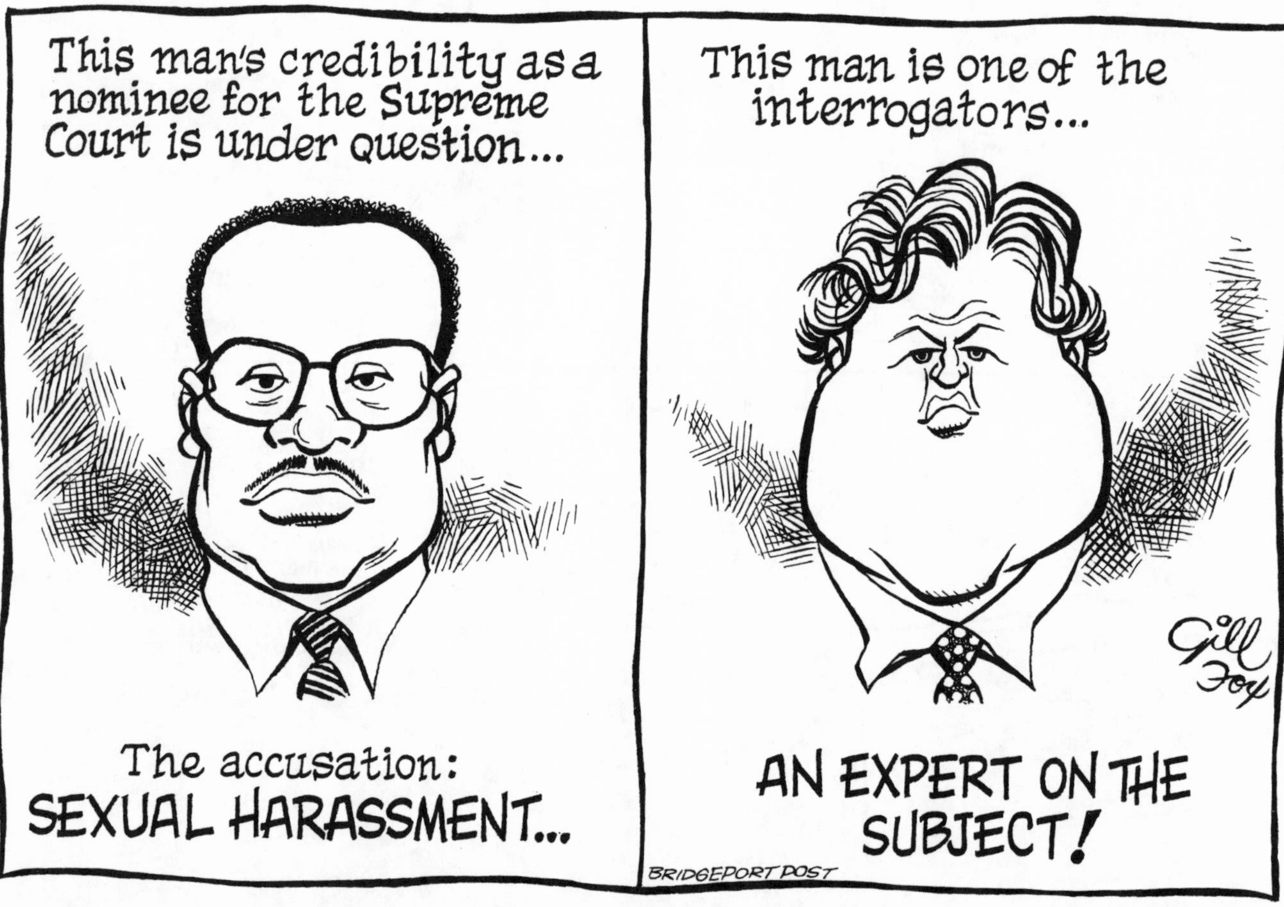

This man's credibility as a nominee for the Supreme Court is under question...
The accusation:
SEXUAL HARASSMENT...
This man is one of the interrogators...
AN EXPERT ON THE SUBJECT!
Gill Fox
BRIDGEPORT POST

GILL FOX
Courtesy Bridgeport Post

Supreme Court Hearings

Clarence Thomas was nominated by President Bush in early July to fill the vacancy on the U.S. Supreme Court created by the retirement of Justice Thurgood Marshall. Thomas was assistant secretary for civil rights at the Department of Education and later chairman of the Equal Employment Opportunity Commission. He also had been confirmed by the Senate for an appellate judgeship where he was serving when nominated for the high court.

Because he was a conservative and probably would tilt the court even further to the right, a bitter confirmation fight ensued. Just when it appeared he would be confirmed, Anita Hill, a young law professor, almost derailed the nomination. Hill testified that she had been sexually harassed in an extremely course manner by Thomas ten years earlier when she had worked for him.

The entire nation viewed the proceedings on television, and the Senate was blamed for sloppy handling of the hearings. Although Thomas eventually was confirmed, most viewers – including those who opposed Thomas as well as those who supported him – were outraged by the affair. Many objected to Sen. Ted Kennedy's sitting on the panel in judgment of someone accused of sexual harassment, given the senator's personal history.

Thomas's view of abortion was the central issue of the confirmation battle.

LAMBERT DER
Courtesy Greenville News

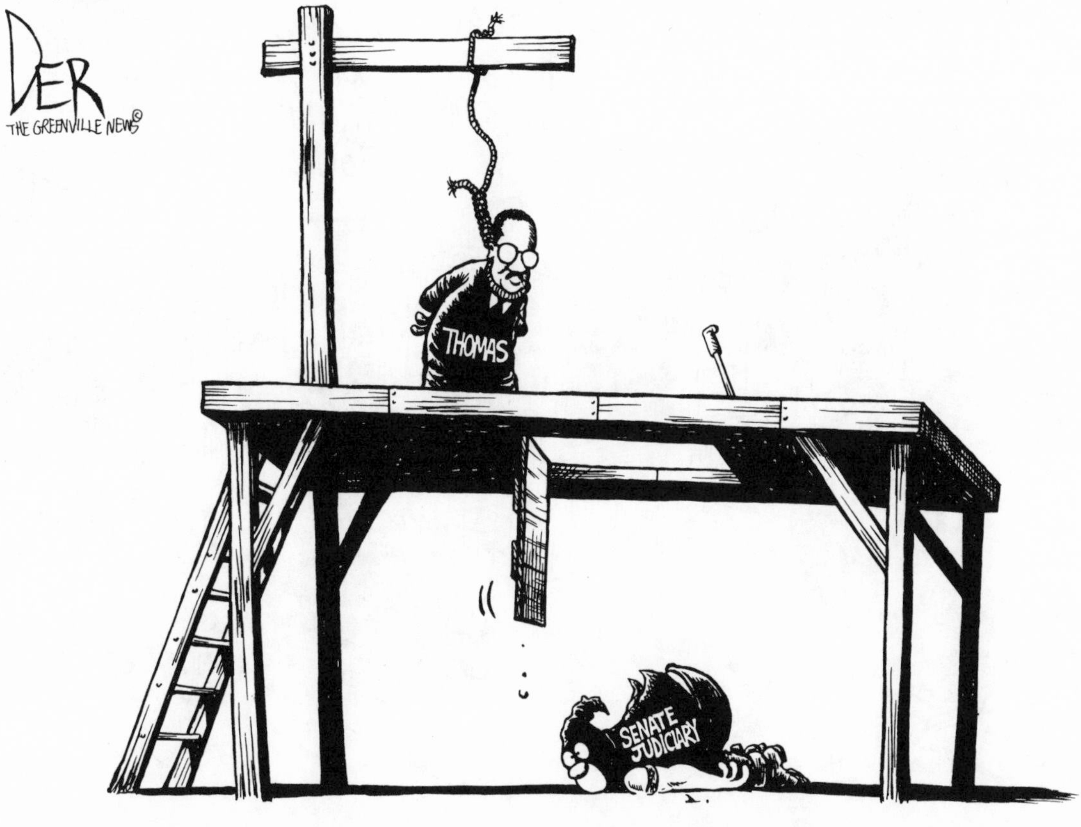
DER
THE GREENVILLE NEWS©
THOMAS
SENATE JUDICIARY

DANA SUMMERS
Courtesy Orlando Sentinel

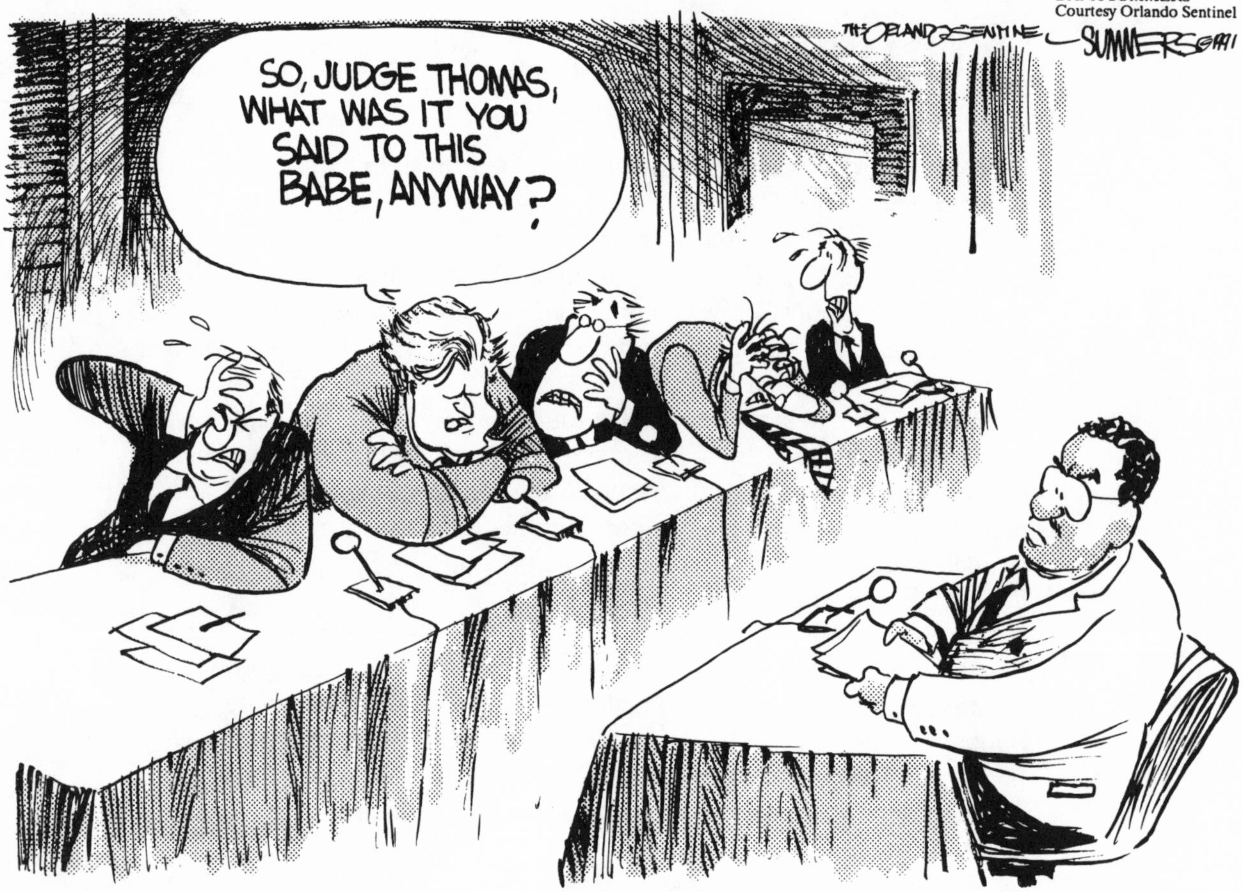
THE ORLANDO SENTINEL SUMMERS ©1991
SO, JUDGE THOMAS, WHAT WAS IT YOU SAID TO THIS BABE, ANYWAY?

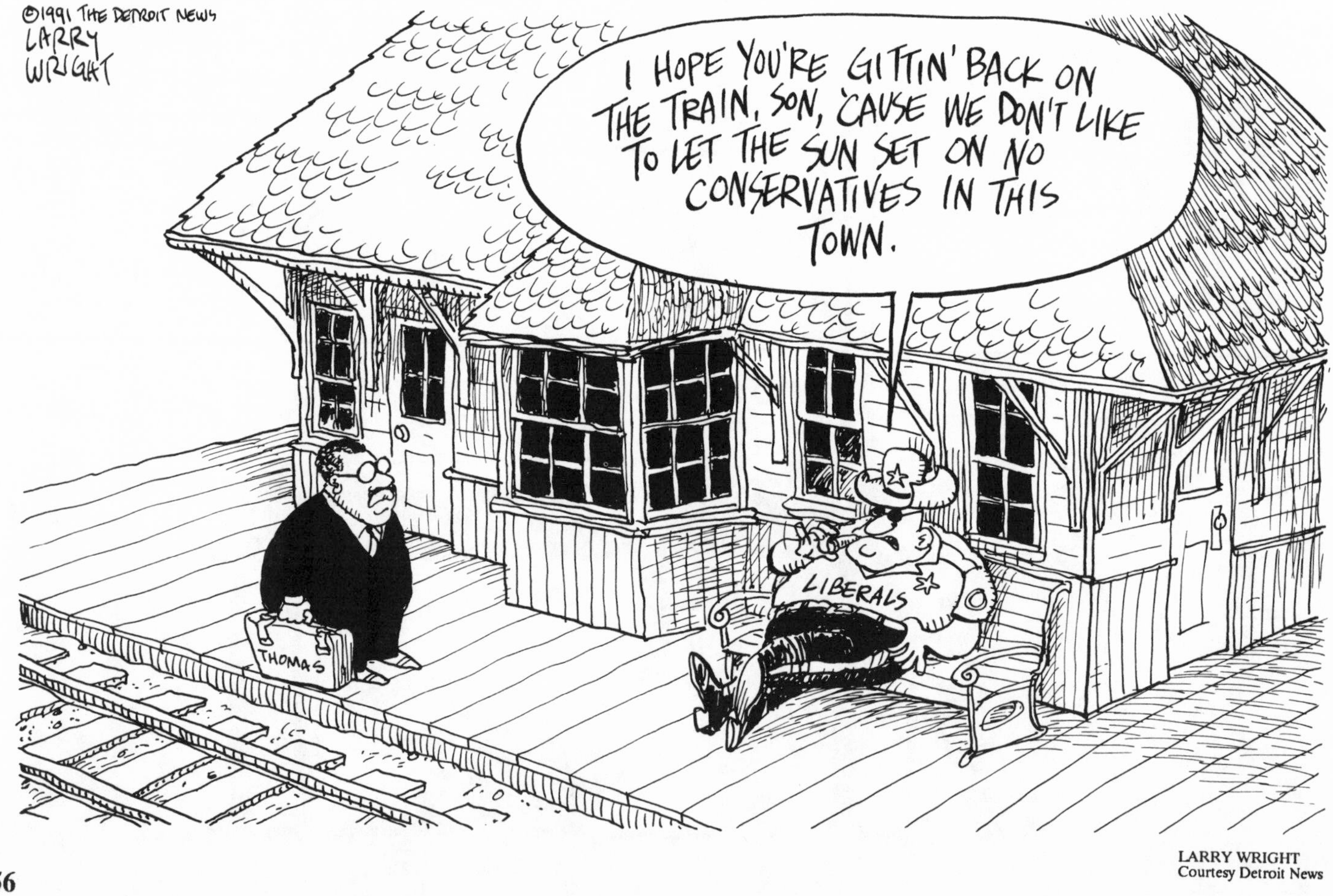
©1991 THE DETROIT NEWS LARRY WRIGHT
I HOPE YOU'RE GITTIN' BACK ON THE TRAIN, SON, 'CAUSE WE DON'T LIKE TO LET THE SUN SET ON NO CONSERVATIVES IN THIS TOWN.
THOMAS
LIBERALS

LARRY WRIGHT
Courtesy Detroit News

S. C. RAWLS
Courtesy NEA

HILL
CAN YOU IMAGINE? WE ALMOST LYNCHED A FINE MAN LIKE CLARENCE THOMAS!!!

CLARENCE THOMAS IS ON THE SUPREME COURT...
REMEMBER, THIS WEEKEND SET YOUR CLOCKS BACK 50 YEARS.
UNITED FEATURE SYN ©1991 DAYTON DAILY NEWS

MIKE PETERS
Courtesy Dayton Daily News

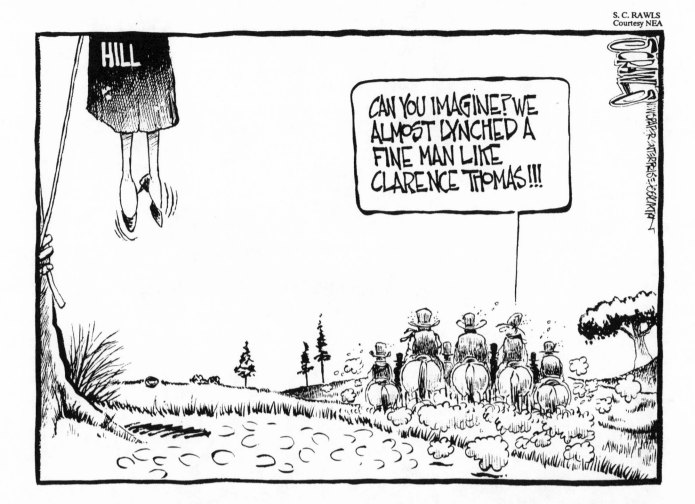

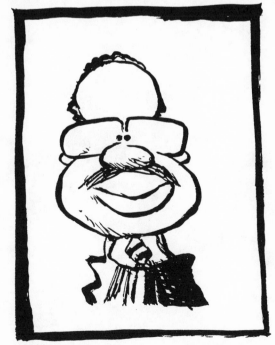

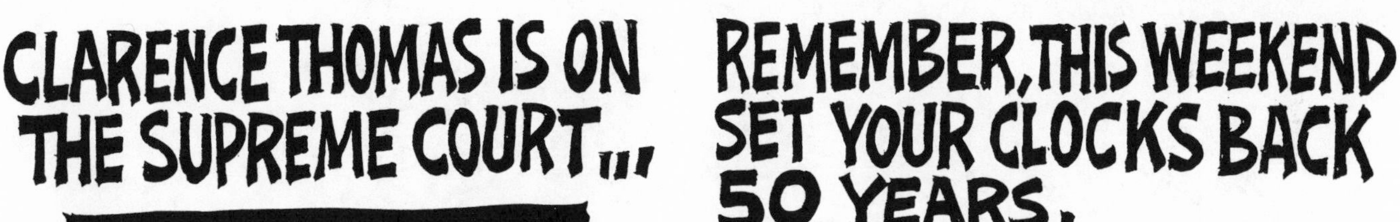

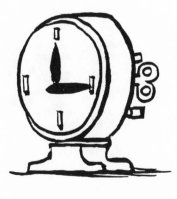

CAM CARDOW
Courtesy Regina Leader Post

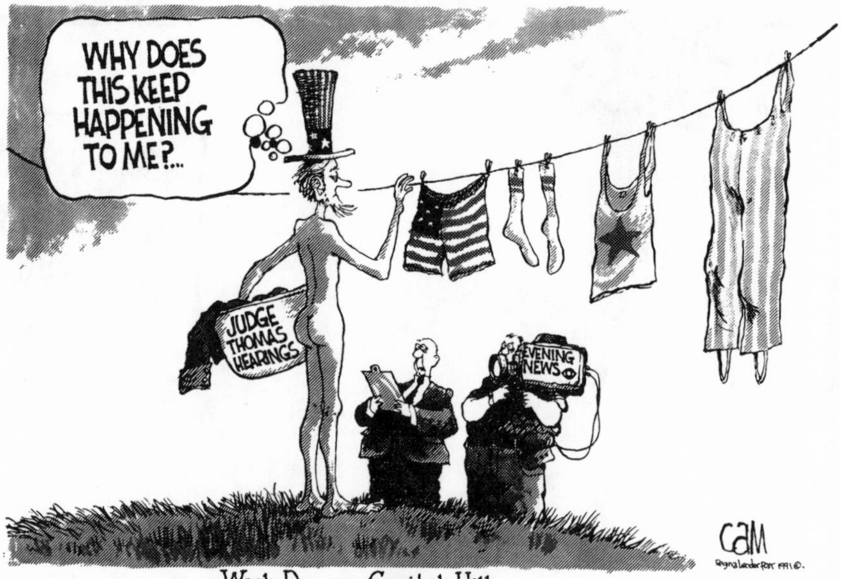
WHY DOES THIS KEEP HAPPENING TO ME?...
JUDGE THOMAS HEARINGS
EVENING NEWS
CAM

Wash Day on Capital Hill...

JERRY FEARING
Courtesy St. Paul Pioneer Press-Dispatch

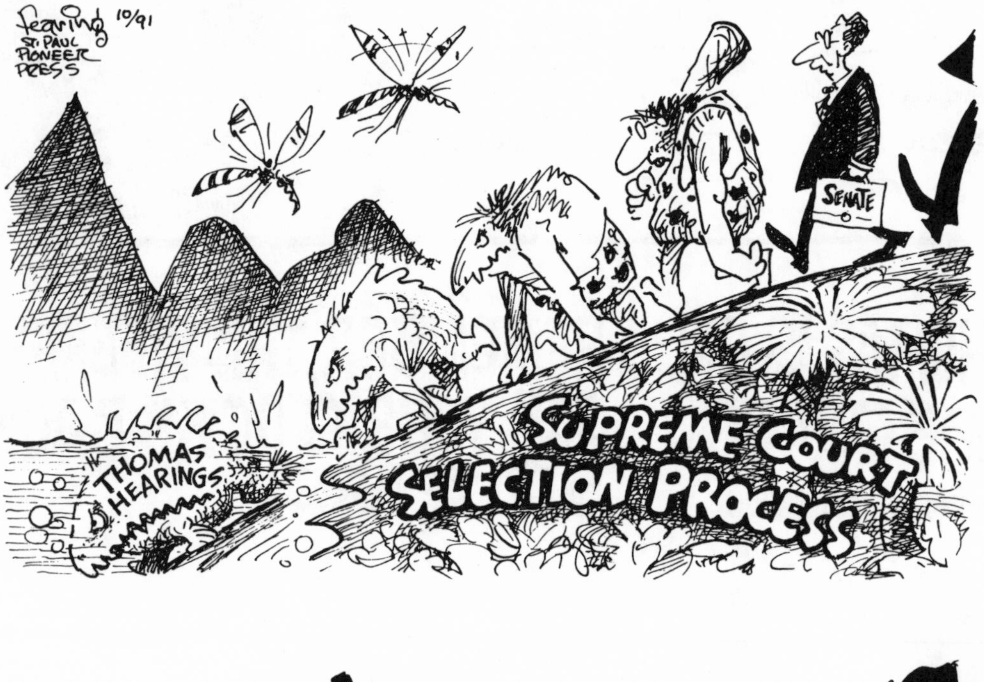
Fearing 10/91 ST. PAUL PIONEER PRESS
SENATE
THOMAS HEARINGS
SUPREME COURT SELECTION PROCESS

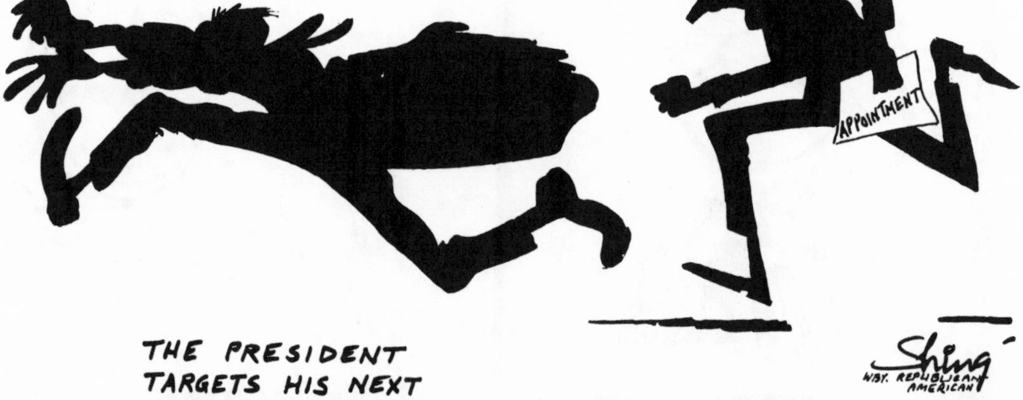
APPOINTMENT
Shing WBY. REPUBLICAN AMERICAN

THE PRESIDENT TARGETS HIS NEXT SUPREME COURT CANDIDATE.

J. R. SHINGLETON
Courtesy Waterbury Republican-American

DENNIS DRAUGHON
Courtesy Scranton Times

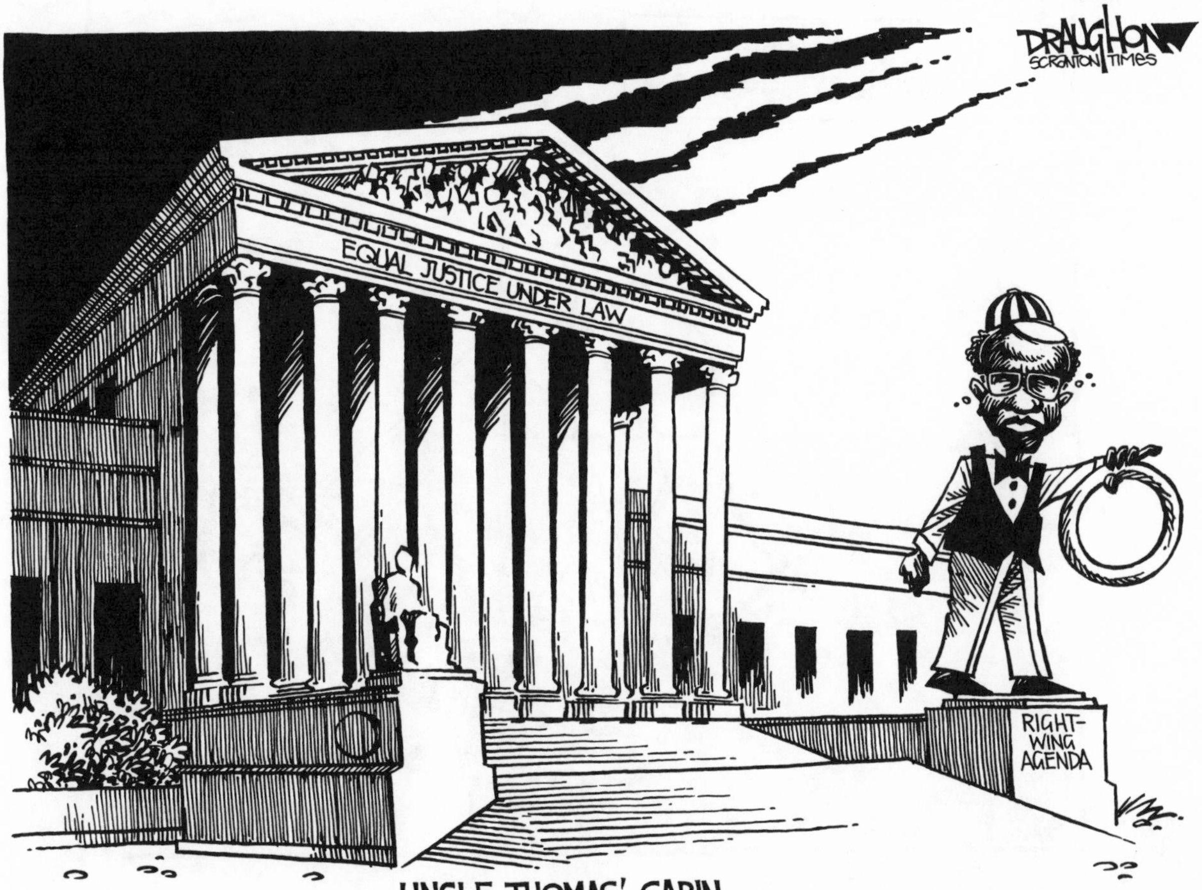
DRAUGHON SCRANTON TIMES
EQUAL JUSTICE UNDER LAW
RIGHT-WING AGENDA

UNCLE THOMAS' CABIN...

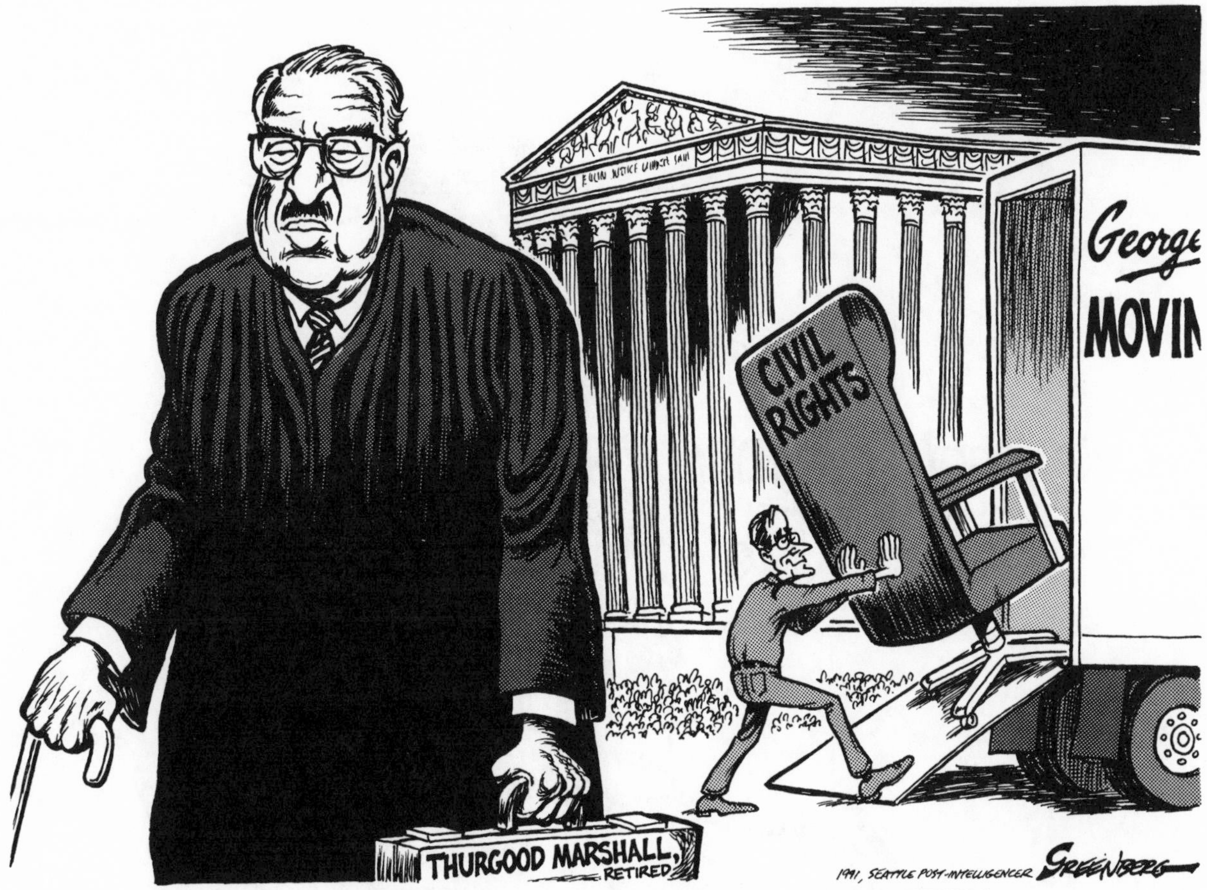
George
MOVIN
CIVIL RIGHTS
THURGOOD MARSHALL, RETIRED
1991, SEATTLE POST-INTELLIGENCER GREENBERG

STEVE GREENBERG
Courtesy Seattle Post-Intelligencer

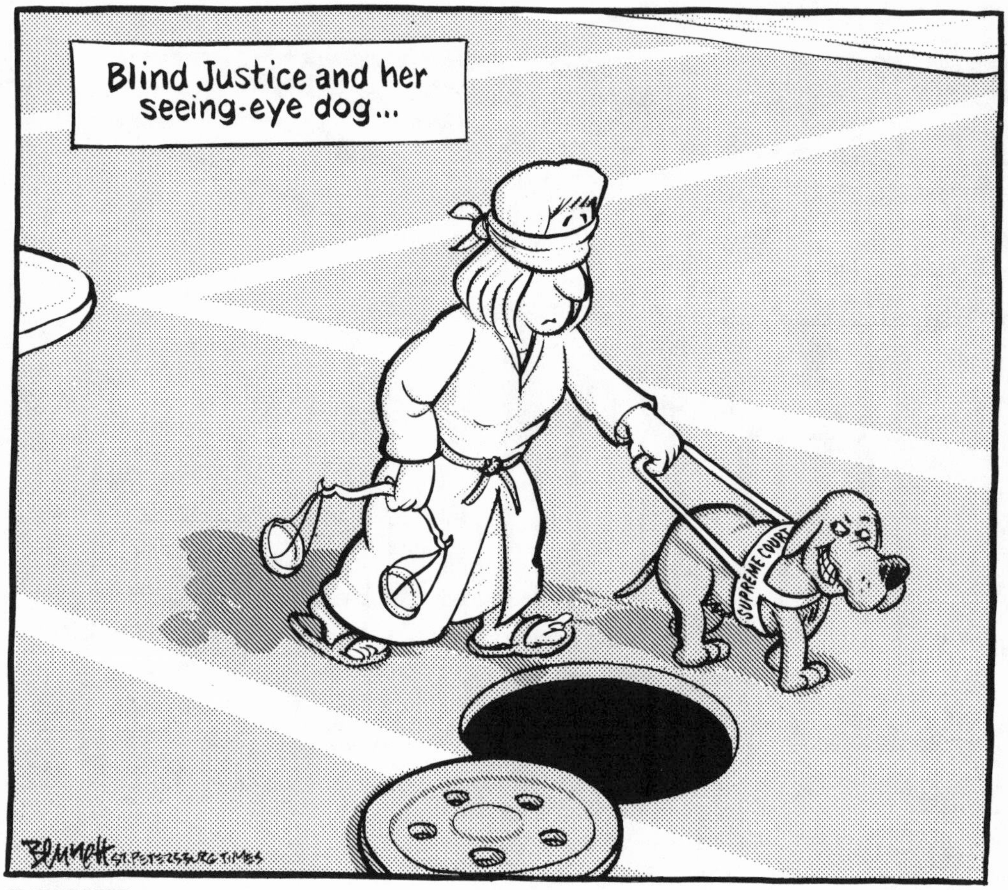
Blind Justice and her seeing-eye dog...
SUPREME COURT
Bennett ST. PETERSBURG TIMES

CLAY BENNETT
Courtesy St. Petersburg Times

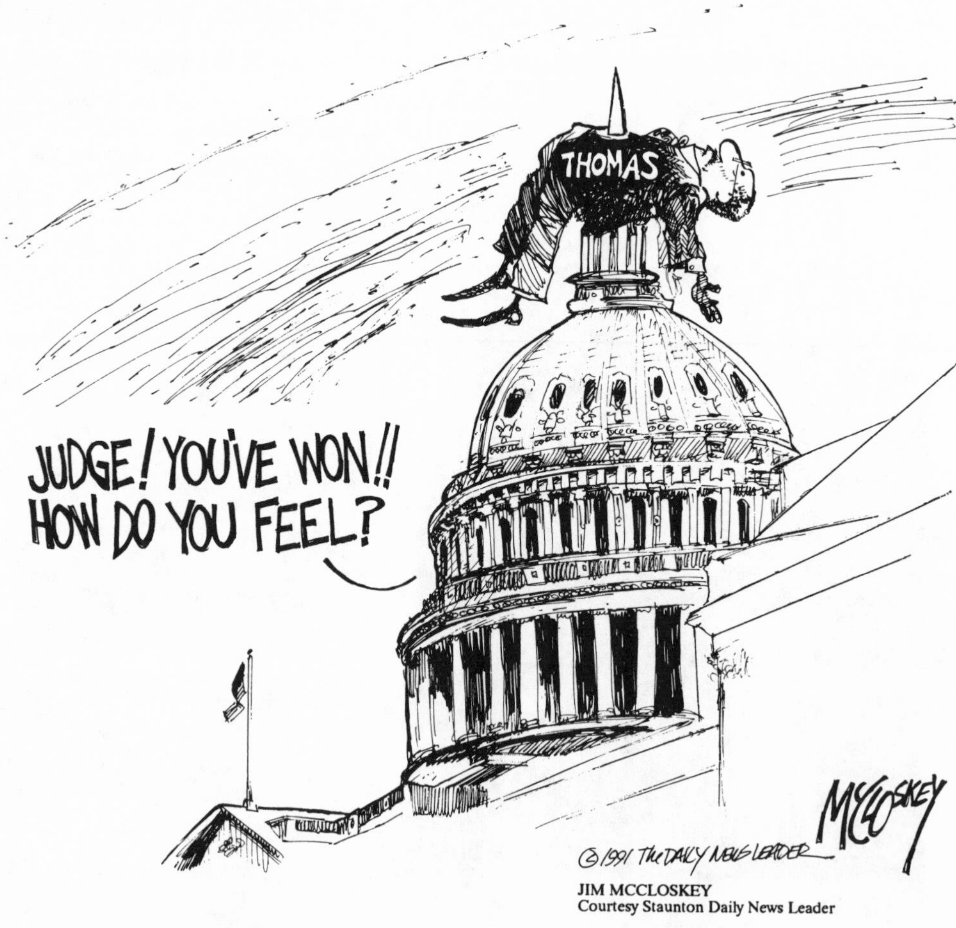
THOMAS
JUDGE! YOU'VE WON!! HOW DO YOU FEEL?
McCLOSKEY
© 1991 The DAILY NEWS LEADER

JIM MCCLOSKEY
Courtesy Staunton Daily News Leader

JEFF MACNELLY
Courtesy Chicago Tribune and
Tribune Media Services

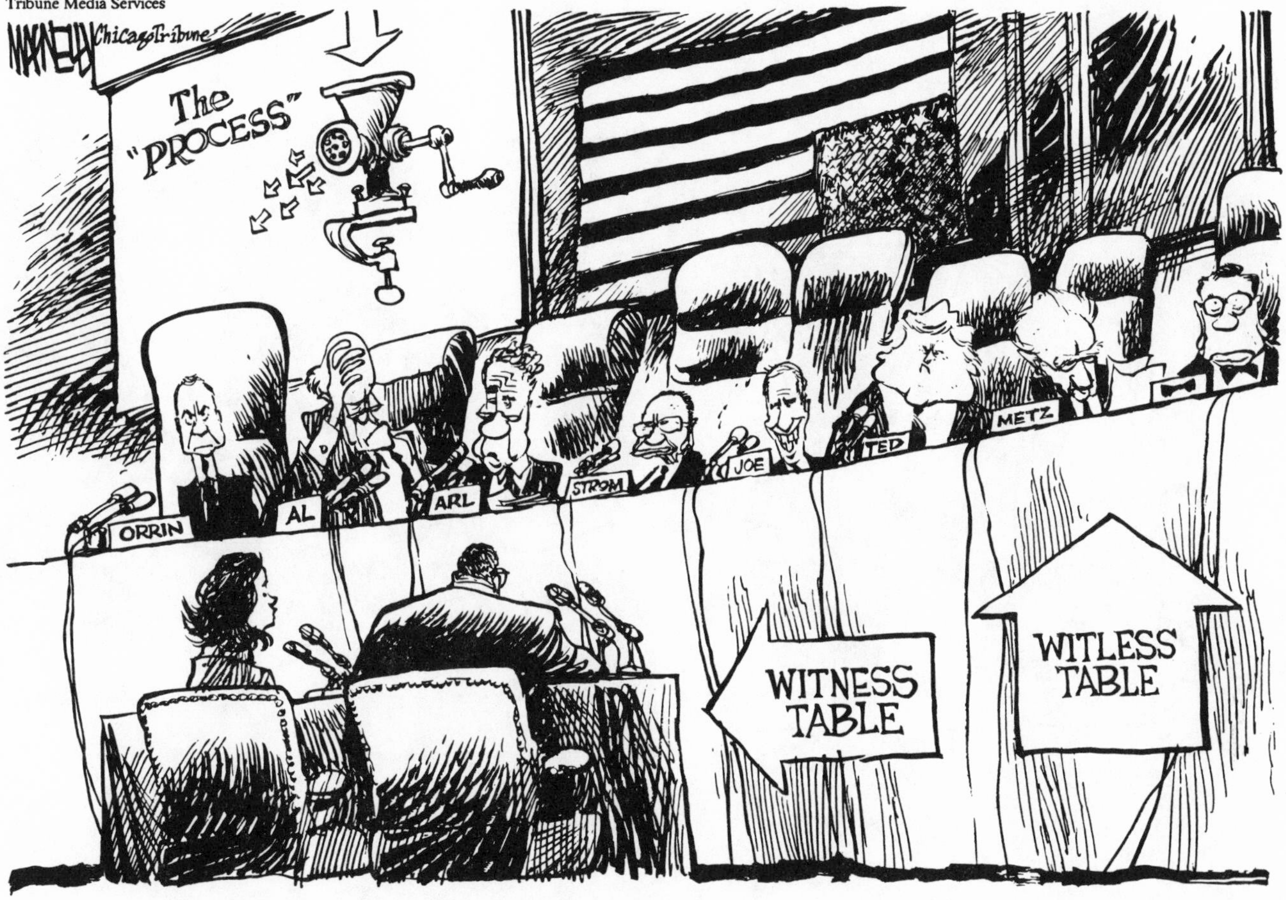
MACNELLY ChicagoTribune
The "PROCESS"
ORRIN
AL
ARL
STROM
JOE
TED
METZ
WITNESS TABLE
WITLESS TABLE

BOB ENGLEHART
Courtesy Hartford Courant

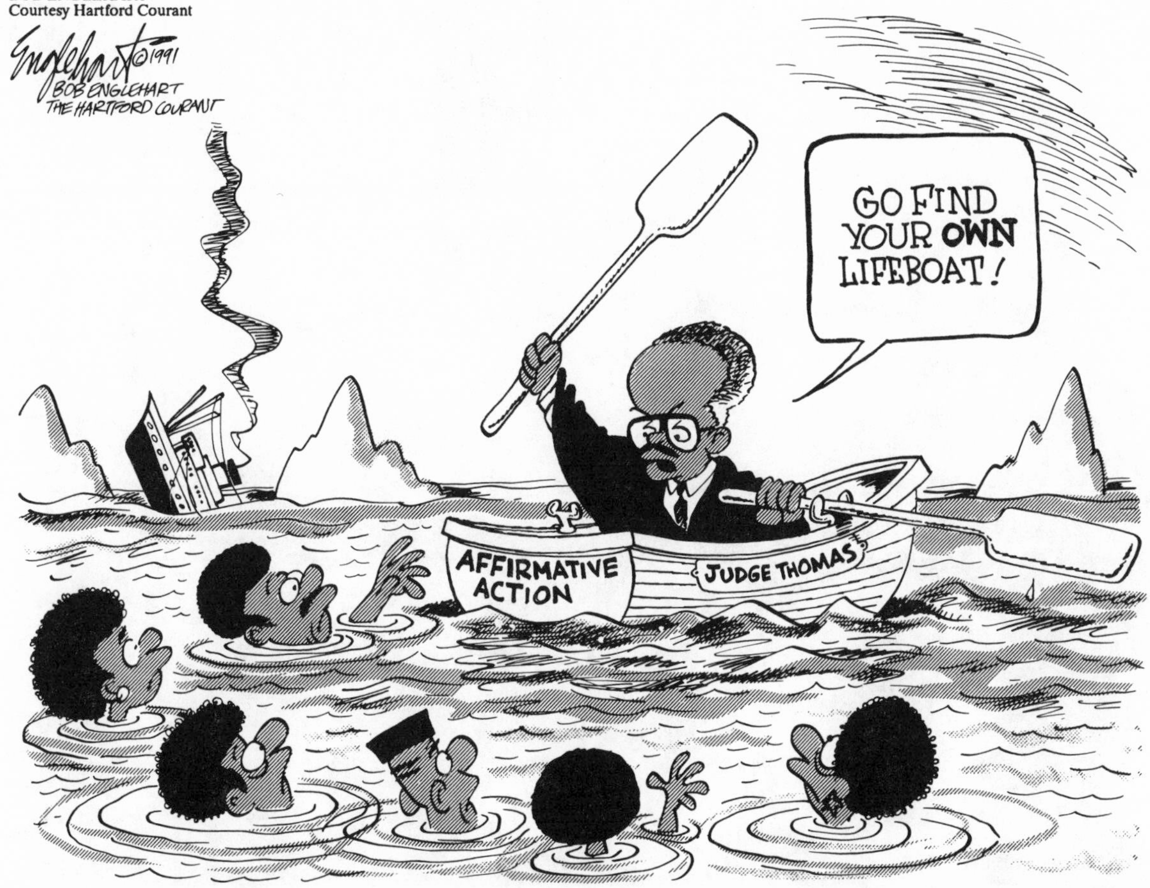
Englehart ©1991
BOB ENGLEHART
THE HARTFORD COURANT
GO FIND YOUR **OWN** LIFEBOAT!
AFFIRMATIVE ACTION
JUDGE THOMAS

BRIAN DUFFY
Courtesy Des Moines Register

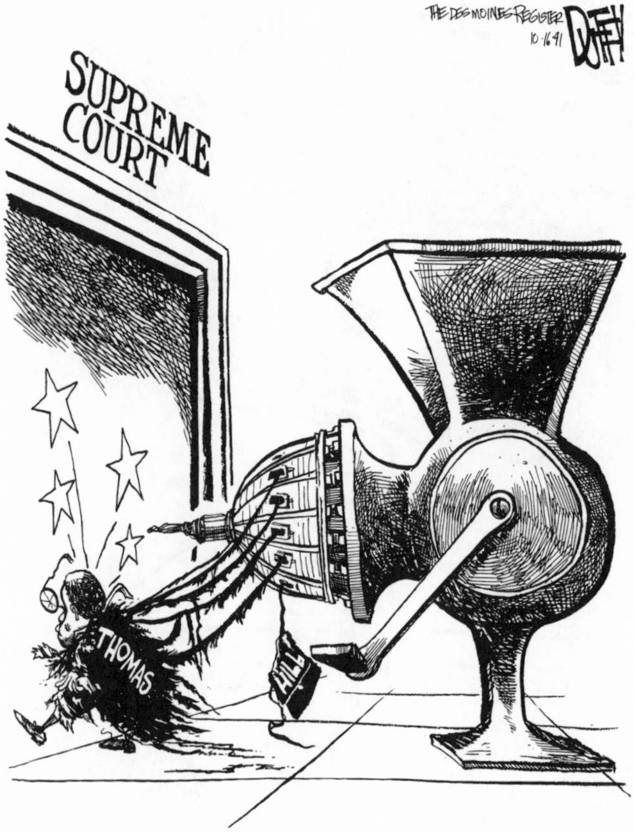
THE DES MOINES REGISTER 10-16-91 DUFFY
SUPREME COURT
THOMAS
HILL

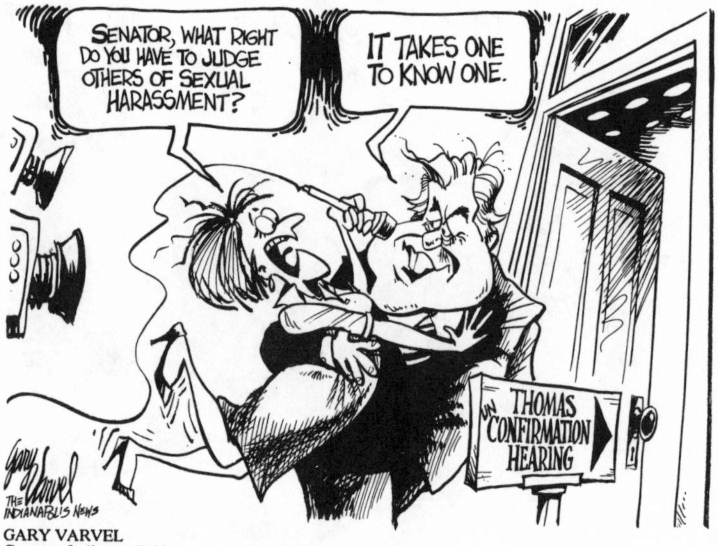
SENATOR, WHAT RIGHT DO YOU HAVE TO JUDGE OTHERS OF SEXUAL HARASSMENT?
IT TAKES ONE TO KNOW ONE.
THOMAS UN CONFIRMATION HEARING

GARY VARVEL
Courtesy Indianapolis News

CHRIS OBRION
Courtesy Potomac News

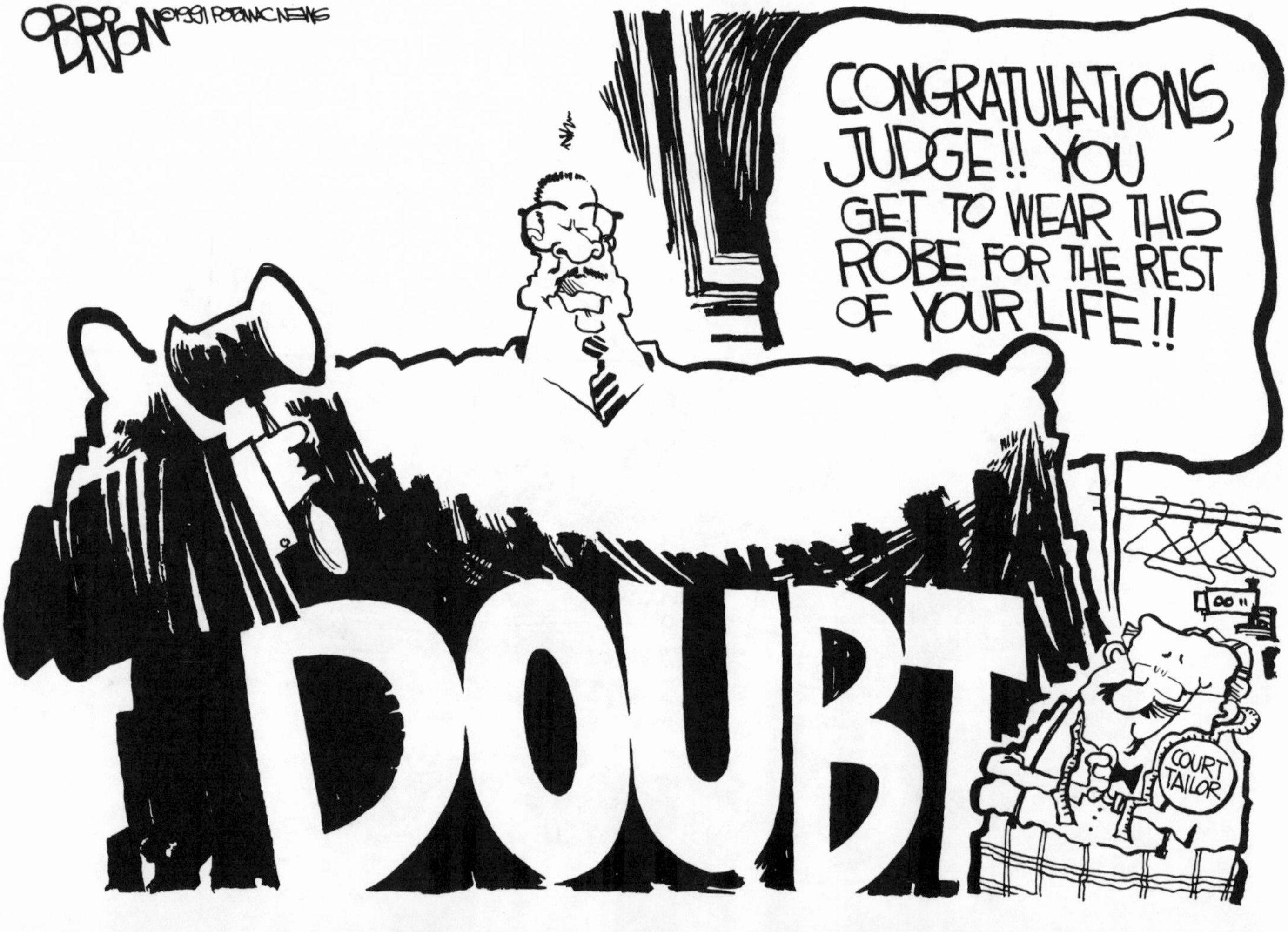
OBRION ©1991 POTOMAC NEWS
CONGRATULATIONS, JUDGE!! YOU GET TO WEAR THIS ROBE FOR THE REST OF YOUR LIFE!!
DOUBT
COURT TAILOR

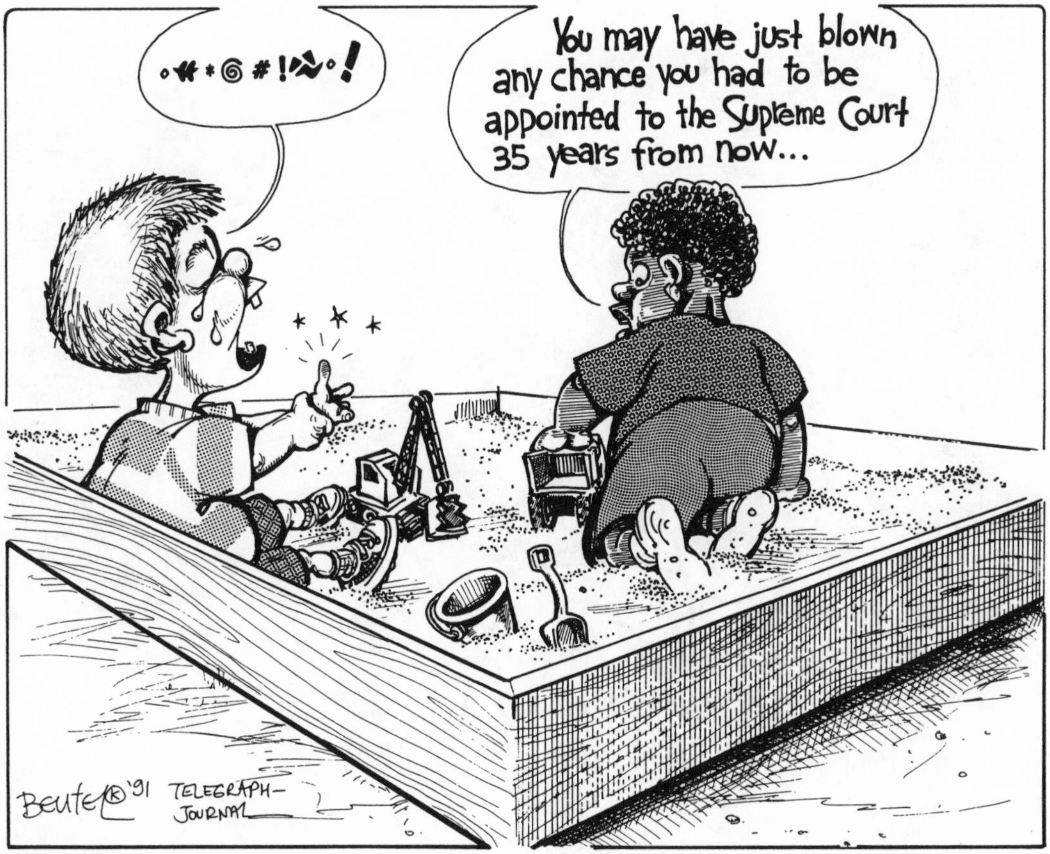
You may have just blown any chance you had to be appointed to the Supreme Court 35 years from now...
BEUTEL ©'91 TELEGRAPH-JOURNAL

JOSH BEUTEL
Courtesy New Brunswick Telegraph-Journal

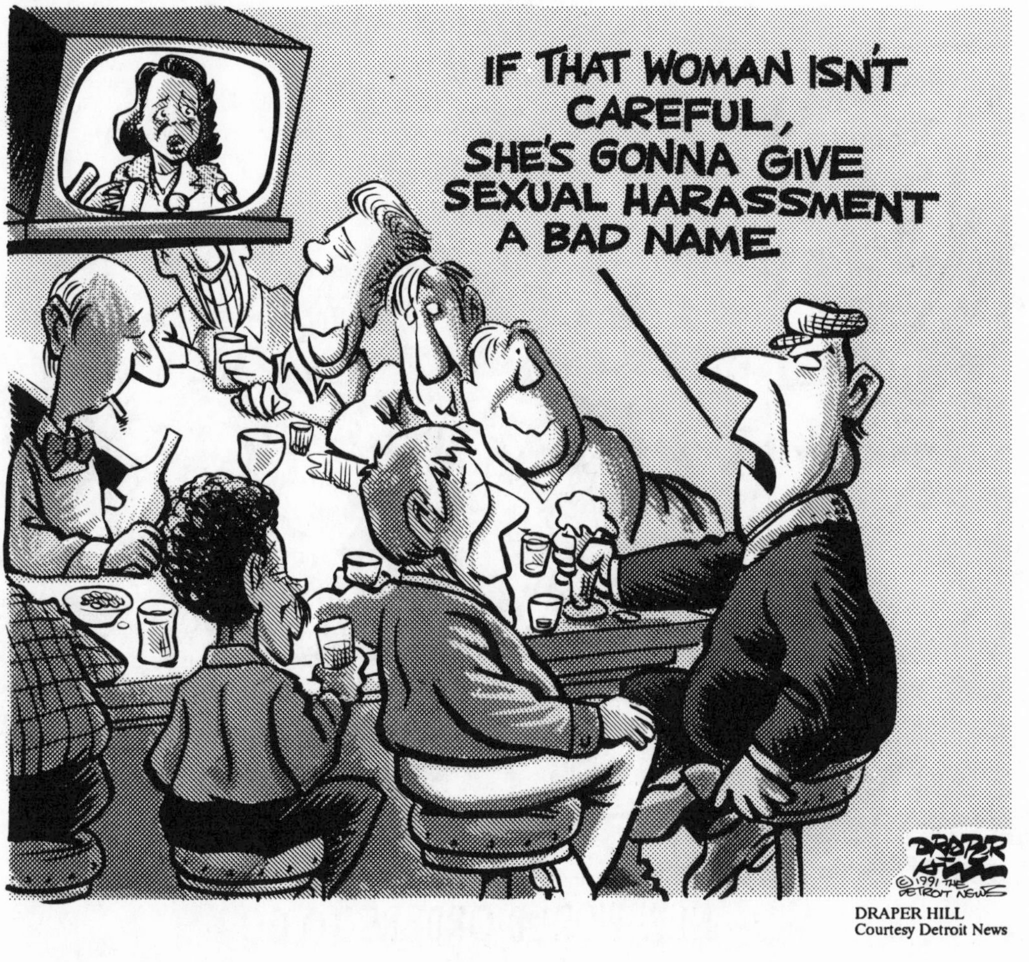
IF THAT WOMAN ISN'T CAREFUL, SHE'S GONNA GIVE SEXUAL HARASSMENT A BAD NAME.
©1991 THE DETROIT NEWS

DRAPER HILL
Courtesy Detroit News

BRUCE TINSLEY
Courtesy Washington Times

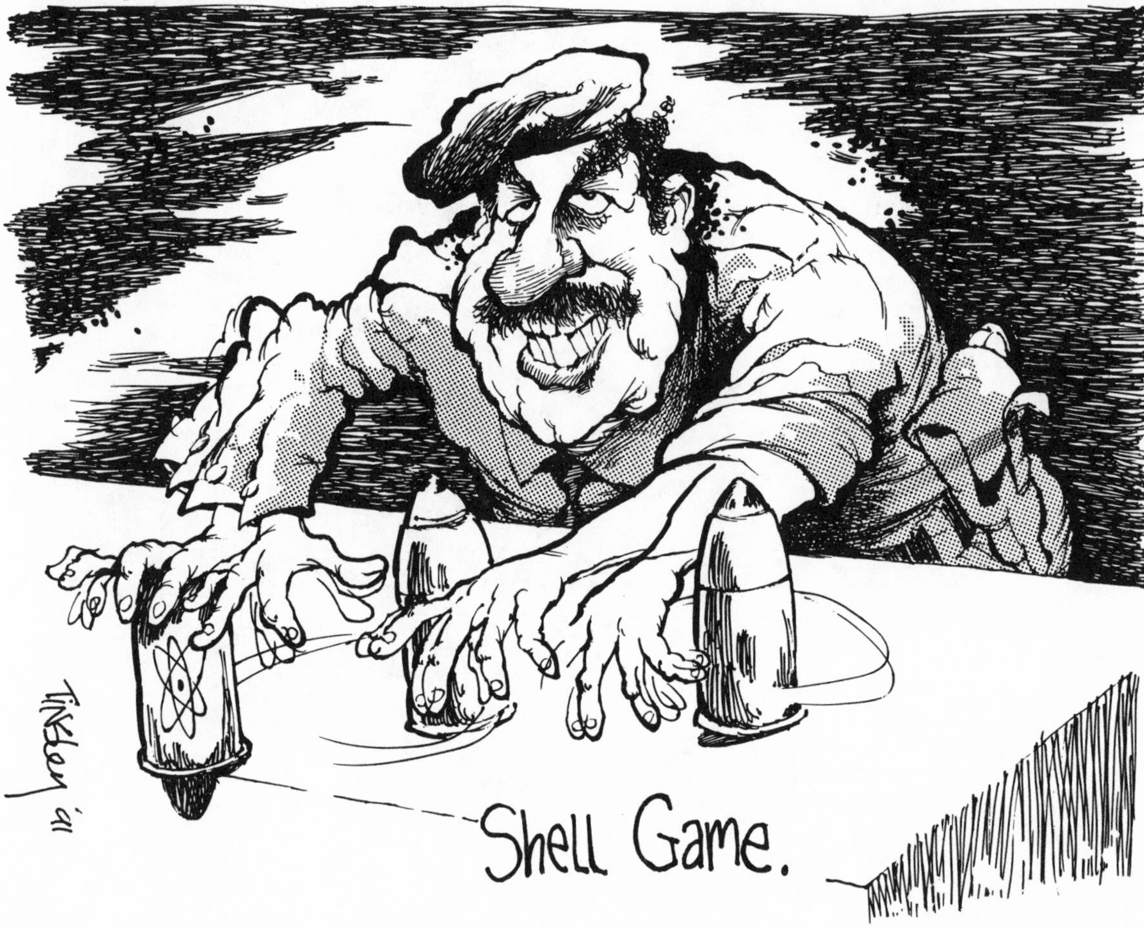
TINSLEY '91
Shell Game.

DAVID SWANN
Courtesy Huntsville Times (Ala.)

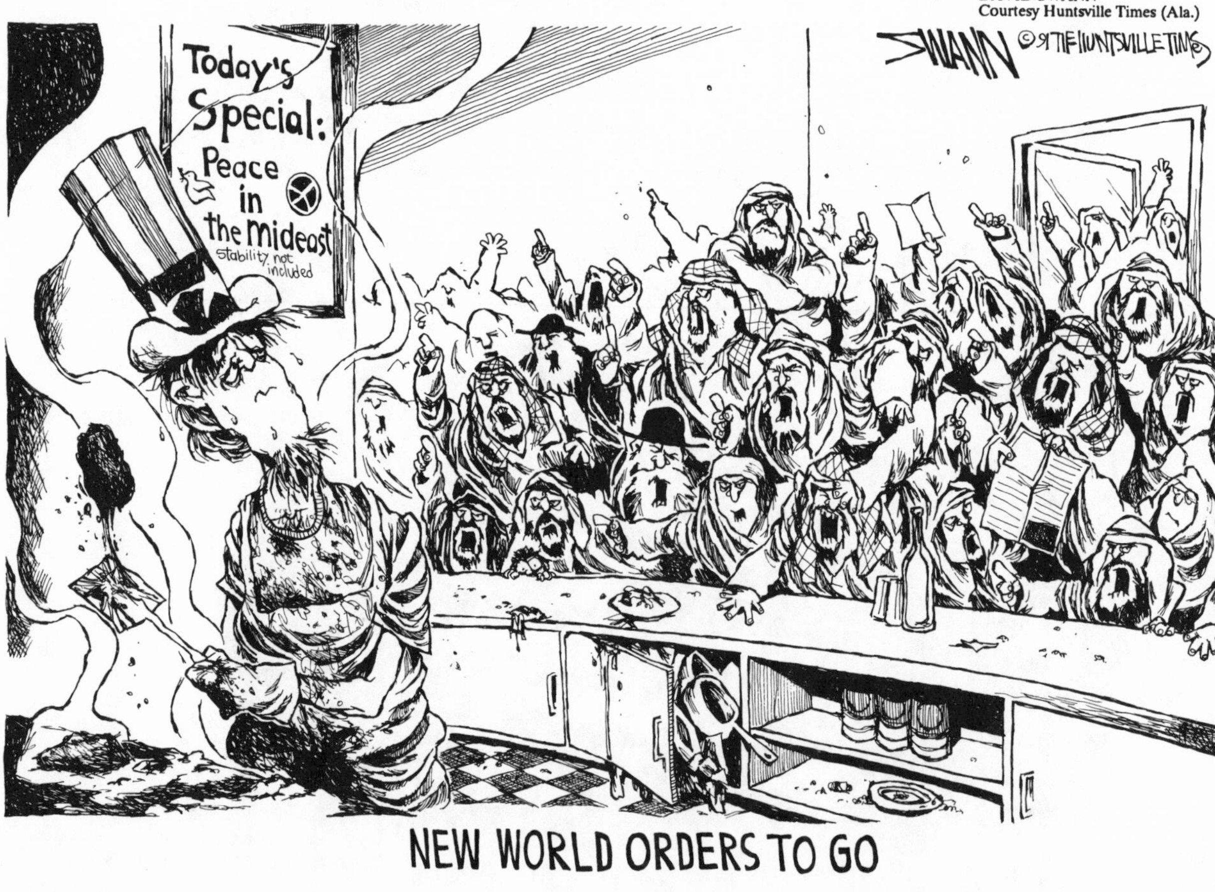
SWANN ©91 THE HUNTSVILLE TIMES
Today's Special:
Peace in the mideast
stability not included

NEW WORLD ORDERS TO GO

The Mideast

After eight months of shuttle diplomacy, Secretary of State James Baker put together a historic peace conference between Arabs and Israel. It marked the first direct negotiations between the age-old enemies. The Palestine Liberation Organization, which backed Saddam Hussein in the Gulf War, was barred from participation. The talks continued into 1992, and all observers agreed that genuine peace was a shaky prospect at best.

The "hostage era" finally ended in 1991, with the release of fourteen men held in Lebanon by various Arab factions, including Americans Edward Tracy, Thomas Sutherland, Joseph Cicippio, Alann Steen, Jesse Turner, and Terry Anderson.

After Saddam Hussein unleashed his troops to slaughter Kurds in the mountains of Iraq, the U.S. stationed a military task force along the Turkish border in an attempt to protect them.

MISSION: IMPOSSIBLE
YOUR MISSION MR. BAKER IS TO BRING PEACE TO THE MIDDLE EAST. GOOD LUCK, JIM. THIS PHONE BOOTH SELF-DESTRUCTS IN FIVE SECONDS...
TELEPHONE
TNT
DANBY ©1991
BANGOR NEWS

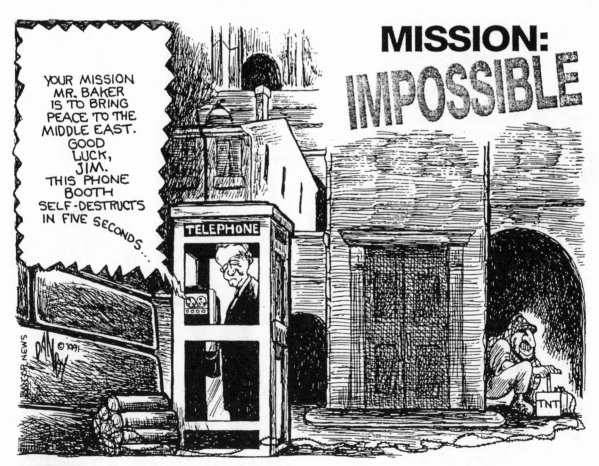

GEORGE DANBY
Courtesy Bangor Daily News

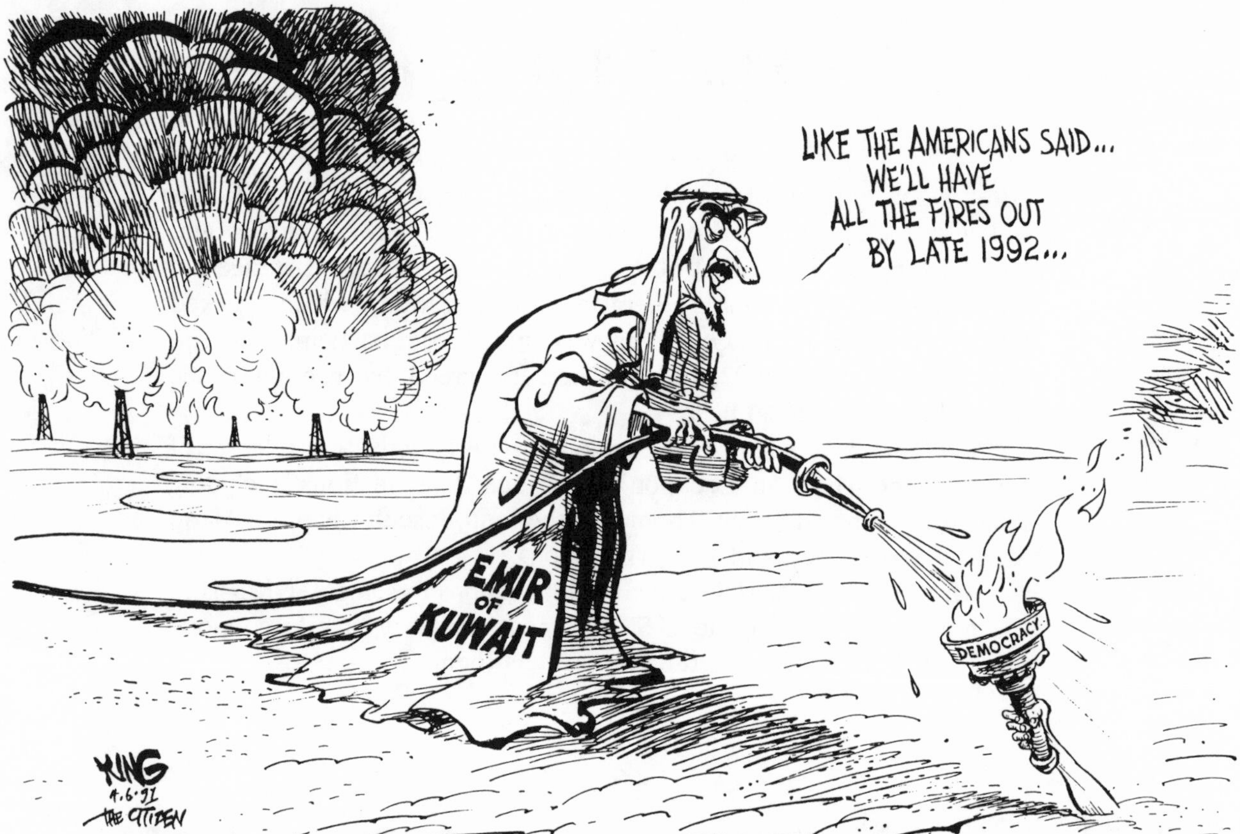
LIKE THE AMERICANS SAID... WE'LL HAVE ALL THE FIRES OUT BY LATE 1992...
EMIR OF KUWAIT
DEMOCRACY
KING 4.6.91 THE CITIZEN

ALAN KING
Courtesy Ottawa Citizen

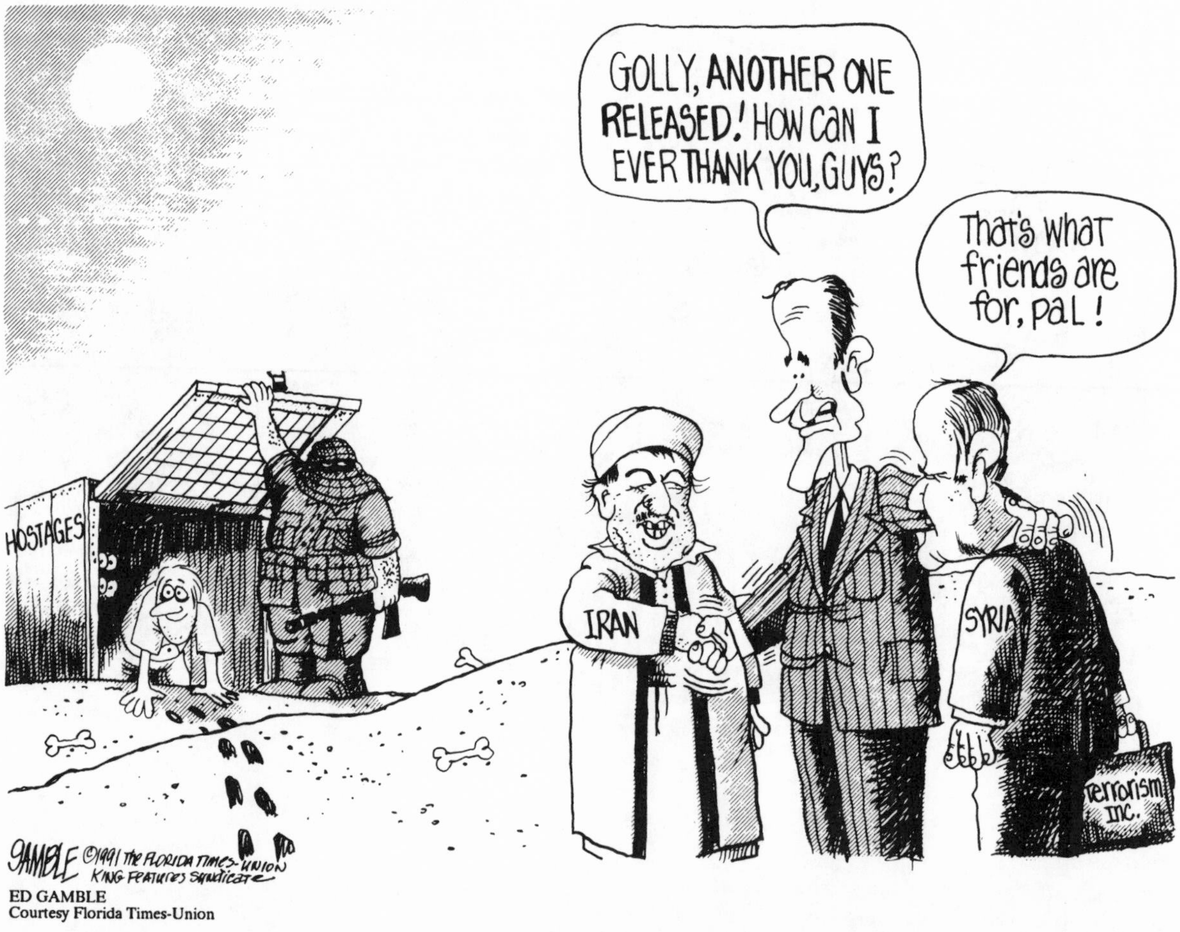
GOLLY, ANOTHER ONE RELEASED! HOW CAN I EVER THANK YOU, GUYS?
That's what friends are for, pal!
HOSTAGES
IRAN
SYRIA
terrorism INC.
GAMBLE ©1991 The Florida Times-Union King Features Syndicate

ED GAMBLE
Courtesy Florida Times-Union

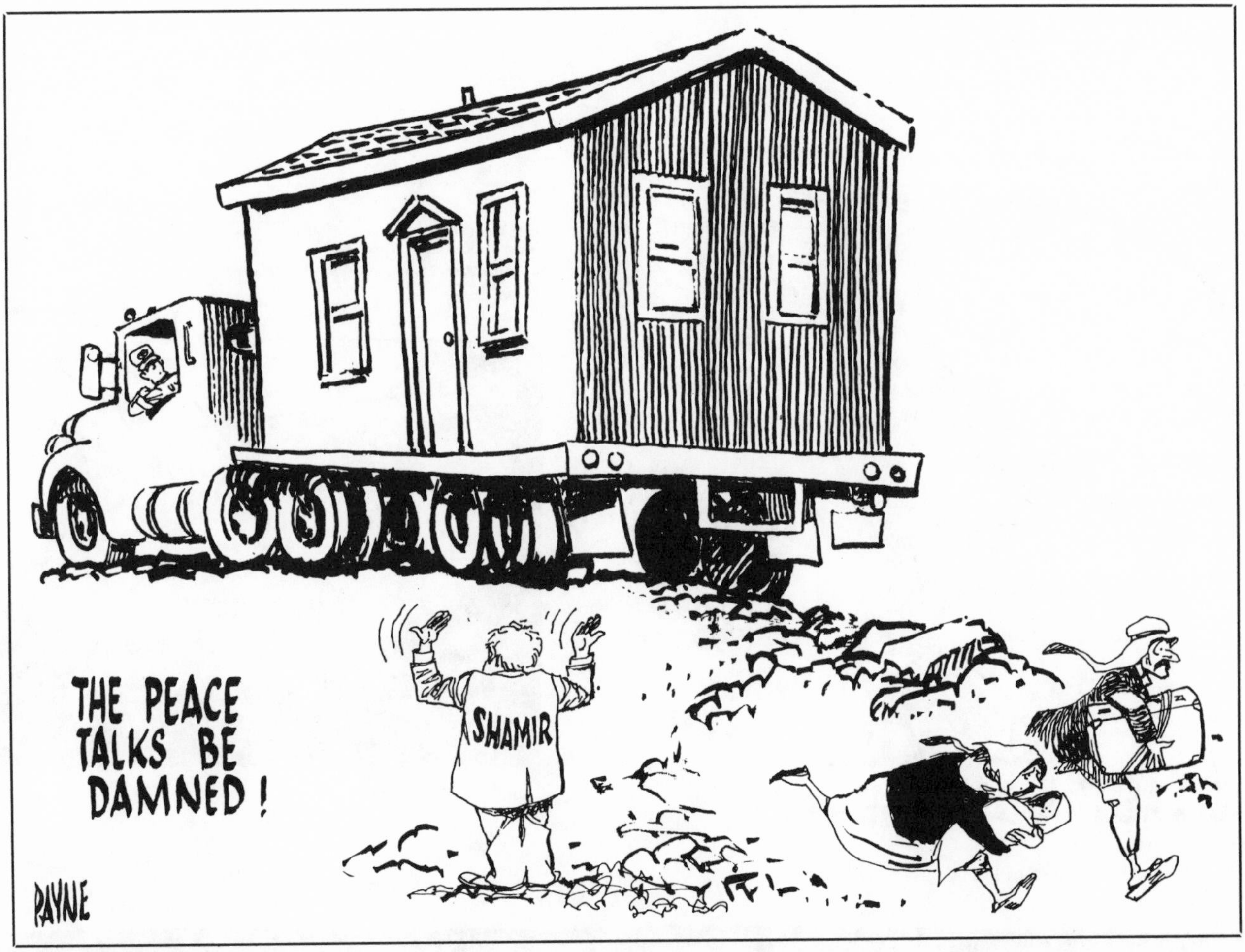
THE PEACE
TALKS BE
DAMNED!
SHAMIR
PAYNE

EUGENE PAYNE
Courtesy Charlotte Observer

MIKE KEEFE
Courtesy Denver Post

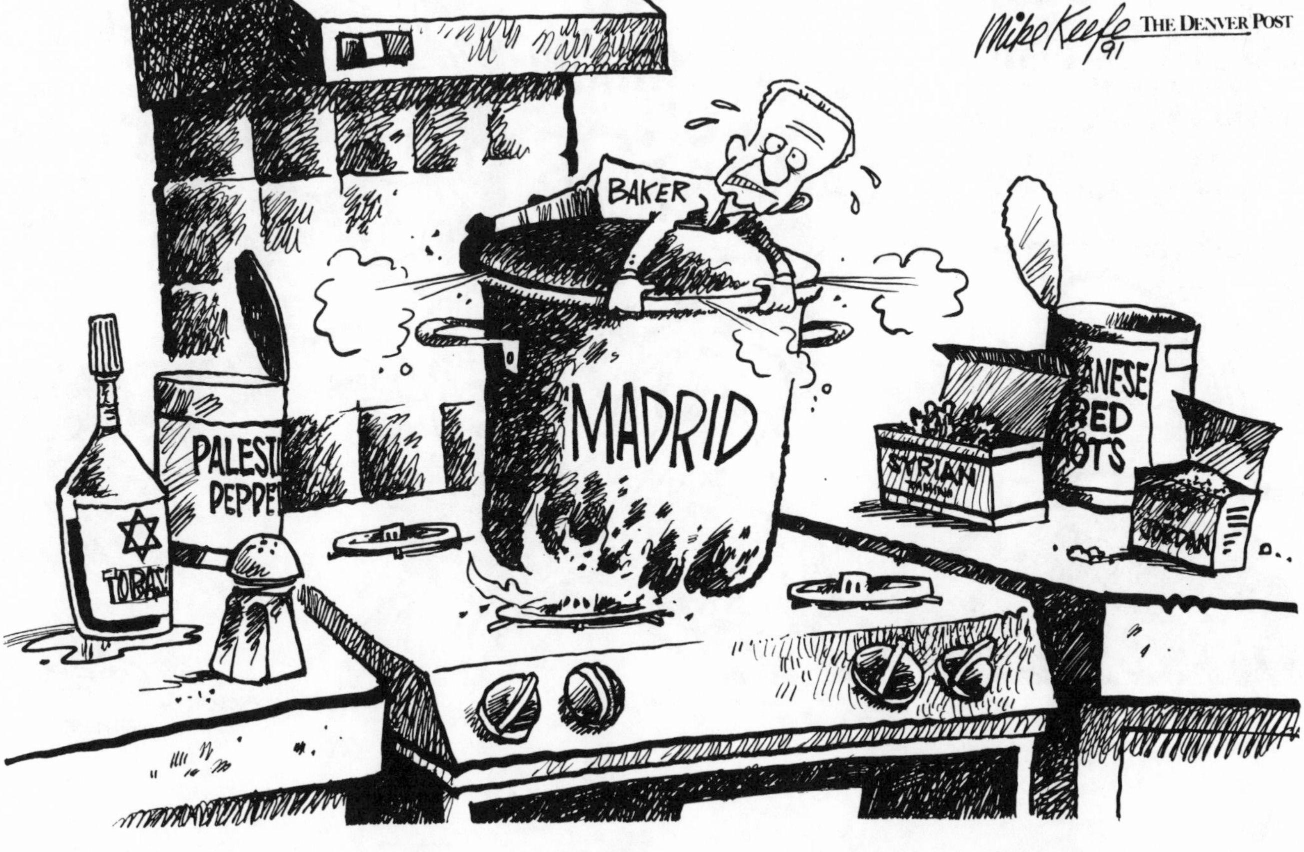
Mike Keefe 91 THE DENVER POST
BAKER
MADRID
SYRIAN
JORDAN

CHIP BECK
Courtesy Northern Virginia Sun
and Associated Features

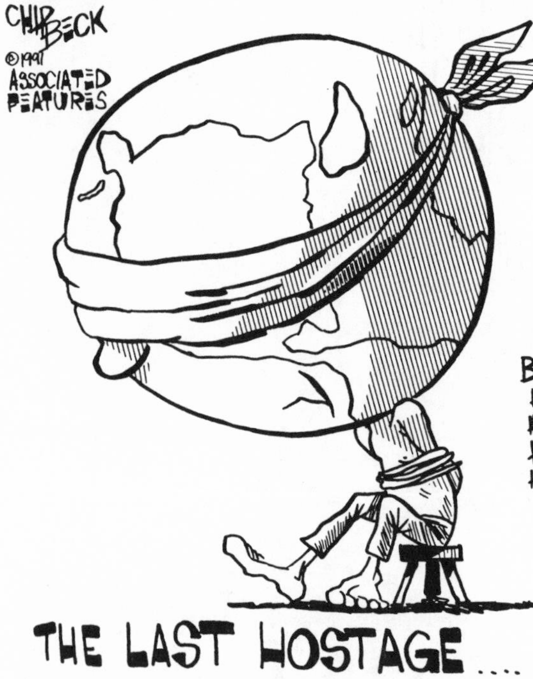
CHIP BECK
©1991
ASSOCIATED
FEATURES
BEIRUT - 1984
..1990...1991
THE LAST HOSTAGE....

BILL GARNER
Courtesy Washington Times

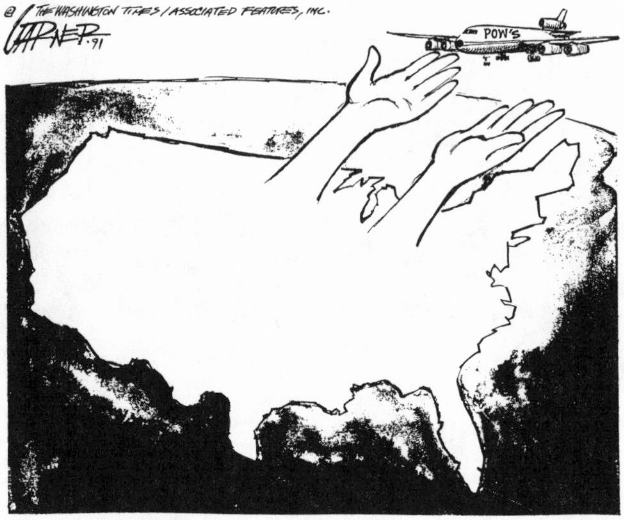
© THE WASHINGTON TIMES / ASSOCIATED FEATURES, INC.
GARNER '91
POW'S

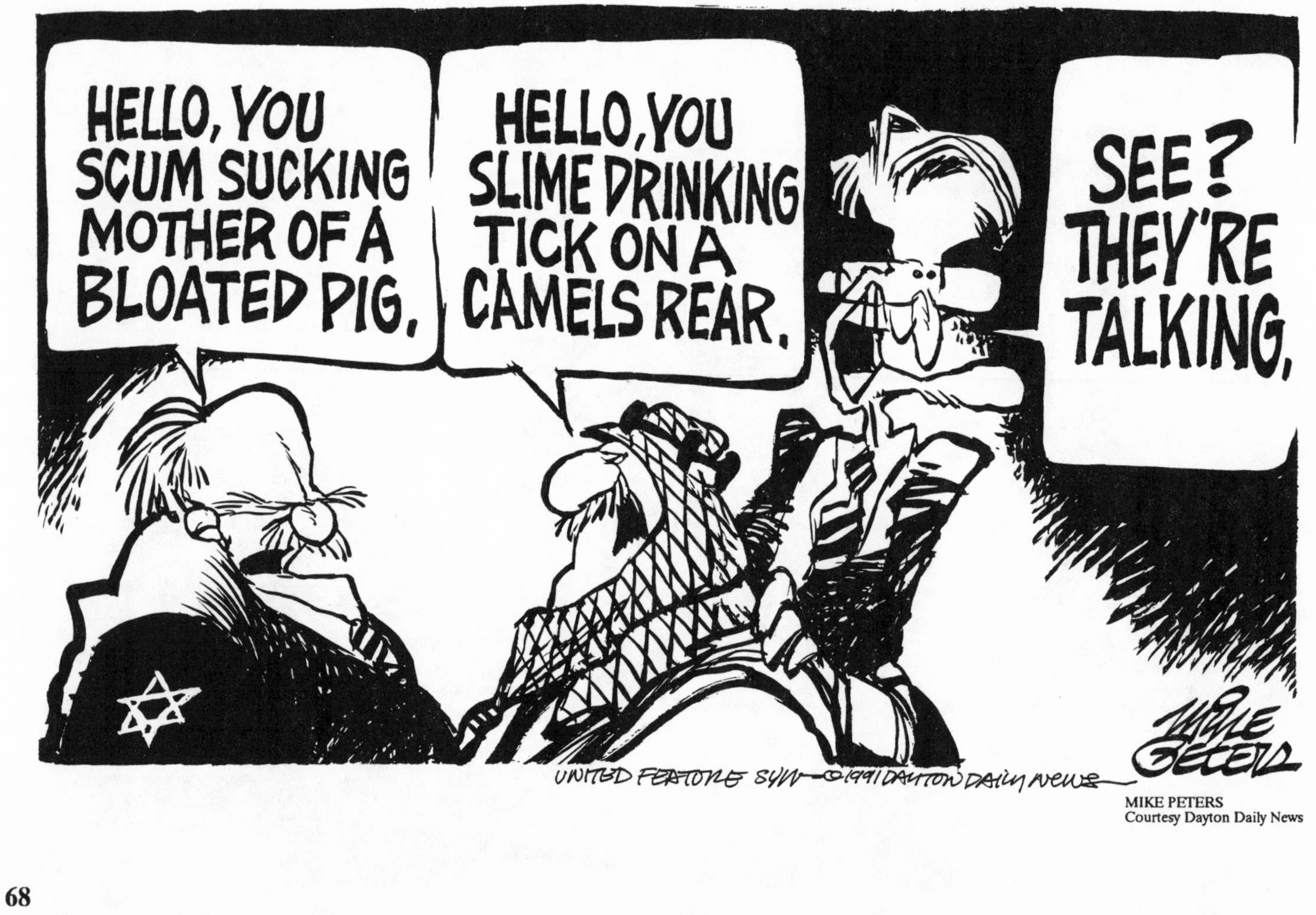
HELLO, YOU SCUM SUCKING MOTHER OF A BLOATED PIG.
HELLO, YOU SLIME DRINKING TICK ON A CAMELS REAR.
SEE? THEY'RE TALKING.
MIKE PETERS
UNITED FEATURE SYN ©1991 DAYTON DAILY NEWS

MIKE PETERS
Courtesy Dayton Daily News

JERRY HOLBERT
Courtesy Boston Herald

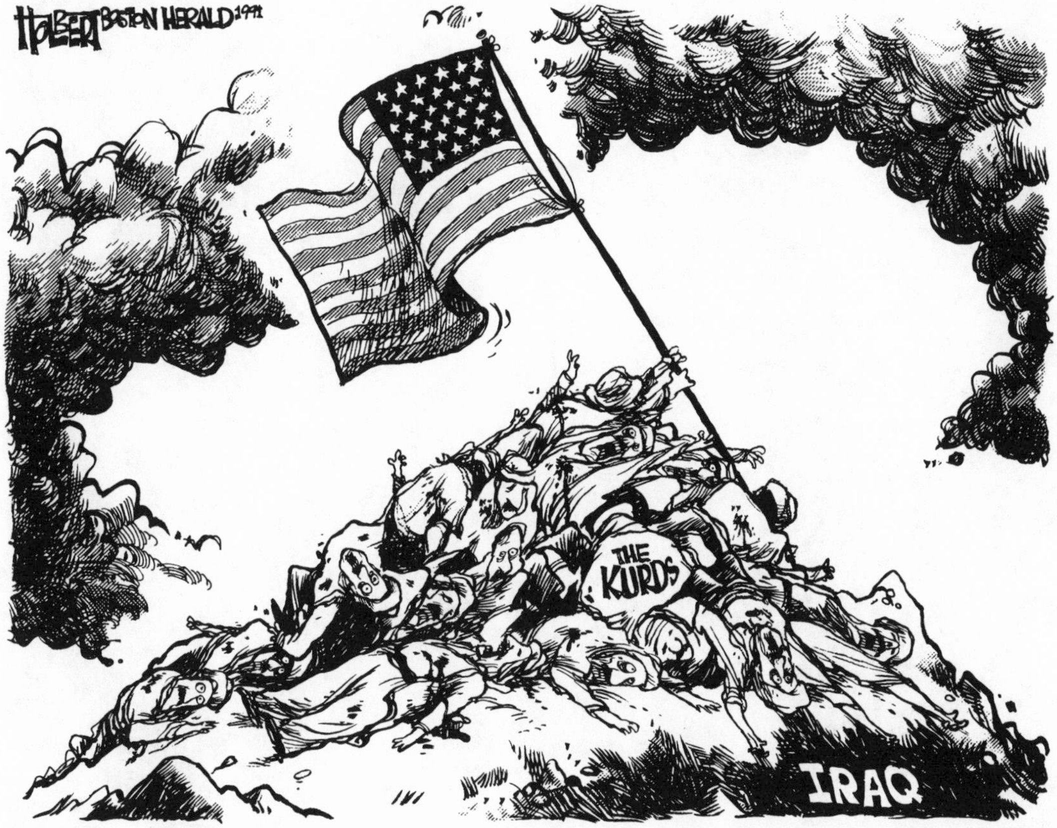
HOLBERT BOSTON HERALD 1991
THE KURDS
IRAQ

TIM HARTMAN
Courtesy Valley News Dispatch (Pa.)

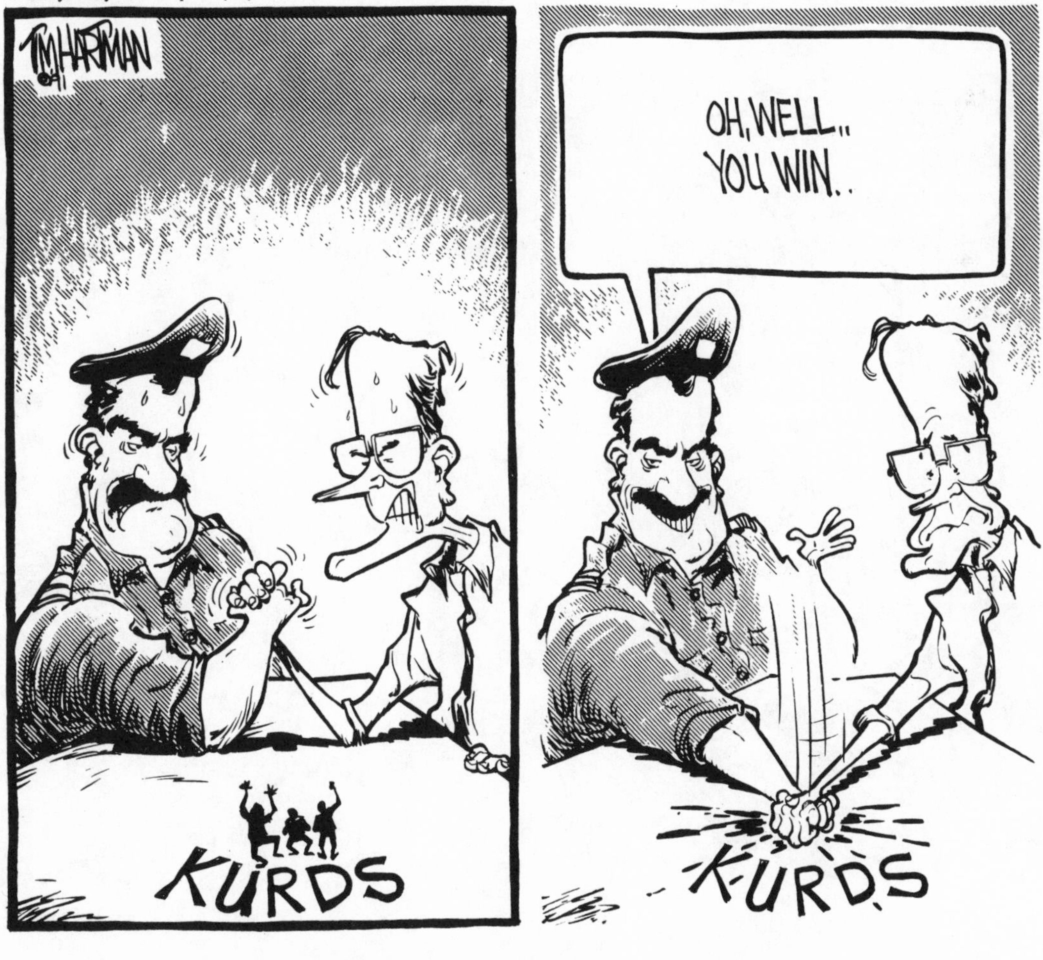
TIM HARTMAN ©91
KURDS
OH, WELL.. YOU WIN..
KURDS

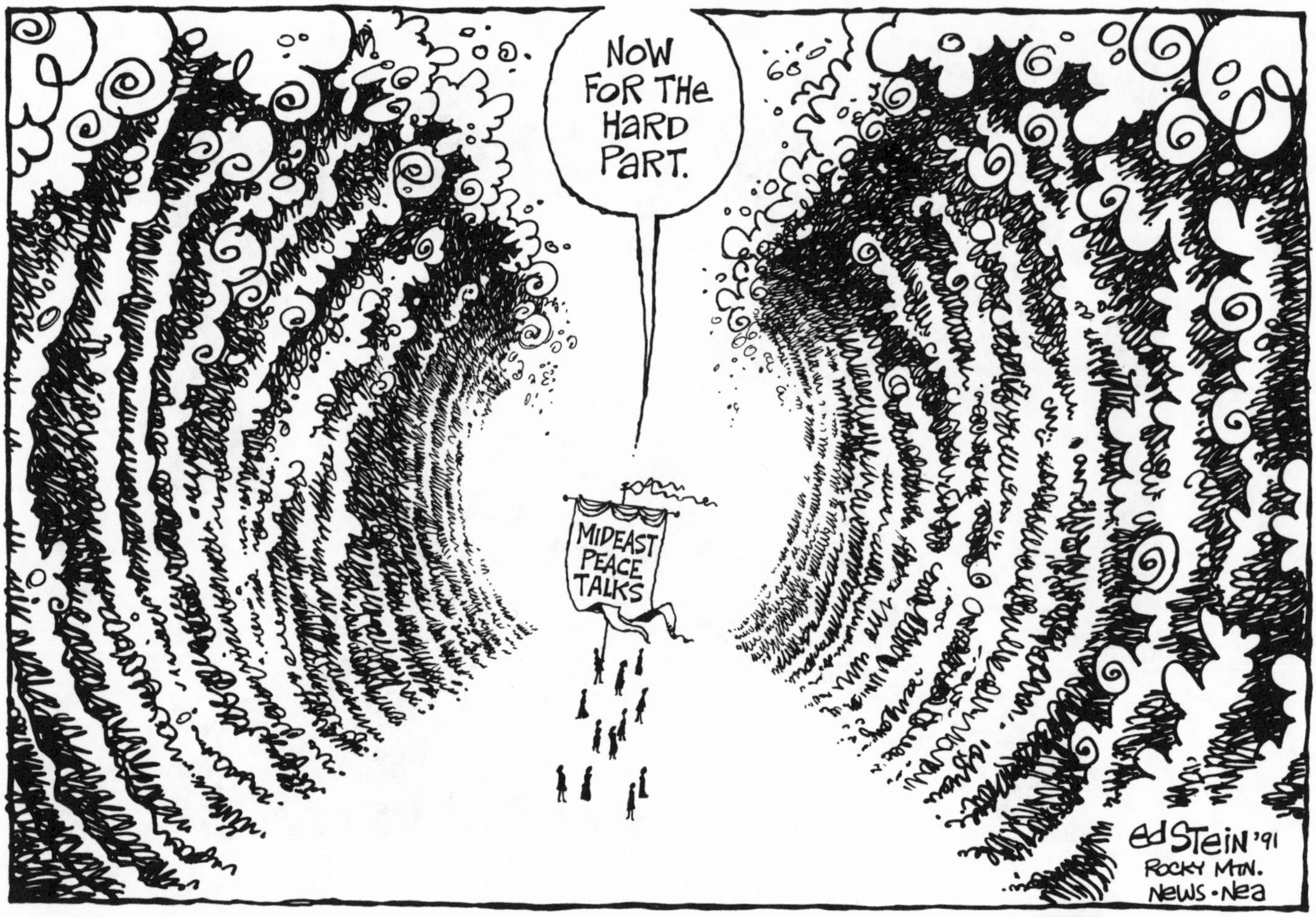
NOW FOR THE HARD PART.
MIDEAST PEACE TALKS
ed STEIN '91 ROCKY MTN. NEWS • NEA

ED STEIN
Courtesy Rocky Mountain News and NEA

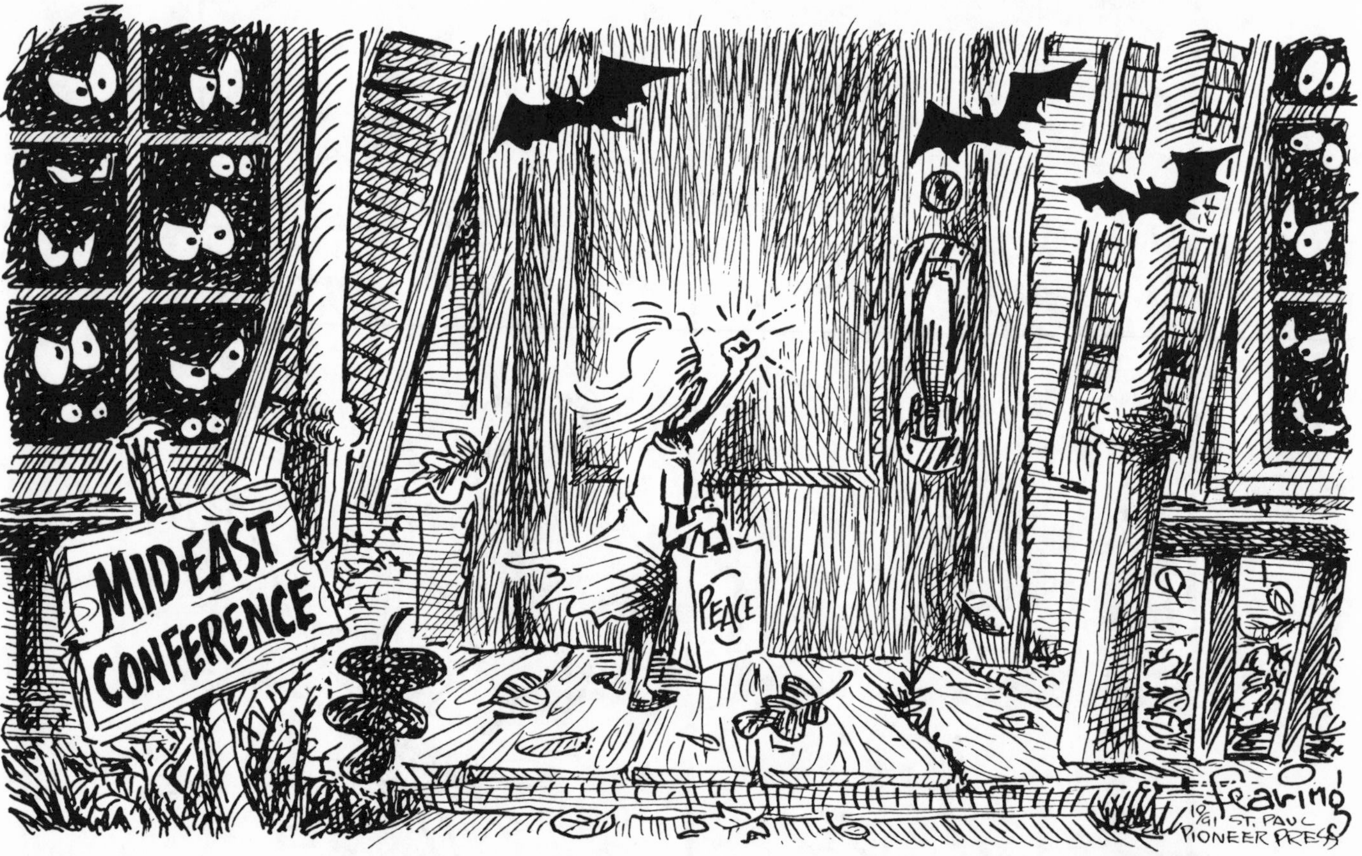
MID-EAST CONFERENCE
PEACE
FEARING 10/91 ST. PAUL PIONEER PRESS

JERRY FEARING
Courtesy St. Paul Pioneer Press-Dispatch

GARY MARKSTEIN
Courtesy Tribune Newspapers

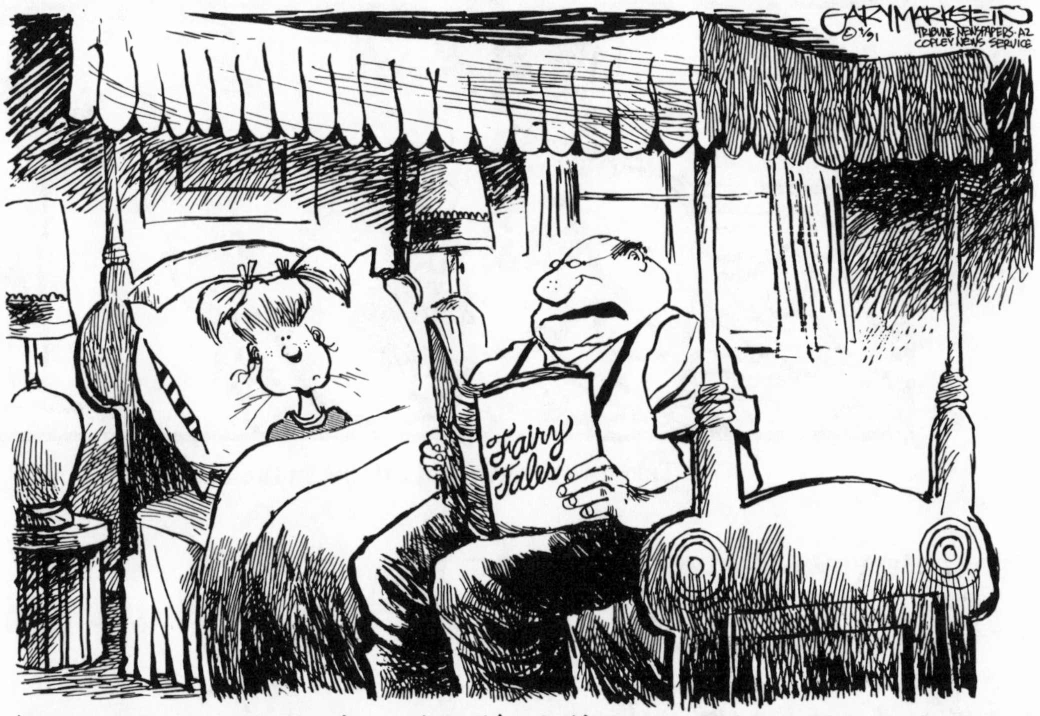
Fairy Tales

"BAKER'S PEACE PLAN WAS LOVED BY EVERYONE: ARAFAT SOUGHT ARAB-ISRAELI PEACE, SHAMIR STOPPED THE WEST BANK SETTLEMENTS, THE PALESTINIANS GOT A HOMELAND AND EVERYONE LIVED HAPPILY EVER AFTER..."

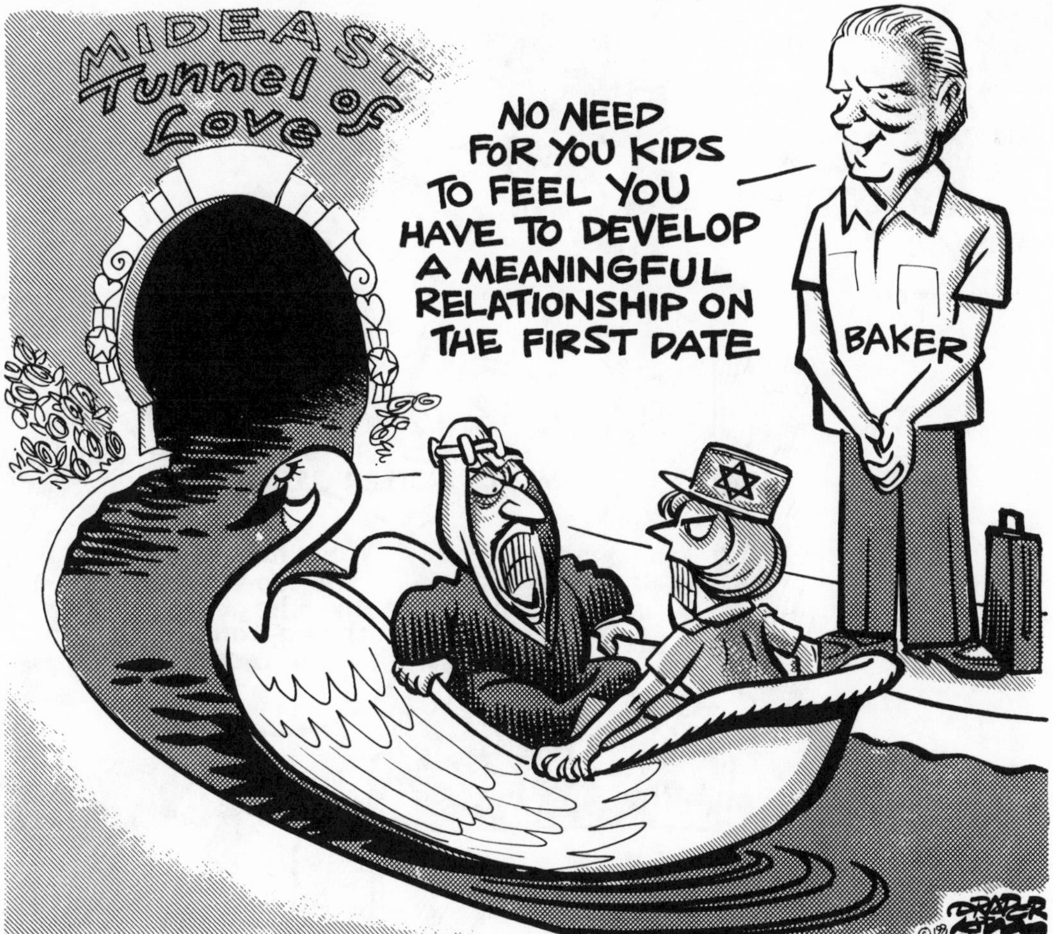
MIDEAST Tunnel of Love
NO NEED FOR YOU KIDS TO FEEL YOU HAVE TO DEVELOP A MEANINGFUL RELATIONSHIP ON THE FIRST DATE
BAKER

DRAPER HILL
Courtesy Detroit News

TOM CURTIS
Courtesy National Review

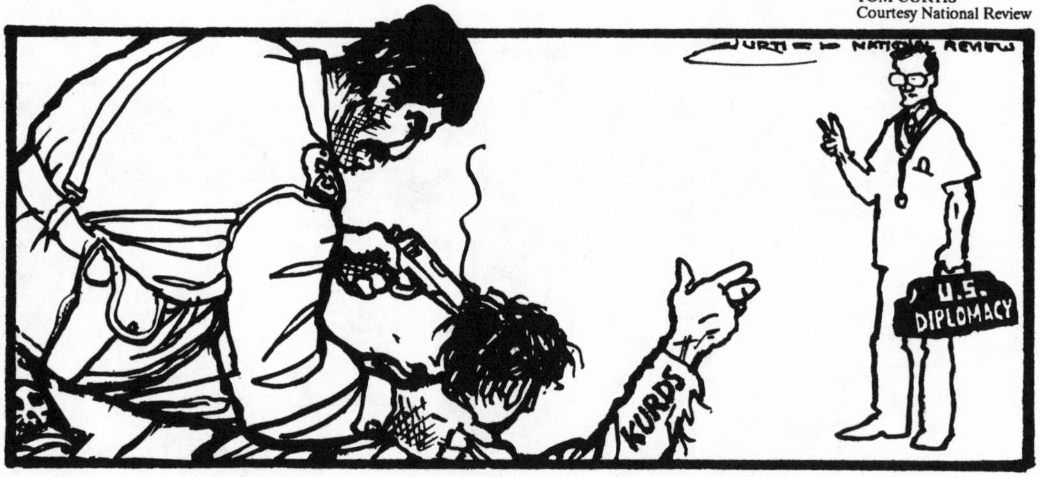
CURTIS NATIONAL REVIEW
U.S. DIPLOMACY
KURDS

"Take two aspirin and call me in the morning."

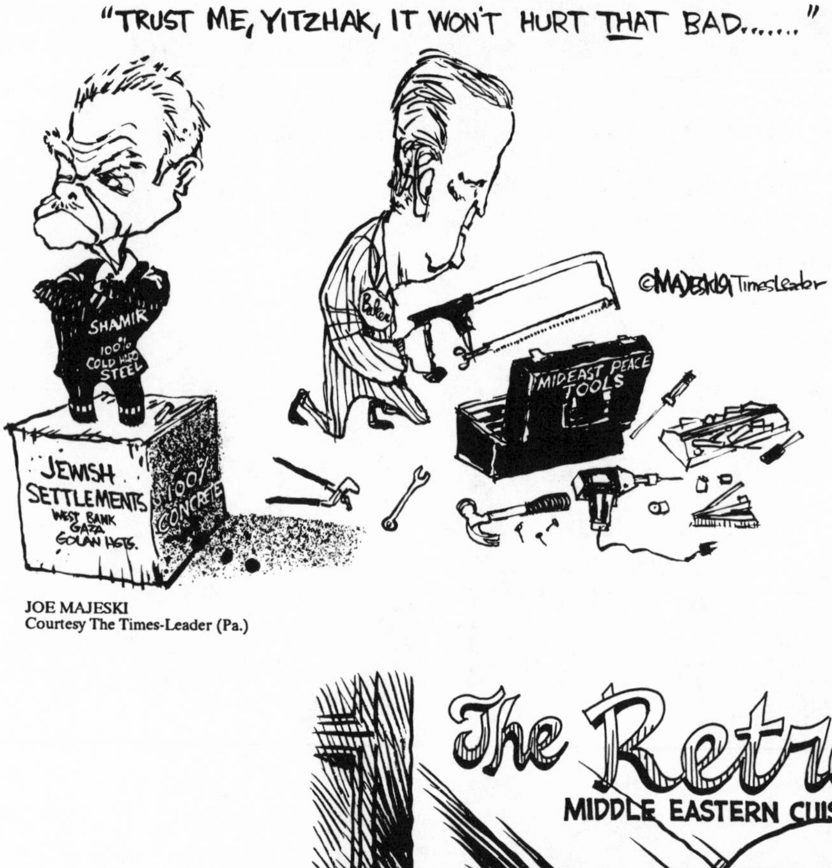
"TRUST ME, YITZHAK, IT WON'T HURT THAT BAD......"
SHAMIR
100% COLD H2O STEEL
JEWISH SETTLEMENTS
WEST BANK
GAZA
GOLAN HGTS.
100% CONCRETE
Baker
MIDEAST PEACE TOOLS
©MAJESKI91 TimesLeader

JOE MAJESKI
Courtesy The Times-Leader (Pa.)

JIMMY MARGULIES
Courtesy The Record (N.J.) and
North America Syndicate

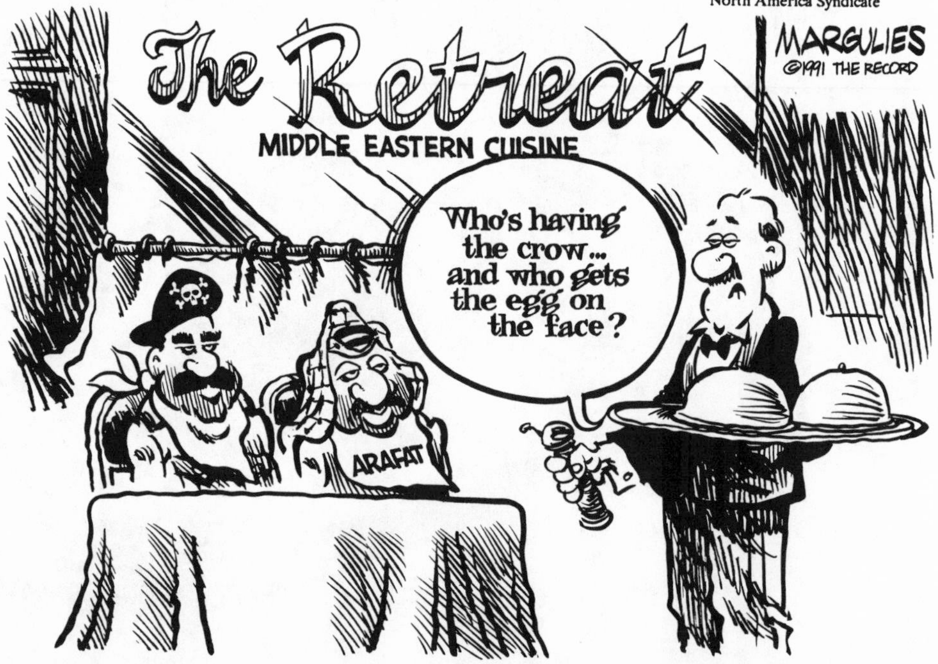
The Retreat
MIDDLE EASTERN CUISINE
MARGULIES
©1991 THE RECORD
Who's having the crow... and who gets the egg on the face?
ARAFAT

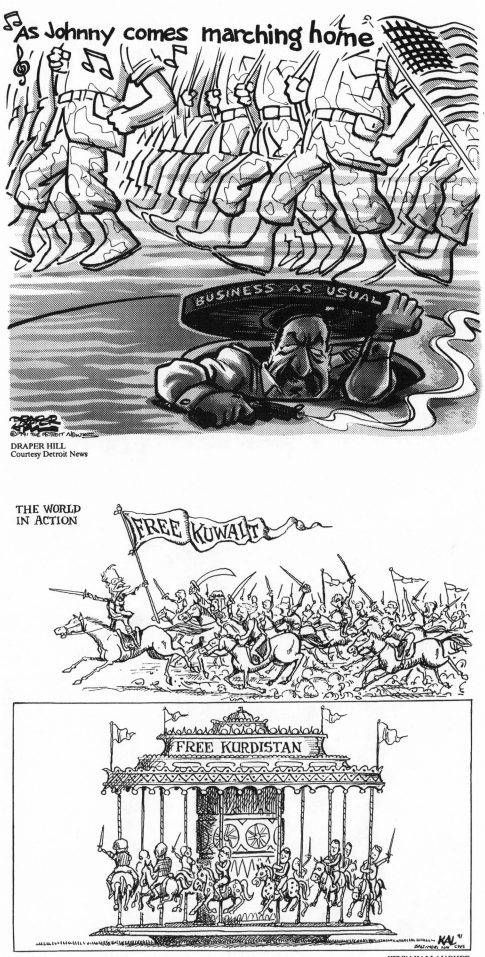

As Johnny comes marching home
BUSINESS AS USUAL
DRAPER HILL
©1991 THE DETROIT NEWS

DRAPER HILL
Courtesy Detroit News

THE WORLD
IN ACTION
FREE KUWAIT
FREE KURDISTAN
KAL '91
BALTIMORE SUN CWS

KEVIN KALLAUGHER
Courtesy Baltimore Sun

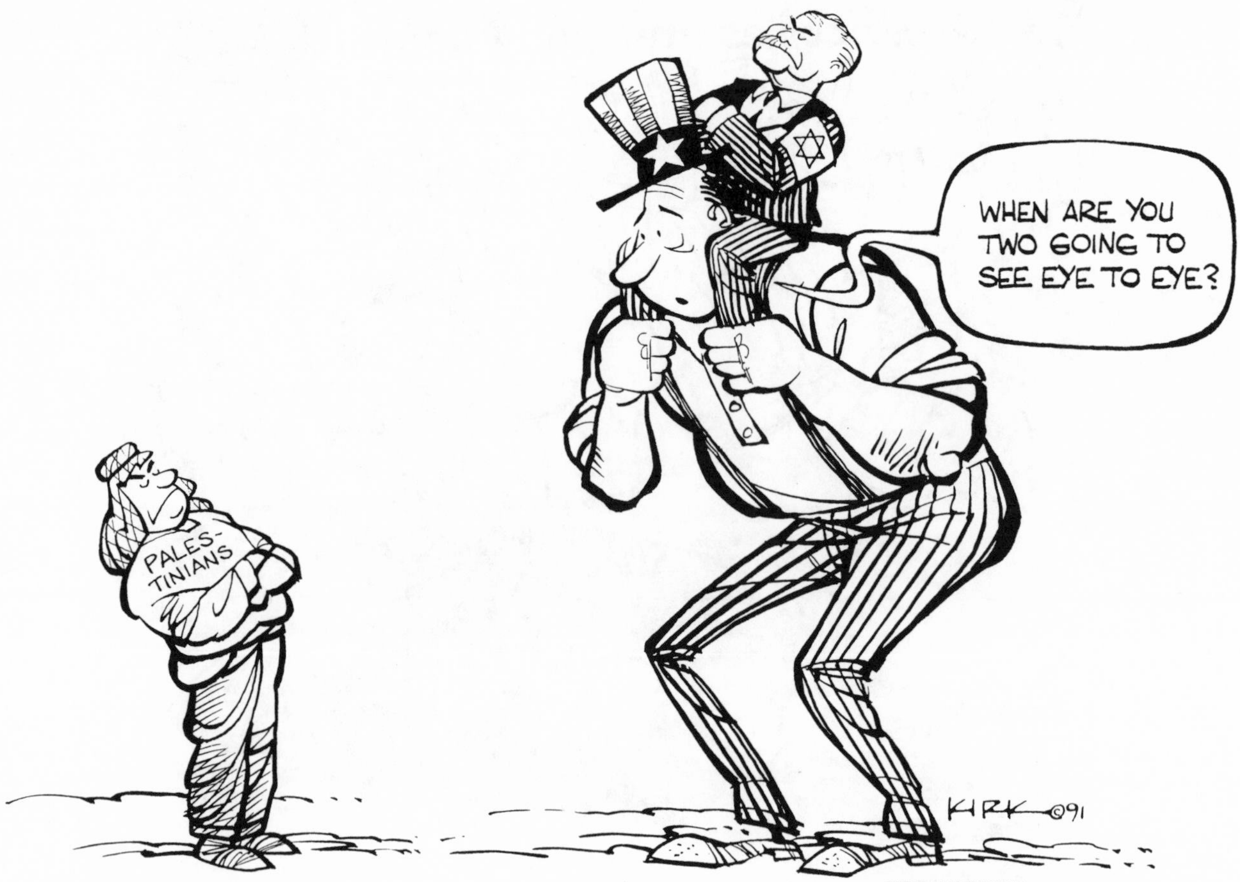
WHEN ARE YOU TWO GOING TO SEE EYE TO EYE?
PALES-TINIANS
KIRK ©91

KIRK ANDERSON
Courtesy Madison (Wis.) Capital Times

KELLY CAMPBELL
Courtesy Break Magazine

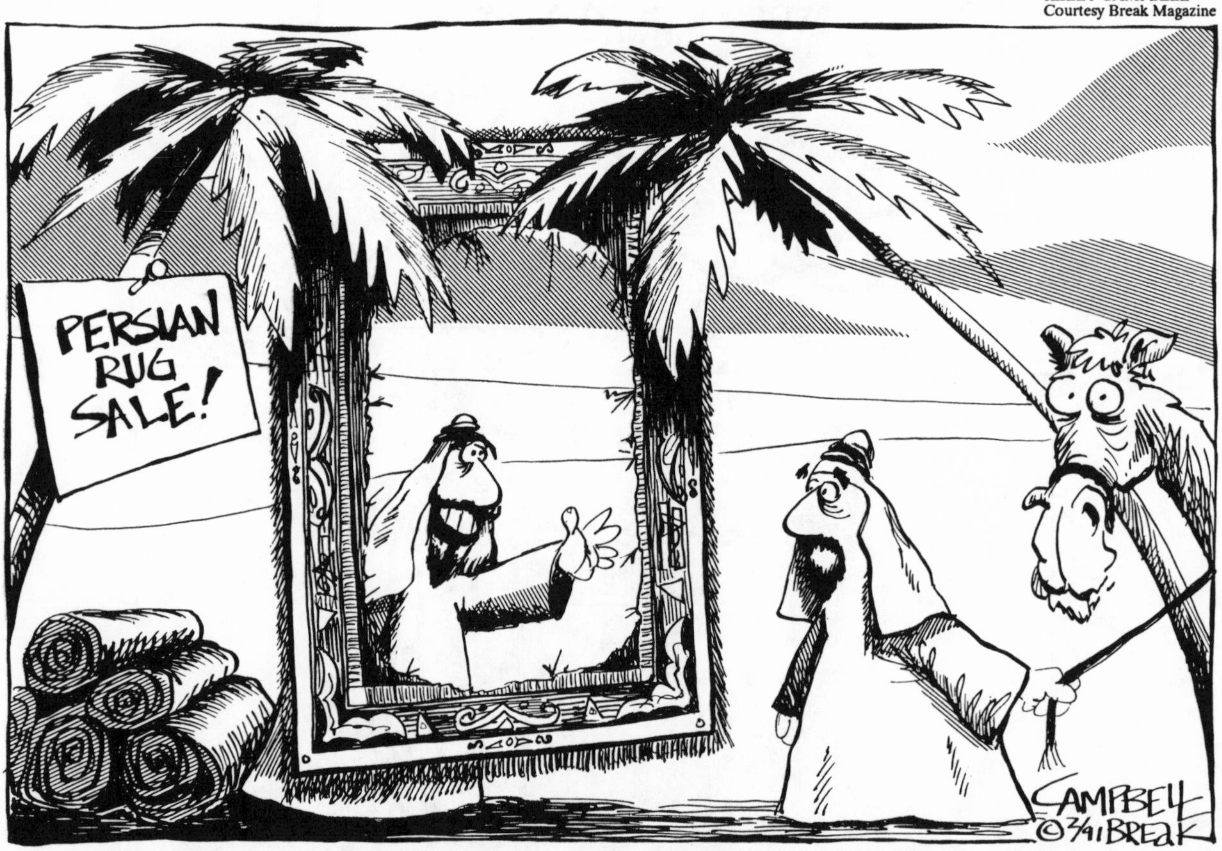
PERSIAN RUG SALE!
CAMPBELL ©3/91 BREAK

I'LL GIVE YOU A GREAT DEAL ON THIS ONE, IT WAS CARPET BOMBED!

The Economy

During 1991, the U.S. economy continued to worsen. Polls showed that consumer confidence in the government's economic policies was at the lowest point since 1980. In fact, business failures in the current recession were nearly five times as high as in the 1980 recession. By year's end, more than 1.9 million jobs had been lost since the slowdown began in mid-1990.

Repeated reductions in the Federal Reserve's key discount rate seemed to have failed to revive the sick economy. Although blue-collar jobs had dropped steadily during the 1970s and 1980s, the present recession added white-collar workers to out-of-work rolls, with more than 854,000 white-collar jobs lost. Many of the losses seemed permanent as high-tech jobs moved overseas and businesses tightened their belts.

State and local governments were hurt by the loss of tax dollars and laid off additional thousands of workers. Many cities turned to higher taxes as a solution to the decline in revenues.

Pan American Airways, the pioneer of commercial aviation, went out of business in early December, and General Motors announced that it would close twenty-one factories by 1994. Experts predicted that the economy would expand slightly by late 1992, but most expected sluggish growth for many months to come.

ROB ROGERS
Courtesy Pittsburgh Press

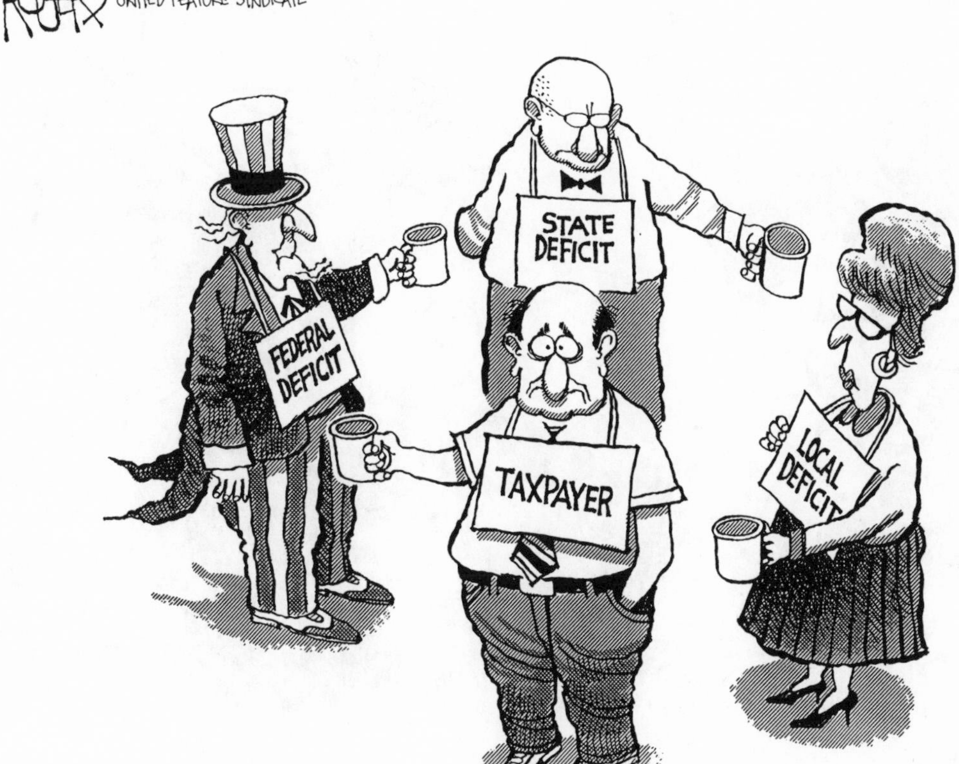
ROGERS
©1991 THE PITTSBURGH PRESS
UNITED FEATURE SYNDICATE
STATE DEFICIT
FEDERAL DEFICIT
TAXPAYER
LOCAL DEFICIT

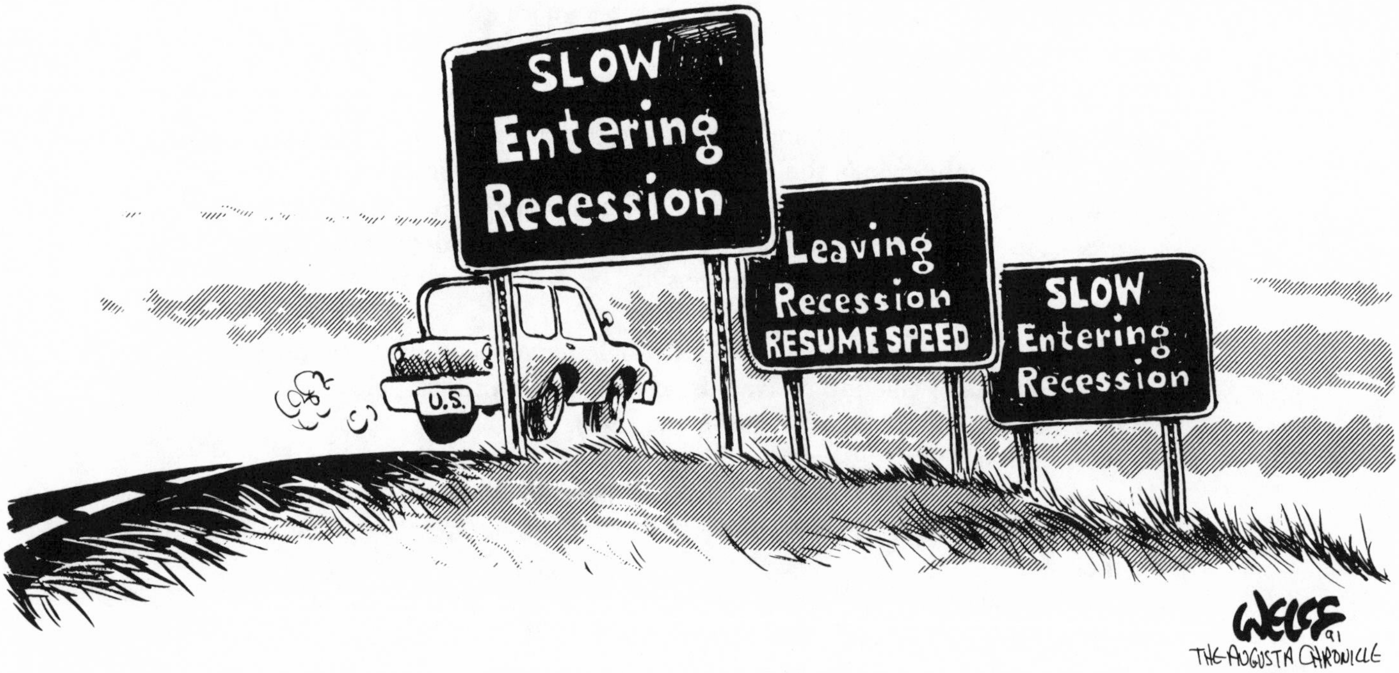
SLOW
Entering
Recession
Leaving
Recession
RESUME SPEED
SLOW
Entering
Recession
U.S.
THE AUGUSTA CHRONICLE

CLYDE WELLS
Courtesy Augusta Chronicle

GENE BASSET
Courtesy Atlanta Journal

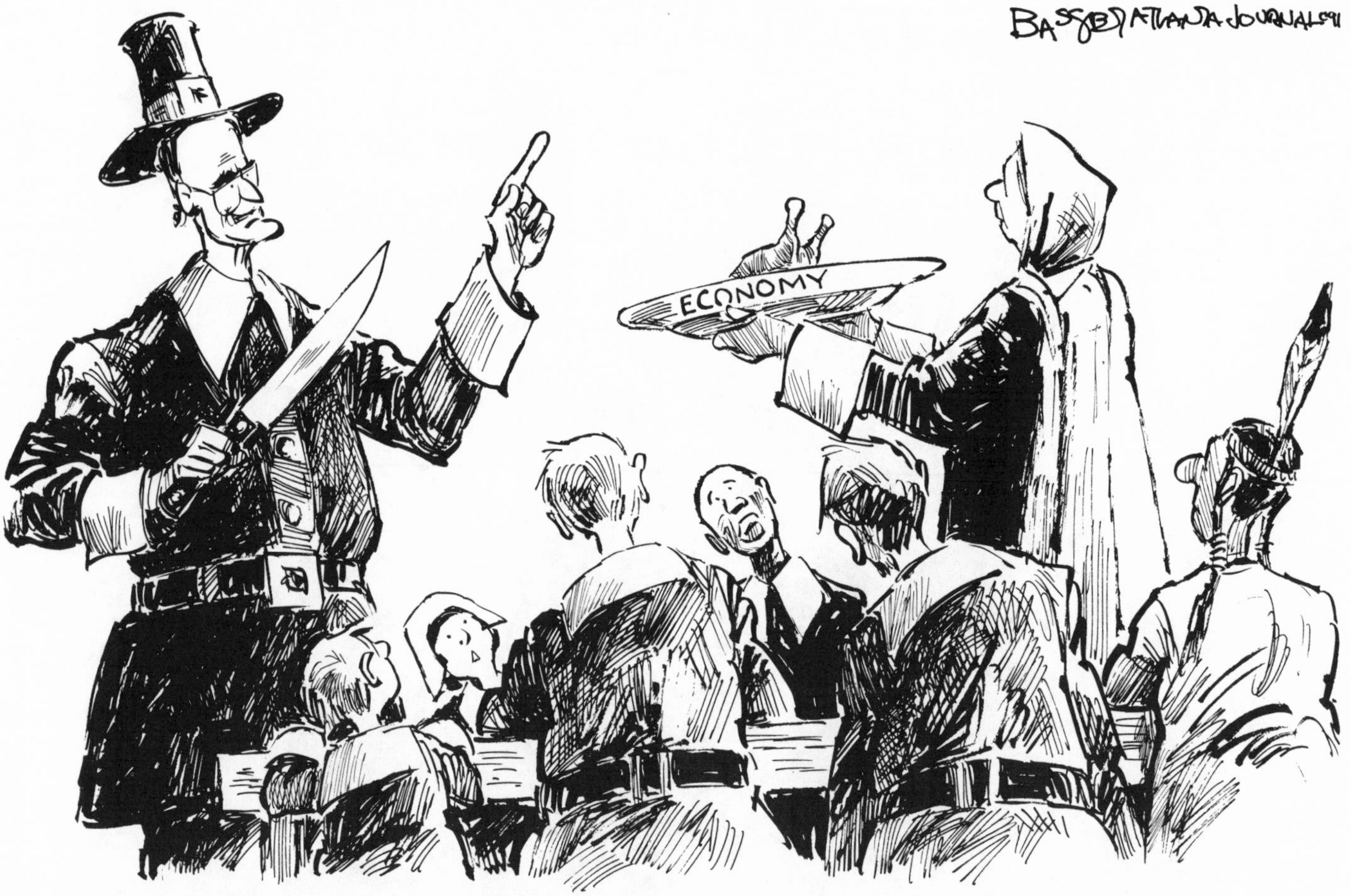
ECONOMY

"WITH SUSTAINED GROWTH, NEXT YEAR LOOKS EVEN BETTER."

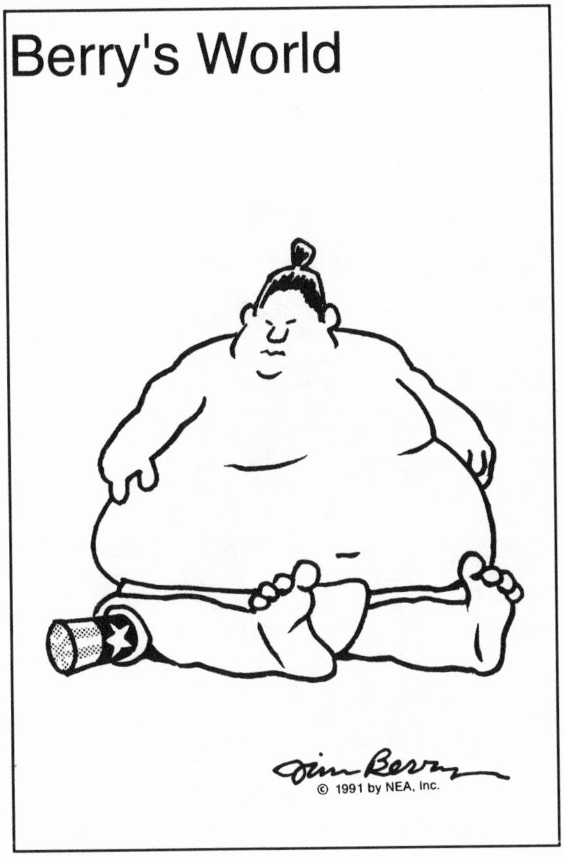
Berry's World
© 1991 by NEA, Inc.

JIM BERRY
Courtesy NEA

AL LIEDERMAN
Courtesy Rothco

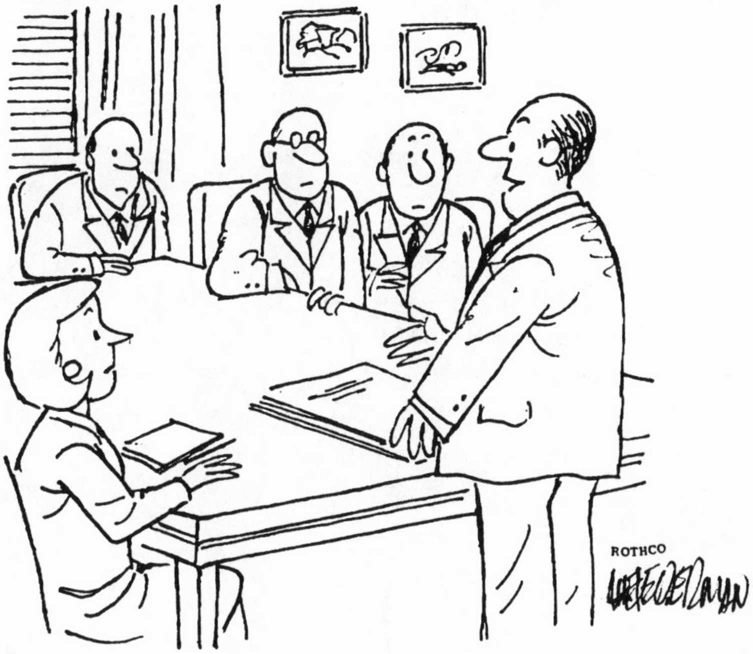
ROTHCO

" SINCE WE LICKED THE PRODUCTION PROBLEM AND FIXED OUR LABOR SITUATION, WE HAVE DECIDED TO CLOSE THE PLANT!"

LARRY WRIGHT
Courtesy Detroit News

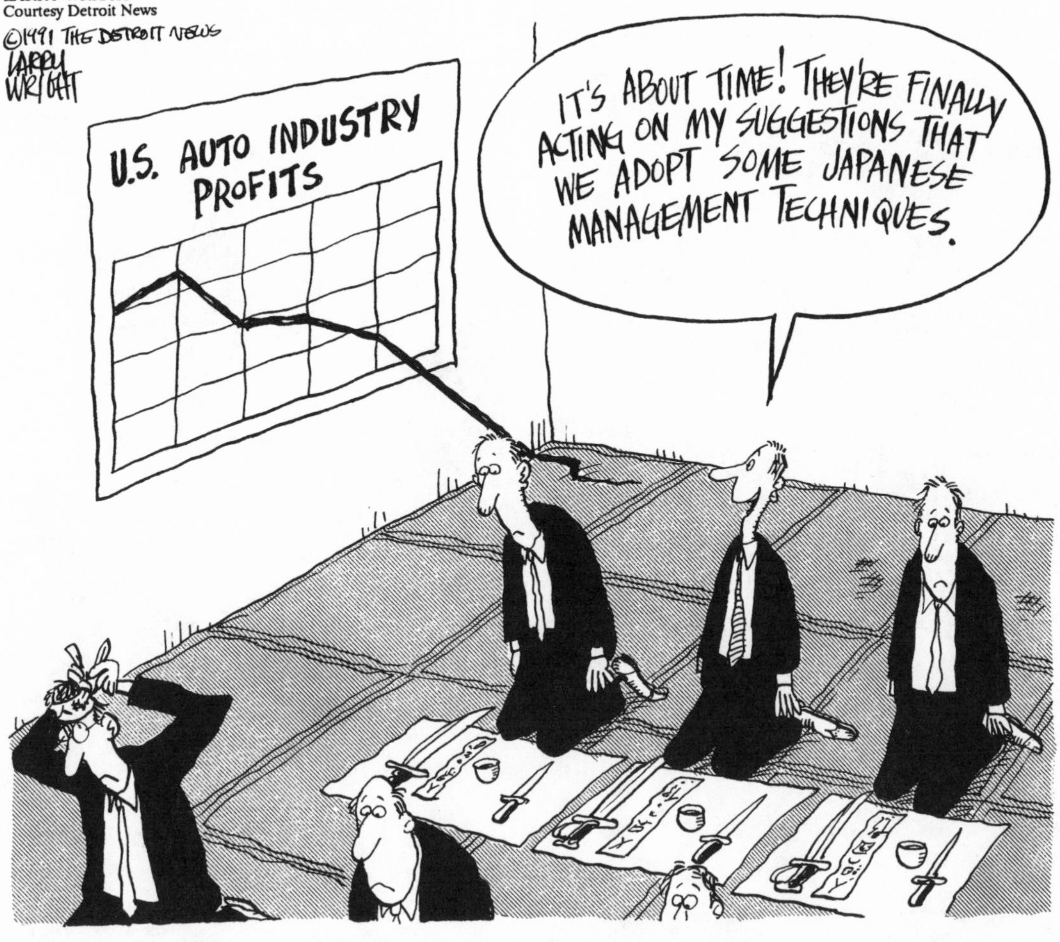
©1991 THE DETROIT NEWS
LARRY WRIGHT
U.S. AUTO INDUSTRY PROFITS
IT'S ABOUT TIME! THEY'RE FINALLY ACTING ON MY SUGGESTIONS THAT WE ADOPT SOME JAPANESE MANAGEMENT TECHNIQUES.

DICK WALLMEYER
Courtesy Long Beach Press-Telegram

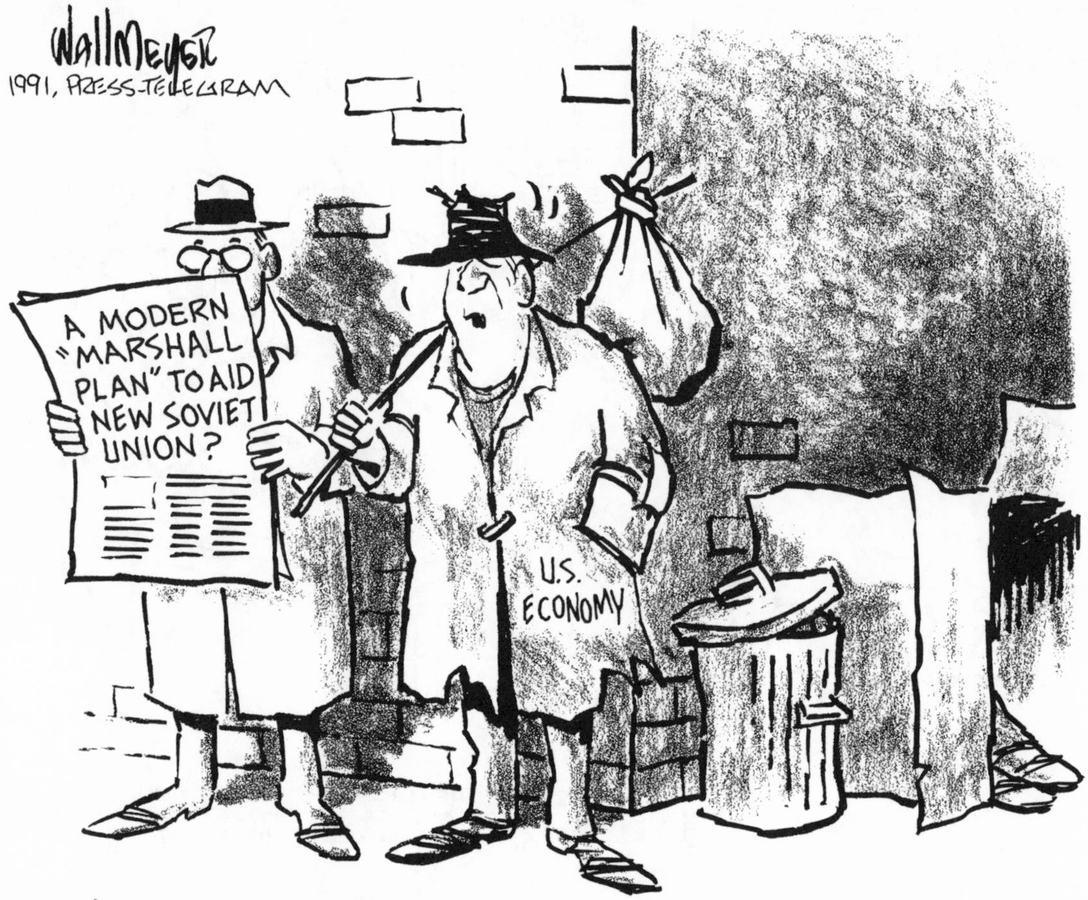
Wallmeyer
1991, PRESS-TELEGRAM
A MODERN "MARSHALL PLAN" TO AID NEW SOVIET UNION?
U.S. ECONOMY

"I'M STILL WAITING FOR A BUSH PLAN."

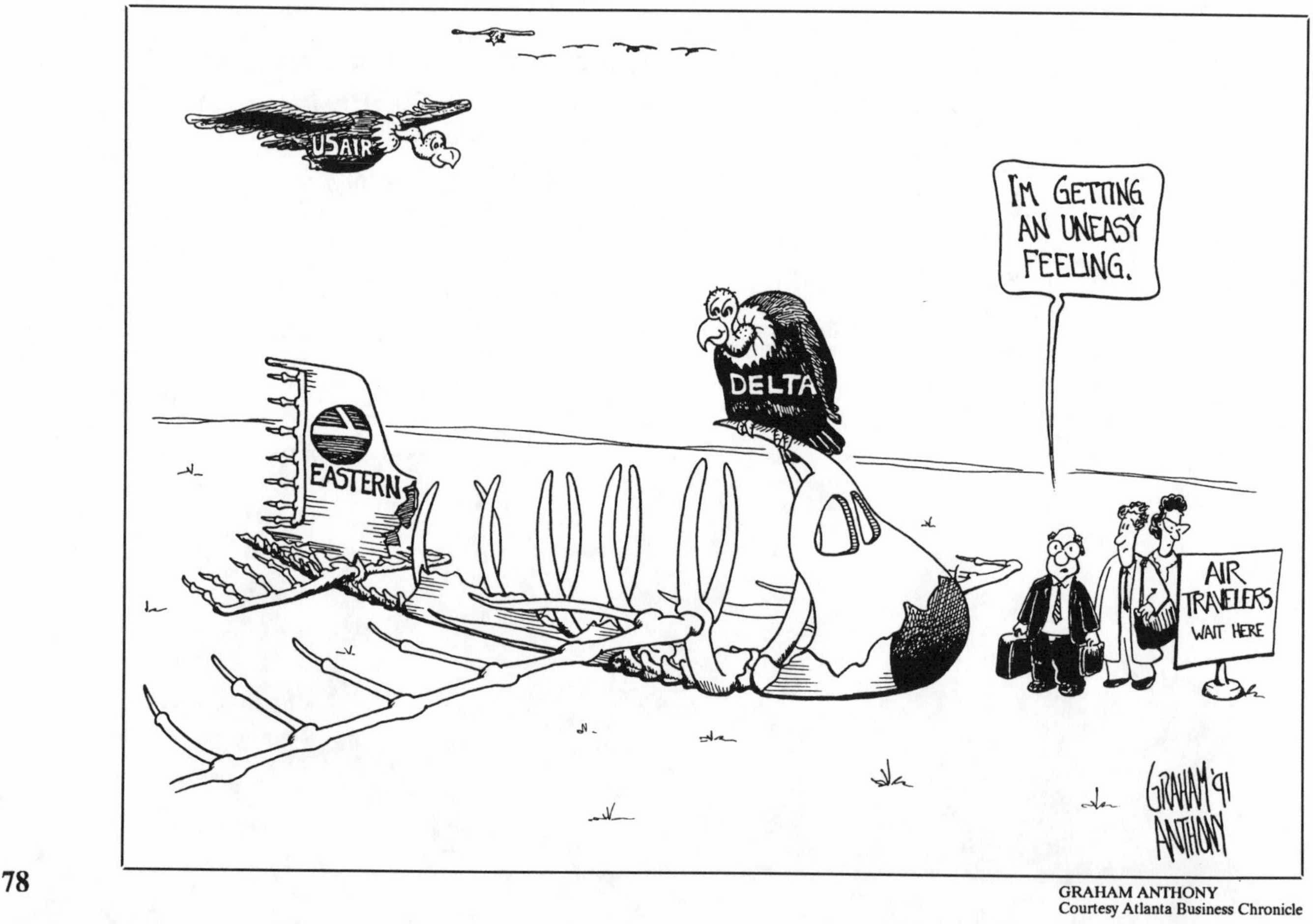
USAIR
I'M GETTING AN UNEASY FEELING.
DELTA
EASTERN
AIR TRAVELERS WAIT HERE
GRAHAM '91 ANTHONY

GRAHAM ANTHONY
Courtesy Atlanta Business Chronicle

PAUL FELL
Courtesy Lincoln Journal

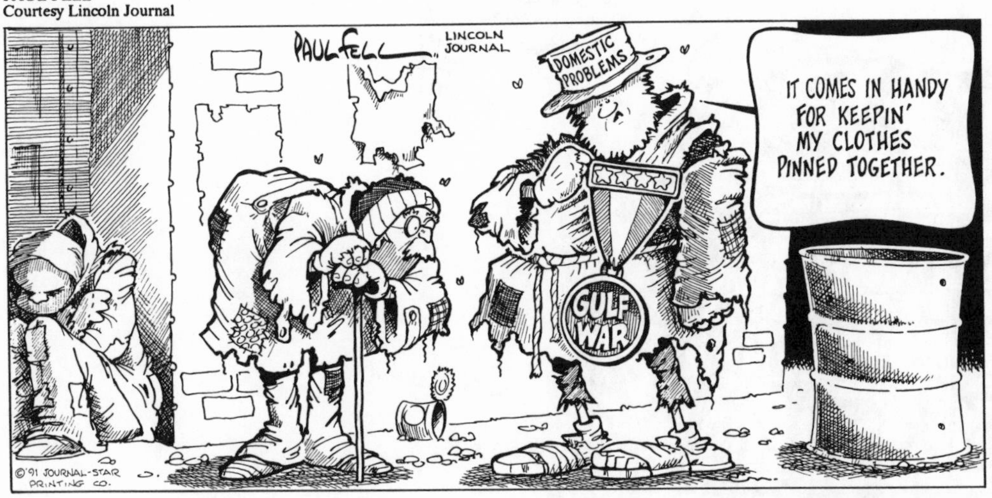
PAUL FELL LINCOLN JOURNAL
DOMESTIC PROBLEMS
GULF WAR
IT COMES IN HANDY FOR KEEPIN' MY CLOTHES PINNED TOGETHER.
©'91 JOURNAL-STAR PRINTING CO.

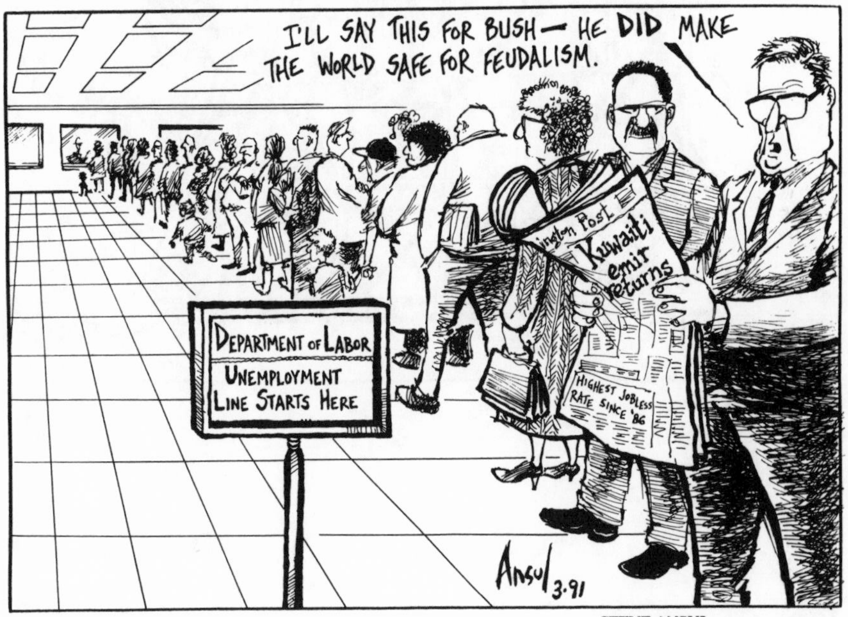
I'LL SAY THIS FOR BUSH — HE DID MAKE THE WORLD SAFE FOR FEUDALISM.
Kuwaiti emir returns
HIGHEST JOBLESS RATE SINCE '86
DEPARTMENT OF LABOR
UNEMPLOYMENT LINE STARTS HERE
Ansul 3·91

STEVE ANSUL
Courtesy Wilmington News Journal

ROGER SCHILLERSTROM
Courtesy Crain Communications

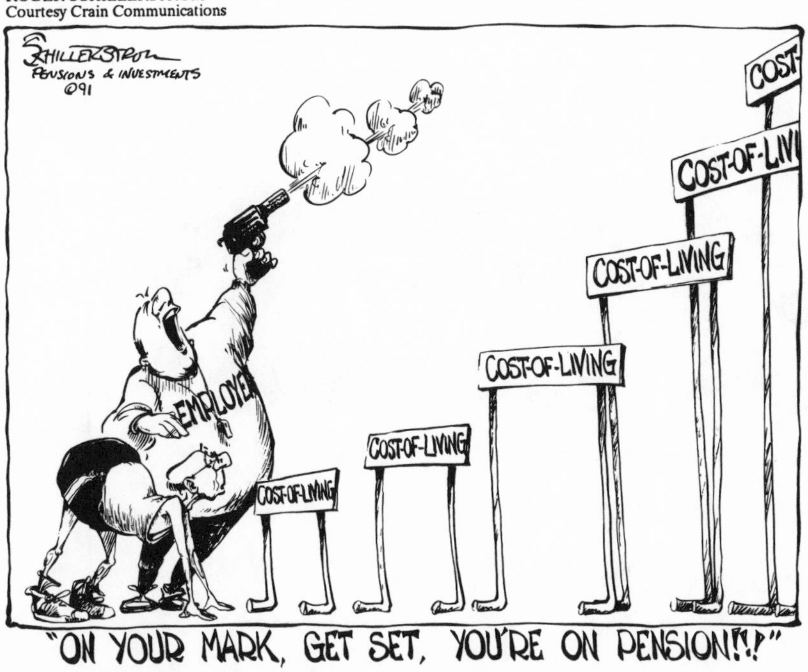
SCHILLERSTROM
PENSIONS & INVESTMENTS ©91
EMPLOYEE
COST-OF-LIVING
COST-OF-LIVING
COST-OF-LIVING
COST-OF-LIVING
COST-OF-LIV
COST-

"ON YOUR MARK, GET SET, YOU'RE ON PENSION!!!"

BRIAN DUFFY
Courtesy Des Moines Register

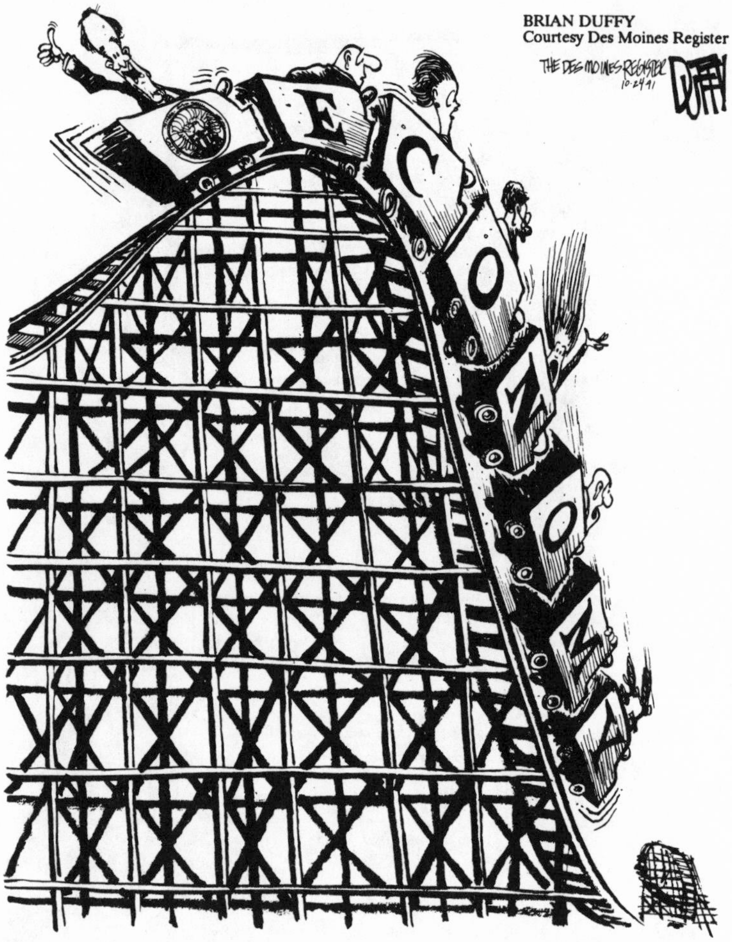
THE DES MOINES REGISTER 10-24-91 DUFFY
ECONOMY

JOE HOFFECKER
Courtesy Cincinnati Business Courier

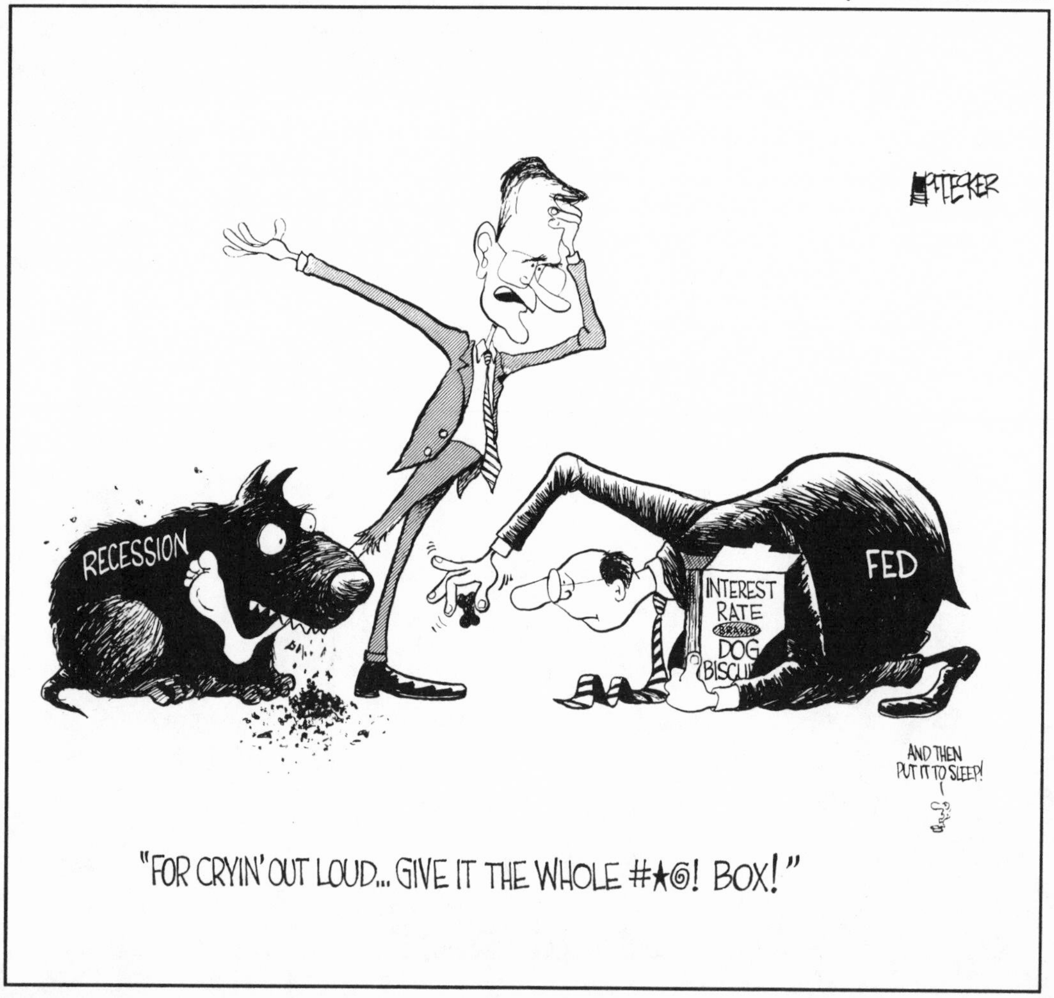
HOFFECKER
RECESSION
FED
INTEREST RATE BRAND DOG BISCUI
AND THEN PUT IT TO SLEEP!
"FOR CRYIN' OUT LOUD... GIVE IT THE WHOLE #★@! BOX!"

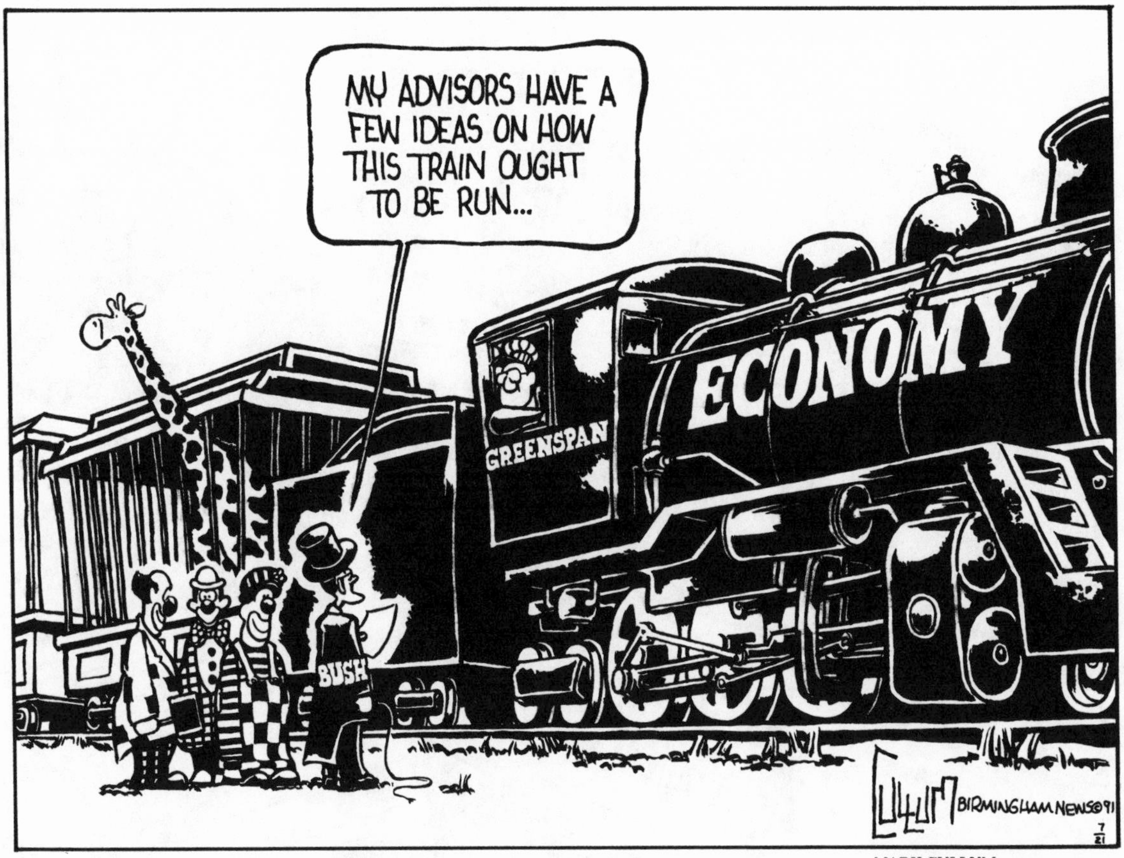

MY ADVISORS HAVE A FEW IDEAS ON HOW THIS TRAIN OUGHT TO BE RUN...
ECONOMY
GREENSPAN
BUSH
CULLUM BIRMINGHAM NEWS©91
7/21

MARK CULLUM
Courtesy Birmingham News

JOHN SPENCER
Courtesy Philadelphia Business Journal

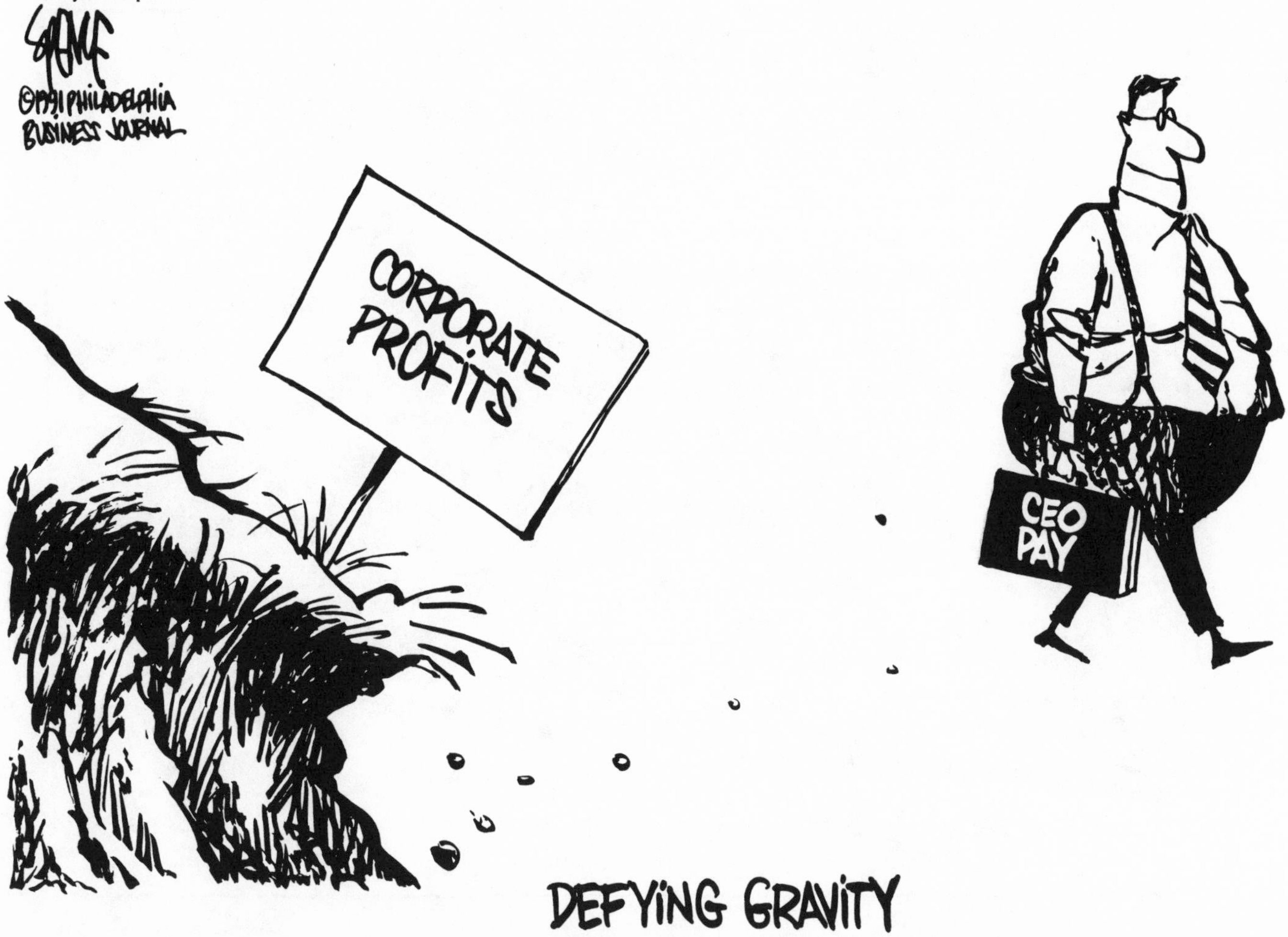

©1991 PHILADELPHIA BUSINESS JOURNAL
CORPORATE PROFITS
CEO PAY
DEFYING GRAVITY

JEFF STAHLER
Courtesy Cincinnati Post

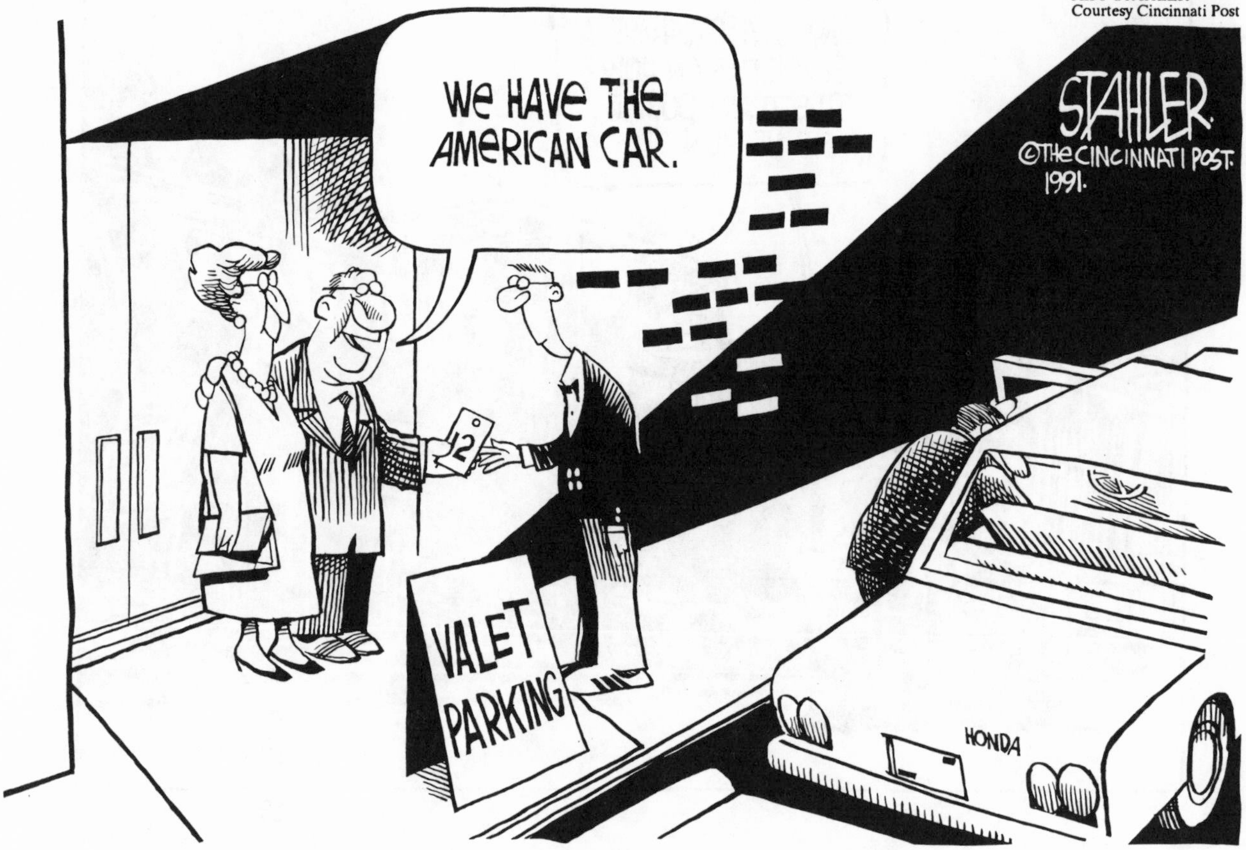
WE HAVE THE AMERICAN CAR.
STAHLER
©THE CINCINNATI POST 1991
VALET PARKING
'12
HONDA

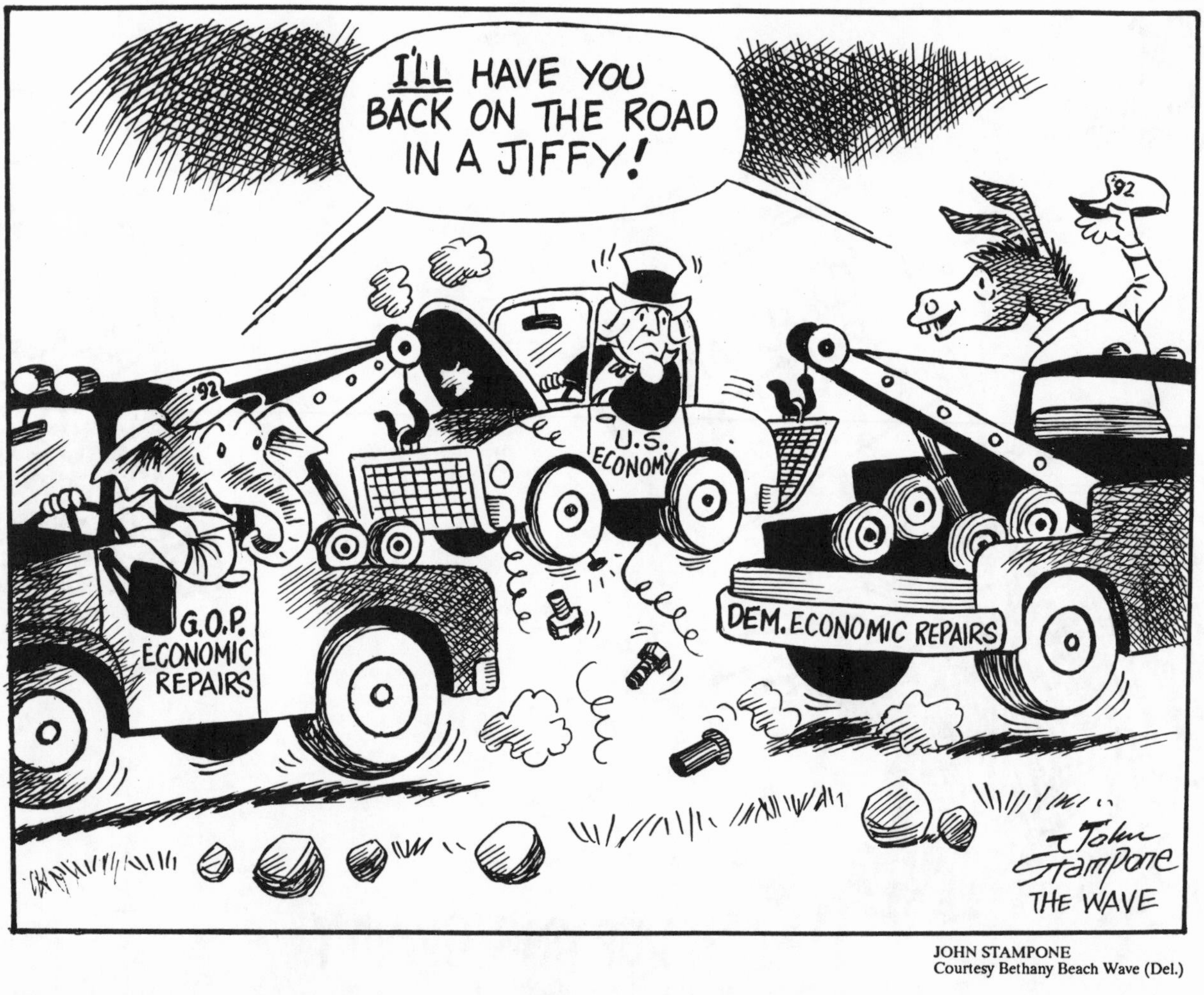
I'LL HAVE YOU BACK ON THE ROAD IN A JIFFY!
'92
U.S. ECONOMY
G.O.P. ECONOMIC REPAIRS
DEM. ECONOMIC REPAIRS
John Stampone
THE WAVE

JOHN STAMPONE
Courtesy Bethany Beach Wave (Del.)

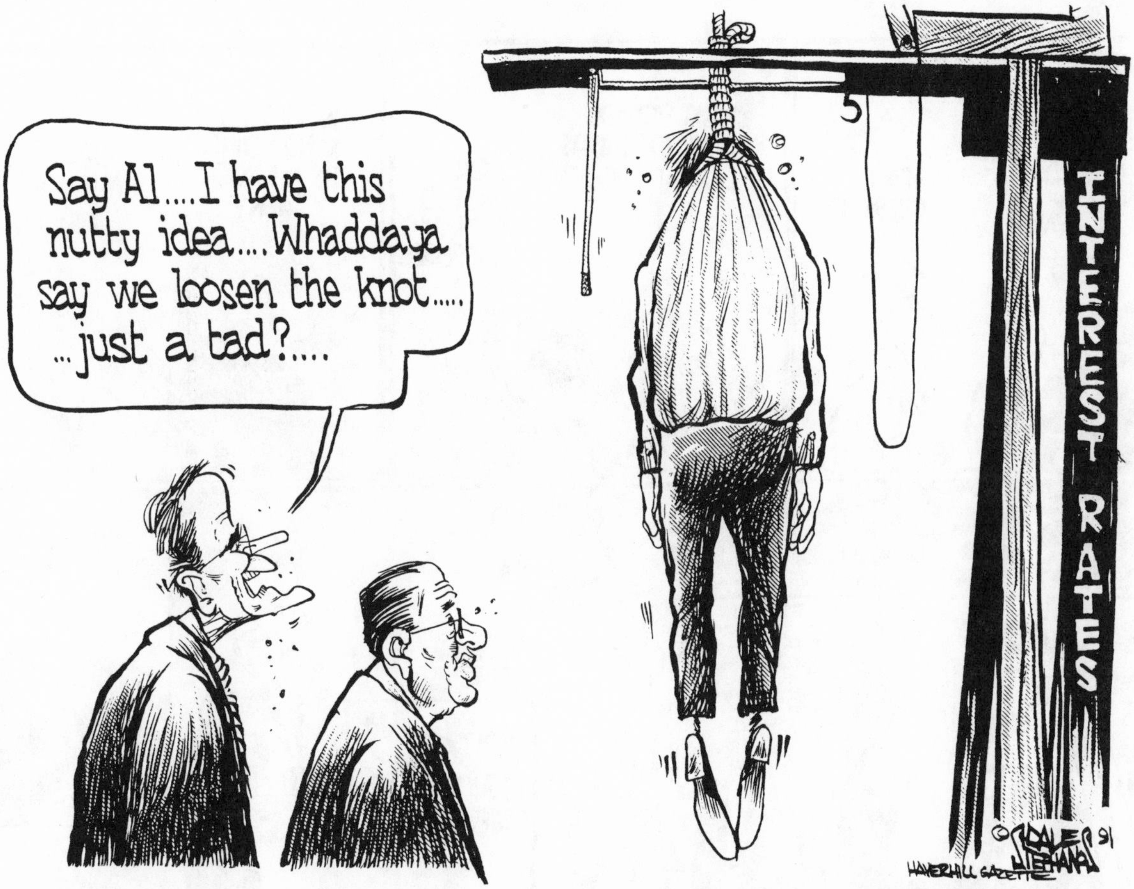
Say Al....I have this nutty idea.....Whaddaya say we loosen the knot..... ...just a tad?.....
5
INTEREST RATES
HAVERHILL GAZETTE

DALE STEPHANOS
Courtesy Haverhill Gazette (Mass.)

BUBBA FLINT
Courtesy Ft. Worth Star-Telegram

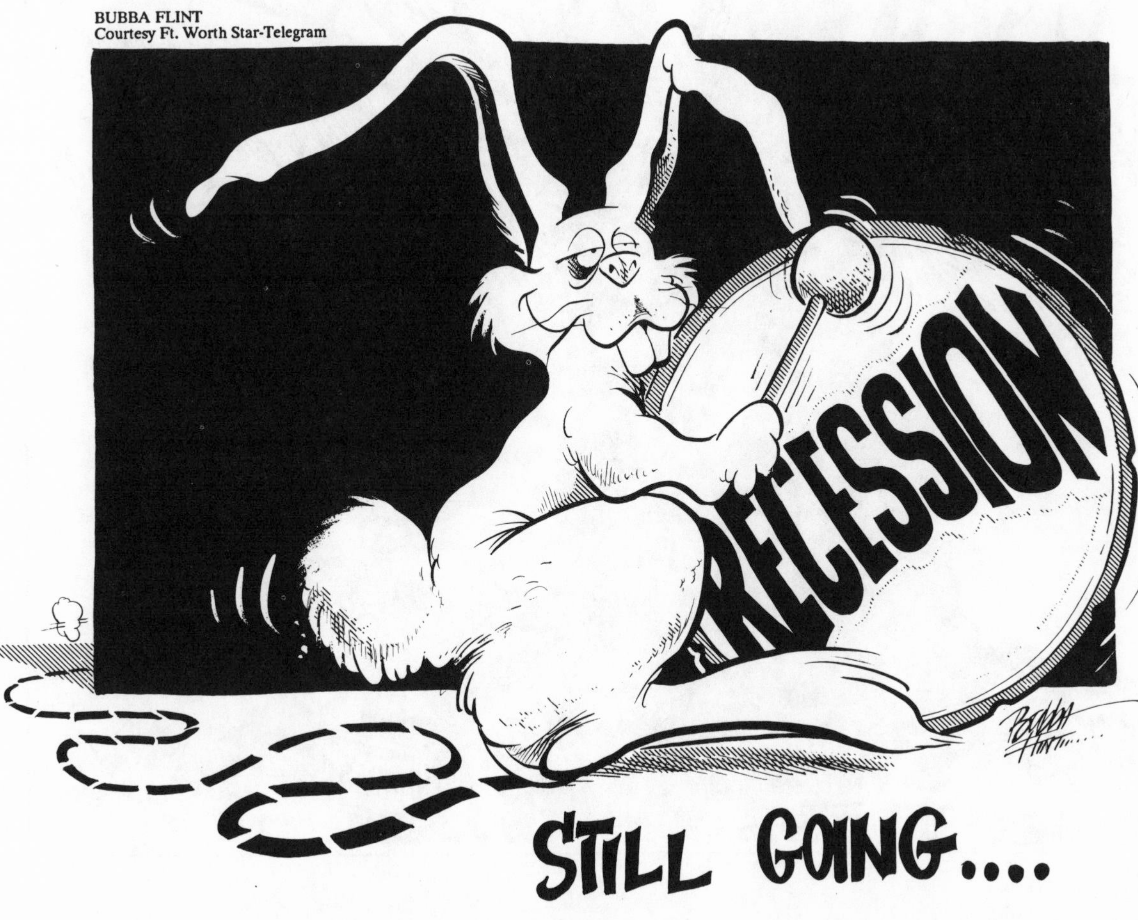
RECESSION
STILL GOING....

JACK OHMAN
Courtesy Portland Oregonian

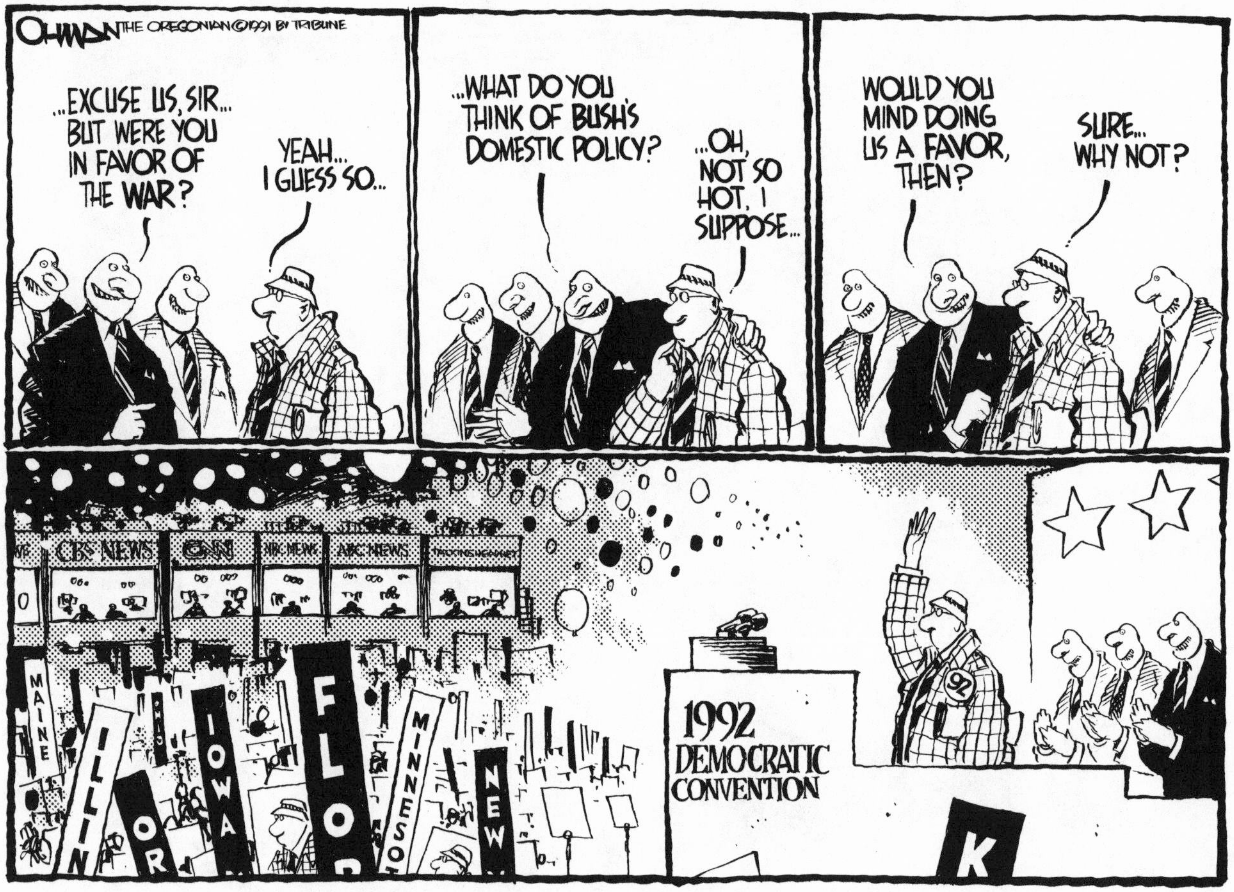
OHMAN THE OREGONIAN ©1991 BY TRIBUNE
...EXCUSE US, SIR... BUT WERE YOU IN FAVOR OF THE WAR?
YEAH... I GUESS SO...
...WHAT DO YOU THINK OF BUSH'S DOMESTIC POLICY?
...OH, NOT SO HOT, I SUPPOSE...
WOULD YOU MIND DOING US A FAVOR, THEN?
SURE... WHY NOT?
CBS NEWS
CNN
NBC NEWS
ABC NEWS
MAINE
ILLIN
OR
IOWA
FLO
MINNESO
NEW
92
1992 DEMOCRATIC CONVENTION
K

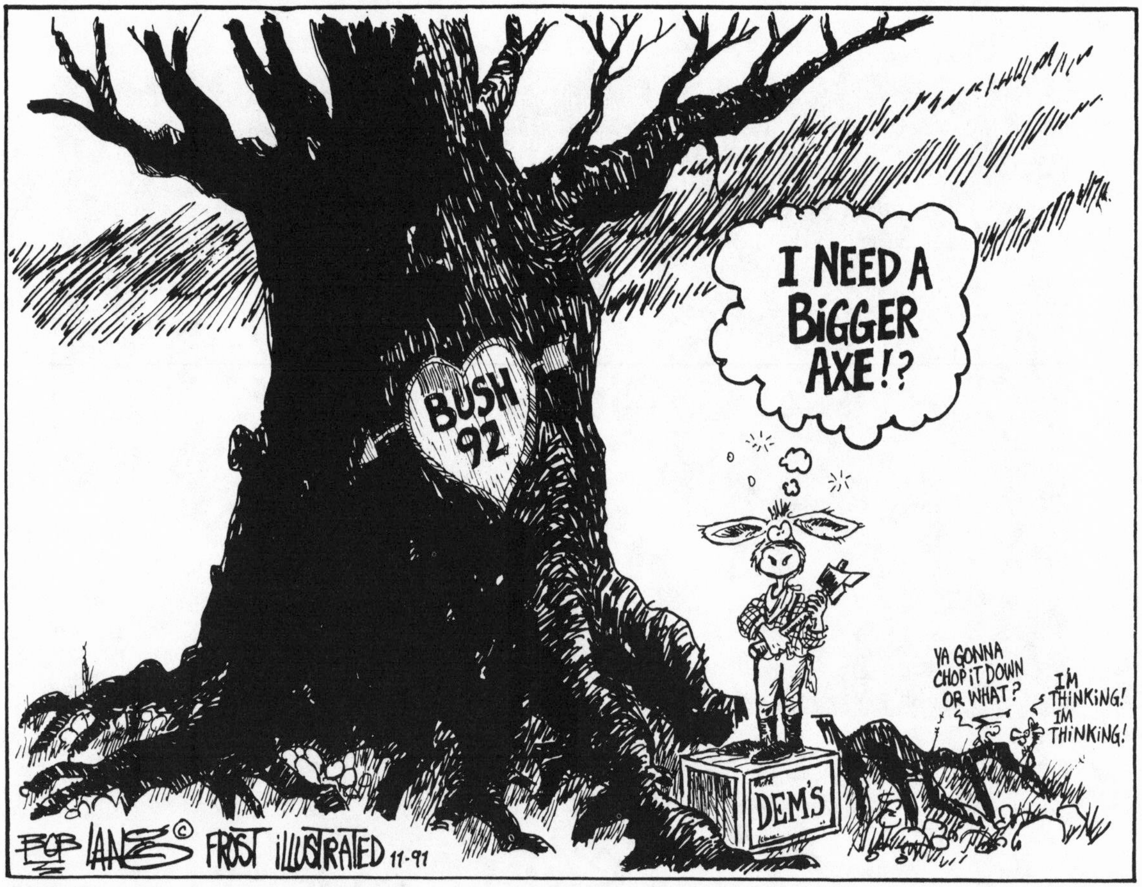
I NEED A BIGGER AXE!?
BUSH 92
DEM'S
YA GONNA CHOP IT DOWN OR WHAT?
I'M THINKING! I'M THINKING!
BOB LANG © FROST ILLUSTRATED 11-91

BOB LANG
Courtesy Frost Illustrated

Politics

In the months immediately following America's resounding victory in the Persian Gulf War, President Bush no doubt could have been reelected in a landslide. But as the months went by and the country found itself deeply mired in recession, the Democrats began to see a glimmer of hope. Former Sen. Paul Tsongas of Massachusetts threw his hat into the ring early, and was followed by Gov. Bill Clinton of Arkansas, Sen. Tom Harkin of Iowa, former Gov. Jerry Brown of California, Sen. Bob Kerrey of Nebraska, and Gov. Doug Wilder of Virginia.

New York Gov. Mario Cuomo commanded the most attention, however, as a Democratic possibility. The media followed him for months expecting an announcement, but the governor tarried. Finally, when he appeared to be on the verge of entering the race, he announced he would not run. He said his first responsibility was to the state of New York, which faced desperate financial problems. The state budget had nearly doubled during Cuomo's nine-year tenure while the population remained static, and the 1992 deficit was pegged at $3.6 billion.

By the end of 1991, with domestic problems mounting for President Bush, the Democrats were still searching for a strong leader to serve as standard bearer in the race.

DICK LOCHER
Courtesy Chicago Tribune

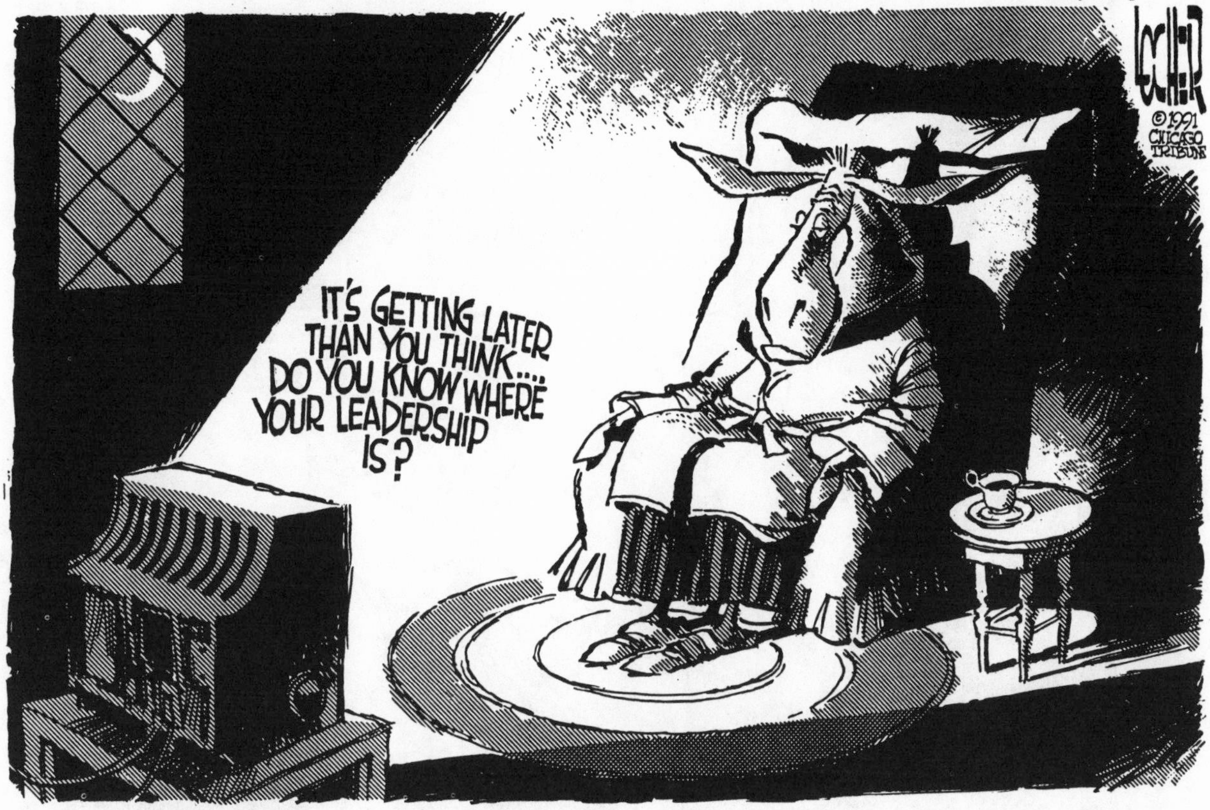
LOCHER
©1991 CHICAGO TRIBUNE
IT'S GETTING LATER THAN YOU THINK.... DO YOU KNOW WHERE YOUR LEADERSHIP IS?

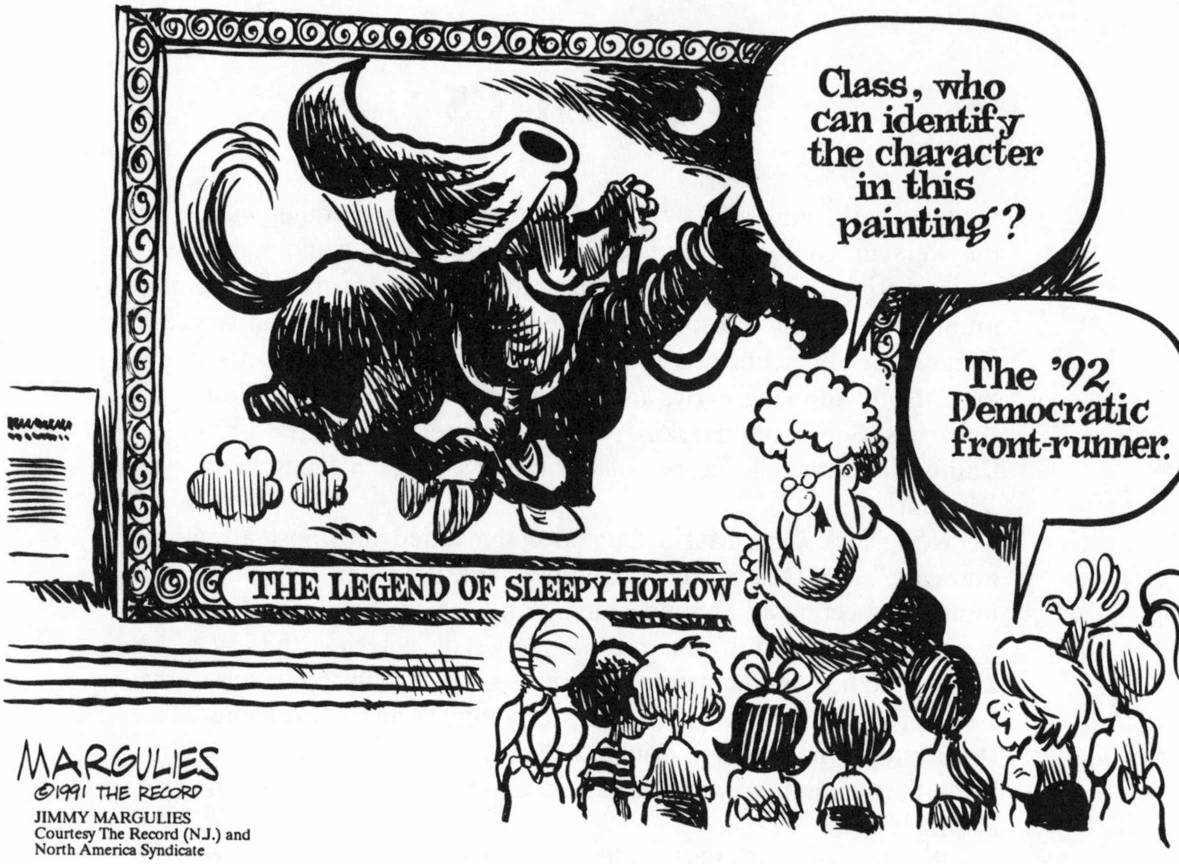
Class, who can identify the character in this painting?
The '92 Democratic front-runner.
THE LEGEND OF SLEEPY HOLLOW
MARGULIES ©1991 THE RECORD

JIMMY MARGULIES
Courtesy The Record (N.J.) and North America Syndicate

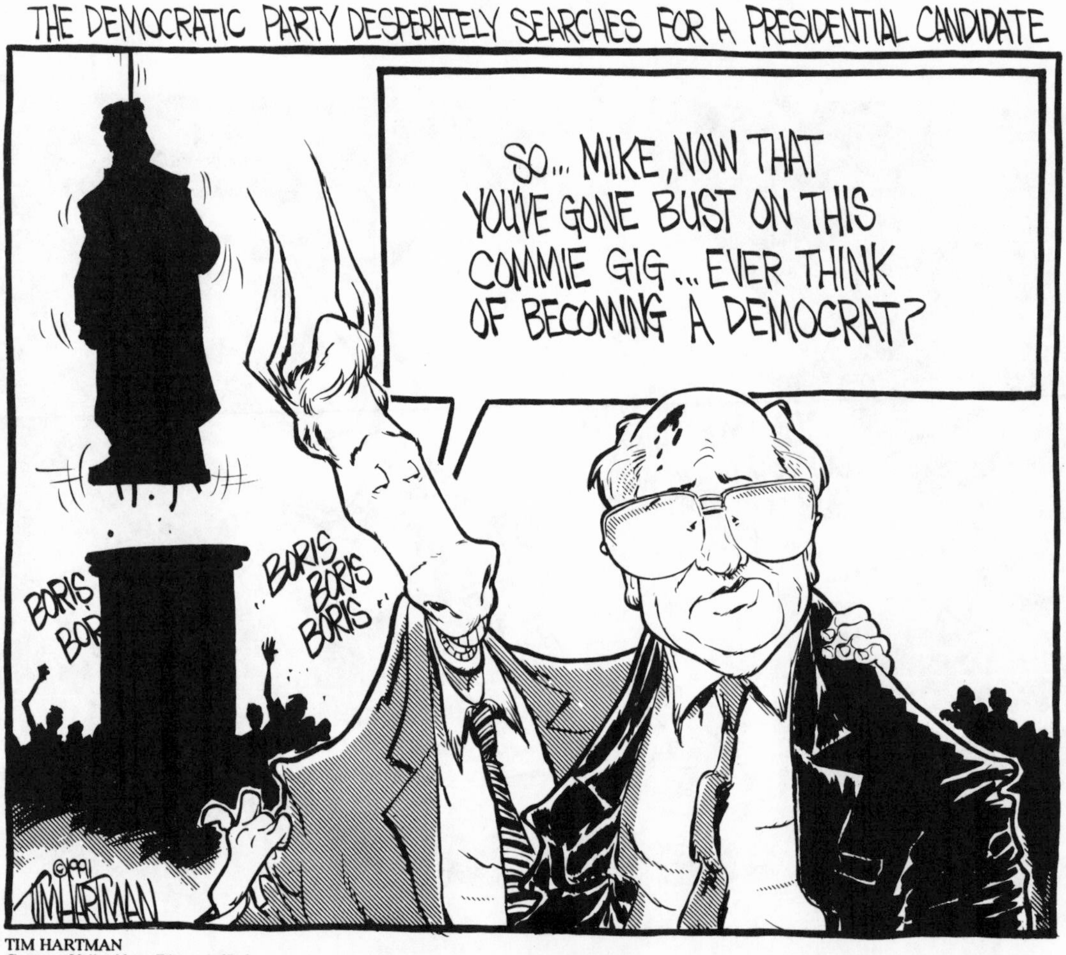
THE DEMOCRATIC PARTY DESPERATELY SEARCHES FOR A PRESIDENTIAL CANDIDATE
SO... MIKE, NOW THAT YOU'VE GONE BUST ON THIS COMMIE GIG... EVER THINK OF BECOMING A DEMOCRAT?
BORIS BOR
...BORIS BORIS BORIS...
©1991 TIM HARTMAN

TIM HARTMAN
Courtesy Valley News Dispatch (Pa.)

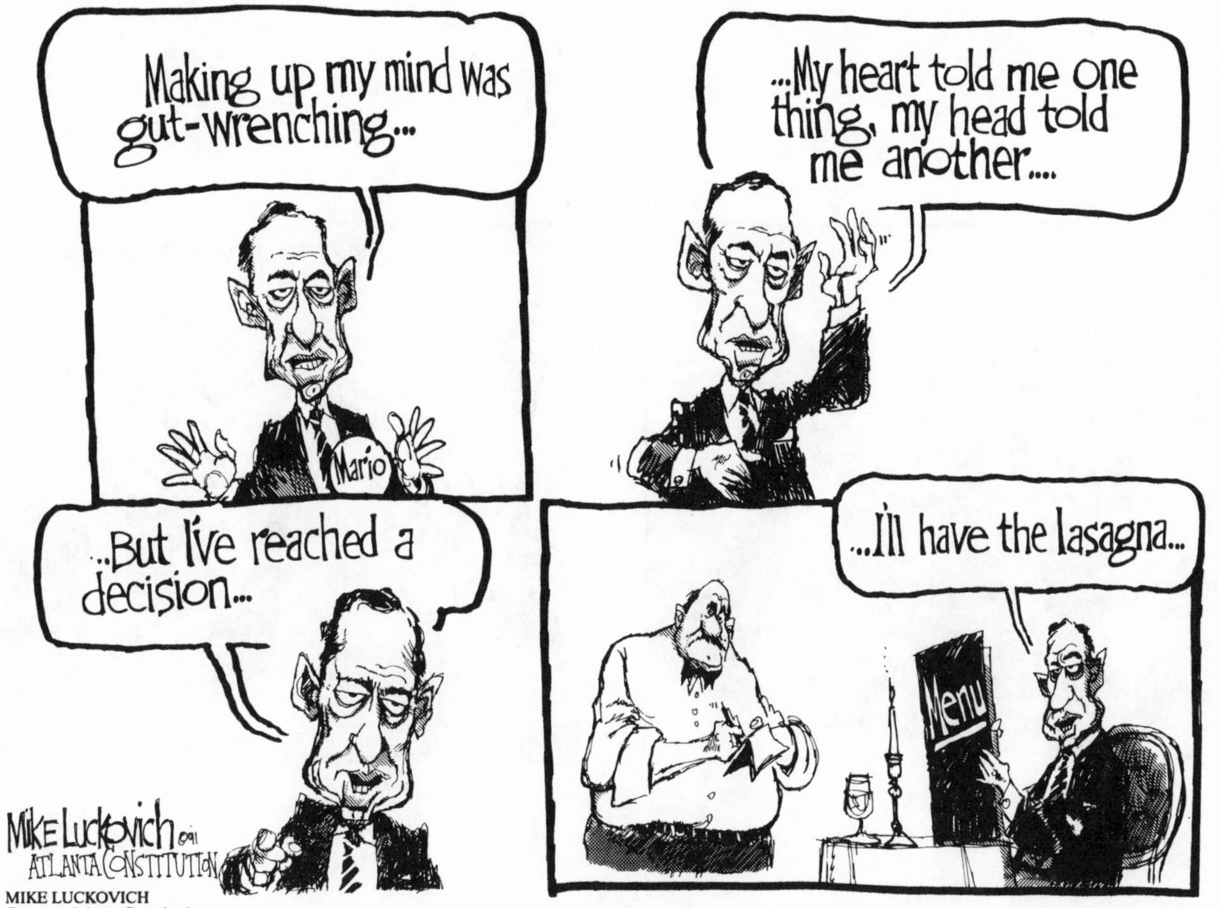
Making up my mind was gut-wrenching...
Mario
...My heart told me one thing, my head told me another....
...But I've reached a decision...
...I'll have the lasagna...
Menu
MIKE LUCKOVICH
ATLANTA CONSTITUTION

MIKE LUCKOVICH
Courtesy Atlanta Constitution

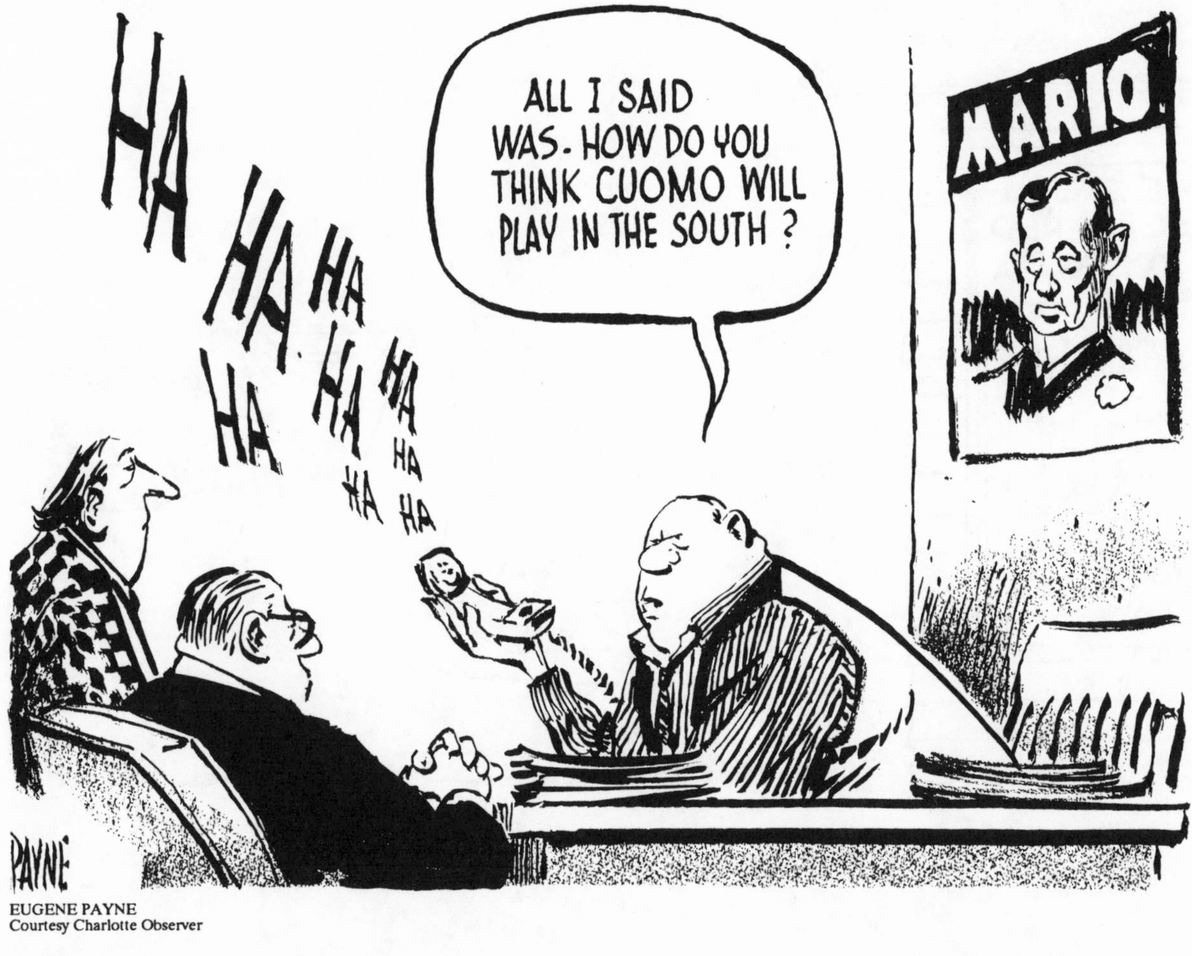
HA HA HA HA HA HA HA HA HA HA HA
ALL I SAID WAS. HOW DO YOU THINK CUOMO WILL PLAY IN THE SOUTH ?
MARIO
PAYNE

EUGENE PAYNE
Courtesy Charlotte Observer

TOM BECK
Courtesy Journal Standard (Ill.)

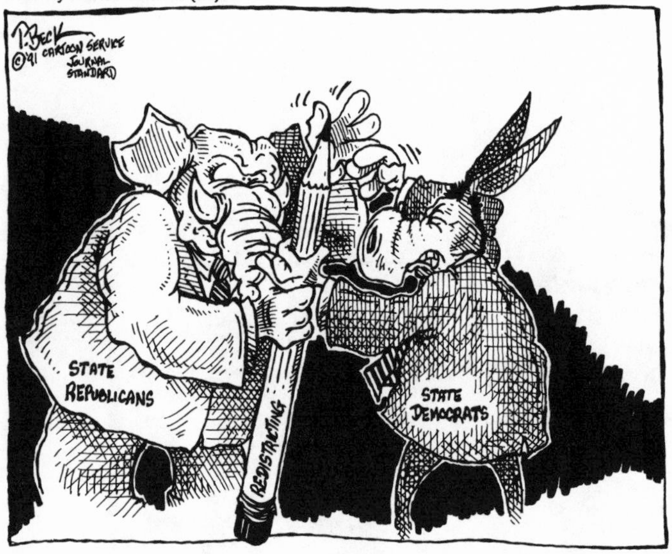
STATE REPUBLICANS
REDISTRICTING
STATE DEMOCRATS

ERIC SMITH
Courtesy Capital Gazette Newspapers

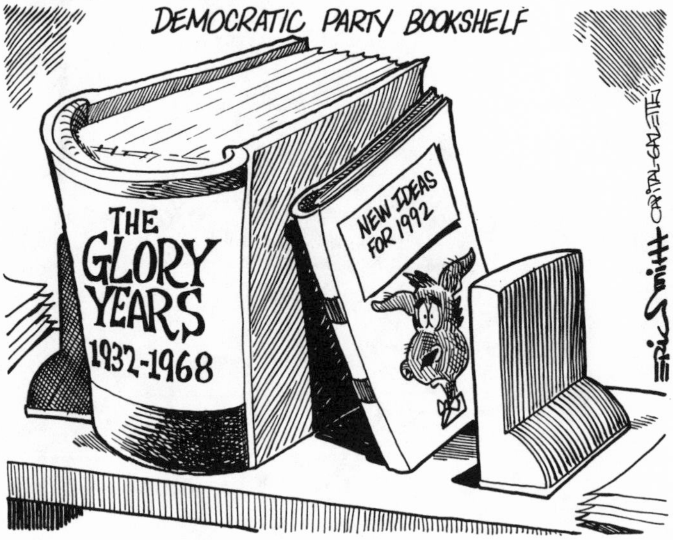
DEMOCRATIC PARTY BOOKSHELF
THE GLORY YEARS 1932-1968
NEW IDEAS FOR 1992

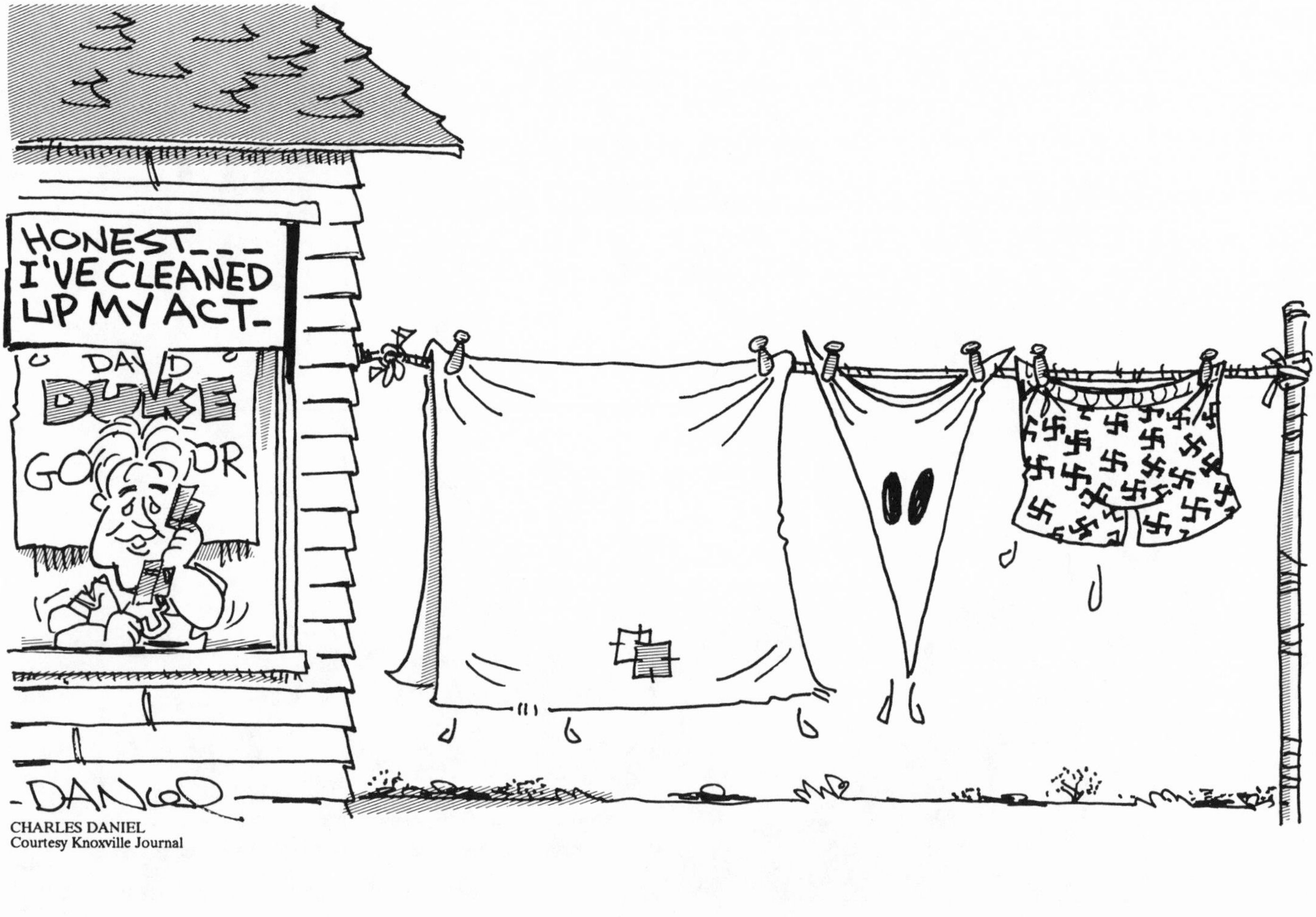
HONEST_ _ _ I'VE CLEANED UP MY ACT_
DAVID DUKE GOVERNOR

CHARLES DANIEL
Courtesy Knoxville Journal

REX BABIN
Courtesy Times Union (N.Y.)

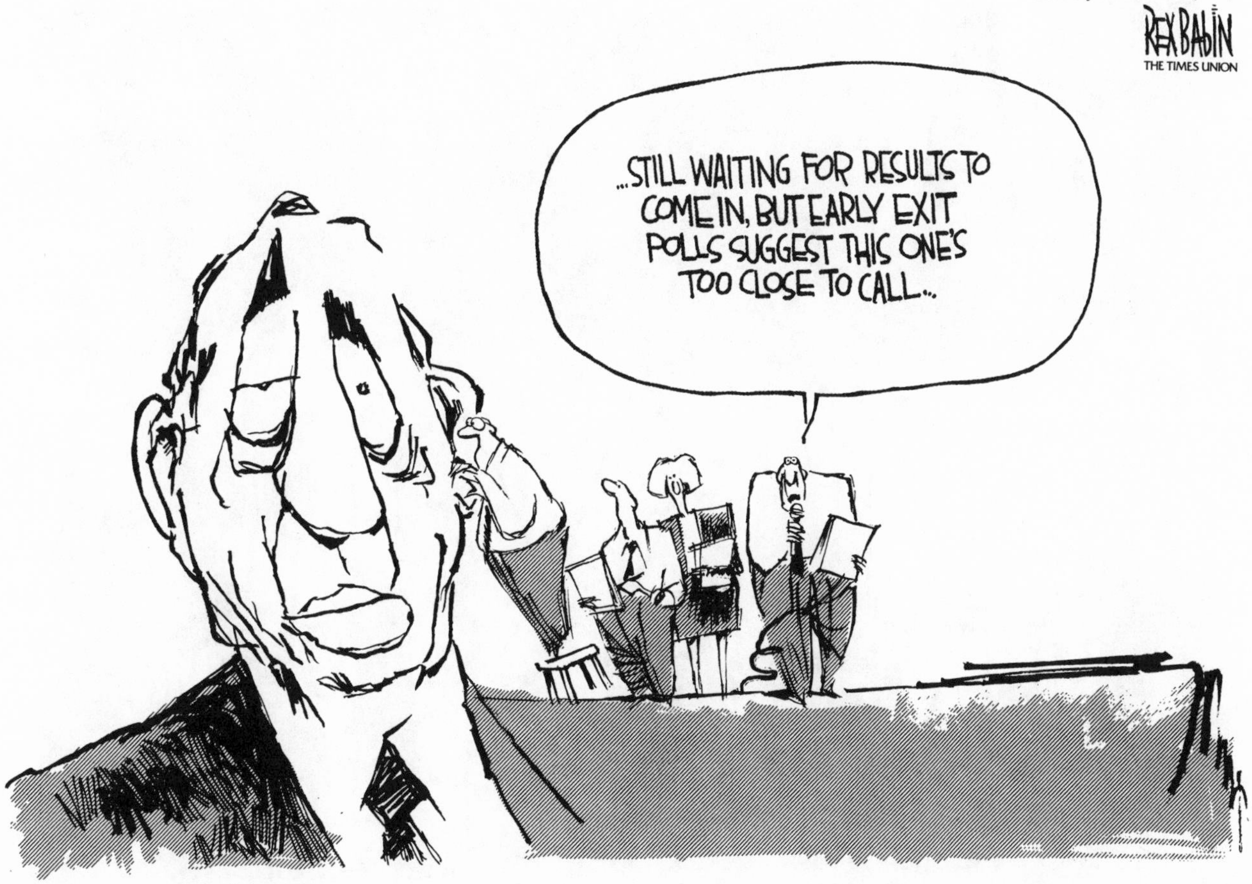
REX BABIN THE TIMES UNION
...STILL WAITING FOR RESULTS TO COME IN, BUT EARLY EXIT POLLS SUGGEST THIS ONE'S TOO CLOSE TO CALL...

FRANK CAMMUSO
Courtesy Syracuse Herald-Journal

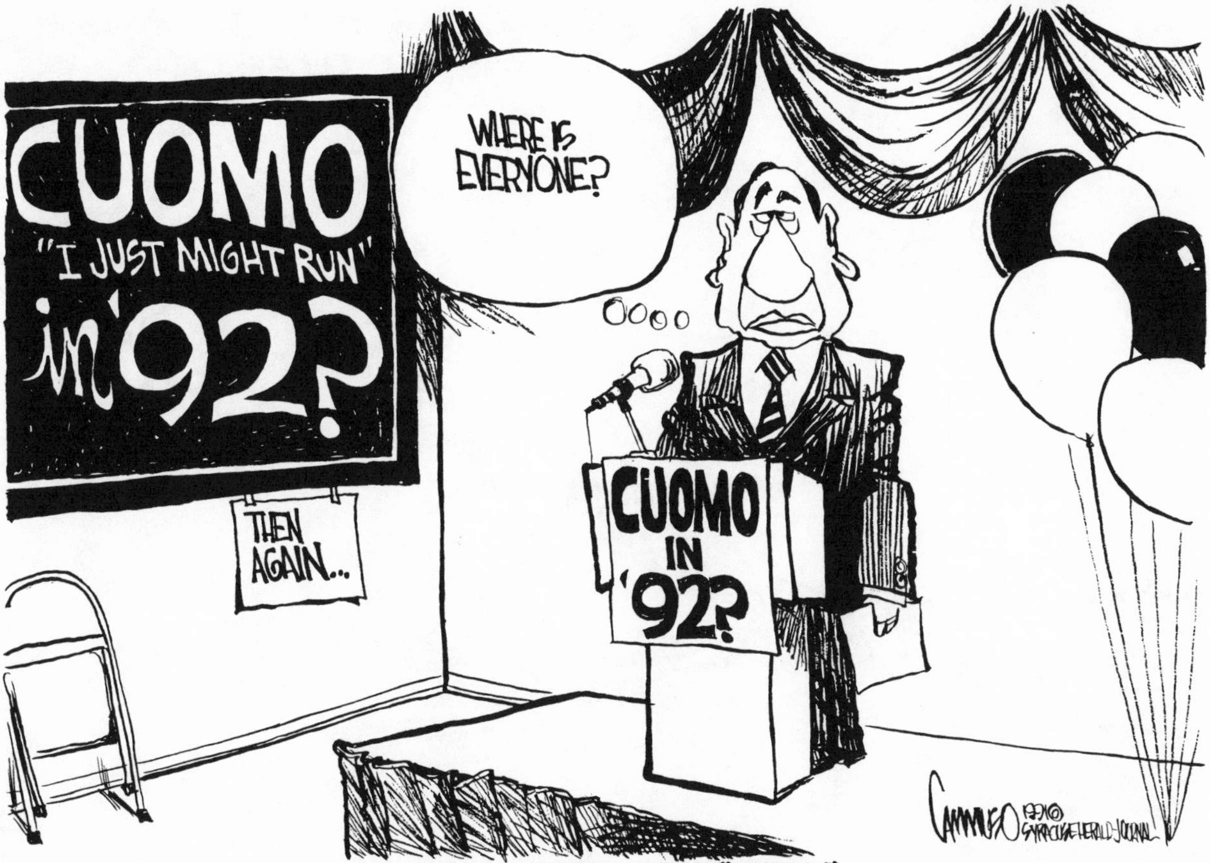
CUOMO "I JUST MIGHT RUN" in '92?
THEN AGAIN...
WHERE IS EVERYONE?
Oooo
CUOMO IN '92?
CAMMUSO SYRACUSE HERALD-JOURNAL

THE BOY WHO CRIED "MAYBE".

WALT HANDELSMAN
Courtesy Times-Picayune (N.O.)

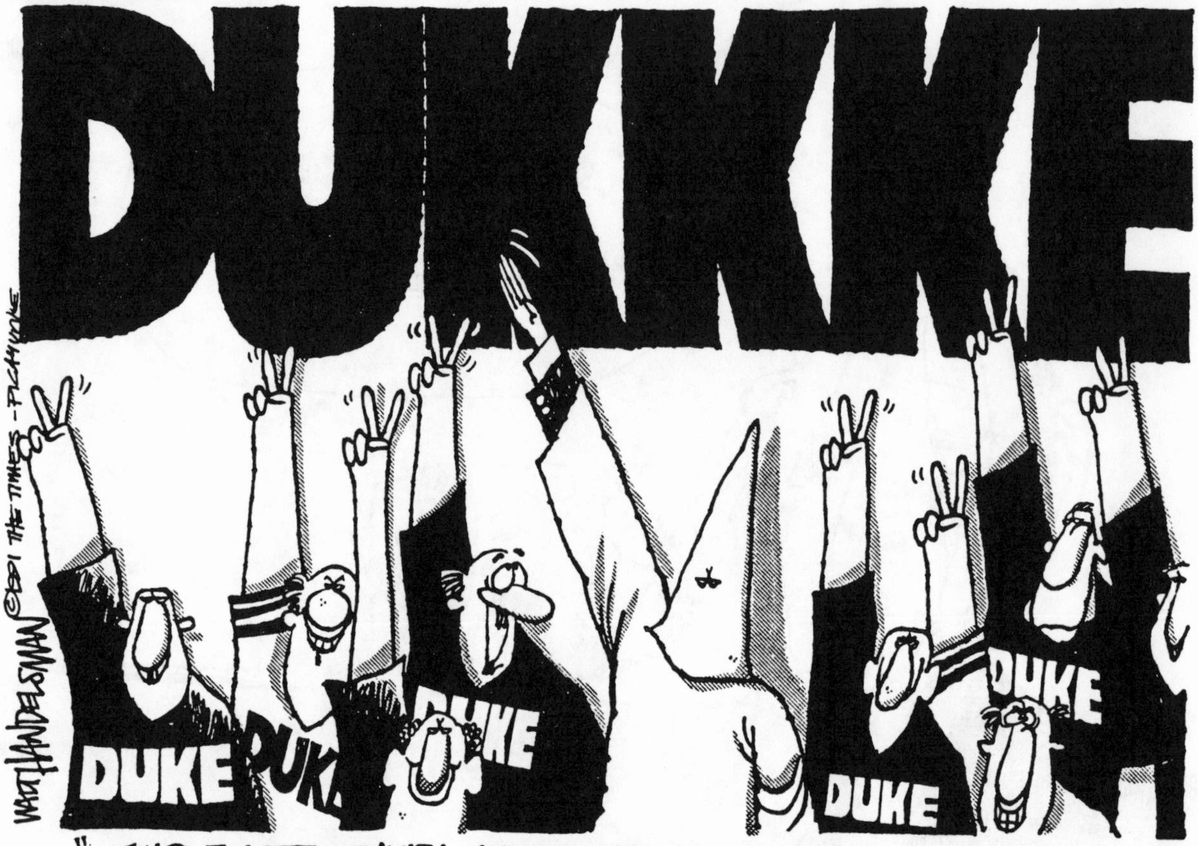
DUKKKE
DUKE
DUKE
DUKE
DUKE
DUKE
WALT HANDELSMAN ©1991 THE TIMES-PICAYUNE

"... TWO FINGERS, DAVID!.. JUST USE TWO FINGERS!.. LIKE THIS..."

DANA SUMMERS
Courtesy Orlando Sentinel

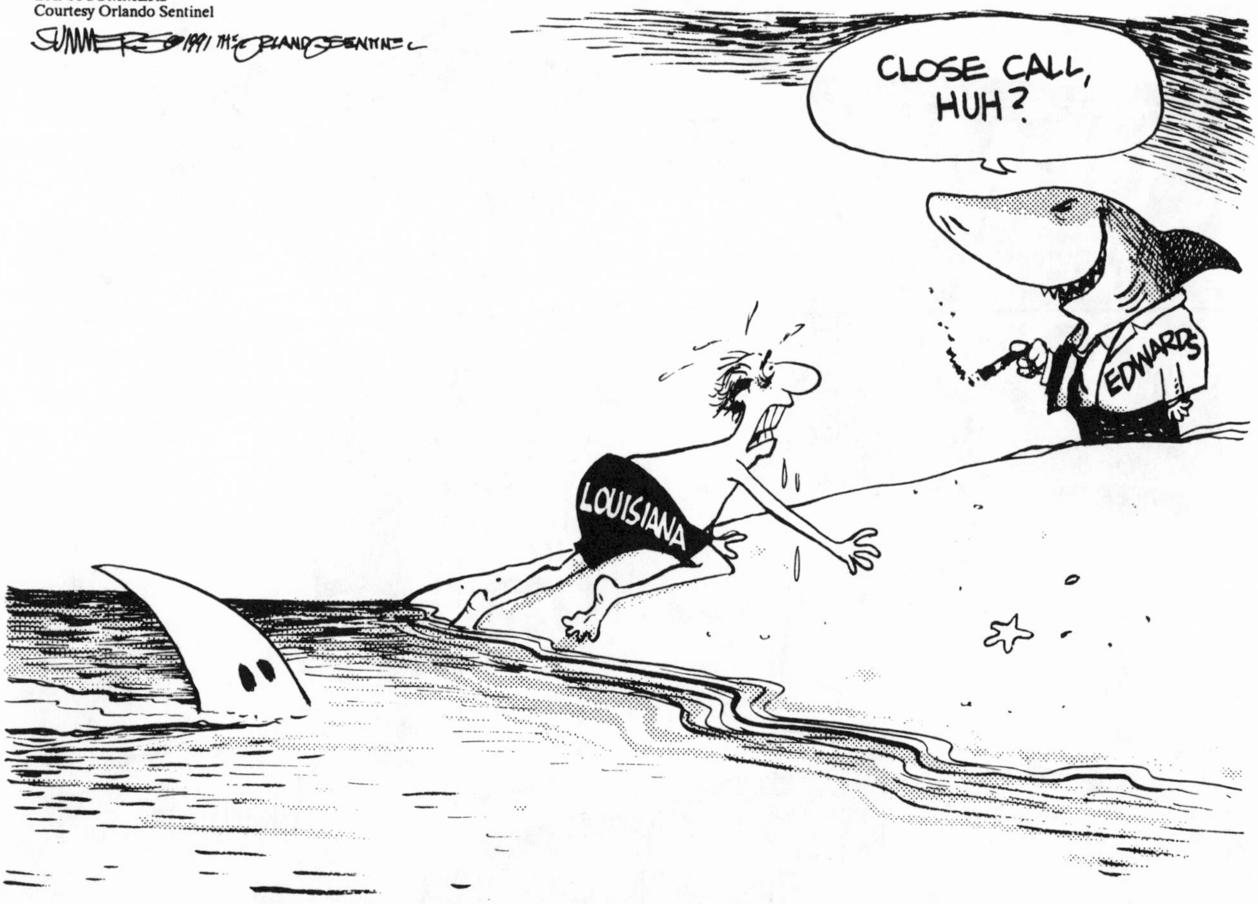
SUMMERS ©1991 THE ORLANDO SENTINEL
CLOSE CALL, HUH?
EDWARDS
LOUISIANA

JIMMY MARGULIES
Courtesy The Record (N.J.) and
North America Syndicate

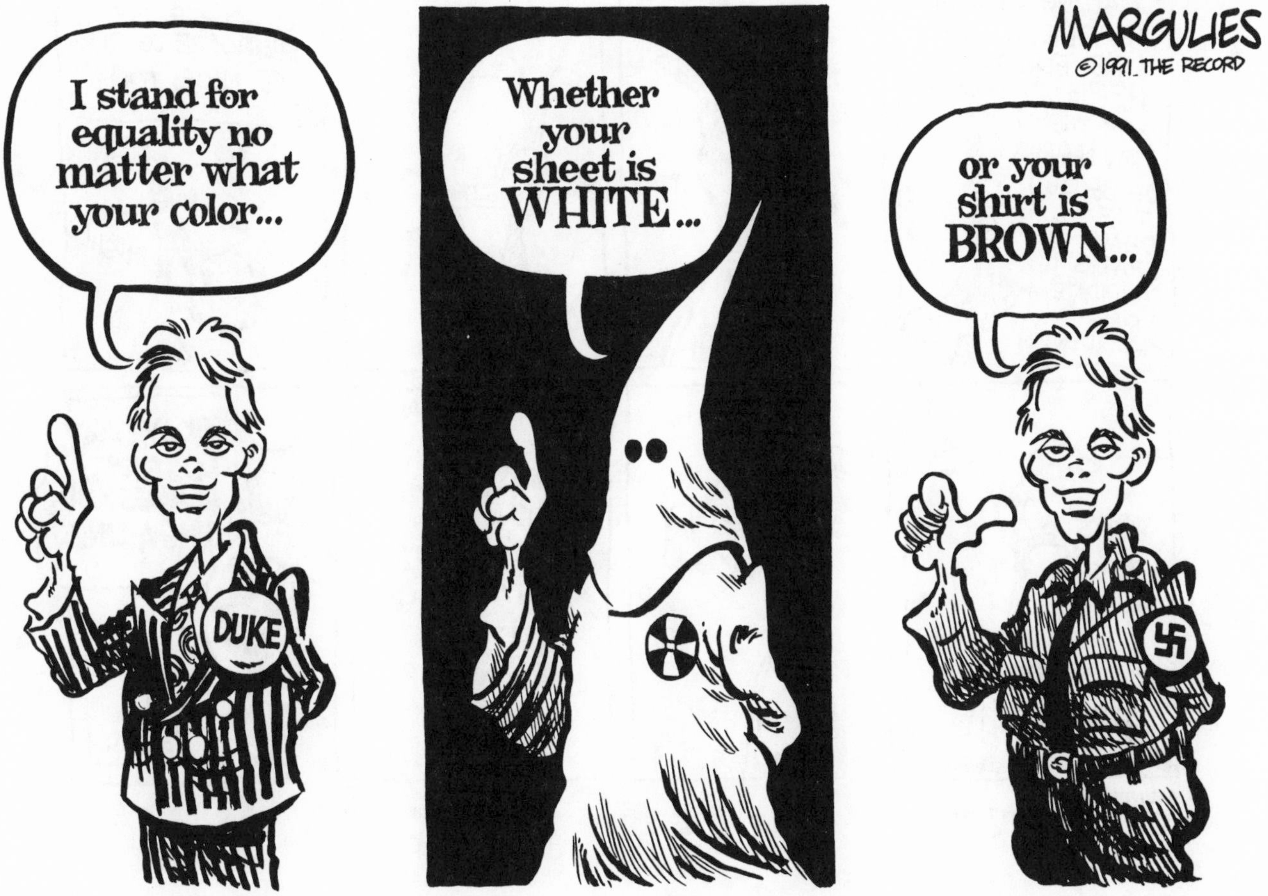
MARGULIES
© 1991 THE RECORD
I stand for equality no matter what your color...
Whether your sheet is WHITE...
or your shirt is BROWN...
DUKE

RICHARD CROWSON
Courtesy Wichita Eagle

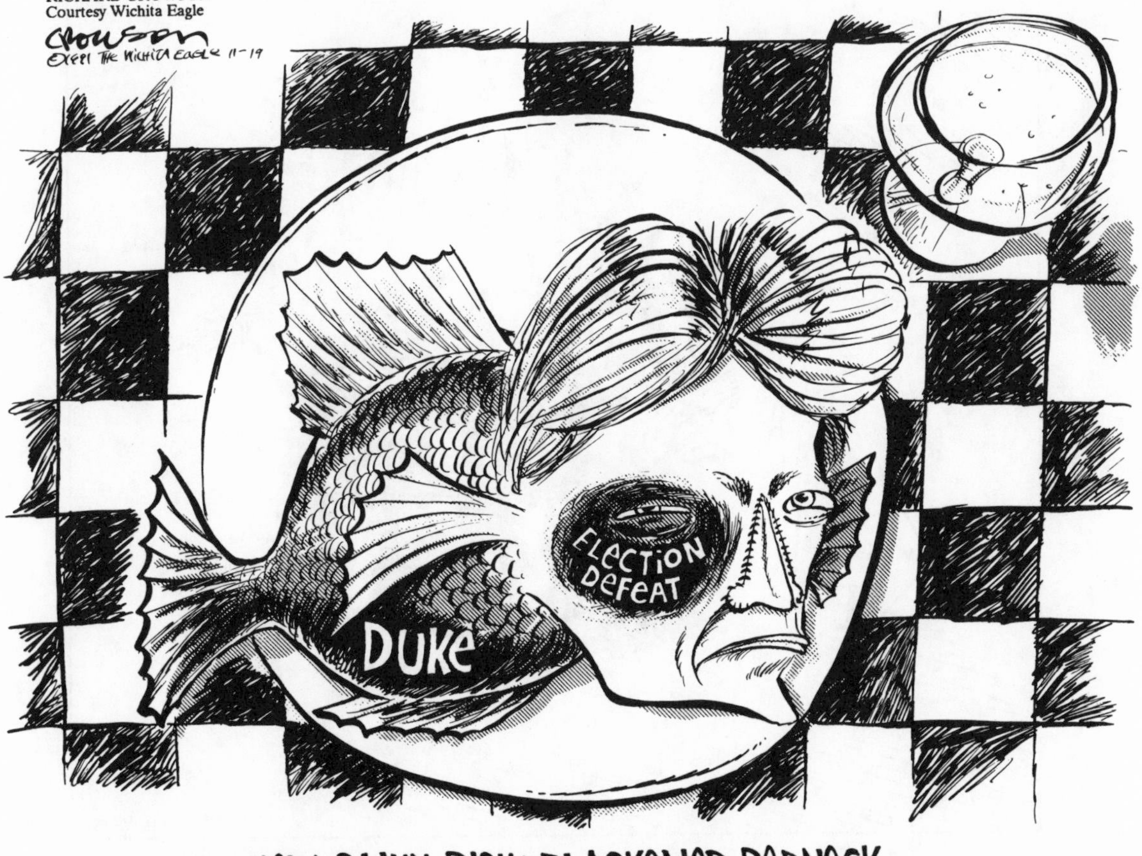
CROWSON
©1991 THE WICHITA EAGLE 11-19
ELECTION DEFEAT
DUKE

NEW CAJUN DISH: BLACKENED REDNECK

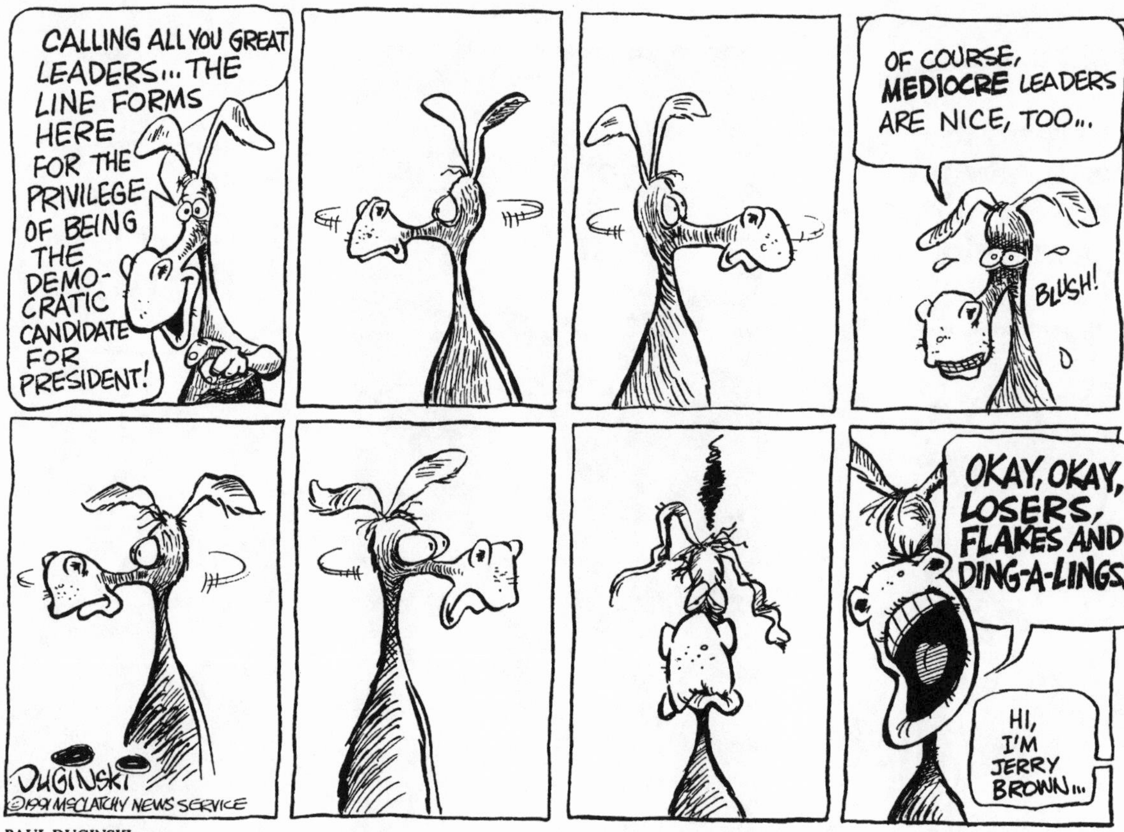
CALLING ALL YOU GREAT LEADERS... THE LINE FORMS HERE FOR THE PRIVILEGE OF BEING THE DEMO-CRATIC CANDIDATE FOR PRESIDENT!
OF COURSE, MEDIOCRE LEADERS ARE NICE, TOO...
BLUSH!
OKAY, OKAY, LOSERS, FLAKES AND DING-A-LINGS!!
HI, I'M JERRY BROWN...
DUGINSKI
©1991 McCLATCHY NEWS SERVICE

PAUL DUGINSKI
Courtesy McClatchy News Service

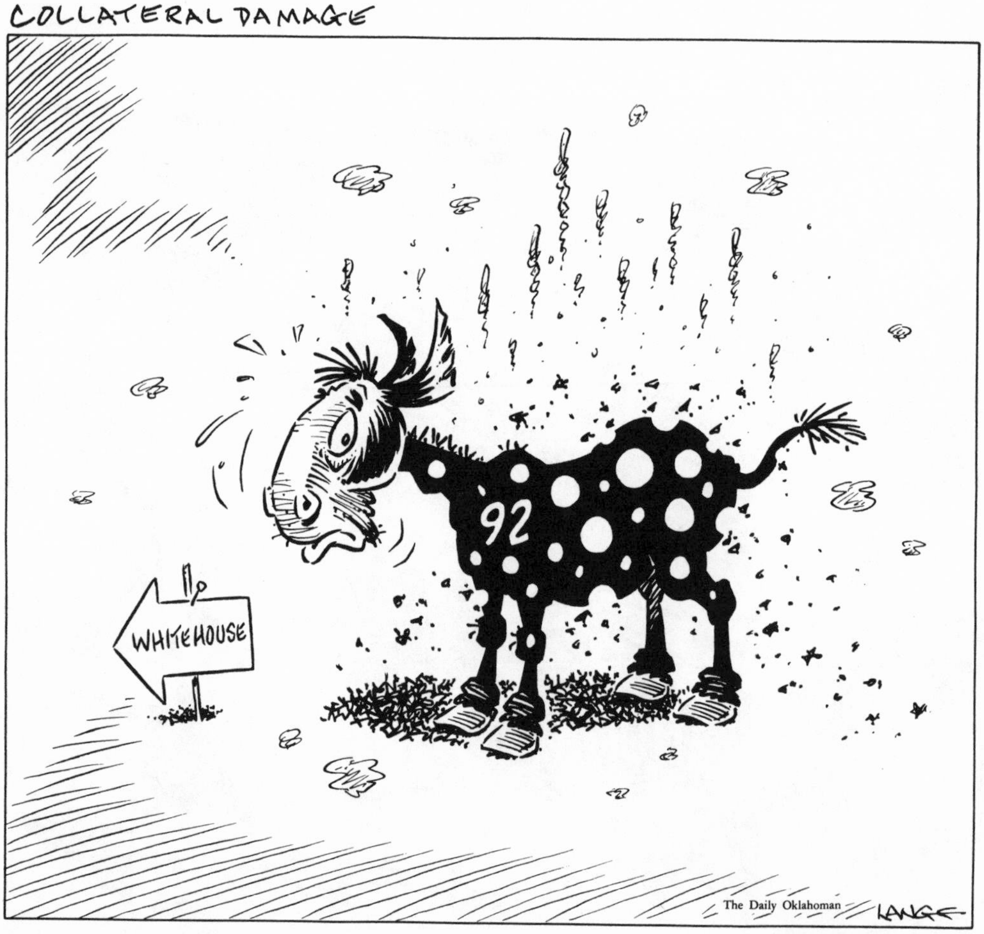
COLLATERAL DAMAGE
92
WHITEHOUSE
The Daily Oklahoman
LANGE

JIM LANGE
Courtesy Daily Oklahoman

WILLIE HORTON ADS
RACIAL POLITICS
"QUOTA" RHETORIC FERTILIZER
RACIAL POLITICS
WICKS
©THE SIGNAL 1991
RACIAL POLITICS
RACIAL POLITICS
DUKE

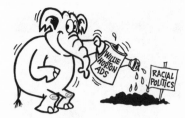

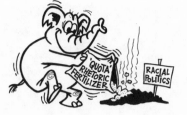

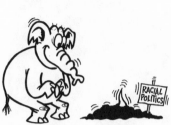

RANDY WICKS
Courtesy Valencia Signal (Calif.)

COME ON, OLD GIRL... JUST A BIT FURTHER!
SOCIALIST UTOPIA
REDISTRIBUTION OF WEALTH PLANS
ENVIRONMENTAL PROGRAMS
HOUSING PLANS
PUBLIC EDUCATION PLANS
NATIONAL HEALTH CARE PLAN
U.S. LIBERALS
DEMS
SOVIETS
ASAY ©
COLORADO SPRINGS GAZETTE TELEGRAPH

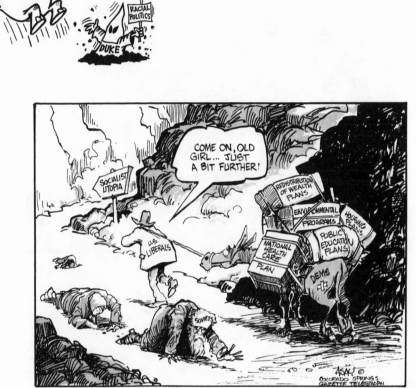

CHUCK ASAY
Courtesy Colorado Springs Gazette Telegraph

JOHN COLE
Courtesy Durham Herald-Sun

JOHN COLE THE HERALD-SUN
CASEY
IRAN ARMS DEAL
GATES
WHAT? ME WORRY?

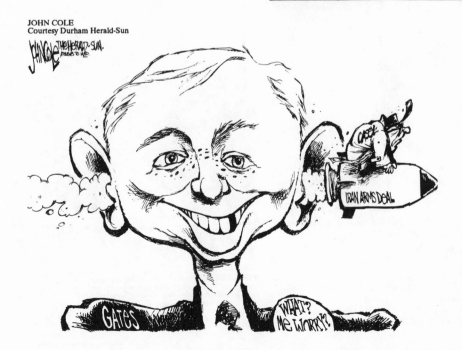

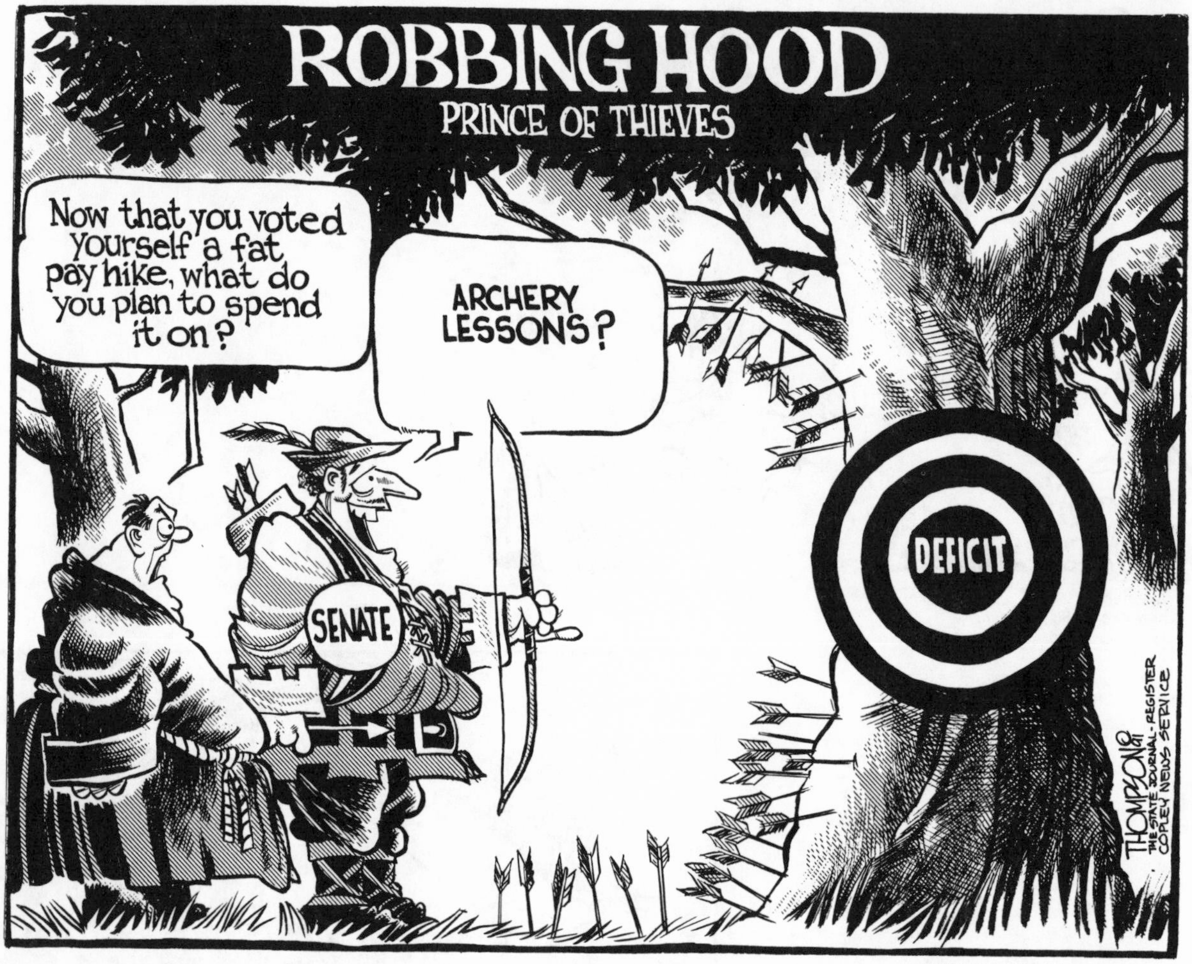
ROBBING HOOD
PRINCE OF THIEVES
Now that you voted yourself a fat pay hike, what do you plan to spend it on?
ARCHERY LESSONS?
SENATE
DEFICIT
THOMPSON '91 THE STATE JOURNAL-REGISTER COPLEY NEWS SERVICE

MIKE THOMPSON
Courtesy State Journal-Register (Ill.)

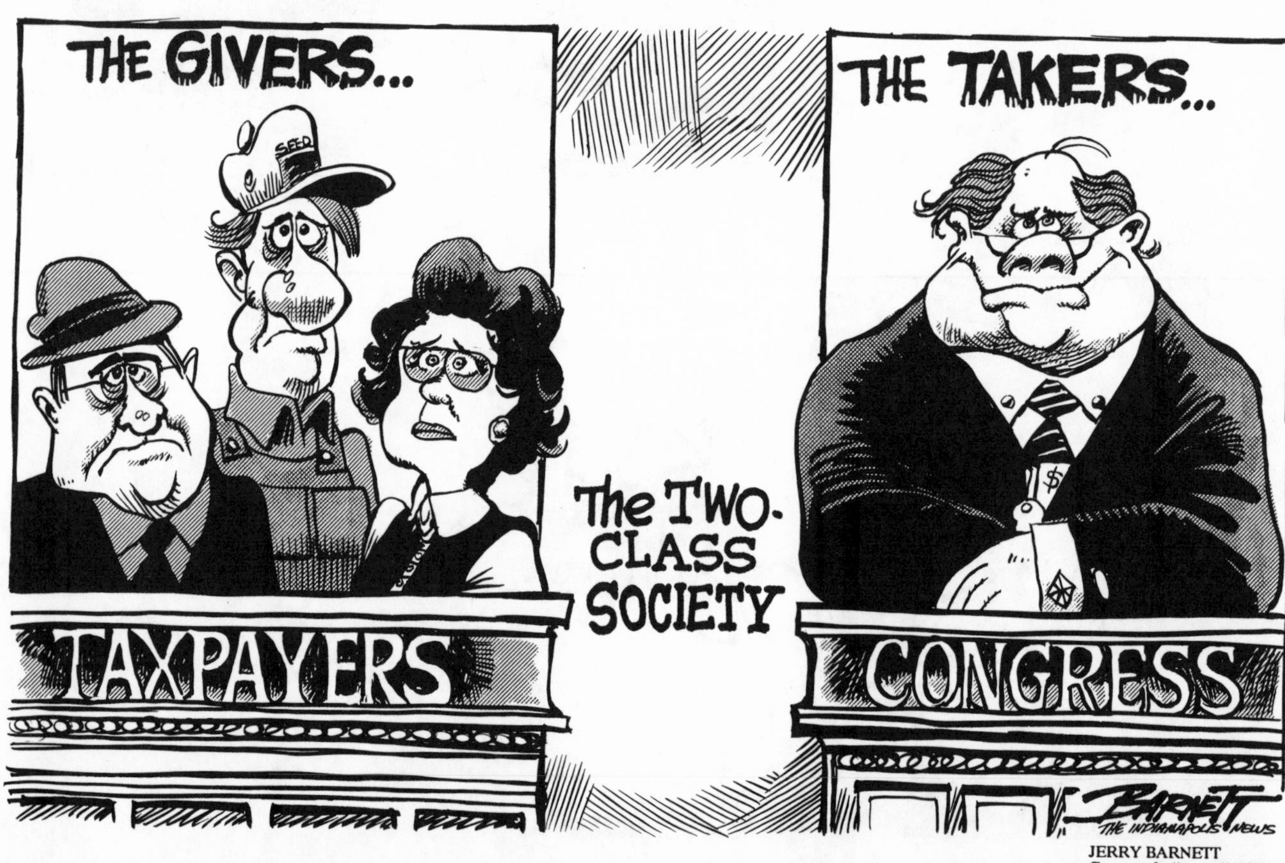
THE GIVERS...
THE TAKERS...
The TWO-CLASS SOCIETY
TAXPAYERS
CONGRESS
BARNETT THE INDIANAPOLIS NEWS

JERRY BARNETT
Courtesy Indianapolis News

Congress

The U.S. Congress usually moves at a snail's pace – but not always. In July, under the cover of late-night darkness and with the swiftness of an attacking animal, the honorables voted themselves a $23,200 pay raise. The entire matter took only one hour and three minutes. Voter anger erupted as various citizen groups heightened the call for limiting the terms of officeholders.

In early October, news broke that members of Congress owed some $300,000 in overdue bills to the House restaurant. Furthermore, the House bank had quietly handled 8,331 bad checks written by congressmen, including some for thousands of dollars that amounted to interest-free loans. Some of the biggest names in the House were cited as being guilty of writing rubber checks, including Speaker Tom Foley and Majority Leader Richard Gephardt.

Because of the changing world situation, Congress set about to trim defense spending. But new pork barrel projects claimed the interest of many members, and the ballooning national deficit was expected to reach $348 billion for 1992.

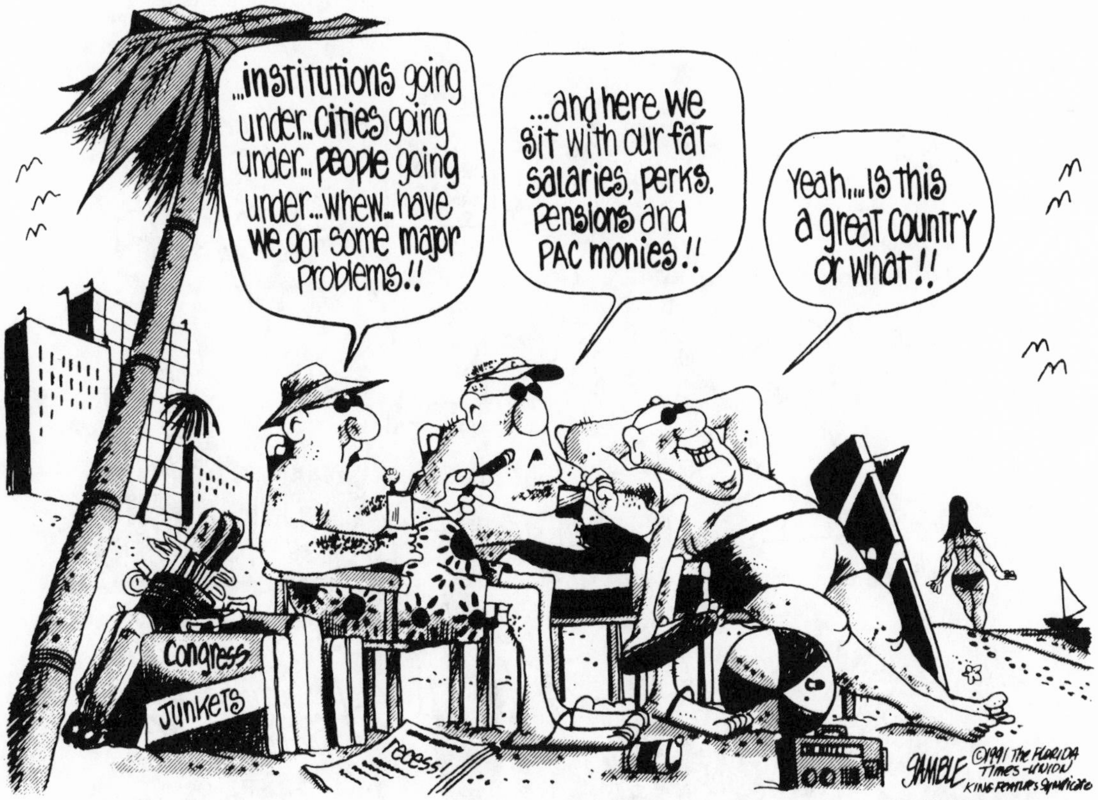
...institutions going under.. cities going under... people going under...whew.. have we got some major problems!!
...and here we sit with our fat salaries, perks, pensions and PAC monies!!
Yeah,...is this a great country or what!!
Congress
Junkets
recess!
GAMBLE ©1991 The Florida Times-Union King Features Syndicate

ED GAMBLE
Courtesy Florida Times-Union

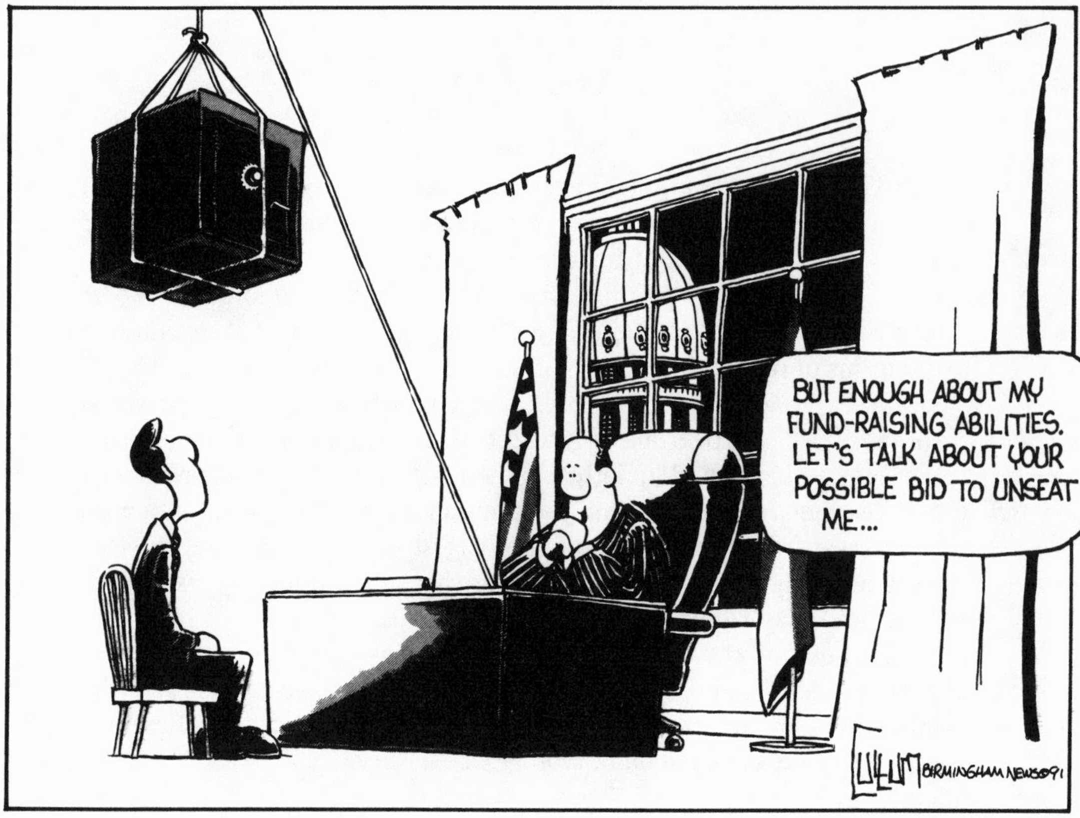
BUT ENOUGH ABOUT MY FUND-RAISING ABILITIES. LET'S TALK ABOUT YOUR POSSIBLE BID TO UNSEAT ME...
CULLUM BIRMINGHAM NEWS©91

MARK CULLUM
Courtesy Birmingham News

TOM ENGELHARDT
Courtesy St. Louis Post-Dispatch

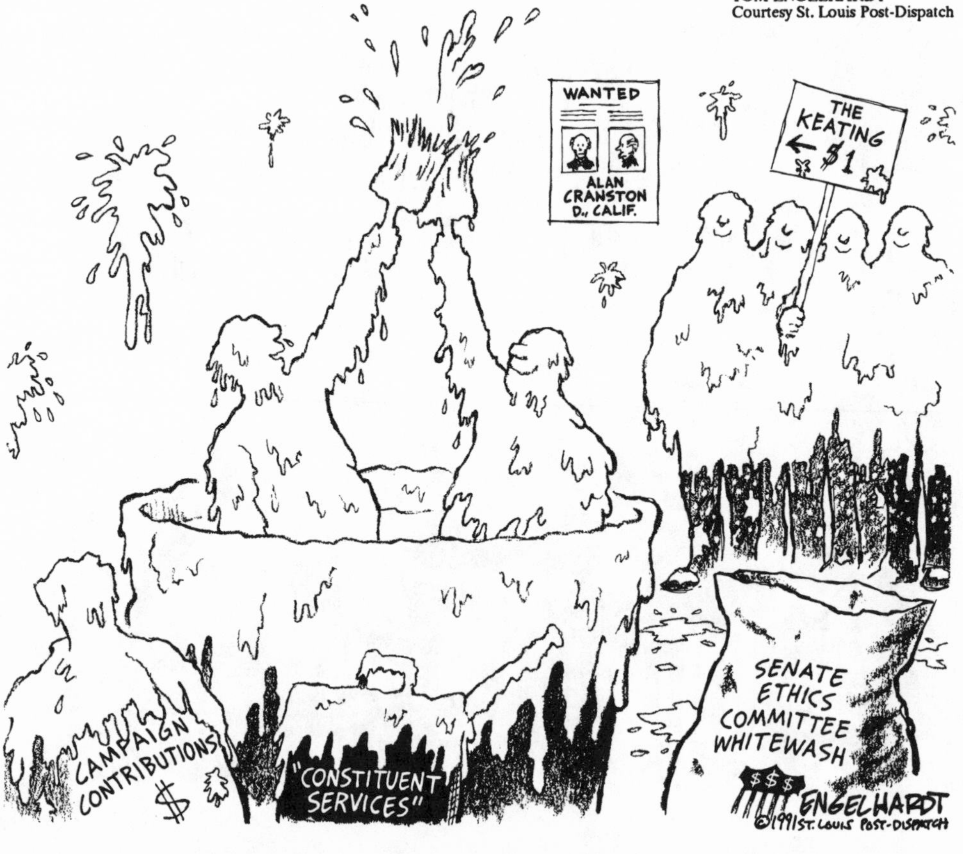
WANTED
ALAN CRANSTON D., CALIF.
THE KEATING ← $1
CAMPAIGN CONTRIBUTIONS
$
"CONSTITUENT SERVICES"
SENATE ETHICS COMMITTEE WHITEWASH
$$$
ENGELHARDT ©1991 ST. LOUIS POST-DISPATCH

'It Was A Tough Chore, But We Managed To Cover Just About Everything'

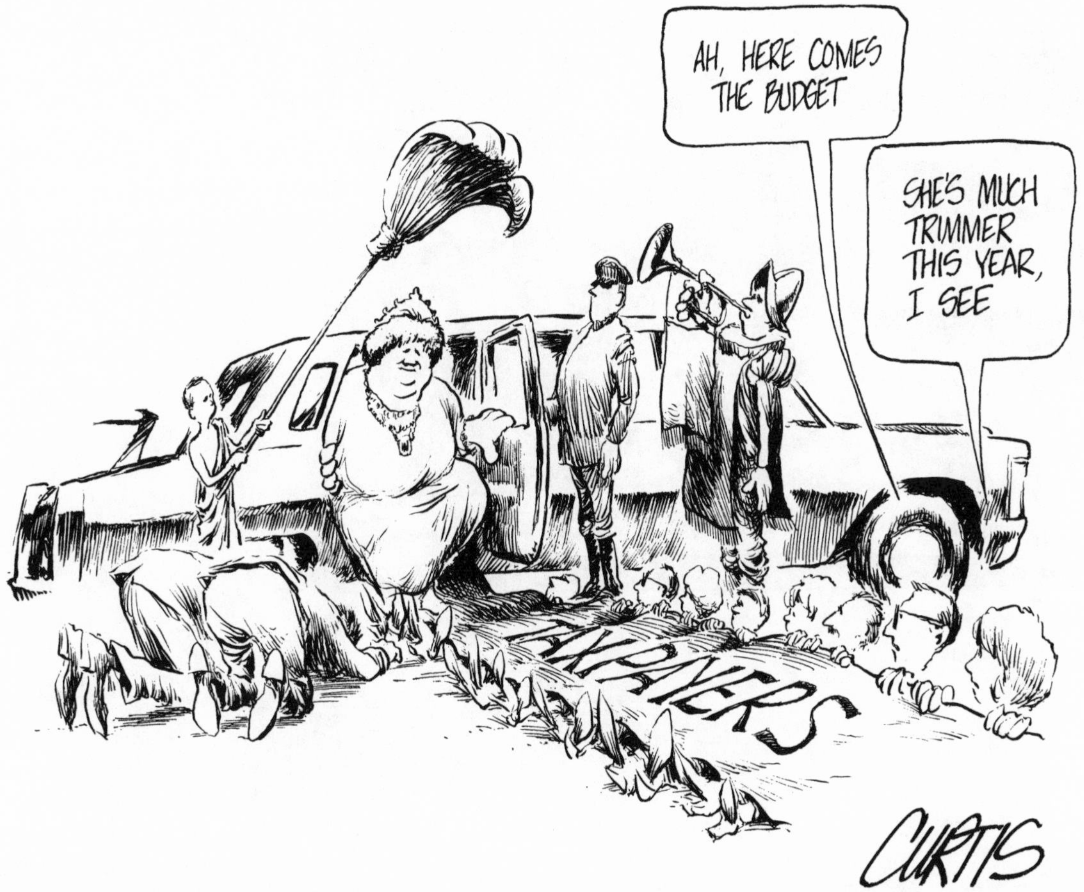
AH, HERE COMES THE BUDGET
SHE'S MUCH TRIMMER THIS YEAR, I SEE
TAXPAYERS
CURTIS

CHRIS CURTIS
Courtesy Alexandria Gazette Packet

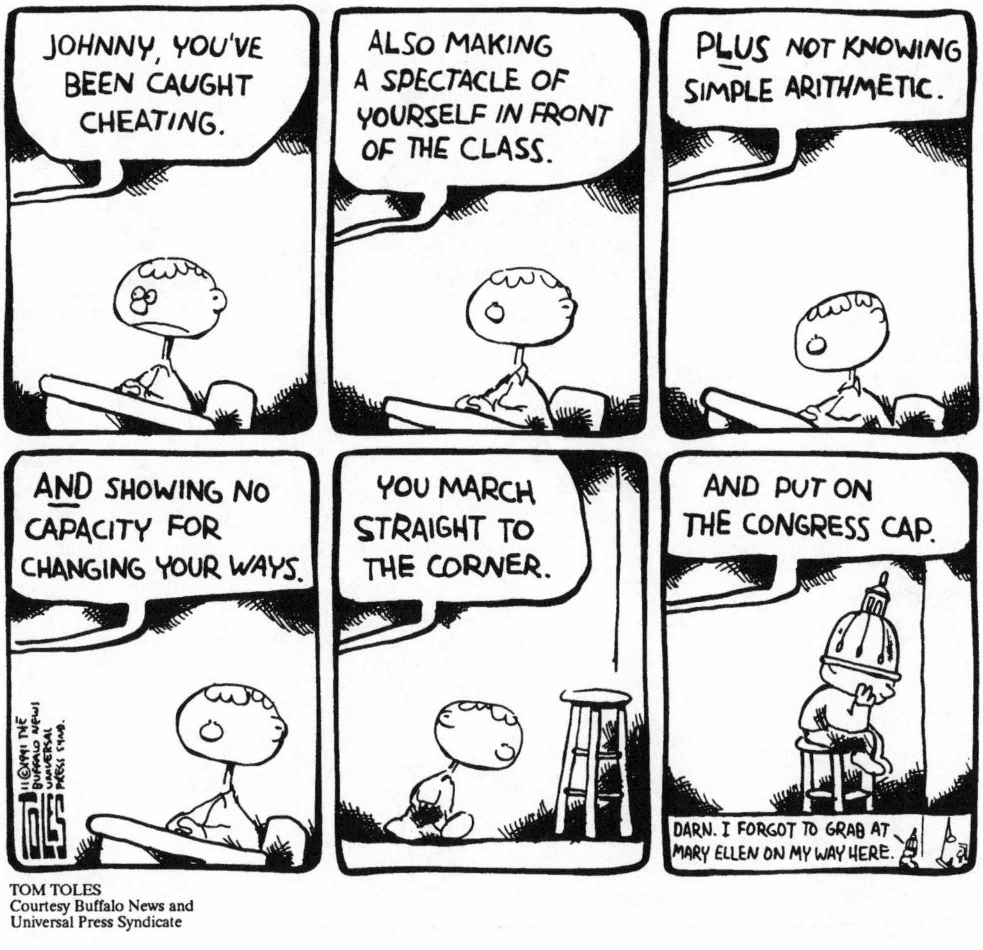
JOHNNY, YOU'VE BEEN CAUGHT CHEATING.
ALSO MAKING A SPECTACLE OF YOURSELF IN FRONT OF THE CLASS.
PLUS NOT KNOWING SIMPLE ARITHMETIC.
AND SHOWING NO CAPACITY FOR CHANGING YOUR WAYS.
YOU MARCH STRAIGHT TO THE CORNER.
AND PUT ON THE CONGRESS CAP.
DARN. I FORGOT TO GRAB AT MARY ELLEN ON MY WAY HERE.
TOLES

TOM TOLES
Courtesy Buffalo News and
Universal Press Syndicate

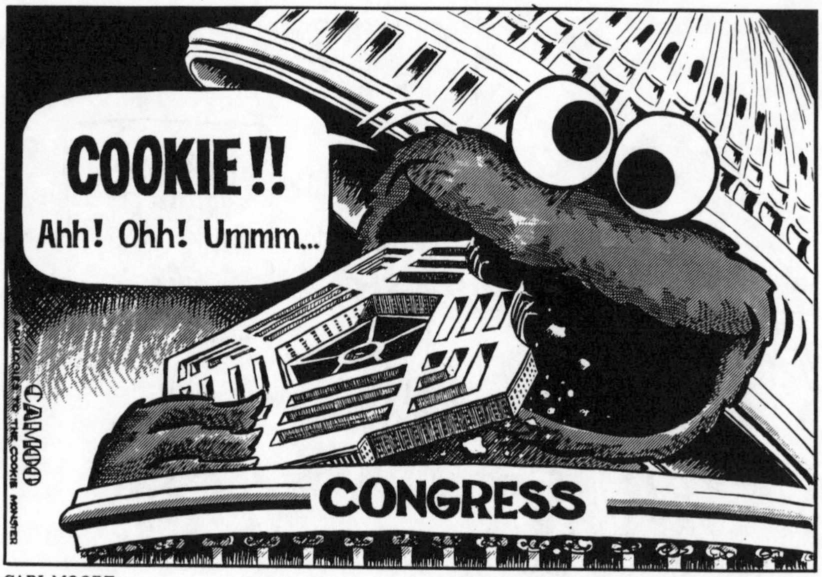
COOKIE!!
Ahh! Ohh! Ummm...
CONGRESS
APOLOGIES TO THE COOKIE MONSTER
CARL MOORE
Courtesy National Review

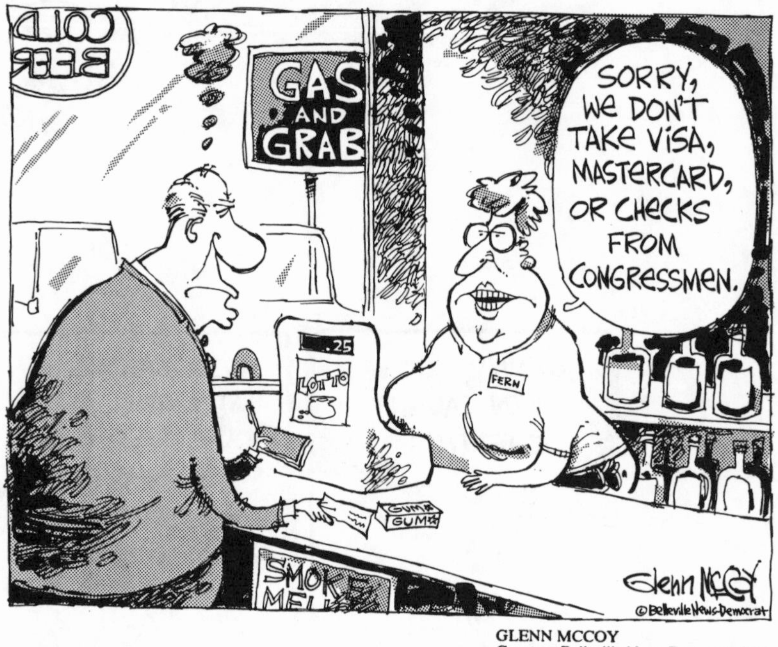
GAS AND GRAB
SORRY, WE DON'T TAKE VISA, MASTERCARD, OR CHECKS FROM CONGRESSMEN.
FERN
LOTTO
GUM
Glenn McCoy
©Belleville News-Democrat
GLENN MCCOY
Courtesy Belleville News-Democrat (Ill.)

STEVE LINDSTROM
Courtesy Duluth News-Tribune

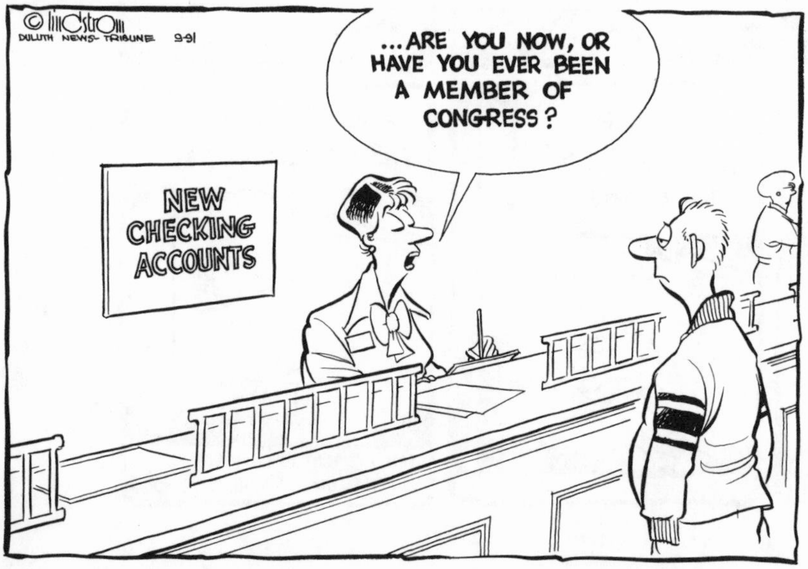
DULUTH NEWS-TRIBUNE 9-91
...ARE YOU NOW, OR HAVE YOU EVER BEEN A MEMBER OF CONGRESS?
NEW CHECKING ACCOUNTS

WILLIAM COSTELLO
Courtesy Lowell Sun

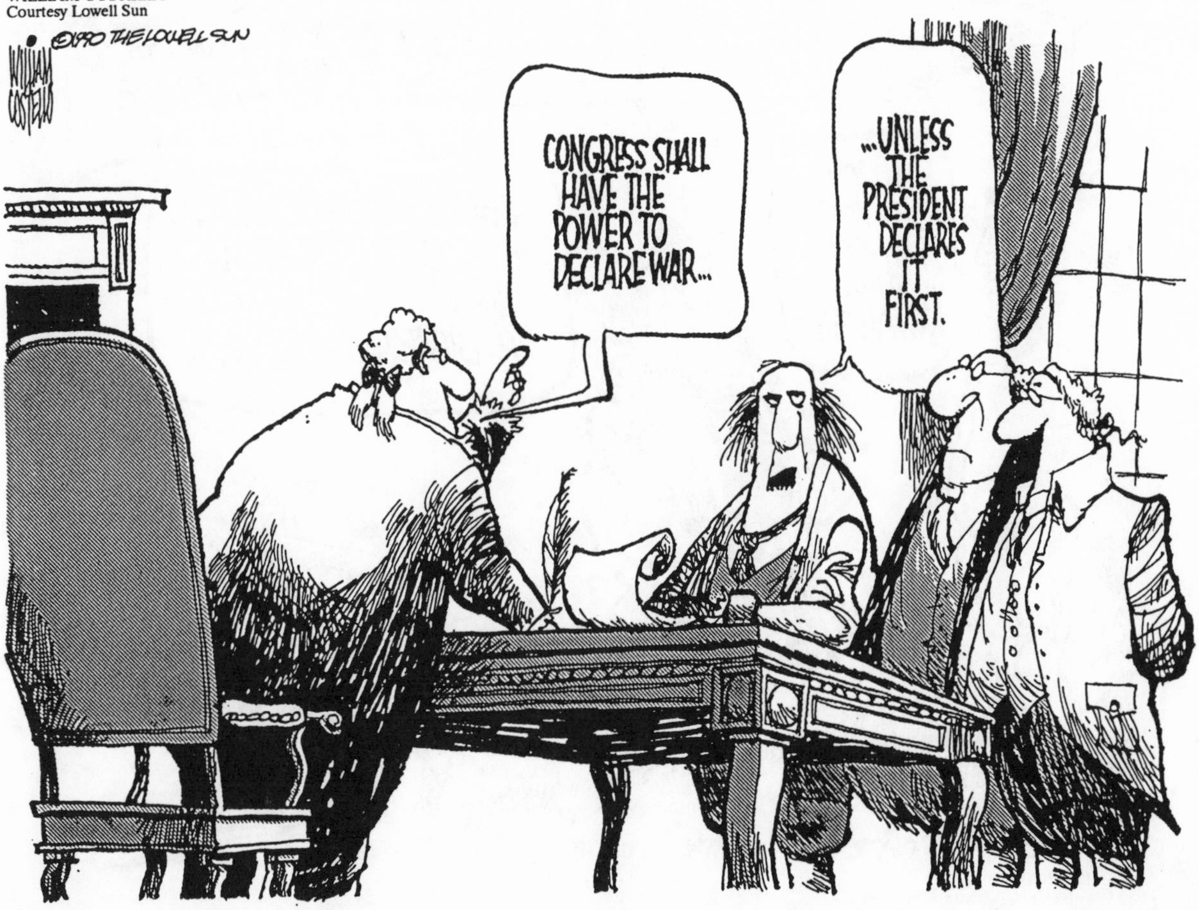
©1990 THE LOWELL SUN
WILLIAM COSTELLO
CONGRESS SHALL HAVE THE POWER TO DECLARE WAR...
...UNLESS THE PRESIDENT DECLARES IT FIRST.

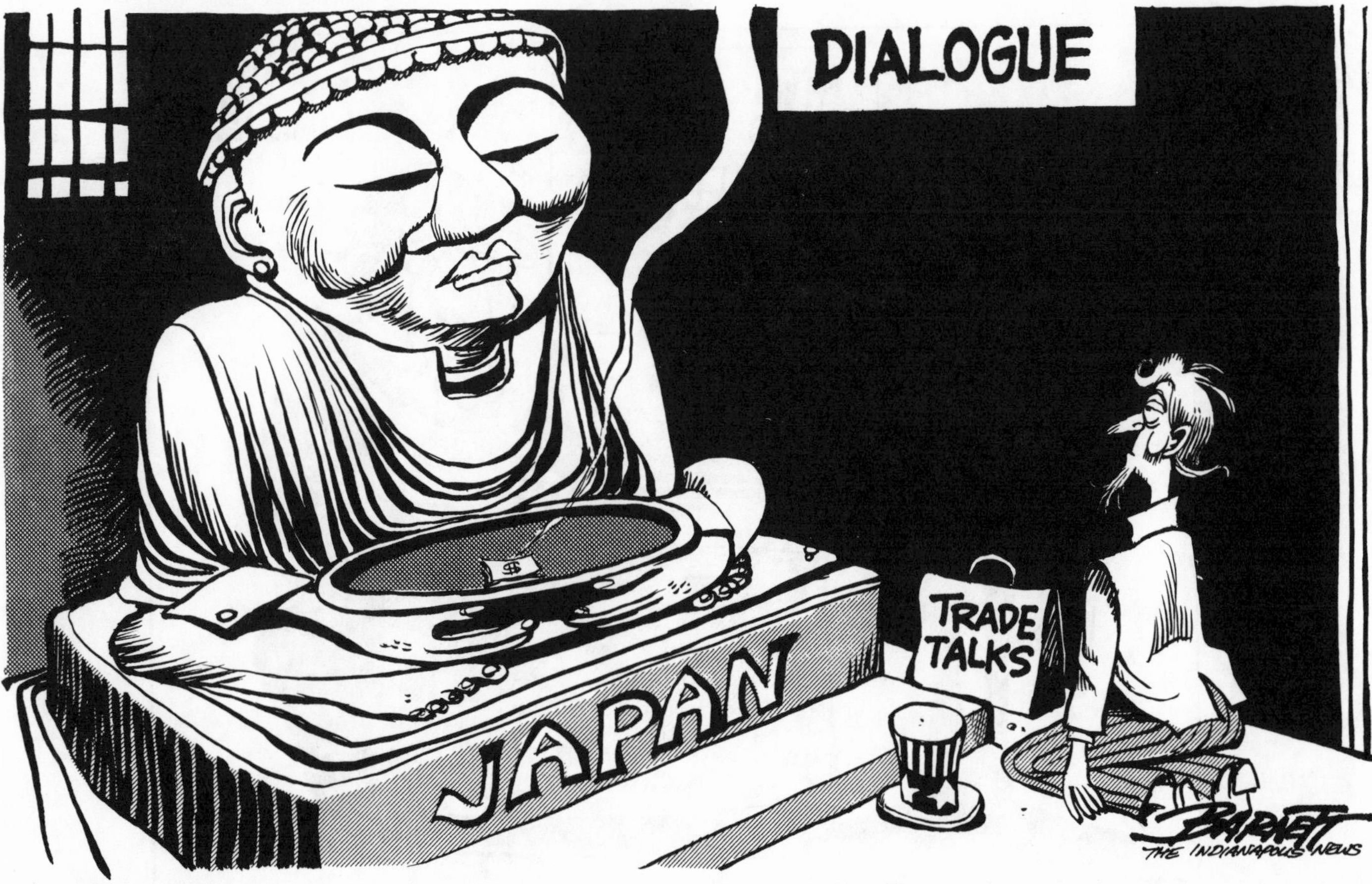
DIALOGUE
JAPAN
TRADE TALKS
BARNETT
THE INDIANAPOLIS NEWS

JERRY BARNETT
Courtesy Indianapolis News

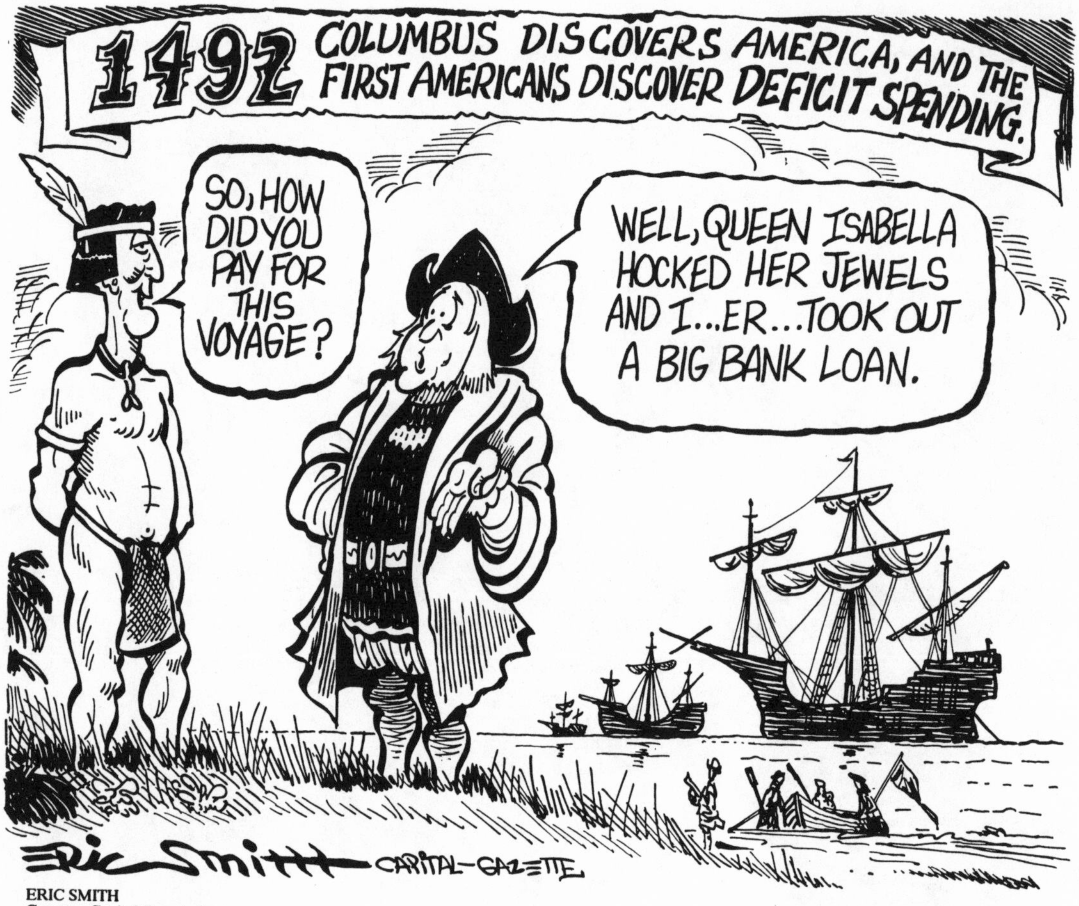
1492 COLUMBUS DISCOVERS AMERICA, AND THE FIRST AMERICANS DISCOVER DEFICIT SPENDING.
SO, HOW DID YOU PAY FOR THIS VOYAGE?
WELL, QUEEN ISABELLA HOCKED HER JEWELS AND I...ER...TOOK OUT A BIG BANK LOAN.
CAPITAL-GAZETTE

ERIC SMITH
Courtesy Capital Gazette Newspapers

HANK MCCLURE
Courtesy Lawton Constitution

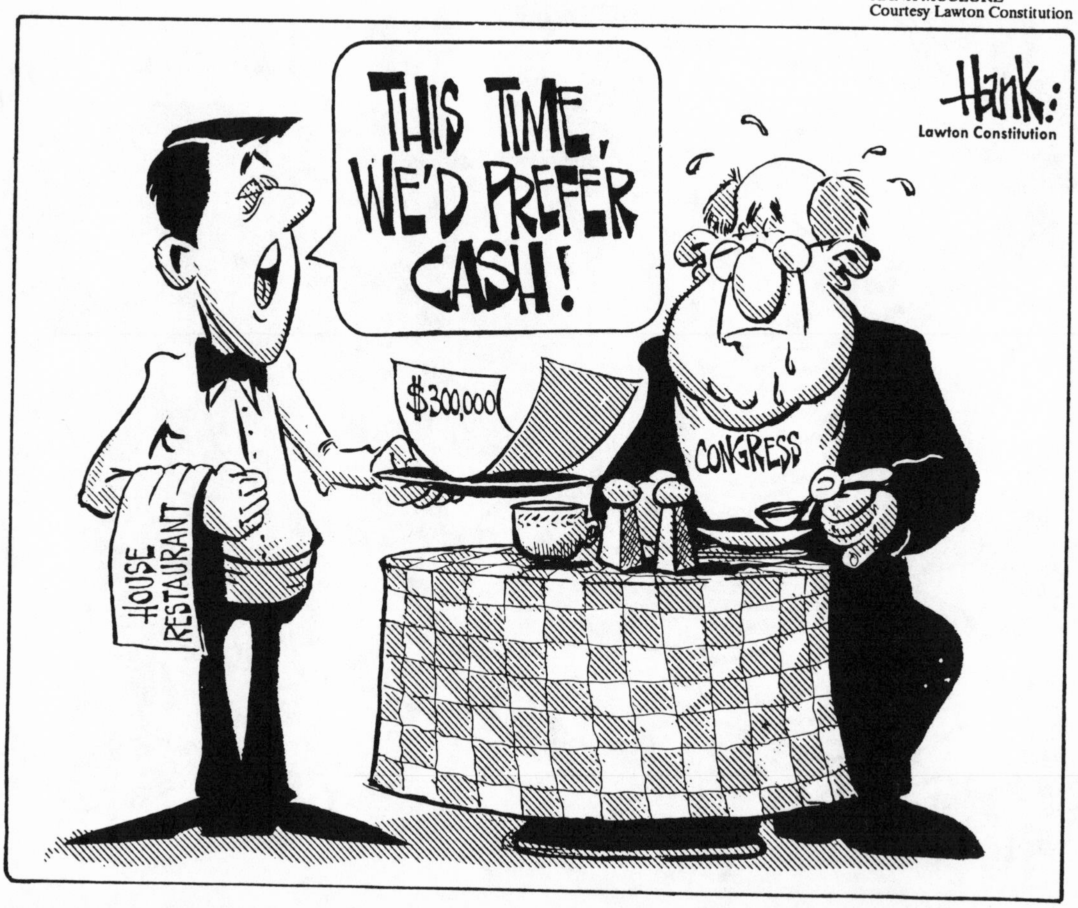
Hank
Lawton Constitution
THIS TIME, WE'D PREFER CASH!
$300,000
CONGRESS
HOUSE RESTAURANT

RANDY BISH
Courtesy Greensburg Tribune-Review

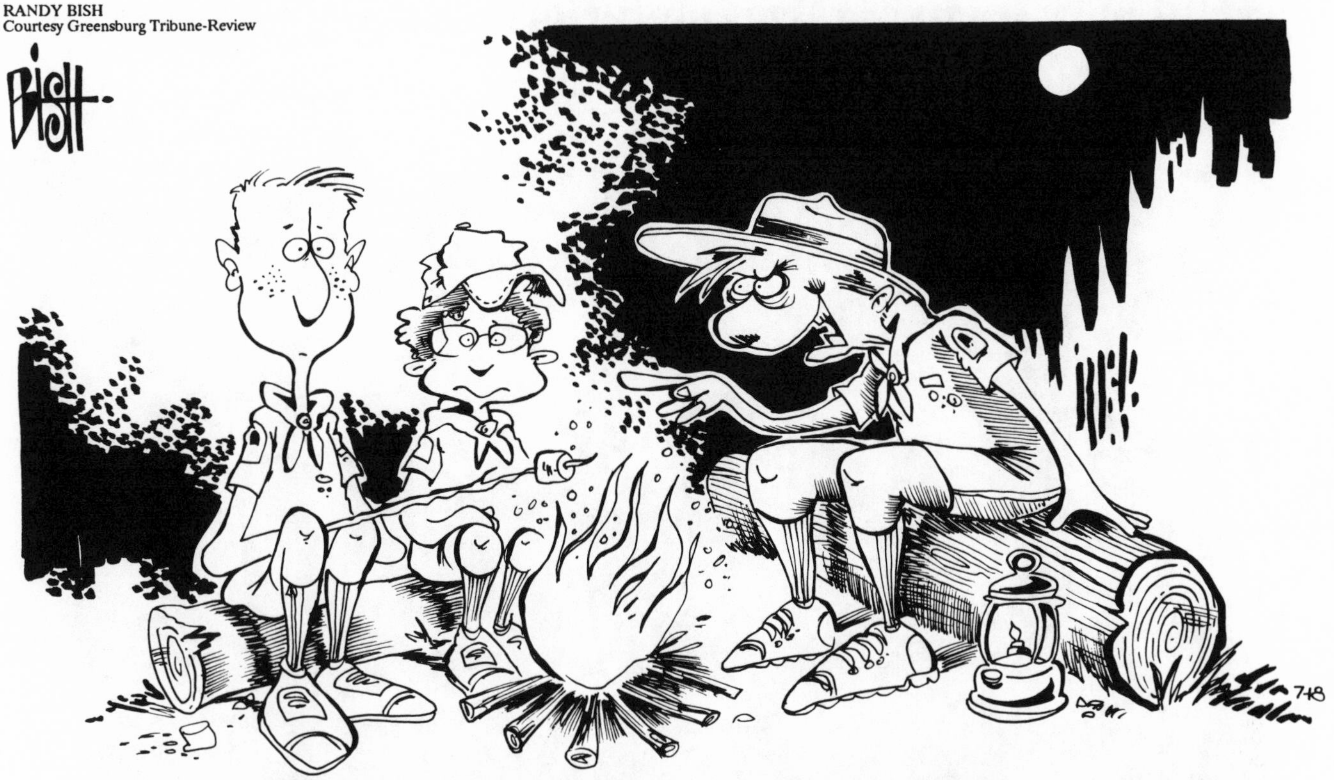

OH SURE-THAT HEADLESS WOODSMAN STORY IS PLENTY SCARY-BUT WAIT TILL I TELL YOU HOW SENATORS GET RAISES

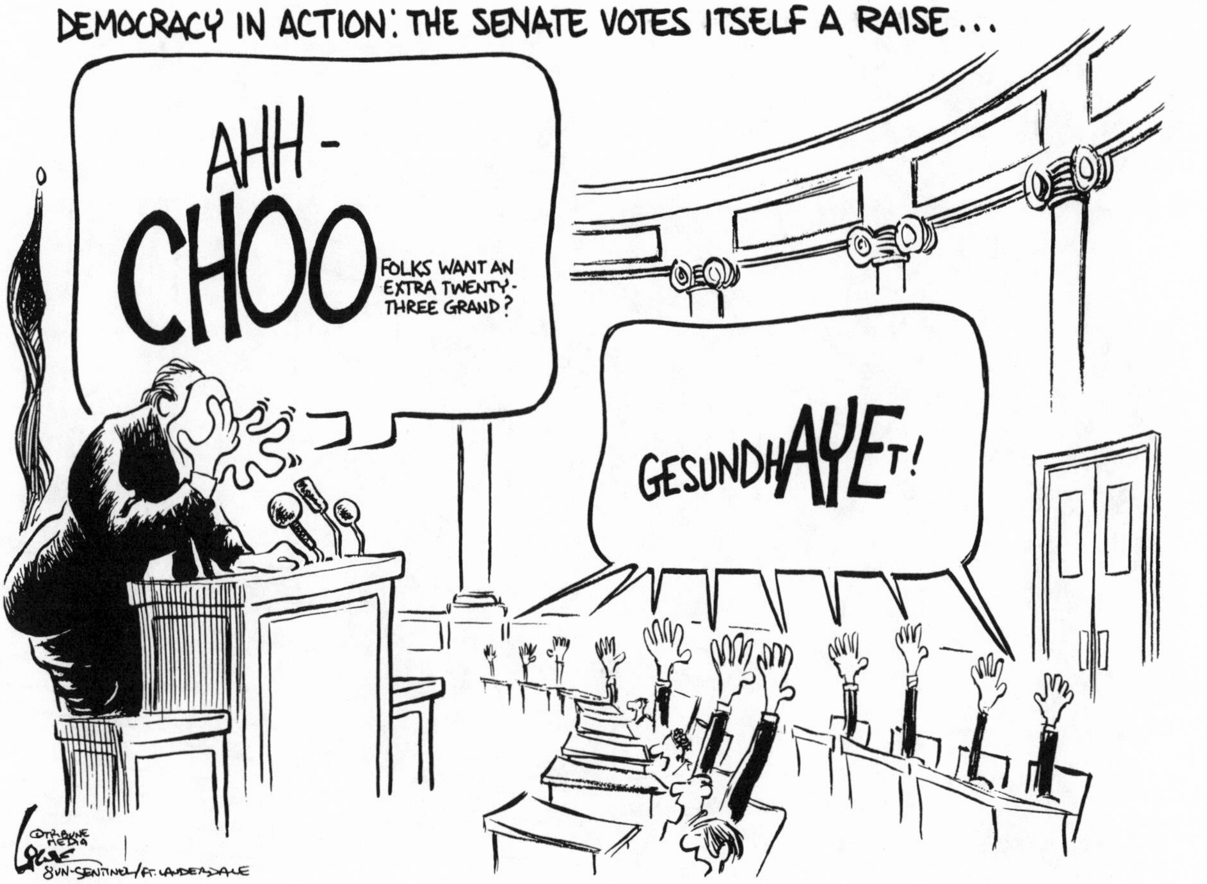
DEMOCRACY IN ACTION: THE SENATE VOTES ITSELF A RAISE...
AHH-CHOO
FOLKS WANT AN EXTRA TWENTY-THREE GRAND?
GESUNDHAYEt!

CHAN LOWE
Courtesy The News/Sun-Sentinel (Fla.)

The only form of term limitation favored by Congress...

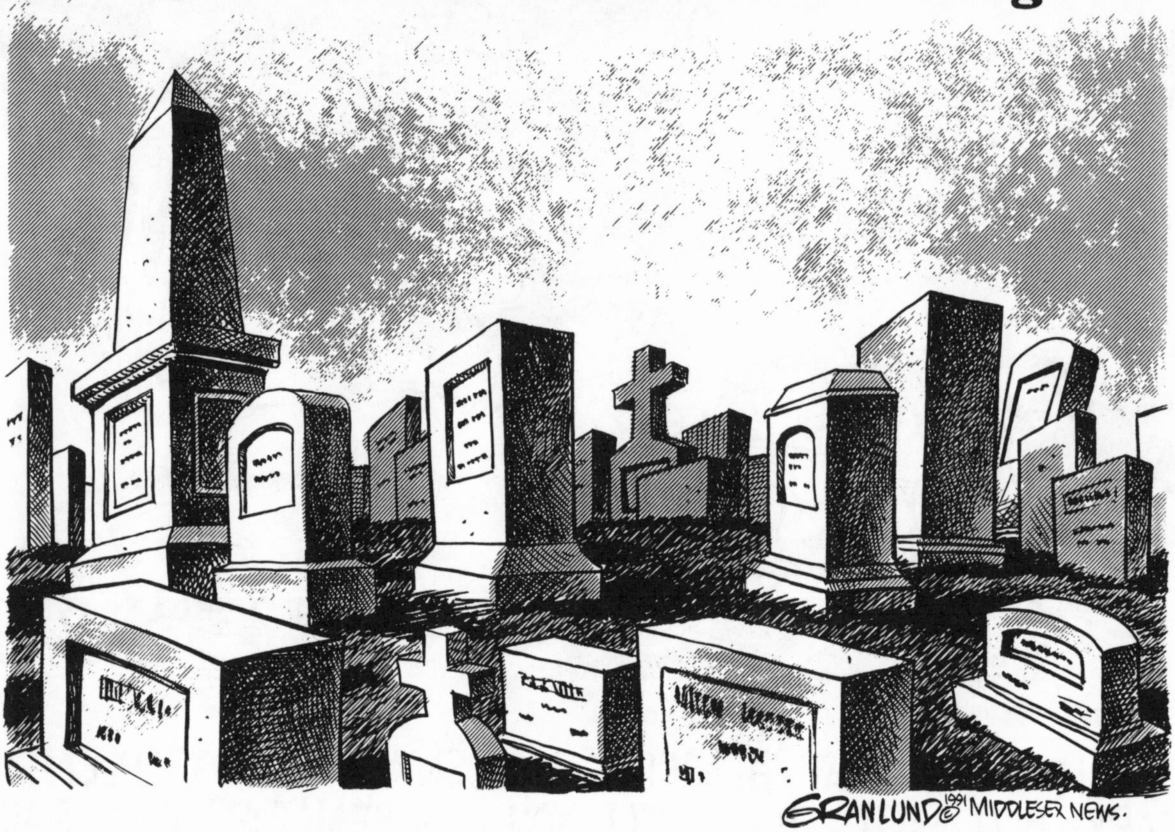
GRANLUND ©1991 MIDDLESEX NEWS.

DAVID GRANLUND
Courtesy Middlesex News

BRUCE BEATTIE
Courtesy Daytona Beach News-Journal

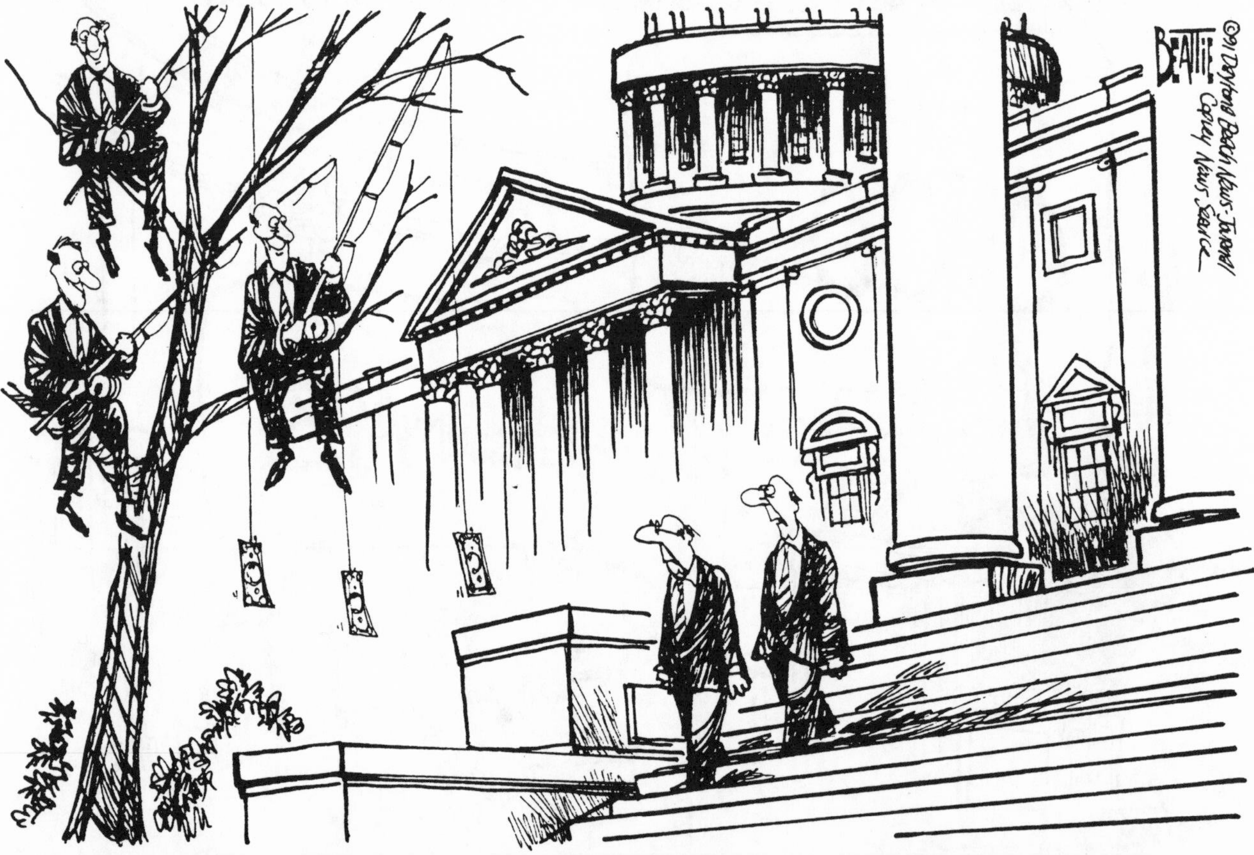
BEATTIE
©91 Daytona Beach News-Journal
Copley News Service

"I don't think lobbyists are taking our attempts at ethics reform seriously."

Foreign Affairs

Yugoslavia as it had existed since 1918 came to an end in 1991 as the country slid into civil war. Separatist sentiment overflowed in the western, economically well-off republics of Slovenia and Croatia, which seek to retain ties with Serbia and other republics only in a loose confederation. After Croatia and Slovenia declared their independence on June 25, more than 7,000 were killed in the fighting that followed.

The drug trial of former Panama strongman Manuel Noriega got under way in Miami. The trial was good theater, but questions were raised about the cost – in cold cash to the government and in reduced sentences handed out to witnesses against Noriega. Imelda Marcos returned to the Philippines in November, declaring that she had "no political agenda." She is expected to run for president even though she faces eighty criminal suits stemming from charges her family looted the national treasury. The U.S. began pulling troops out of the Philippines after negotiations to renew leases for American bases there broke down.

An assassin's bomb killed Indian prime minister Rajiv Gandhi in May, and thousands of others died in the resulting religious and caste warfare.

Although Japan gets 70 percent of its oil from the Persian Gulf, it grudgingly contributed only $13 billion to the war against Iraq. Japan also was rocked by stock scandals that undermined investor confidence.

GLEN FODEN
Courtesy Patuxent Pub. Co.

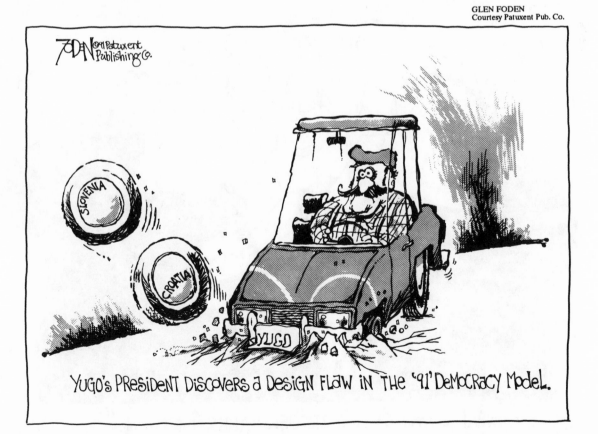

FODEN ©91 Patuxent Publishing Co.
SLOVENIA
CROATIA
YUGO
YUGO'S PRESIDENT DISCOVERS A DESIGN FLAW IN THE '91' DEMOCRACY MODEL.

ETTA HULME
Courtesy Ft. Worth Star-Telegram

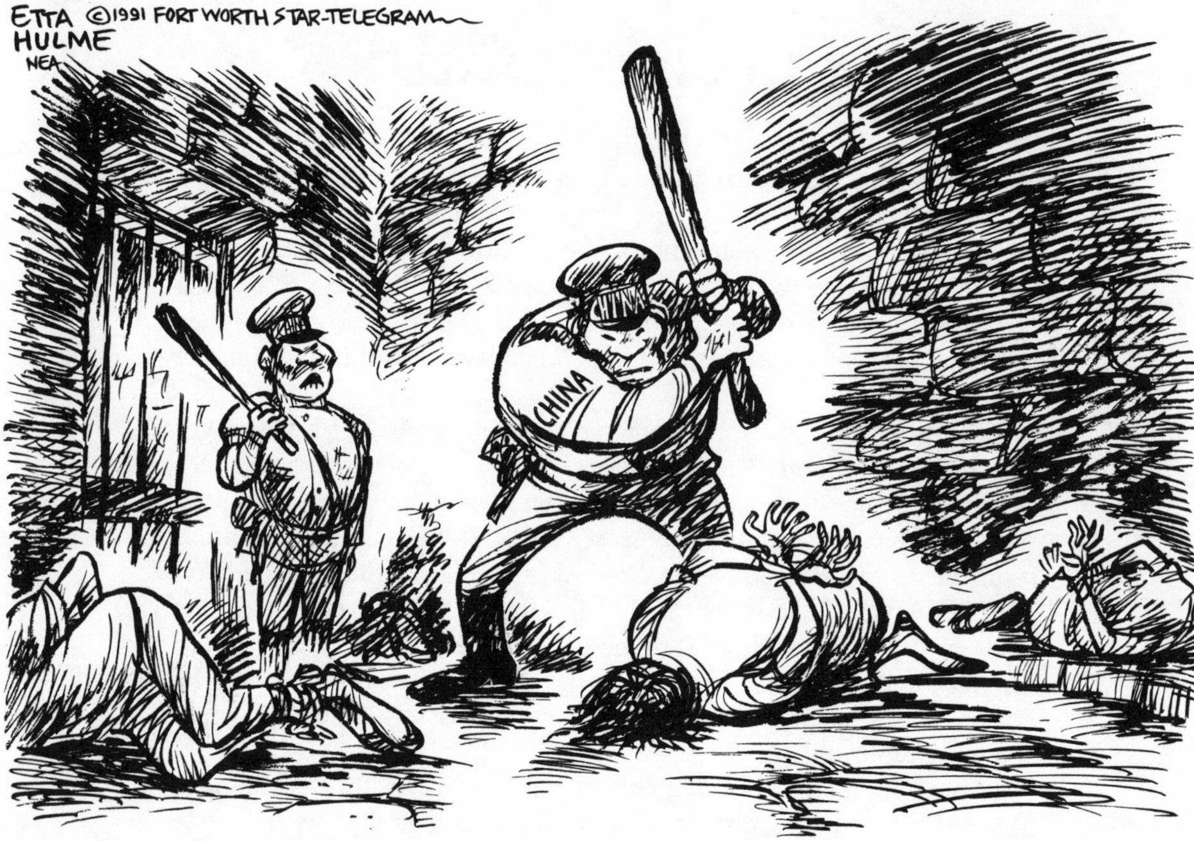
ETTA ©1991 FORT WORTH STAR-TELEGRAM
HULME
NEA
CHINA
CHINA

"IF YOU'LL FINISH UP HERE, I'LL PUT ON THE TEA FOR SECRETARY OF STATE JAMES A. BAKER 3d."

TOM GIBB
Courtesy Altoona Mirror

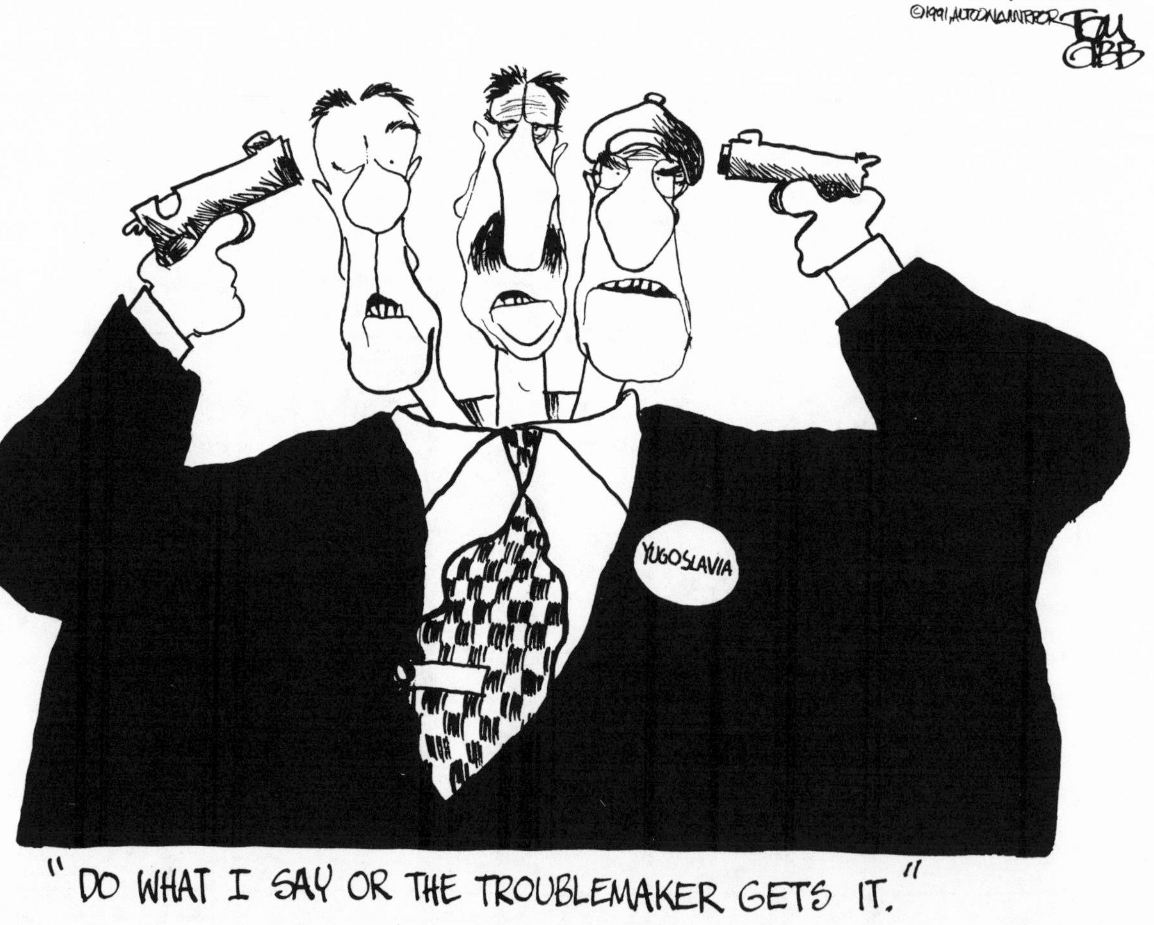
©1991, ALTOONA MIRROR
TOM GIBB
YUGOSLAVIA

"DO WHAT I SAY OR THE TROUBLEMAKER GETS IT."

GEN. IMELDA MARCARTHUR: "I HAVE RETURNED!"
BABALIK KA RIN, UPANG AKO AY ALIWIN...*
*"YOU'LL RETURN TO ME IN ORDER TO COMFORT ME..." – FILIPINO DITTY
el dani ©1991 NY FILIPINO REPORTER

DANI AGUILA
Courtesy Filipino Reporter

YUGO
SLOVENIA
CROATIA

D. MURPHY
Courtesy Vancouver Province

YUGOSLAVIAN CEASEFIRE...

JFTODD '91©

JIM TODD
Courtesy Southam Syndicate

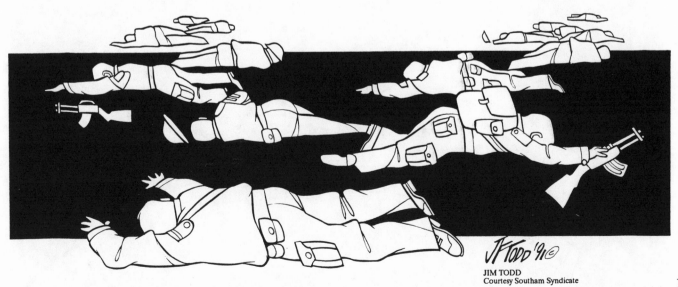

ETTA HULME
Courtesy Ft. Worth Star-Telegram

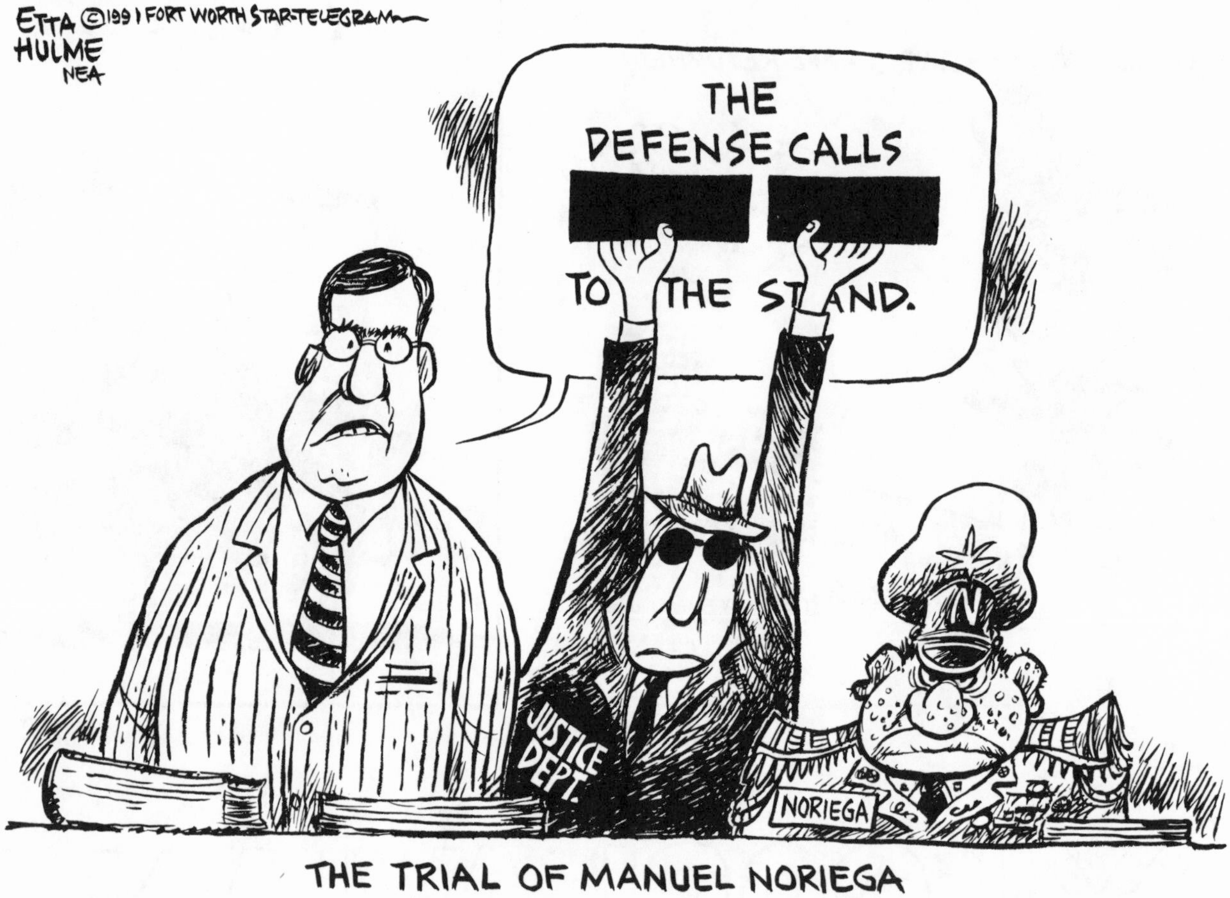
ETTA HULME ©1991 FORT WORTH STAR-TELEGRAM NEA
THE DEFENSE CALLS [redacted] [redacted] TO THE STAND.
JUSTICE DEPT.
NORIEGA
THE TRIAL OF MANUEL NORIEGA

ROB ROGERS
Courtesy Pittsburgh Press

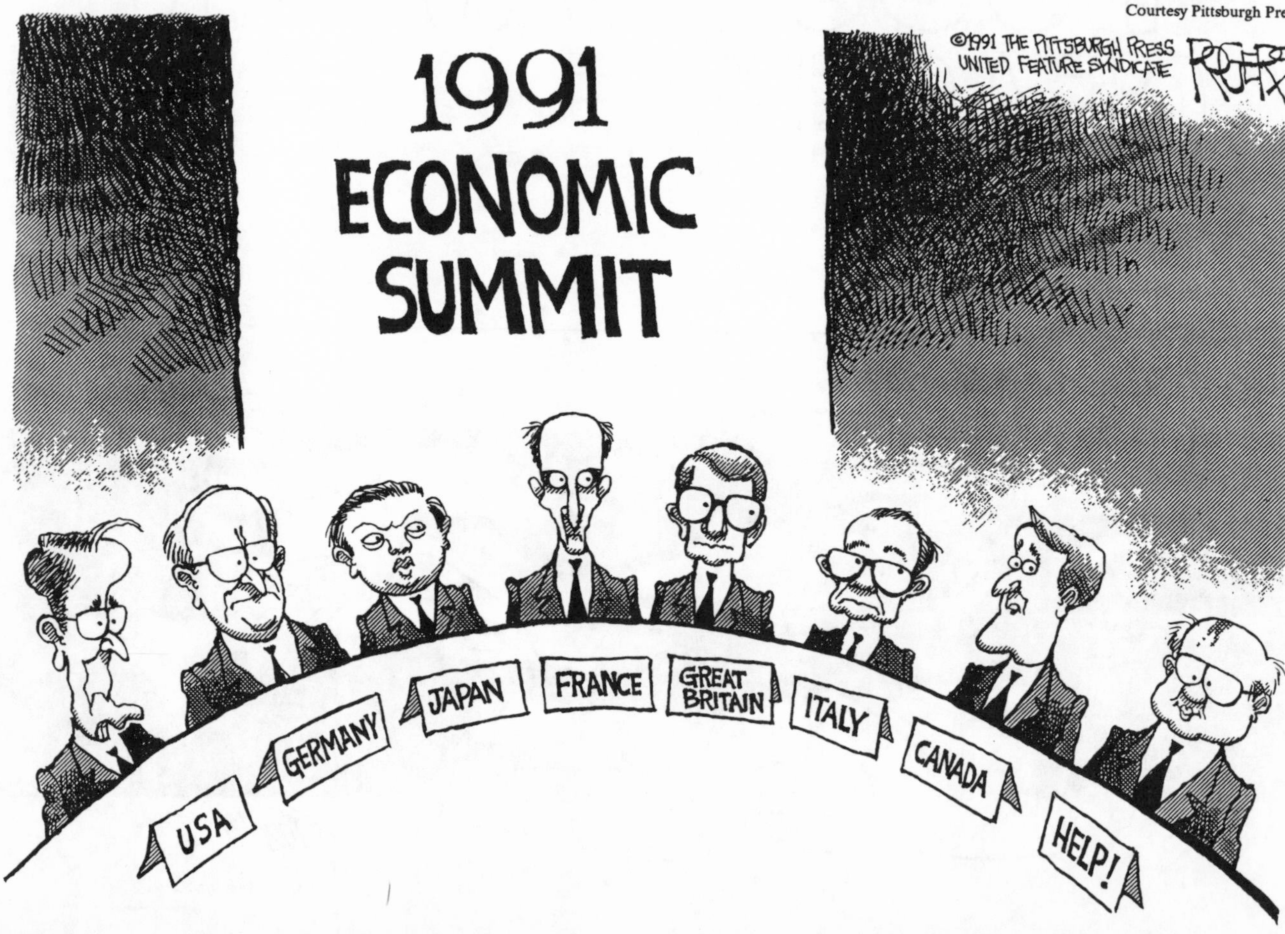
©1991 THE PITTSBURGH PRESS UNITED FEATURE SYNDICATE ROGERS
1991 ECONOMIC SUMMIT
USA
GERMANY
JAPAN
FRANCE
GREAT BRITAIN
ITALY
CANADA
HELP!

AND NOW BACK TO THE WAR
AFRICAN FAMINE
MURPHY
THE PROVINCE

D. MURPHY
Courtesy Vancouver Province

SEEMS LIKE ONLY YESTERDAY GEN. MacARTHUR WALKED ASHORE...
...TO THE "ETERNAL" GRATITUDE OF THE PHILIPPINE PEOPLE...
McLEOD

JACK MCLEOD
Courtesy Navy Times

ELECTIONS INDIA

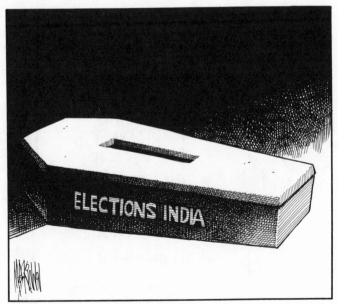

BRUCE MACKINNON
Courtesy Halifax Chronicle-Herald

LIBERTY OR DEATH
FRESQUET

LAZARO FRESQUET
Courtesy El Nuevo (Miami)

THIS 8.5 BILLION CHECK TO THE UNITED STATES... DO I CHARGE THAT TO NATIONAL SECURITY OR PUBLIC RELATIONS ?
ACCOUNTS PAYABLE
JAPAN
DANZIGER
The Christian Science Monitor
Los Angeles Times Syndicate

JEFF DANZIGER
Courtesy Christian Science Monitor

INDIA
MAN LIVES FREELY ONLY BY HIS READINESS TO DIE, IF NEED BE, AT THE HANDS OF HIS BROTHER...
MOHANDAS K. GANDHI
RAJIV GANDHI
1944-1991
KOVALIC
©1991 WISC STATE JOURNAL

JOHN KOVALIC
Courtesy Wisconsin State Journal

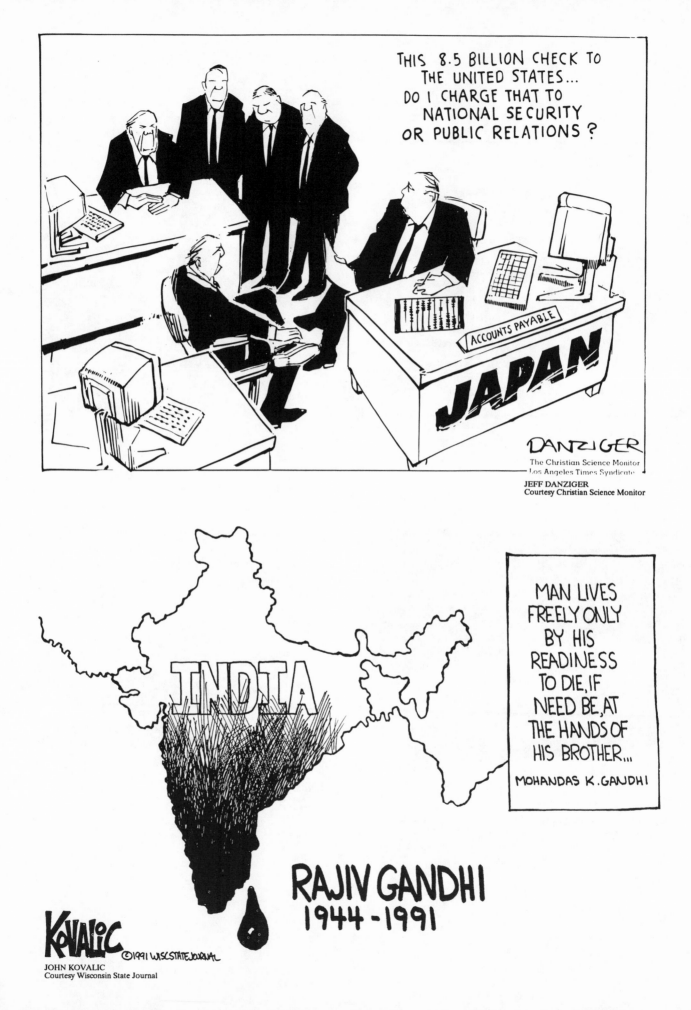

FRED CURATOLO
Courtesy Edmonton Sun

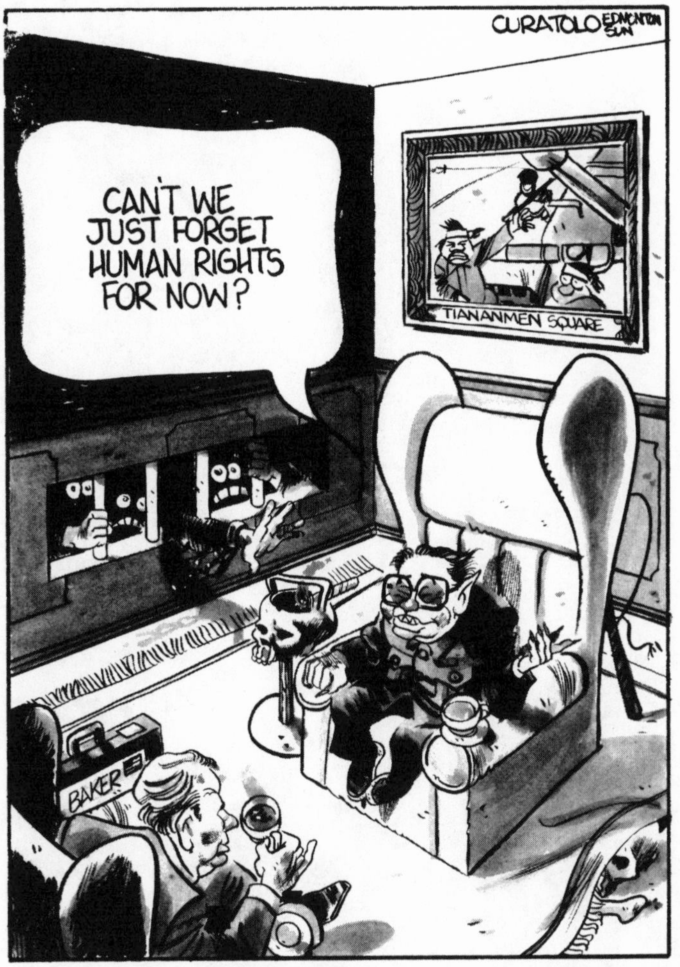
CURATOLO EDMONTON SUN
CAN'T WE JUST FORGET HUMAN RIGHTS FOR NOW?
TIANANMEN SQUARE
BAKER

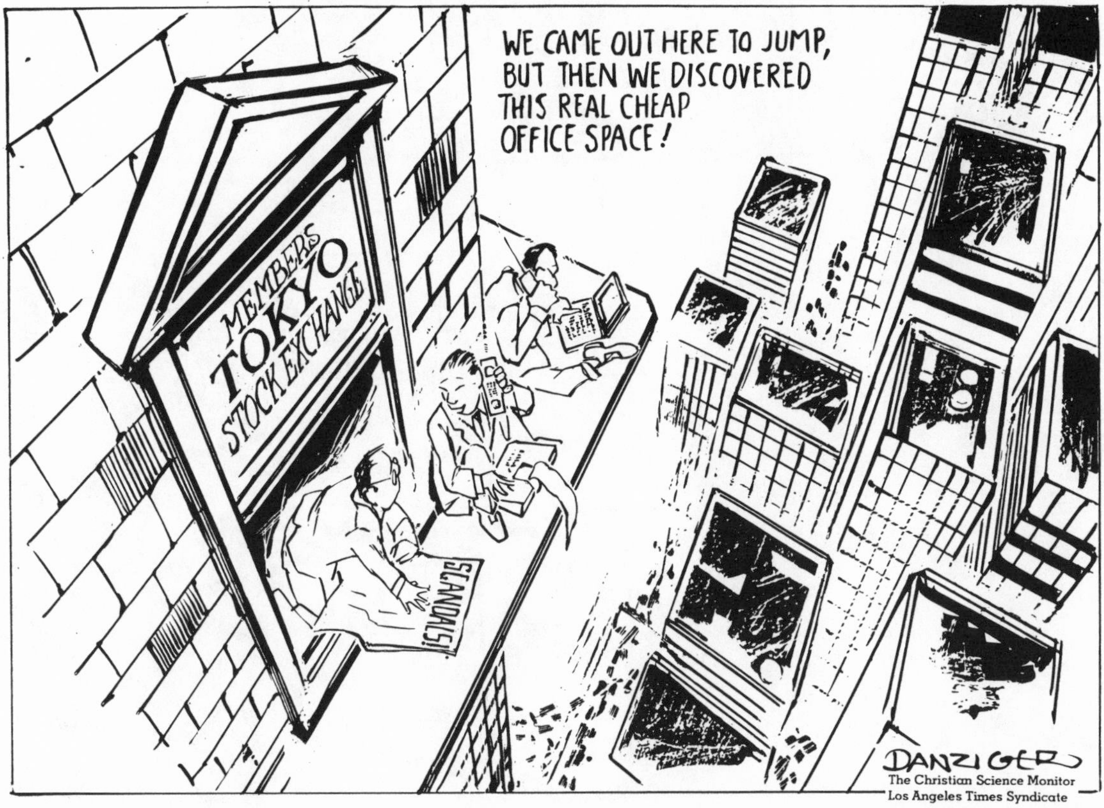
WE CAME OUT HERE TO JUMP, BUT THEN WE DISCOVERED THIS REAL CHEAP OFFICE SPACE!
MEMBERS TOKYO STOCK EXCHANGE
SCANDALS!
DANZIGER
The Christian Science Monitor
Los Angeles Times Syndicate

JEFF DANZIGER
Courtesy Christian Science Monitor

DID YOU HEAR THAT? THE STOCK MARKET IS SOARING AND THE JOBLESS RATE HAS DIPPED!
WALL ST. BULLISH
WITH THE EMPHASIS ON BULL!
CANTONE ROTHCO SYND.

VIC CANTONE
Courtesy N.Y. Daily News

ROBERT ARIAIL
Courtesy The State (S.C.)

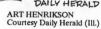

THERE ARE THOUSANDS OF THEM, GEORGE - THEY'RE COLD AND HUNGRY AND THEY FEEL YOU'VE DESERTED THEM. YOU HAVE A MORAL OBLIGATION TO HELP THESE HOMELESS PEOPLE!
YOU'RE RIGHT, BARBARA. IT'S TIME I GOT SERIOUS ABOUT HELPING THE KURDS!

AFFORDABLE HOUSING? HAVE YOU TRIED THE OTHER SUBURBS?
ARTHUR HENRIKSON
DAILY HERALD

ART HENRIKSON
Courtesy Daily Herald (Ill.)

The Poor

Census reports released in December documented the fact that poverty and income inequality in the U.S. rose to the highest level in a quarter of a century. Welfare and assistance programs reached record highs, with one in ten Americans now receiving food stamps.

Since the current recession began, forty states have reduced benefits for aid to families with dependent children. Thirty states also cut short-term assistance to the poor, and twenty states reduced aid to the homeless.

A big-city survey showed that requests for emergency shelter were up 13 percent and emergency food appeals rose 26 percent. With a tight federal budget and large deficits in many states, the outlook for the poor in 1992 appeared bleak indeed.

JEFF BRANCH
Courtesy San Antonio Express-News

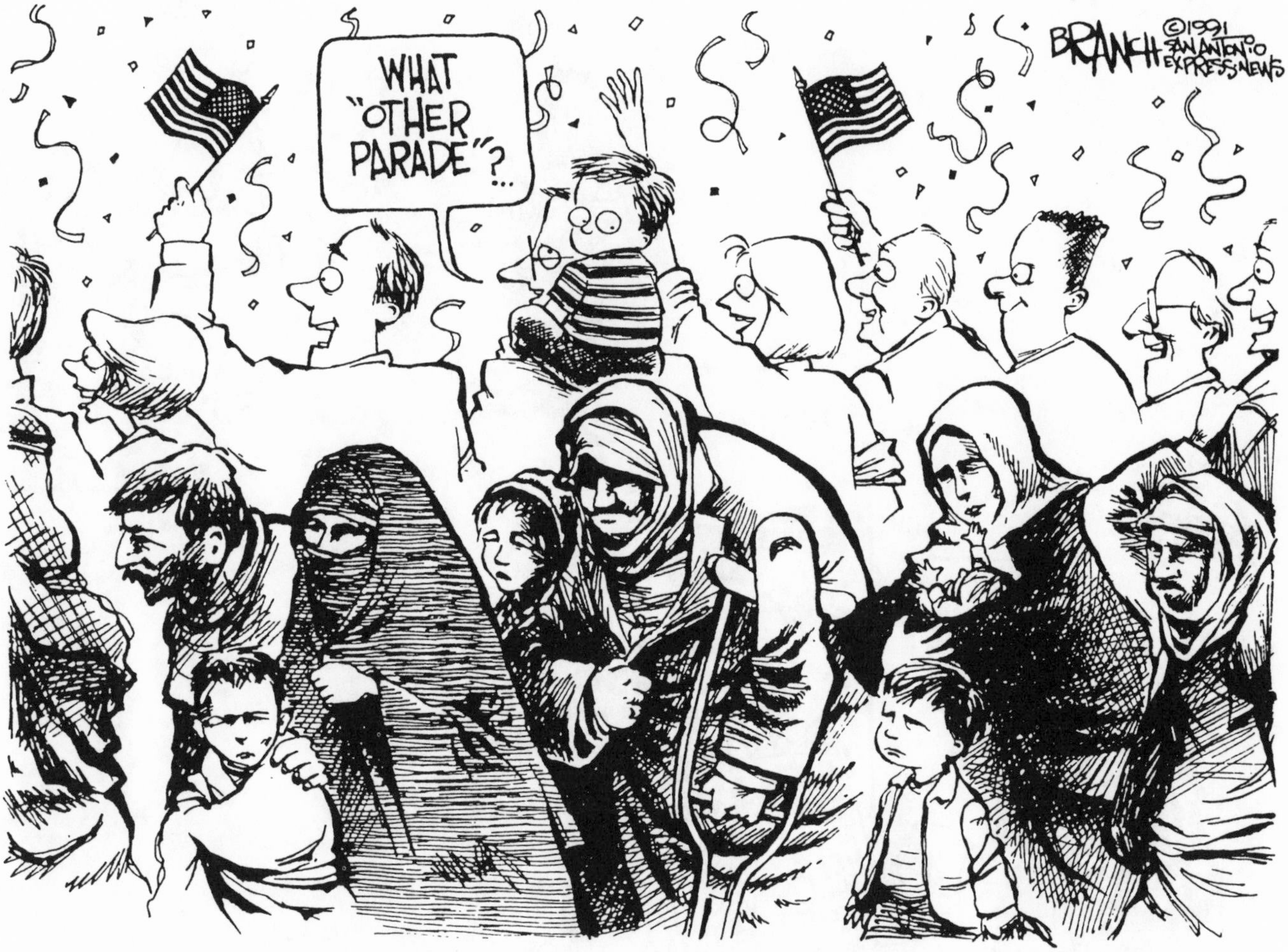
WHAT "OTHER PARADE"?...
BRANCH ©1991 SAN ANTONIO EXPRESS-NEWS

THERE'LL BE LOTS OF HALF-EATEN FOOD THROWN AWAY, TOO. WE'LL HAVE A FEAST!
MAYBE AFTER THE PARADE WE CAN GRAB ENOUGH OF THOSE YELLOW RIBBONS TO FILL THIS GROCERY SACK. IT'LL MAKE US A NICE PILLOW!
MOM... IS CONFETTI GOOD TO EAT?
HOME SWEET HOME
DESERT STORM VICTORY PARADES
WASHINGTON $12 MIL.
GRAHAME
© 1991 SPENCER NEWSPAPERS

NEIL GRAHAME
Courtesy Spencer Newspapers

Foreign Policy Test...
WHICH GROUP IS MOST LIKELY TO BE RESCUED BY THE COMBINED MIGHT OF THE ARMIES OF THE NEW WORLD ORDER?
A.
B.
OIL
OIL
STEVE HILL OKLAHOMA GAZETTE

STEVE HILL
Courtesy Oklahoma Gazette

CLIFF LEVERETTE
Courtesy Leverette Syndicate

LEVERETTE ©1991
THIS IS MY CORNER. BEAT IT!
HOMELESS PLEASE HELP
NATIONAL ENDOWMENT FOR THE ARTS HELP.
PORTRAITS $5000.00
CHARGE IT

MOSCOW
CHINA
ISRAEL
IRAQ
IRAN
AFGHANISTAN
PAKISTAN
INDIA
SAUDI ARABIA
ADEN
AFRICA
NIGHTLY NEWS
ALGY ©91

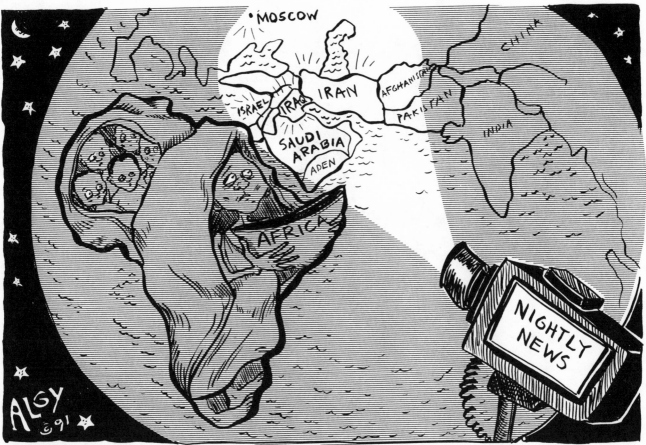

LINDA GODFREY
Courtesy Janesville Gazette
and Walworth County Week (Wis.)

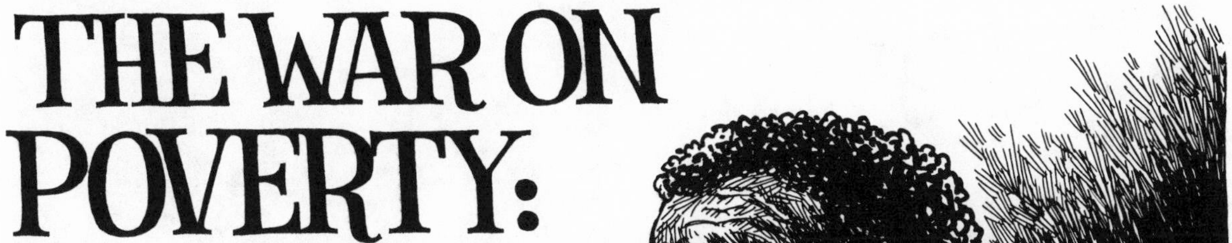

THE WAR ON POVERTY:
MY COUNTRY FOUGHT IRAQ AND ALL I GOT WAS THIS STUPID T-SHIRT
DRAUGHON
SCRANTON TIMES

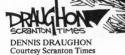

DENNIS DRAUGHON
Courtesy Scranton Times

DICK WRIGHT
Courtesy Providence Journal-Bulletin

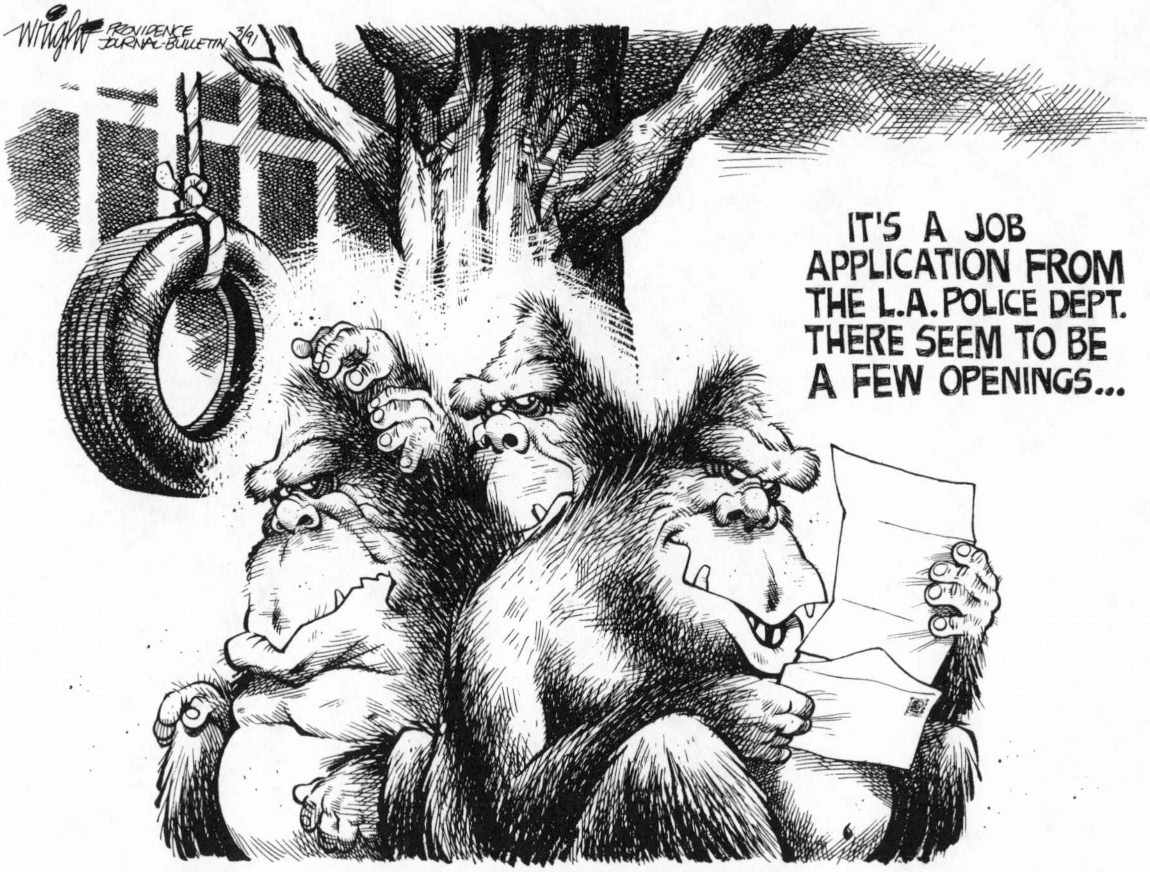
WRIGHT PROVIDENCE JOURNAL-BULLETIN 3/91
IT'S A JOB APPLICATION FROM THE L.A. POLICE DEPT. THERE SEEM TO BE A FEW OPENINGS...

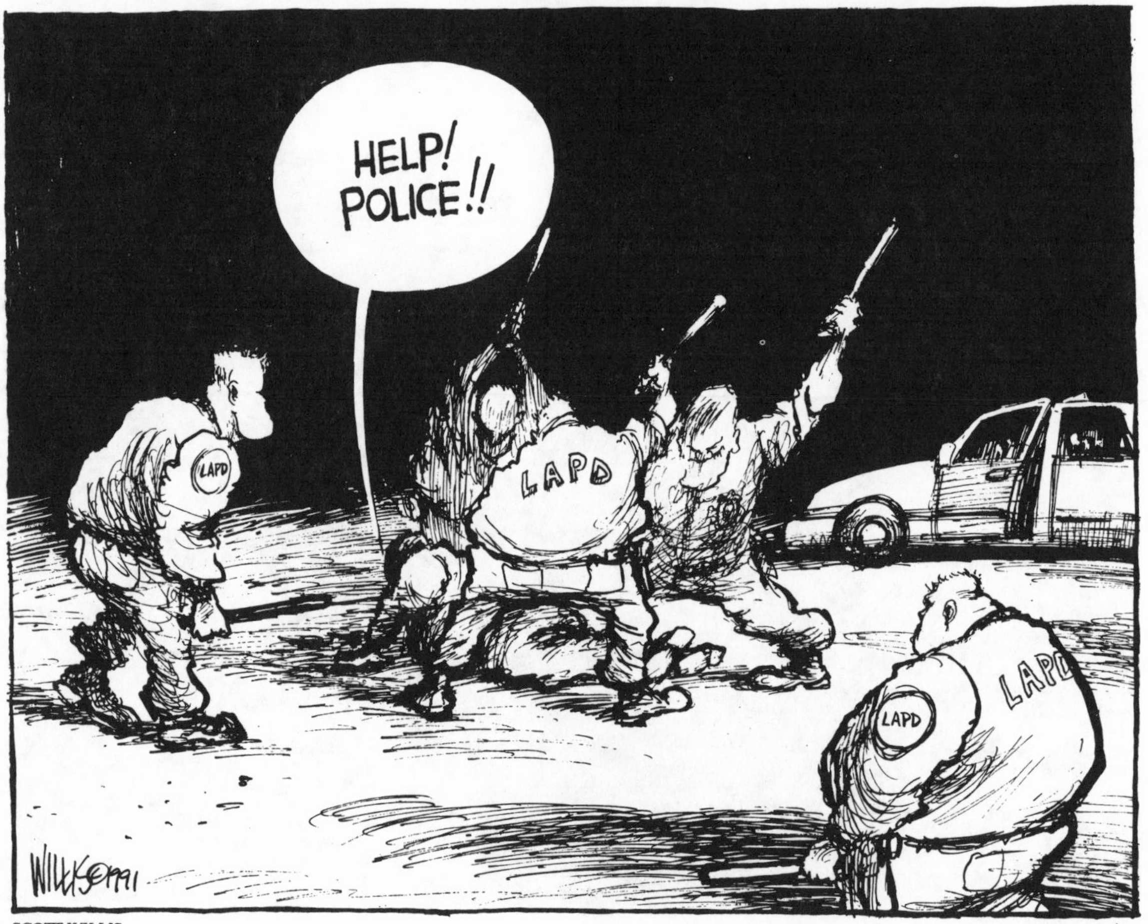
HELP! POLICE!!
LAPD
LAPD
LAPD
LAPD
WILLIS©1991

SCOTT WILLIS
Courtesy San Jose Mercury

Crime and Drugs

Crime remained very much a part of American life during the year. Every 100 hours more young people die on the streets of America than were killed in the Persian Gulf War. During the first half of the year, violent crime rose 5 percent over 1990. Robbery increased by 9 percent while murder was up 5 percent.

Four Los Angeles police officers were captured on a two-minute videotape in March beating a defenseless black man while twelve other officers watched. The incident spawned a nationwide scrutiny of police brutality. On the other side of the coin, sixty-five police officers were slain in the line of duty during the year, and forty-three more were killed in work-related accidents.

U.S. drug czar Bob Martinez reported that the number of drug abusers in the U.S. had dropped 43 percent to 23 million in the past five years. Signs point to a comeback, however, of the drug heroin, and police in fifteen large cities counted a record 1,500 thriving open-air drug markets.

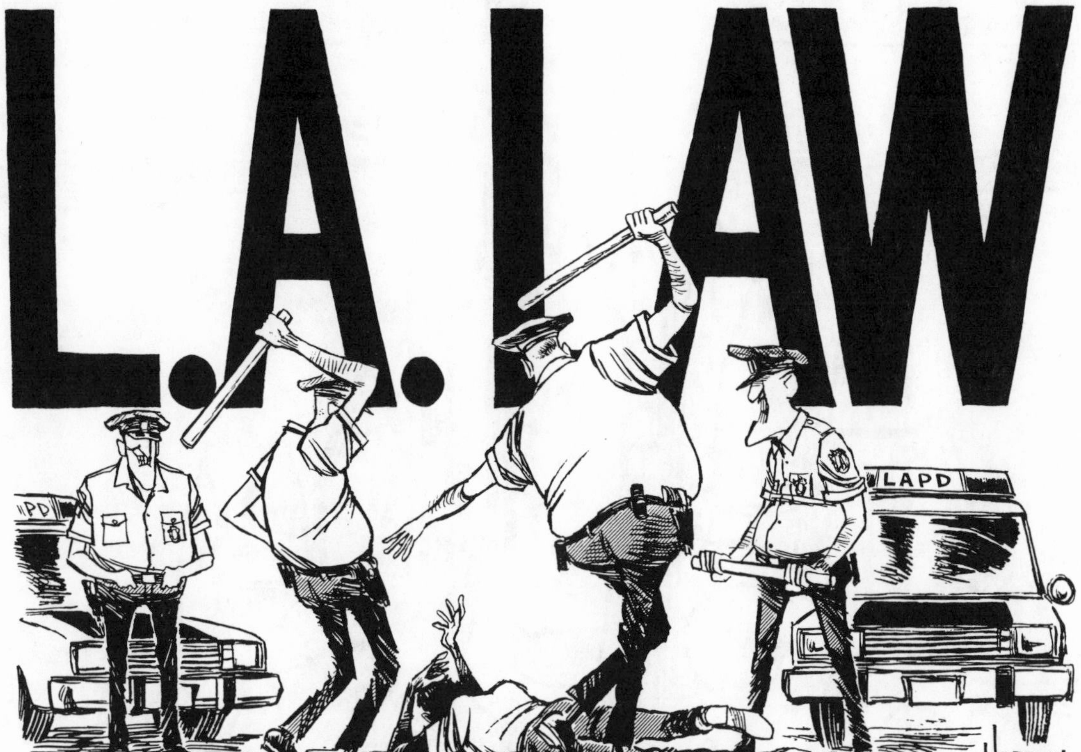
L.A. LAW
LAPD
PD
HORSEY
©1991 SEATTLE POST-INTELLIGENCER - NORTH AMERICA SYNDICATE

DAVID HORSEY
Courtesy Seattle Post-Intelligencer

RICHARD CROWSON
Courtesy Wichita Eagle

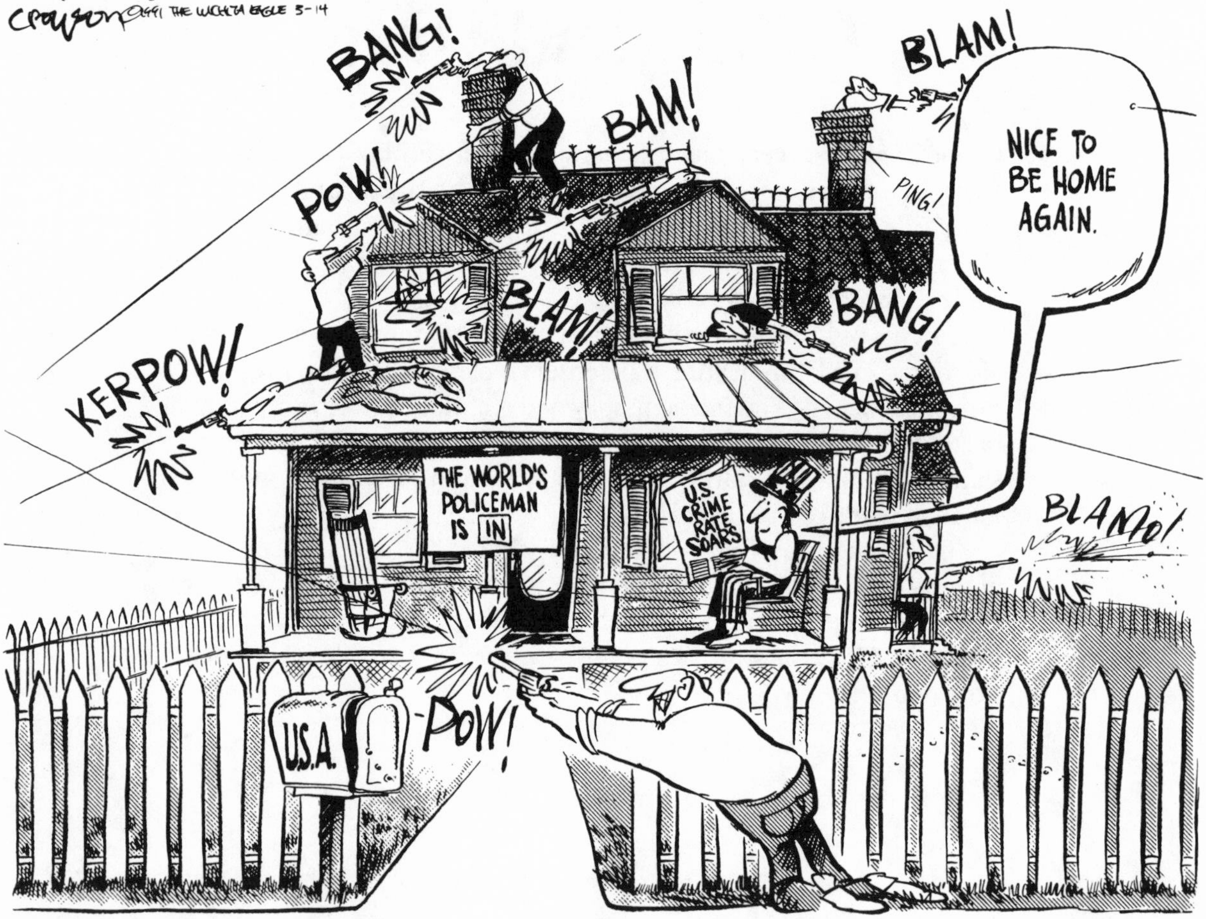
CROWSON ©1991 THE WICHITA EAGLE 3-14
BANG!
POW!
BAM!
BLAM!
NICE TO BE HOME AGAIN.
PING!
BLAM!
BANG!
KERPOW!
THE WORLD'S POLICEMAN IS IN
U.S. CRIME RATE SOARS
BLAM!
U.S.A.
POW!

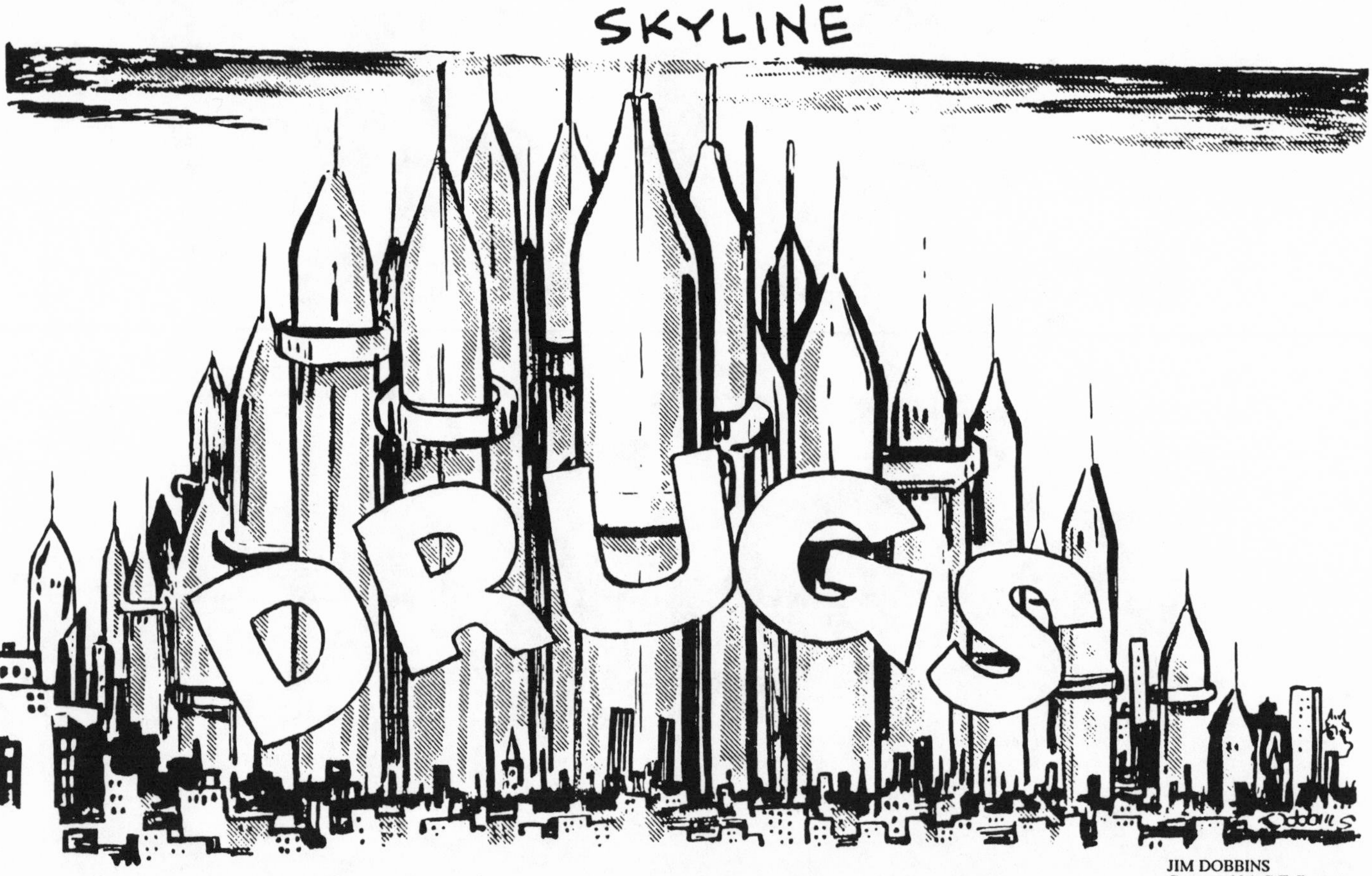
SKYLINE
DRUGS
DOBBINS

JIM DOBBINS
Courtesy N.A.G.E. Reporter

WAYNE STROOT
Courtesy Hastings Tribune (Neb.)

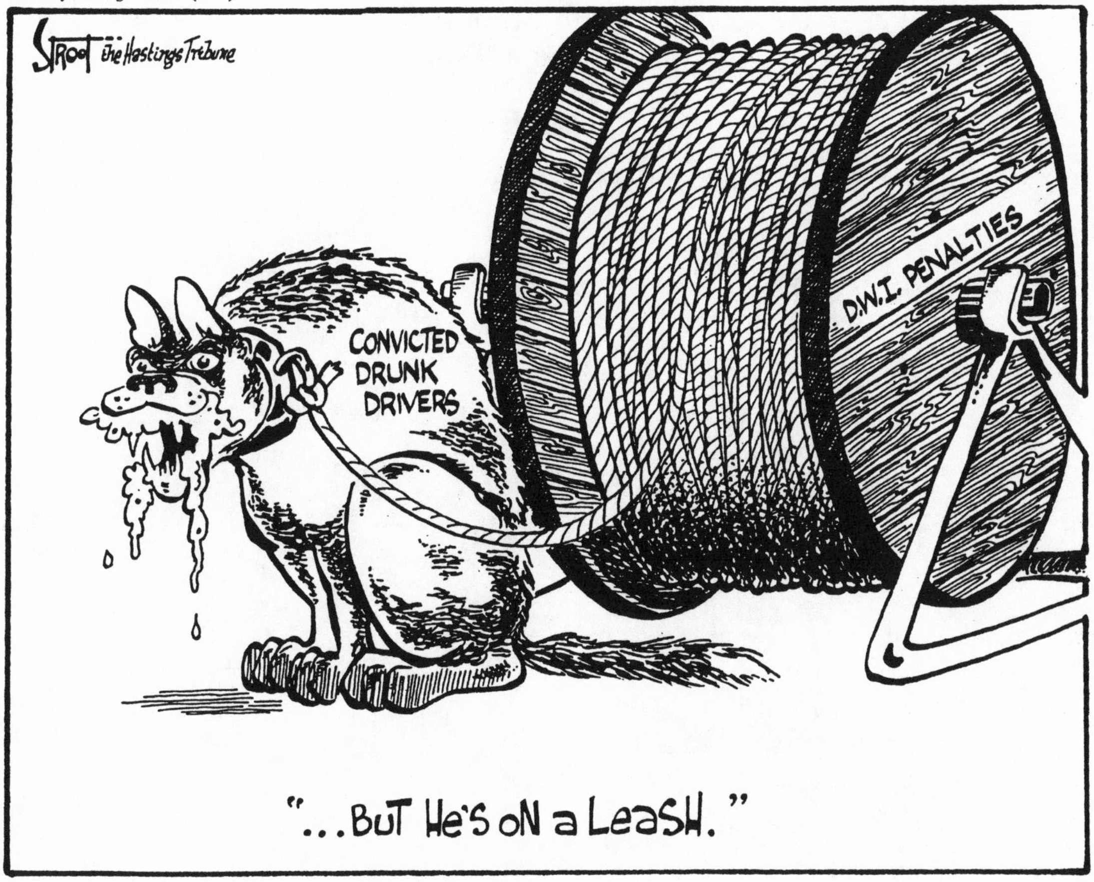
STROOT the Hastings Tribune
CONVICTED DRUNK DRIVERS
D.W.I. PENALTIES
"...BUT HE'S ON A LEASH."

ROD WARREN
Courtesy Bakersfield Californian

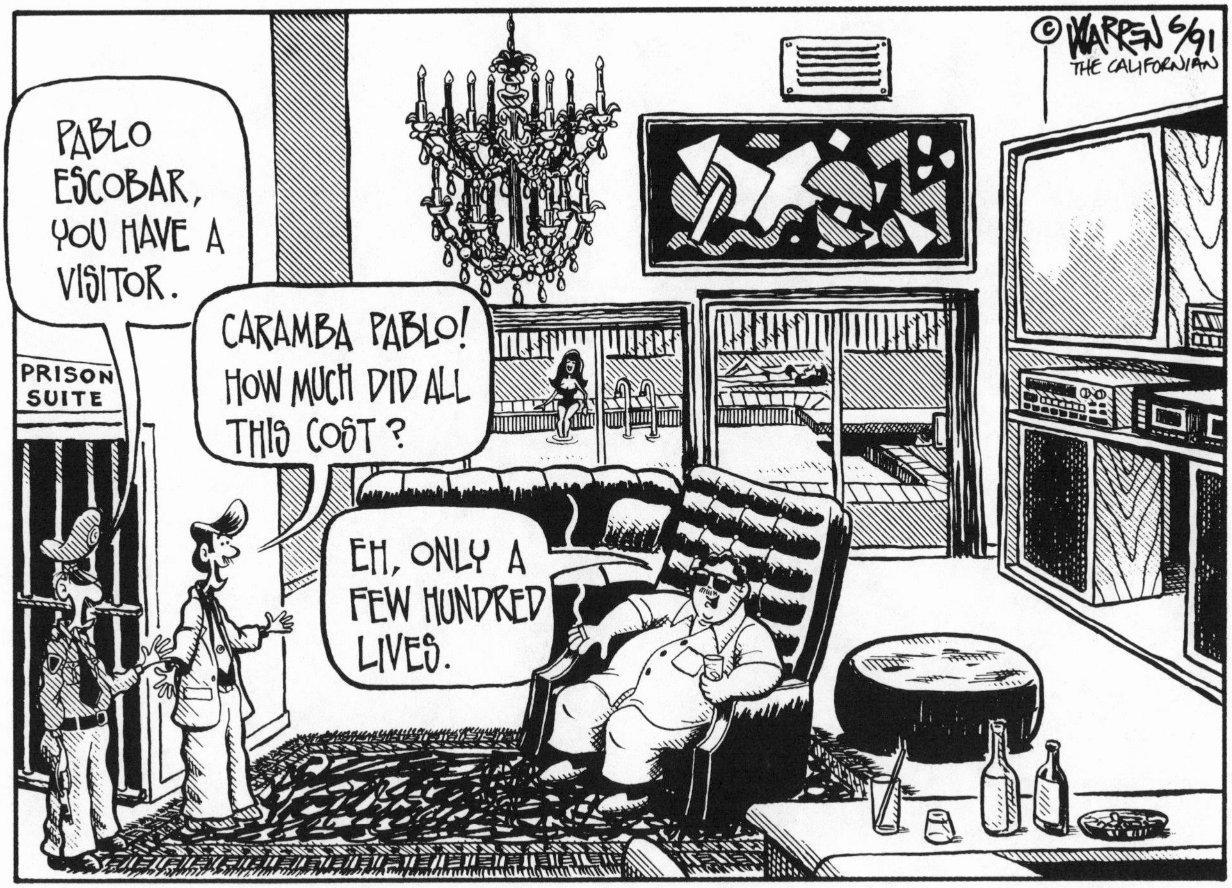
© WARREN 6/91 THE CALIFORNIAN
PABLO ESCOBAR, YOU HAVE A VISITOR.
PRISON SUITE
CARAMBA PABLO! HOW MUCH DID ALL THIS COST?
EH, ONLY A FEW HUNDRED LIVES.

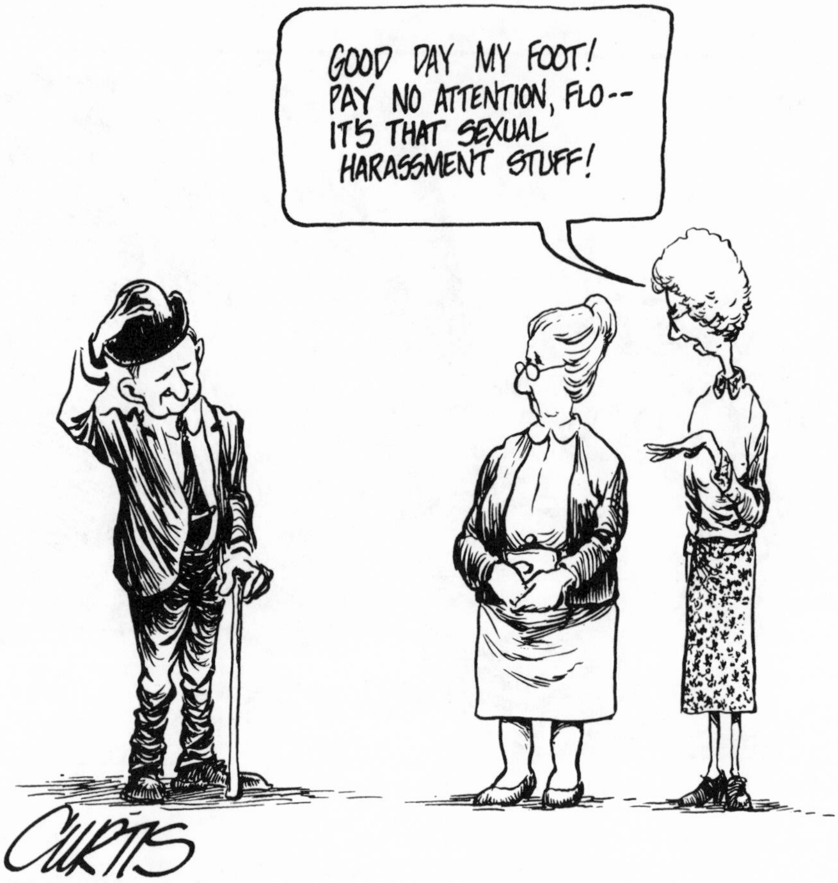
GOOD DAY MY FOOT! PAY NO ATTENTION, FLO-- IT'S THAT SEXUAL HARASSMENT STUFF!
CURTIS

CHRIS CURTIS
Courtesy Washington Times

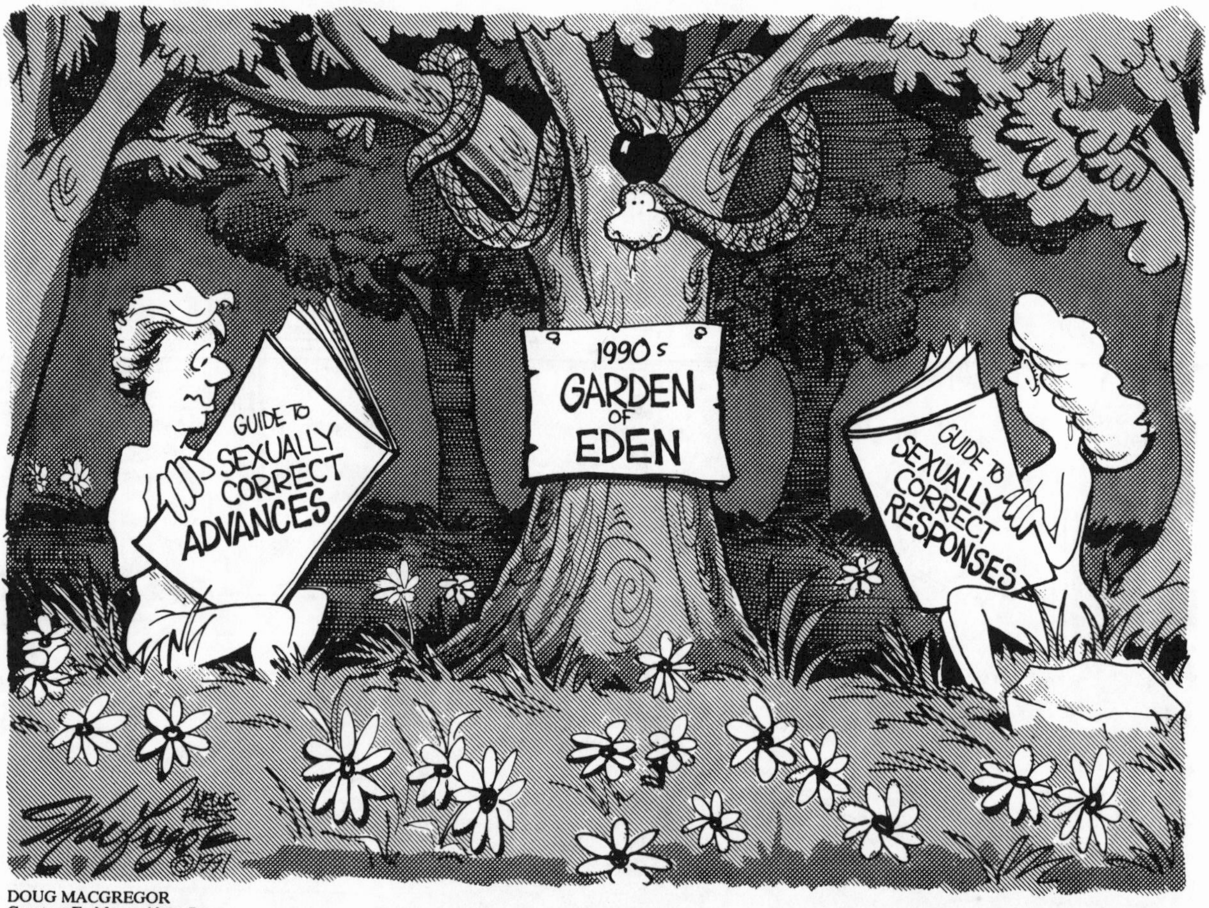
GUIDE TO SEXUALLY CORRECT ADVANCES
1990s GARDEN OF EDEN
GUIDE TO SEXUALLY CORRECT RESPONSES

DOUG MACGREGOR
Courtesy Ft. Meyers News-Press

Women's Issues

The U.S. Justice Department intervened when a prolonged confrontation occurred at an abortion clinic in Wichita, Kansas between members of an anti-abortion group, Operation Rescue, and visitors to the clinic. Over 2,000 arrests were made, and in August the Justice Department filed a brief in court contending that the federal courts had no jurisdiction in the matter.

The Clarence Thomas Supreme Court hearings focused the spotlight on one of the biggest issues involving women – sexual harassment. It got the attention of the legislators and other politicians who previously had given the issue scant attention, and it also got the attention of men in the workplace.

Despite more than twenty years of struggle for equal pay and job opportunity, women still earn less than their male counterparts in virtually every field. A barrier remains in place to inhibit women who attempt to push beyond middle management. Only 3 of every 100 top executive positions in the largest U.S. companies are held by women. It is a matter women's groups no doubt will focus on in the future.

BOB GORRELL
Courtesy Richmond News

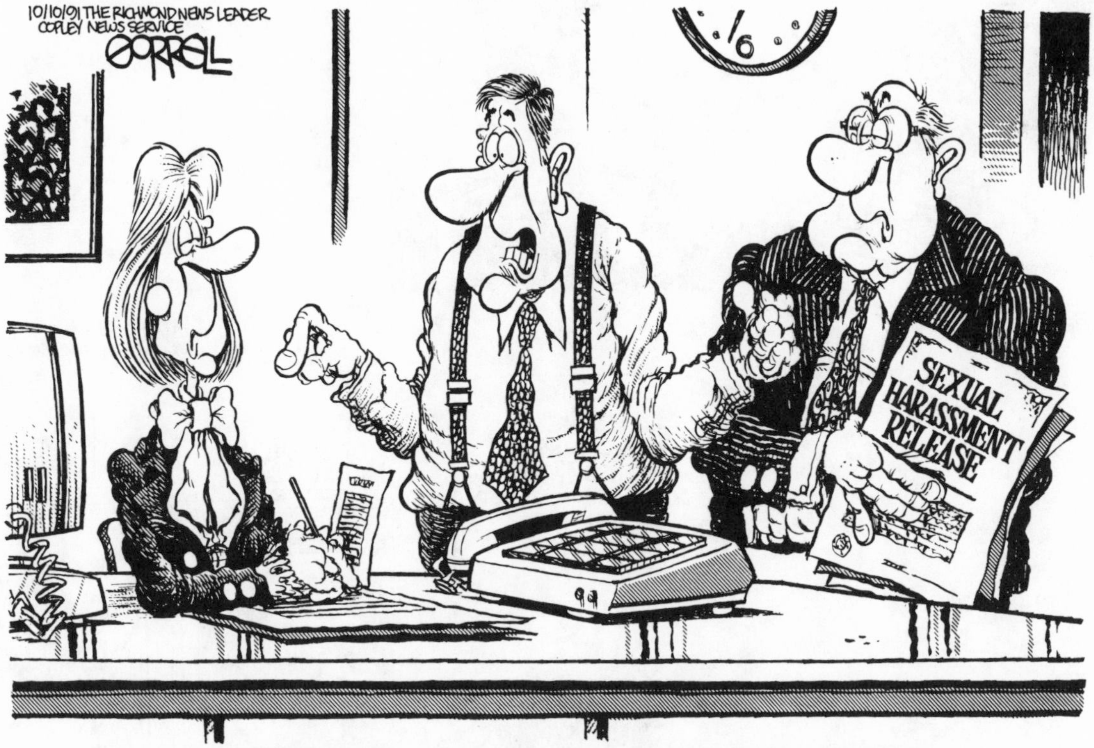

10/10/91 THE RICHMOND NEWS LEADER
COPLEY NEWS SERVICE
GORRELL
SEXUAL HARASSMENT RELEASE

"BEFORE I COMPLIMENT YOU ON THAT NEW BLOUSE YOU'RE WEARING, MY ATTORNEY HAS A FEW PAPERS WE'D LIKE YOU TO SIGN . . . !"

SHE SEZ JIMMY CARTER HARASSED HER IN HIS HEART BACK IN '75-
DANIEL

CHARLIE DANIEL/© 1991, The Knoxville Journal

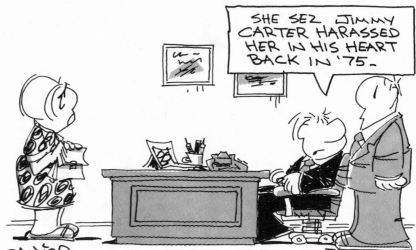

CHARLES DANIEL
Courtesy Knoxville Journal

WOULD YOU LIKE YOUR BUNS TOASTED MISS HILL? *OOPS* ER-UH-I MEAN...

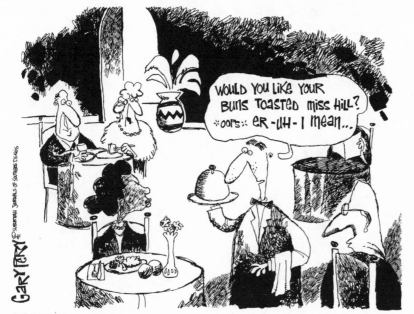

GARY PERCY
Courtesy Belleville Journal (Ill.)

CHAN LOWE
Courtesy The News/Sun-Sentinel (Fla.)

WHAT'S THIS "GLASS CEILING" NONSENSE?? THE DOORS OF OPPORTUNITY ARE OPEN TO EVERYONE!
WHITE MALES
WOMEN & MINORITIES
CORPORATE AMERICA

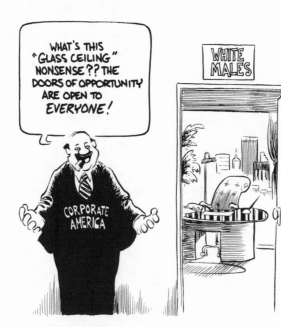

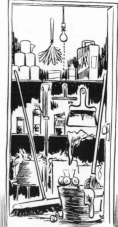

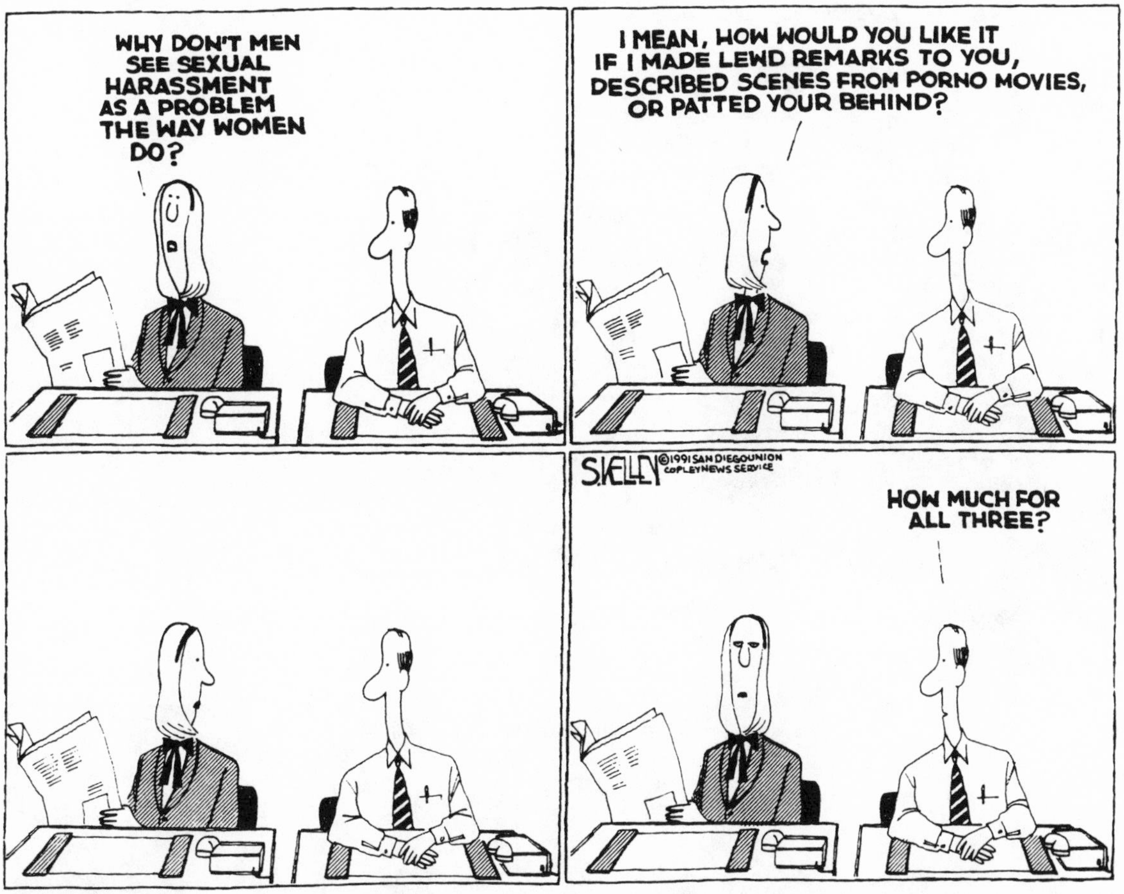
WHY DON'T MEN SEE SEXUAL HARASSMENT AS A PROBLEM THE WAY WOMEN DO?
I MEAN, HOW WOULD YOU LIKE IT IF I MADE LEWD REMARKS TO YOU, DESCRIBED SCENES FROM PORNO MOVIES, OR PATTED YOUR BEHIND?
S.KELLEY ©1991 SAN DIEGO UNION COPLEY NEWS SERVICE
HOW MUCH FOR ALL THREE?

STEVE KELLEY
Courtesy San Diego Union

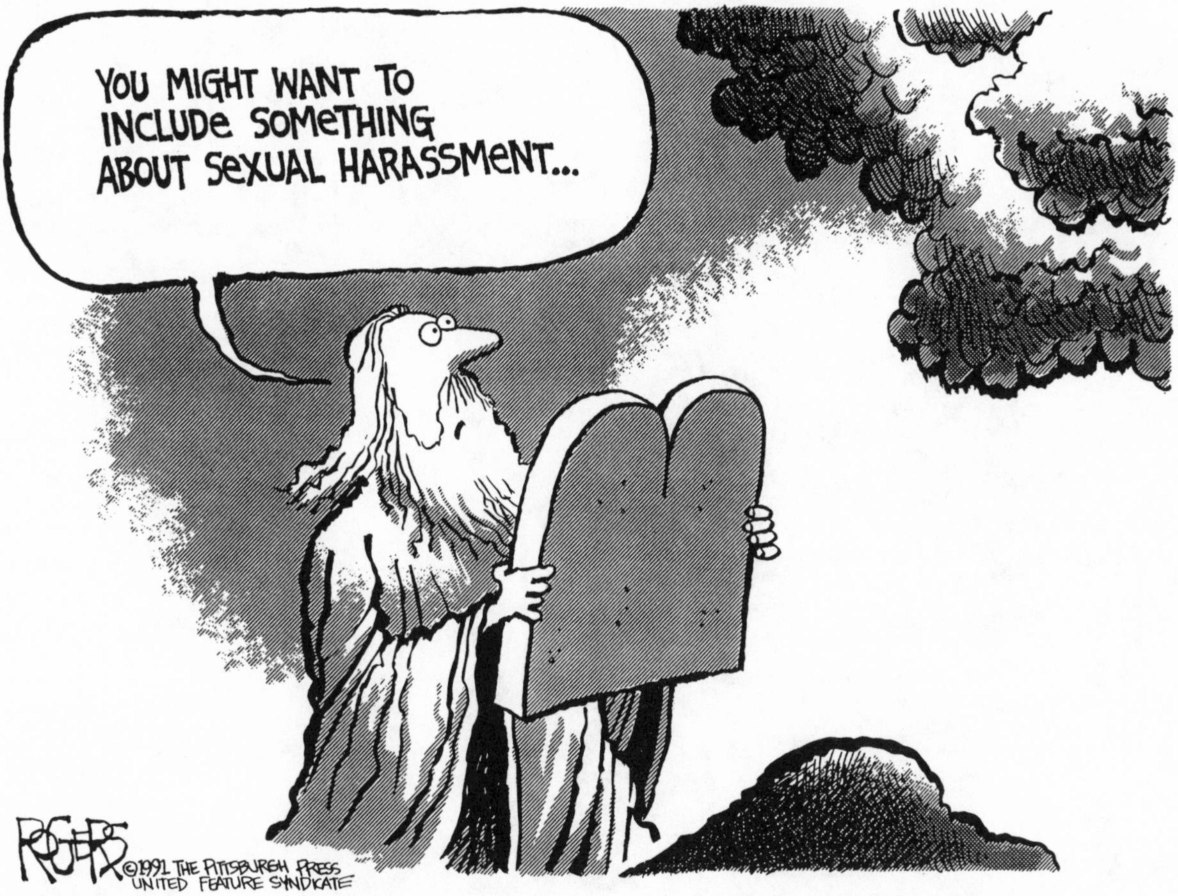
YOU MIGHT WANT TO INCLUDE SOMETHING ABOUT SEXUAL HARASSMENT...
ROGERS ©1991 THE PITTSBURGH PRESS UNITED FEATURE SYNDICATE

ROB ROGERS
Courtesy Pittsburgh Press

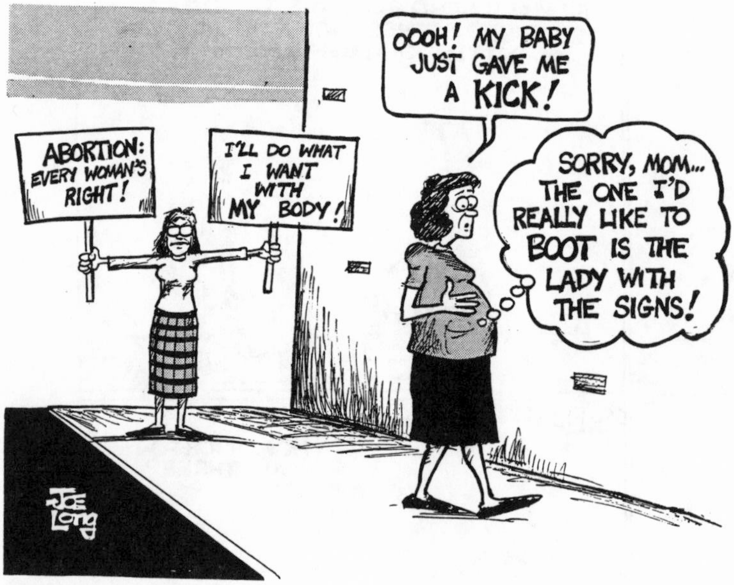
ABORTION: EVERY WOMAN'S RIGHT!
I'LL DO WHAT I WANT WITH MY BODY!
OOOH! MY BABY JUST GAVE ME A KICK!
SORRY, MOM... THE ONE I'D REALLY LIKE TO BOOT IS THE LADY WITH THE SIGNS!
JOE LONG

JOE LONG
Courtesy Little Falls Evening Times (N.Y.)

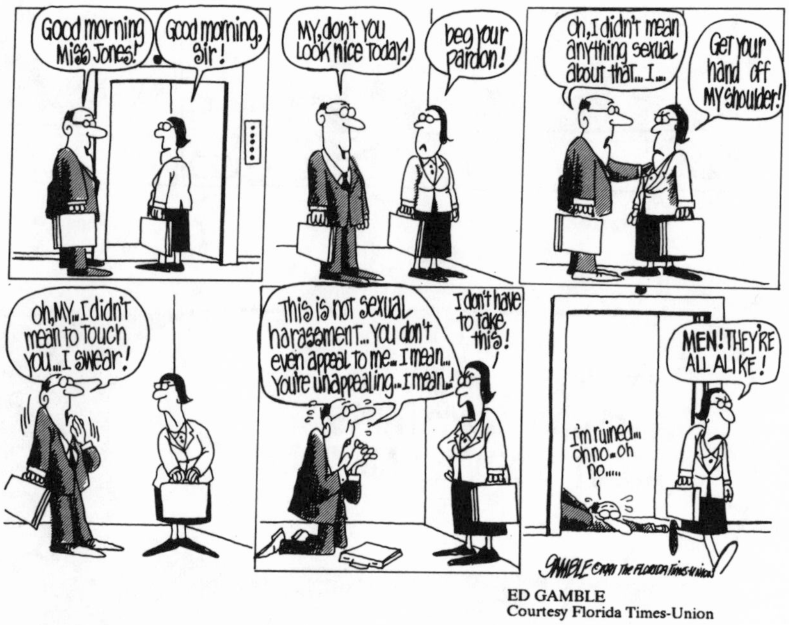
Good morning Miss Jones!
Good morning, sir!
My, don't you look nice today!
beg your pardon!
Oh, I didn't mean anything sexual about that... I...
Get your hand off my shoulder!
Oh, my... I didn't mean to touch you... I swear!
This is not sexual harassment... You don't even appeal to me... I mean... You're unappealing... I mean...!
I don't have to take this!
I'm ruined... oh no... oh no.....
MEN! THEY'RE ALL ALIKE!
GAMBLE

ED GAMBLE
Courtesy Florida Times-Union

RAY OSRIN
Courtesy Cleveland Plain Dealer

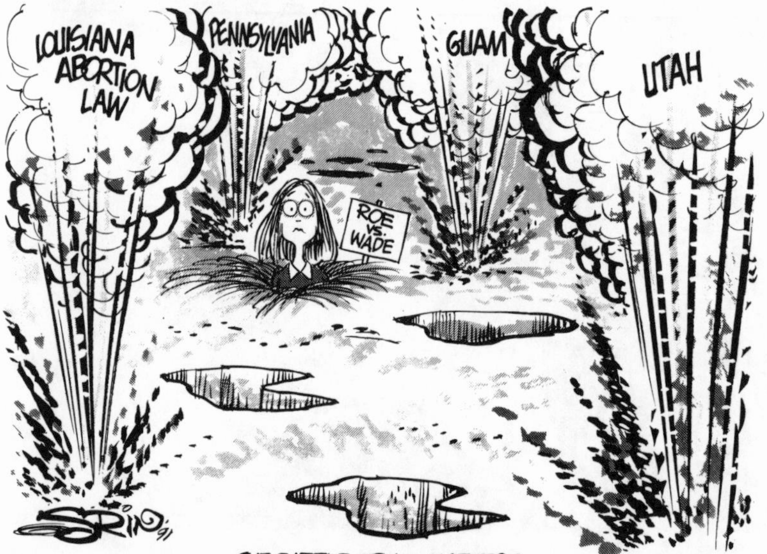
LOUISIANA ABORTION LAW
PENNSYLVANIA
GUAM
UTAH
ROE VS. WADE
OSRIN '91

THE BATTLE OF ALL MOTHERS

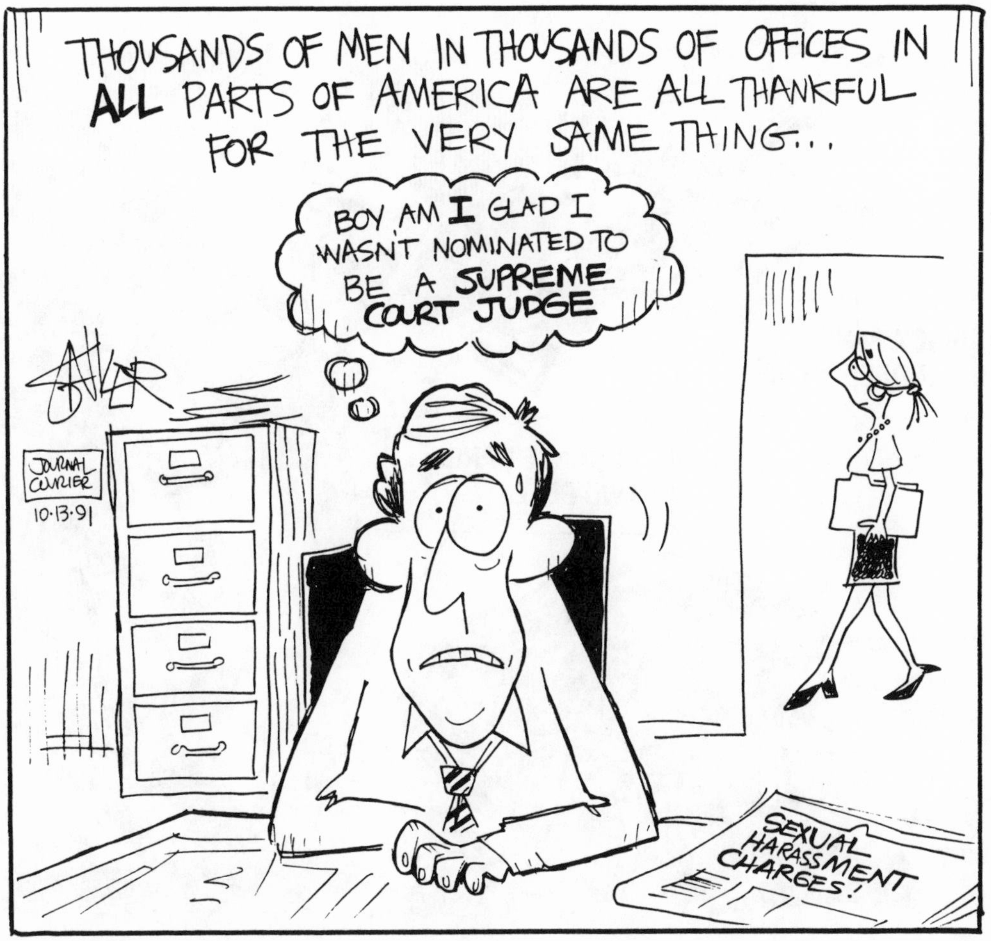
THOUSANDS OF MEN IN THOUSANDS OF OFFICES IN ALL PARTS OF AMERICA ARE ALL THANKFUL FOR THE VERY SAME THING...
BOY AM I GLAD I WASN'T NOMINATED TO BE A SUPREME COURT JUDGE
JOURNAL COURIER
10·13·91
SEXUAL HARASSMENT CHARGES!

DAVE SATTLER
Courtesy Journal and Courier (Ind.)

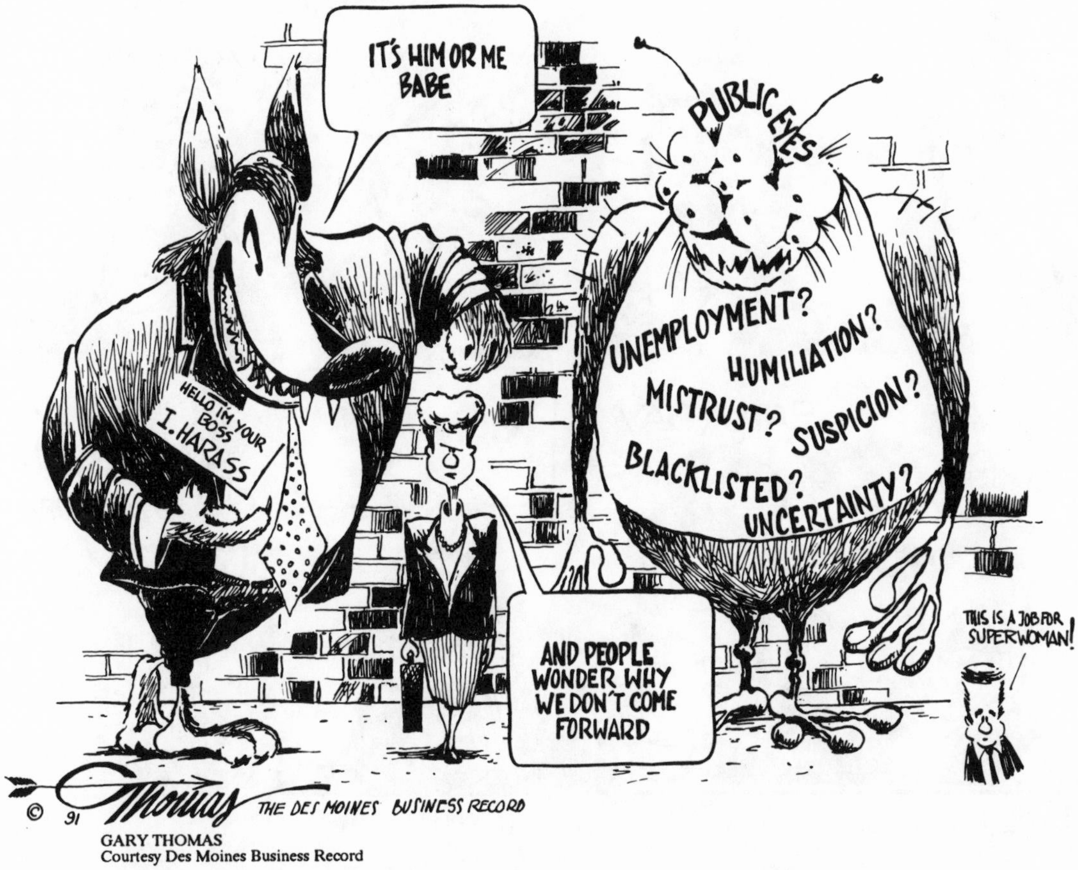
IT'S HIM OR ME BABE
PUBLIC EYES
HELLO I'M YOUR BOSS I. HARASS
UNEMPLOYMENT?
HUMILIATION?
MISTRUST?
SUSPICION?
BLACKLISTED?
UNCERTAINTY?
AND PEOPLE WONDER WHY WE DON'T COME FORWARD
THIS IS A JOB FOR SUPERWOMAN!
© 91 THOMAS
THE DES MOINES BUSINESS RECORD

GARY THOMAS
Courtesy Des Moines Business Record

TOM DARCY
Courtesy Newsday

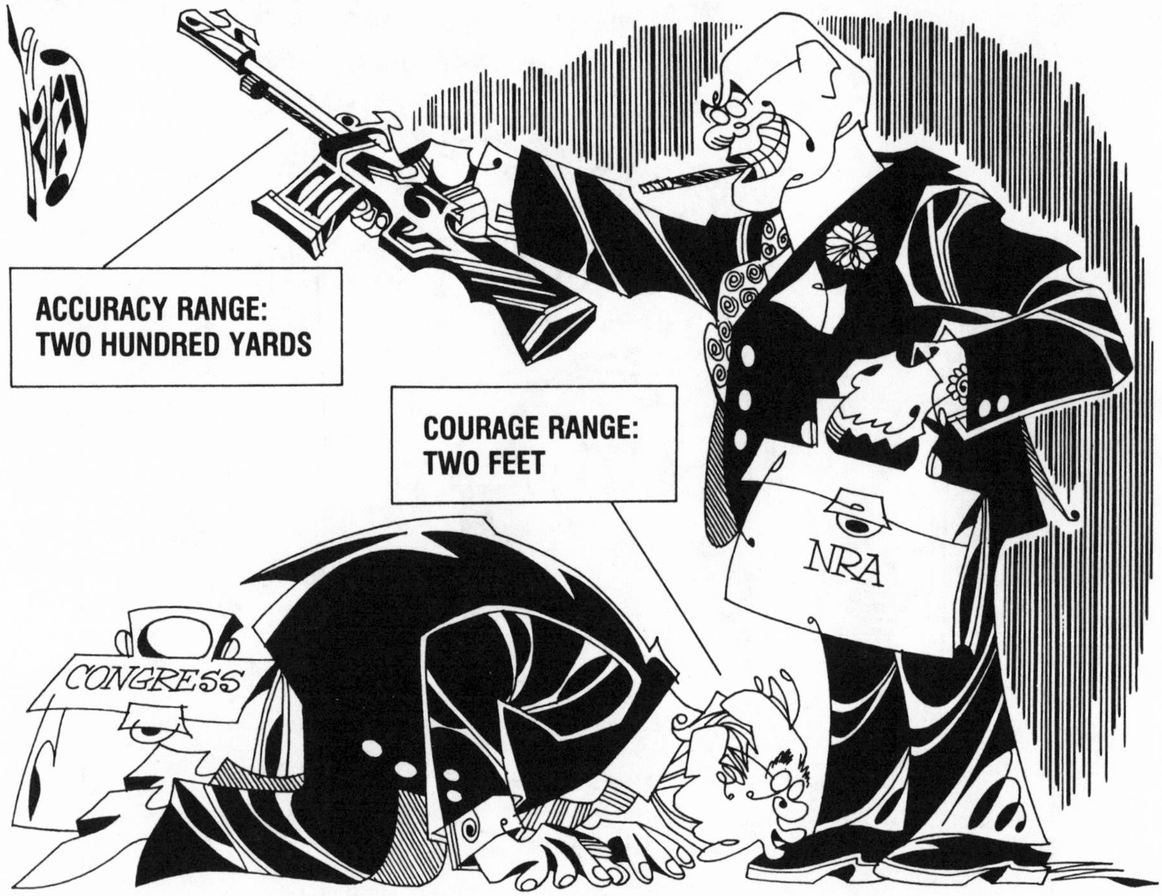
ACCURACY RANGE: TWO HUNDRED YARDS
COURAGE RANGE: TWO FEET
NRA
CONGRESS

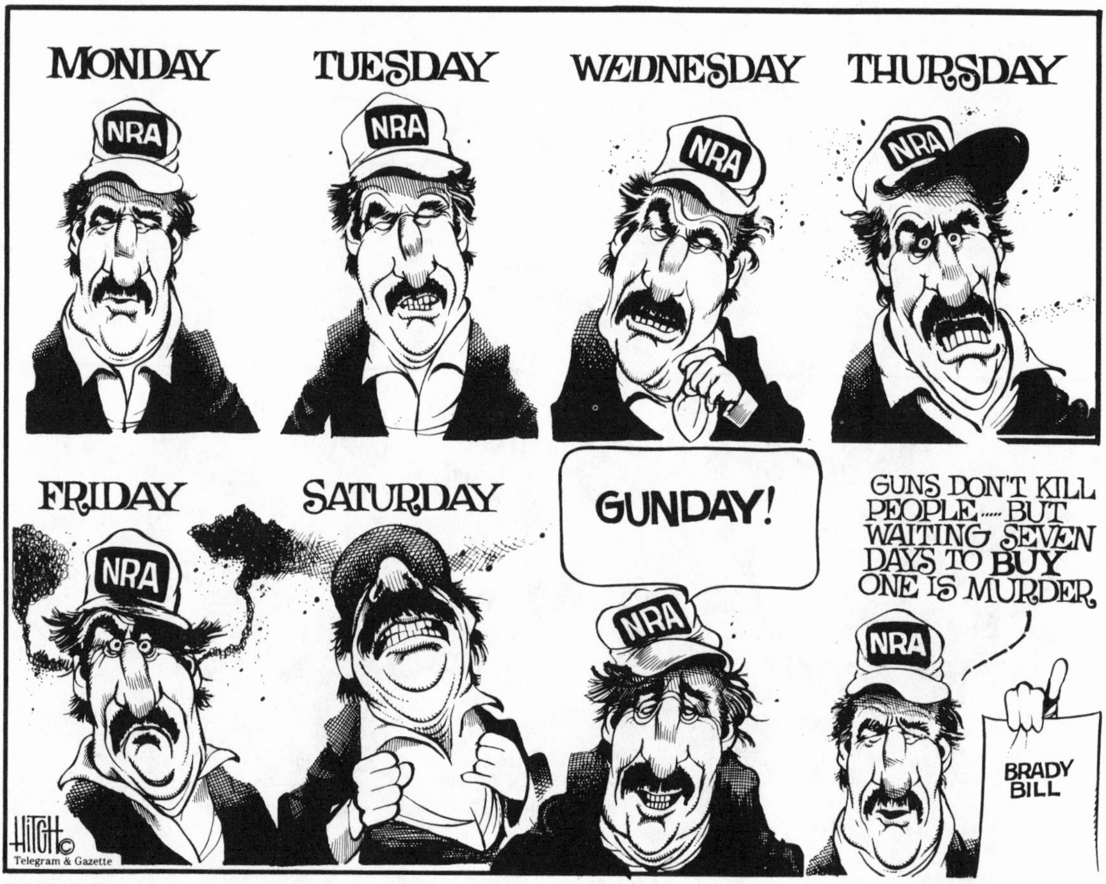
MONDAY
TUESDAY
WEDNESDAY
THURSDAY
NRA
NRA
NRA
NRA
FRIDAY
SATURDAY
NRA
GUNDAY!
NRA
GUNS DON'T KILL PEOPLE..... BUT WAITING SEVEN DAYS TO BUY ONE IS MURDER
NRA
BRADY BILL
HITCH ©
Telegram & Gazette

DAVID HITCH
Courtesy Worcester Telegram & Gazette

Gun Control

Teenagers are killing each other across the U.S. at an alarming pace, and the death rate continued to climb during 1991. Arguments that once were settled with fists are now decided with guns. Every 100 hours more youths die on the streets than were killed in the Persian Gulf War. This homicide rate is more than eleven times higher for blacks than for whites, and most of it is black on black.

The clear trend in 1991 was toward more powerful weapons, such as 9mm semiautomatic pistols, which could be purchased for $300 to $700 on the streets. Cheaper but still deadly guns could be bought for around $50. As more gangs surfaced across the country, more guns found their way into the streets. Gang-related killings accounted for about 35 percent of all homicides.

The House in May passed the Brady Handgun Violence Prevention Act, which provides for a seven-day waiting period on purchases of handguns, so that police can check for criminal records of prospective buyers. The National Rifle Association opposed the bill, but conservatives such as Richard Nixon and Ronald Reagan joined a growing number of police officers in endorsing it. James Brady, for whom the bill is named, was seriously wounded ten years ago in an assassination attempt on Reagan.

MIKE PETERS
Courtesy Dayton Daily News

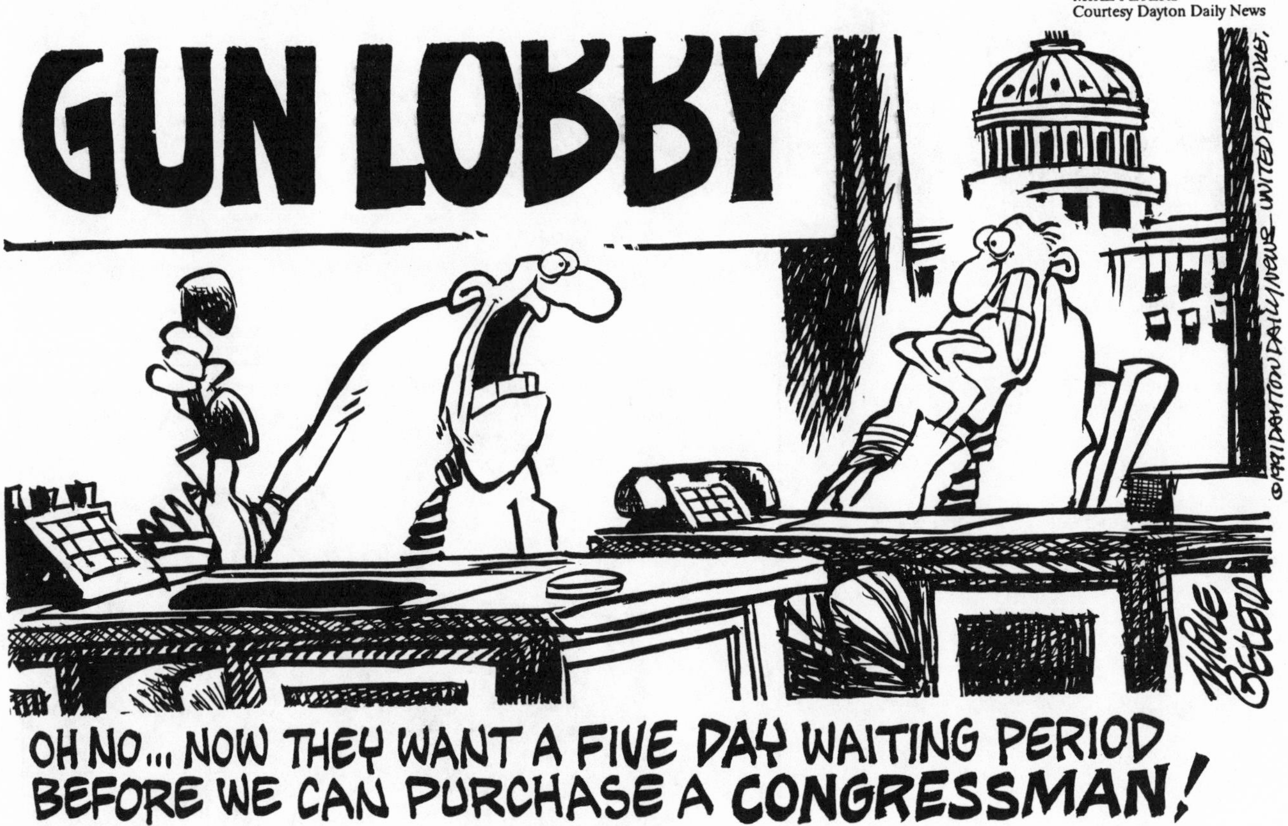

GUN LOBBY
©1991 DAYTON DAILY NEWS - UNITED FEATURES
OH NO... NOW THEY WANT A FIVE DAY WAITING PERIOD BEFORE WE CAN PURCHASE A CONGRESSMAN!

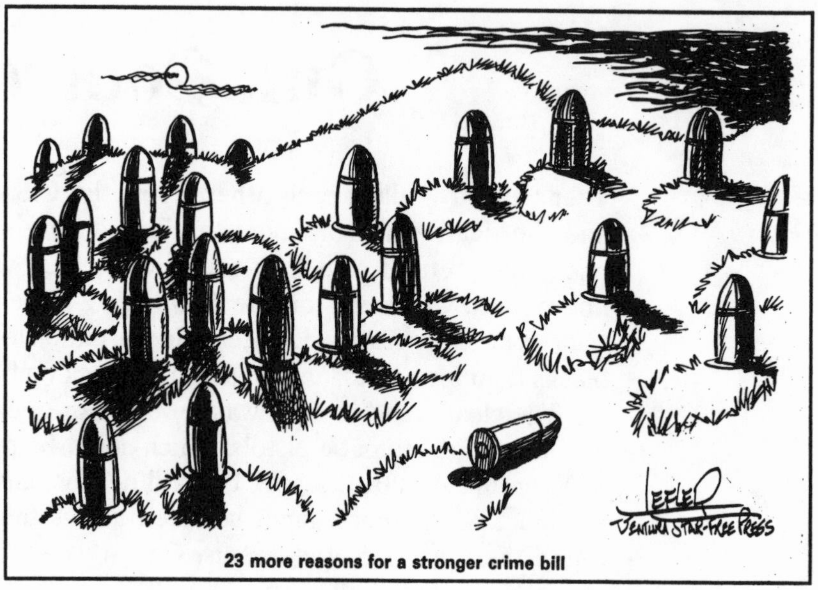
LEFLER
Ventura Star-Free Press
23 more reasons for a stronger crime bill

JERRY LEFLER
Courtesy Ventura County Star-Free Press

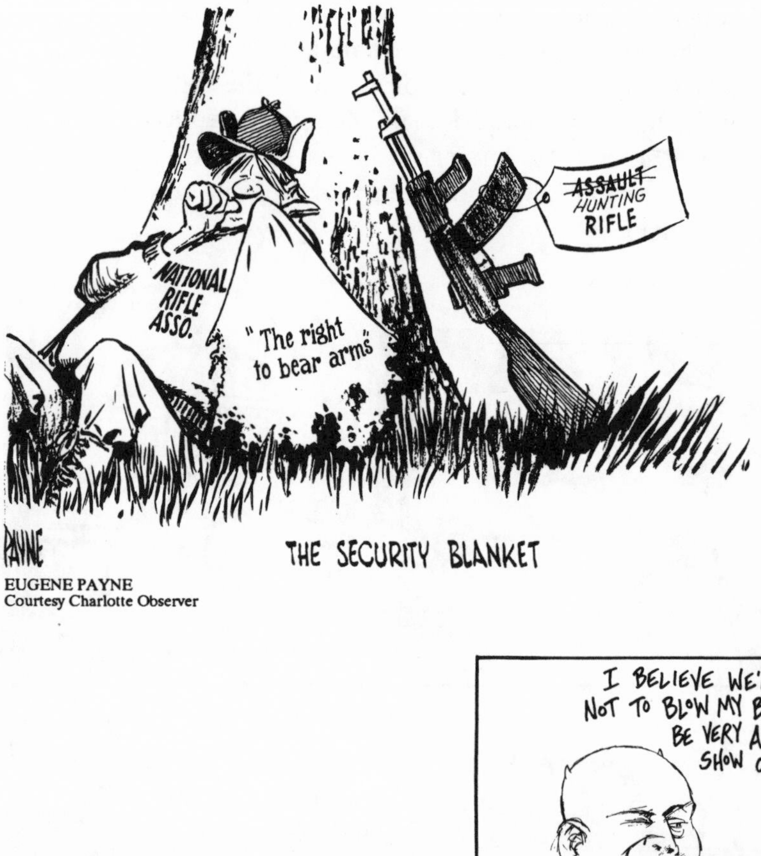
ASSAULT
HUNTING
RIFLE
NATIONAL
RIFLE
ASSO.
"The right to bear arms"
PAYNE
THE SECURITY BLANKET

EUGENE PAYNE
Courtesy Charlotte Observer

STEVE ANSUL
Courtesy Wilmington News Journal

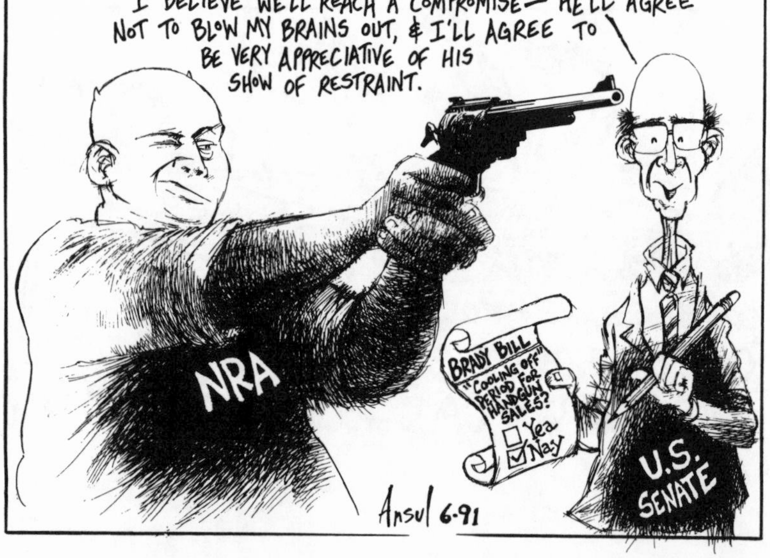
I BELIEVE WE'LL REACH A COMPROMISE— HE'LL AGREE NOT TO BLOW MY BRAINS OUT, & I'LL AGREE TO BE VERY APPRECIATIVE OF HIS SHOW OF RESTRAINT.
NRA
BRADY BILL
"COOLING OFF" PERIOD FOR HANDGUN SALES?
Yea
Nay
U.S. SENATE
Ansul 6-91

JACK HIGGINS
Courtesy Chicago Sun-Times

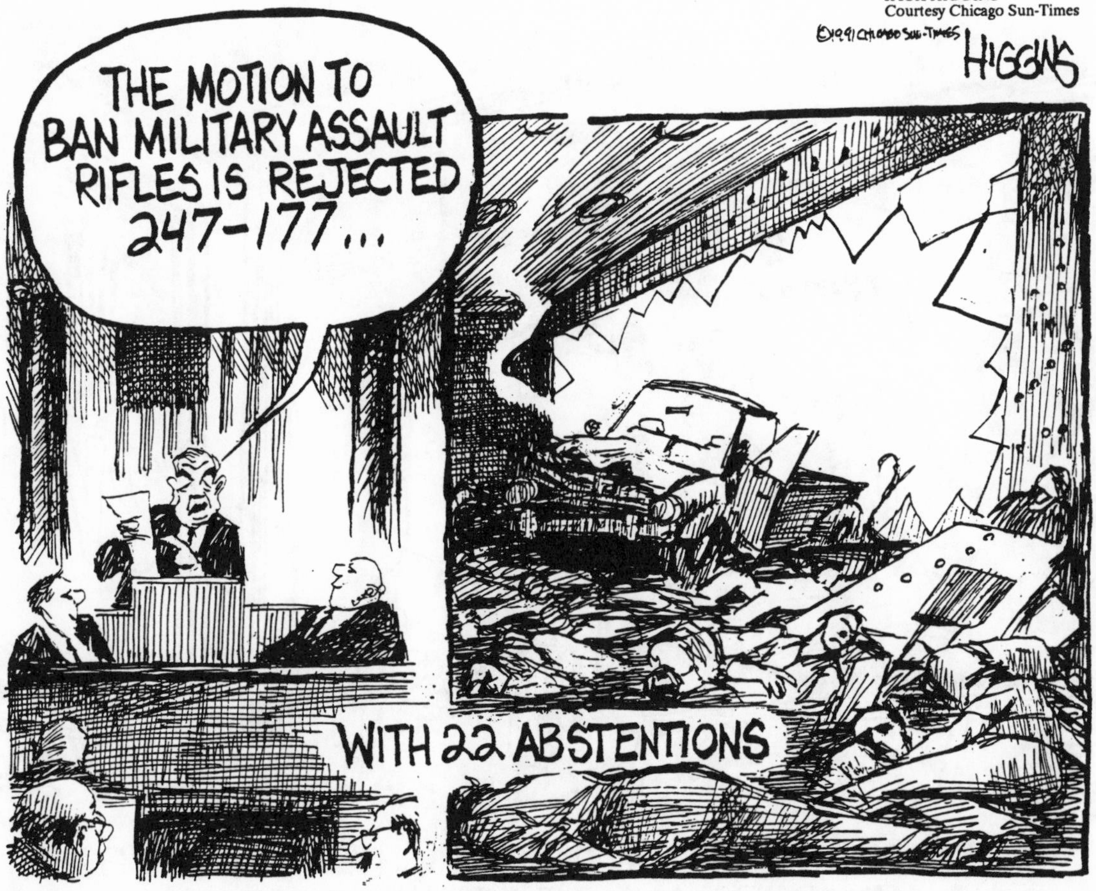
©1991 CHICAGO SUN-TIMES
HIGGINS
THE MOTION TO BAN MILITARY ASSAULT RIFLES IS REJECTED 247-177...
WITH 22 ABSTENTIONS

BRUCE PLANTE
Courtesy Chattanooga Times and
Extra Newspapers Features

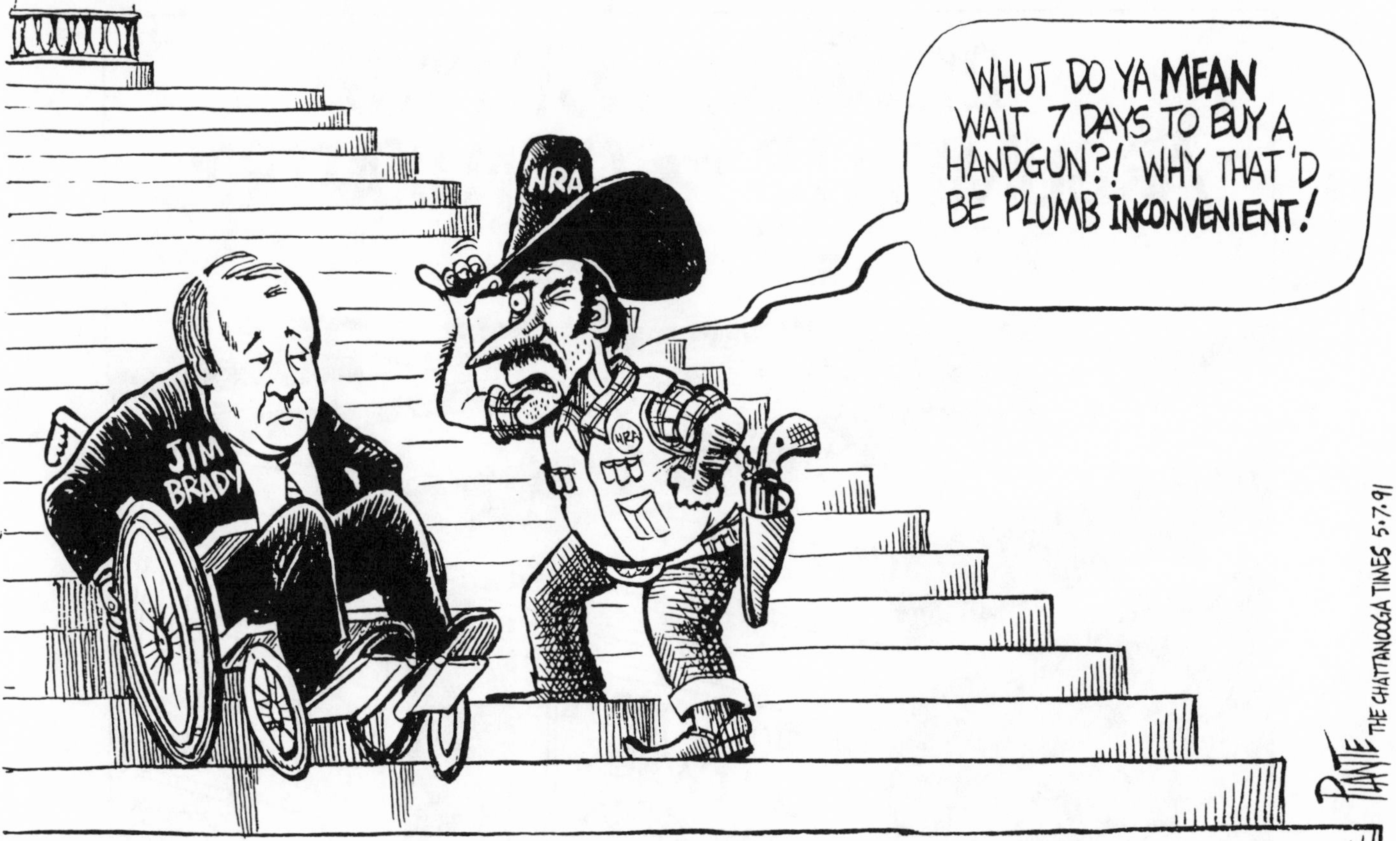
WHUT DO YA MEAN WAIT 7 DAYS TO BUY A HANDGUN?! WHY THAT'D BE PLUMB INCONVENIENT!
NRA
NRA
JIM BRADY
PLANTE
THE CHATTANOOGA TIMES 5.7.91

MALCOLM MAYES
Courtesy Edmonton Journal

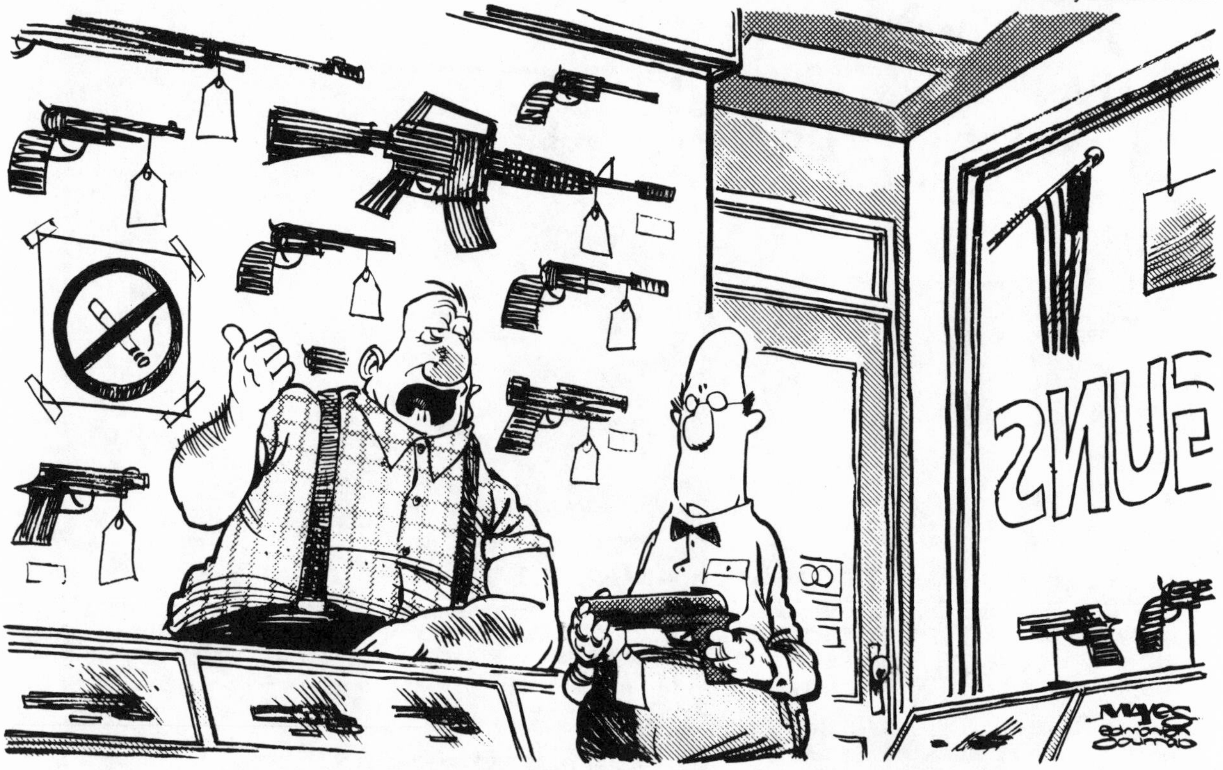
GUNS
MAYES Edmonton Journal

"I'VE BANNED CIGARETTES IN THE SHOP.... IT'S FRIGHTENING HOW MANY PEOPLE A YEAR THOSE THINGS KILL."

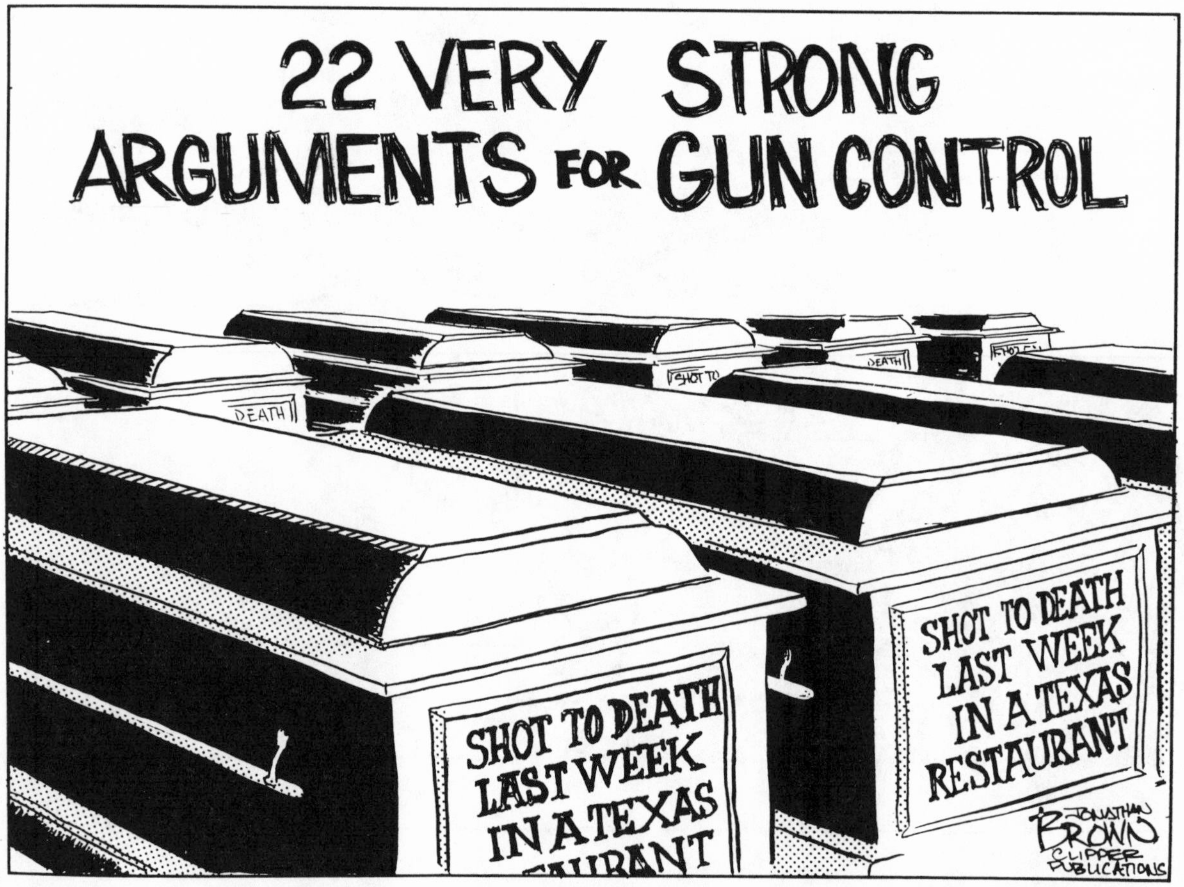
22 VERY STRONG ARGUMENTS FOR GUN CONTROL
DEATH
SHOT TO
SHOT TO DEATH LAST WEEK IN A TEXAS RESTAURANT
SHOT TO DEATH LAST WEEK IN A TEXAS RESTAURANT
JONATHAN BROWN CLIPPER PUBLICATIONS

JONATHAN BROWN
Courtesy Davis County Clipper (Utah)

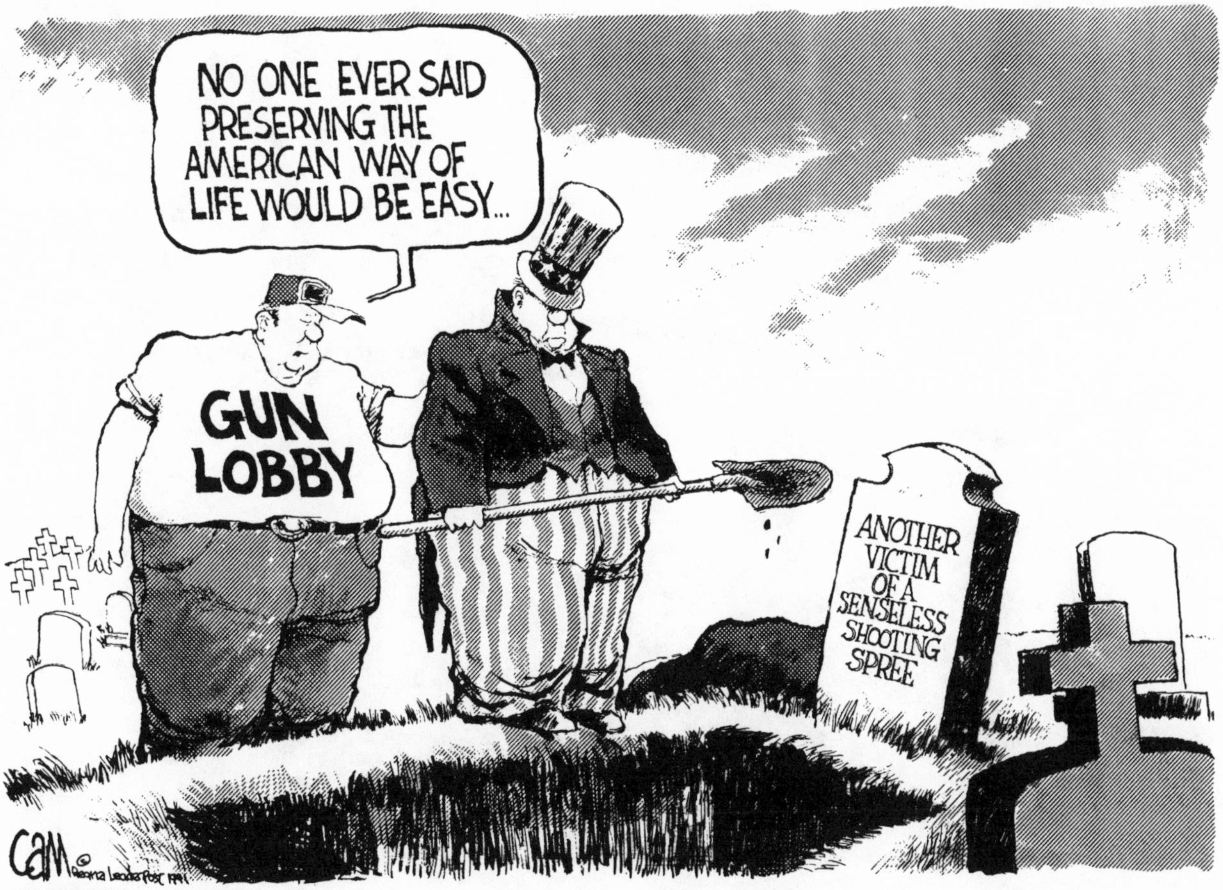
NO ONE EVER SAID PRESERVING THE AMERICAN WAY OF LIFE WOULD BE EASY...
GUN LOBBY
ANOTHER VICTIM OF A SENSELESS SHOOTING SPREE
CAM

CAM CARDOW
Courtesy Regina Leader Post

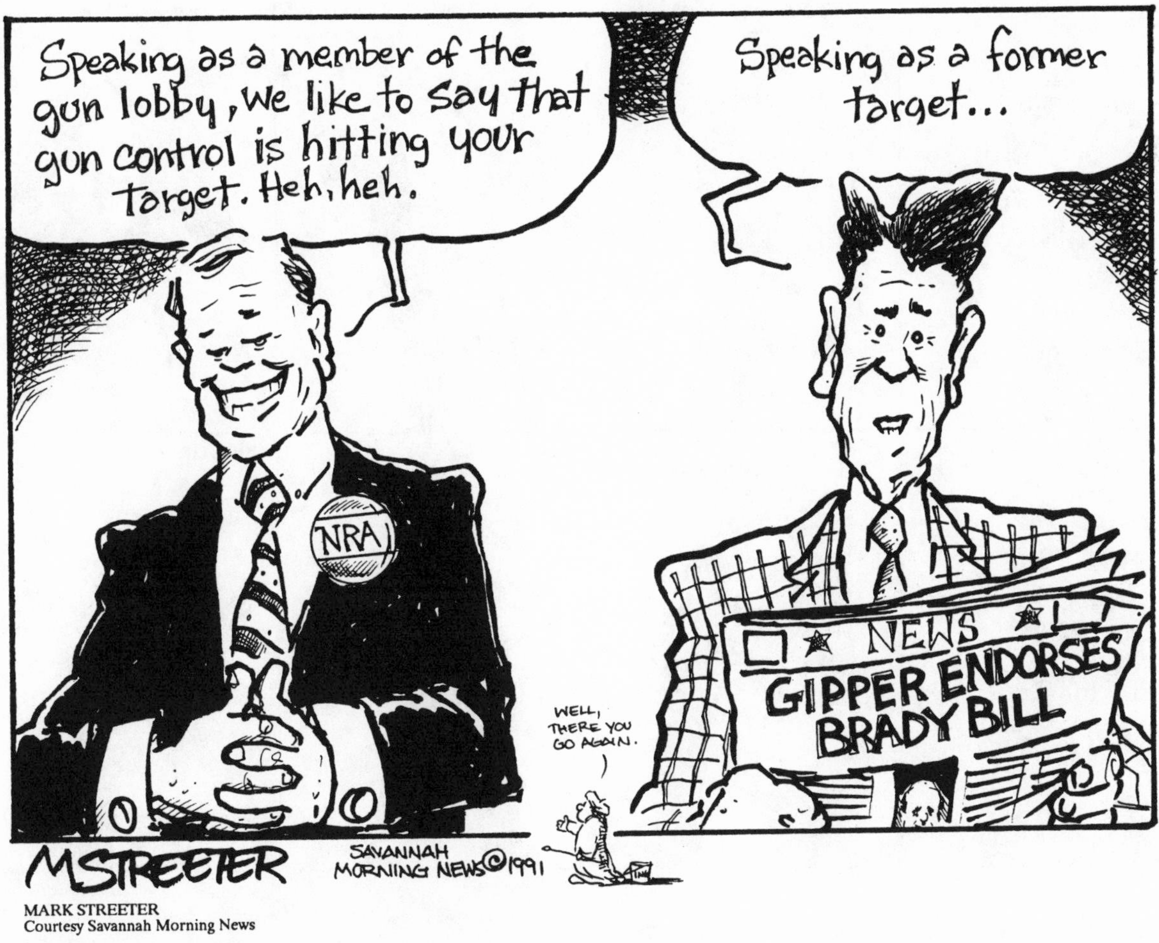
Speaking as a member of the gun lobby, we like to say that gun control is hitting your target. Heh, heh.
Speaking as a former target...
NRA
NEWS
GIPPER ENDORSES BRADY BILL
WELL, THERE YOU GO AGAIN.
MSTREETER
SAVANNAH MORNING NEWS©1991

MARK STREETER
Courtesy Savannah Morning News

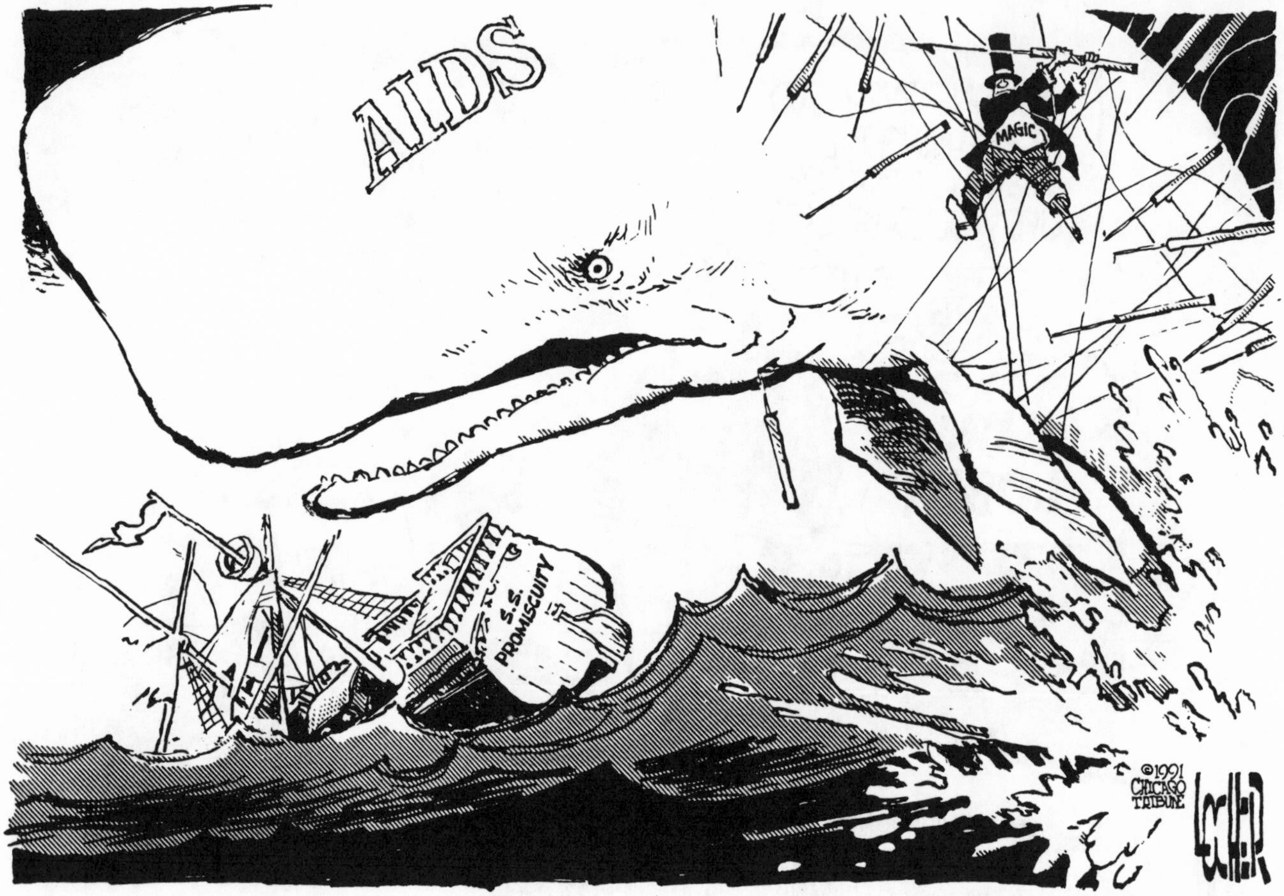
AIDS
MAGIC
S.S. PROMISCUITY
©1991 CHICAGO TRIBUNE
LOCHER

DICK LOCHER
Courtesy Chicago Tribune

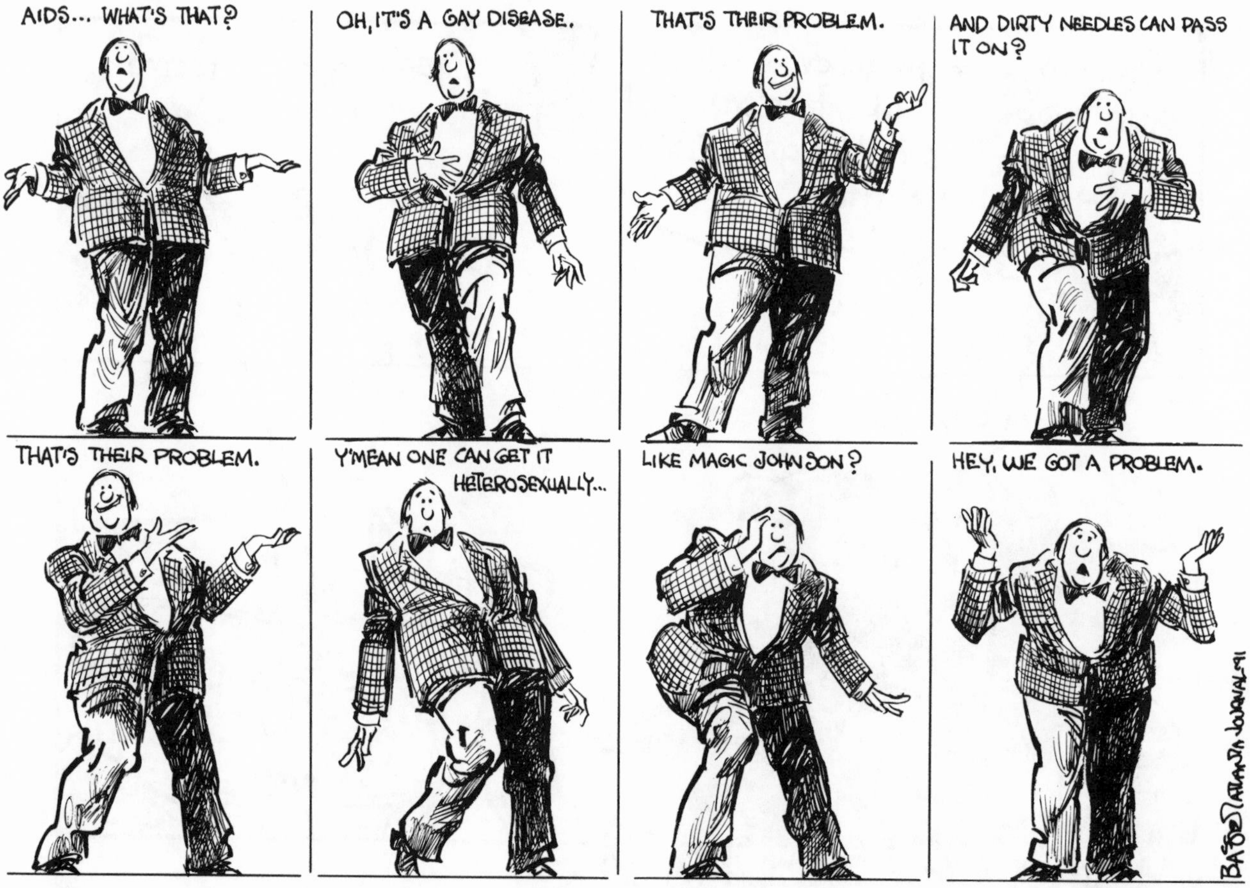
AIDS... WHAT'S THAT?
OH, IT'S A GAY DISEASE.
THAT'S THEIR PROBLEM.
AND DIRTY NEEDLES CAN PASS IT ON?
THAT'S THEIR PROBLEM.
Y'MEAN ONE CAN GET IT HETEROSEXUALLY...
LIKE MAGIC JOHNSON?
HEY, WE GOT A PROBLEM.

GENE BASSET
Courtesy Atlanta Journal

Health Issues

The nation was stunned in November when professional basketball star Magic Johnson announced he was quitting the game. Johnson said he had contracted the HI virus, which causes AIDS. He indicated the virus had been acquired through sexual contact and began campaigning to alert young people about the deadly infection. Nearly 200,000 Americans have contracted the disease, and some 126,000 have died. Johnson at first spoke out in behalf of "safe sex," but later amended his warning to include an admonition that really safe sex meant abstinence outside of marriage.

Medical groups announced their opposition to strict standards for AIDS-infected doctors and nurses, contending there is only one known case of a health-care worker having transmitted the virus to a patient. Nevertheless, federal officials were working to develop guidelines for infected health-care workers.

The cost of health care continued to outpace every other category of living expenses for Americans, with almost 14 percent of the gross national product being spent for medical treatment and medicine. That figure is nearly three times what is spent on defense. Many doctors have ceased performing certain types of operations because of runaway malpractice suits and spiraling damage awards.

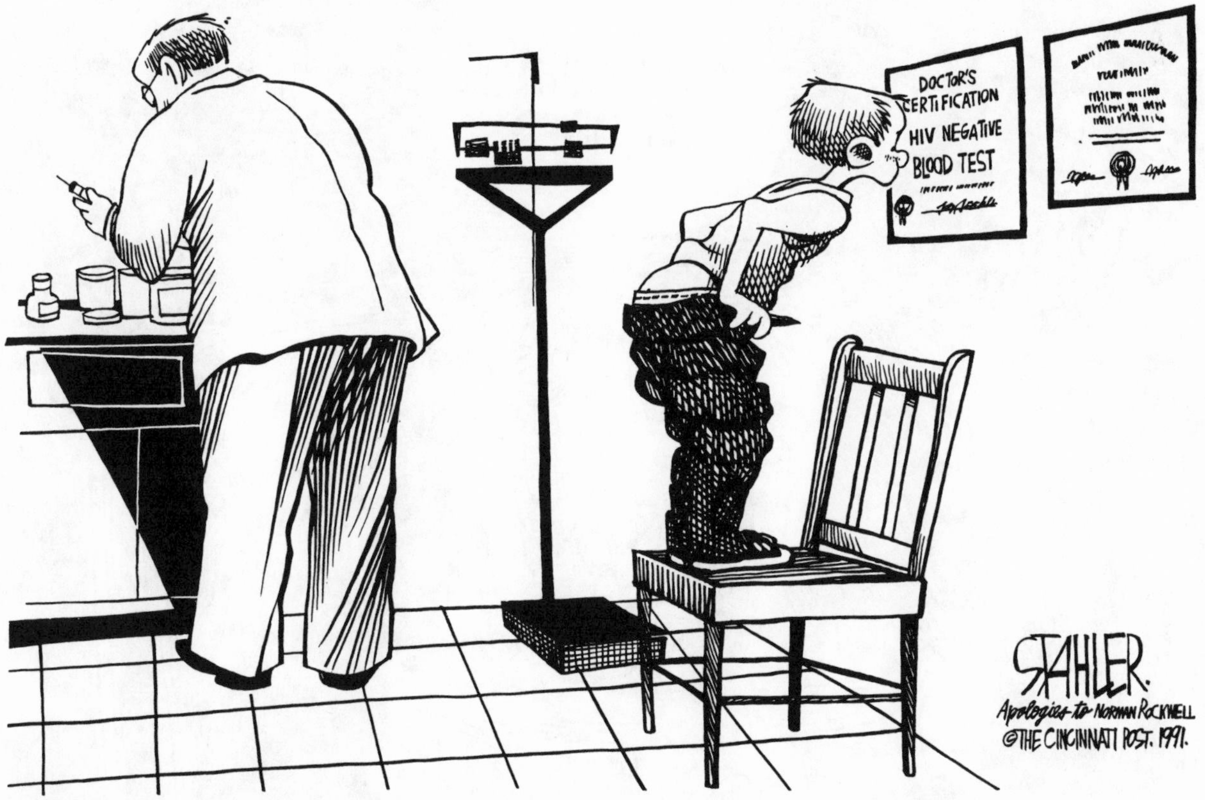
DOCTOR'S CERTIFICATION
HIV NEGATIVE
BLOOD TEST
STAHLER.
Apologies to NORMAN ROCKWELL
©THE CINCINNATI POST. 1991.

JEFF STAHLER
Courtesy Cincinnati Post

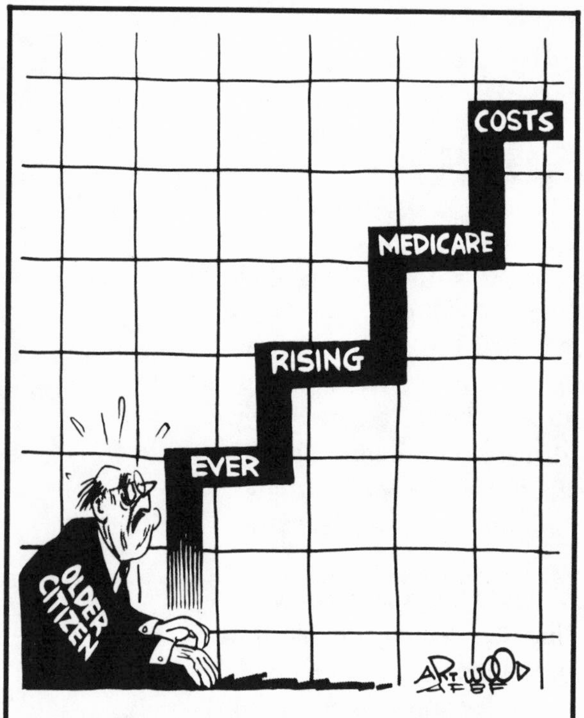
COSTS
MEDICARE
RISING
EVER
OLDER CITIZEN
ART WOOD

"You mean that I've got to climb that?"

ART WOOD
Courtesy Farm Bureau News

AL LIEDERMAN
Courtesy Rothco

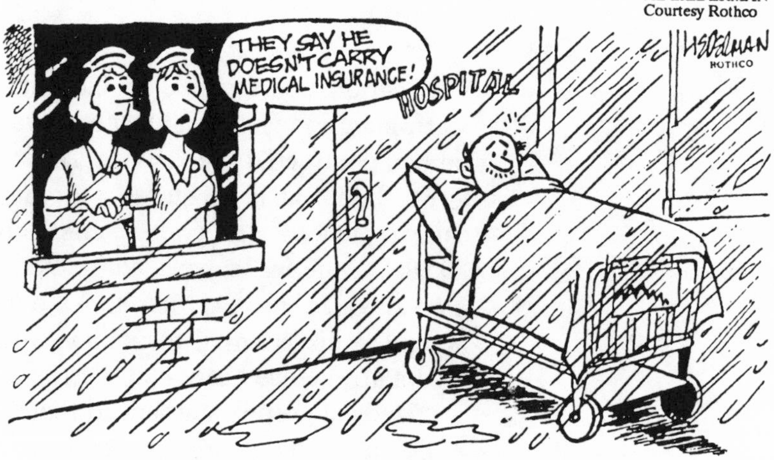
THEY SAY HE DOESN'T CARRY MEDICAL INSURANCE!
HOSPITAL
LIEDERMAN
ROTHCO

UNINSURED HOSPITAL PATIENTS FOUND MORE LIKELY TO DIE —REPORT

BOB DORNFRIED
Courtesy Fairfield Citizen (Conn.)

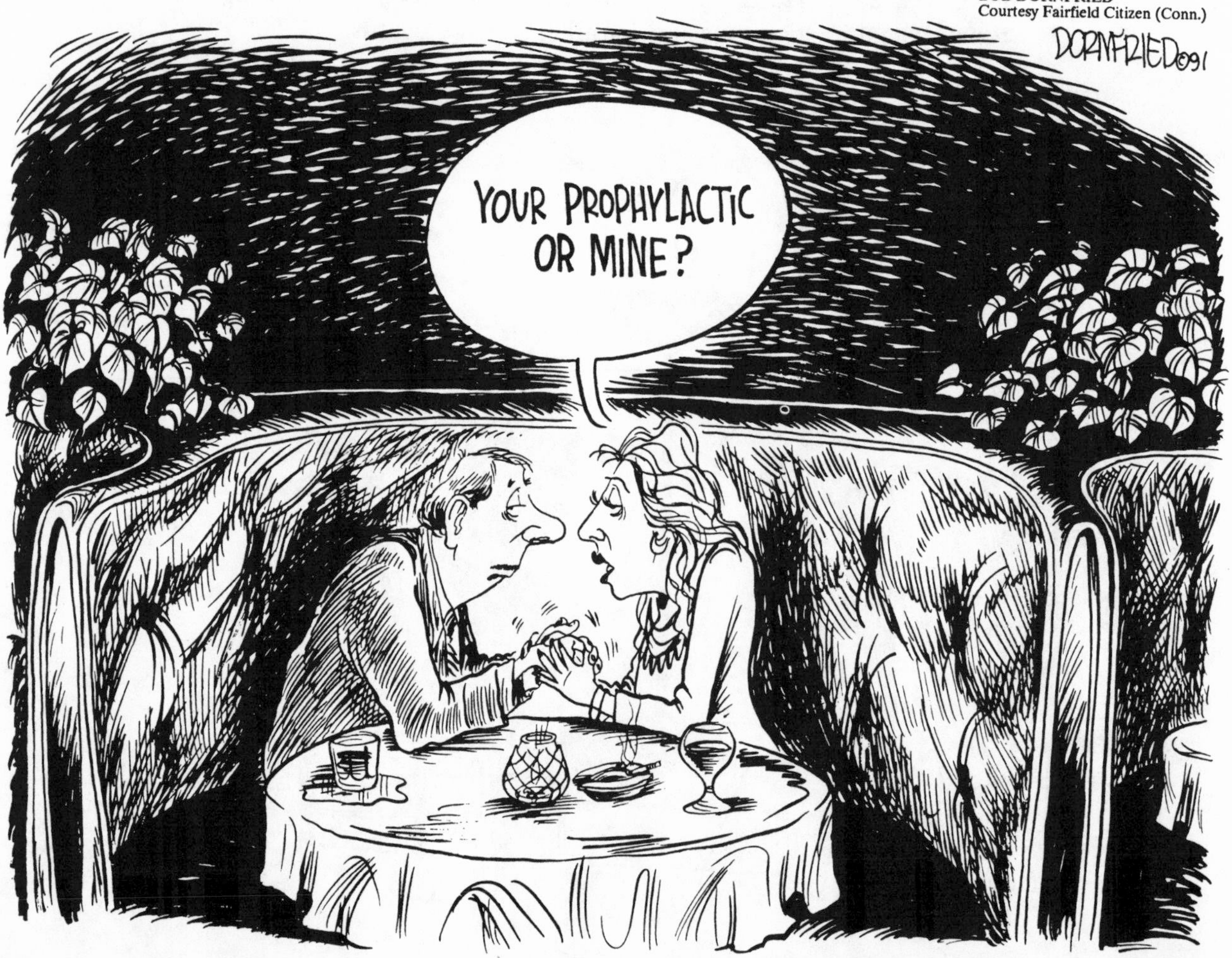
DORNFRIED©91
YOUR PROPHYLACTIC OR MINE?

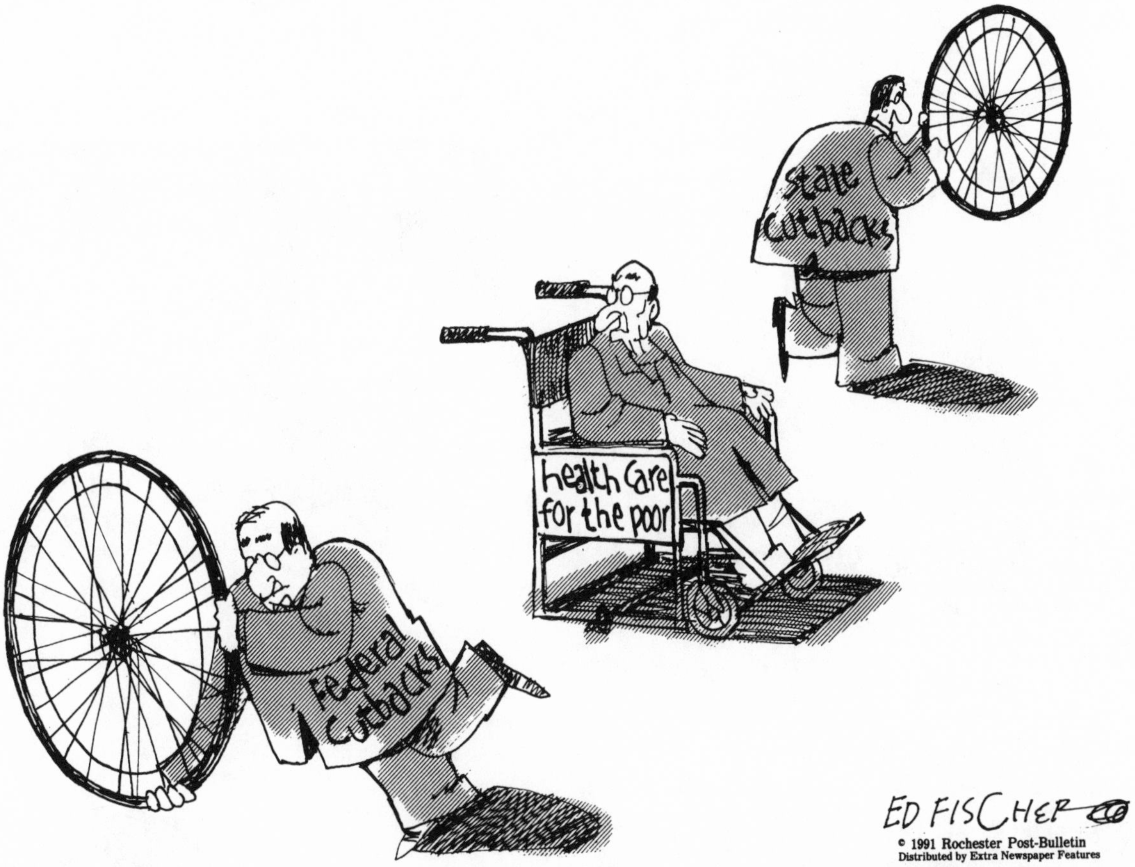
State Cutbacks
Health Care for the poor
Federal Cutbacks
ED FISCHER
© 1991 Rochester Post-Bulletin
Distributed by Extra Newspaper Features

ED FISCHER
Courtesy Rochester Post-Bulletin

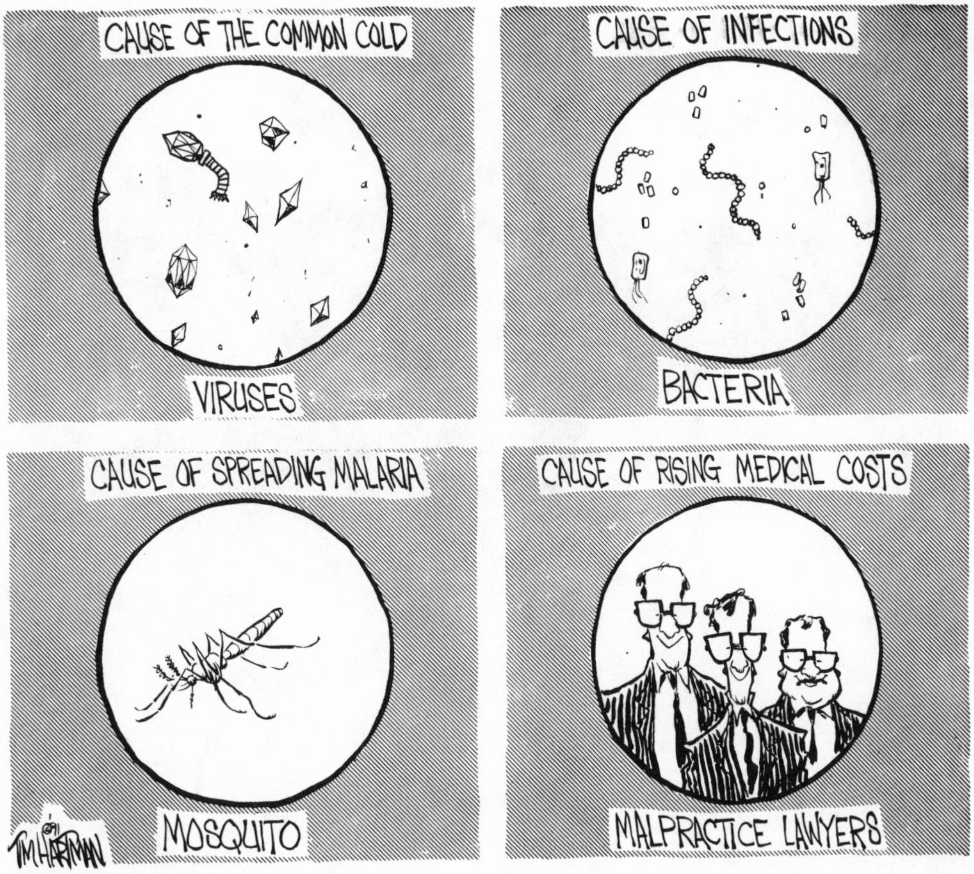
CAUSE OF THE COMMON COLD
VIRUSES
CAUSE OF INFECTIONS
BACTERIA
CAUSE OF SPREADING MALARIA
MOSQUITO
CAUSE OF RISING MEDICAL COSTS
MALPRACTICE LAWYERS
TIM HARTMAN

TIM HARTMAN
Courtesy Valley News Dispatch (Pa.)

CLIFF LEVERETTE
Courtesy Leverette Syndicate

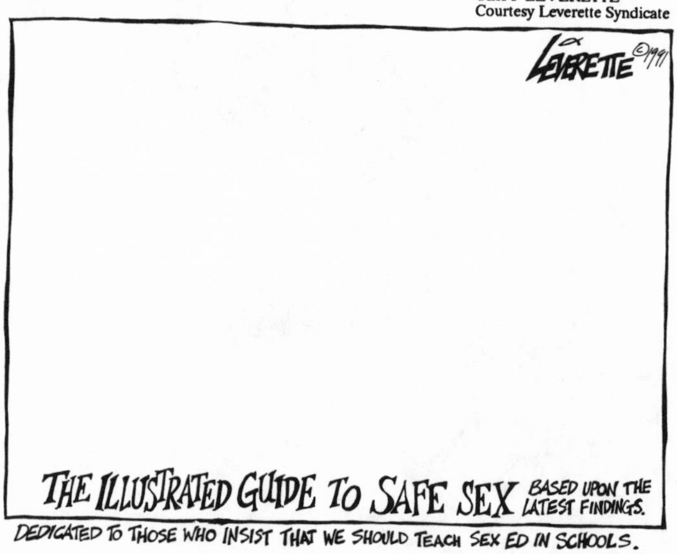
LEVERETTE ©1991
THE ILLUSTRATED GUIDE TO SAFE SEX BASED UPON THE LATEST FINDINGS.
DEDICATED TO THOSE WHO INSIST THAT WE SHOULD TEACH SEX ED IN SCHOOLS.

HY ROSEN
Courtesy Albany Times-Union

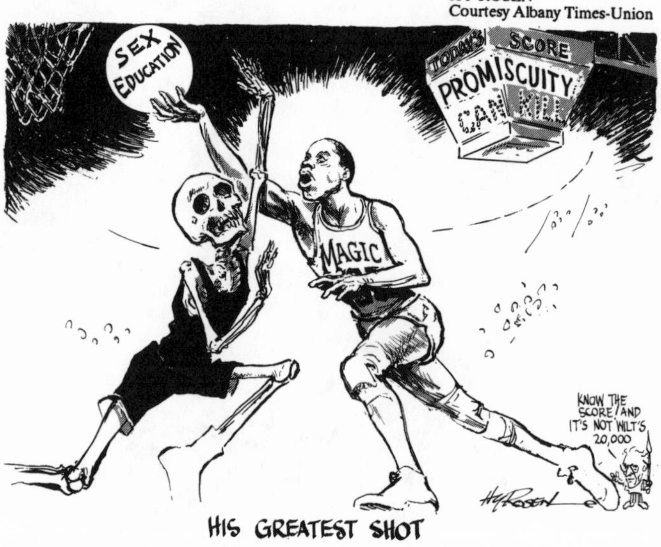
SEX EDUCATION
TODAY'S SCORE
PROMISCUITY CAN KILL
MAGIC
KNOW THE SCORE AND IT'S NOT WILT'S 20,000
HY ROSEN
HIS GREATEST SHOT

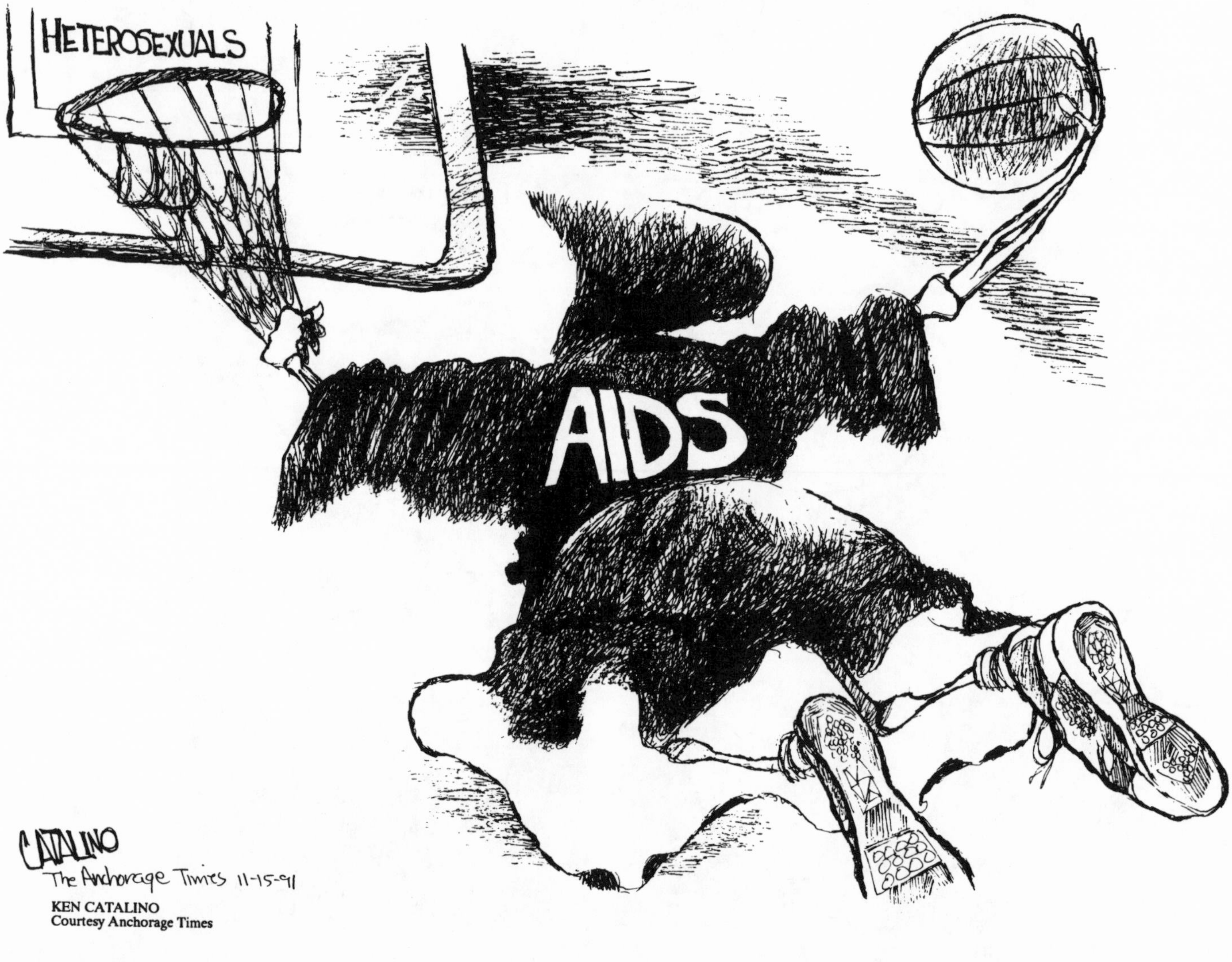
HETEROSEXUALS
AIDS
CATALINO
The Anchorage Times 11-15-91

KEN CATALINO
Courtesy Anchorage Times

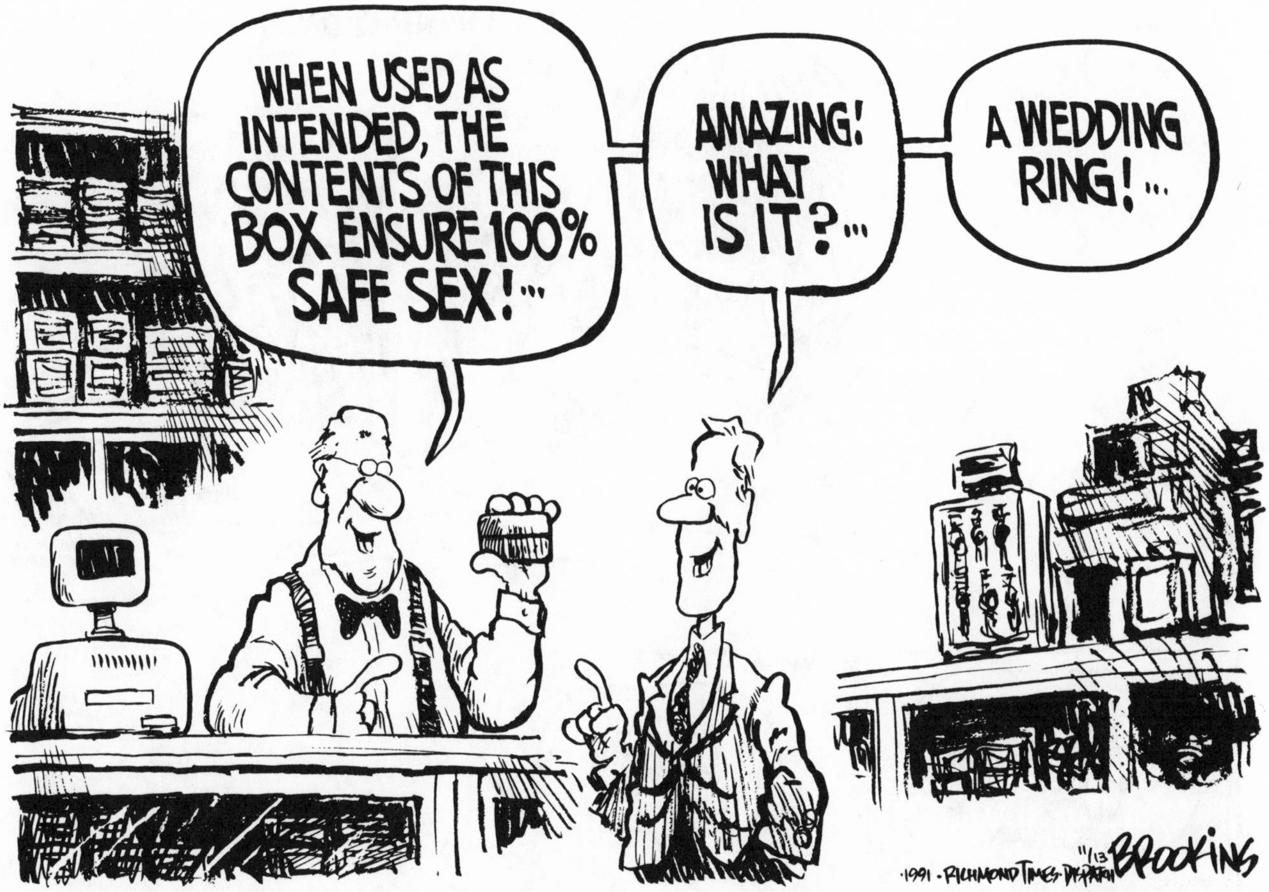
WHEN USED AS INTENDED, THE CONTENTS OF THIS BOX ENSURE 100% SAFE SEX!...
AMAZING! WHAT IS IT?...
A WEDDING RING!...
·1991 · RICHMOND TIMES-DISPATCH 11/13 BROOKINS

GARY BROOKINS
Courtesy Richmond Times-Dispatch

DOUGLAS REGALIA
Courtesy San Ramon Valley Times (Calif.)

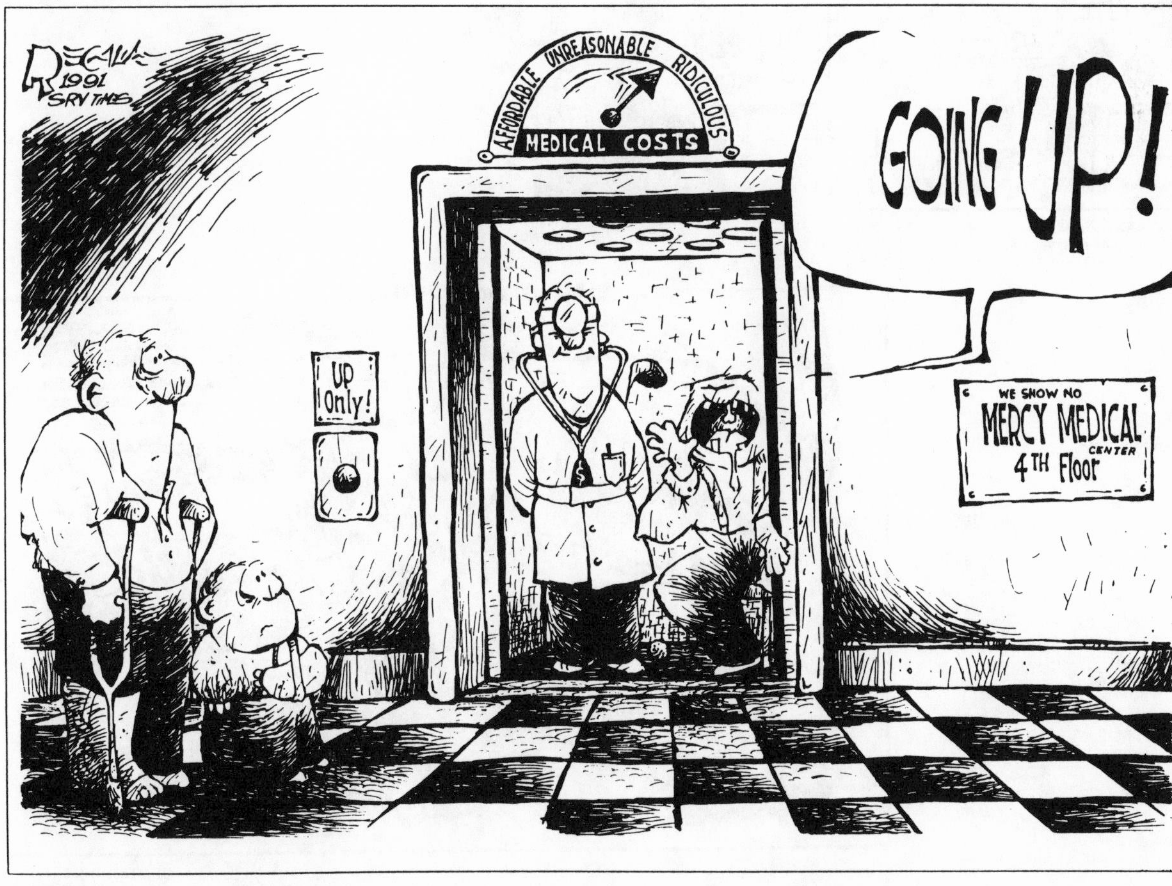
REGALIA 1991 SRV TIMES
AFFORDABLE
UNREASONABLE
RIDICULOUS
MEDICAL COSTS
GOING UP!
UP Only!
WE SHOW NO
MERCY MEDICAL CENTER
4TH Floor

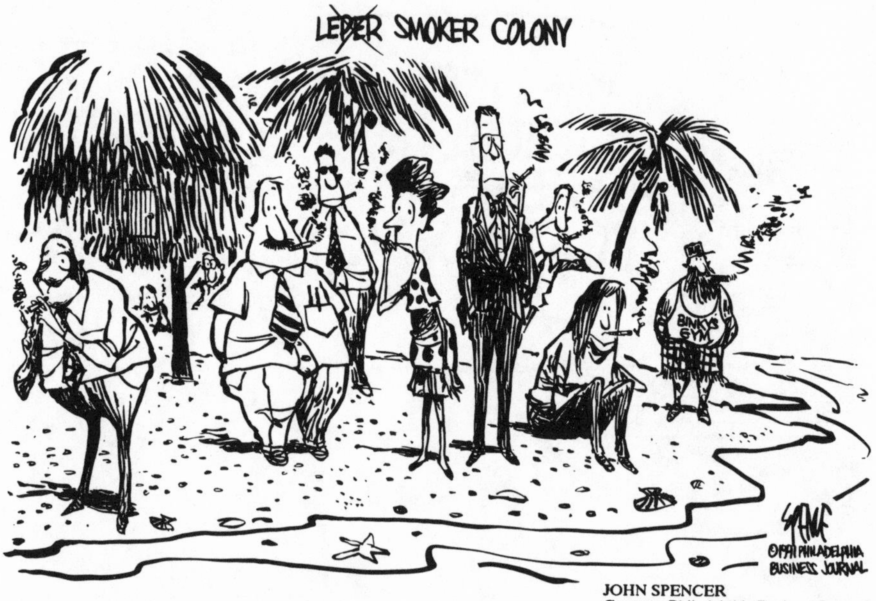
LEPER SMOKER COLONY
BINKY'S GYM
©1991 PHILADELPHIA BUSINESS JOURNAL
JOHN SPENCER
Courtesy Philadelphia Business Journal

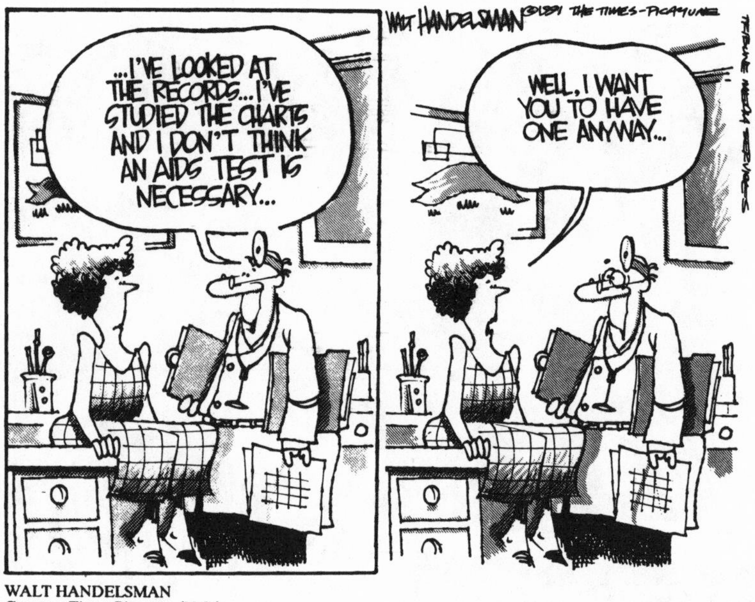
WALT HANDELSMAN ©1991 THE TIMES-PICAYUNE
...I'VE LOOKED AT THE RECORDS...I'VE STUDIED THE CHARTS AND I DON'T THINK AN AIDS TEST IS NECESSARY...
WELL, I WANT YOU TO HAVE ONE ANYWAY...
TRIBUNE MEDIA SERVICES
WALT HANDELSMAN
Courtesy Times-Picayune (N.O.)

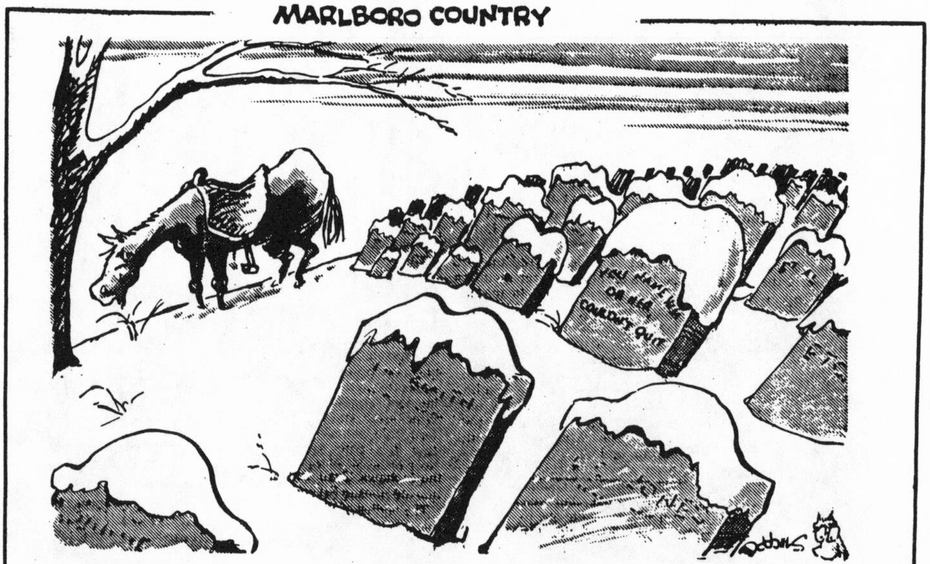
MARLBORO COUNTRY
JIM DOBBINS
Courtesy N.A.G.E. Reporter

THE PRESIDENT SAYS US KIDS ARE OUT OF SHAPE. WE'RE FAT... UNHEALTHY... WELL, I DON'T AGREE.
EVERY DAY I PLAY FOOTBALL, BASEBALL, OR BASKETBALL FOR AT LEAST TWO HOURS.
IN FACT, I PLAY EVERY SPORT THERE IS... EXCEPT POLO.
NINTENDO DOESN'T MAKE THAT ONE YET.

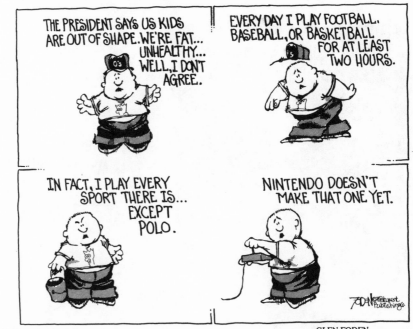

GLEN FODEN
Courtesy Patuxent Pub. Co.

ABSTINENCE?? GET REAL, POP__THIS IS THE 90's___ SAFE SEX IS THE WAY_
DID YOU HAVE THAT LITTLE TALK WITH JUNIOR?
!
DANIEL

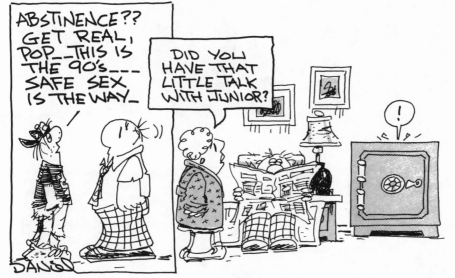

CHARLES DANIEL
Courtesy Knoxville Journal

AIDS VICTIMS... WE'RE HATED... FEARED... SHUNNED...
SCORNED AS THE DREGS... THE SCUM OF THE EARTH... DESERVING OUR FATE...!
BUT SUDDENLY, OVERNIGHT, THERE'S NEW UNDERSTANDING... SYMPATHY... HOPE...!
IT'S MAGIC!
©1991 THE CHARLOTTE OBSERVER KEVIN SIERS

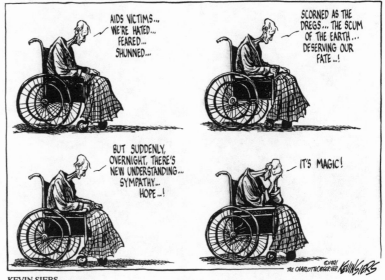

KEVIN SIERS
Courtesy Charlotte Observer

JEFF BRANCH
Courtesy San Antonio Express-News

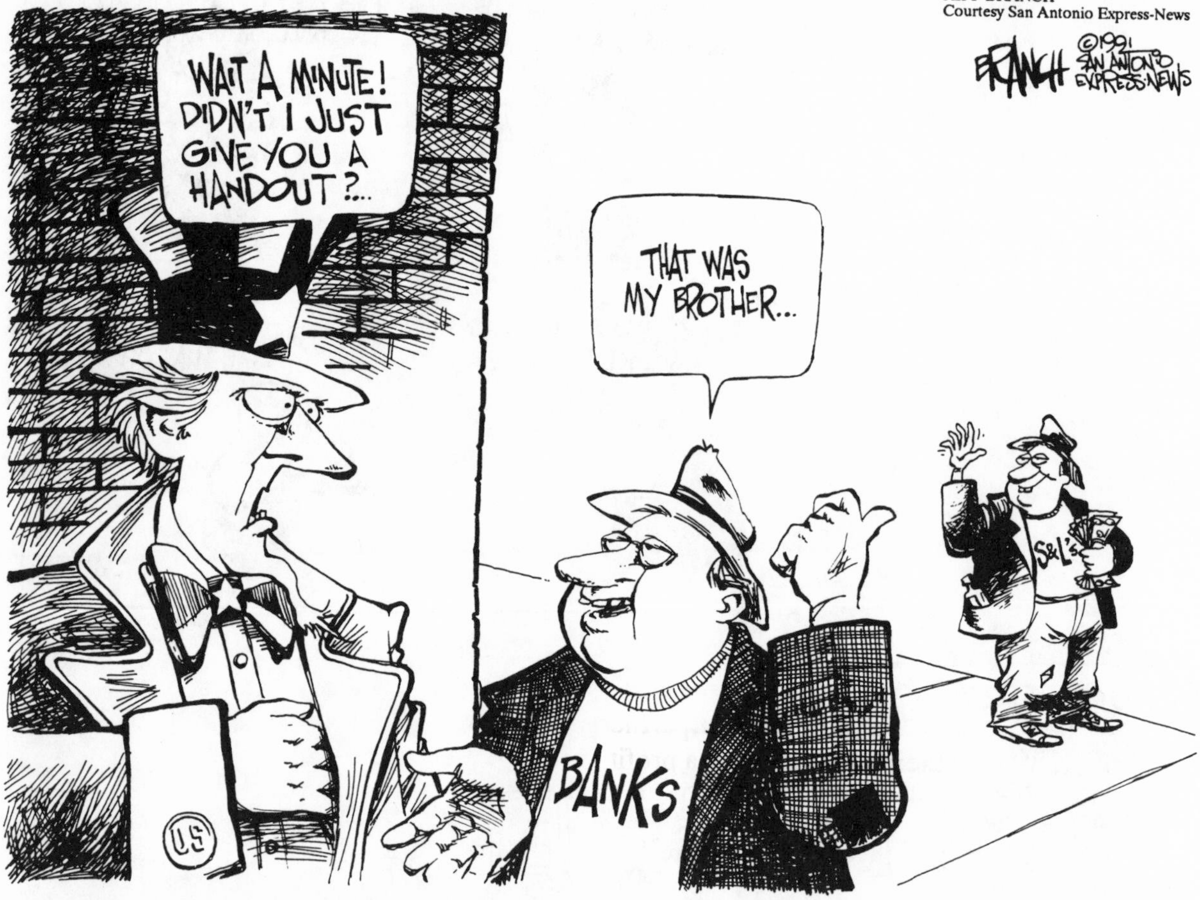
BRANCH ©1991 SAN ANTONIO EXPRESS-NEWS
WAIT A MINUTE! DIDN'T I JUST GIVE YOU A HANDOUT?...
THAT WAS MY BROTHER...
US
BANKS
S&L's

JEFF PARKER
Courtesy Orlando Business Journal

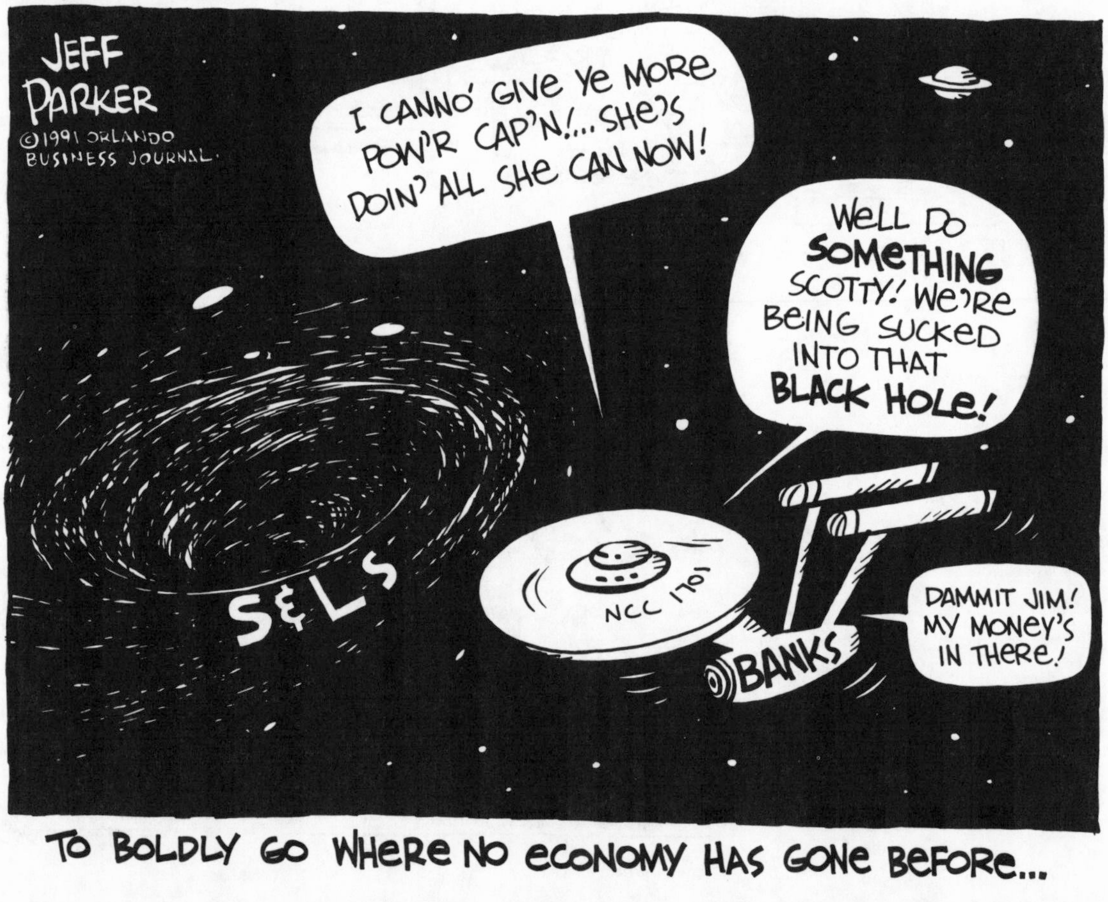
JEFF PARKER ©1991 ORLANDO BUSINESS JOURNAL
I CANNO' GIVE YE MORE POW'R CAP'N!... SHE'S DOIN' ALL SHE CAN NOW!
WELL DO SOMETHING SCOTTY! WE'RE BEING SUCKED INTO THAT BLACK HOLE!
S&LS
NCC 1701
BANKS
DAMMIT JIM! MY MONEY'S IN THERE!
TO BOLDLY GO WHERE NO ECONOMY HAS GONE BEFORE...

Financial Institutions

The growing bank crisis in 1991 began to resemble the savings and loan fiasco in some areas of the country. The immediate problem is that the assets of many large U.S. banks are worth less than their liabilities. Many bank loans made in the booming 1980s began to turn bad as more and more borrowers were unable to meet their obligations. As a result, a steady stream of banks have failed.

In the ongoing savings and loan mess, the federal government took control of $355.1 billion in loans and assets. At year's end, only $213.7 billion had been recovered through collections and sales of real estate ranging from office buildings to golf courses.

Clark Clifford, eighty-four-year-old former secretary of defense and advisor to Democratic presidents, found himself entangled in the Bank of Credit and Commerce International investigation. It appeared that he may not have told Federal Reserve regulators all he knew about BCCI's illegal control of the Washington bank holding company of which he was chairman. BCCI fraud is estimated at some $10 billion worldwide. Clifford and partner Robert Altman are alleged to have sold their bank stock for a profit of $9.8 million.

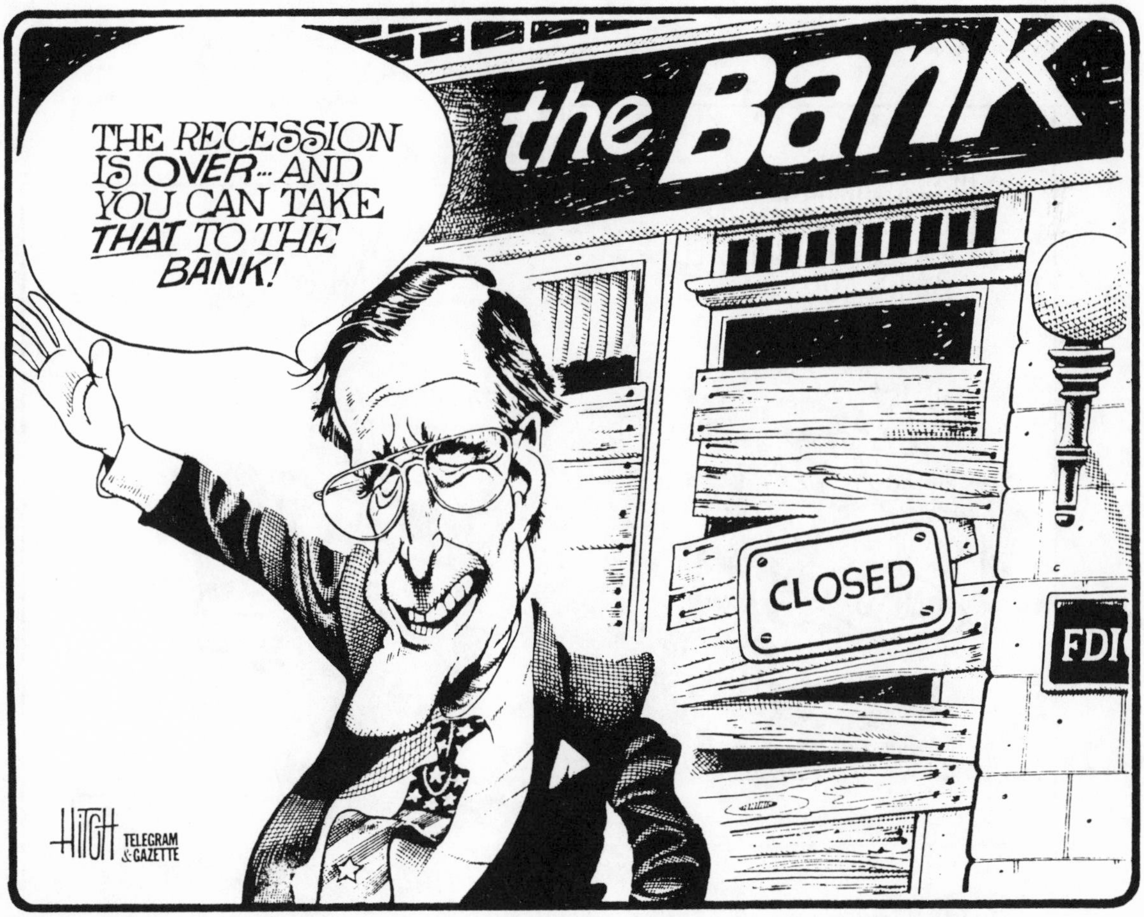
THE RECESSION IS OVER... AND YOU CAN TAKE THAT TO THE BANK!
the Bank
CLOSED
FDI
HITCH
TELEGRAM & GAZETTE

DAVID HITCH
Courtesy Worcester Telegram & Gazette

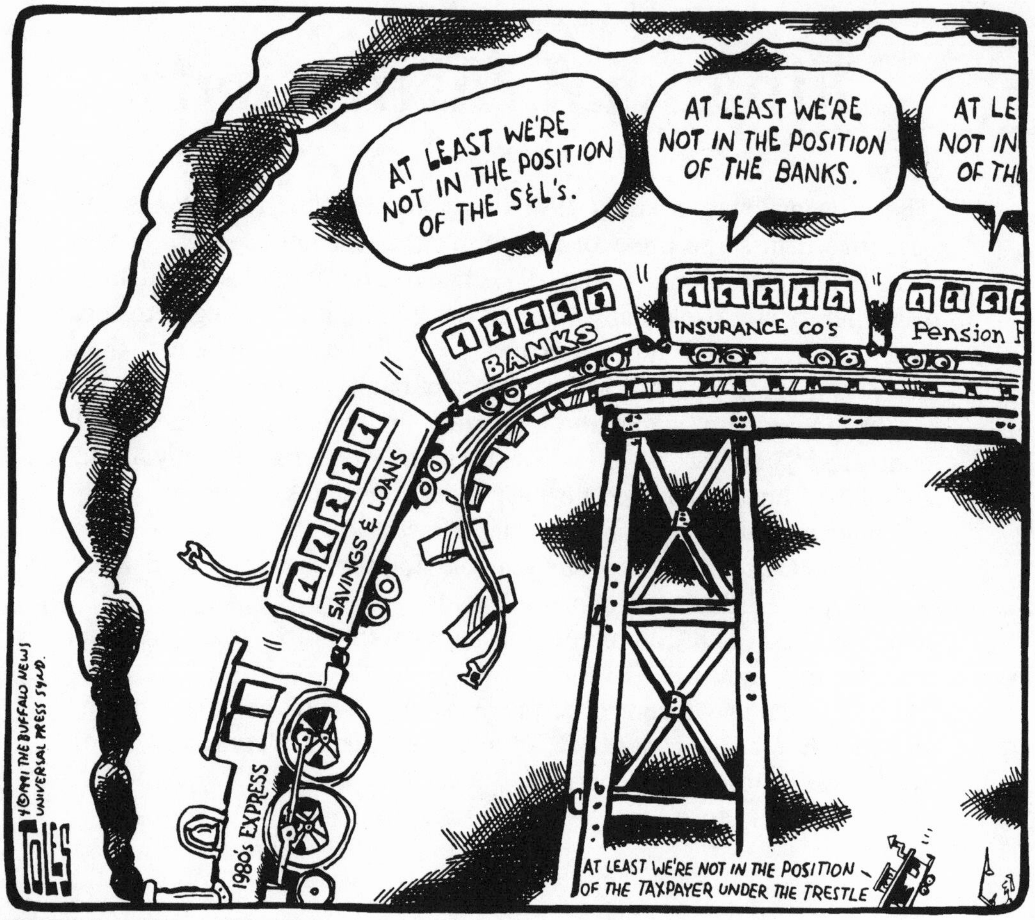
AT LEAST WE'RE NOT IN THE POSITION OF THE S&L's.
AT LEAST WE'RE NOT IN THE POSITION OF THE BANKS.
AT LE NOT IN OF TH
BANKS
INSURANCE CO's
Pension F
SAVINGS & LOANS
1980's EXPRESS
AT LEAST WE'RE NOT IN THE POSITION OF THE TAXPAYER UNDER THE TRESTLE
©1991 THE BUFFALO NEWS UNIVERSAL PRESS SYND.
TOLES

TOM TOLES
Courtesy Buffalo News and
Universal Press Syndicate

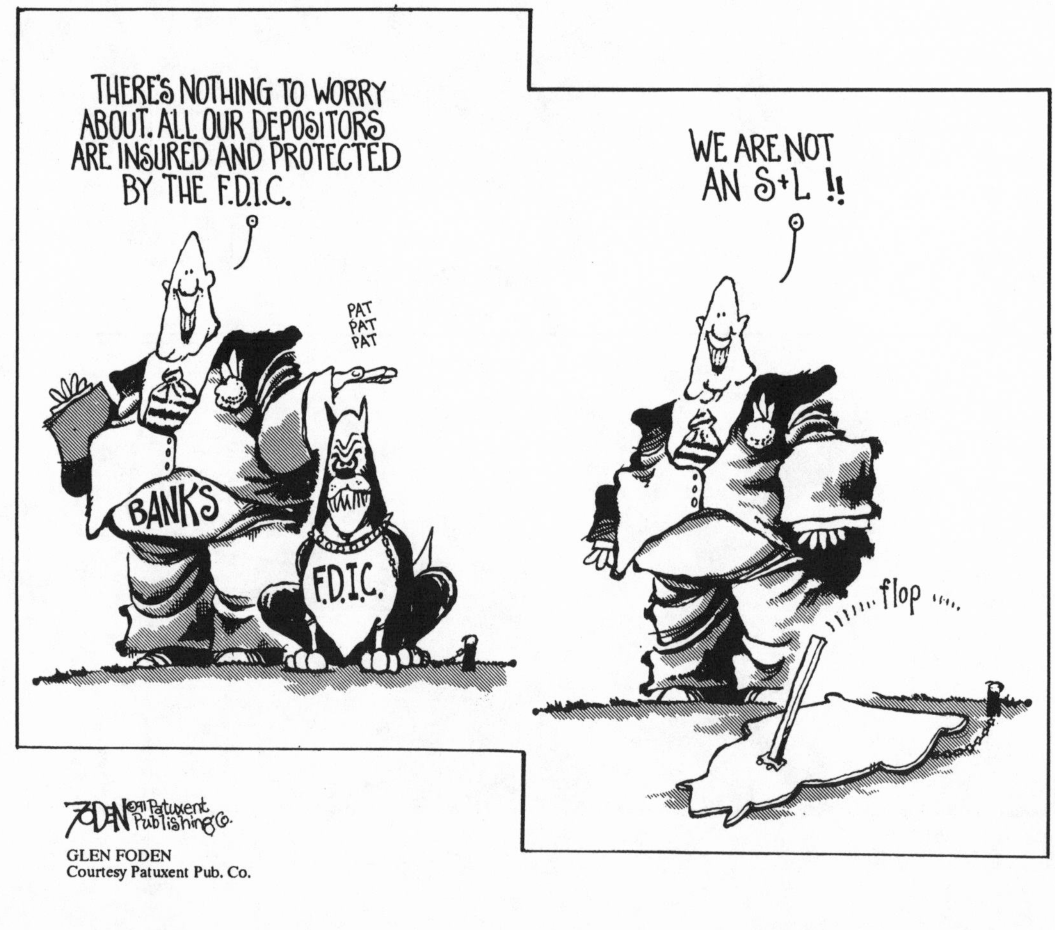
THERE'S NOTHING TO WORRY ABOUT. ALL OUR DEPOSITORS ARE INSURED AND PROTECTED BY THE F.D.I.C.
PAT PAT PAT
BANKS
F.D.I.C.
WE ARE NOT AN S+L !!
flop
FODEN ©91 Patuxent Publishing Co.

GLEN FODEN
Courtesy Patuxent Pub. Co.

CRAIG MACINTOSH
Courtesy Minneapolis Star-Tribune

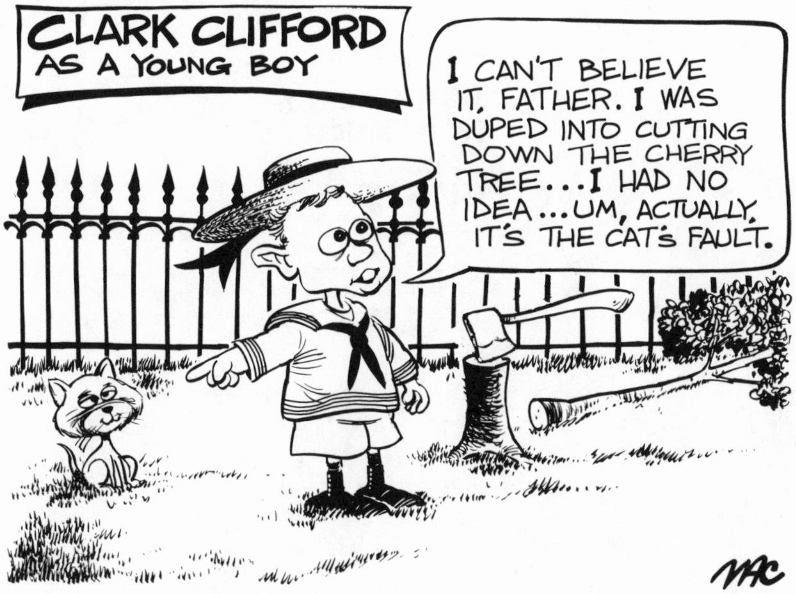
CLARK CLIFFORD AS A YOUNG BOY
I CAN'T BELIEVE IT, FATHER. I WAS DUPED INTO CUTTING DOWN THE CHERRY TREE...I HAD NO IDEA...UM, ACTUALLY, IT'S THE CAT'S FAULT.
MAC

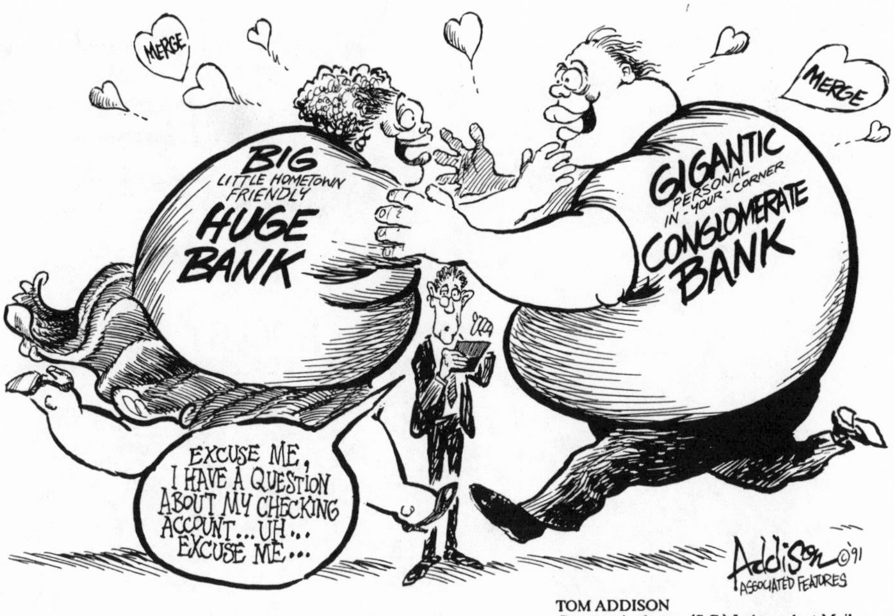
MERGE
MERGE
BIG LITTLE HOMETOWN FRIENDLY HUGE BANK
GIGANTIC PERSONAL IN-YOUR-CORNER CONGLOMERATE BANK
EXCUSE ME, I HAVE A QUESTION ABOUT MY CHECKING ACCOUNT...UH... EXCUSE ME...
Addison ©'91 ASSOCIATED FEATURES

TOM ADDISON
Courtesy Anderson (S.C.) Independent Mail and Associated Features Syndicate

J. R. ROSE
Courtesy Warren Sentinel (Va.)

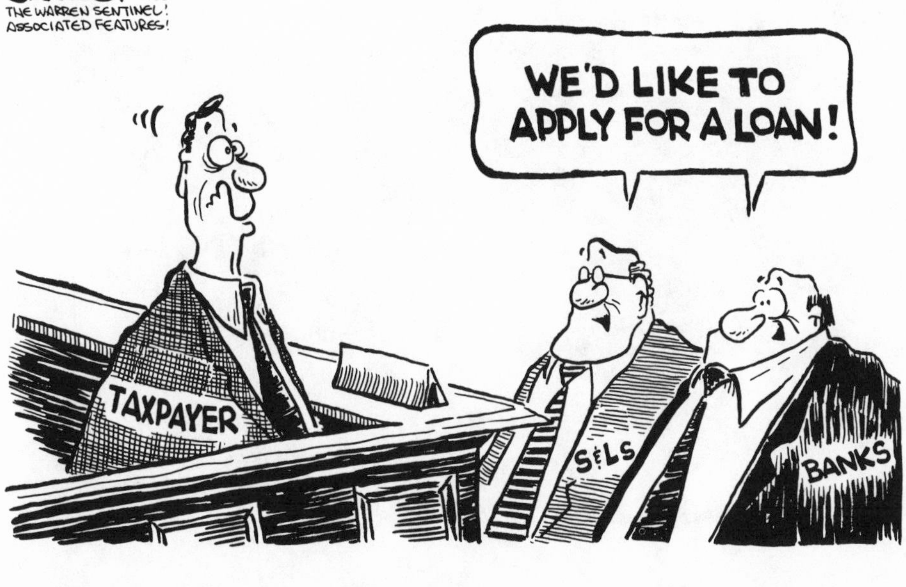
JRROSE! ©1991 THE WARREN SENTINEL! ASSOCIATED FEATURES!
WE'D LIKE TO APPLY FOR A LOAN!
TAXPAYER
S&LS
BANKS

STEVE KELLEY
Courtesy San Diego Union

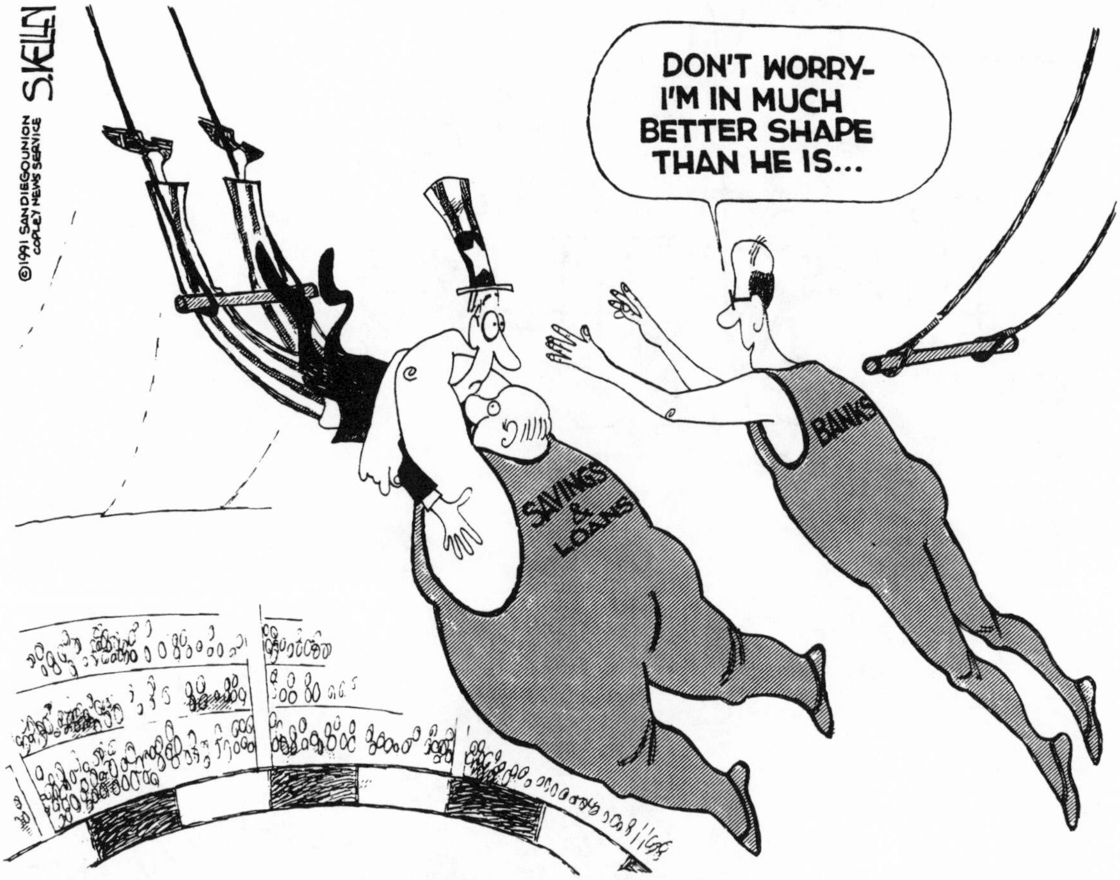
S.KELLEY
©1991 SANDIEGOUNION COPLEY NEWS SERVICE
DON'T WORRY- I'M IN MUCH BETTER SHAPE THAN HE IS...
SAVINGS & LOANS
BANKS

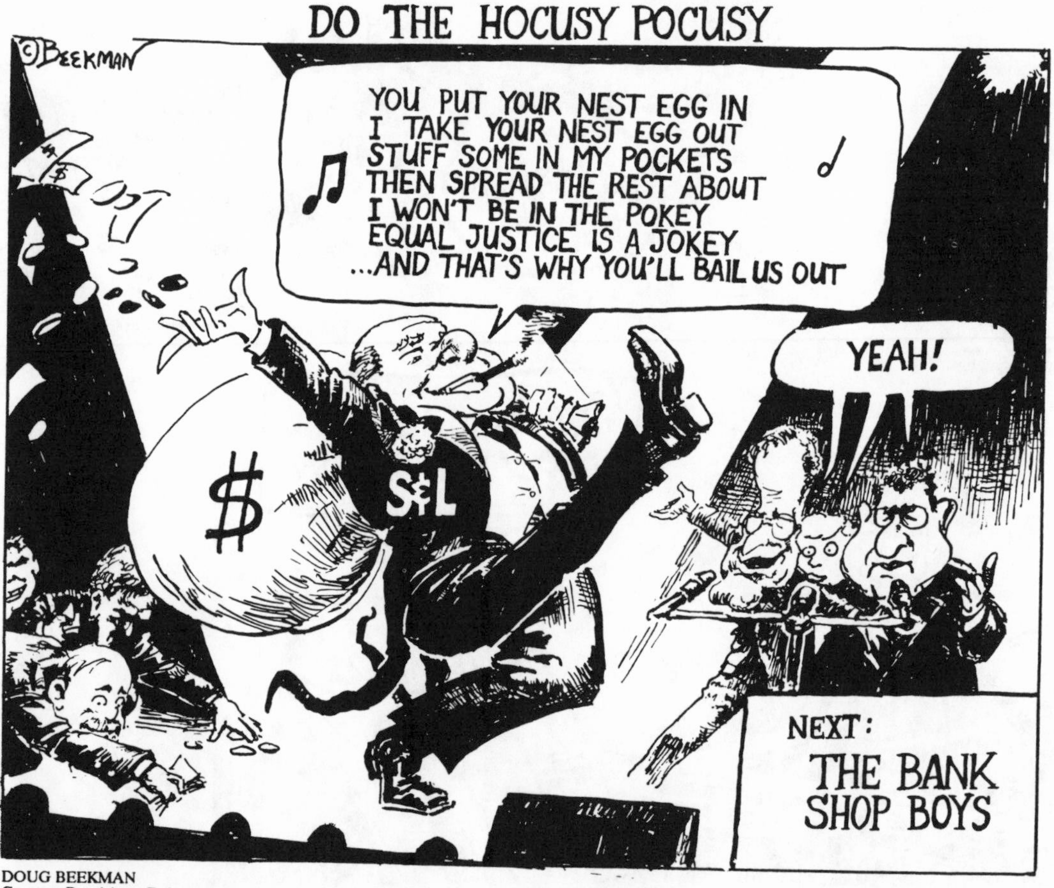
DO THE HOCUSY POCUSY
©BEEKMAN
YOU PUT YOUR NEST EGG IN
I TAKE YOUR NEST EGG OUT
STUFF SOME IN MY POCKETS
THEN SPREAD THE REST ABOUT
I WON'T BE IN THE POKEY
EQUAL JUSTICE IS A JOKEY
...AND THAT'S WHY YOU'LL BAIL US OUT
YEAH!
$
S&L
NEXT: THE BANK SHOP BOYS

DOUG BEEKMAN
Courtesy Brattleboro Reformer

Senator Kennedy

Sen. Edward Kennedy of Massachusetts found himself in the news again in 1991, this time as a key figure in a highly publicized rape case in Florida. The senator's nephew, William Kennedy Smith, was charged with rape in Palm Beach, where he had been visiting with his uncle and his cousin, Patrick. Senator Kennedy apparently had awakened the two young men sometime after midnight and invited them to go out with him to a bar.

Later, at a night spot called Au Bar, Smith met a thirty-one-year-old woman, the stepdaughter of a millionaire. The two danced and eventually drove back to the Kennedy home where, after a walk on the beach, the alleged rape took place. The trial was covered by network television and was watched by millions of viewers across the country. Senator Kennedy was called to the stand and questioned about events leading up to the incident, particularly about exactly when he first heard of the charges. It was never clearly established whether he had known of the charges before he left for Washington the next day. Smith's defense cost an estimated $1 million, and it took only seventy-seven minutes for the jury to return a verdict of "not guilty."

Senator Kennedy's reputation for drinking and womanizing seemed to be hurting him politically, and in a surprising speech at Harvard he took responsibility for "faults in the conduct of my private life."

MIKE LUCKOVICH
Courtesy Atlanta Constitution

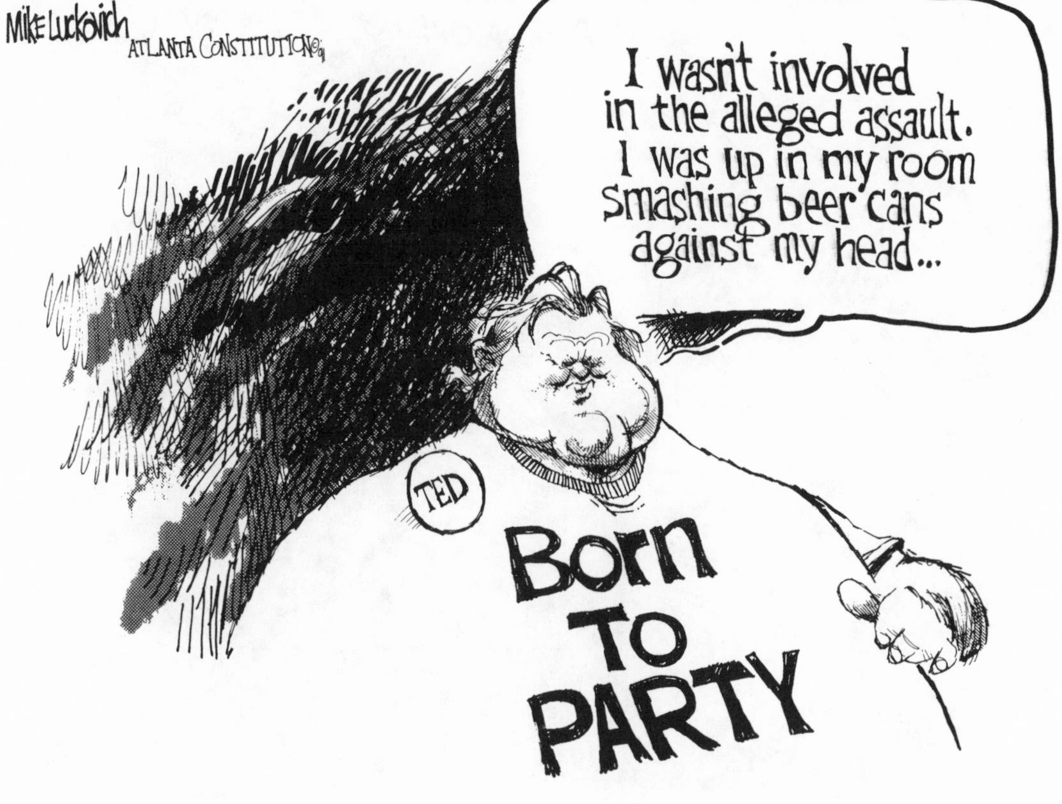
Mike Luckovich
ATLANTA CONSTITUTION
I wasn't involved in the alleged assault. I was up in my room smashing beer cans against my head...
TED
Born TO PARTY

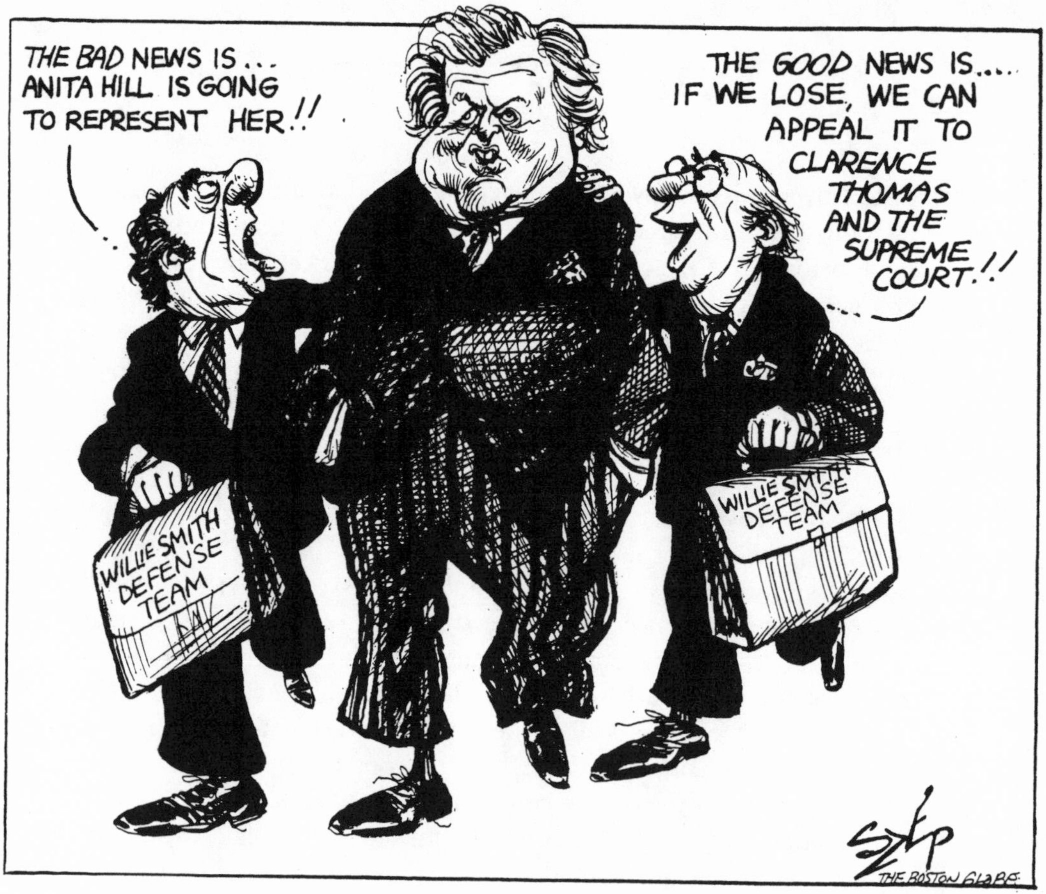
THE BAD NEWS IS...
ANITA HILL IS GOING TO REPRESENT HER.!!
THE GOOD NEWS IS.... IF WE LOSE, WE CAN APPEAL IT TO CLARENCE THOMAS AND THE SUPREME COURT.!!
WILLIE SMITH DEFENSE TEAM
WILLIE SMITH DEFENSE TEAM
SZEP
THE BOSTON GLOBE

PAUL SZEP
Courtesy Boston Globe

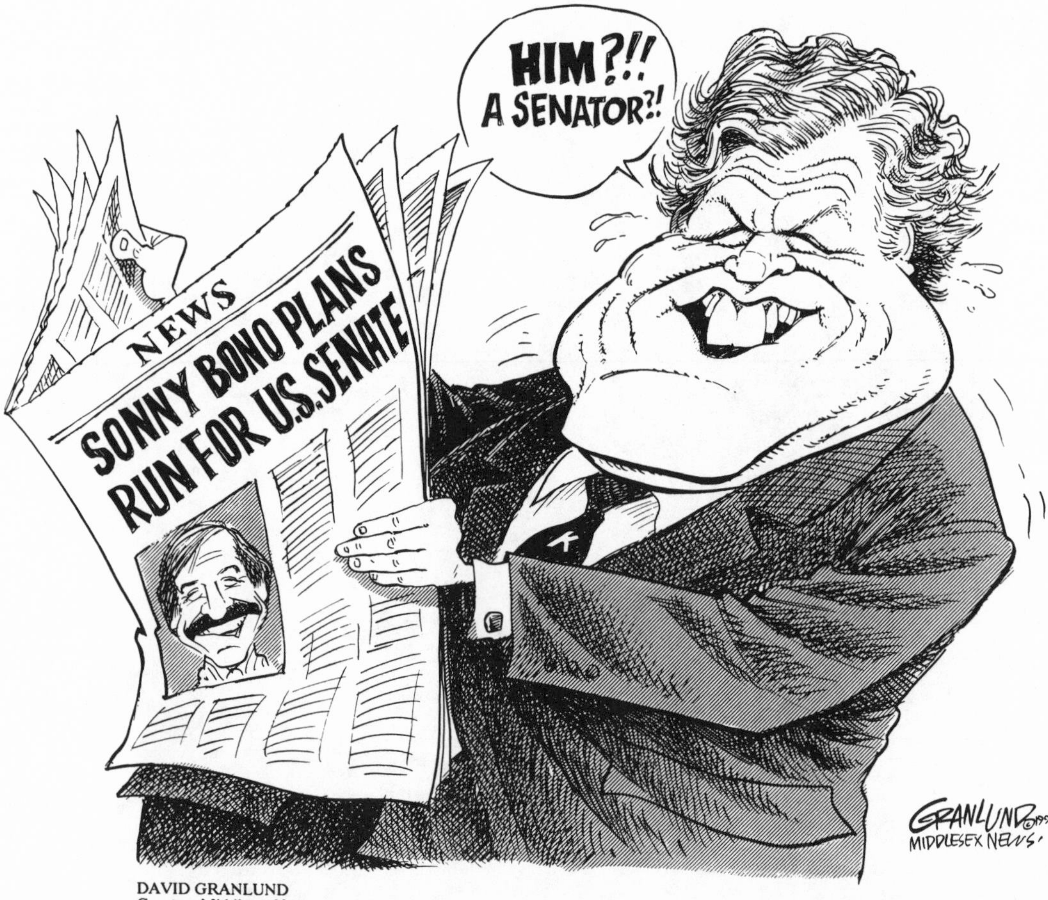
HIM?!!
A SENATOR?!
NEWS
SONNY BONO PLANS RUN FOR U.S. SENATE
GRANLUND ©1991
MIDDLESEX NEWS

DAVID GRANLUND
Courtesy Middlesex News

YOU HAVE TO BELIEVE ME!! I DIDN'T DO ANYTHING WRONG!!
PALM BEACH COURTHOUSE
ALL I DID WAS GO OUT DRINKING AND TRY TO HUSTLE CHICKS!!!
I'M INNOCENT I TELL YA!!!!
NO ONE'S ACCUSING YOU OF ANYTHING, TED...
KIRK
©1991 The (Toledo) Blade

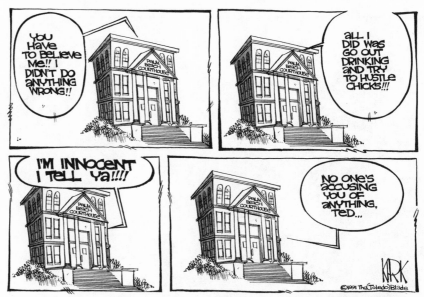

KIRK WALTERS
Courtesy Toledo Blade

GARY BROOKINS
Courtesy Richmond Times-Dispatch

BROOKINS 1991 · RICHMOND TIMES-DISPATCH 8/2
MASSACHUSETTS
POLLS

...HELLO?... ANITA HILL? HOW'D YOU LIKE TO COME OVER TO THE SENATE FOR A LITTLE... UH... DEBRIEFING ?
DEMS

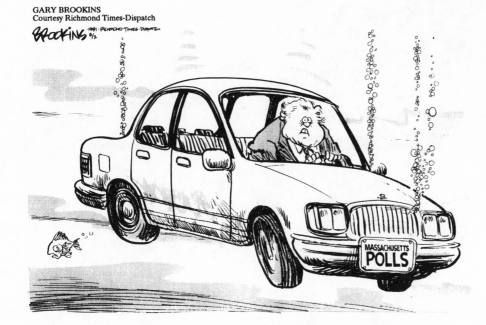

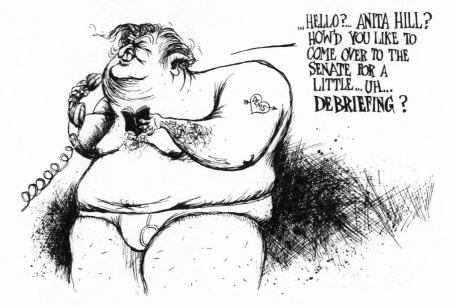

MIKE SHELTON
Courtesy Orange County Register
and King Features Syndicate

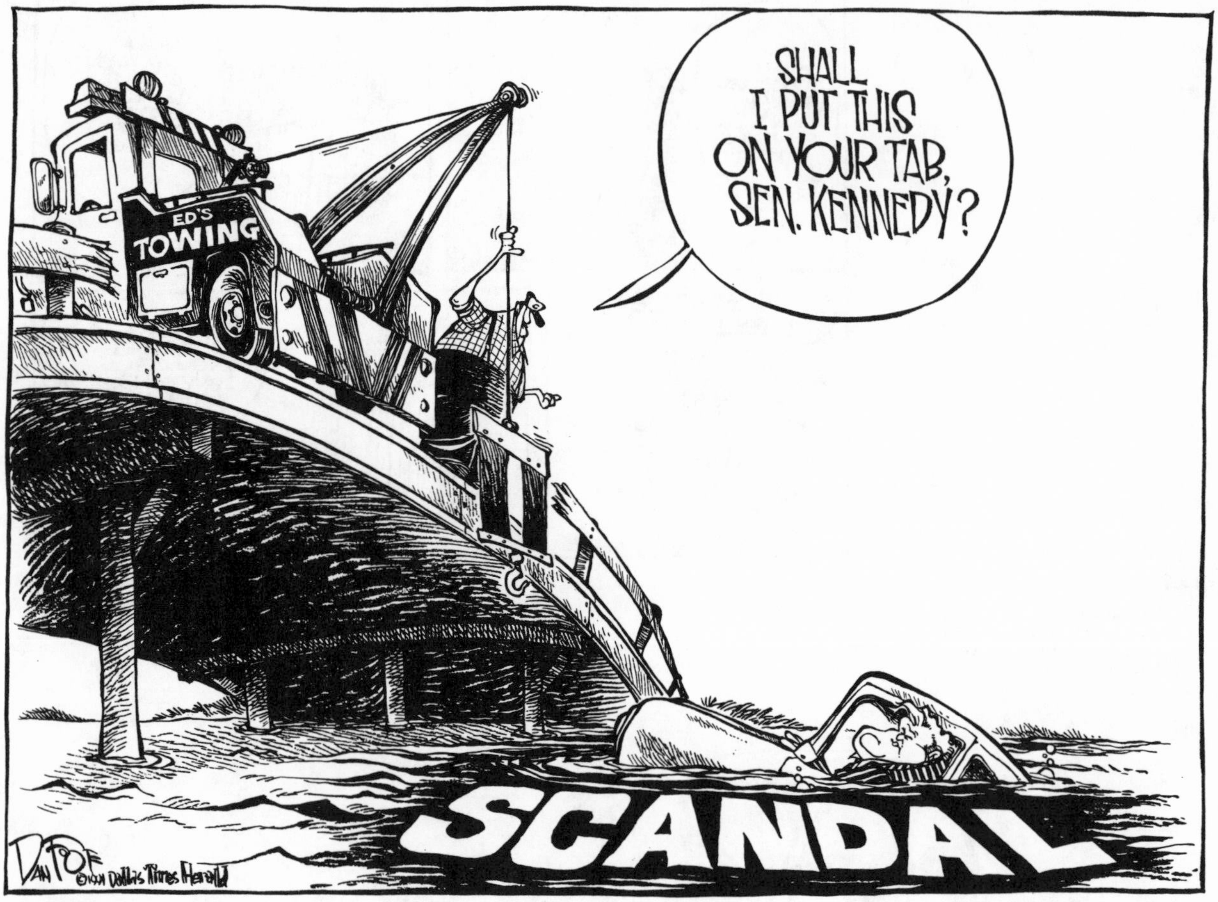
SHALL I PUT THIS ON YOUR TAB, SEN. KENNEDY?
ED'S TOWING
SCANDAL

DAN FOOTE
Courtesy Dallas Times Herald

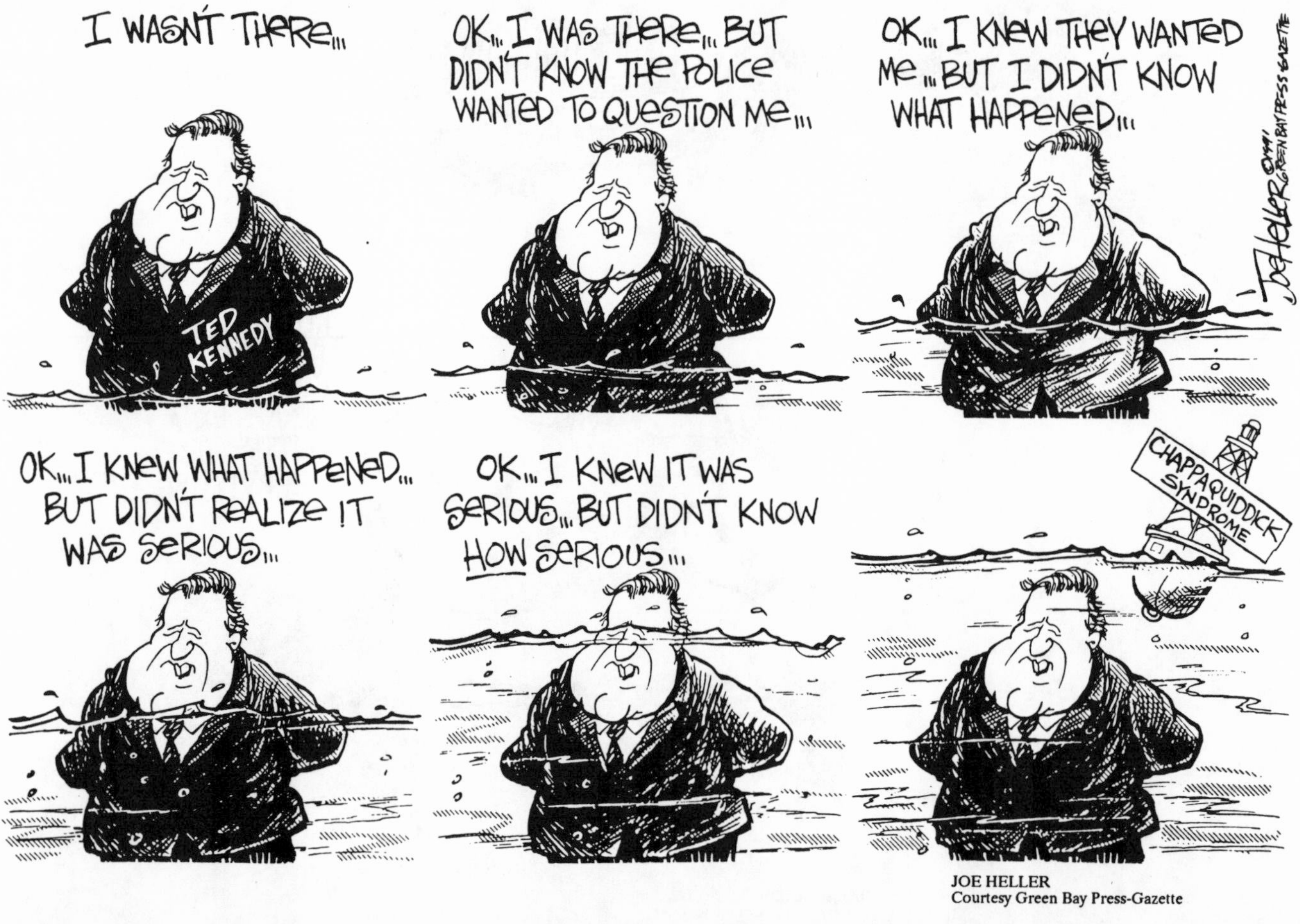
I WASN'T THERE...
TED KENNEDY
OK... I WAS THERE... BUT DIDN'T KNOW THE POLICE WANTED TO QUESTION ME...
OK... I KNEW THEY WANTED ME... BUT I DIDN'T KNOW WHAT HAPPENED...
OK... I KNEW WHAT HAPPENED... BUT DIDN'T REALIZE IT WAS SERIOUS...
OK... I KNEW IT WAS SERIOUS... BUT DIDN'T KNOW HOW SERIOUS...
CHAPPAQUIDDICK SYNDROME

JOE HELLER
Courtesy Green Bay Press-Gazette

BOB GORRELL
Courtesy Richmond News

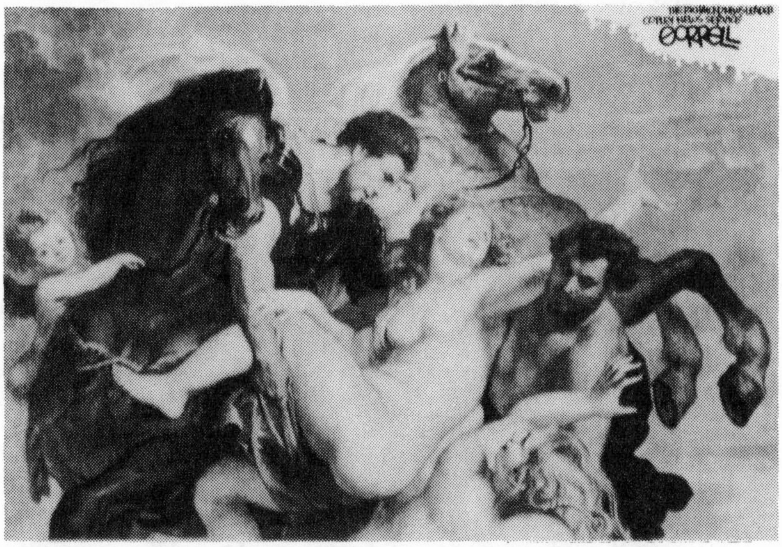
GORRELL

"SO. . . . IS THIS YOUR FIRST VISIT TO THE KENNEDY COMPOUND?"

DICK WRIGHT
Courtesy Providence Journal-Bulletin

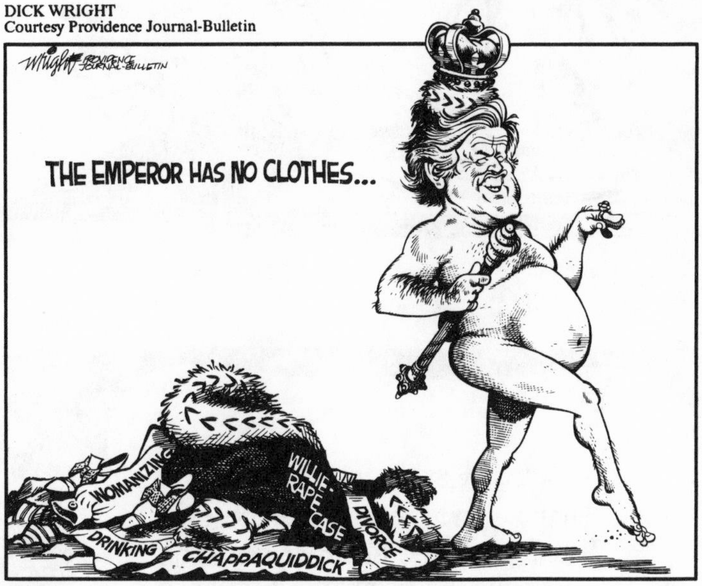
THE EMPEROR HAS NO CLOTHES...
WOMANIZING
WILLIE-RAPE-CASE
DIVORCE
DRINKING
CHAPPAQUIDDICK

KEN CATALINO
Courtesy Anchorage Times

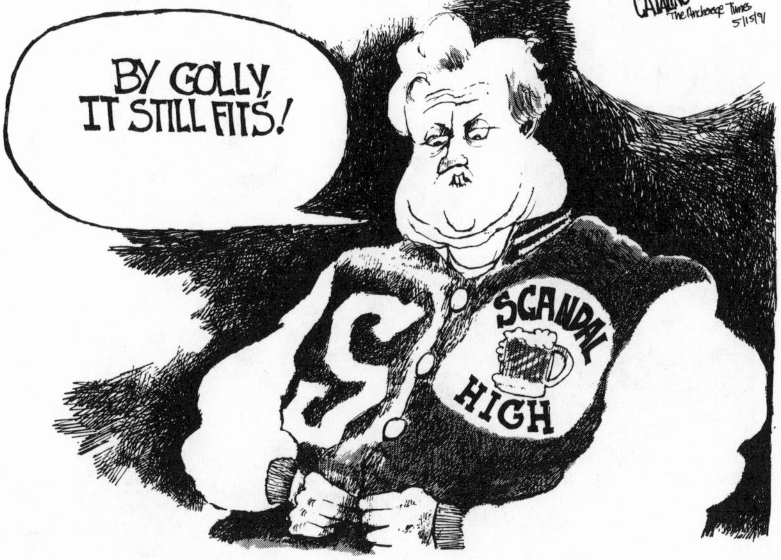
CATALINO The Anchorage Times 5/15/91
BY GOLLY, IT STILL FITS!
S
SCANDAL HIGH

DAVID HORSEY
Courtesy Seattle Post-Intelligencer

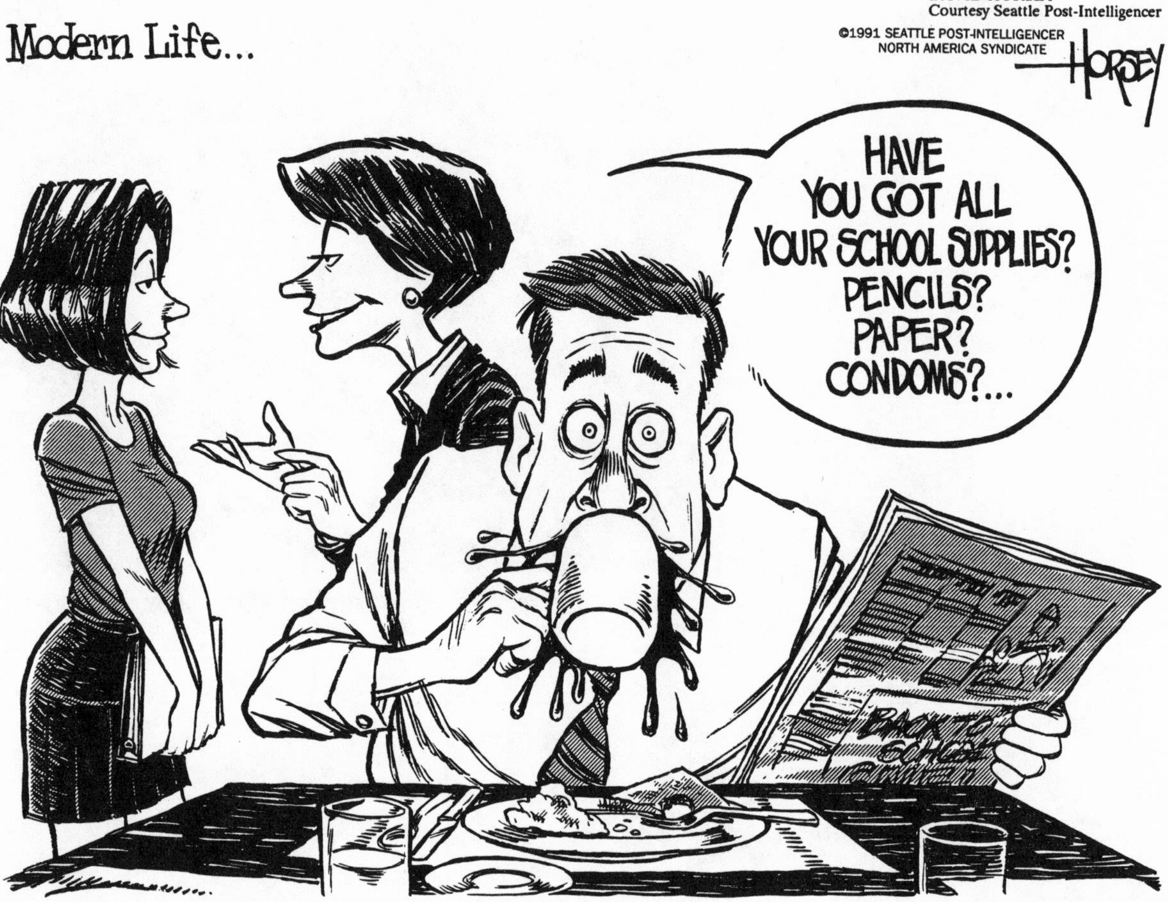
Modern Life...
©1991 SEATTLE POST-INTELLIGENCER
NORTH AMERICA SYNDICATE
HORSEY
HAVE YOU GOT ALL YOUR SCHOOL SUPPLIES? PENCILS? PAPER? CONDOMS?...

MICHAEL RAMIREZ
Courtesy Memphis Commercial Appeal

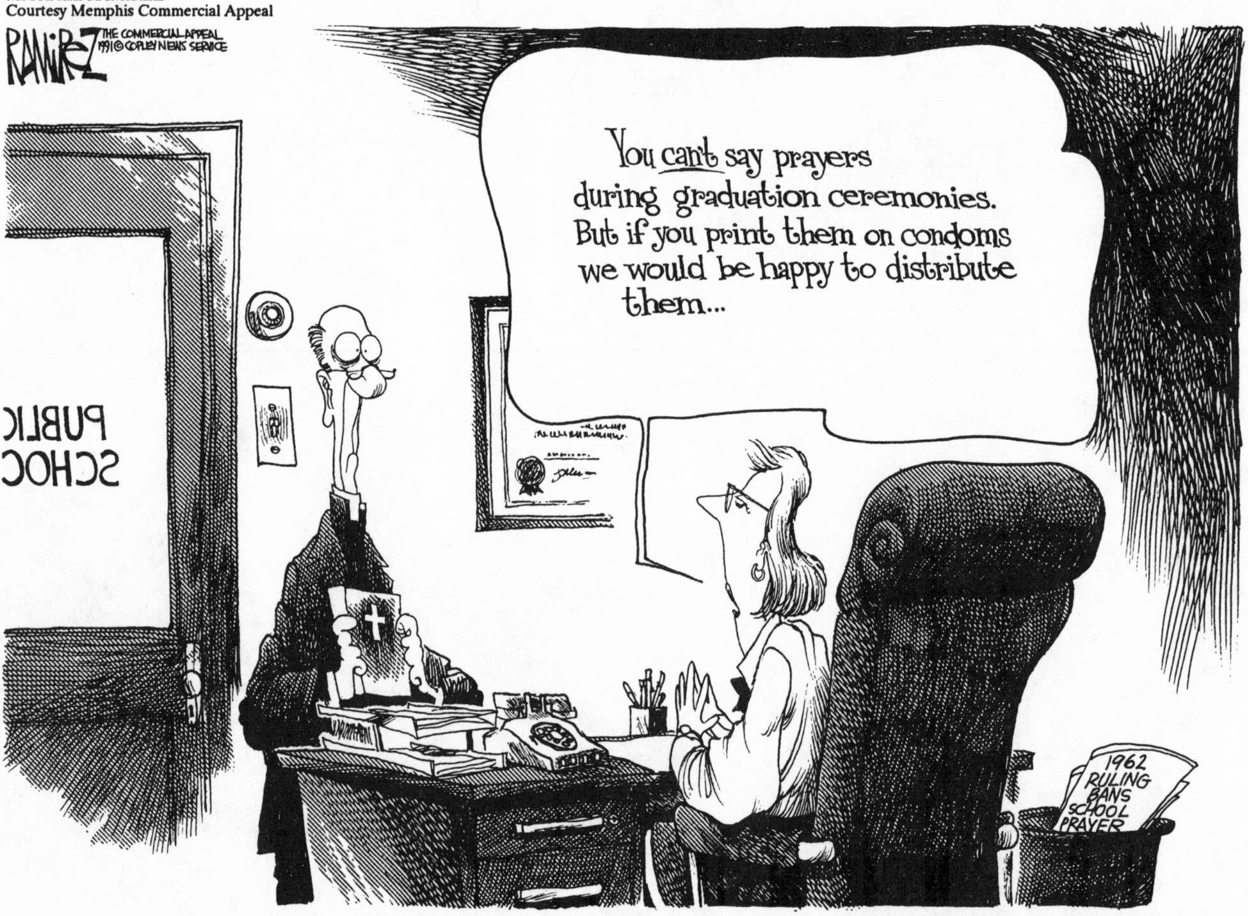
RAMIREZ
THE COMMERCIAL APPEAL 1991 © COPLEY NEWS SERVICE
You can't say prayers during graduation ceremonies. But if you print them on condoms we would be happy to distribute them...
PUBLIC SCHOC
1962 RULING BANS SCHOOL PRAYER

Education

Federal and state governments continued to search for answers to education problems in the U.S. Polls in 1991 indicated that parents believe schoolchildren in America are not getting as good an education as are the youth of Japan and Germany. Test scores seem to confirm that view.

Florida announced plans to turn to private companies to manage an entire school system. Other states were beginning to monitor more closely what was being taught in their schools and how it was being done.

President Bush's chief architect for repairing education is Chester Finn, Jr., a professor of education and public policy at Vanderbilt University. He is working on a new plan for schools that Bush plans to push in 1992. Despite some reforms by teachers and local governments, public schools still are not teaching the basic skills and work habits required in the modern world. School administrators across the country continued the call for more funds during the year.

New York City jolted conservatives–and a lot of liberals, as well–when it announced that condoms would be dispensed free in its public schools to students who asked for them. The measure was said to be an effort to combat sexually transmitted diseases, mainly AIDS, which has been spreading at an alarming rate. Others viewed it as one more sign of an overly permissive society.

IS IT TOTALLY AWESOME OR WHAT, THAT MTV'S BEEN ON TEN YEARS?... TEN YEARS! I'LL BET NOTHIN' GOOD'S EVER BEEN AROUND THAT LONG BEFORE...
MOTLEY CRUDE
MARK TWAIN
HERMAN MELVILLE
WILLA CATHER
CHARLOTTE & EMILY BRONTE
JOHN STEINBECK
The Works of WILLIAM SHAKESPEARE
PLATO
THE WORKS OF CHARLES DICKENS
JEFF KOTERBA 1991 Omaha World-Herald

JEFF KOTERBA
Courtesy Omaha World-Herald

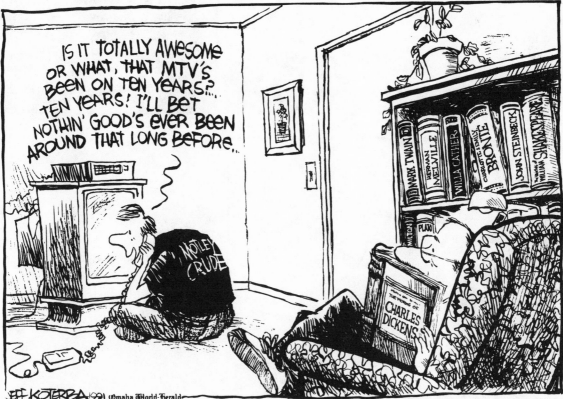

FRANK CAMMUSO
Courtesy Syracuse Herald-Journal

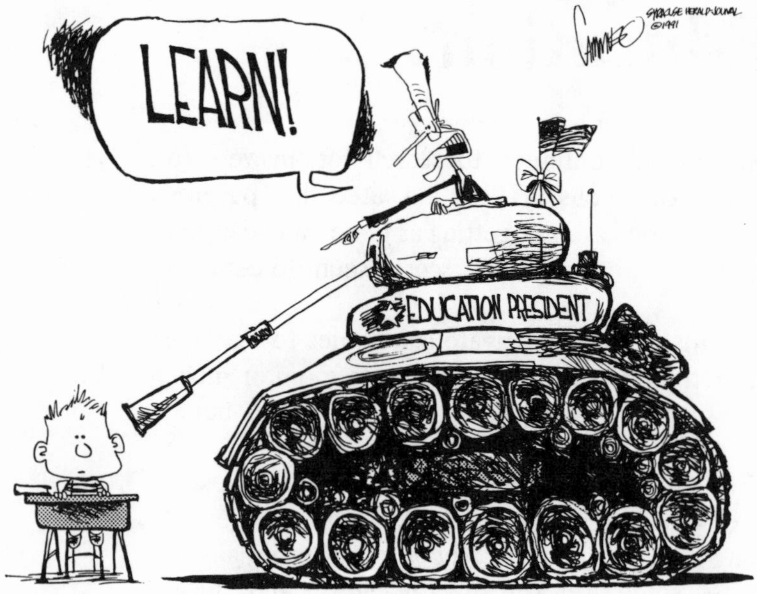
LEARN!
EDUCATION PRESIDENT

PETER B. WALLACE
Courtesy Boston Herald

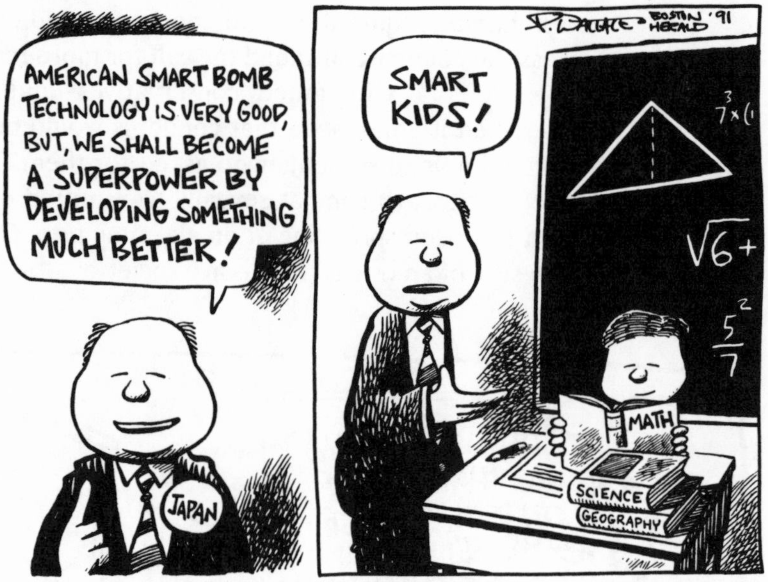
AMERICAN SMART BOMB TECHNOLOGY IS VERY GOOD, BUT, WE SHALL BECOME A SUPERPOWER BY DEVELOPING SOMETHING MUCH BETTER!
JAPAN
SMART KIDS!
MATH
SCIENCE
GEOGRAPHY

SCOTT WILLIS
Courtesy San Jose Mercury

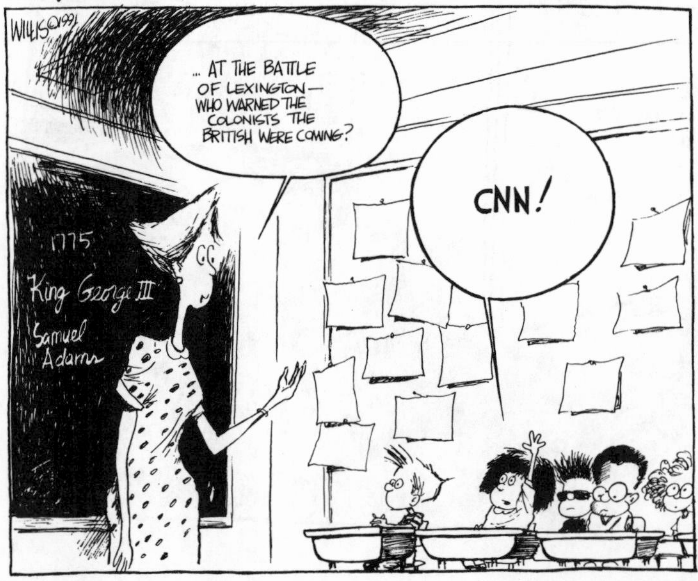
... AT THE BATTLE OF LEXINGTON— WHO WARNED THE COLONISTS THE BRITISH WERE COMING?
CNN!
1775
King George III
Samuel Adams

BRUCE BEATTIE
Courtesy Daytona Beach News-Journal

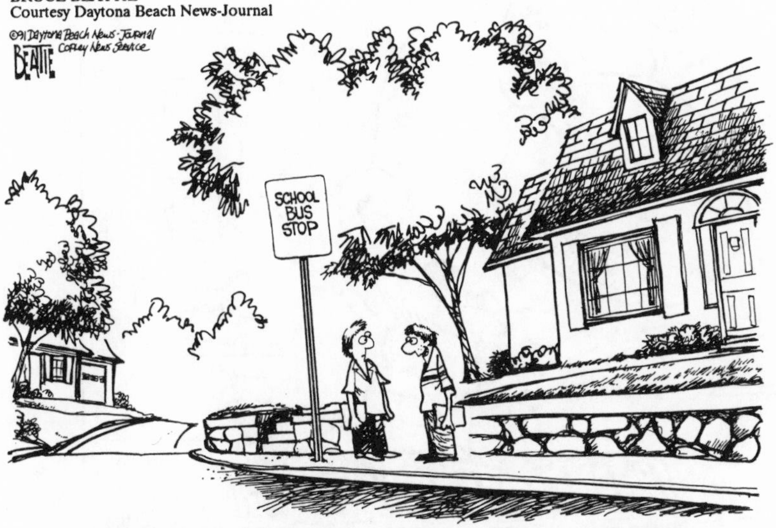
SCHOOL BUS STOP
BEATTIE

"I hope they revamp the U.S. education system. I want to be able to operate all the neat products the Japanese will be selling us in 20 years!"

DAVID DONAR
Courtesy Macomb Daily (Miss.)

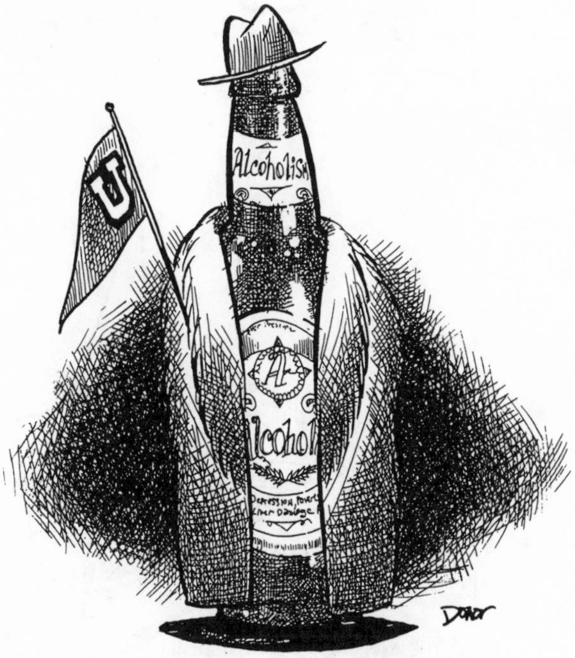
U
Alcoholism
Alcohol
Donar

BIG MAN ON CAMPUS

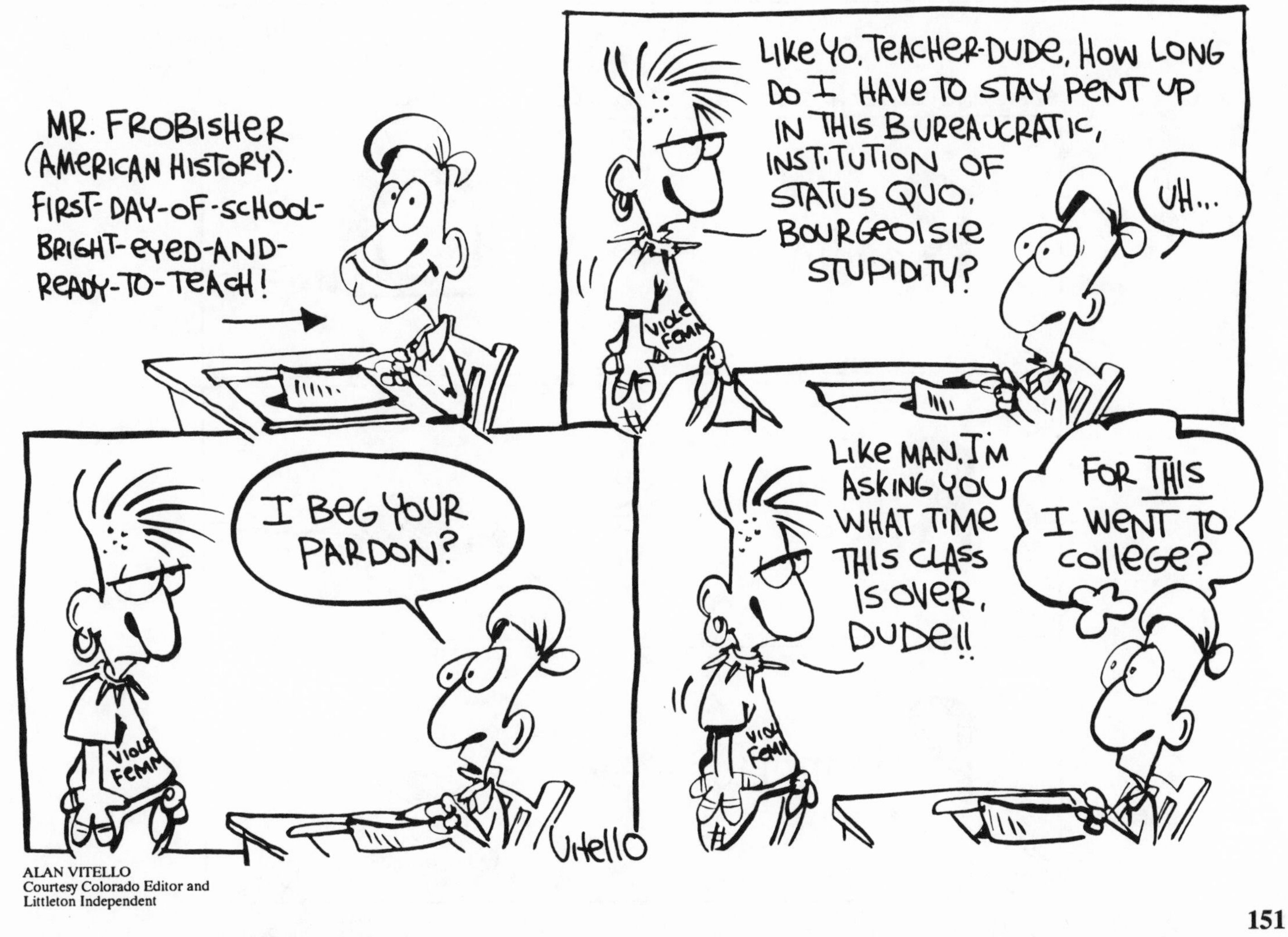
MR. FROBISHER (AMERICAN HISTORY). FIRST-DAY-OF-SCHOOL-BRIGHT-EYED-AND-READY-TO-TEACH!
LIKE YO, TEACHER-DUDE, HOW LONG DO I HAVE TO STAY PENT UP IN THIS BUREAUCRATIC, INSTITUTION OF STATUS QUO, BOURGEOISIE STUPIDITY?
UH...
I BEG YOUR PARDON?
LIKE MAN, I'M ASKING YOU WHAT TIME THIS CLASS IS OVER, DUDE!!
FOR THIS I WENT TO COLLEGE?
Vitello

ALAN VITELLO
Courtesy Colorado Editor and
Littleton Independent

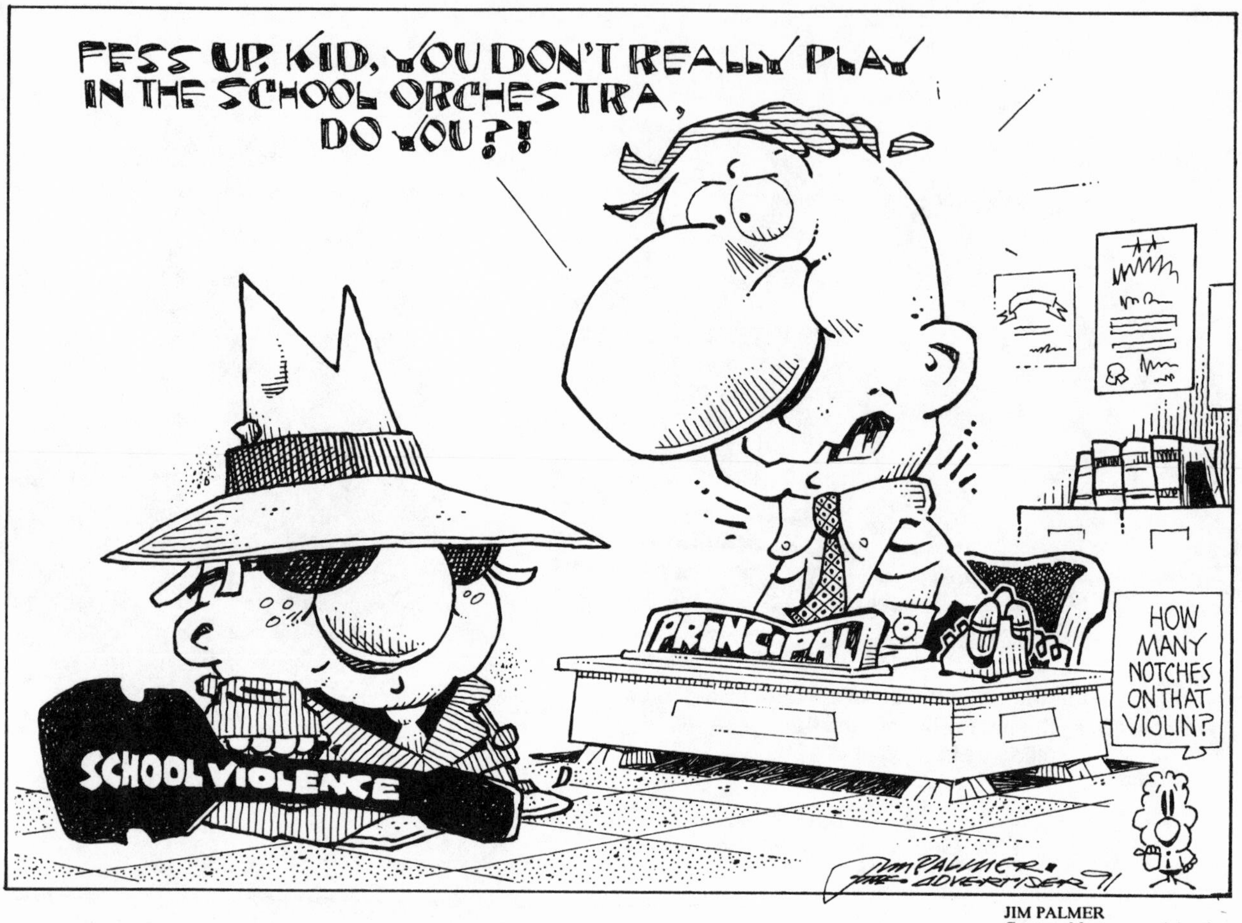
FESS UP, KID, YOU DON'T REALLY PLAY IN THE SCHOOL ORCHESTRA, DO YOU?!
PRINCIPAL
HOW MANY NOTCHES ON THAT VIOLIN?
SCHOOL VIOLENCE
JIM PALMER THE ADVERTISER 91

JIM PALMER
Courtesy Montgomery Advertiser

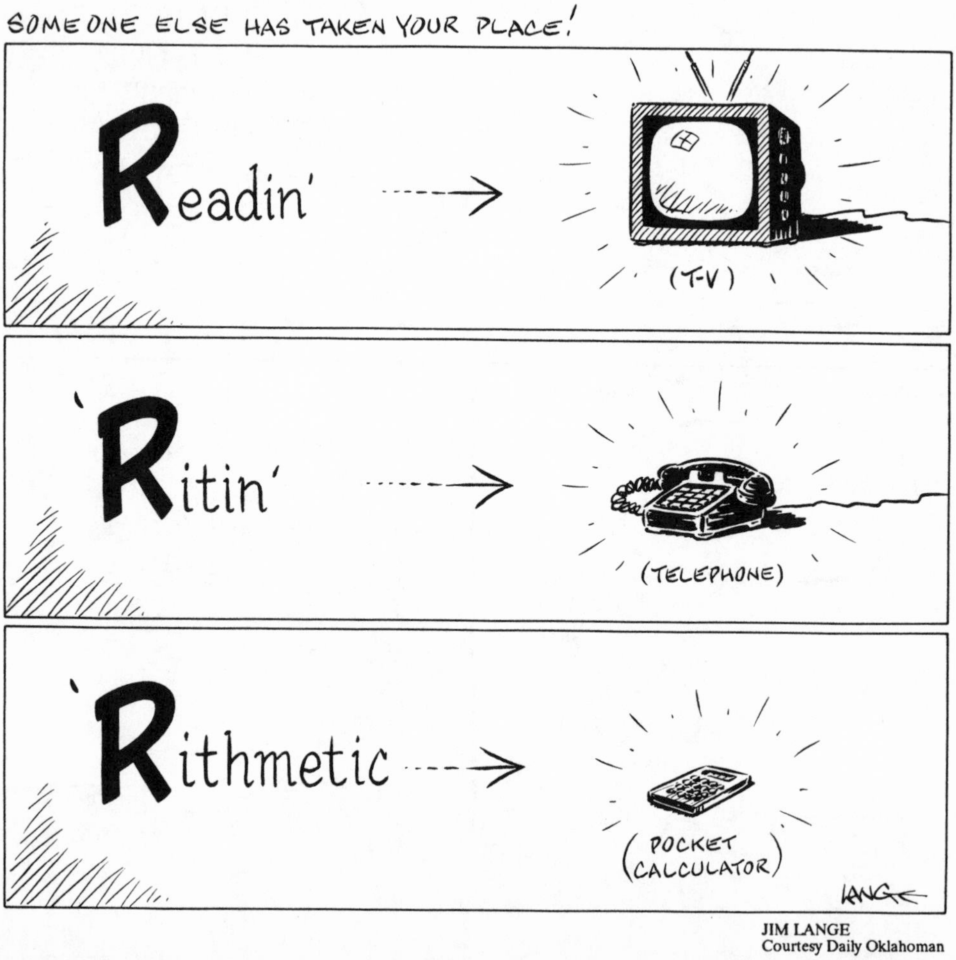
SOMEONE ELSE HAS TAKEN YOUR PLACE!
Readin'
(T-V)
'Ritin'
(TELEPHONE)
'Rithmetic
(POCKET CALCULATOR)
LANGE

JIM LANGE
Courtesy Daily Oklahoman

The Environment

After decades of programs to control urban pollution, nearly 100 American cities still fall short of the Environmental Protection Agency's health standards for clean air. Los Angeles has until the year 2010 to bring its dangerous ozone levels down to the federal government's standards. Despite the latest emission-control systems on new cars, the automobile remains the primary source of urban pollution.

Of the 6,000 garbage dumps operating in 1991, about half will be closed by 1996 as stricter environmental standards go into effect. New landfills are not opening as fast as they once did because of these strict new standards, and the cost of getting rid of garbage is rising rapidly.

Debate continued during the year on the so-called greenhouse effect, and whether or not the earth is cooling off. Concern also focused on reported holes in the ozone layer. Many scientists argue forcefully that these problems are not serious and that nature will take care of them over time. Other experts warn that time is running out on both problems.

KEVIN KALLAUGHER
Courtesy Baltimore Sun

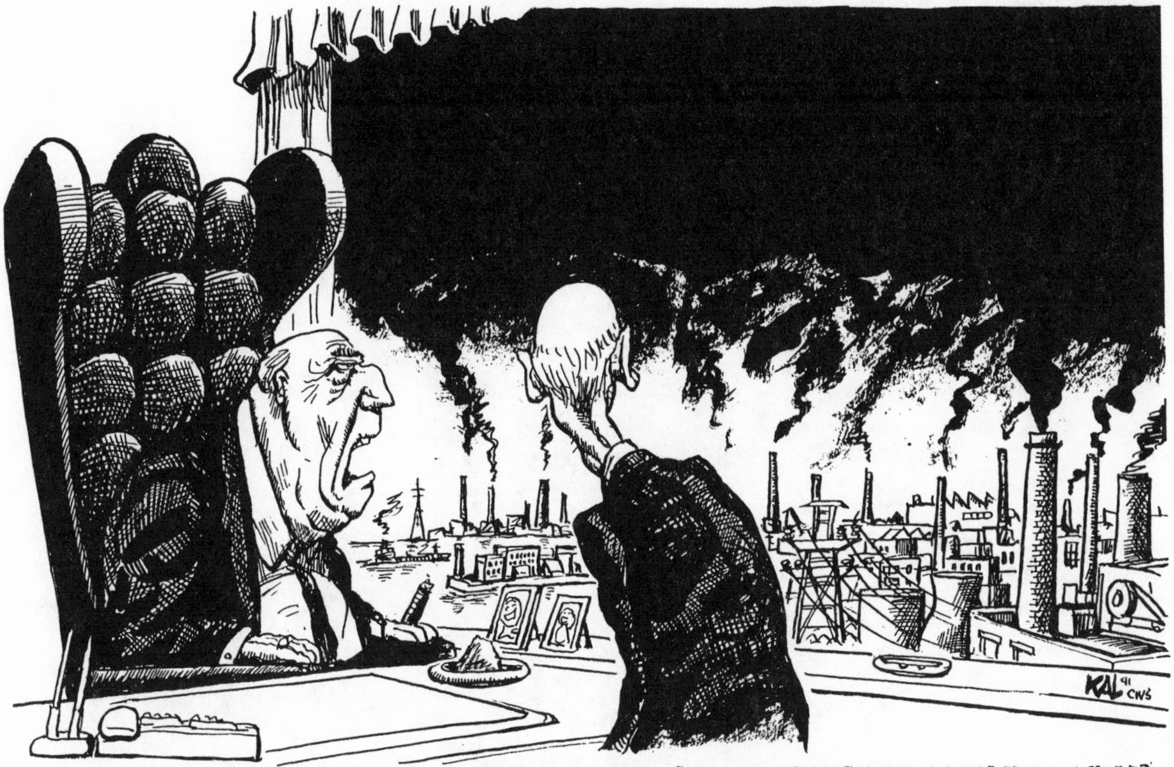
KAL '91 CWS

ALL THESE SCIENTISTS DO IS COMPLAIN ABOUT THE OZONE LAYER. LOOK OUT THERE, SMITHSON, DO YOU SEE A HOLE?

VIC CANTONE
Courtesy N.Y. Daily News

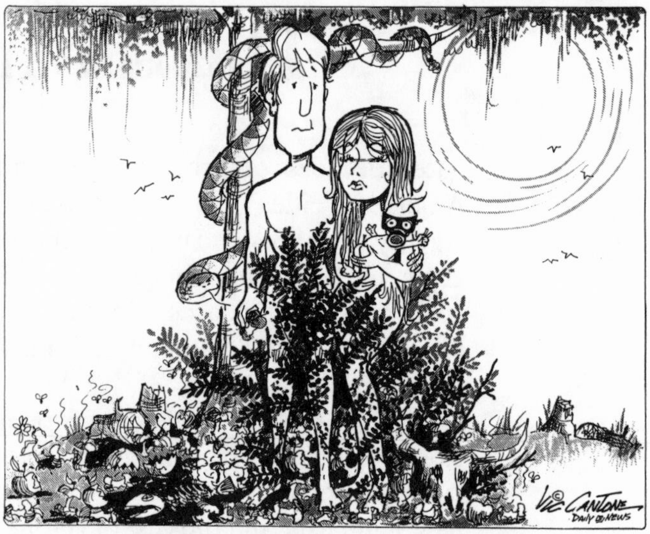
VIC CANTONE
Daily News

YESTERDAY, TODAY AND TOMORROW.

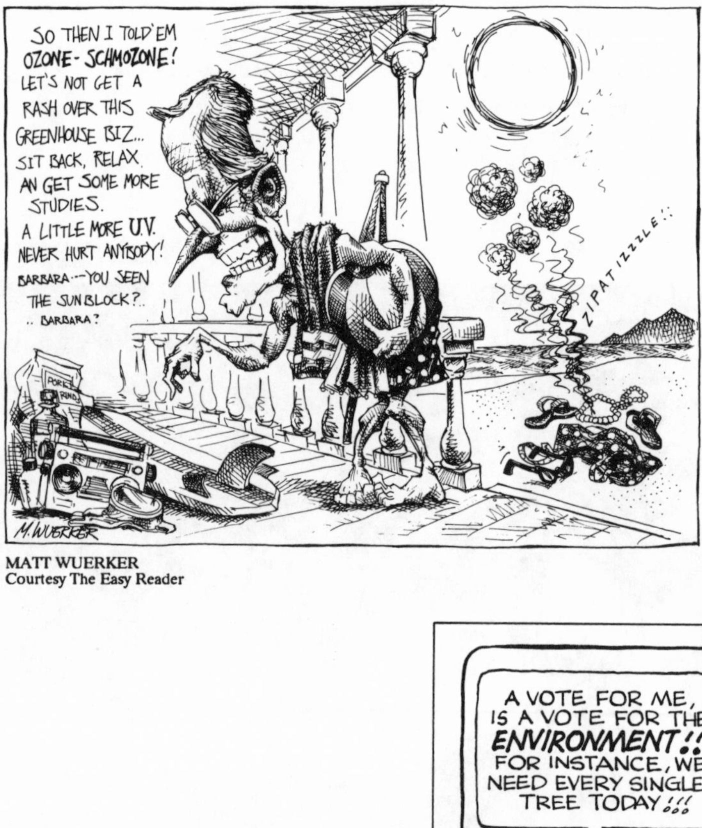
SO THEN I TOLD'EM OZONE-SCHMOZONE! LET'S NOT GET A RASH OVER THIS GREENHOUSE BIZ... SIT BACK, RELAX AN GET SOME MORE STUDIES. A LITTLE MORE U.V. NEVER HURT ANYBODY! BARBARA---YOU SEEN THE SUN BLOCK?.. BARBARA?
ZIPATIZZZLE!!
M. WUERKER

MATT WUERKER
Courtesy The Easy Reader

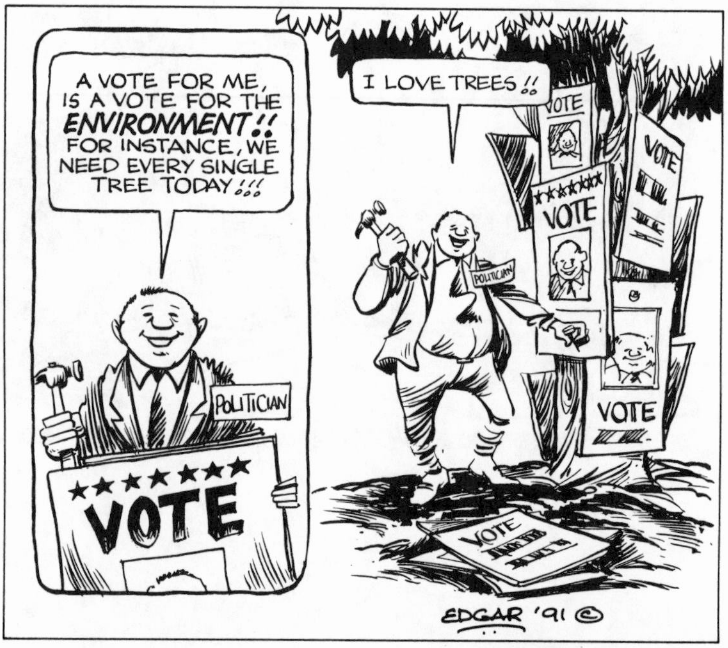
A VOTE FOR ME, IS A VOTE FOR THE ENVIRONMENT!! FOR INSTANCE, WE NEED EVERY SINGLE TREE TODAY!!!
I LOVE TREES!!
POLITICIAN
VOTE
VOTE
EDGAR '91 ©

EDGAR D'SOUZA
Courtesy Sparta Independent (N.J.)

JERRY BUCKLEY
Courtesy Express Newspapers

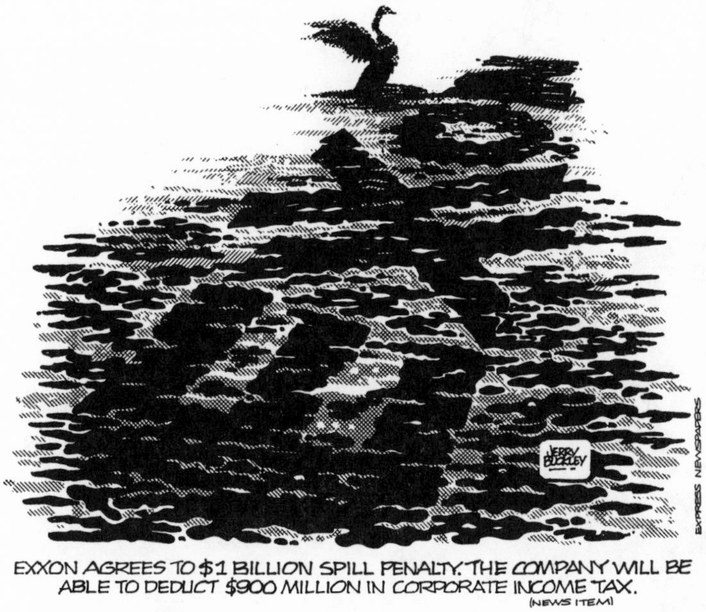
JERRY BUCKLEY
EXPRESS NEWSPAPERS
EXXON AGREES TO $1 BILLION SPILL PENALTY. THE COMPANY WILL BE ABLE TO DEDUCT $900 MILLION IN CORPORATE INCOME TAX.
(NEWS ITEM)

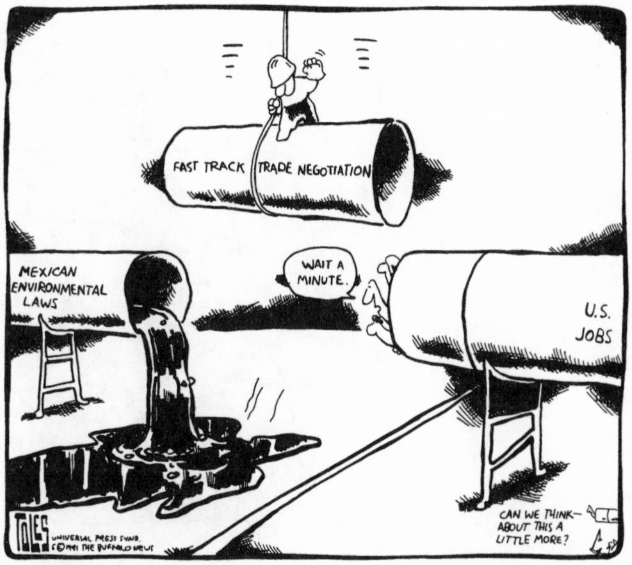
FAST TRACK
TRADE NEGOTIATION
MEXICAN ENVIRONMENTAL LAWS
WAIT A MINUTE.
U.S. JOBS
CAN WE THINK— ABOUT THIS A LITTLE MORE?
TOLES

TOM TOLES
Courtesy Buffalo News and
Universal Press Syndicate

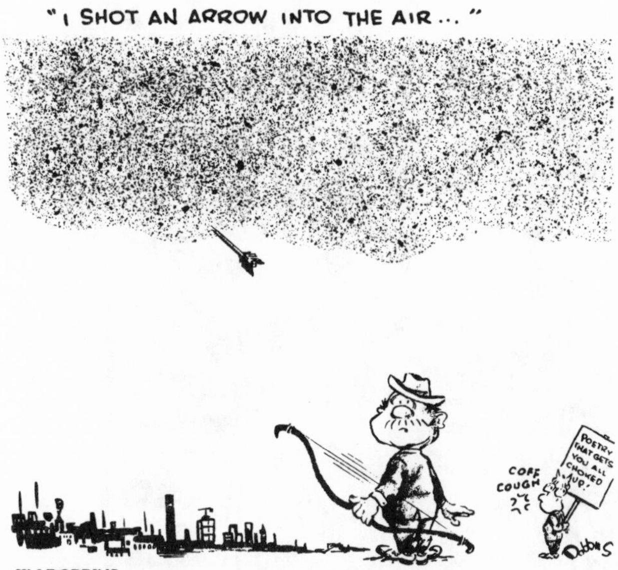
"I SHOT AN ARROW INTO THE AIR..."
COFF COUGH
POETRY THAT GETS YOU ALL CHOKED UP.
DOBBINS

JIM DOBBINS
Courtesy N.A.G.E. Reporter

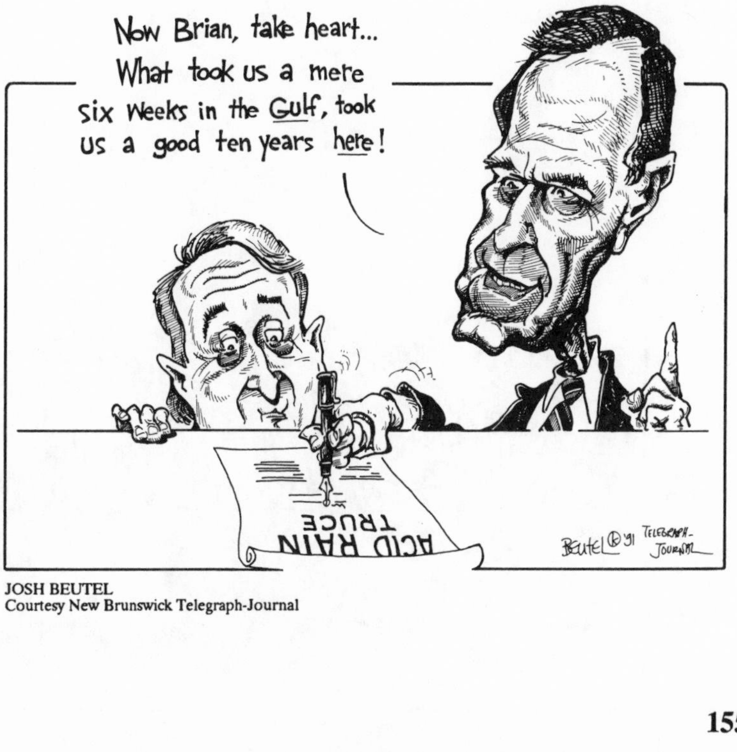
Now Brian, take heart... What took us a mere six weeks in the Gulf, took us a good ten years here!
ACID RAIN TRUCE
BEUTEL '91 TELEGRAPH-JOURNAL

JOSH BEUTEL
Courtesy New Brunswick Telegraph-Journal

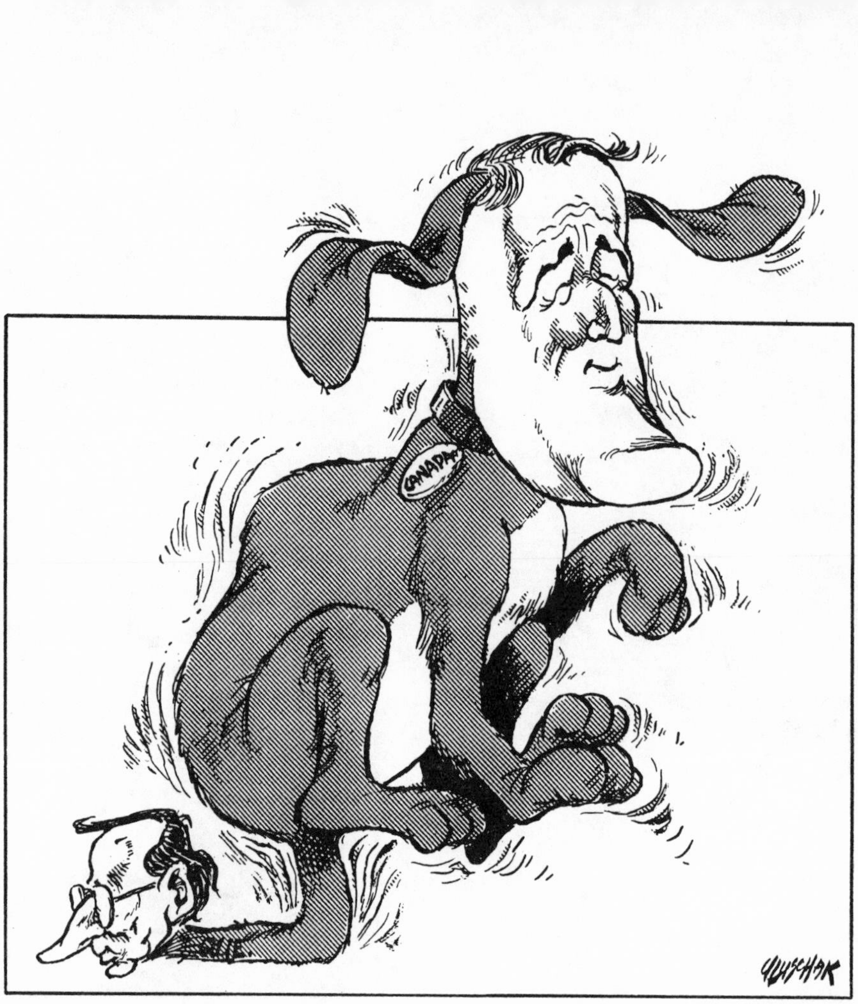
CANADA
ULUSCHAK

EDD ULUSCHAK
Courtesy Miller Features

DENNY PRITCHARD
Courtesy Ottawa Citizen

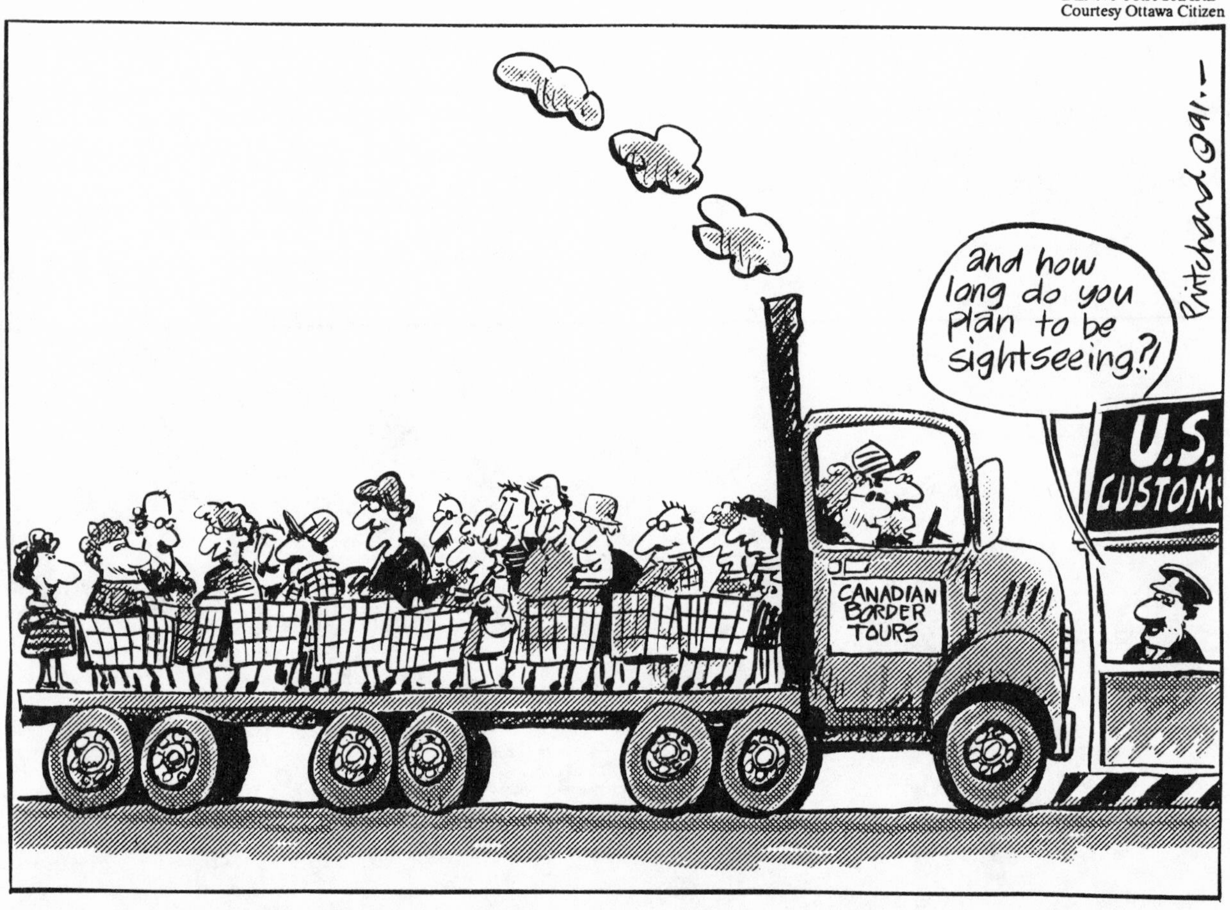
and how long do you plan to be sightseeing?!
Pritchard ©91.-
U.S. CUSTOMS
CANADIAN BORDER TOURS

Canada

It did not make the front pages like the splintering of the Soviet Union, but Canada, too, in 1991 struggled with its own separatist movement. Prime Minister Brian Mulroney labored hard much of the year to put together political reforms that would dissuade Quebec from seceding from Canada to form a new French-speaking nation. The result may be a referendum by the citizens of Quebec in 1992. Of the 6.8 million residents of Quebec, 83 percent speak French and many believe they do not need to be a part of Canada to prosper. Quebec already has its own income tax and civil law.

Two English-speaking provinces voted against the 1990 Meech Lake Accord, which would have amended the Canadian Constitution to recognize Quebec as a "distinct society" and given it more control over its own affairs. The vote inflamed independence fever throughout Quebec. Many people, including top business leaders, cautioned, however, that a vote to go it alone could be costly for Quebec.

Inflation cut the buying power of Canadian workers, and a recession forced business to tighten its belt. Unions pushed their demands with strikes, one of which stopped the mail, causing loud protests from pensioners who did not receive their checks. Indians continued to protest the cutting of trees on what they believe to be their land, and more businesses moved across the border to the U.S.

ROY PETERSON
Courtesy Vancouver Sun

Your problem is that, as a non~Quebecer, you think like an English~Canadian.

Your problem is that, as a Canadian, I think like a Canadian.

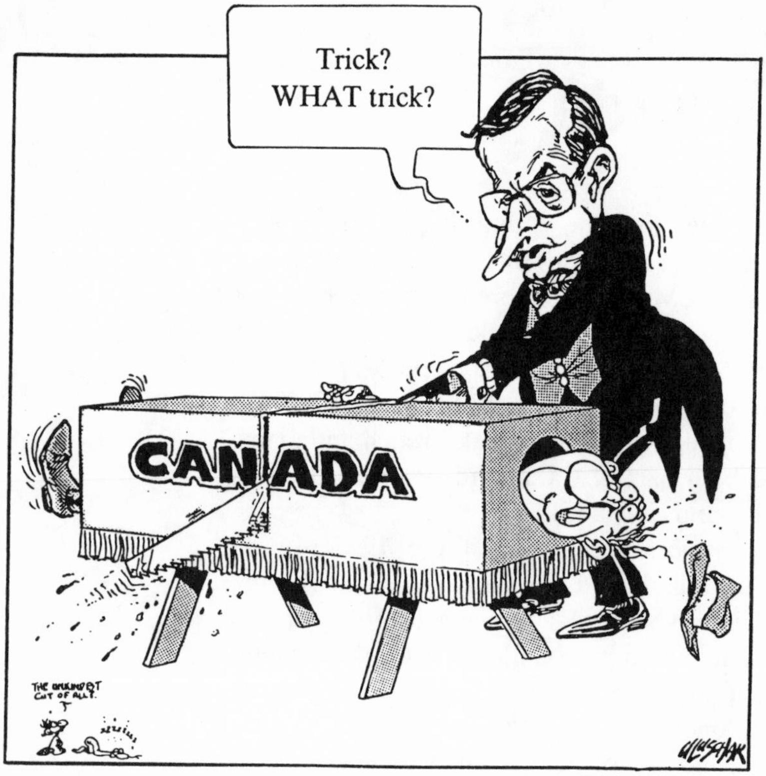
Trick?
WHAT trick?
CANADA
THE UNKINDEST CUT OF ALL.
ULUSCHAK

EDD ULUSCHAK
Courtesy Miller Features

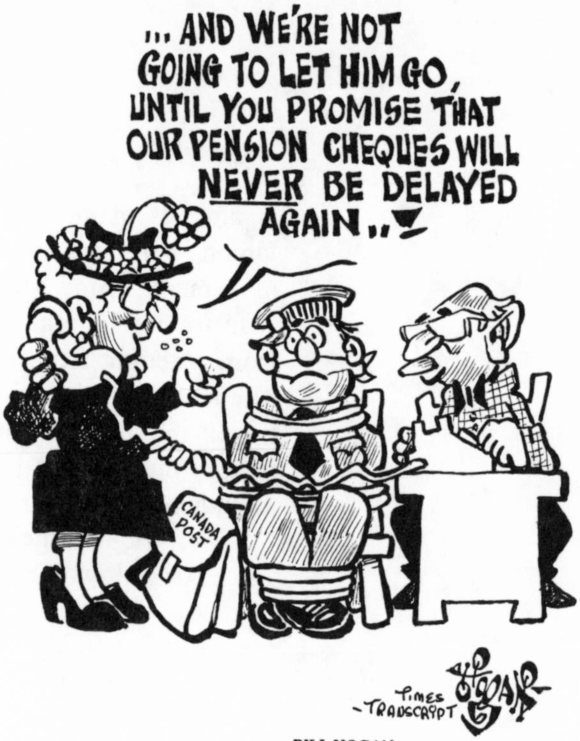
... AND WE'RE NOT GOING TO LET HIM GO, UNTIL YOU PROMISE THAT OUR PENSION CHEQUES WILL NEVER BE DELAYED AGAIN..!
CANADA POST
TIMES - TRANSCRIPT
HOGAN

BILL HOGAN
Courtesy Times-Transcript (N. Bruns.)

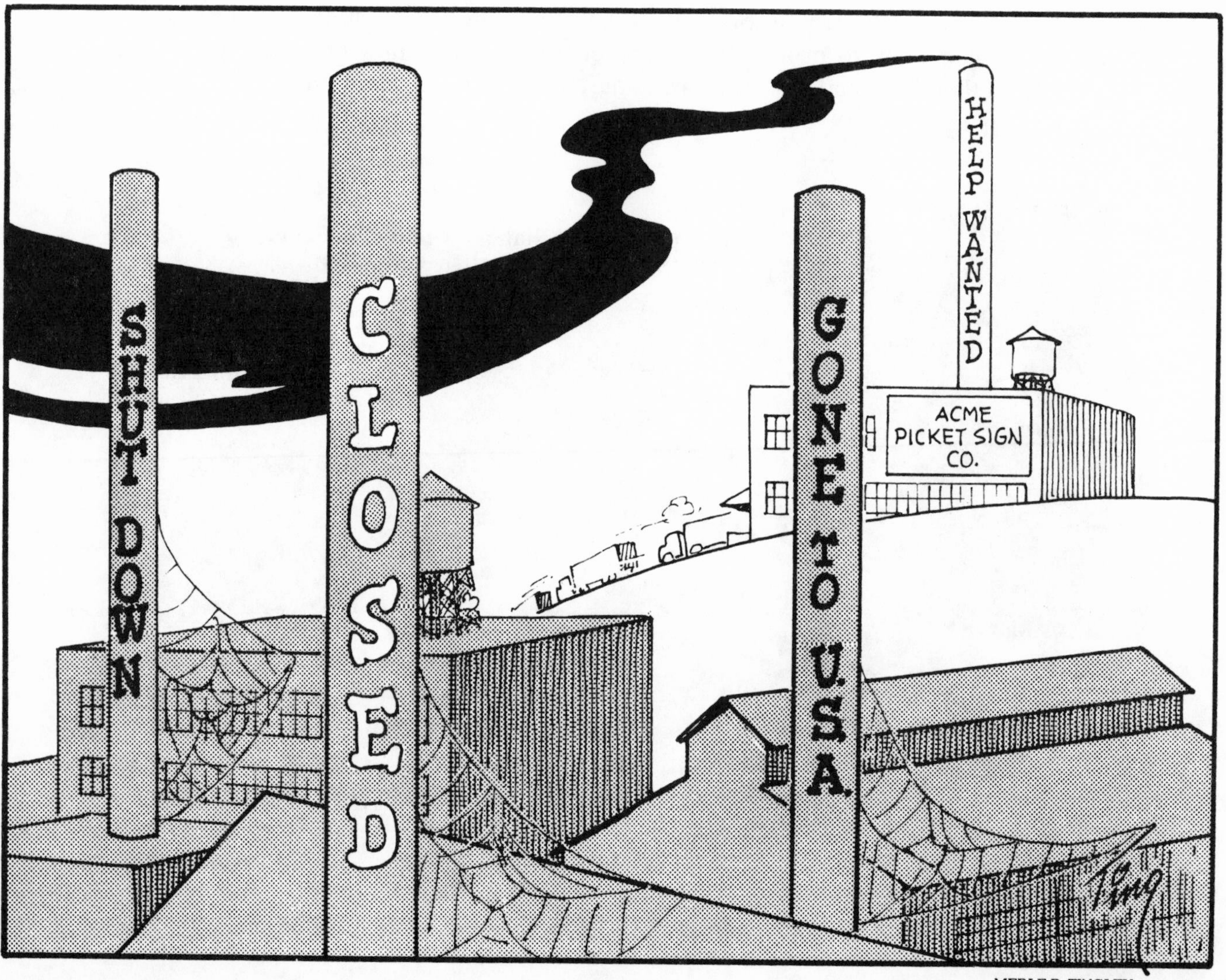
SHUT DOWN
CLOSED
GONE TO U.S.A.
HELP WANTED
ACME PICKET SIGN CO.
Ting

MERLE R. TINGLEY
Courtesy London Free Press (Ont.)

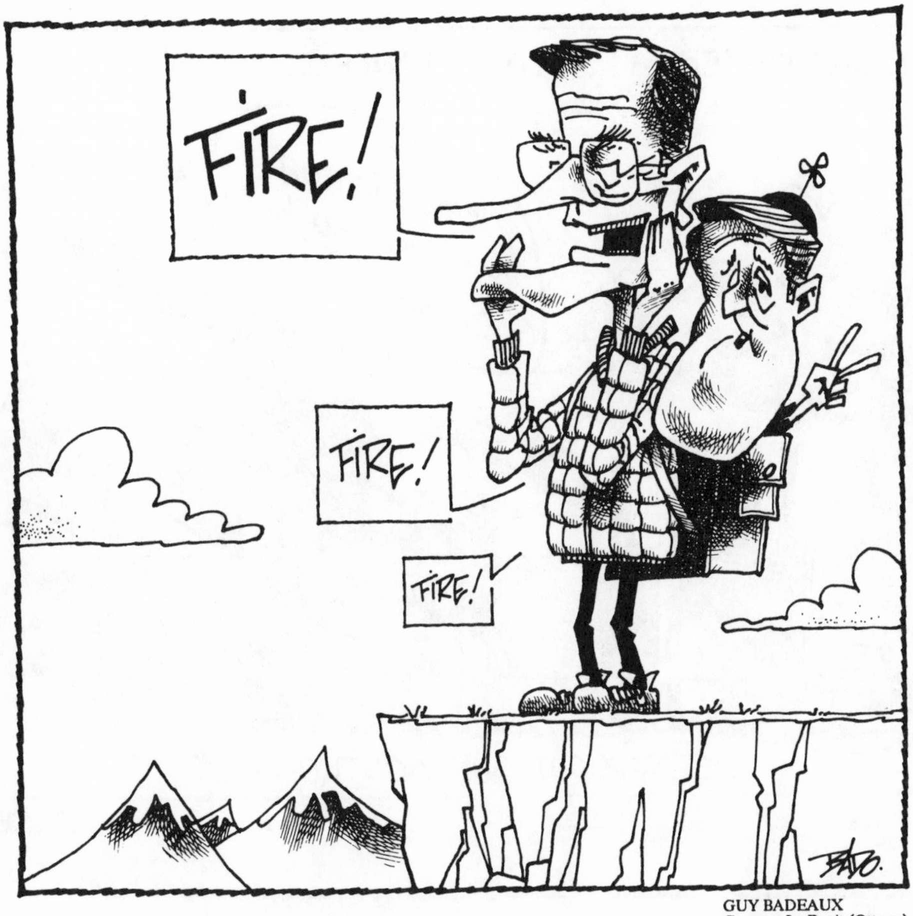
FIRE!
FIRE!
FIRE!
BADO.

GUY BADEAUX
Courtesy Le Droit (Ottawa)

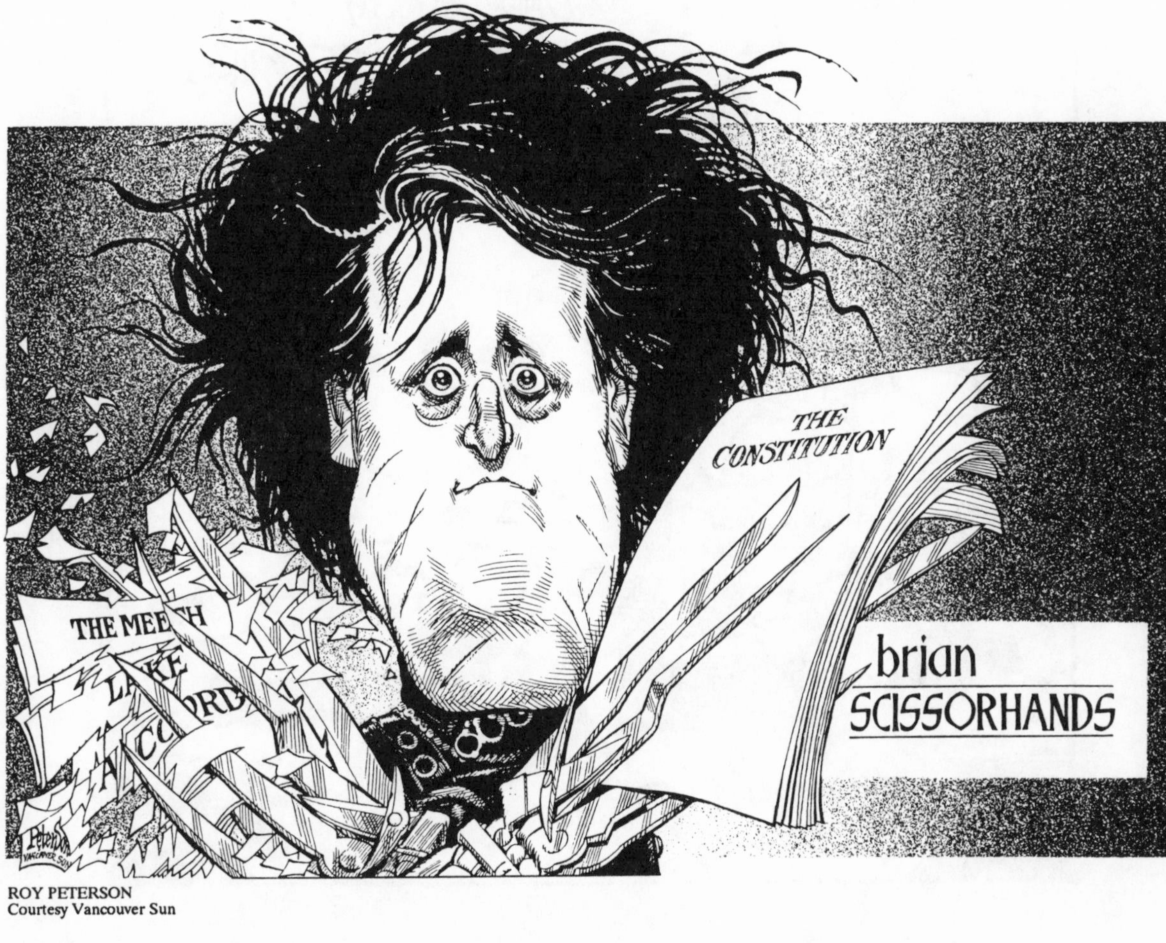
THE CONSTITUTION
THE MEECH LAKE ACCORD
brian
SCISSORHANDS

ROY PETERSON
Courtesy Vancouver Sun

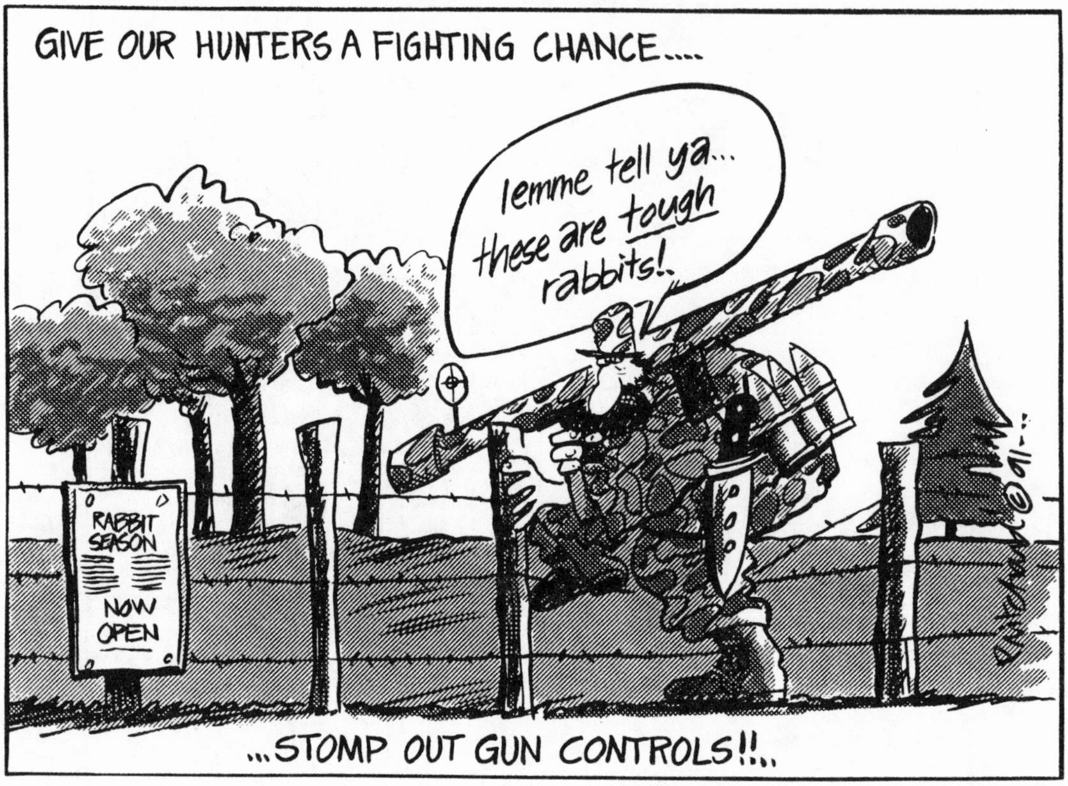
GIVE OUR HUNTERS A FIGHTING CHANCE....
lemme tell ya... these are tough rabbits!
RABBIT SEASON NOW OPEN
...STOMP OUT GUN CONTROLS!!..

DENNY PRITCHARD
Courtesy Ottawa Citizen

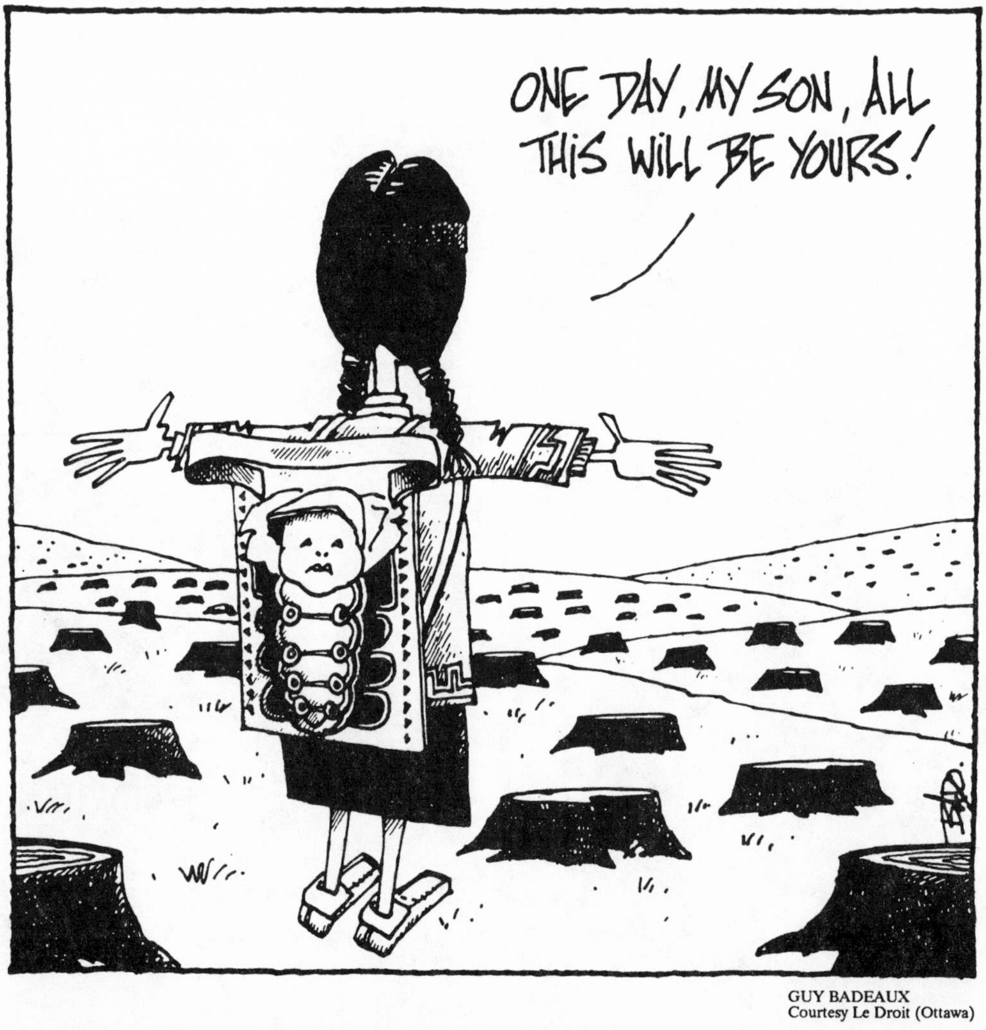
ONE DAY, MY SON, ALL THIS WILL BE YOURS!

GUY BADEAUX
Courtesy Le Droit (Ottawa)

Sports

In 1991, at the age of forty-four, Nolan Ryan of the Texas Rangers pitched the seventh no-hitter of his career, eighteen years after recording his first. Ryan struck out a record 383 batters in 1973 and was the first major leaguer to reach a career total of 5,000 strikeouts.

Baseball cards continued to grow as big business during the year. These cards change hands in memorabilia shops and card shows regularly held in malls and hotels across the country. Collectors look for pristine cards and seek those of rookies who someday may develop into superstars. A Nolan Ryan rookie card, for example, is now worth $1,400, while Tom Seaver's 1967 Topps card is valued at $1,100. The highest ever paid for a card was $451,000 for one of old-time great Honus Wagner, a shortstop for the Pittsburgh Pirates.

Sports salaries and earnings continued to skyrocket during the year. Heavyweight boxing champion Evander Holyfield reportedly earned $19.5 million in 1991, while Mike Tyson is said to have earned $14.8 million. Jose Canseco of the Oakland A's received $3.5 million, quarterback Joe Montana of the San Francisco '49ers signed for $13 million for four years, and New York Knicks star Patrick Ewing took home $4.6 million. In 1990, thirty-seven athletes earned more than $3 million each for playing their sport. That number no doubt will grow when final figures are in for 1991.

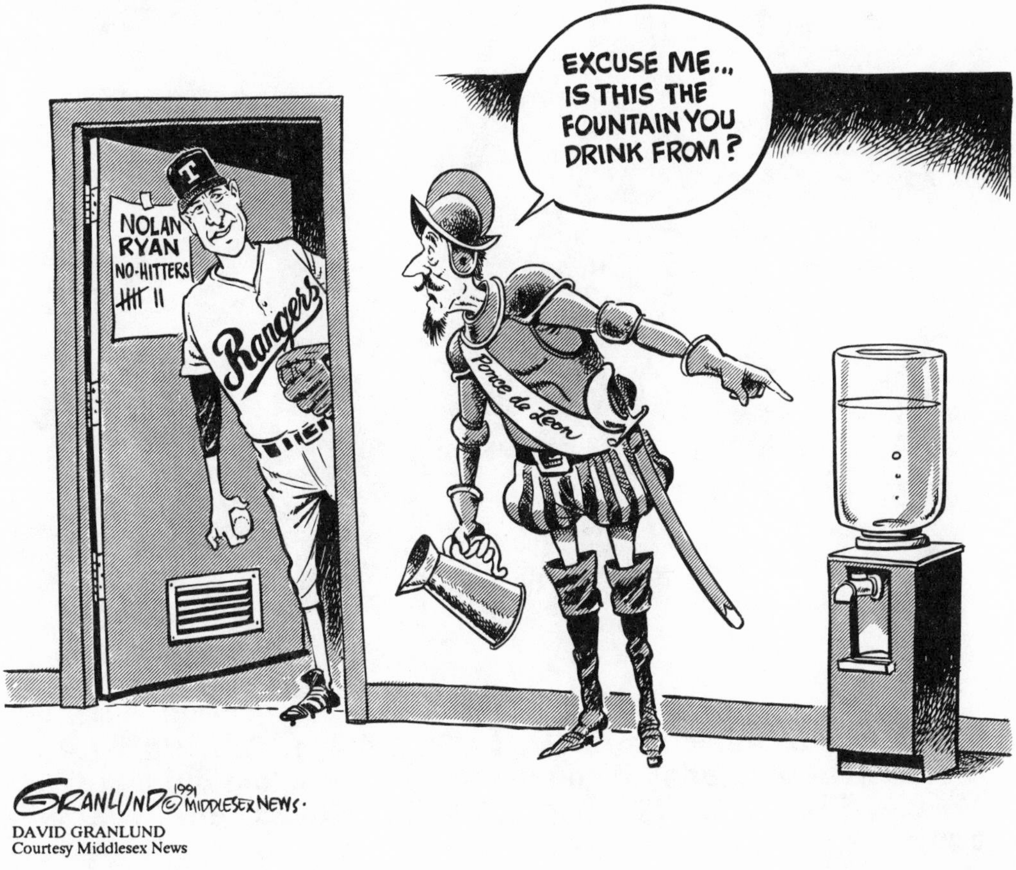
EXCUSE ME... IS THIS THE FOUNTAIN YOU DRINK FROM?
NOLAN RYAN NO-HITTERS
Rangers
Ponce de Leon
GRANLUND © 1991 MIDDLESEX NEWS.

DAVID GRANLUND
Courtesy Middlesex News

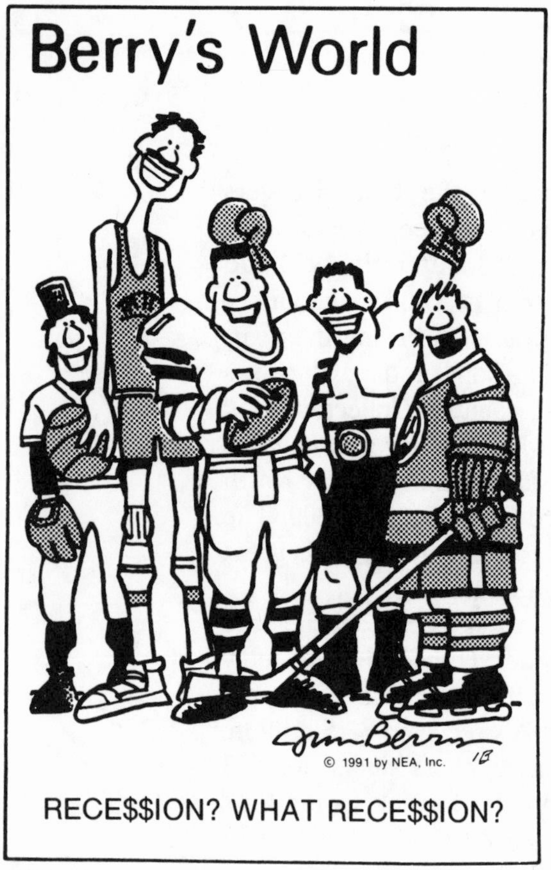
Berry's World
© 1991 by NEA, Inc.
RECE$$ION? WHAT RECE$$ION?

JIM BERRY
Courtesy NEA

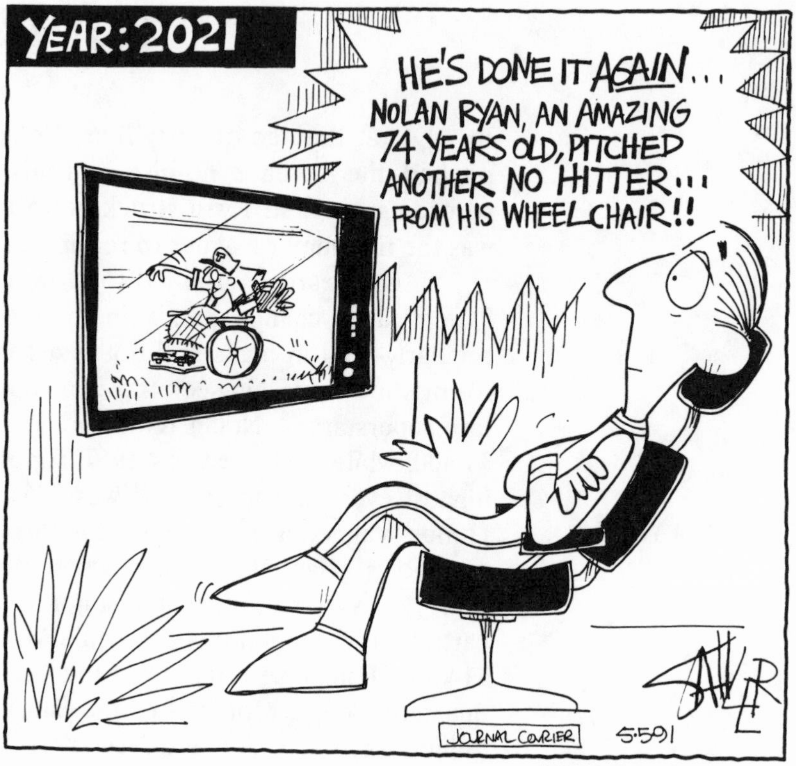
YEAR: 2021
HE'S DONE IT AGAIN... NOLAN RYAN, AN AMAZING 74 YEARS OLD, PITCHED ANOTHER NO HITTER!!! FROM HIS WHEELCHAIR!!
JOURNAL COURIER
5-5-91

DAVE SATTLER
Courtesy Journal and Courier (Ind.)

JOE LONG
Courtesy Little Falls Evening Times (N.Y.)

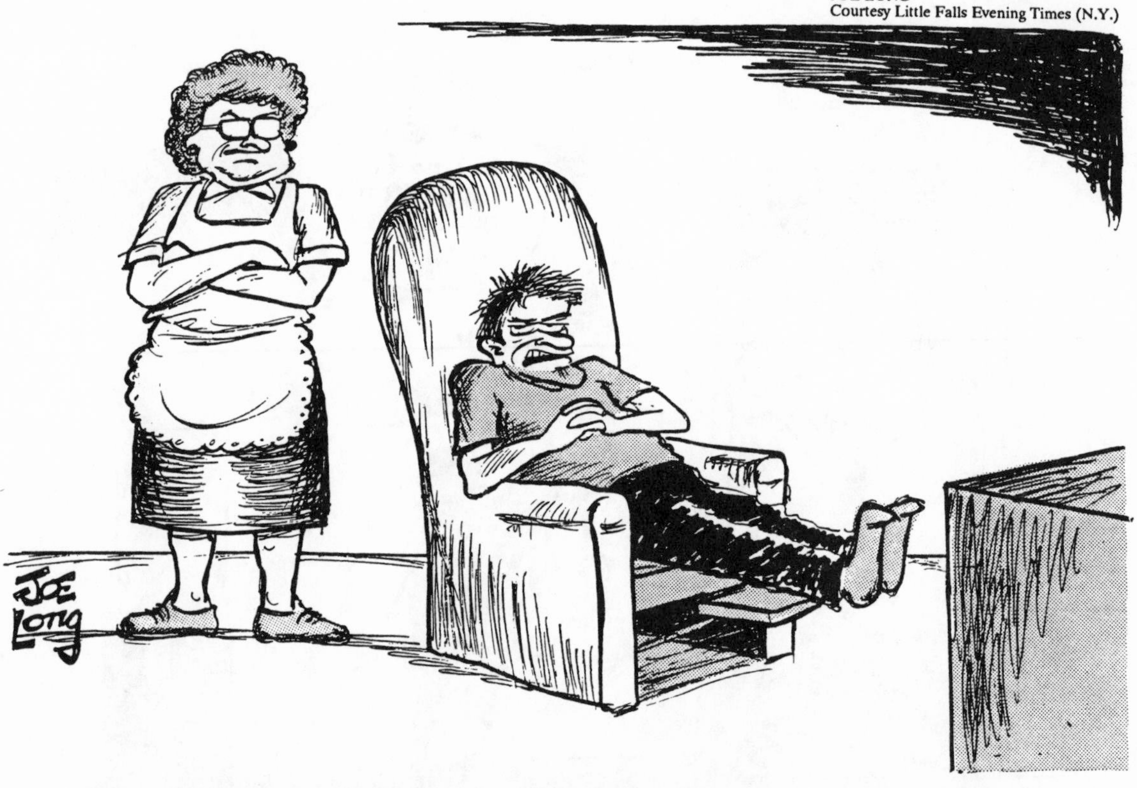
JOE LONG

"I know you think I'm a FAILURE, Mom. But, I'd be a MILLIONAIRE today if you didn't make me toss out all my old BASEBALL CARDS and COMIC BOOKS twenty years ago!"

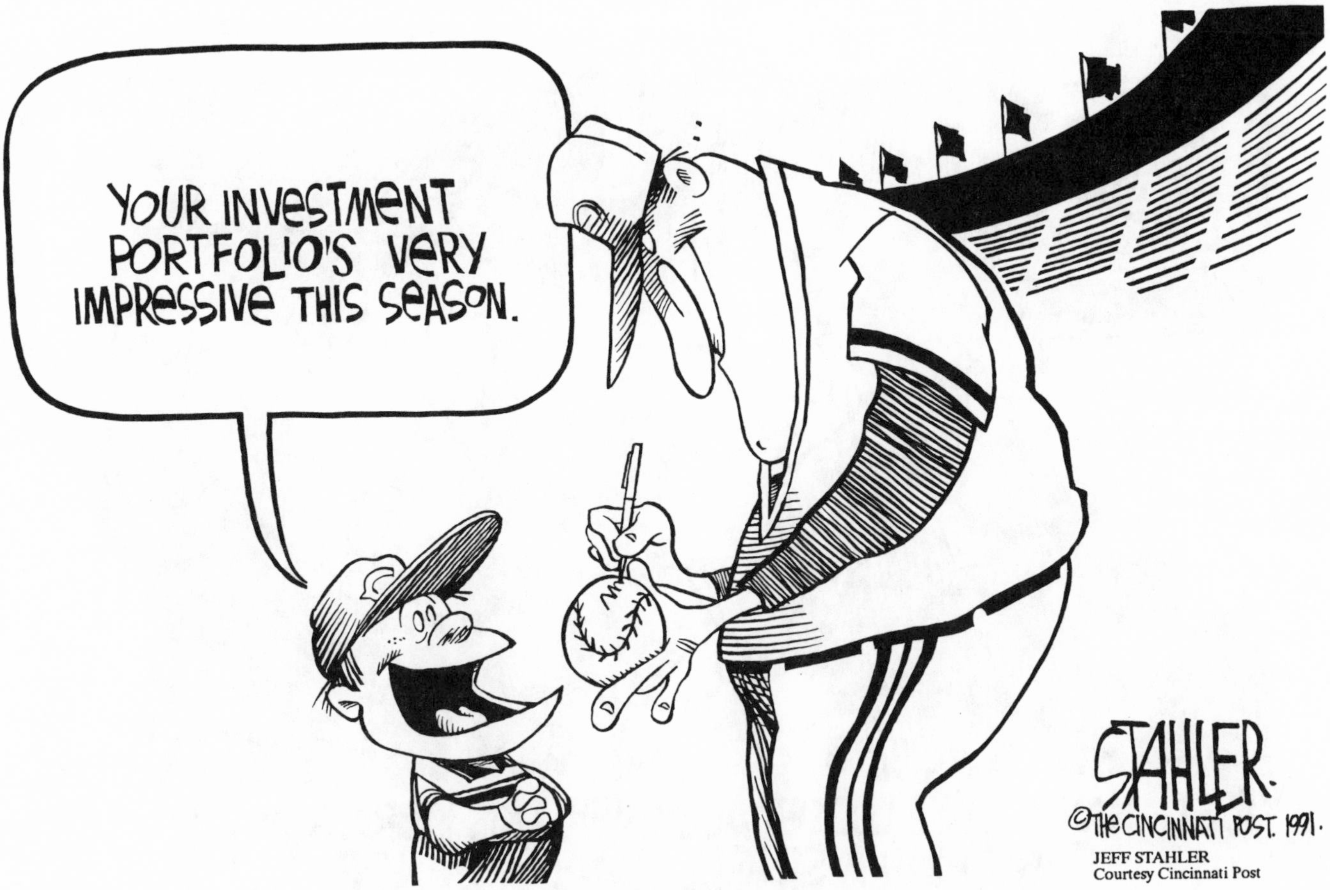
YOUR INVESTMENT PORTFOLIO'S VERY IMPRESSIVE THIS SEASON.
STAHLER.
©THE CINCINNATI POST. 1991.

JEFF STAHLER
Courtesy Cincinnati Post

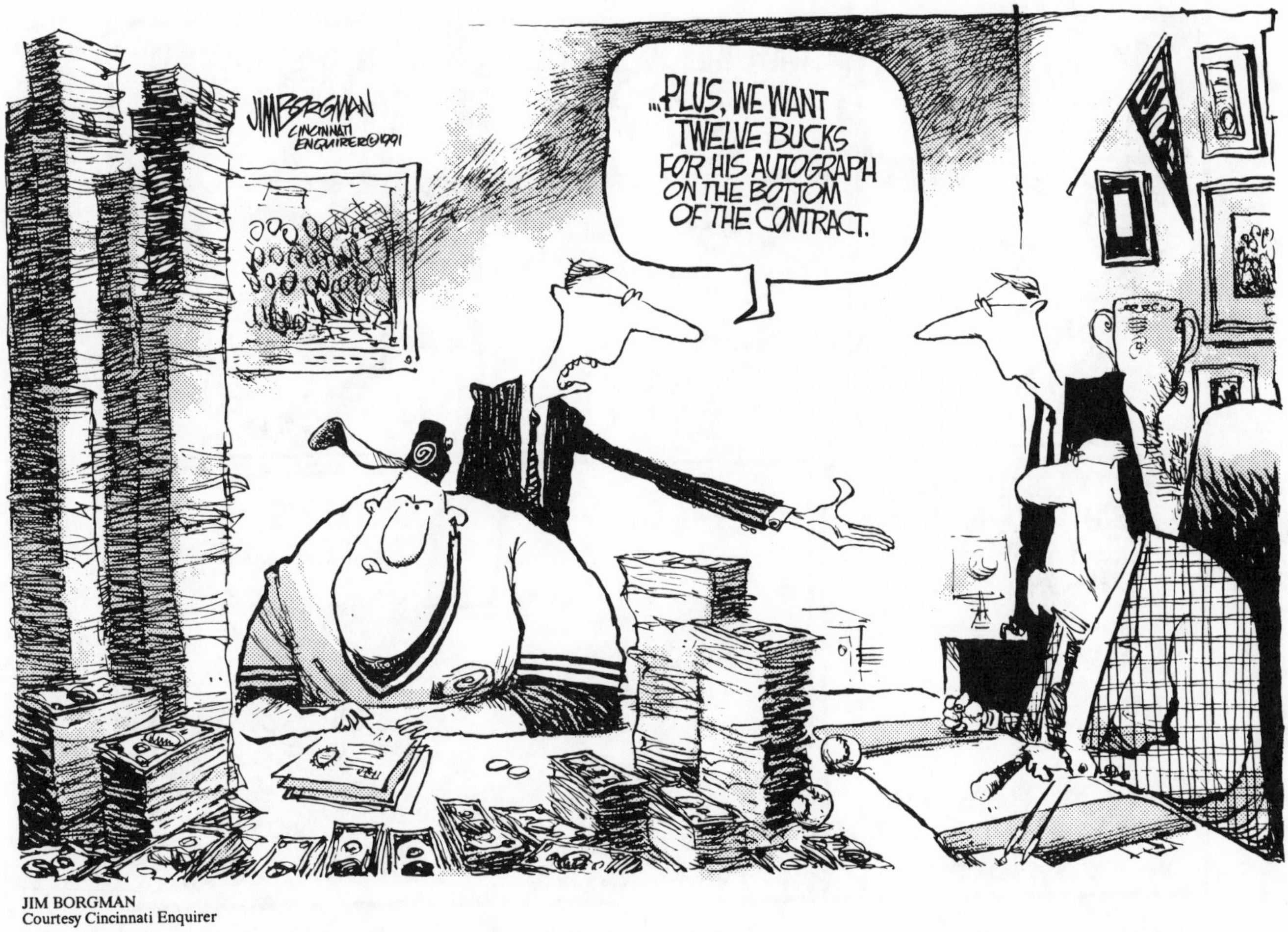
JIMBORGMAN
CINCINNATI ENQUIRER©1991
...PLUS, WE WANT TWELVE BUCKS FOR HIS AUTOGRAPH ON THE BOTTOM OF THE CONTRACT.

JIM BORGMAN
Courtesy Cincinnati Enquirer

GARY BROOKINS
Courtesy Richmond Times-Dispatch

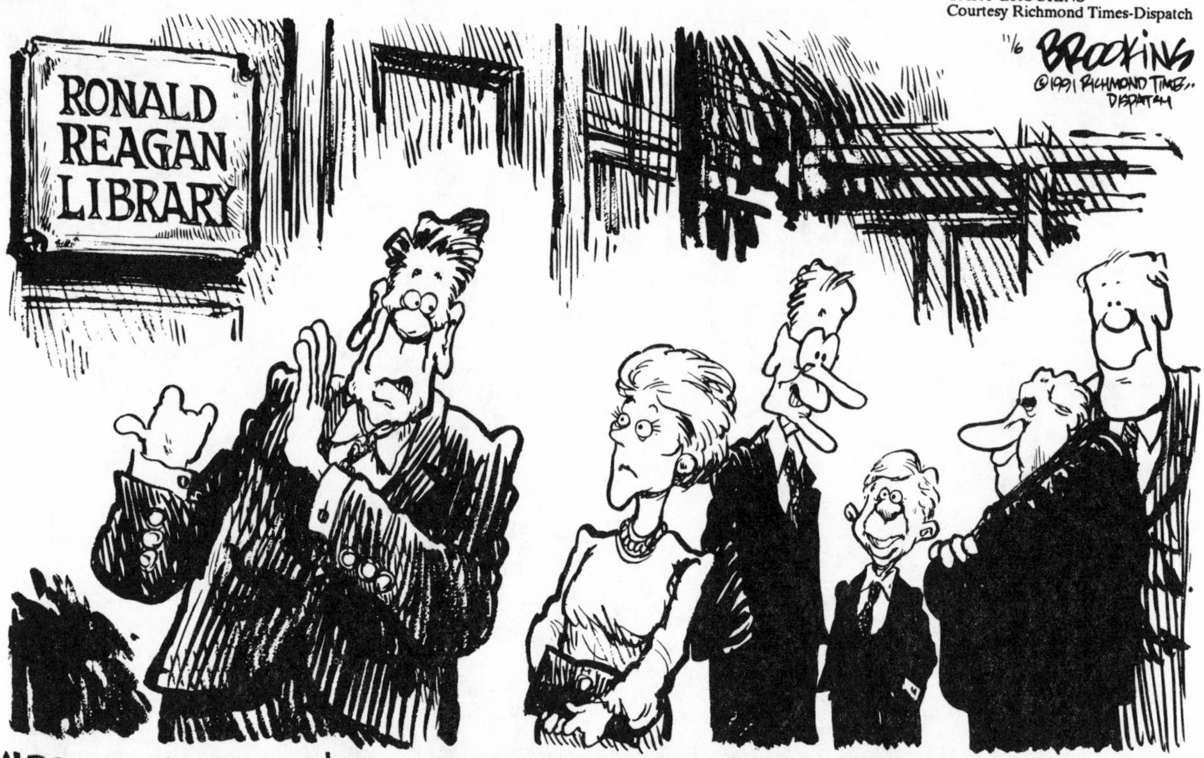

RONALD REAGAN LIBRARY
BROOKINS
©1991 RICHMOND TIMES-DISPATCH

"PSST... NANCY... I'VE LOOKED ALL OVER THIS LIBRARY AND I CAN'T FIND A SINGLE ZANE GREY NOVEL!..."

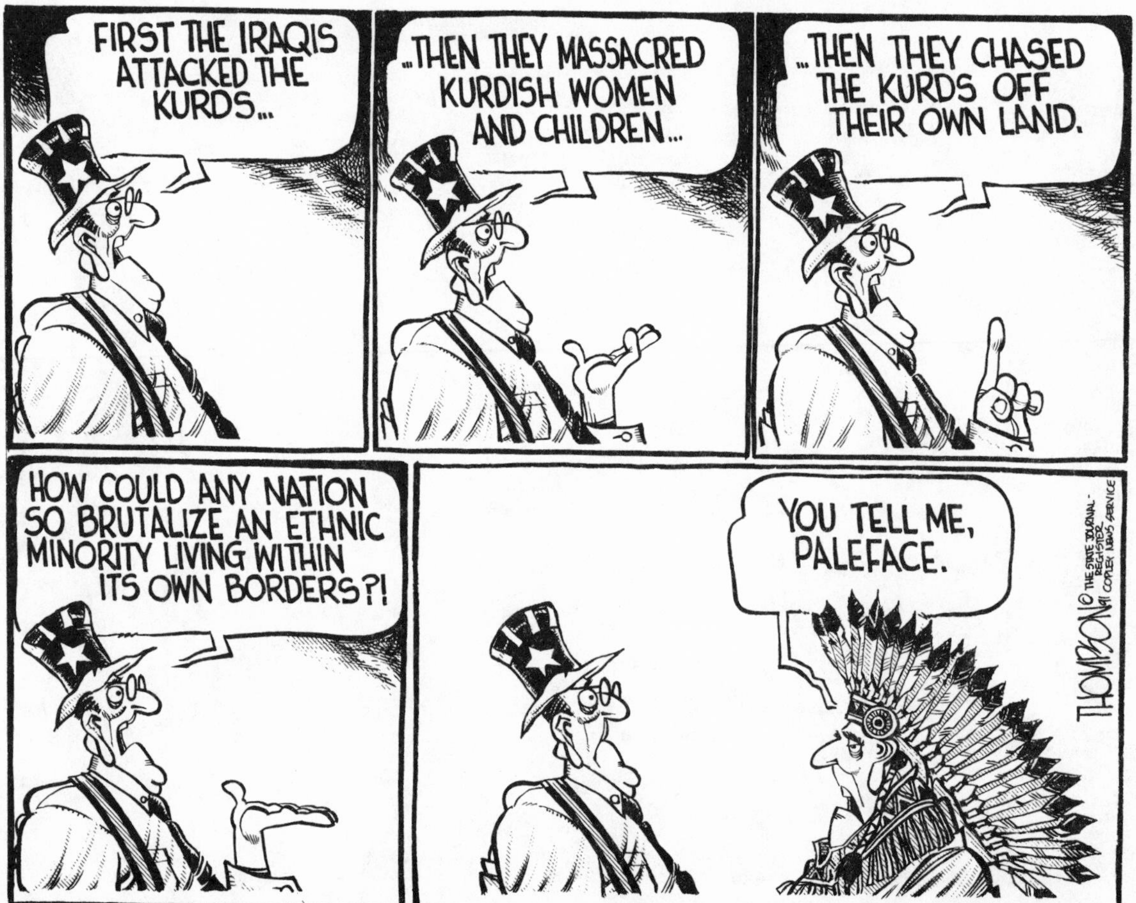

FIRST THE IRAQIS ATTACKED THE KURDS...
...THEN THEY MASSACRED KURDISH WOMEN AND CHILDREN...
...THEN THEY CHASED THE KURDS OFF THEIR OWN LAND.
HOW COULD ANY NATION SO BRUTALIZE AN ETHNIC MINORITY LIVING WITHIN ITS OWN BORDERS?!
YOU TELL ME, PALEFACE.
THOMPSON

MIKE THOMPSON
Courtesy State Journal-Register (Ill.)

. . . and Other Issues

Throughout the country in 1991, people complained about high taxes. But the outlook for the next few years, especially for state and local entities, is for even more tax increases. New York and California have been hard hit because of overspending, but other states are studying ways to increase revenues to balance their budgets. Many states and cities still complain about the short census count, which affects the amount of federal funds received through a variety of programs. The government admits that at least 5 million people were missed in the count.

CNN led the way in reporting the Persian Gulf War and consistently outpaced the three major networks in reporting breaking news. The U.S. Supreme Court refused to review the Iran-Contra case against Oliver North after a lower court had earlier overturned his convictions. The U.S. Postal Service failed in an attempt to raise rates once again, and President Bush joined the other four living presidents at the opening of the Ronald Reagan Library in California.

Many celebrities passed away during 1991, including Gene Roddenberry, Tennessee Ernie Ford, James Roosevelt, Vaughn Shoemaker, Theodor Geisel (Dr. Seuss), Red Grange, Harry Reasoner, Redd Foxx, Ralph Bellamy, Robert Maxwell, and jazz trumpeter Miles Davis.

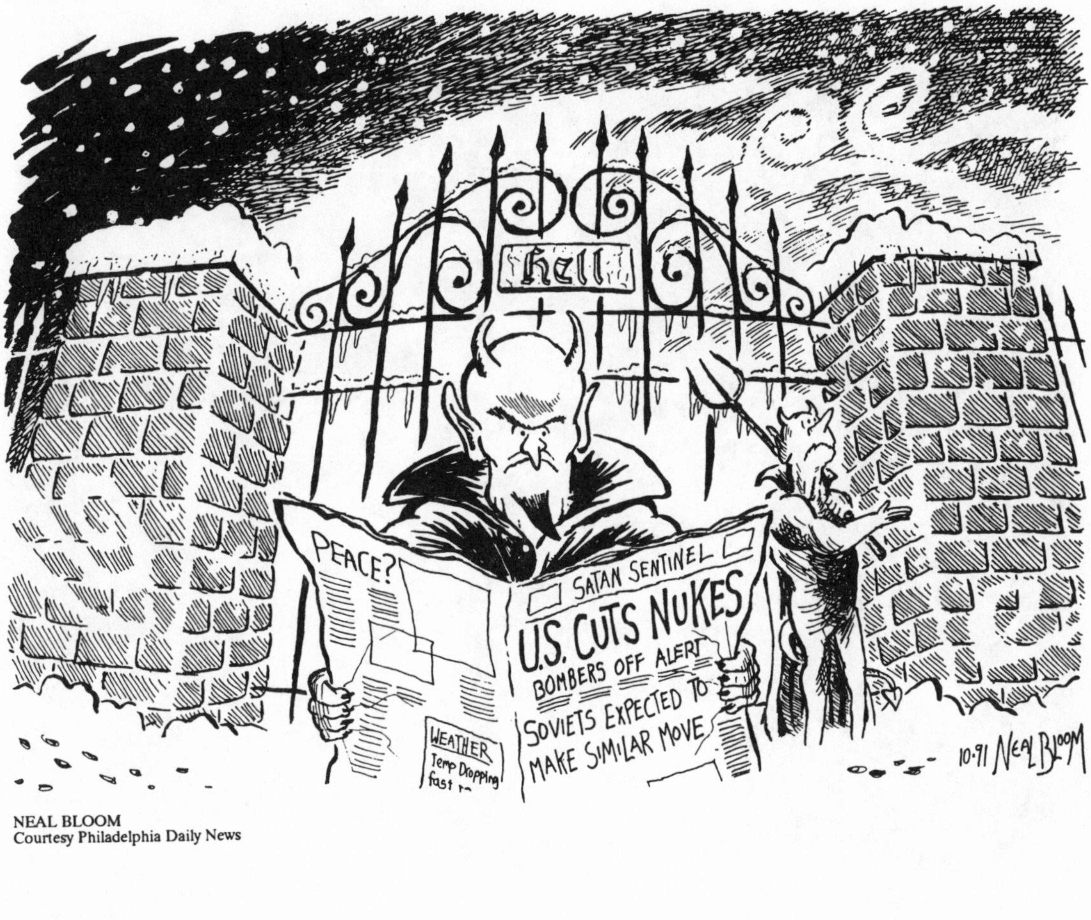
Hell
PEACE?
SATAN SENTINEL
U.S. CUTS NUKES
BOMBERS OFF ALERT
SOVIETS EXPECTED TO MAKE SIMILAR MOVE
WEATHER
Temp Dropping fast
10·91 NEAL BLOOM

NEAL BLOOM
Courtesy Philadelphia Daily News

KEVIN SIERS
Courtesy Charlotte Observer

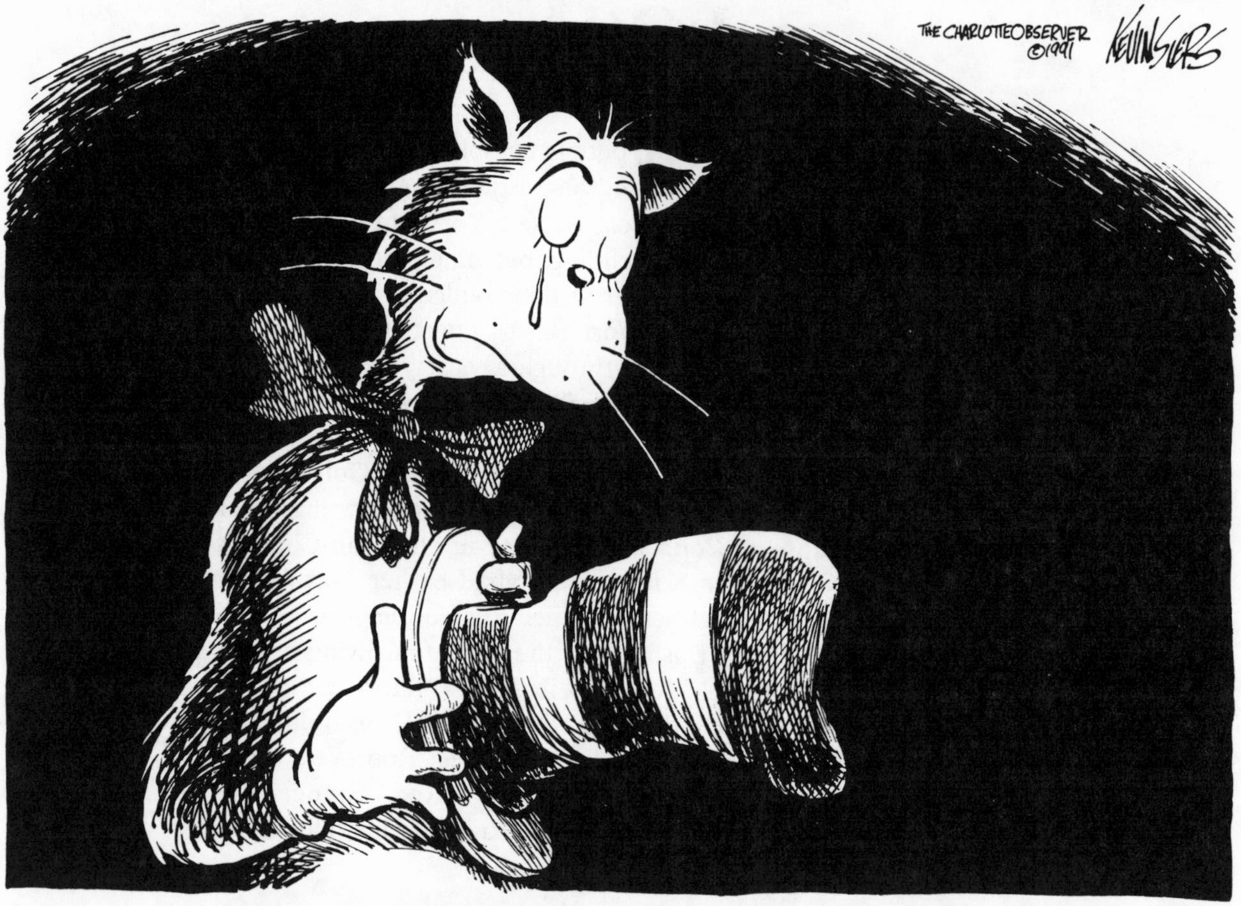

THE CHARLOTTE OBSERVER ©1991
KEVIN SIERS

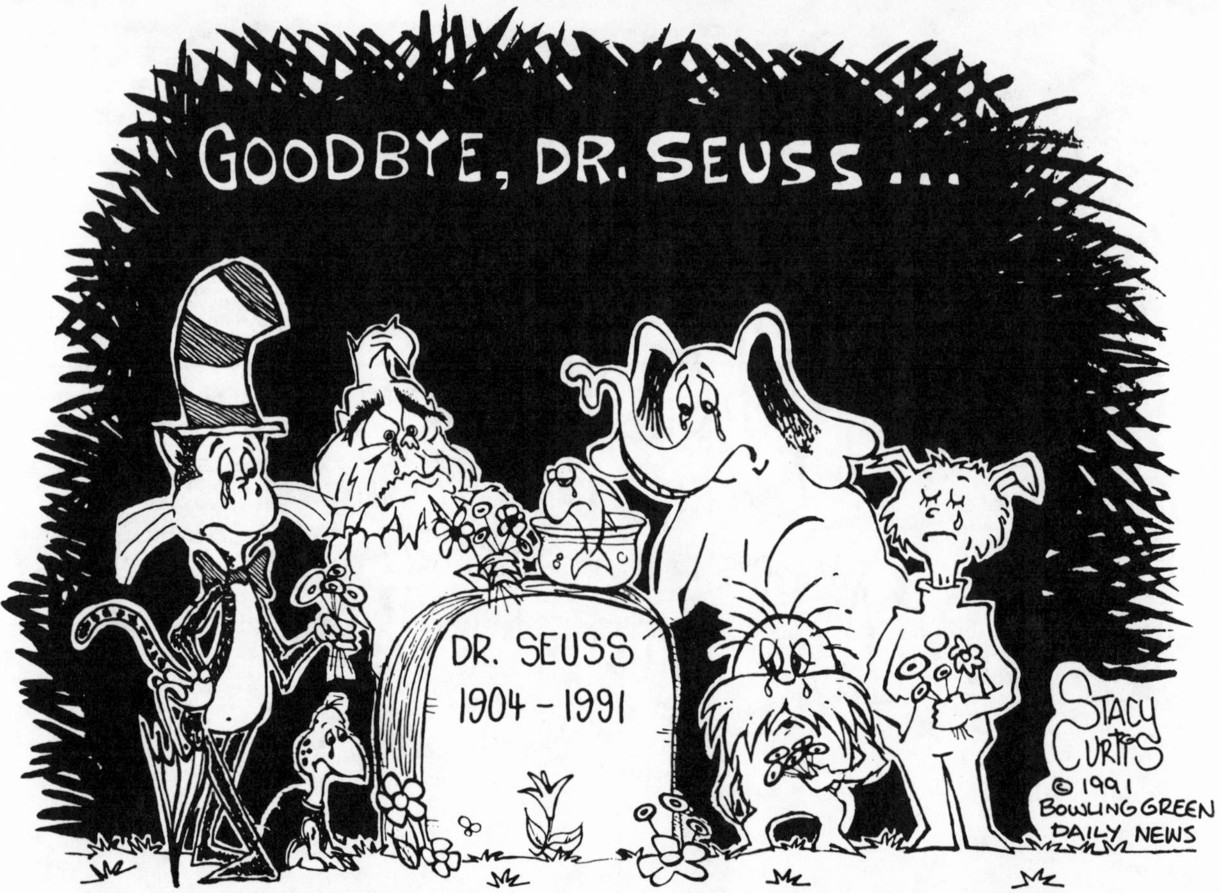

GOODBYE, DR. SEUSS ...
DR. SEUSS
1904 - 1991
STACY CURTIS
© 1991 BOWLING GREEN DAILY NEWS

STACY CURTIS
Courtesy Bowling Green Daily News

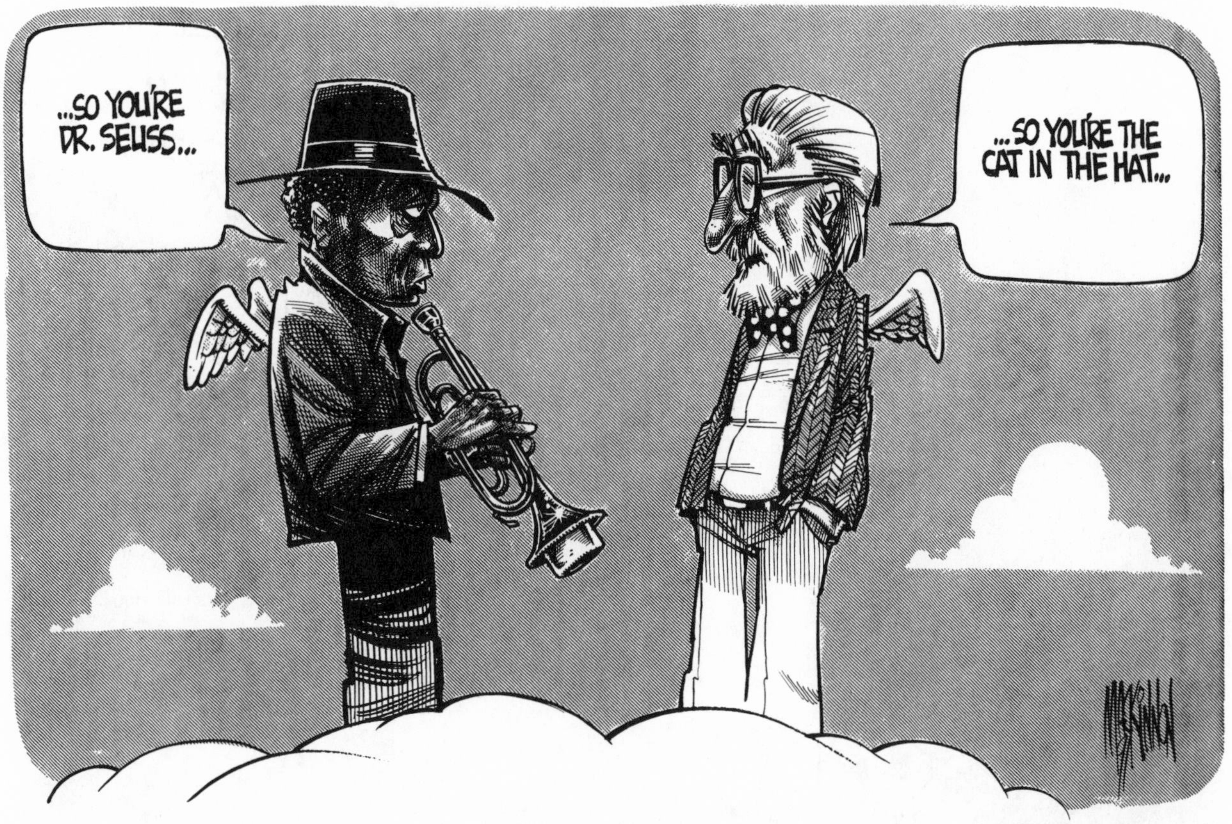
...SO YOU'RE DR. SEUSS...
...SO YOU'RE THE CAT IN THE HAT...

BRUCE MACKINNON
Courtesy Halifax Chronicle-Herald

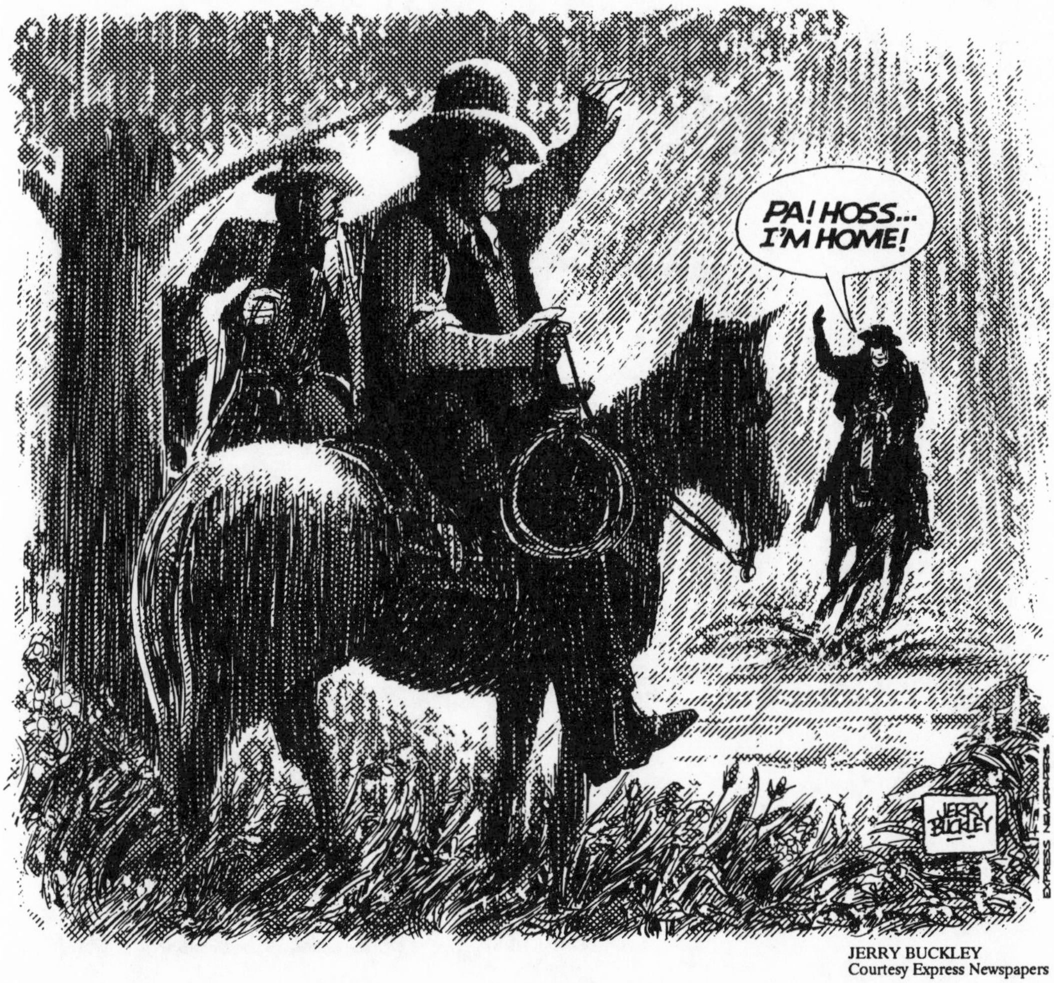
PA! HOSS... I'M HOME!
JERRY BUCKLEY

JERRY BUCKLEY
Courtesy Express Newspapers

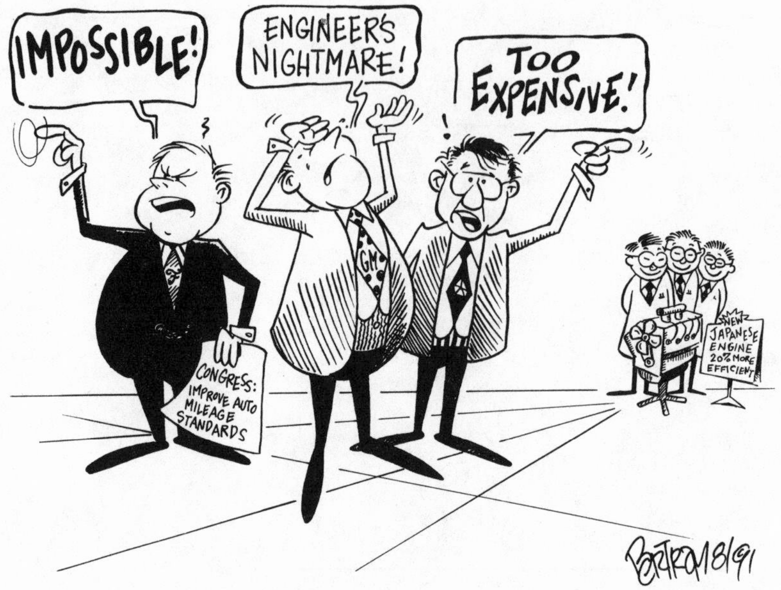
IMPOSSIBLE!
ENGINEER'S NIGHTMARE!
TOO EXPENSIVE!
CONGRESS: IMPROVE AUTO MILEAGE STANDARDS
GM
NEW
JAPANESE ENGINE 20% MORE EFFICIENT
BERTRAM 8/91

JIM BERTRAM
Courtesy St. Cloud Times

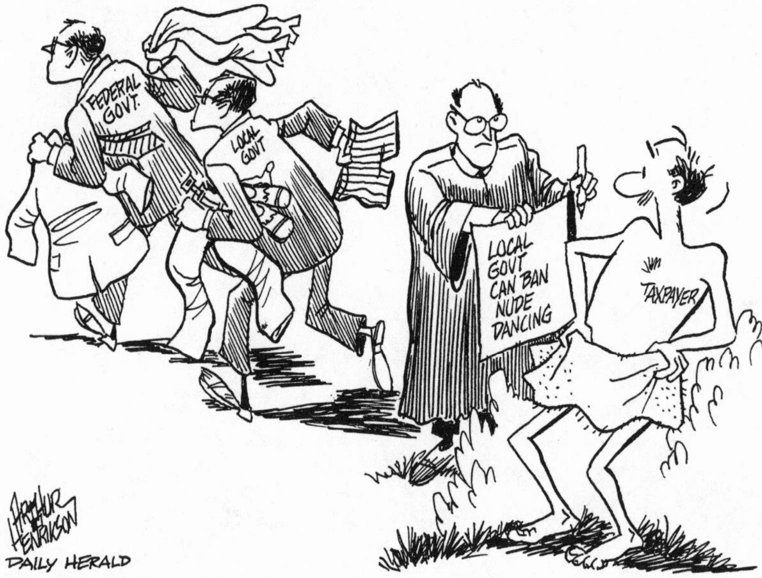
FEDERAL GOVT.
LOCAL GOVT
LOCAL GOVT CAN BAN NUDE DANCING
TAXPAYER
ARTHUR HENRIKSON
DAILY HERALD

ART HENRIKSON
Courtesy Daily Herald (Ill.)

VIC HARVILLE
Courtesy Arkansas Democrat-Gazette

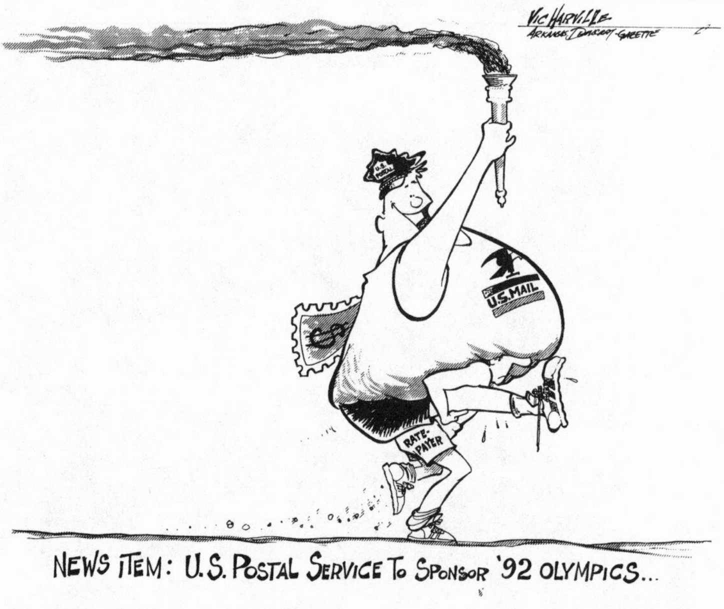
VIC HARVILLE
U.S. MAIL
RATE-PAYER
NEWS ITEM: U.S. POSTAL SERVICE TO SPONSOR '92 OLYMPICS...

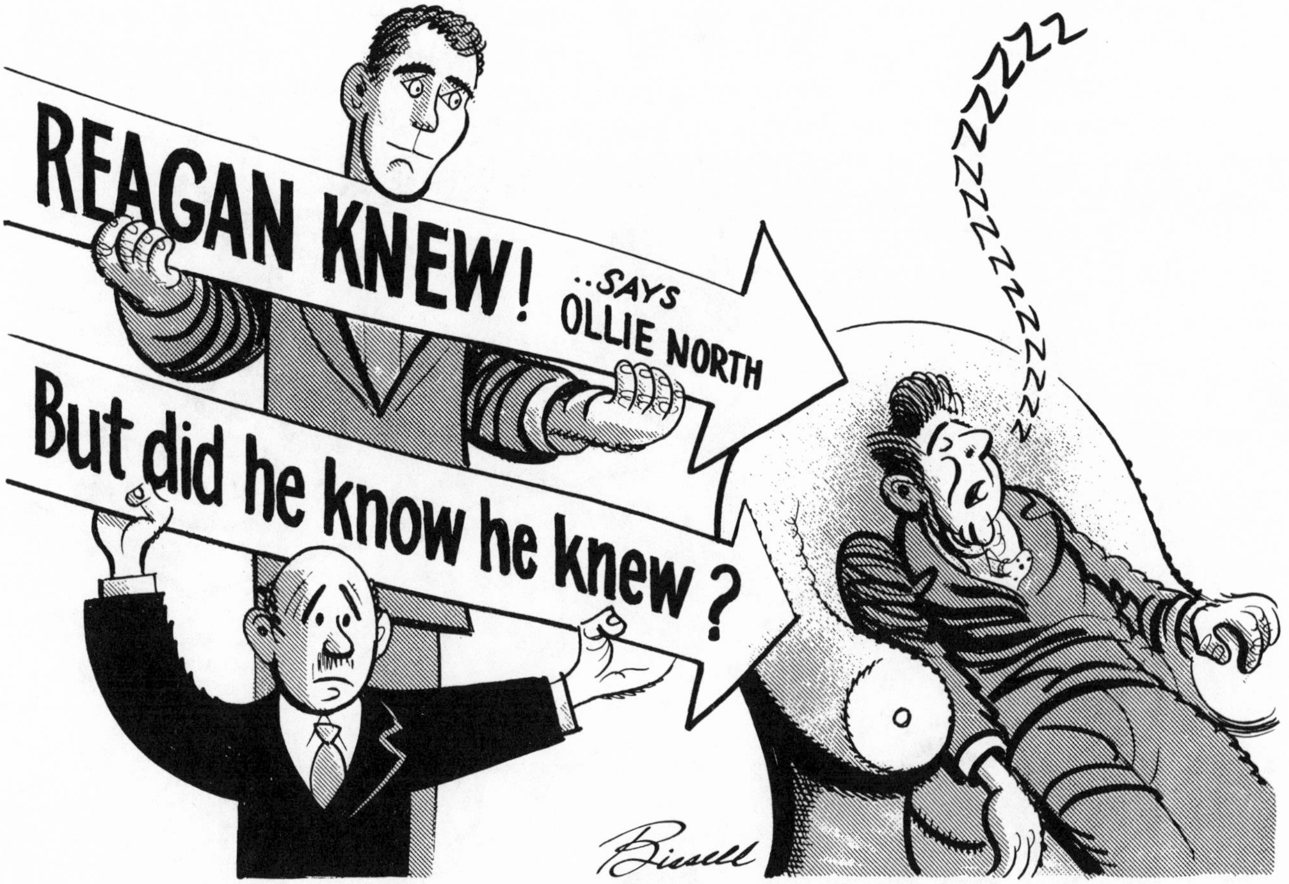
REAGAN KNEW!
..SAYS OLLIE NORTH
But did he know he knew ?
ZZZZZZZZZZZZZZZZZ
Bissell

CHARLES BISSELL
Courtesy The Tennessean

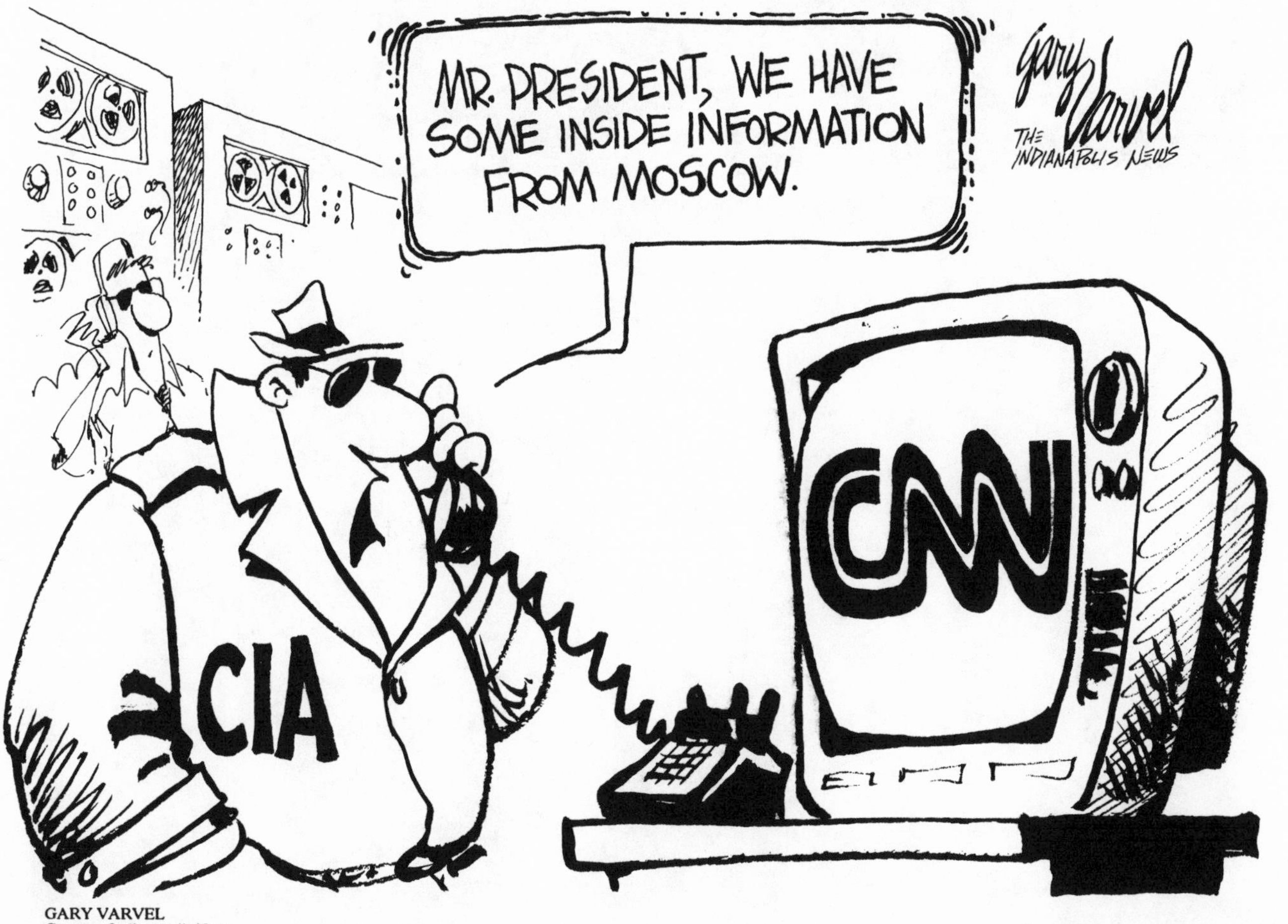
MR. PRESIDENT, WE HAVE SOME INSIDE INFORMATION FROM MOSCOW.
Gary Varvel
THE INDIANAPOLIS NEWS
CNN
CIA

GARY VARVEL
Courtesy Indianapolis News

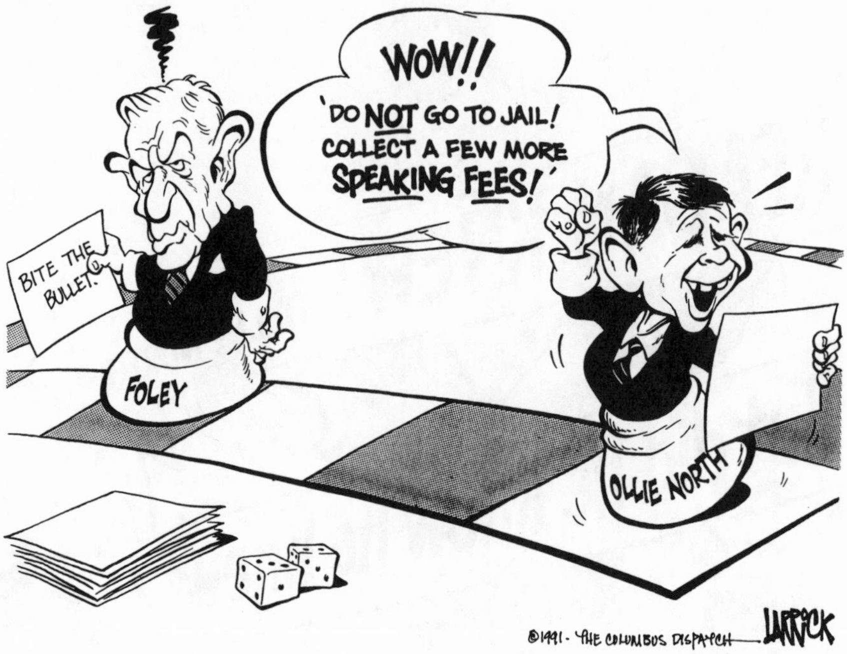

WOW!!
'DO NOT GO TO JAIL! COLLECT A FEW MORE SPEAKING FEES!'
BITE THE BULLET!
FOLEY
OLLIE NORTH
©1991 - THE COLUMBUS DISPATCH
LARRICK

JAMES LARRICK
Courtesy Columbus Dispatch

TOM CURTIS
Courtesy National Review

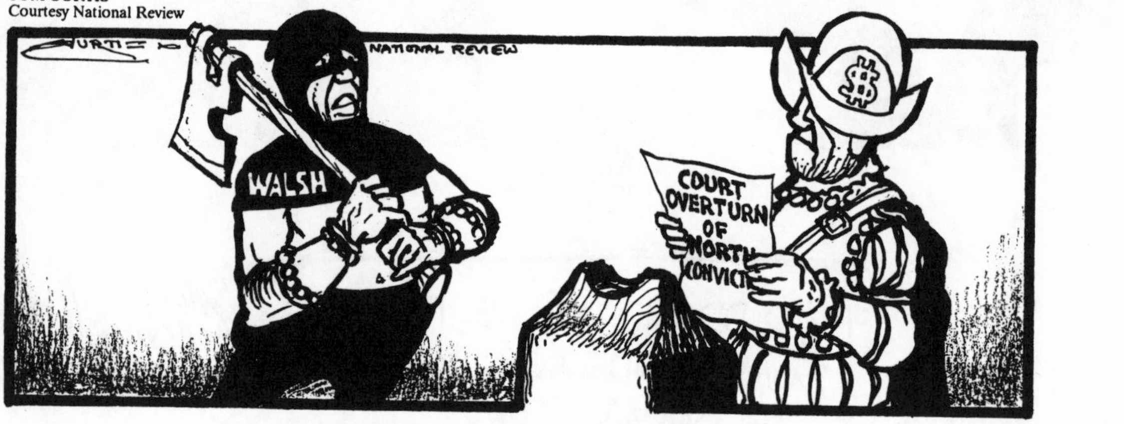

CURTIS
NATIONAL REVIEW
WALSH
COURT OVERTURN OF NORTH CONVICT

"Quick! Send out another invitation!"

CRAIG M. TERRY
Courtesy N.W. Florida Daily News

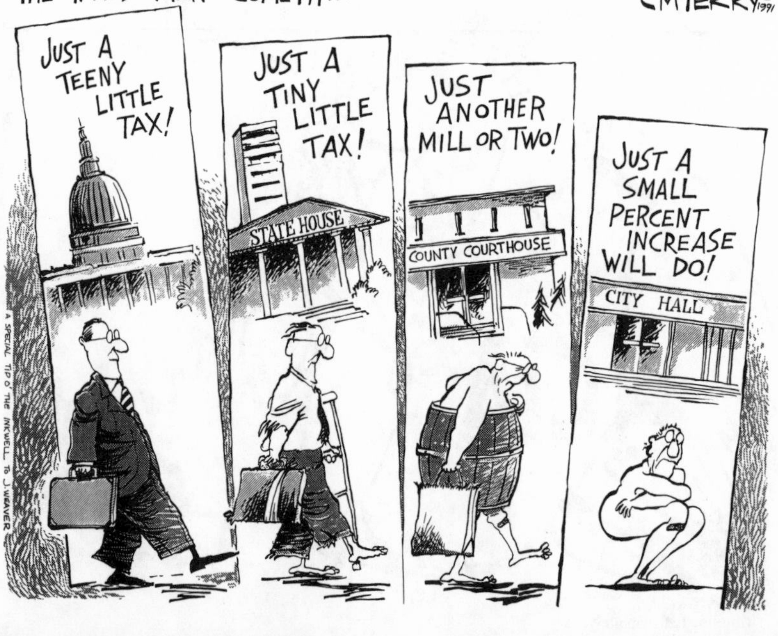

THE TAXED MAN COMETH...
NORTHWEST FLORIDA DAILY NEWS
CMTERRY© 1991
JUST A TEENY LITTLE TAX!
JUST A TINY LITTLE TAX!
STATE HOUSE
JUST ANOTHER MILL OR TWO!
COUNTY COURTHOUSE
JUST A SMALL PERCENT INCREASE WILL DO!
CITY HALL

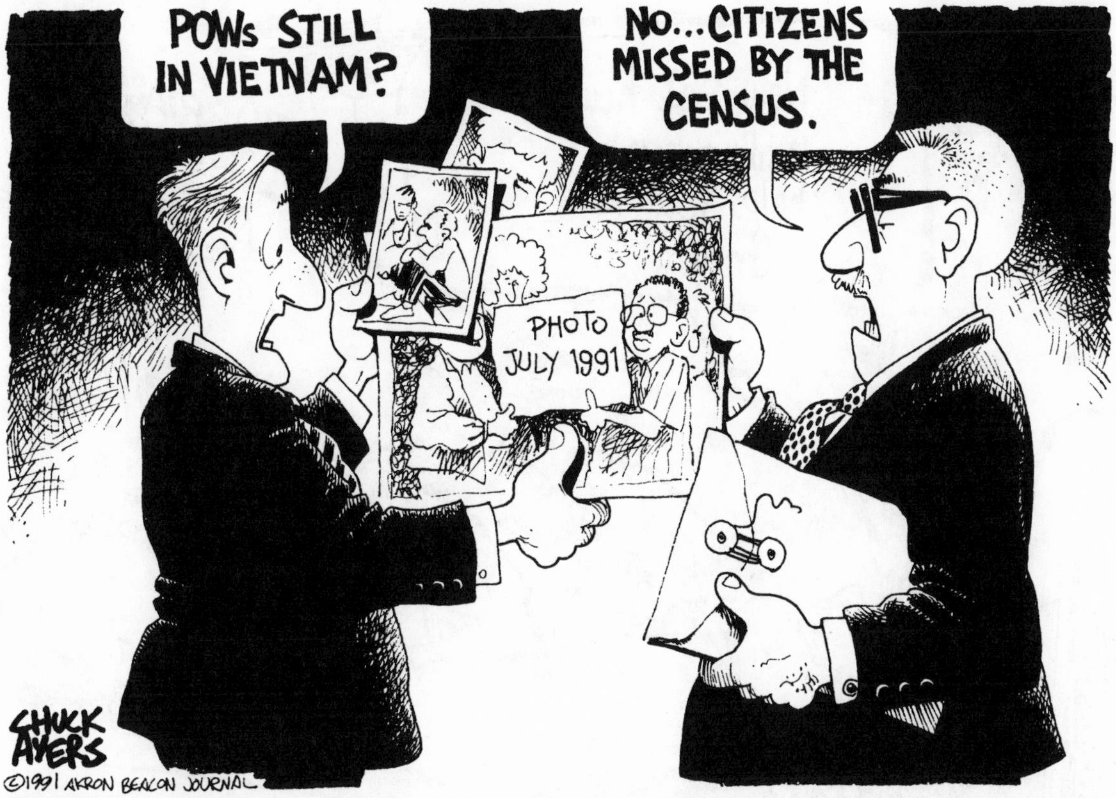
POWs STILL IN VIETNAM?
NO... CITIZENS MISSED BY THE CENSUS.
PHOTO JULY 1991
CHUCK AYERS
©1991 AKRON BEACON JOURNAL

CHUCK AYERS
Courtesy Akron Beacon Journal

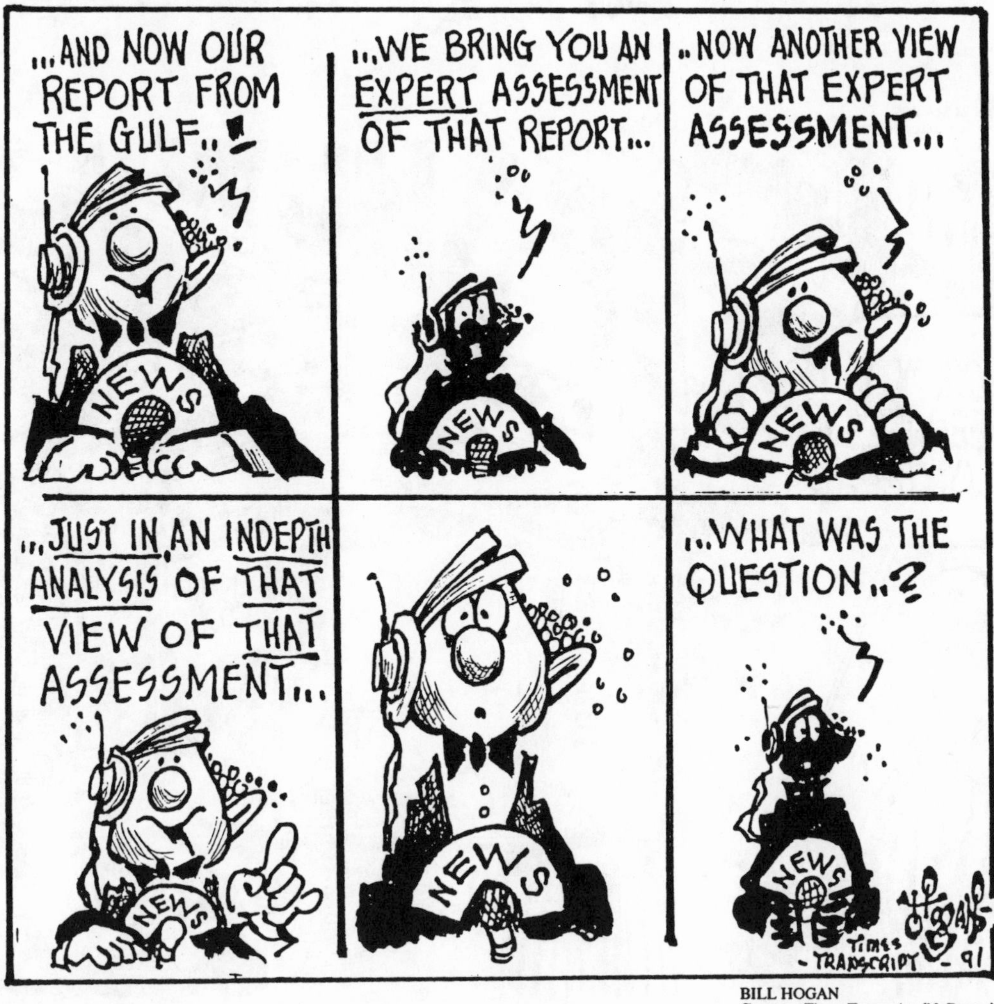
...AND NOW OUR REPORT FROM THE GULF..!
NEWS
...WE BRING YOU AN EXPERT ASSESSMENT OF THAT REPORT...
NEWS
..NOW ANOTHER VIEW OF THAT EXPERT ASSESSMENT...
NEWS
...JUST IN, AN INDEPTH ANALYSIS OF THAT VIEW OF THAT ASSESSMENT...
NEWS
NEWS
...WHAT WAS THE QUESTION..?
NEWS
TIMES - TRANSCRIPT - 91

BILL HOGAN
Courtesy Times-Transcript (N. Bruns.)

STEVE MCBRIDE
Courtesy Independence Daily Reporter (Kan.)

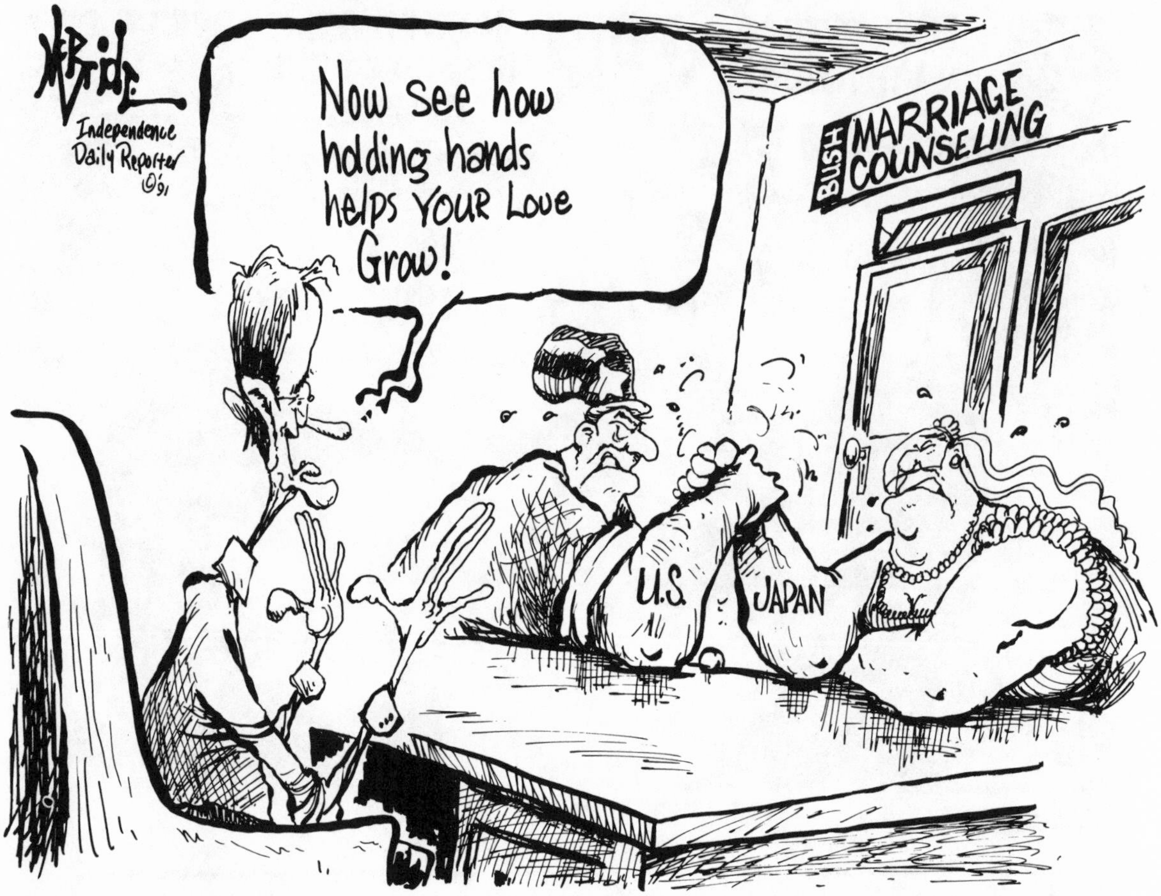
McBride Independence Daily Reporter ©'91
Now see how holding hands helps YOUR Love Grow!
BUSH MARRIAGE COUNSELING
U.S.
JAPAN

MALCOLM MAYES
Courtesy Edmonton Journal

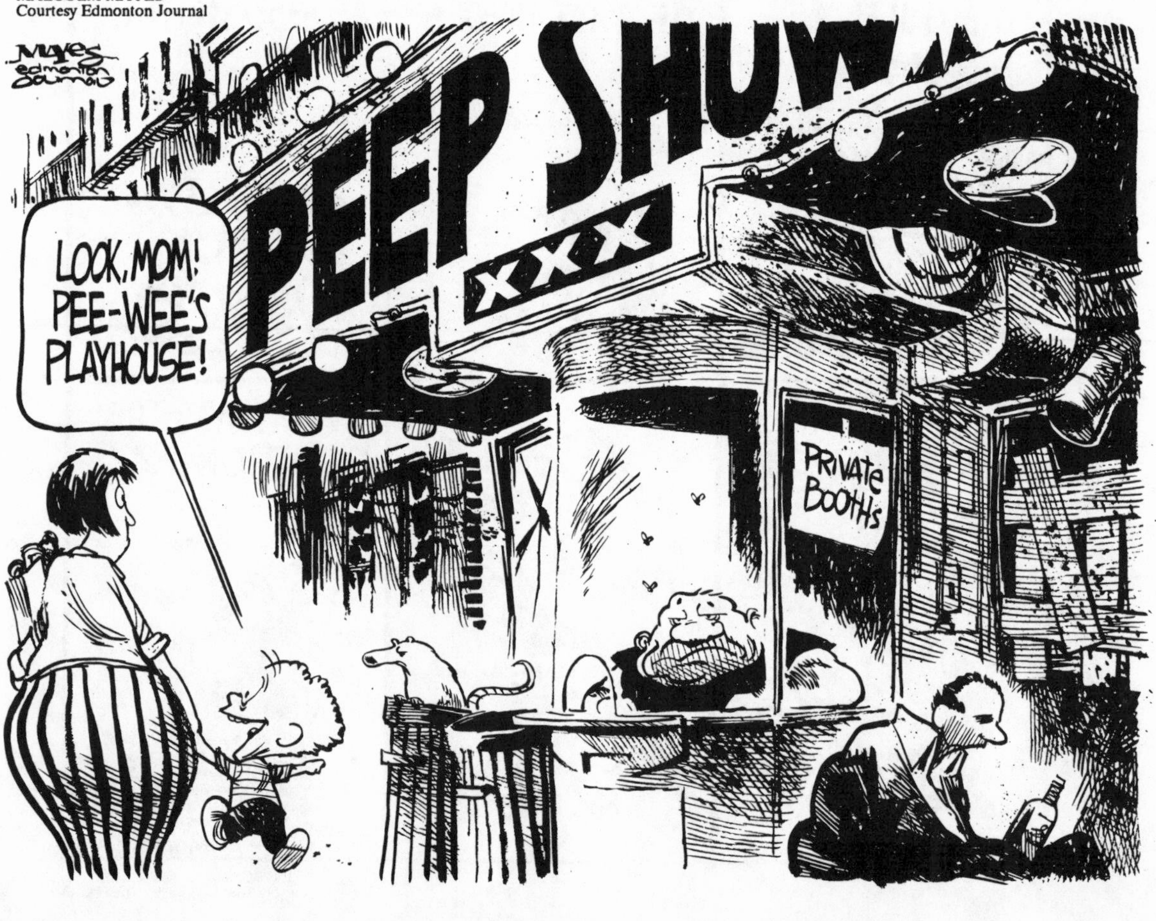
MAYES Edmonton Journal
PEEP SHOW
XXX
LOOK, MOM! PEE-WEE'S PLAYHOUSE!
Private BOOTHS

Past Award Winners

NATIONAL SOCIETY OF PROFESSIONAL JOURNALISTS AWARD
(Formerly Sigma Delta Chi Award)

1942 – Jacob Burck, Chicago Times
1943 – Charles Werner, Chicago Sun
1944 – Henry Barrow, Associated Press
1945 – Reuben L. Goldberg, New York Sun
1946 – Dorman H. Smith, NEA
1947 – Bruce Russell, Los Angeles Times
1948 – Herbert Block, Washington Post
1949 – Herbert Block, Washington Post
1950 – Bruce Russell, Los Angeles Times
1951 – Herbert Block, Washington Post, and
        Bruce Russell, Los Angeles Times
1952 – Cecil Jensen, Chicago Daily News
1953 – John Fischetti, NEA
1954 – Calvin Alley, Memphis Commercial Appeal
1955 – John Fischetti, NEA
1956 – Herbert Block, Washington Post
1957 – Scott Long, Minneapolis Tribune
1958 – Clifford H. Baldowski, Atlanta Constitution
1959 – Charles G. Brooks, Birmingham News
1960 – Dan Dowling, New York Herald-Tribune
1961 – Frank Interlandi, Des Moines Register
1962 – Paul Conrad, Denver Post
1963 – William Mauldin, Chicago Sun-Times
1964 – Charles Bissell, Nashville Tennessean
1965 – Roy Justus, Minneapolis Star
1966 – Patrick Oliphant, Denver Post
1967 – Eugene Payne, Charlotte Observer
1968 – Paul Conrad, Los Angeles Times
1969 – William Mauldin, Chicago Sun-Times
1970 – Paul Conrad, Los Angeles Times
1971 – Hugh Haynie, Louisville Courier-Journal
1972 – William Mauldin, Chicago Sun-Times
1973 – Paul Szep, Boston Globe
1974 – Mike Peters, Dayton Daily News
1975 – Tony Auth, Philadelphia Enquirer
1976 – Paul Szep, Boston Globe
1977 – Don Wright, Miami News
1978 – Jim Borgman, Cincinnati Enquirer
1979 – John P. Trever, Albuquerque Journal
1980 – Paul Conrad, Los Angeles Times
1981 – Paul Conrad, Los Angeles Times
1982 – Dick Locher, Chicago Tribune
1983 – Rob Lawlor, Philadelphia Daily News
1984 – Mike Lane, Baltimore Evening Sun
1985 – Doug Marlette, Charlotte Observer
1986 – Mike Keefe, Denver Post
1987 – Paul Conrad, Los Angeles Times
1988 – Jack Higgins, Chicago Sun-Times
1989 – Don Wright, Palm Beach Post
1990 – Jeff MacNelly, Chicago Tribune

NATIONAL HEADLINERS CLUB AWARD

1938 – C. D. Batchelor, New York Daily News
1939 – John Knott, Dallas News
1940 – Herbert Block, NEA
1941 – Charles H. Sykes, Philadelphia Evening Ledger
1942 – Jerry Doyle, Philadelphia Record
1943 – Vaughn Shoemaker, Chicago Daily News
1944 – Roy Justus, Sioux City Journal
1945 – F. O. Alexander, Philadelphia Bulletin
1946 – Hank Barrow, Associated Press
1947 – Cy Hungerford, Pittsburgh Post-Gazette
1948 – Tom Little, Nashville Tennessean
1949 – Bruce Russell, Los Angeles Times
1950 – Dorman Smith, NEA
1951 – C. G. Werner, Indianapolis Star
1952 – John Fischetti, NEA
1953 – James T. Berryman and
        Gib Crocket, Washington Star
1954 – Scott Long, Minneapolis Tribune
1955 – Leo Thiele, Los Angeles Mirror-News
1956 – John Milt Morris, Associated Press
1957 – Frank Miller, Des Moines Register
1958 – Burris Jenkins, Jr., New York Journal-American
1959 – Karl Hubenthal, Los Angeles Examiner
1960 – Don Hesse, St. Louis Globe-Democrat
1961 – L. D. Warren, Cincinnati Enquirer
1962 – Franklin Morse, Los Angeles Mirror
1963 – Charles Bissell, Nashville Tennessean
1964 – Lou Grant, Oakland Tribune
1965 – Merle R. Tingley, London (Ont.) Free Press
1966 – Hugh Haynie, Louisville Courier-Journal
1967 – Jim Berry, NEA
1968 – Warren King, New York News
1969 – Larry Barton, Toledo Blade
1970 – Bill Crawford, NEA
1971 – Ray Osrin, Cleveland Plain Dealer
1972 – Jacob Burck, Chicago Sun-Times
1973 – Ranan Lurie, New York Times
1974 – Tom Darcy, Newsday
1975 – Bill Sanders, Milwaukee Journal
1976 – No award given
1977 – Paul Szep, Boston Globe
1978 – Dwane Powell, Raleigh News and Observer
1979 – Pat Oliphant, Washington Star
1980 – Don Wright, Miami News
1981 – Bill Garner, Memphis Commercial Appeal
1982 – Mike Peters, Dayton Daily News
1983 – Doug Marlette, Charlotte Observer
1984 – Steve Benson, Arizona Republic
1985 – Bill Day, Detroit Free Press
1986 – Mike Keefe, Denver Post
1987 – Mike Peters, Dayton Daily News
1988 – Doug Marlette, Charlotte Observer
1989 – Walt Handelsman, Scranton Times
1990 – Robert Ariail, The State
1991 – Jim Borgman, Cincinnati Enquirer

PULITZER PRIZE

1922 – Rollin Kirby, New York World
1923 – No award given
1924 – J. N. Darling, New York Herald Tribune
1925 – Rollin Kirby, New York World
1926 – D. R. Fitzpatrick, St. Louis Post-Dispatch
1927 – Nelson Harding, Brooklyn Eagle
1928 – Nelson Harding, Brooklyn Eagle
1929 – Rollin Kirby, New York World
1930 – Charles Macauley, Brooklyn Eagle
1931 – Edmund Duffy, Baltimore Sun
1932 – John T. McCutcheon, Chicago Tribune
1933 – H. M. Talburt, Washington Daily News
1934 – Edmund Duffy, Baltimore Sun
1935 – Ross A. Lewis, Milwaukee Journal
1936 – No award given
1937 – C. D. Batchelor, New York Daily News
1938 – Vaughn Shoemaker, Chicago Daily News
1939 – Charles G. Werner, Daily Oklahoman
1940 – Edmund Duffy, Baltimore Sun
1941 – Jacob Burck, Chicago Times
1942 – Herbert L. Block, NEA
1943 – Jay N. Darling, New York Herald Tribune
1944 – Clifford K. Berryman, Washington Star
1945 – Bill Mauldin, United Features Syndicate
1946 – Bruce Russell, Los Angeles Times
1947 – Vaughn Shoemaker, Chicago Daily News
1948 – Reuben L. ("Rube") Goldberg, New York Sun
1949 – Lute Pease, Newark Evening News
1950 – James T. Berryman, Washington Star
1951 – Reginald W. Manning, Arizona Republic
1952 – Fred L. Packer, New York Mirror
1953 – Edward D. Kuekes, Cleveland Plain Dealer
1954 – Herbert L. Block, Washington Post
1955 – Daniel R. Fitzpatrick, St. Louis Post-Dispatch
1956 – Robert York, Louisville Times
1957 – Tom Little, Nashville Tennessean
1958 – Bruce M. Shanks, Buffalo Evening News
1959 – Bill Mauldin, St. Louis Post-Dispatch
1960 – No award given
1961 – Carey Orr, Chicago Tribune
1962 – Edmund S. Valtman, Hartford Times
1963 – Frank Miller, Des Moines Register
1964 – Paul Conrad, Denver Post
1965 – No award given
1966 – Don Wright, Miami News
1967 – Patrick B. Oliphant, Denver Post
1968 – Eugene Gray Payne, Charlotte Observer
1969 – John Fischetti, Chicago Daily News
1970 – Thomas F. Darcy, Newsday
1971 – Paul Conrad, Los Angeles Times
1972 – Jeffrey K. MacNelly, Richmond News Leader
1973 – No award given
1974 – Paul Szep, Boston Globe
1975 – Garry Trudeau, Universal Press Syndicate
1976 – Tony Auth, Philadelphia Enquirer
1977 – Paul Szep, Boston Globe
1978 – Jeff MacNelly, Richmond News Leader
1979 – Herbert Block, Washington Post
1980 – Don Wright, Miami News
1981 – Mike Peters, Dayton Daily News
1982 – Ben Sargent, Austin American-Statesman
1983 – Dick Locher, Chicago Tribune
1984 – Paul Conrad, Los Angeles Times
1985 – Jeff MacNelly, Chicago Tribune
1986 – Jules Feiffer, Universal Press Syndicate

1987 – Berke Breathed, Washington Post Writers Group
1988 – Doug Marlette, Atlanta Constitution
1989 – Jack Higgins, Chicago Sun-Times
1990 – Tom Toles, Buffalo News
1991 – Jim Borgman, Cincinnati Enquirer

NATIONAL NEWSPAPER AWARD / CANADA

1949 – Jack Boothe, Toronto Globe and Mail
1950 – James G. Reidford, Montreal Star
1951 – Len Norris, Vancouver Sun
1952 – Robert La Palme, Le Devoir, Montreal
1953 – Robert W. Chambers, Halifax Chronicle-Herald
1954 – John Collins, Montreal Gazette
1955 – Merle R. Tingley, London Free Press
1956 – James G. Reidford, Toronto Globe and Mail
1957 – James G. Reidford, Toronto Globe and Mail
1958 – Raoul Hunter, Le Soleil, Quebec
1959 – Duncan Macpherson, Toronto Star
1960 – Duncan Macpherson, Toronto Star
1961 – Ed McNally, Montreal Star
1962 – Duncan Macpherson, Toronto Star
1963 – Jan Kamienski, Winnipeg Tribune
1964 – Ed McNally, Montreal Star
1965 – Duncan Macpherson, Toronto Star
1966 – Robert W. Chambers, Halifax Chronicle-Herald
1967 – Raoul Hunter, Le Soleil, Quebec
1968 – Roy Peterson, Vancouver Sun
1969 – Edward Uluschak, Edmonton Journal
1970 – Duncan Macpherson, Toronto Daily Star
1971 – Yardley Jones, Toronto Star
1972 – Duncan Macpherson, Toronto Star
1973 – John Collins, Montreal Gazette
1974 – Blaine, Hamilton Spectator
1975 – Roy Peterson, Vancouver Sun
1976 – Andy Donato, Toronto Sun
1977 – Terry Mosher, Montreal Gazette
1978 – Terry Mosher, Montreal Gazette
1979 – Edd Uluschak, Edmonton Journal
1980 – Vic Roschkov, Toronto Star
1981 – Tom Innes, Calgary Herald
1982 – Blaine, Hamilton Spectator
1983 – Dale Cummings, Winnipeg Free Press
1984 – Roy Peterson, Vancouver Sun
1985 – Ed Franklin, Toronto Globe and Mail
1986 – Brian Gable, Regina Leader Post
1987 – Raffi Anderian, Ottawa Citizen
1988 – Vance Rodewalt, Calgary Herald
1989 – Cameron Cardow, Regina Leader-Post
1990 – Roy Peterson, Vancouver Sun

FISCHETTI AWARD

1982 – Lee Judge, Kansas City Times
1983 – Bill DeOre, Dallas Morning News
1984 – Tom Toles, Buffalo News
1985 – Scott Willis, Dallas Times-Herald
1986 – Doug Marlette, Charlotte Observer
1987 – Dick Locher, Chicago Tribune
1988 – Arthur Bok, Akron Beacon-Journal
1989 – Lambert Der, Greenville News
1990 – Jeff Stahler, Cincinnati Post
1991 – Mike Keefe, Denver Post

Index

INDEX